Communications in Computer and Information Science 1663

More information about this series at https://link.springer.com/bookseries/7899

Xiaofeng Chen · Xinyi Huang ·
Mirosław Kutyłowski (Eds.)

Security and Privacy in Social Networks and Big Data

8th International Symposium, SocialSec 2022 Xi'an, China, October 16–18, 2022 Proceedings

Springer

Editors
Xiaofeng Chen
Xidian University
Xi'an, China

Xinyi Huang
Fujian Normal University
Fuzhou, China

Mirosław Kutyłowski
Wrocław University of Science and Technology
Wrocław, Poland

ISSN 1865-0929 ISSN 1865-0937 (electronic)
Communications in Computer and Information Science
ISBN 978-981-19-7241-6 ISBN 978-981-19-7242-3 (eBook)
https://doi.org/10.1007/978-981-19-7242-3

This Springer imprint is published by the registered company Springer Nature Singapore Pte Ltd.
The registered company address is: 152 Beach Road, #21-01/04 Gateway East, Singapore 189721, Singapore

Preface

The 8th International Symposium on Security and Privacy in Social Networks and Big Data (SocialSec 2022) was held during October 16–18, 2022, in Xi'an, China.

This year the conference received 106 submissions. These papers were evaluated on the basis of their significance, novelty, and technical quality, as well as on their practical impact or their level of advancement of the field's foundations. Each paper was assigned to at least three referees. Finally, the Program Committee selected 23 papers to be included in the conference program (resulting in an acceptance rate of 21.7%). The revised papers were not subject to editorial review and the authors bear full responsibility for the contents. The submission and review processes were supported by the EasyChair system. Besides the paper presentations, we were honored to have eight keynote speakers: Elisa Bertino, Moti Yung, Xuemin Lin, Jinjun Chen, Yan Zhang, Xinghua Li, Jin Li, and Zheli Liu, who enhanced the conference's program by delivering illuminating talks.

There is a long list of people who volunteered their time and energy to put together and organize the conference, and who deserve special thanks. Firstly, we would like to thank the authors of all papers (both accepted and rejected) for submitting their papers to this conference. Secondly, we must thank all the members of the Program Committee and the external reviewers for all their hard work in evaluating the papers. We are also very grateful to all the people whose work ensured a smooth organization process. Finally, a number of institutes deserve thanks as well for their great support: the State Key Laboratory of Integrated Services Networks (ISN), NSCLab, and the Xi'an Data Security and Privacy Preservation ISTC Base. The conference was partially sponsored by the China 111 Project (No. B16037).

July 2022

Xiaofeng Chen
Xinyi Huang
Mirosław Kutyłowski

Organization

Organizing Committee

Honorary Chairs

Elisa Bertino	Purdue University, USA
Hui Li	Xidian University, China
Jianfeng Ma	Xidian University, China

General Chairs

Zilong Wang	Xidian University, China
Yong Yu	Xi'an University of Posts and Telecommunications, China
Zonghua Zhang	Huawei France Research Center, France

Program Co-chairs

Xiaofeng Chen	Xidian University, China
Xinyi Huang	Fujian Normal University, China
Mirosław Kutyłowski	Wrocław University of Science and Technology, Poland

Publicity Co-chairs

Chao Chen	James Cook University, Australia
Debiao He	Wuhan University, China
Xiaoyu Zhang	Xidian University, China

Steering Committee Chair

Yang Xiang	Swinburne University of Technology, Australia

Organization Committee Members

Shichong Tan	Xidian University, China
Guohua Tian	Xidian University, China
Jiaojiao Wu	Xidian University, China

Program Committee

Shaoying Cai	Hunan University, China
Jiageng Chen	Central China Normal University, China
Rongmao Chen	National University of Defense Technology, China
Kai Chen	Chinese Academy of Sciences, China
Jintai Ding	University of Cincinnati, USA
Changyu Dong	Newcastle University, UK
Steven Furnell	University of Nottingham, UK
Shuai Han	Shanghai Jiao Tong University, China
Sajad Homayoun	Technical University of Denmark, Denmark
Qiong Huang	South China Agricultural University, China
Sokratis Katsikas	Norwegian University of Science and Technology, Norway
Jingwei Li	University of Electronic Science and Technology of China, China
Wenjuan Li	The Hong Kong Polytechnic University, China
Joseph Liu	Monash University, Australia
Shigang Liu	Swinburne University of Technology, Australia
Ximeng Liu	Fuzhou University, China
Shengli Liu	Shanghai Jiao Tong University, China
Jian Lou	Xidian University, China
Bo Luo	University of Kansas, USA
Xiapu Luo	The Hong Kong Polytechnic University, China
Xu Ma	Qufu Normal University, China
Yuantian Miao	Swinburne University of Technology, Australia
Jianting Ning	Fujian Normal University, China
Lei Pan	Swinburne University of Technology, Australia
Javier Parra-Arnau	Universitat Politècnica de Catalunya, Spain
Gerardo Pelosi	Politecnico di Milano, Italy
Saiyu Qi	Xi'an Jiaotong University, China
Seonghan Shin	National Institute of Advanced Industrial Science and Technology, Japan
Siwei Sun	University of Chinese Academy of Sciences, China
Hung-Min Sun	National Tsing Hua University, China
Shi-Feng Sun	Shanghai Jiao Tong University, China
Zhiyuan Tan	Edinburgh Napier University, UK
Haibo Tian	Sun Yat-sen University, China
Zhibo Wang	Zhejiang University, China
Ding Wang	Peking University, China

Contents

Cryptography and its Applications

Improved (t,n)-Threshold Proxy Signature Scheme

Yaodong Zhang[1(✉)] and Feng Liu[2]

[1] School of Computer Science and Technology, Shandong Technology and Business University, Yantai 264005, China
zhangyd136@163.com

[2] School of Mathematics and Information Science, Shandong Technology and Business University, Yantai 264005, China

Abstract. With the increasing maturity of (t, n) threshold signatures and proxy signatures, (t, n) threshold proxy signatures have been increasingly studied. The (t, n) threshold proxy signature scheme allows t or more proxy signers in a proxy group to sign messages on behalf of the original signer, but less than t signers cannot. In this paper, by studying a (t, n) threshold proxy signature scheme, we find that their scheme cannot resist forgery attack and does not meet the requirements of anonymity and traceability. Therefore, we propose an improved (t, n) threshold proxy signature scheme which remedies the security problems mentioned above. It is proved by analysis that our scheme not only can resist forgery attack, collusion attack and public-key substitute attack, but also has anonymity, distinguishability, and traceability. Moreover, the improved signature scheme is ultimately somewhat lower in terms of computational complexity.

Keywords: Proxy signature · Threshold proxy signature · Forgery attack · Traceability · Anonymity

1 Introduction

The study of threshold signatures became more and more popular after Desmedt and Frankels [1] first proposed the (t, n) threshold signature scheme in 1991, which refers to a signature group consisting of n members, and a combination of greater than or equal to t members in the group can sign a message on behalf of the group [2–7]. Thereafter, (t, n) threshold proxy signatures were created in order to distribute the rights of proxy signers and decentralize the custody of proxy keys. The (t, n) threshold proxy signature refers to dividing the signature key into multiple sub-keys, and distributing them to multiple proxy signers. Each proxy signer uses his own sub-key to generate partial proxy signature, and

Supported by the National Natural Science Foundation of China, Grant Nos. 61771294, 61202475.

X. Chen et al. (Eds.): SocialSec 2022, CCIS 1663, pp. 3–14, 2022.
https://doi.org/10.1007/978-981-19-7242-3_1

a valid threshold proxy signature can be generated when the number of partial proxy signatures is greater than or equal to the threshold value t.

In 1999, based on Kim et al.'s scheme [8], Sun et al. proposed a scheme [9] that can eliminate the drawback that the verifier cannot determine whether the proxy group key is legitimate. In 2001, Hsu et al. [10] found that Sun et al.'s scheme [9] does not resist collusion attack, so Hsu et al. proposed a threshold proxy signature scheme with a known signer that is non-repudiation. Later, Yang et al. [11] improved the scheme of Hsu et al. to further improve the security of the scheme. However, in 2009, Hu et al. [12] found that Yang et al.'s scheme [11] did not resist the frame attack and public-key substitute attack, and Hu et al. improved Yang et al.'s scheme. In 2017, Liu et al. [13] improved Hu et al.'s scheme [12] so that the scheme could confirm the actual signer.

In this paper, by analyzing the scheme of Liu et al. [13], we find that their scheme cannot resist forgery attack and does not provide anonymity and traceability to the signature members. In order to solve the above problems, we propose an improved signature scheme based on Liu et al.'s scheme. Our main contributions are as follows:

1. We achieve the anonymity of our proposed signature scheme by changing the composition of polynomial parameters and expanding the number of members who know the secret number among members in the Proxy Share and Key Generation.
2. We achieve the traceability of our proposed signature scheme by constructing Lagrange polynomials about public information.
3. We achieve the distinguishability of our proposed signature scheme by adding both the original signer and proxy signers public key in the final signature.
4. Based on the discrete logarithm problem and the secure Hash function algorithm, we solve the problem of forgery attack and collusion attack of our signature scheme.

2 Briefly Review of Liu's Scheme

In this section we briefly introduce the Liu et al.'s scheme [13]: Initialization Phase, Proxy Key Generation Phase, Proxy Signature Generation Phase, and Proxy Signature Verification Phase. Finally, we analyze the security problems in the Liu et al.'s scheme and present our solution in the next section.

2.1 Initialization Phase

p, q are two secure large prime numbers and satisfy $q|p-1$, g is a generating element of order q on Z_q^*, and $H(x), F(x)$ are two secure one-way hash functions. Original signer generates the authorization certificate m_w, which includes the identity of the original signer and the proxy signer, the threshold value t, the proxy privileges and other information. CA is the third-party certification authority, CA requires the original signer P_0 and proxy signers in group G offer the Zero-Knowledge Proof of their private key about their public key [12].

2.2 Proxy Key Generation Phase

Suppose the original signer P_0 and the proxy signature group $G = \{P_1, P_2, \cdots, P_n\}$. P_0 performs the following steps:

1. P_0 choose a $k \in Z_q^*$, and broadcasts $K = g^k \ modp$.
2. P_0 computes
$$\sigma_0 = (x_0 H(m_w, K) + k) \ modq \tag{1}$$
and publishes $\sigma = \sigma_0/t$.
3. P_i receives σ, checks
$$g^{t \times \sigma} = K {y_0}^{H(m_w,K)} \ modp \tag{2}$$
Let $G_p = (P_1, P_2, \cdots, P_t)$ be the actual proxy signers and ASID be the collection of identities of all users in G_p.
4. P_i chooses number $c_i \in Z_q^*$, broadcasts $C_i = g^{c_i} \ modp$ and generates a $(t-1)$ degree ploynomial $f_i(x) = (c_i + \sigma) + b_{i,1}x + \cdots + b_{i,t-1}x^{t-1} \ modq$ with random coefficients $b_{i,j} \in Z_q^*$. P_i computes $f_i(v_j)$ where v_j is the public identifier for P_j, and sends $f_i(v_j)$ to P_j via a secure channel. P_i broadcasts $r_{i,j} = g^{b_{i,j}} \ modp$.
5. P_j validate all the $f_i(v_j)$ sent from P_i by checking the equation
$$g^{\sum_{i=i,i\neq j}^{t} f_i(v_j)} = \prod_{i=1,i\neq j}^{t} C_i({y_0}^{H(m_w,K)}K)^{t-1} \prod_{l=1,l\neq j}^{t} \prod_{m=1}^{t-1} {r_{i,m}}^{v_j^m} \ modp \tag{3}$$
If it is hold, P_j computes $\sigma_j = f(v_j) = \sum_{i=1}^{t} f_i(v_j)$, else P_j validates all $f_i(v_j)$ in sequence by the equation
$$g^{f_i(v_j)} = C_i y_0^{H(m_w,K)} K \prod_{m=1}^{t-1} {r_{i,m}}^{(v_j)^m} \ modp \tag{4}$$

2.3 Proxy Signature Generation Phase

Let m be the signing message.

1. P_i selects $k_i \in Z_q^*$ and broadcasts $w_i = g^{k_i} \ modp$.
2. After receiving w_j from P_j each P_i computes
$$s_i = k_i W + (\sigma_i \prod_{j=1,j\neq i}^{t} \frac{v_j}{v_j - v_i} + x_i H(m_w, K)) F(W, m, ASID) \ modq \tag{5}$$
where $W = \prod_{i=1}^{t} w_i \ modp$.
3. P_i computes $\gamma_i = g^{\sigma_i} \ modp$ and sends (s_i, w_i, K, γ_i) to DC.
4. After receiving all the partial signatures (s_i, w_i, K, γ_i) of P_i in G_p, DC checks whether the following equation holds
$$g^{s_i} = {w_i}^{W} ({\gamma_i}^{\prod_{j=1,j\neq i}^{t} \frac{v_j}{v_j - v_i}} {y_i}^{H(m_w,K)})^{F(W,m,ASID)} \ modp \tag{6}$$
5. If it does, DC computes $S = \sum_{i=1}^{t} s_i \ modq$, and sends the proxy signature $(S, W, K, m_w, ASID, C)$ and the signing message m to the verifier.

2.4 Proxy Signature Verification Phase

After receiving the proxy signature $(S, W, K, m_w, ASID, C)$. Since

$$S = \sum_{i=1}^{t} w_i + (\sum_{i=1}^{t} c_i + \sigma_0 + \sum_{i=1}^{t} x_i H(m_w, K))F(W, m, ASID) \ modq$$
$$= \sum_{i=1}^{t} w_i + (\sum_{i=1}^{t} c_i + k + \sum_{i=0}^{t} x_i H(m_w, K))F(W, m, ASID) \ modq$$

so the verifier can check whether the following equation holds or not.

$$g^S = W^W (C \times K \times \prod_{i=0}^{t} y_i{}^{H(m_w,K)})^{F(W,m,ASID)} \ modp \quad (7)$$

If the equation holds, the signature is a valid signature cooperatively generated by the signers in G_p.

3 Analysis of Liu's Scheme

In 2017, Liu et al. [13] improved the Hu et al.'s signature scheme [12] so that the improved scheme can identify the actual proxy signer. In this section, we analyze the scheme of Liu et al. and find that their scheme is not resistant to forgery attack and does not provide anonymity and traceability to the signature members.

3.1 Equation Error

The analysis of the scheme of Liu et al. reveals an error in the proxy share generation equation in their scheme, as follows.

$$\begin{aligned}
g^{\sum_{i=i,i\neq j}^{t} f_i(v_j)} &= \prod_{i=1,i\neq j}^{t} C_i(y_0{}^{H(m_w,K)}K)^{t-1} \prod_{l=1,l\neq j}^{t} \prod_{m=1}^{t-1} r_{i,m}{}^{v_j{}^m} \\
&= \prod_{i=1,i\neq j}^{t} C_i(g^{t\times\sigma})^{t-1} \prod_{l=1,l\neq j}^{t} \prod_{m=1}^{t-1} r_{i,m}{}^{v_j{}^m} \\
&= \prod_{i=1,i\neq j}^{t} C_i(g^{\sigma_0})^{t-1} \prod_{l=1,l\neq j}^{t} g^{\sum_{m=1}^{t-1} b_{i,m} v_j{}^m} \\
&\neq \prod_{i=1,i\neq j}^{t} C_i(g^{\sigma_0})^{t^{-1}} g^{\sum_{m=1}^{t-1} b_{i,m} v_j{}^m} \\
&= \prod_{i=1,i\neq j}^{t} g^{C_i+\sigma+\sum_{m=1}^{t-1} b_{i,m} v_j{}^m} \\
&= g^{\sum_{i=i,i\neq j}^{t} f_i(v_j)} \ modp
\end{aligned}$$

As stated in the original, if this equation does not hold, then P_i confirms that all $f_i(v_j)$ through the Eq. (4). However, after analysis, it was found that the equation also contains errors:

$$\begin{aligned} g^{f_i(v_j)} &= C_i {y_0}^{H(m_w,K)} K \prod_{m=1}^{t-1} {r_{i,m}}^{(v_j)^m} \\ &= g^{c_i} g^{t \times \sigma} g^{\sum_{m=1}^{t-1} b_{i,m} {v_j}^m} \\ &= g^{c_i + t\times\sigma + b_{i,1} v_j + \cdots + b_{i,t-1} {v_j}^{t-1}} \\ &\neq g^{c_i + \sigma + b_{i,1} v_j + \cdots + b_{i,t-1} {v_j}^{t-1}} \\ &= g^{f_i(v_j)} \ modp \end{aligned}$$

So, even if the correct $f_i(v_j)$ does not pass the verification of P_j so that P_j's proxy share cannot be generated, which ultimately results in proxy signatures not being generated.

3.2 Forgery Attack

It is assumed that the proxy shares of the Liu et al.'s scheme can be generated correctly. In this paper, we construct a forgery attack based on the frame attack proposed in the Hu et al.'s scheme [12], it is shown that the Liu et al. scheme [13] cannot resist this forgery attack. The specific steps are as follows.

1. The original signer P_0 randomly chooses $\alpha, \beta, \gamma \in Z_q^*$, computes: $W' = g^{\alpha} \ modp$, $K' = g^{\beta} \ modp$, $C' = g^{\gamma} (\prod_{i=0}^{t} {y_i}^{H(m_w,K')})^{-1} \ modp$.
2. Since $(g, m_w, H, y_i, ASID)$ is public information, P_0 constructs the equation:

$$\begin{aligned} S' &= \alpha W' + (\beta + \gamma) F(W', m', ASID) \ modq \\ g^{S'} &= g^{\alpha W'} g^{(\beta+\gamma) F(W', m', ASID)} \\ &= W'^{W'} (K'C' \prod_{i=0}^{t} {y_i}^{H(m_w,K')})^{F(W',m',,ASID)} \ modq \end{aligned}$$

That is, $(C', K', S', W', m_w, ASID)$ satisfies the verification equation. Thus, a malicious original signer P_0 can forge a valid threshold proxy signature for any message m' without the knowledge of the actual proxy signature group.

3.3 No Anonymity

The anonymity of a threshold proxy signature scheme means that the verifier can only know that the signature was generated by the signature group and does not know exactly which members of the group signed it. In Liu et al.'s scheme [13], the verifier who wants to verify the correctness of the signature must know the actual signature signers, otherwise there is no way to compute $\prod_{i=0}^{t} {y_i}^{H(m_w,K)}$. As long as the verifier knows the actual signature signers, the scheme is not anonymous.

4 Improved Scheme

After analyzing the signature scheme of Liu et al. in Sect. 3, we improve their scheme in this section so that the improved scheme not only can resist forgery attack, collusion attack and public-key substitute attack, but also has anonymity, distinguishability and traceability. Our improved scheme consists of four parts: System Initialization, Proxy Share and Key Generation, Proxy Signature Generation, and Proxy Signature Verification.

4.1 System Initialization

The system parameters are the same as those in Sect. 2.1, but there are some differences in our new scheme: we just use one secure one-way hash function $h(x)$, and we define PSID is the set of identities of all proxy members in the proxy group, $ID_i(i = 0, 1, \ldots, n)$ is a unique identifier for each member. CA is the third-party certification authority, and DC is the partial proxy signature composer.

Assume that P_0 is the original signer and the proxy signature group is $G = \{P_1, P_2, \ldots, P_n\}$. P_0 randomly selects $x_0 \in Z_q^*$ as his private key, the public key is $y_0 = g^{x_0}\ modp$ and certified by CA. P_i randomly selects $x_i \in Z_q^*$ as his private key, the public key is $y_i = g^{x_i}\ modp$ and certified by CA.

CA requires P_0 and P_i to provide a zero-knowledge proof of the private key to the public key:

1. CA randomly selects e, computes $E = g^e\ modp$, and sends E to P_0, P_i.
2. P_0, P_i compute $Y_0 = E^{x_0}\ modp$ and $Y_i = E^{x_i}\ modp$ respectively and send them to CA.
3. CA verifies $y_0^e = Y_0$, $y_i^e = Y_i$. If it holds, the verification is successful.

4.2 Proxy Share and Key Generation

In this part, the proxy signer gets the proxy share and generates its own proxy key.

1. P_0 randomly selects $k \in Z_q^*$, computes $K = g^k\ modp$, $\sigma_0 = t\sigma = x_0 h(m_w, K) + kK\ modq$, and sends (m_w, K, σ) to $P_i \in G$. P_i receives (m_w, K, σ) and verifies
$$g^{t\sigma} = K^K {y_0}^{h(m_w,K)}\ modp \tag{8}$$
If the verification is successful, P_i takes σ as his own proxy share.
2. P_i randomly selects $v_i \in Z_q^*$, computes $V_i = g^{v_i}\ modp$, and broadcasts V_i to $P_j(j = 1, 2, \ldots, n, j \neq i)$.
3. P_i randomly selects a $(t-1)$ degree ploynomial $f_i(x) = a_{i,o} + a_{i,1}x + \cdots + a_{i,t-1}x^{t-1}\ modq$, $a_{i,0} = x_i h(m_w, PSID)$, $a_{i,m} \in Z_q^*(m = 1, 2, \ldots, t-1)$. P_i broadcasts $A_{i,m} = g^{a_{i,m}}\ modp$, computes $\lambda_{i,j} = f_i(ID_j)\ modq$, and sends $\lambda_{i,j}$ to $P_j \in G$ via a secure channel.

4. P_i verifies following equation after receiving $\lambda_{j,i}$ from the other $n-1$ members.
$$g^{\lambda_{j,i}} = {y_j}^{h(m_w,PSID)} \prod_{m=1}^{t-1} {A_{j,m}}^{{ID_i}^m} \ modp \tag{9}$$
If the equation holds, P_i accepts $\lambda_{j,i}$, computes $\lambda_i = \sum_{j=1}^{n} \lambda_{j,i} \ modq$, $Q_i = g^{\lambda_i} \ modp$, and broadcasts Q_i.
5. P_i takes $X_i = \sigma + \lambda_i + v_i$ as the proxy private key and the corresponding public key as $Y_i = g^{X_i} \ modp$.

4.3 Proxy Signature Generation

Without loss of generality, let $D = \{P_1, P_2, \ldots, P_t\}$ be the t actual proxy signer that is delegated by the original signer P_0 to generate the proxy signature, m is the message to be signed.

1. P_i randomly selects $r_i \in Z_q^*$, computes and broadcasts $R_i = g^{r_i} \ modp$. After P_i receives $t-1$ copies of R_j, computes $R = \prod_{i=1}^{t} R_i \ modp$, $V = \prod_{i=1}^{t} V_i \ modp$ and
$$s_i = r_i + h(R, PSID, m)(\sigma + \lambda_i C_i + v_i) \ modq \tag{10}$$
where $C_i = \prod_{j=1, j \neq i}^{t} \frac{-ID_j}{ID_i - ID_j}$, $(i = 1, 2, \ldots, t)$, P_i sends (s_i, C_i) to DC.
2. After DC receives (s_i, C_i), takes (s_i, C_i) into the following equation:
$$g^{s_i t} = {R_i}^t (K^K {y_0}^{h(m_w,K)} {Q_i}^{tC_i} {V_i}^t)^{h(R,PSID,m)} \ modp \tag{11}$$
If the equation holds, the partial proxy signature is proven to be valid. DC performs the following steps.
3. DC computes $S = \sum_{i=1}^{t} s_i \ modq$, and constructs the Lagrange polynomial $g(y)$ using the t-pair (y_i, ID_i) and saves it secretly.
$$g(y) = \sum_{i=1}^{t} ID_i \prod_{j=1, j \neq i}^{t} \frac{yg^{s't} - y_j g^{s_j t}}{y_i g^{s_i t} - y_j g^{s_j t}}, s' \in \{s_1, s_2, \ldots, s_t\} \tag{12}$$
This polynomial is used to trace the actual signature members in case of post-facto disputes. DC sends $(S, R, K, V, PSID, m_w)$ to verifier.

4.4 Proxy Signature Verification

After receiving the threshold proxy signature $(S, R, K, V, PSID, m_w)$, the verifier takes it into the following equation to verify validity.
$$g^S = R(K^K {y_0}^{h(m_w,K)} V \prod_{i=1}^{n} {y_i}^{h(m_w,PSID)})^{h(R,PSID,m)} \ modp \tag{13}$$
If the equation holds, the verifier considers the sent threshold proxy signature valid.

5 Analysis of Improvement Scheme

In this section, we will analyze the correctness and security of our improved signature scheme.

5.1 Scheme Correctness

1. Correctness of proxy share and key generation phase:

$$\begin{aligned} g^{\lambda_{j,i}} &= g^{f_j(ID_i)} \\ &= g^{x_j h(m_w,PSID)+a_{j,1}ID_i+\cdots+a_{j,t-1}ID_i{}^{t-1}} \\ &= y_j{}^{h(m_w,PSID)} \prod_{m=1}^{t-1} A_{j,m}{}^{ID_i{}^m} \ modp \end{aligned}$$

2. Correctness of proxy signature generation phase:

$$\begin{aligned} g^{s_i t} &= g^{r_i t+h(R.PSID,m)(t\sigma+\lambda_i C_i t+v_i t)} \\ &= R_i{}^t g^{h(R,PSID,m)(\sigma_0+\lambda_i C_i t+v_i t)} \\ &= R_i{}^t (K^K y_0{}^{h(m_w,K)} Q_i{}^{tC_i} V_i{}^t)^{h(R,PSID,m)} \ modp \end{aligned}$$

3. Correctness of proxy signature verification phase:

$$\begin{aligned} g^S = g^{\sum_{i=1}^t s_i} &= g^{\sum_{i=1}^t (r_i+h(R,PSID,m)(\sigma+\lambda_i C_i+v_i))} \\ &= \prod_{i=1}^t g^{r_i} g^{\sum_{i=1}^t (\sigma+\lambda_i C_i+v_i)h(R,PSID,m)} \\ &= R(g^{\sum_{i=1}^t \sigma} g^{\sum_{i=1}^t \sum_{j=1}^n f_j(ID_i)\prod_{j=1,j\neq i}^t \frac{-ID_j}{ID_i-ID_j}} \prod_{i=1}^t g^{v_i})^{h(R,PSID,m)} \\ &= R(K^K y_0{}^{h(m_w,K)} V g^{\sum_{j=1}^n f_j(o)})^{h(R,PSID,m)} \\ &= R(K^K y_0{}^{h(m_w,K)} V \prod_{j=1}^n y_i{}^{h(m_w,PSID)})^{h(R,PSID,m)} \ modp \end{aligned}$$

5.2 Scheme Security

In general, the security of a threshold proxy signature means that the signature scheme is resistant to forgery attack, collusion attack, public-key substitute attack, and is anonymous, distinguishable, and traceable.

1. Resistant to forgery attack:
   We have assumed three scenarios of forgery attacks.
   - If the adversary tries to fake σ' to cheat P_i, because $\sigma_0 = t\sigma = x_0 h(m_w, K) + kK \ modq$, it is impossible for an adversary to forge σ' without knowing the P_0's private key and make σ' satisfy $g^{t\sigma} = K^K y_0{}^{h(m_w,K)} \ modp$. Trying to find σ directly from this equation faces the discrete logarithm problem.

- P_0 cannot forge the threshold proxy signature of P_i. Because the difficulty of P_0 trying to derive the (S', R', K', V') is equivalent to solving the discrete logarithm problem. In addition, R' is protected under the secure one-way hash function $h()$. Therefore, the original signer P_0 cannot forge any valid threshold proxy of information m'.
- The adversary cannot forge the threshold proxy signature. Because P_i's proxy private key X_i and P_i's private key x_i are used in the threshold signature process, an adversary trying to get them faces solving the discrete logarithm problem, so our scheme is resistant to forgery.

2. Resistant to collusion attack:
Greater than or equal to t members of the proxy group conspire to construct the Lagrange polynomial $f(x)$, there exists $f(x) = \sum_{i=1}^{n} f_i(x)\ modq = a_0 + a_1x + \cdots + a_{t-1}x^{t-1}\ modq$ and $\lambda_i = f(ID_i)\ modq$. Since ID_i is public information, the malicious collusion members can obtain the λ_i of other members, but since v_i in $s_i = r_i + h(R, PSID, m)(\sigma + \lambda_i C_i + v_i)\ modq$ is a secret value, the proxy private key of P_i cannot be obtained and the malicious collusion members cannot impersonate other members to generate partial proxy signatures.
3. Resistant to public-key substitute attack:
Based on the public key substitution attack proposed by JiGuo Li and ZhenFu Cao [14], without loss of generality, we suppose P_1 wants to sign any message m' on behalf of the signing members via a public-key substitute attack. $\alpha, \beta, \gamma, K' \in Z_q^*$ are randomly taken by P_1 and P_1 computes:

$$R' = g^{\alpha}\ modp$$
$$V' = g^{\gamma}\ modp$$
$$S' = \alpha + (\beta + x_1 h(m_w, K') + \gamma)h(R', PSID, m')\ modq$$
$$y_1' = (g^{\beta} {y_1}^{h(m_W, PSID)} {y_0}^{-h(m_w, K')} K'^{-K'} \prod_{i=2}^{n} {y_i}^{-h(m_w, PSID)})^{-h(m_w, PSID)}\ modp$$

P_1 wants to replace his public key y_1' to CA after the computation is completed. If the replacement is successful.

$$g^{S'} = R'({y_0}^{h(mw, K')} K'^{K'} \prod_{i=2}^{n} {y_i}^{h(m_w, PSID)} {y_1'}^{h(m_w, PSID)} V')^{h(R', PSID, m')}\ modp$$

But replacing the public key to CA requires providing a zero-knowledge proof of the private key to the public key. P_1 only computes y_1' and does not compute x_1' from $y_1' = g^{x_1'}\ modp$, so P_1 cannot perform the public-key substitute attack.
4. Anonymity:
From the threshold proxy signature verification equation, it can be seen that the $\prod_{i=1}^{n} {y_i}^{h(m_w, PSID)}$ used in the verification equation is the product of the public keys of all proxy group members. Thus our scheme achieves anonymity for the actual signature members.

5. Distinguishability:
   From the threshold proxy signature verification equation, it is clear that the equation contains both the public key of the original signer P_0 and the public keys of all proxy signers. In addition, the authorization proxy certificate m_w contains the information of the original signer and the proxy signer, so our scheme is distinguishable.
6. Traceability:
   Threshold proxy signatures are sometimes faced with situations where a dispute arises after the signature has been signed, and it is necessary to reveal the identity of the participating signature members. Our scheme builds Lagrange polynomial based on the public information (y_i, ID_i) of the actual proxy signers in group D.

$$g(y) = \sum_{i=1}^{t} ID_i \prod_{j=1, j\neq i}^{t} \frac{yg^{s't} - y_j g^{s_j t}}{y_i g^{s_i t} - y_j g^{s_j t}}, s' \in \{s_1, s_2, \ldots, s_t\}$$

   Tracking of participating signature members is achieved by this polynomial.

5.3 Scheme Performance

In this section, we compare the computational complexity of our improved signature scheme with that of Liu et al.'s scheme and show the results in Table 1. For the convenience of representation, we analyze the complexity with the following notation.

T_e the time for one exponentiation computation.
T_m the time for one modular multiplication computation.
T_h the time for hash function computation.
T_i the time for one inverse computation.

Table 1. Comparison of computational complexity.

	Proxy share generation	Proxy signature generation	Proxy signature verification
Liu et al.'s scheme	$(t^2 + 3t + 5)T_e + (3t^2 + 2nt - 3n + 3)T_m + 3T_h + 2T_i$	$(5t + 2)T_e + (2t^2 + t)T_m + 4T_h + (2t - 2)T_i$	$4T_e + (t + 3)T_m + 2T_h$
The improved scheme	$(2t + 5)T_e + (2nt + 3t - 3n - 1)T_m + 3T_h + T_i$	$(7t + 1)T_e + (2t^2 + 9t - 3)T_m + 3T_h + t^2T_i$	$5T_e + (n + 3)T_m + 3T_h$

By analyzing the data in Table 1, it is clear that: our improved signature scheme has significantly lower computational complexity in the proxy share generation part than Liu et al.'s scheme. The computational complexity in the proxy signature generation part is higher than Liu et al.'s scheme, because our improved scheme adds Lagrange tracing equation as well as achieves anonymity in the proxy signature generation part.

6 Conclusions

In this paper, we firstly analyze the security of Liu et al.'s signature scheme, pointing out that their scheme suffers from verification equation errors and we find that their scheme cannot resist forgery attack and does not meet the requirements of anonymity, distinguishability and traceability.

Secondly, we propose an improved (t, n) threshold proxy signature scheme based on the scheme of Liu et al. By analyzing our improved signature scheme, we demonstrate that our scheme not only can resist forgery attack, collusion attack and public-key substitute attack, but also has anonymity, distinguishability, and traceability.

Finally, after the computational complexity comparison, our improved signature scheme has lower computational complexity in the proxy share generation part than the scheme of Liu et al. In the proxy signature generation part, the computational complexity of our improved signature scheme is higher than that of Liu et al.'s scheme due to the addition of the Lagrange tracing equation, but our scheme is much safer and more practical than Liu et al.'s.

Acknowledgements. This work was supported by the National Natural Science Foundation of China (Research on the theory and application of quantum coherent resources (No. 61771294)), the National Natural Science Foundation of China (Design and security proof of leak-tolerant public key encryption (No. 61202475)).

References

1. Desmedt, Y., Frankel, Y.: Shared generation of authenticators and signatures. In: Feigenbaum, J. (ed.) CRYPTO 1991. LNCS, vol. 576, pp. 457–469. Springer, Heidelberg (1992). https://doi.org/10.1007/3-540-46766-1_37
2. Zhao, L.S., Liu, J.M.: (t, n) threshold digital signature scheme with traceable signers against conspiracy attacks. In: 2013 5th International Conference on Intelligent Networking and Collaborative Systems, pp. 649–651. IEEE (2013)
3. Gu, K., Wang, Y., Wen, S.: Traceable threshold proxy signature. J. Inf. Sci. Eng. **33**(1), 63–79 (2017)
4. Wang, X., Ning, Z., Wang, W., Yang, Y.: Anti-conspiracy attack threshold signature model and protocol paper retracted. Int. J. Wirel. Mob. Comput. **17**(3), 300–306 (2019)
5. Kurek, R.: Efficient forward-secure threshold signatures. In: Aoki, K., Kanaoka, A. (eds.) IWSEC 2020. LNCS, vol. 12231, pp. 239–260. Springer, Cham (2020). https://doi.org/10.1007/978-3-030-58208-1_14
6. Duong, D.H., Tran, H.T., Susilo, W., et al.: An efficient multivariate threshold ring signature scheme. Comput. Stand. Interfaces **74**, 103489 (2021)
7. Guo, R., Cheng, X.: Cryptanalysis and improvement of a (t, n) threshold group signature scheme. Quantum Inf. Process. **21**(1), 1–9 (2022)

8. Kim, S., Park, S., Won, D.: Proxy signatures, revisited. In: Han, Y., Okamoto, T., Qing, S. (eds.) ICICS 1997. LNCS, vol. 1334, pp. 223–232. Springer, Heidelberg (1997). https://doi.org/10.1007/BFb0028478
9. Sun, H.M.: An efficient nonrepudiable threshold proxy signature scheme with known signers. Comput. Commun. **22**(8), 717–722 (1999)
10. Hsu, C.L., Wu, T.S., Wu, T.C.: New nonrepudiable threshold proxy signature scheme with known signers. J. Syst. Softw. **58**(2), 119–124 (2001)
11. Yang, C.Y., Tzeng, S.F., Hwang, M.S.: On the efficiency of nonrepudiable threshold proxy signature scheme with known signers. J. Syst. Softw. **73**(3), 507–514 (2004)
12. Hu, J., Zhang, J.: Cryptanalysis and improvement of a threshold proxy signature scheme. Comput. Stand. Interfaces **31**(1), 169–173 (2009)
13. Liu, D., Wang, L., Wang, C., Huo, P.: A nonrepudiable threshold proxy signature scheme against forgery attack. In: Proceedings of the 2017 International Conference on Cryptography, Security and Privacy, pp. 76–80 (2017)
14. Li, J.G., Cao, Z.F.: Improvement of a threshold proxy signature scheme. J. Comput. Res. Dev. **39**(11), 515–518 (2002)

Algorithm Substitution Attacks on Identity-Based Encryption

Yifei Wang, Yuliang Lin(✉), Yi Wang(✉), Wei Peng(✉), and Lin Liu(✉)

School of Computer, National University of Defense Technology, Changsha, China
{wangyifei_20,linyuliang21,wangyi14,wpeng,liulin16}@nudt.edu.cn

Abstract. Algorithm substitution attack (ASA) was proposed by Bellare *et al.* at CRYPTO 2014 and has been studied in the context of various cryptographic primitives so far. In this work, we turn to study ASAs on identity-based encryption (IBE) scheme which has been widely considered as a useful encryption tool. We first provide ASAs models to capture the attacks against IBE and then present concrete ASAs on two IBE schemes where the key extraction algorithm and encryption algorithm are effectively subverted respectively. Our work shows that ASA on IBE could be dangerous and thus the proposal of effective countermeasures is highly desirable to deploy IBE securely in the real-world applications.

Keywords: Identity-based encryption · Algorithm substitution attack · Hash function

1 Introduction

The security of cryptographic primitives is usually proved under certain models that capture real-world attacks. Thus, security models are meaningful only if all possible attacks are well-considered. Typical security models implicitly assume that cryptographic implementations are honest while in 2013 the Snowden revelation showed that cryptosystems might deviate from their legitimate specifications and such kind of new attacks could completely render the typical provable security failure.

In fact, the studies on such attacks have been studied several decades ago. In 1996, Adam Young and Moti Yung [7] presented the so-called SETUP mechanism. A powerful attacker can embed such a mechanism in a cryptographic device that is used in a black-box manner so that the secret information inside the device could be leaked to the outside world in an undetectable way. Later, they extended the attack to get secret information without a subliminal channel and named it Kleptography [8], which means that the attacker can get the information he wants exclusively, securely and subliminally. In a word, the attacker aims to steal the secret information without being detected by the security analysts via modifying the implementation of underlying algorithms maliciously.

X. Chen et al. (Eds.): SocialSec 2022, CCIS 1663, pp. 15–31, 2022.
https://doi.org/10.1007/978-981-19-7242-3_2

1.1 Algorithm Substitution Attack

The Snowden revelation rekindled the researchers' attention on such hazardous subversion attack. In 2014, Mihir Bellare *et al.* [9] proposed the notion of Algorithm Substitution Attack (ASA) and presented two concrete ASAs on symmetric encryption: IV-replacement and biased ciphertext attacks. The subverted encryption algorithms generate ciphertext along with a subversion key such that the attacker knowing this key can recover secret information from subverted ciphertexts. Besides, the subverted algorithm should be indistinguishable from the original version to anyone except for the attacker [10]. In 2015, Giuseppe Ateniese *et al.* [11] introduced two ASAs on signature schemes. In these attacks, the attacker can extract the signing key from signatures using a pseudo-random function.

Most of ASAs on encryption scheme only consider the subversion of the encryption algorithm. In 2019, Marcel Armour and Bertram Poettering [12] proposed two ASAs subverting the decryption algorithm of AEAD. One is a passive attack, and the other is active. The attacker could recover the secret key by collecting the decryption results of subverted decryption algorithm. In 2020, Rongmao Chen *et al.* [13] presented an ASA on public-key encryption algorithm and showed that it is more dangerous for ASAs on public-key encryption schemes.

At present, public-key encryption schemes are also widely used in our daily life. The security of public-key encryption schemes against such attacks also needs to be studied. While there are few pieces of research on algorithm substitution attacks on public-key encryption schemes. This motivates us to study ASA on a concrete public-key encryption scheme. A case in point is an identity-based encryption scheme.

1.2 Identity-Based Encryption

The idea of an Identity-Based Encryption (IBE) scheme was first proposed by Adi Shamir [1]. He proposed to use a trusted key generation center to distribute keys to users. The key is calculated by the Private Key Generator (PKG), using the user's identity information that is publicly available. The PKG is viewed as a trusted key generation center. This is why IBE scheme differs from other public-key encryption schemes. On the basis of this, many IBE schemes have been proposed, such as BF-IBE scheme [2], BB-IBE scheme [4,5], Waters-IBE scheme [6], and so on [3].

However, we cannot ensure that the PKG is honest. If the PKG is tempered by an algorithm substitution attack, it is easy for the attacker to get the secret key and even recover the message. Therefore, it is necessary to study the form of ASA and find an effective attack on IBE scheme. This will help us to look for solutions of protecting the scheme from ASA.

1.3 Our Work

Inspired by [12] and [13,14], we consider subverting algorithms in identity-based encryption(IBE) scheme. The subversion attacks use a computational hash function with smooth entropy to change the way of choosing random and then recover the key or the message through the hash function. In this paper, we consider subverting two algorithms in IBE scheme. One is key extraction algorithm, the other is encryption algorithm. At last, we give two instantiations of IBE scheme under the algorithm substitution attack. The attacker could subvert the two algorithms separately in IBE scheme, and then he uses the subverted information leaked by the scheme to successfully recover the key or the message.

2 Preliminaries

Notation. Let $\{0,1\}^l$ be the finite set S of strings of length l. For an element $s \in \{0,1\}^l$, we have $|s| = l$. s_i denotes the i-th bit of s. $s \leftarrow\!\!\$\, S$ denotes that s is randomly chosen from S. Let (u_i) be a vector and $(u_{i,j})$ be a matrix. Let $\mathcal{A}$ be an adversary running an algorithm, $b \leftarrow \mathcal{A}^{\mathcal{O}(\cdot)}(x)$ denotes that with input x and access to oracle $\mathcal{O}$ the output of the algorithm is b.

Hash Function with Smooth Entropy. Smooth entropy allows us to extract a random from a uniform distribution by an algorithm. In this way, we can get a random which can be calculated by the algorithm however looks like randomly chosen from a distribution. We say that H is a hash function with smooth entropy if for any PPT adversary $\mathcal{B}$, the advantage that $\mathcal{B}$ wins the game SE is negligible, defined as follows:

$$\mathsf{Adv}^{\mathsf{se}}_{\mathcal{B},\mathsf{H}}(\lambda) = \left|2\Pr\left[\mathsf{SE}^{\mathcal{B}}_{\mathsf{H}} = \mathsf{true}\right] - 1\right| \leq \mathsf{negl}(\lambda).$$

The game SE is described in Fig. 1.

$\mathsf{SE}^{\mathcal{B}}_{\mathsf{H}}$	$\mathcal{O}_{\mathsf{se}}(x)$
$b \leftarrow\!\!\$\, \{0,1\}$	**if** $b = 0, y \leftarrow \mathsf{H}(x)$
$b' \leftarrow \mathcal{B}^{\mathcal{O}_{\mathsf{se}}(\cdot)}$	**else** $y \leftarrow\!\!\$\, \mathbb{Z}_q$
return $b' = b$	**return** y

Fig. 1. Hash function with smooth entropy

Bilinear Groups. We denote $\mathbb{G}_1$ and $\mathbb{G}_2$ are cyclic groups of prime order q. $\hat{e} : \mathbb{G}_1 \times \mathbb{G}_1 \rightarrow \mathbb{G}_2$ is a bilinear map between the two groups. P is a generator of $\mathbb{G}_1$. The map $\hat{e} : \mathbb{G}_1 \times \mathbb{G}_1 \rightarrow \mathbb{G}_2$ has the following properties:

- Bilinear: $\hat{e} : \mathbb{G}_1 \times \mathbb{G}_1 \rightarrow \mathbb{G}_2$ is bilinear, *if* $\forall P, Q \in \mathbb{G}_1, \forall a, b \in \mathbb{Z}_q$, $\hat{e}(aP, bQ) = \hat{e}(P,Q)^{ab}$.
- Non-degenerate: $\exists P \in \mathbb{G}_1$, s.t. $\hat{e}(P,P) \neq 1$.
- Computable: $\forall P, Q \in \mathbb{G}_1$, $\hat{e}(P,Q)$ can be computed by an efficient algorithm.

BDH (Bilinear Diffie-Hellman) Parameter Generator. We denote $\mathcal{IG}$ as a BDH parameter generator that runs in polynomial time. Let $\mathcal{IG}$ be a randomized algorithm that takes a security parameter λ as input and outputs two groups $\mathbb{G}_1, \mathbb{G}_2$ of the same prime order q and a map $\hat{e} : \mathbb{G}_1 \times \mathbb{G}_1 \rightarrow \mathbb{G}_2$. It is written as $(\mathbb{G}_1, \mathbb{G}_2, \hat{e}) \leftarrow \mathcal{IG}(1^\lambda)$, and is used in the algorithm Set in IBE scheme.

Decisional Bilinear Diffie-Hellman Problem (DBDH). There are two tuples $(P, aP, bP, \hat{e}(P,P)^{ab})$ and $(P, aP, bP, \hat{e}(P,P)^{z})$, where a, b, z are uniformly and randomly chosen from $\mathbb{Z}_q$. Given a tuple of them, it is hard to distinguish the value is whether $\hat{e}(P,P)^{ab}$ or $\hat{e}(P,P)^{z}$.

Identity-Based Encryption Scheme (IBE). There are four algorithms in an IBE scheme, denoted as $\mathsf{IBE} = (\mathsf{IBE.Setup}, \mathsf{IBE.Ext}, \mathsf{IBE.Enc}, \mathsf{IBE.Dec})$.

- $\mathsf{IBE.Setup}(\lambda)$: Takes as input a security parameter λ and runs PKG, outputs public system parameters params and secret master-key msk.
- $\mathsf{IBE.Ext}(\mathsf{msk}, \mathsf{ID})$: Takes as input msk, the identity ID, outputs the private key d_{ID}.
- $\mathsf{IBE.Enc}(\mathsf{ID}, m)$: Takes as input ID, the message m, outputs the ciphertext C
- $\mathsf{IBE.Dec}(d_{\mathsf{ID}}, C)$: Takes as input d_{ID} and C, outputs the message m or $\perp$.

CORRECTNESS. An IBE scheme satisfies correctness if for any $\lambda \in \mathbb{N}$, any params and msk output by $\mathsf{IBE.Setup}(\lambda)$, any identity ID, and any message m, we have $\mathsf{IBE.Dec}(\mathsf{IBE.Ext}(\mathsf{msk}, \mathsf{ID}), \mathsf{IBE.Enc}(\mathsf{ID}, m)) = m$.

SECURITY. An IBE scheme is secure against an adaptive chosen-plaintext attack (IND-ID-CPA), if for any PPT adversary $\mathcal{A}$, we have

$$\mathsf{Adv}^{\mathsf{cpa}}_{\mathsf{IBE},\mathcal{A}}(\lambda) = \left| 2 \cdot \Pr \left[b' = b : \begin{array}{c} b \leftarrow_{\$} \{0,1\} \\ (m_0, m_1) \leftarrow \mathcal{A}^{\mathcal{O}_{ke}(\mathsf{ID}_i)}(\lambda, \mathsf{params}) \\ c \leftarrow \mathsf{IBE.Enc}(\mathsf{ID}^*, m_b) \\ b' \leftarrow \mathcal{A}(\lambda, \mathsf{params}, c) \end{array} \right] - 1 \right| \leq \mathsf{negl}(\lambda).$$

The adversary with access to key extraction oracle $\mathcal{O}_{ke}$ can make any key extraction queries except for $\mathsf{ID}_i = \mathsf{ID}^*$.

3 ASA Model of IBE Scheme

In this section, we first give models of algorithm substitution attack on IBE scheme. Then we describe definitions of the properties that the subverted algorithm satisfies. The IBE scheme has the possibility of leaking information due to its randomness in the key extraction and encryption algorithms. So we consider subverting key extraction algorithm and encryption algorithm in a IBE scheme respectively. When they are subverted respectively, they are both undetectable, and it is easy for the attacker to recover the key or message successfully by using the information leaked by the scheme.

Let $\mathsf{IBE} = (\mathsf{IBE.Setup}, \mathsf{IBE.Ext}, \mathsf{IBE.Enc}, \mathsf{IBE.Dec})$ be an honest IBE scheme. We propose a subverted IBE scheme under algorithm substitution attack which is denoted as $\widetilde{\mathsf{IBE}} = (\mathcal{BK}, \mathsf{IBE.Setup}, \widetilde{\mathsf{IBE.Ext}}, \widetilde{\mathsf{IBE.Enc}}, \mathsf{IBE.Dec})$. The subverted algorithms in the scheme are defined as follows:

- $\widetilde{\mathsf{IBE}}.\mathsf{Ext}(\mathsf{msk},\mathsf{ID},\mathsf{bk})$: Takes as input master-key msk, an identity ID and a backdoor bk, outputs the subverted private key $\tilde{d_{\mathsf{ID}}}$, where msk is obtained by the algorithm IBE.Setup in unsubverted IBE scheme.
- $\widetilde{\mathsf{IBE}}.\mathsf{Enc}(\mathsf{ID},m,\mathsf{bk})$: Takes as input an ID, a message m and a backdoor bk, outputs the subverted ciphertext $\tilde{C}$, where params are obtained by the algorithm IBE.Setup in unsubverted IBE scheme.

$\mathcal{BK}$ is a finite backdoor set. The attacker could randomly select a backdoor bk from $\mathcal{BK}$ and keep bk to himself. In a concrete IBE scheme, the key extraction algorithm and encryption algorithm are subverted respectively, but the setup algorithm and decryption algorithm are still the original algorithms in the subverted IBE scheme. The subversion is symmetric because of the same backdoor used in subverting and recovering.

3.1 Subverting Key Extraction Algorithm

Definition 1 (Undetectability for Extraction). *We say that a subverted algorithm* $\widetilde{\mathsf{IBE}}.\mathsf{Ext}$ *is undetectable if for any* PPT *detector* $\mathcal{D}$, *the advantage that* $\mathcal{D}$ *returns the right bit in the game* DET *is negligible.*

The game DET is described in Fig. 2. And the advantage that $\mathcal{D}$ returns the right bit in the game is defined as follows:

$$\mathsf{Adv}^{\mathrm{det}}_{\mathcal{D},\mathsf{IBE},\widetilde{\mathsf{IBE}}}(\lambda) = \left|2\Pr\left[\mathsf{DET}^{\mathcal{D}}_{\mathsf{IBE},\widetilde{\mathsf{IBE}}}(\lambda) = \mathsf{true}\right] - 1\right|.$$

$\mathsf{DET}^{\mathcal{D}}_{\mathsf{IBE},\widetilde{\mathsf{IBE}}}(\lambda)$	$\mathcal{O}_{\mathsf{ext}}(\mathsf{ID})$
$b \leftarrow\$ \{0,1\}$	**if** $b = 1, d_{\mathsf{ID}} \leftarrow \mathsf{IBE.Ext}(\mathsf{msk},\mathsf{ID})$
$\mathsf{msk} \leftarrow \mathsf{IBE.Setup}(\lambda)$	**else** $d_{\mathsf{ID}} \leftarrow \widetilde{\mathsf{IBE}}.\mathsf{Ext}(\mathsf{msk},\mathsf{ID},\mathsf{bk})$
$\mathsf{bk} \leftarrow\$ \mathcal{BK}$	**return** d_{ID}
$b' \leftarrow \mathcal{D}^{\mathcal{O}_{\mathsf{ext}}(\cdot)}$	
return $b' = b$	

Fig. 2. Game used to detect the subversion of the key extraction algorithm

Definition 2 (Master-key Recovery). *We say that an attacker can recover the master-key with the subverted algorithm* $\widetilde{\mathsf{IBE}}.\mathsf{Ext}$ *if for any* PPT *adversary* $\mathcal{A}$, *the advantage that* $\mathcal{A}$ *returns the master-key correctly in the game* KR *is non-negligible.*

The game KR is described in Fig. 3. And the advantage that $\mathcal{A}$ returns the master-key correctly in the game is defined as follows:

$$\mathsf{Adv}^{\mathrm{kr}}_{\mathcal{A},\widetilde{\mathsf{IBE}}}(\lambda) = \Pr\left[\mathsf{KR}^{\mathcal{A}}_{\widetilde{\mathsf{IBE}}}(\lambda) = \mathsf{true}\right].$$

$\mathsf{KR}^{\mathcal{A}}_{\widetilde{\mathsf{IBE}}}(\lambda)$	$\mathcal{O}_{\mathsf{ext}}(\mathsf{ID})$
$\mathsf{msk} \leftarrow \mathsf{IBE.Setup}(\lambda)$	$\tilde{d_{\mathsf{ID}}} \leftarrow \widetilde{\mathsf{IBE}}.\mathsf{Ext}(\mathsf{msk}, \mathsf{ID}, \mathsf{bk})$
$\mathsf{bk} \leftarrow\!\!\$\ \mathcal{BK}$	**return** $\tilde{d_{\mathsf{ID}}}$
$\mathsf{msk}' \leftarrow \mathcal{A}^{\mathcal{O}_{\mathsf{ext}}(\cdot)}(\mathsf{bk})$	
return $\mathsf{msk}' = \mathsf{msk}$	

Fig. 3. Game used to denote master-key recovery

3.2 Subverting Encryption Algorithm

Definition 3 (Undetectability for Encryption). *We say that a subverted algorithm* $\widetilde{\mathsf{IBE}}.\mathsf{Enc}$ *is undetectable if for any* PPT *detector* $\mathcal{D}$*, the advantage that* $\mathcal{D}$ *returns the right bit in the game* DET *is negligible.*

The game DET is described in Fig. 4. And the advantage that $\mathcal{D}$ returns the right bit in the game is defined as follows:

$$\mathsf{Adv}^{\mathsf{det}}_{\mathcal{D},\mathsf{IBE},\widetilde{\mathsf{IBE}}}(\lambda) = \left| 2\Pr\left[\mathsf{DET}^{\mathcal{D}}_{\mathsf{IBE},\widetilde{\mathsf{IBE}}}(\lambda) = \mathsf{true}\right] - 1 \right|.$$

$\mathsf{DET}^{\mathcal{D}}_{\mathsf{IBE},\widetilde{\mathsf{IBE}}}(\lambda)$	$\mathcal{O}_{\mathsf{enc}}(\mathsf{ID}, m)$
$b \leftarrow\!\!\$\ \{0,1\}$	**if** $b = 1, C \leftarrow \mathsf{IBE.Enc}(\mathsf{ID}, m)$
$\mathsf{params} \leftarrow \mathsf{IBE.Setup}(\lambda)$	**else** $C \leftarrow \widetilde{\mathsf{IBE}}.\mathsf{Enc}(\mathsf{ID}, m, \mathsf{bk})$
$\mathsf{bk} \leftarrow\!\!\$\ \mathcal{BK}$	**return** C
$b' \leftarrow \mathcal{D}^{\mathcal{O}_{\mathsf{enc}}(\cdot)}(\mathsf{params})$	
return $b' = b$	

Fig. 4. Game used to detect the subversion of the encryption algorithm

Definition 4 (Ciphertext Distinguishability). *We say that the original algorithm* $\mathsf{IBE.Enc}$ *and the subverted algorithm* $\widetilde{\mathsf{IBE}}.\mathsf{Enc}$ *are distinguishable in the view of an attacker if for any* PPT *adversary* $\mathcal{A}$*, the advantage that* $\mathcal{A}$ *returns the right bit in the game* CD *is non-negligible.*

The game CD is described in Fig. 5. And the advantage that $\mathcal{A}$ returns the right bit in the game is defined as follows:

$$\mathsf{Adv}^{\mathsf{cd}}_{\mathcal{A},\mathsf{IBE},\widetilde{\mathsf{IBE}}}(\lambda) = \left| 2\Pr\left[\mathsf{CD}^{\mathcal{A}}_{\mathsf{IBE},\widetilde{\mathsf{IBE}}}(\lambda) = \mathsf{true}\right] - 1 \right|.$$

$\mathsf{CD}^{\mathcal{A}}_{\mathsf{IBE},\widetilde{\mathsf{IBE}}}(\lambda)$	$\mathcal{O}_{\mathsf{enc}}(\mathsf{ID}, m)$
$b \leftarrow\$ \{0,1\}$	**if** $b = 1, C \leftarrow \mathsf{IBE.Enc}(\mathsf{ID}, m)$
$\mathsf{params} \leftarrow \mathsf{IBE.Setup}(\lambda)$	**else** $C \leftarrow \widetilde{\mathsf{IBE}}.\mathsf{Enc}(\mathsf{ID}, m, \mathsf{bk})$
$\mathsf{bk} \leftarrow\$ \mathcal{BK}$	**return** C
$b' \leftarrow \mathcal{A}^{\mathcal{O}_{\mathsf{enc}}(\cdot)}(\mathsf{params}, \mathsf{bk})$	
return $b' = b$	

Fig. 5. Game used to denote ciphertext distinguishability

Definition 5 (Message Recovery). *We say that an attacker can recover the message from the subverted algorithm* $\widetilde{\mathsf{IBE}}.\mathsf{Enc}$ *if for any* PPT *adversary* $\mathcal{A}$, *the advantage that* $\mathcal{A}$ *returns the message correctly in the game* MR *is non-negligible.*

The game MR is described in Fig. 6. And the advantage that $\mathcal{A}$ returns the message correctly in the game is defined as follows:

$$\mathsf{Adv}^{\mathrm{mr}}_{\mathcal{A},\widetilde{\mathsf{IBE}}}(\lambda) = \Pr\left[\mathsf{MR}^{\mathcal{A}}_{\widetilde{\mathsf{IBE}}}(\lambda) = \mathsf{true}\right]$$

$\mathsf{MR}^{\mathcal{A}}_{\widetilde{\mathsf{IBE}}}(\lambda)$	$\mathcal{O}_{\mathsf{enc}}(\mathsf{ID})$
$m \leftarrow\$ \{0,1\}^n$	$\tilde{C} \leftarrow \widetilde{\mathsf{IBE}}.\mathsf{Enc}(\mathsf{ID}, m, \mathsf{bk})$
$\mathsf{params} \leftarrow \mathsf{IBE.Setup}(\lambda)$	**return** $\tilde{C}$
$\mathsf{bk} \leftarrow\$ \mathcal{BK}$	
$m' \leftarrow \mathcal{A}^{\mathcal{O}_{\mathsf{enc}}(\cdot)}(\mathsf{params}, \mathsf{bk})$	
return $m' = m$	

Fig. 6. Game used to denote message recovery

4 Instantiations

In this section, we mount ASAs on two classical IBE schemes. We will subvert the key extraction and encryption algorithms in each IBE scheme separately and show that subversions are effective. One is Waters-IBE scheme [6]. The other is BB-IBE scheme [5]. The two schemes are both IND-ID-CPA secure under the DBDH assumption. The reason why we attack them is that randoms are used both in the key extraction algorithm and encryption algorithm. In addition, the number of randoms is different in the two schemes. In fact, Waters-IBE scheme is a modification of BB-IBE scheme. BB-IBE scheme converts an identity to a vector, while Waters-IBE scheme uses a string as an identity and stores the sequence number of a bit which is equal to 1 in an identity space. We consider subversions of Waters-IBE scheme first and then apply the similar approach to BB-IBE scheme.

4.1 ASA on Waters-IBE Scheme

Waters-IBE scheme, denoted as $\mathsf{W} = (\mathsf{W.Setup}, \mathsf{W.Ext}, \mathsf{W.Enc}, \mathsf{W.Dec})$, was presented by Brent Waters [6]. The details are shown in Fig. 7. We can see that both W.Ext and W.Enc have randomness, so it could be subverted in an undetectable method to leak secret information and an attacker could recover the master-key or message from the exfiltrated information.

$\mathsf{W.Setup}(\lambda)$	$\mathsf{W.Ext}(g_2^\alpha, \mathsf{ID})$
$(\mathbb{G}_1, \mathbb{G}_2, \hat{e}) \leftarrow \mathcal{IG}(1^\lambda)$	$\mathsf{ID} \leftarrow\!\$ \{0,1\}^n$
$g \leftarrow\!\$ \mathbb{G}_1, g_2 \leftarrow\!\$ \mathbb{G}_1, u' \leftarrow\!\$ \mathbb{G}_1$	**for** $i = 1, \ldots, n$
$\alpha \leftarrow\!\$ \mathbb{Z}_q, g_1 = g^\alpha$	**if** $\mathsf{ID}_i = 1$ **then** $i \in \mathcal{ID}$
for $i = 1, \ldots, n$	$r \leftarrow\!\$ \mathbb{Z}_q$
$u_i \leftarrow\!\$ \mathbb{G}_1,\ U = (u_i)$	$d_{\mathsf{ID}} = (g_2^\alpha (u' \prod_{i \in \mathcal{ID}} u_i)^r, g^r)$
$\mathsf{params} = (g, g_1, g_2, u', U), \mathsf{msk} = g_2^\alpha$	
$\mathsf{W.Enc}(\mathsf{ID}, m)$	$\mathsf{W.Dec}(d_{\mathsf{ID}}, C)$
$t \leftarrow\!\$ \mathbb{Z}_q$	*parse* C *as* (C_1, C_2, C_3)
$C = (\hat{e}(g_1, g_2)^t m, g^t, (u' \prod_{i \in \mathcal{ID}} u_i)^t)$	*parse* d_{ID} *as* (d_1, d_2)
	$C_1 \dfrac{\hat{e}(d_2, C_3)}{\hat{e}(d_1, C_2)} = m$

Fig. 7. Waters-IBE scheme

We consider subverting the key extraction algorithm W.Ext first. The subverted algorithm $\widetilde{\mathsf{W}}.\mathsf{Ext}$ is shown in Algorithm 1. We show that $\widetilde{\mathsf{W}}.\mathsf{Ext}$ is undetectable when utilizing hash function with smooth entropy [15,16].

Theorem 1. *The subverted algorithm $\widetilde{\mathsf{W}}.\mathsf{Ext}$ described in Algorithm 1 is undetectable if* H *is a hash function with smooth entropy. Let $\mathcal{D}$ be a* PPT *detector in Fig. 2, we can build an SE adversary $\mathcal{B}$ such that*

$$\mathsf{Adv}^{\mathrm{det}}_{\mathcal{D},\mathsf{W},\widetilde{\mathsf{W}}}(\lambda) \leq 2\mathsf{Adv}^{\mathrm{se}}_{\mathcal{B},\mathsf{H}}(\lambda) \leq \mathsf{negl}(\lambda).$$

Proof. We construct a detector $\mathcal{D}$ plays the game DET against the undetectability of $\widetilde{\mathsf{W}}.\mathsf{Ext}$. Let $\mathsf{W_i}$ be an event that $\mathcal{D}$ wins in $\mathsf{Game_i}$. Let $\Pr[\mathsf{W_i}]$ be the

Algorithm 1. $\widetilde{\mathsf{W}}.\mathsf{Ext}(\mathsf{ID}, g_2^{\alpha}, \mathsf{bk})$

Input: identity ID, master-key g_2^{α}, backdoor bk
Output: subverted private key $\tilde{d_{\mathsf{ID}}}$

initialize $Map : \{0,1\}^n \rightarrow \mathbb{Z}$
initialize $\mathsf{H} : Dom(\mathsf{bk}) \times \{0,1\}^n \times \mathbb{Z} \rightarrow \mathbb{Z}_q$
$\mathsf{bk} \leftarrow_\$ \mathcal{BK}$
if $\mathsf{ID} \in Dom(Map)$:
then $r \leftarrow_\$ \mathsf{H}(\mathsf{bk}, \mathsf{ID}, Map[\mathsf{ID}])$, $Map[\mathsf{ID}] \leftarrow Map[\mathsf{ID}] + 1$
else $Map[\mathsf{ID}] \leftarrow 0$, $r \leftarrow_\$ \mathsf{H}(\mathsf{bk}, \mathsf{ID}, 0)$
for $i = 1, \ldots, n$
if $\mathsf{ID}_i = 1 \mathbf{then} i \in \mathcal{ID}$
$\tilde{d_{\mathsf{ID}}} \leftarrow (g_2^{\alpha}(u' \prod_{i \in \mathcal{ID}} u_i)^r, g^r)$

probability that $\mathcal{D}$ wins in $\mathsf{Game_i}$. The details of the two games are given as follows.

- $\mathsf{Game_0}$: It is the initial game described in Fig. 2. So, we have

$$\mathsf{Adv}^{\mathsf{det}}_{\mathcal{D},\mathsf{W},\widetilde{\mathsf{W}}}(\lambda) = |2\Pr[\mathsf{W_0}] - 1|.$$

- $\mathsf{Game_1}$: Same as $\mathsf{Game_0}$ except that when $b = 0$, in $\widetilde{\mathsf{W}}.\mathsf{Ext}$, we replace the hash function H with a random choice from $\mathbb{Z}_q$. So it is truly random in the view of the detector. Then we have

$$\Pr[\mathsf{W_1}] = \frac{1}{2}.$$

Besides, we can use $\mathcal{D}$ to build an SE adversary $\mathcal{B}$ who plays the game SE and outputs the same as $\mathcal{D}$. We can use the Difference Lemma to obtain

$$|\Pr[\mathsf{W_0}] - \Pr[\mathsf{W_1}]| \leq \mathsf{Adv}^{\mathsf{se}}_{\mathcal{B},\mathsf{H}}(\lambda).$$

In the view of the detector, it is indistinguishable between $\mathsf{Game_0}$ and $\mathsf{Game_1}$ due to the entropy smoothing hash function, namely, the detector cannot detect the subversion of W.Ext. Putting the above together, we have:

$$\begin{aligned}\mathsf{Adv}^{\mathsf{det}}_{\mathcal{D},\mathsf{W},\widetilde{\mathsf{W}}}(\lambda) &:= |2\Pr[\mathsf{W_0}] - 1| \\ &= |2\Pr[\mathsf{W_0}] - 2\Pr[\mathsf{W_1}] + 2\Pr[\mathsf{W_1}] - 1| \\ &\leq 2|\Pr[\mathsf{W_0}] - \Pr[\mathsf{W_1}]| + |2\Pr[\mathsf{W_1}] - 1| \\ &\leq 2\mathsf{Adv}^{\mathsf{se}}_{\mathcal{B},\mathsf{H}}(\lambda)\end{aligned}$$

□

Theorem 2. *The subverted algorithm* $\widetilde{\mathsf{W}}.\mathsf{Ext}$ *in Algorithm 1 is master-key recoverable, if* H *is a hash function with smooth entropy. Let* $\mathcal{A}$ *be an adversary who plays the game* KR*, then we have*

$$\mathsf{Adv}^{\mathrm{kr}}_{\mathcal{A},\widetilde{\mathsf{W}}}(\lambda) = 1$$

Proof. We assume that in game KR, the adversary $\mathcal{A}$ makes a private key query and obtains the subverted private key $\tilde{d_{\mathsf{ID}}}$ corresponding to the identity ID he queries. The backdoor bk is only known to $\mathcal{A}$ and params is public. Parse $\tilde{d_{\mathsf{ID}}}$ as $(\tilde{d_1}, \tilde{d_2})$. Then $\mathcal{A}$ has $\tilde{d_1}$ which contains the master-key and is calculated by a random r. If $\mathcal{A}$ knows the calculation of the random r, then he can use the known information to recover the master-key through

$$\frac{\tilde{d_1}}{(u' \prod_{i \in \mathcal{ID}} u_i)^r} = g_2^{\alpha}.$$

Since H is known to $\mathcal{A}$, $\mathcal{A}$ can obtain the random r by the calculation of H. Then we have $\Pr\left[\mathsf{KR}^{\mathcal{A}}_{\widetilde{\mathsf{W}}}(\lambda) = \mathsf{true}\right] = 1$, and the theorem follows. □

We notice that there is a random in encryption algorithm $\mathsf{W.Enc}$. It is similar to the key extraction algorithm $\mathsf{W.Ext}$, so we could use the same idea to subvert $\mathsf{W.Enc}$. The subverted algorithm $\widetilde{\mathsf{W}}.\mathsf{Enc}$ is shown in Algorithm 2. Similar to $\widetilde{\mathsf{W}}.\mathsf{Ext}$, we can prove that $\widetilde{\mathsf{W}}.\mathsf{Enc}$ is an undetectable subversion of $\mathsf{W.Enc}$ and is message recoverable.

Algorithm 2. $\widetilde{\mathsf{W}}.\mathsf{Enc}(\mathsf{ID}, m, \mathsf{bk})$

Input: identity ID, message m, backdoor bk
Output: subverted ciphertext $\tilde{C}$

initialize $Map : \{0,1\}^n \to \mathbb{Z}$
initialize $\mathsf{H} : Dom(\mathsf{bk}) \times \{0,1\}^n \times \mathbb{Z} \to \mathbb{Z}_q$
$\mathsf{bk} \leftarrow_{\$} \mathcal{BK}$
if $\mathsf{ID} \in Dom(Map)$:
then $t \leftarrow_{\$} \mathsf{H}(\mathsf{bk}, \mathsf{ID}, Map[\mathsf{ID}])$, $Map[\mathsf{ID}] \leftarrow Map[\mathsf{ID}] + 1$
else $Map[\mathsf{ID}] \leftarrow 0$, $t \leftarrow_{\$} \mathsf{H}(\mathsf{bk}, \mathsf{ID}, 0)$
$\tilde{C} \leftarrow (\hat{e}(g_1, g_2)^t m, g^t, (u' \prod_{i \in \mathcal{ID}} u_i)^t)$

Theorem 3. *The subverted algorithm* $\widetilde{\mathsf{W}}.\mathsf{Enc}$ *described in Algorithm 2 is an undetectable subversion of* $\mathsf{W.Enc}$ *if* H *is a hash function with smooth entropy. Let* $\mathcal{D}$ *be a* PPT *detector in Fig. 4, we can build an SE adversary* $\mathcal{B}$ *such that*

$$\mathsf{Adv}^{\mathrm{det}}_{\mathcal{D},\mathsf{W},\widetilde{\mathsf{W}}}(\lambda) \leq 2\mathsf{Adv}^{\mathrm{se}}_{\mathcal{B},\mathsf{H}}(\lambda) \leq \mathsf{negl}(\lambda).$$

Proof. Same as the proof of Theorem 1 expect that we construct a detector $\mathcal{D}$ plays the game DET against the undetectability of $\widetilde{\mathsf{W}}.\mathsf{Enc}$. The details of the two games are given as follows.

- Game_0: Described in Fig. 4. We have $\Pr[\mathsf{W}_0] = \Pr\left[\mathsf{DET}^{\mathcal{D}}_{\mathsf{W},\widetilde{\mathsf{W}}} = \mathsf{true}\right]$, then
$$\mathsf{Adv}^{\mathrm{det}}_{\mathcal{D},\mathsf{W},\widetilde{\mathsf{W}}}(\lambda) = |2\Pr[\mathsf{W}_0] - 1|.$$
- Game_1: Same as Game_0 except that when $b = 0$, in $\widetilde{\mathsf{W}}.\mathsf{Enc}$, we replace the hash function H with a random choice from $\mathbb{Z}_q$. So it is truly random in the view of the detector. Then we have
$$\Pr[\mathsf{W}_1] = \frac{1}{2}.$$
Same as the above, we build an SE adversary $\mathcal{B}$. We can use the Difference Lemma to obtain $|\Pr[\mathsf{W}_0] - \Pr[\mathsf{W}_1]| \leq \mathsf{Adv}^{\mathsf{se}}_{\mathcal{B},\mathsf{H}}(\lambda)$. In the view of the detector, it is indistinguishable between Game_0 and Game_1 due to the entropy smoothing hash function, namely the detector cannot detect the subversion of W.Enc. Putting the above together, we have:
$$\begin{aligned}\mathsf{Adv}^{\mathrm{det}}_{\mathcal{D},\mathsf{W},\widetilde{\mathsf{W}}}(\lambda) &:= |2\Pr[\mathsf{W}_0] - 1| \\ &= |2\Pr[\mathsf{W}_0] - 2\Pr[\mathsf{W}_1] + 2\Pr[\mathsf{W}_1] - 1| \\ &\leq 2|\Pr[\mathsf{W}_0] - \Pr[\mathsf{W}_1]| + |2\Pr[\mathsf{W}_1] - 1| \\ &\leq 2\mathsf{Adv}^{\mathsf{se}}_{\mathcal{B},\mathsf{H}}(\lambda)\end{aligned}$$

□

An adversary can recover the message based on the property of ciphertext distinguishability.

Theorem 4. *The subverted algorithm* $\widetilde{\mathsf{W}}.\mathsf{Enc}$ *is distinguishable from* W.Enc *in the view of an attacker, if* H *is a computational hash function with smooth entropy. Let* $\mathcal{A}$ *be an adversary who plays the game* CD*, then we have*
$$\mathsf{Adv}^{\mathrm{cd}}_{\mathcal{A},\mathsf{W},\widetilde{\mathsf{W}}}(\lambda) = 1$$

Proof. Since H is computational and is known to the adversary, $\mathcal{A}$ can calculate a subverted ciphertext $\tilde{C}$ by himself. When $\mathcal{A}$ makes a query of identity ID and message m, the challenger returns a ciphertext C to him, he can tell the difference between $\tilde{C}$ and C and return the right guessing bit b'. So we have $\Pr\left[\mathsf{CD}^{\mathcal{A}}_{\mathsf{W},\widetilde{\mathsf{W}}}(\lambda) = \mathsf{true}\right] = 1$. Then the theorem follows. □

Theorem 5. *The subverted algorithm* $\widetilde{\mathsf{W}}.\mathsf{Enc}$ *in Algorithm 2 is message recoverable, if* H *is a computational hash function with smooth entropy. Let* $\mathcal{A}$ *be an adversary who plays the game* MR*, then we have*
$$\mathsf{Adv}^{\mathrm{mr}}_{\mathcal{A},\widetilde{\mathsf{W}}}(\lambda) = 1$$

Proof. We assume that in game MR, $\mathcal{A}$ makes a ciphertext query and obtains the subverted ciphertext $\tilde{C}$ corresponding to the identity ID he queries. The backdoor bk is only known to the adversary and params is public. Parse $\tilde{C}$ as $(\tilde{C_1}, \tilde{C_2}, \tilde{C_3})$, then the adversary has $\tilde{C_1}$ which contains the message and is calculated by a random t. Since H is computational and is known to the adversary, $\mathcal{A}$ can get the random t by the calculation of H, then he can use the known information to recover the message through

$$\frac{\tilde{C_1}}{\hat{e}(g_1, g_2)^t} = m.$$

Then we have $\Pr\left[\mathsf{MR}^{\mathcal{A}}_{\widetilde{\mathsf{W}}}(\lambda) = \mathsf{true}\right] = 1$, and the theorem follows. □

4.2 ASA on BB-IBE Scheme

BB-IBE scheme was presented by Dan Boneh and Xavier Boyen [5], shown in Fig. 8. We denote the scheme as $\mathsf{BB} = (\mathsf{BB.Setup}, \mathsf{BB.Ext}, \mathsf{BB.Enc}, \mathsf{BB.Dec})$. We notice that they use a matrix when calculating the private key while Waters uses a vector. Besides, they denoted a family of hash functions as $\{\mathsf{H}_k : \{0,1\}^w \rightarrow \Sigma^n\}_{k\in\mathcal{K}}$, where Σ is an alphabet and $|\Sigma| = s$.

$\mathsf{BB.Setup}(\lambda)$

- $(\mathbb{G}_1, \mathbb{G}_2, \hat{e}) \leftarrow \mathcal{IG}(1^\lambda)$
- $g \leftarrow\!\!\$\ \mathbb{G}_1^*, g_2 \leftarrow\!\!\$\ \mathbb{G}_1$
- $\alpha \leftarrow\!\!\$\ \mathbb{Z}_q, g_1 = g^\alpha$
- $\Sigma = \{1, \ldots, s\}$
- $k \leftarrow\!\!\$\ \mathcal{K},\ \mathsf{H}_k : \{0,1\}^w \rightarrow \Sigma^n$
- **for** $i = 1, \ldots, n$
  - **for** $j = 1, \ldots, s$
    - $u_{i,j} \leftarrow\!\!\$\ \mathbb{G}_1,\ U = (u_{i,j})$
- $\mathsf{params} = (g, g_1, g_2, U, k), \mathsf{msk} = g_2^\alpha$

$\mathsf{BB.Ext}(g_2^\alpha, \mathsf{ID})$

- $\mathsf{ID} \leftarrow\!\!\$\ \{0,1\}^w$
- $\boldsymbol{a} = \mathsf{H}_k(\mathsf{ID}) = a_1 \ldots a_n$
- $r_1, \ldots r_n \leftarrow\!\!\$\ \mathbb{Z}_q$
- $d_{\mathsf{ID}} = (g_2^\alpha \prod_{i=1}^{n} u_{i,a_i}^{r_i}, g^{r_1}, \ldots, g^{r_n})$

$\mathsf{BB.Enc}(\ \mathsf{ID}, m)$

- $\boldsymbol{a} = \mathsf{H}_k(\mathsf{ID}) = a_1 \ldots a_n$
- $t \leftarrow\!\!\$\ \mathbb{Z}_q$
- $C = (\hat{e}(g_1, g_2)^t m, g^t, u_{1,a_1}^t, \ldots, u_{n,a_n}^t)$

$\mathsf{BB.Dec}(d_{\mathsf{ID}}, C)$

- *parse* C *as* $(A, B, C_1, \ldots, C_n)$
- *parse* d_{ID} *as* $(d_0, d_1, \ldots, d_n)$
- $A \cdot \frac{\prod_{j=1}^{n} \hat{e}(C_j, d_j)}{\hat{e}(B, d_0)} = m$

Fig. 8. BB-IBE scheme

We consider subverting the algorithm $\mathsf{BB.Ext}$ first. The subverted algorithm $\widetilde{\mathsf{BB.Ext}}$ is shown in Algorithm 3. Since there are n randoms in the scheme, we use two hash functions with smooth entropy, H_1 to generate the first random and H_2 to generate the rest $n-1$ randoms by iteration.

Algorithm 3. $\widetilde{\mathsf{BB}}.\mathsf{Ext}(\mathsf{ID}, g_2^{\alpha}, \mathsf{bk})$

Input: identity ID, master-key g_2^{α}, backdoor bk
Output: subverted private key $\tilde{d_{\mathsf{ID}}}$

initialize $\mathsf{Map} : \{0,1\}^w \to \mathbb{Z}$
initialize $\mathsf{H}_1 : Dom(\mathsf{bk}) \times \{0,1\}^w \times \mathbb{Z} \to \mathbb{Z}_q$, $\mathsf{H}_2 : Dom(\mathsf{bk}) \times \mathbb{Z}_q \to \mathbb{Z}_q$
$\mathsf{bk} \leftarrow_{\$} \mathcal{BK}$
if $\mathsf{ID} \in Dom(Map)$:
then $r_1 \leftarrow_{\$} \mathsf{H}_1(\mathsf{bk}, \mathsf{ID}, Map[\mathsf{ID}])$, $Map[\mathsf{ID}] \leftarrow Map[\mathsf{ID}] + 1$
else $Map[\mathsf{ID}] \leftarrow 0$, $r_1 \leftarrow_{\$} \mathsf{H}_1(\mathsf{bk}, \mathsf{ID}, 0)$
for $j = 2, .., n$:
$r_j \leftarrow \mathsf{H}_2(\mathsf{bk}, r_{j-1})$
$a = \mathsf{H}_k(\mathsf{ID}) = (a_1, ..., a_n)$
$\tilde{d_{\mathsf{ID}}} \leftarrow (g_2^{\alpha} \prod_{i=1}^{n} u_{i,a_i}^{r_i}, g^{r_1}, ..., g^{r_n})$

Theorem 6. *The subverted algorithm $\widetilde{\mathsf{BB}}.\mathsf{Ext}$ described in Algorithm 3 is an undetectable subversion of* BB.Ext *if H_1 and H_2 are hash functions with smooth entropy. Let $\mathcal{D}$ be a* PPT *detector in Fig. 2, we can build two SE adversaries $\mathcal{B}_1$ and $\mathcal{B}$ such that*

$$\mathsf{Adv}^{\mathrm{det}}_{\mathcal{D},\mathsf{BB},\widetilde{\mathsf{BB}}}(\lambda) \le 2\mathsf{Adv}^{\mathrm{se}}_{\mathcal{B}_1,\mathsf{H}_1}(\lambda) + 2(n-1)\mathsf{Adv}^{\mathrm{se}}_{\mathcal{B},\mathsf{H}_2}(\lambda) \le \mathsf{negl}(\lambda).$$

Proof. We construct a detector $\mathcal{D}$ plays the game DET against the undetectability of $\widetilde{\mathsf{BB}}.\mathsf{Ext}$. Let $\mathsf{W_i}$ be an event that $\mathcal{D}$ wins in $\mathsf{Game_i}$. Let $\Pr[\mathsf{W_i}]$ be the probability that $\mathcal{D}$ wins in $\mathsf{Game_i}$. The details of the games are given as follows.

- $\mathsf{Game_0}$: Described in Fig. 2. We have $\Pr[\mathsf{W_0}] = \Pr\left[\mathsf{DET}^{\mathcal{D}}_{\mathsf{BB},\widetilde{\mathsf{BB}}}(\lambda) = \mathsf{true}\right]$, then

$$\mathsf{Adv}^{\mathrm{det}}_{\mathcal{D},\mathsf{BB},\widetilde{\mathsf{BB}}}(\lambda) = |2\Pr[\mathsf{W_0}] - 1|.$$

- $\mathsf{Game_1}$: Same as $\mathsf{Game_0}$ except that when $b = 0$, in $\widetilde{\mathsf{BB}}.\mathsf{Ext}$, we replace the hash function H_1 with a random choice from $\mathbb{Z}_q$. Then we can use $\mathcal{D}$ to build an SE adversary $\mathcal{B}_1$ who plays the game SE against H_1 and outputs the same as $\mathcal{D}$. We can use the Difference Lemma to obtain

$$|\Pr[\mathsf{W_0}] - \Pr[\mathsf{W_1}]| \le \mathsf{Adv}^{\mathrm{se}}_{\mathcal{B}_1,\mathsf{H}_1}(\lambda).$$

- Game_2: Same as Game_1 except that when $b = 0$, in $\widetilde{\mathsf{BB}}.\mathsf{Ext}$, we replace the hash function H_2 with $n-1$ random choices from $\mathbb{Z}_q$. So it is truly random in the view of the detector. Then we have

$$\Pr[\mathsf{W}_2] = \frac{1}{2}.$$

Then we use $\mathcal{D}$ to build an SE adversary $\mathcal{B}_2$ against H_2. Based on Game_1, we introduce a sequence of n hybrid games, called Hybrid 1, Hybrid 2, ..., Hybrid n. In Hybrid k, we let the first $k-1$ values randomly chosen from $\mathbb{Z}_q$ and the rest $n-k+1$ calculated by H_2. Let p_k be the probability that $\mathcal{B}_2$ wins in Hybrid k. We notice that Hybrid 1 is equal to $\mathcal{B}_2$ outputs 1 in game SE and Hybrid n is equal to $\mathcal{B}_2$ outputs 0 in game SE, so we have

$$\mathsf{Adv}^{\mathsf{se}}_{\mathcal{B}_2,\mathsf{H}_2}(\lambda) = |p_1 - p_n|.$$

We build an adversary $\mathcal{B}$ that plays a role of challenger to $\mathcal{B}_2$ and outputs the same as $\mathcal{B}_2$. $\mathcal{B}$ first chose a random w from a set $\{2,\ldots,n\}$, when he receives r_j from the challenger, he set the first $w-2$ are randomly chosen from $\mathbb{Z}_q$, $r_w = r_j$, and the rest $n-w$ are calculated by H_2. Then we have $\Pr[\mathsf{W}_1|w=k] = p_{k-1}$ and $\Pr[\mathsf{W}_2|w=k] = p_k$. Therefore,

$$\Pr[\mathsf{W}_1] = \sum_{k=2}^{n} \Pr[\mathsf{W}_1|w=k]\Pr[w=k] = \frac{1}{n-1}\sum_{k=2}^{n} p_{k-1}$$

$$\Pr[\mathsf{W}_2] = \sum_{k=2}^{n} \Pr[\mathsf{W}_2|w=k]\Pr[w=k] = \frac{1}{n-1}\sum_{k=2}^{n} p_{k}$$

$$\begin{aligned}\mathsf{Adv}^{\mathsf{se}}_{\mathcal{B},\mathsf{H}_2}(\lambda) &= |\Pr[\mathsf{W}_1] - \Pr[\mathsf{W}_2]| \\ &= \left|\frac{1}{n-1}\sum_{k=2}^{n} p_{k-1} - \frac{1}{n-1}\sum_{k=2}^{n} p_k\right| \\ &= \frac{1}{n-1}|p_1 - p_n|\end{aligned}$$

We have $\mathsf{Adv}^{\mathsf{se}}_{\mathcal{B}_2,\mathsf{H}_2}(\lambda) = |p_1 - p_n| = (n-1)\mathsf{Adv}^{\mathsf{se}}_{\mathcal{B},\mathsf{H}_2}(\lambda)$. Putting the above together, we have:

$$\begin{aligned}\mathsf{Adv}^{\mathsf{det}}_{\mathcal{D},\mathsf{BB},\widetilde{\mathsf{BB}}}(\lambda) &:= |2\Pr[\mathsf{W}_0] - 1| \\ &= |2\Pr[\mathsf{W}_0] - 2\Pr[\mathsf{W}_1] + 2\Pr[\mathsf{W}_1] - 2\Pr[\mathsf{W}_2] + 2\Pr[\mathsf{W}_2] - 1| \\ &\le 2|\Pr[\mathsf{W}_0] - \Pr[\mathsf{W}_1]| + 2|\Pr[\mathsf{W}_1] - \Pr[\mathsf{W}_2]| + |2\Pr[\mathsf{W}_2] - 1| \\ &\le 2\mathsf{Adv}^{\mathsf{se}}_{\mathcal{B}_1,\mathsf{H}_1}(\lambda) + 2(n-1)\mathsf{Adv}^{\mathsf{se}}_{\mathcal{B},\mathsf{H}_2}(\lambda)\end{aligned}$$

□

Theorem 7. *The subverted algorithm* $\widetilde{\mathsf{BB}}.\mathsf{Ext}$ *in Algorithm 3 is master-key recoverable, if* H_1 *and* H_2 *are computational hash functions with smooth entropy. Let* $\mathcal{A}$ *be an adversary who plays the game* KR, *then we have*

$$\mathsf{Adv}^{\mathsf{kr}}_{\mathcal{A},\widetilde{\mathsf{BB}}}(\lambda) = 1$$

Proof. We assume that in game KR, $\mathcal{A}$ makes a private key query and obtains the subverted private key $\widetilde{d_{\mathsf{ID}}}$ corresponding to the identity ID he queries. The backdoor bk is only known to the adversary and params is public. Parse $\widetilde{d_{\mathsf{ID}}}$ as $(\tilde{d}_0, \tilde{d}_1, \ldots, \tilde{d}_n)$, then the adversary has $\tilde{d}_0$ which contains the master-key and is calculated by randoms $(r_1, \ldots, r_n)$. Since H_1 and H_2 are computational and known to the adversary, $\mathcal{A}$ can get the randoms $(r_1, \ldots, r_n)$ by the calculation of H_1 and H_2. Then he can use the known information to recover the master-key through

$$\frac{\tilde{d}_0}{\prod_{i=1}^{n} u_{i,a_i}^{r_i}} = g_2^{\alpha}.$$

Then we have $\Pr\left[\mathsf{KR}^{\mathcal{A}}_{\widetilde{\mathsf{BB}}}(\lambda) = \mathsf{true}\right] = 1$, and the theorem follows. □

The random t in algorithm $\mathsf{BB}.\mathsf{Enc}$ is uniformly distributed in the same set $\mathbb{Z}_q$ as in Waters-IBE, so that we could use the same idea to subvert $\mathsf{BB}.\mathsf{Enc}$. It is described in Algorithm 4. The analyses of the properties of the subverting algorithm $\widetilde{\mathsf{BB}}.\mathsf{Enc}$ are the same as $\widetilde{\mathsf{W}}.\mathsf{Enc}$ in Waters-IBE.

Algorithm 4. $\widetilde{\mathsf{BB}}.\mathsf{Enc}(\mathsf{ID}, m, \mathsf{bk})$

Input: identity ID, message m, backdoor bk
Output: subverted ciphertext $\tilde{C}$

initialize $\mathsf{Map} : \{0,1\}^w \to \mathbb{Z}$
initialize $\mathsf{H}_1 : Dom(\mathsf{bk}) \times \{0,1\}^w \times \mathbb{Z} \to \mathbb{Z}_q$
$\boldsymbol{a} = \mathsf{H}_k(\mathsf{ID}) = (a_1, ..., a_n)$
$\mathsf{bk} \leftarrow_{\$} \mathcal{BK}$
if $\mathsf{ID} \in Dom(Map)$:
 then $t \leftarrow_{\$} \mathsf{H}_1(\mathsf{bk}, \mathsf{ID}, Map[\mathsf{ID}])$, $Map[\mathsf{ID}] \leftarrow Map[\mathsf{ID}] + 1$
else $Map[\mathsf{ID}] \leftarrow 0$, $t \leftarrow_{\$} \mathsf{H}_1(\mathsf{bk}, \mathsf{ID}, 0)$
$\tilde{C} \leftarrow (\hat{e}(g_1, g_2)^t m, g^t, u_{1,a_1}^t, \ldots, u_{n,a_n}^t)$

---

5 Conclusion

Through the algorithm substitution attack on specific IBE schemes, we notice that it is very easy for an attacker to subvert the algorithms in the scheme and make the scheme leak secret information. In addition, the attacker can effectively recover the key or the message. For the attacker, he can distinguish whether the information is subverted. Then he could use the information to recover the secret he wants. In the view of the users, the subversion is undetectable and the subverted information is valid. The attack is very dangerous and may be used in our daily life. Our next work is to study some possible defences such as unique ciphertext, cryptographic reverse firewall, etc. Based on this, we try to find an effective way in the future, aiming to protect IBE scheme from leaking secret information even though it is already subverted by ASA.

Acknowledgements. The work is supported by the National Natural Science Foundation of China (Grant No. 62122092 and Grant No. 62032005). The work of Lin Liu is supported by the National Natural Science Foundation of China (Grant No. 62102430) and the Natural Science Foundation of Hunan Province, China (Grant No. 2021JJ40688), and the Science Research Plan Program by NUDT (Grant No. ZK22-50).

References

1. Shamir, A.: Identity-Based Cryptosystems and Signature Schemes. Springer, Berlin, Heidelberg (1984). https://doi.org/10.1007/3-540-39568-7_5
2. Boneh, D., Franklin, M.: Identity-based encryption from the Weil pairing. In: Kilian, J. (ed.) CRYPTO 2001. LNCS, vol. 2139, pp. 213–229. Springer, Heidelberg (2001). https://doi.org/10.1007/3-540-44647-8_13
3. Cocks, C.: An identity based encryption scheme based on quadratic residues. In: Honary, B. (ed.) Cryptography and Coding 2001. LNCS, vol. 2260, pp. 360–363. Springer, Heidelberg (2001). https://doi.org/10.1007/3-540-45325-3_32
4. Dan, B., Boyen, X.: Efficient Selective-ID Secure Identity-Based Encryption Without Random Oracles. Springer, Berlin, Heidelberg (2004). https://doi.org/10.1007/978-3-540-24676-3_14
5. Boneh, D., Boyen, X.: Secure identity based encryption without random oracles. In: Franklin, M. (ed.) CRYPTO 2004. LNCS, vol. 3152, pp. 443–459. Springer, Heidelberg (2004). https://doi.org/10.1007/978-3-540-28628-8_27
6. Waters, B.: Efficient identity-based encryption without random oracles. In: Cramer, R. (ed.) EUROCRYPT 2005. LNCS, vol. 3494, pp. 114–127. Springer, Heidelberg (2005). https://doi.org/10.1007/11426639_7
7. Young, A., Yung, M.: The dark side of black-box cryptography or: should we trust capstone? In: Koblitz, N. (ed.) CRYPTO 1996. LNCS, vol. 1109, pp. 89–103. Springer, Heidelberg (1996). https://doi.org/10.1007/3-540-68697-5_8
8. Young, A., Yung, M.: Kleptography: using cryptography against cryptography. In: Fumy, W. (ed.) EUROCRYPT 1997. LNCS, vol. 1233, pp. 62–74. Springer, Heidelberg (1997). https://doi.org/10.1007/3-540-69053-0_6
9. Bellare, M., Paterson, K.G., Rogaway, P.: Security of symmetric encryption against mass surveillance. In: Garay, J.A., Gennaro, R. (eds.) CRYPTO 2014. LNCS, vol. 8616, pp. 1–19. Springer, Heidelberg (2014). https://doi.org/10.1007/978-3-662-44371-2_1
10. Bellare, M., Jaeger, J., Kane, D.: Mass-surveillance without the state: strongly undetectable algorithm-substitution attacks. ACM (2015)
11. Ateniese, G., Magri, B., Venturi, D.: Subversion-resilient signature schemes. In: Proceedings of the 22nd ACM SIGSAC Conference ACM (2015)

12. Armour, M., Poettering, B.: Subverting decryption in AEAD. In: Albrecht, M. (ed.) IMACC 2019. LNCS, vol. 11929, pp. 22–41. Springer, Cham (2019). https://doi.org/10.1007/978-3-030-35199-1_2
13. Chen, R., Huang, X., Yung, M.: Subvert KEM to break DEM: practical algorithm-substitution attacks on public-key encryption. In: Moriai, S., Wang, H. (eds.) ASIACRYPT 2020. LNCS, vol. 12492, pp. 98–128. Springer, Cham (2020). https://doi.org/10.1007/978-3-030-64834-3_4
14. Dodis, Y., Gennaro, R., Håstad, J., Krawczyk, H., Rabin, T.: Randomness extraction and key derivation using the CBC, cascade and HMAC modes. In: Franklin, M. (ed.) CRYPTO 2004. LNCS, vol. 3152, pp. 494–510. Springer, Heidelberg (2004). https://doi.org/10.1007/978-3-540-28628-8_30
15. Cachin, C., Maurer, U.: Smoothing probability distributions and smooth entropy. IEEE (1997)
16. Cachin, C.: Smooth entropy and Rényi entropy. In: Fumy, W. (ed.) EUROCRYPT 1997. LNCS, vol. 1233, pp. 193–208. Springer, Heidelberg (1997). https://doi.org/10.1007/3-540-69053-0_14

Authenticated Continuous Top-k Spatial Keyword Search on Dynamic Objects

Yetneberk Zenebe Melesew(✉), Jiayi Li, and Yinbin Miao

Xidian University, Xi'an, China
zed.melesew@gmail.com

Abstract. GPS location and simple notification services are becoming more advanced. This advancement enhances spatial keyword search, including content locations and textual descriptions. Cloud users may read the news and watch social media and movies while going outside. Cloud Service Provider (CSP) can handle a wide range of spatial web objects gathered from various sources for saving local computation and storage resources. However, one major issue is that the malicious CSP may provide erroneous query results due to cost concerns, accidents or a hacker attack. The current authentication techniques for the continuous moving object are cumbersome and inadequate for our scenario. We need to check the search results on the user side and verify the query results' correctness and soundness. This paper addresses authenticating those dynamic objects' spatialkeyword searches, whose keywords and locations vary over time. This query benefits several location-aware services, including e-commerce, potential consumer tracking, self-driving stores, and cloud technologies. MIR-tree and MIR*-tree are two novel queries authenticating data structures with low computing and transmission costs. To aid in verifying query results, we provide a verification object and propose ways to generate it. Based on a detailed experimental analysis of real data, our suggested strategies outperform.

Keywords: Safe zone · Spatial-keyword search · Authentication · Query processing

1 Introduction

Spatial keyword query combines location with text search [3,4,21,22]. Such queries produce appropriate geographic web items that match the inputs when given a location and a collection of keywords. Clubs, tourist attractions, resorts, and entertainment services with an internet presence can be considered spatial web objects with locations and text information. Different spatial keyword data searches have been investigated in the past decade. Table 1 shows that most existing research has focused spatial keyword queries on static or moving objects [7,8,12,13,23,24,30,32]. The survey paper [27] studies the classification and thoroughly reviews encrypted data privacy-preserving spatial keyword queries.

X. Chen et al. (Eds.): SocialSec 2022, CCIS 1663, pp. 32–51, 2022.
https://doi.org/10.1007/978-981-19-7242-3_3

Table 1. Comparison to current related studies

Research	Queries status	Objects status	Query support	Authentication
[1]	Streaming	Streaming	Spatial keyword	No
[2,10]	Static	Static	Spatial keyword	No
[7,8,23,32]	Moving	Static	Spatial keyword	No
[6]	Static	Dynamic	Spatial keyword	No
[12,13,24,30]	Static	Moving	Spatial keyword	No
[31]	Moving	Static	Spatial keyword	Yes
[20]	Dynamic	Static	Spatial keyword	Yes
This work	Static	Dynamic	Spatial keyword	Yes

In addition, ordinary things are often dynamic, changing their locations and keywords over time. In this paper, we look at the case of authenticating top-k spatial keyword objects which are dynamic. Consider a collection of queries (static) defined by locations, keywords, and dynamic spatial keyword objects dataset with a change of locations and keywords. The main objective of studying the top-k spatial keywords of dynamic objects is to record the top-k results for each search. The top-k results are evaluated using a scoring function that considers spatial and keyword similarity. Many underlying applications benefit from resolving this issue [6]. (1) Following up on assets: Keywords represent the current status of movable assets (e.g., shared vehicles). (2) Keep track of your location and medications: (3) Tracking wildlife: The objects are wild animals, similar to location and medication watches. Gender, medical condition, and age category are all indicated by keywords. Researchers will watch the herd to see their population and study their migration.

Example 1. Take the following situation, as depicted in Fig. 1, which contains five objects. Assume that the objects are labelled as o_1, o_2, o_3, o_4, and o_5. These are five spatial keyword moving objects, and their queries are q_1, q_2, and q_3. Suppose a query needs to maintain track of everyone within the range query. Within the query keywords, they share at least one term. At time t_1, $R_{q_1}^{t_1} = \{o_3\}$ and $R_{q_2}^{t_1} = \{o_2, o_4\}$ are the top-2 result sets. Each circle denotes a safe zone under which the top two answers remain unaltered as long as the items stay there. Objects o_1, o_3, o_4 are now moving to new positions at time t_2, as small black circles illustrate. The query results are updated to the latest values: $R_{q_1}^{t_2} = \{o_1, o_3\}$, $R_{q_2}^{t_2} = \{o_2\}$, and $R_{q_3}^{t_2} = \{o_4\}$. When the object crosses through the safe zone's border, it updates its position and sends it to CSP. CSP computes and returns a new top-k result for each new coming query. However, CSP is beyond DO's administrative scope and may provide erroneous or wrong query results. Therefore, cloud client-side query authentication, which establishes the soundness and completeness of the query results, is highly desirable.

Authentication methods for many queries have been developed. Continuous top-k Spatial Query (CkSK) queries authentication requires validating spatial

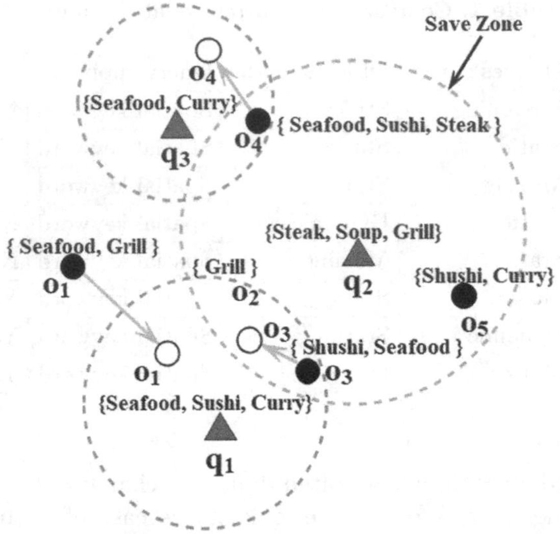

Fig. 1. Example of CkSK query

proximity and text relevancy. As a result, in our situation, all known Authenticated Data Structures (ADS) are either incompatible or ineffective. CkSK query authentication entails checking the top-k results and the associated safe zone. Authentication may fail if non-resulting objects are ignored.

This paper addresses the authentication of those dynamic objects spatial keyword queries whose keywords and locations vary over time. To authenticate CkSK objects, we proposed two authenticating data structures (MIR-tree and MIR*-tree). These algorithms have low computation and transmission costs. We also design a safe zone and verification object construction algorithms. Our contributions include:

- This paper focuses on the CkSK query process, safe zone construction and computation. First, we construct a verification object $\mathcal{VO}$ to check CkSK queries top-k results and the associated safe zones.
- We propose a MIR-tree data structure to authenticate CkSK queries, allowing low computing and transmission costs. We also suggest a nonlinear improved data structure MIR*-tree to minimize communication costs further.
- To assess the effectiveness and resilience of the suggested authentication systems, we undertake comprehensive experiments and security studies.

2 Related Work

2.1 Static Query Authentication

There are two types of static query authentication methods available: Merkle Hash Tree-based and signature chaining approach.

- Merkle Hash Tree-based approach. A standard authentication method built on the Merkle Hash Tree (MHT) [11] is used in several ways [9,16,25,28]. Node digests are produced recursively toward the root node from the leaf node. DO uses a private key to sign the root digest, such as RSA [18]. Devanbu *et al.* used MHT as the search parameter to validate the single-dimensional range query [5]. All MHTs visiting nodes $\mathcal{VO}$ are formed by augmenting all the left-wing digest with the corresponding boundary record R_{i-1} and right-wing digests with a boundary record of R_{j+1} from the root node. The result is valid if $\mathcal{VO}$'s reconstructed root digest matches the encrypted root signature. Subsequently, two MHT disk-based variants are proposed, such as Merkle B-tree [9] and VB-tree [17]. Pang and Mouratidis used MHT to validate a keyword search [16]. In contrast, the Term-MHT creates an MHT for each disc page's posting list entries. Another MHT-inspired solution is MR-tree [25], which relies on R*-tree. MR-tree is an index-based tree structure that can validate random spatial queries.
- Signature chaining-based approaches. In contrast to MHT, signature chaining [15] validates one-dimensional range queries' soundness and completeness. In multi-dimensional index structures, the signature chaining method has been applied [2]. Compared to systems that use MHT, signature chaining techniques have higher storage overhead, index generation costs, and cloud client-side verification time [9].

2.2 Moving Query Authentication

The current moving query authentication method for kNN queries [29] cannot authenticate Moving top-k Spatial Keyword (MkSK) queries. The kNN query safe zone is a Voronoi cell, while MkSK query safe zone is an MW-Voronoi cell [14]. Wei *et al.* introduced digital signature schemes to ensure the integrity of outsourced stream data and proposed an optimal verifiable data streaming protocol with data auditing [19]. However, their work is different from ours. Yung *et al.* explored how to authenticate dynamic range queries [31]. Because the safe zone and the verification set of moving range queries are different from ours, their techniques do not apply to our case.

3 Preliminaries

This section discusses similarity measurement, safe zone definition, and authentication techniques.

3.1 Similarity Measurement

Definition 1 (Rank function). *Suppose we have a query q and an object o; a spatial keyword similarity rank score is defined as:*

$$rank(o, q) = \alpha \cdot simS(o_s, q_s) + (1 - \alpha) \cdot (1 - simT(o_t, q_t)) \quad (1)$$

where $\alpha \in [0, 1]$ is a tuning parameter that balances the importance of spatial distance versus textual relevance. The ranking function $rank(o, q)$ determines the relevance of an object and a query. The object is more relevant to the query if the rank value is small. We normalize $simS(o_s, q_s)$ and $simT(o_t, q_t)$ to [0,1] by utilizing their peak values in the ranking algorithm. We compute the spatial distance $simS$ between two points using the Euclidean distance function and evaluate the textual relevancy $simT$ using the TFIDF function.

$$simT(o_t, q_t) = \sum_{t \in q_t} (tf(t, o_t) \times idf(t)) \tag{2}$$

where $tf(t, o_t)$ is the frequency term and $idf(t)$ is an inverse document frequency. If the context is unambiguous, we employ both ($simT(o_t, q_t)$ and $simT(o, q)$), and ($simS(o_s, q_s)$ and $simS(o, q)$) interchangeably.

3.2 Safe Zone

Safe Zone ($\mathbb{S}Z\,(q_t, k)$) depends on the keyword sets q_t and the value of k. For a given stationary object query q, we have to check its safe region in addition to determining the answer set. If $q'_s \in \mathbb{S}Z\,(q_t, k)$ for a query $q' = (q'_s, q_t, k)$, a moving object query in a new location q' is similar to the query in the initial state q. As a result, we can use $\Re$ to respond to a query in the new location. A safe zone and safe region are interchangeable when the context is apparent. The safe zone is then properly defined as follows:

Definition 2. *Given a set of objects O and a query q, the safe zone of query q is $\mathbb{S}Z = \{q'_s \mid \forall o^* \in \Re, \forall o \in O - \Re, rank\,(q', o^*) \leq rank\,(q', o)\}$, where q'_s is any location of a moving object.*

3.3 Authentication Techniques

- Cryptographic Hash Function. The hash function converts an arbitrary-length message z into a specific size $h(z)$ digest. It has two fundamental properties: (i) collision resistance, i.e., finding two separate messages z_1 and z_2 such that $h(z_1) = h(z_2)$ is difficult; and (ii) irreversibility, i.e., finding a message z such that $h(z) = z$ is challenging to compute.
- Merkle Hash Tree. Merkle hash tree is a data structure that allows data to be authenticated and verified [11].

4 Problem Formulation

In this section, we first describe the system model, threat model, problem formulation and design goal of our system.

4.1 System Model

As demonstrated in Fig. 2, a framework should allow correctness and verification for a continuous top-k spatial keyword search on moving objects. Three entities are involved in the framework: DO, Static Cloud Client, and CSP. The general setup is as follows:

- Data Owner. DO obtains a private key from a reliable key distribution center. DO digitally signs the data by producing signatures using the private key, then sends the dataset, ADS and signatures to CSP.
- Static Cloud Client. The static cloud client (cloud client) issues search queries and verification requests for query results. The cloud client is committed to ensuring that the top-k results are valid and complete using $\mathcal{VO}$ and public key. The root digest is rebuilt and compared to the signed root digest by the cloud client. Verification object $\mathcal{VO}$ consists of all visited leaf node objects, the top-k results, Minimum Bounding Rectangles (MBR), and all pruned nodes digest. If the moving objects leave the safe zone, the cloud client needs to resend an additional request to CSP.
- Cloud Service Provider. CSP returns the query result, which involves the signature and $\mathcal{VO}$, to the stationary cloud client. CSP is also responsible for providing the top-k results for each moving client's top-k spatial keyword query requests (e.g., coupon delivery).

Our system separates the query process from CSP safe zone generation. The system model is shown in Fig. 2, involves the following steps in the query process:

1. X_1: Issue a query
2. X_2: First compute the top-k result, and then compute the safe zone and $\mathcal{VO}$
3. X_3: Return $\mathcal{VO}$
4. X_4: Obtain the top-k results from $\mathcal{VO}$
5. X_5: Verify the top-k result
6. X_6: Check whether the moving objects are inside or outside the safe zone.

4.2 Threat Model

Our system considers a malicious model in which CSP may deviate from a normal protocol execution and alter user-sensitive data. In addition, it may return incorrect results for reducing local data computation and storage overheads. So many security issues are raised. We consider DO and users trustworthy and do not collude with CSP or illegal data users. Furthermore, the transmission routes, access, and authorisation are all assumed to be secure. We examine the following two threat scenarios based on the available information accessible to CSP:

- Ciphertext-Only-Attack Model. CSP is supposed to know the ciphertext of all outsourced data and can see the encrypted trapdoors in the system, but it cannot get the matching plaintext.
- Chosen-Plaintext-Attack Model. In addition to knowing the encrypted spatial data, index, and trapdoor, it is expected that the CSP has access to object ciphertexts for plaintexts of its selection.

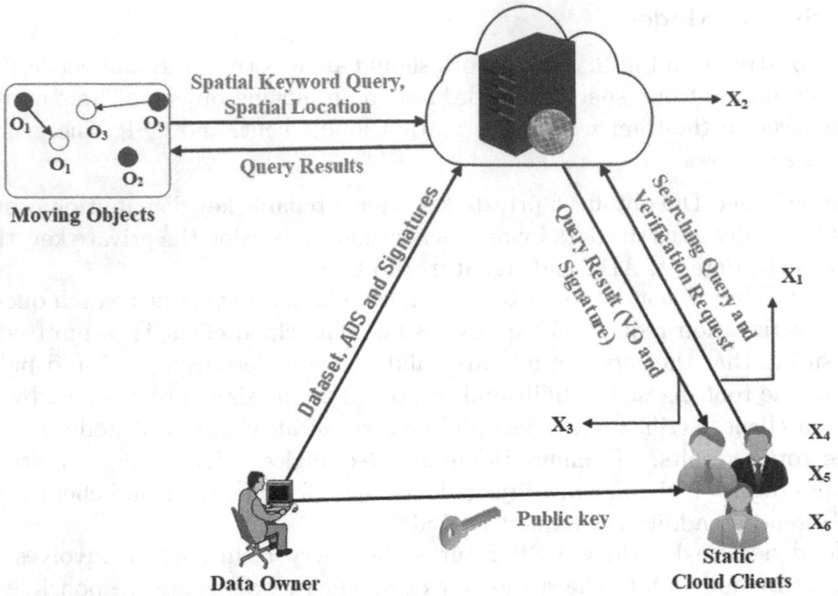

Fig. 2. System model

4.3 Problem Definition

Suppose O is a collection of data, with an object $o \in O$ and a pair $\langle \lambda, t \rangle$, each has a point position $o.\lambda$ and a text description $o.t$. A stationary query $q = \langle q_s, q_t, k \rangle$ includes three arguments. These continually point position changes q_s, keyword collection q_t, and total searched objects k. An object which has a highly relevant description is desirable. As the object moves, for each new location q'_s, its answer set is $\langle \Re, \mathbb{S}Z \rangle$, where $\Re$ is the top-k result set of $q' = (q'_s, q_t, k)$ and $\mathbb{S}Z$ is the corresponding safe zone.

To achieve the authentication of CkSK queries, we have to confirm the validity of the top-k result. When CkSK query q is verified, the user can get the most up-to-date top-k results, even if the object's spatial position alters. The acquired top-k results are acceptable as these objects do not leave the safe zone. An object entering a safe zone border seeks the updated top-k results and the matching safe location.

4.4 Design Goals

To achieve authenticated and privacy-preserving spatial keyword queries, the following conditions must be satisfied by our scheme:

- Authenticated CkSK query. It confirms the top-k result validity, the same as authenticating CkSk queries. Our scheme could ensure the top-k results'

soundness and completeness. The communication cost on the server side should be minimized.
- Document privacy. The dataset and query content are protected under document privacy. So, the plaintext dataset and query should not be made available to CSP or unauthorized parties.

5 Proposed Solution

In this section, we formally propose an authenticated continuous top-k spatial keyword search scheme on dynamic objects. Table 2 contains a summary of symbols notations.

Table 2. Summary of notation

Notation	Description
q	Query or search
o^*, o	Objects
n	Leaf node
$\mathbb{N}$	Non-leaf node
O	Dataset (collection)
str_r	Traversal string
k	Number of requested objects
ω	Keyword collection
X	Keyword weight
Q	A multi-dimensional top-k query
$\Re$	Query result
$\mathcal{VO}$	Verification object
$\mathbb{S}Z$	Safe zone

5.1 Overview

We will introduce how the dominant region constructs and discuss safe zone computation.

Dominant Region Construction. Given two objects (o^* and o) and a query q, the object o^* dominant region over object o is a region such that o^* is a better answer than of o if q is in the region, as defined below.

Definition 3. *Given a query $q = (q_s, q_t, k)$, the dominant region of o^* to o is:*

$$D_{o^*,o} = \{q'_s \mid rank\,(q', o^*) \leq rank\,(q', o)\} \tag{3}$$

where $q' = (q'_s, q_t, k)$.

The next step is to figure out how to depict the dominant region. First, we will go over two notations.

$$\Delta S = simS(q', o^*) - simSt(q', o)$$
$$\Delta T = \frac{1-\alpha}{\alpha}(simT(q', o^*) - simT(q', o)) \tag{4}$$

Based on (1), simS $(q', o^*) \leq$ simS (q', o) if and only if $\Delta S \leq \Delta T$. Thus, we have to $D_{o^*,o} = \{q'_s \mid \Delta S < \Delta T\}$, according to Definition 2. Therefore, the shape of the dominant region can be determined by defining the relationship between ΔT, and simS (o^*, o)as follows in Fig. 3.

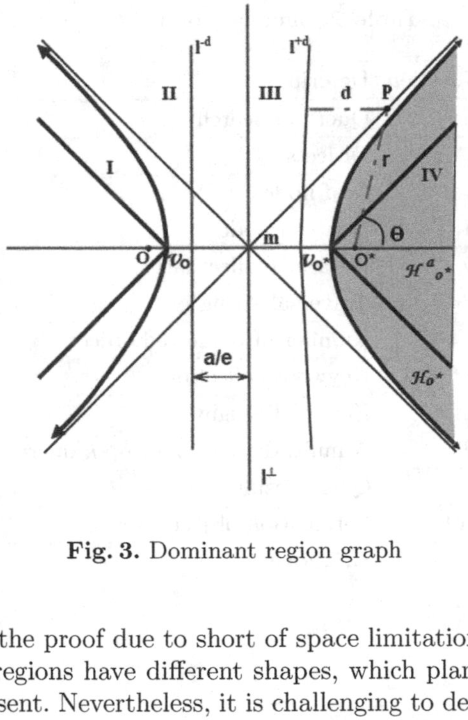

Fig. 3. Dominant region graph

Here we ignore the proof due to short of space limitation.

The dominant regions have different shapes, which planes, half-planes, and half-lines can represent. Nevertheless, it is challenging to depict hyperbola since it is a conic section, as shown in Fig. 3. A matrix or a second-degree polynomial usually expresses a Cartesian coordinate system. However, using such approaches is quite expensive and computing the intersection is inefficient.

Safe Zone Computation. Calculating the dominant areas of o^* to all other objects and computing their intersection is a fundamental approach to computing the safe region. An effective pruning strategy is needed to improve performance, as we propose in Algorithm 1. Consider the following two objects: o_i and o_j. Since $\mathbb{S}Z \subseteq D_{o^*,o_i} \cap D_{o^*,o_j} = D_{o^*,o_i}$, we can prune D_{o^*,o_j} if $D_{o^*,o_i} \subseteq D_{o^*,o_j}$. It is worth noting that determining whether $D_{o^*,o_i} \subseteq D_{o^*,o_j}$ is difficult. We present an alternative way of implementing this concept. Consider the $\mathbb{S}Z' \supseteq \mathbb{S}Z$ area.

Algorithm 1: Index based prunning mothod (O,q)

Require: O: Object collection
  q: A query
Ensure: Safe Region $\mathbb{S}Z$
  o^* = query q best answer
  $\mathbb{S}Z$ = Bounding objects $o \in O$ to the whole plane
  d_{max} = maxBD (o^*, $\mathbb{S}Z$)
  β = priority queue (which is empty)
  Build an IR-tree and insert root into β
while β *is not empty* **do**
  $n = \beta$. dequeue ()
  if $d_{min}(n) \geq d_{max}$ **then**
    if n is a node **then**
      for each child n' of n **do**
        Insert n into β with $d_{min}(n')$
      end for
    end if
  else
    $\mathbb{S}Z = \mathbb{S}Z \cap D_{o^*,n}$
    d_{max} = maxBD (o^*,$\mathbb{S}Z$)
  end if
end while

If $\Re' \subseteq D_{o^*,o}$, for any object o, we can prune object o since $\mathbb{S}Z \subseteq \mathbb{S}Z' \subseteq D_{o^*,o}$, and object o will not affect the safe region.

Safe Zone. Assume the top-1 answering to a query q is o^*. According to the concept of the dominant region, the safe zone is the intersection of the dominating area of o^* with all other objects, i.e. $\mathbb{S}Z = \bigcap_{o \neq o^*} D_{o^*,o}$, as defined in Lemma 1.

Lemma 1. *Given a query q, suppose its top-1 answer is* $o^*, \mathbb{S}Z = \bigcap_{o \neq o^*} D_{o^*,o}$.

After locating the top-1 answer o^*, we compute the dominant area of o^* for each item $o \in O$-o^* in this manner. The intersection of these dominant zones is then computed.

5.2 Authenticated Continuous Top-k Spatial Keyword Search on Dynamic Objects Schemes

Our schemes involve two parts: top-k result authentication and verification. Authentication and verification are two important security features that prevent fraud and other forms of cybercrime. Even though they share the same goal, they are two distinct aspects of cybersecurity. The top-k result authentication requires $\mathcal{VO}$ building, result verification, and testing soundness and completeness. We may classify result verification as a subset of result authentication.

Merkle-IR-Tree. Merkle-IR-Tree (MIR-tree) build on a tree known as IR-tree and is constructed by inserting a succession of digests into each tree node [3], as shown in Fig. 4. Each IR-tree child node combines the spatial distance and text relevance. CkSK search on MIR-tree is demonstrated in Algorithm 2. MIR-tree authenticates the text relevancies in the inverted file associated with every non-leaf node for each post list.

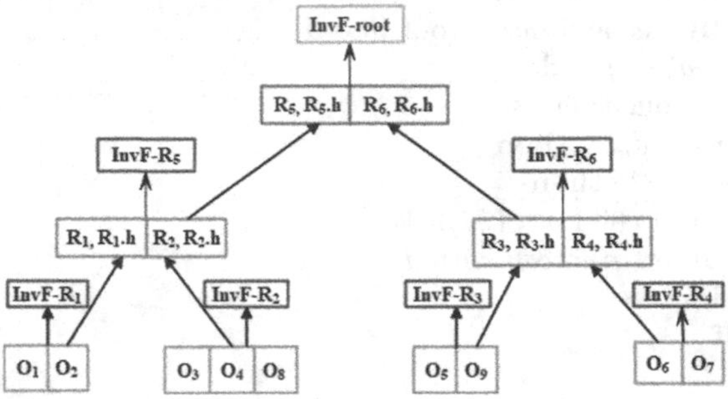

Fig. 4. Merkle IR-tree

Verification Object Construction. By traversing MIR-tree in depth-first, we can calculate the verification object that fulfills the conditions below: A verification object entry is generated and added to $\mathcal{VO}$ if a non-leaf element has a rank value of $rank\_q\,(\varepsilon)$ is greater than $rank\_k$. (i) The child node is processed using Algorithm 3 rather than visiting the sub-tree (lines 6–8). (ii) All items are added to $\mathcal{VO}$ if each node is checked; (line 6). A traversal string str_r is created during $\mathcal{VO}$ construction to monitor MIR-tree search. It includes tree entries and objects appended to $\mathcal{VO}$'s identifiers. Furthermore, the node scope is denoted by the unique tokens '[' and ']' as stated in (lines 1 and 11). Traversal string can prevent duplication of verification object entries. The cloud client receives $\mathcal{VO}$ and the traversal string (str_r).

Top-k Result Authentication. During a top-k result verification, a small $\mathcal{VO}$ with low communication costs and a quick authentication time is required. Separately authenticating the spatial distances and text relevance with the current methods is inefficient [16,25]. The top-k results authentication involves constructing verification objects, result verification, and checking soundness and completeness.

CkSK query authentication's sufficient conditions should involve two separate sub-conditions being fulfilled. Thus are:

– Soundness to a top-k result.

$$\forall o^* \in \Re(o^* \in O) \tag{5}$$

all of the returned results are from DO and satisfy the query criteria.

Algorithm 2: CkSK Search on MIR-tree

```
Require: keyword entry (ω), non-leaf node entry (ε_v), result string (str_r)
Ensure: word string (ω.string), word weight (ω.weight), spatial string
    (Spatial_Str), MBR
  Spatial_Str ← null
  Word_Digest_List(WDL) ← null
  Word_Str_List(WSL) ← null
   MBR ← null
  Spatial_Digest(SD) ← null
  Word_Weight_List(WWL) ← null
for every keywords entry (ω) in query do
    ω.string ← null
    WSL.add(ω.string)
    ω.weight ← −1
    WWL.add(ω.weight)
    ω.digest ← 0
    WDL.add(ω.digest)
end for
while str_r ≠ ∅ do
    ε_v ← str_r.next_Entry()
  if an object denoted by e_v then
      o ← VO.get_Entry(ε_v)
      MBR ← MBR ∪ o.Λ
      MBR ← Spatial_Str |o.id| o.Λ
    for every ω' keyword in {(ω, weight, h_ω'(.))} do
        Get the equivalent ω in WSL and WWL
        ω.string ← ω.string|(o.id, ω'.weight)
        ω.weight ← max(ω.weight, ω'.weight)
    end for
  end if
  if MIR-tree non-leaf entry is represent by ε_v then
      ε ← VO.get_Entry(ε_v)
      MBR ← MBR ∪ ε.Λ
      Spatial_Str ← Spatial_Str |ε.Λ| ε.H
    for every ω' keyword in {(ω, weight, h_ω'(.))} do
        Get the equivalent ω in WSL and WWL
        ω.string ← ω.string|(ω'.weight, h_ω'(.))
        ω.weight ← max(ω.weight, ω'.weight)
    end for
  end if
end while
```

– Completeness to a top-k result.

$$\forall o^* \in \Re, \forall o \in O - \Re, rank\,(q', o^*) \leq rank\,(q', o) \tag{6}$$

Algorithm 3: $\mathcal{VO}$_Construction

```
Require: entry (ε), rank string (rank_k), CkSk query (q)
Ensure: str_r, Verification_ Object_ list
  Annex [ to str_r
for every entry ε in node n do
   if (n == leaf_ node) then
      Add on VO_Entry(ε) to Verification_Object_list
      Annex ε to str_r
     if rank_q (ε) > rank_k then
        Annex ε to str_r
        VO_Entry(ε) to Verification_Object_list
     end if
   else
      VO_Construction (ε,rank_k, q)
   end if
end for
  Annex ] to str_r
  Return str_r and Verification_Object_list
```

no valid top-k result is missing. We demonstrate how our method can validate the top-k result.

Proof of Soundness. Let us consider that one of the objects in the output is a forgery or altered. We know that a collision resistance one-way hash function is used. Algorithm 4 uses the object o and its corresponding word weights and checks whether the reconstructed hash values of word digests and root spatial are against DO signature. The result is discovered, and it is fake.

Proof of Completeness. Suppose o represents one of the top-k items, and n represents the leaf node that contains o. If $\mathcal{VO}$ contains all node n entries, object o is undoubtedly in $\mathcal{VO}$, and the top-k result includes the object. If CSP prunes n, $\mathcal{VO}$ includes the minimum boundary region, n digests, and keyword weights described in Algorithm 2. The user receives $\mathcal{VO}$'s top-k results that do not contain the object o. Suppose the ranking score is accurate and superior to other k-th objects. In that case, the customer will receive violation alerts of incompleteness since the spatial and keyword digests (root hash values) match the decrypted signatures.

Top-k Result Verification. Using $\mathcal{VO}$, the user retrieves and validates the top-k result. Equation (1) calculates the ranking object scores in $\mathcal{VO}$, and the top-k objects rank and receive. The user then recomputes the root word and spatial digests using *str_r* and $\mathcal{VO}$. The data user then compares the recomputed root digests by decrypting the result (Algorithm 2). The primary concept is to rebuild CSP's MIR-tree traversal, ensuring that the items in $\mathcal{VO}$ come from the original MIR-tree. Then, it checks whether the top-k result is accurate by looking at the ranking score.

Algorithm 4: Authentication

Require: Verification_Object, result string (*str_r*), C*k*SK query (q)
Ensure: $MBR, h(Spatial\_Str), WWL, WDL)$
while $str\_r \neq \emptyset$ **do**
  if ϵv is [**then**
    $(wwl, sd, mbr, wdl) \leftarrow$ **Authentication**$(q, str\_r, \mathcal{VO})$
    $MBR \leftarrow MBR \cup$ mbr
    Spatial_Str ← Spatial_Str $|mbr|$sd
    for every ω' keyword in wdl and wwl **do**
      Get the equivalent ω in WSL and WWL
      $\omega.string \leftarrow \omega.string|(\omega'.weight, h_{\omega'}(.))$
      $\omega.weight \leftarrow max(\omega.weight, \omega'.weight)$
    end for
  end if
  if ϵ_v is] **then**
    for every ω' keyword in WDL and WSL **do**
      ω. digest ← h(ω. string)
    end for
    Return $(MBR, h(Spatial\_Str), WWL, WDL)$
  end if
end while

Enhanced MIR*-Tree. The size of the verification object is essential to decrease client/server communication costs and reduce the client-side time for result verification. We then suggest an improved ADS, MIR*-tree, which allows $\mathcal{VO}$ size to be reduced. MIR*-tree digests are calculated differently as compared with MIR-tree digests. The basic idea may be used in any ADS with a tree structure, like MR-tree [25], in which each node contains many entries.

MIR-tree includes multiple word digests for a single spatial digest in every non-leaf entry. A pruned non-leaf entry in $\mathcal{VO}$ has a single spatial digest, X word digests, and MBR, where X is the total keywords query numbers. Thus, for those non-leaf nodes visited in MIR-tree, the $\mathcal{VO}$ may contain additional $Y(X+1)$ digests, where Y represents the total pruned entries amount. Assume that the bytes size to digest is symbolized as S_d, and MBR is denoted as S_X. A non-leaf node ($\mathbb{N}$) contributing to the verification object can be computed as $\mathcal{S}_N = Y[(X+1)S_d + S_X]$, Y may be a considerably high number when a hundred node fanout occurs. When we use a double-precision, a digest S_d may be very big (SHA-512 hash algorithm needs 64 bytes), yet an MBR Sm can only be 32 bytes. As a result, the total digests number determines $\mathcal{VO}$ size.

6 Security Analysis

We examine whether or not our C*k*SK system is secure using the attack model described in Sect. 4.2. The suggested approach assures that scalar products between encrypted vectors can be computed and compared to accomplish spatial keyword queries in the CSP. We assume that the query q and the data object O are d-dimensional. Their ciphertexts, $\bar{q}$ and $\bar{O}$, are $(d+1)$-dimensional, which contain the random numbers δ and γ, to show the suggested scheme's security guarantee without compromising generality.

Theorem 1. *If the adversary does not have each query's random number γ and each corresponding object δ, the suggested system is resistant to the chosen-plaintext attack.*

Proof. Suppose the adversary (i.e., CSP) can deduce a set of queries and their ciphertexts before launching the chosen-plaintext attack. The attacker would use one encrypted pair $\bar{q} = \{M_1^{-1}q', M_2^{-1}q''\}$ in the query processing for each query. According to the proposed technique, the scalar product of encrypted query $\bar{q}$, and any encrypted data $\bar{O} = \{M_1^T O', M_2^T O''\}$ may be calculated using Asymmetric Scalar Inner product Preserving Encryption with Noise (ASPEN) as follows:

$$\begin{aligned} SP(\bar{O},\bar{q}) &= M_1^T O' \cdot M_1^{-1}q' + M_2^T O'' \cdot M_2^{-1}q'' \\ &= (M_1^T O')^T M_1^{-1}q' + (M_2^T O'')^T M_2^{-1}q'' \\ &= (O')^T q' + (O'')^T q'' = \gamma(O^T q + \delta) \end{aligned} \tag{7}$$

In d dimensions of O, the Scalar Product (SP) in (7) has only $d+2$ unknown variables. These unknown variables are the random numbers γ and δ [26]. If the random number γ is identical for all queries, the adversary needs to collect the plaintext-ciphertext pairs of $d+2$ query points and answers the $d+1$ unknowns in O and δ using $d+2$ equations.

7 Performance Evaluation

MIR-tree and MIR*-tree are the proposed solutions. By default, the results number is set to one, two keywords query, speed of the moving object is set to 10 m/s, and fanout for MIR-tree and MIR*-tree is set to 200. We employ disk-based index structures with a 4 KByte page size. The size of the simulated LRU buffer is 256 MB. The tests are run on a Windows server with an Intel(R) Core (TM)i5-8300H CPU running at 2.30 GHz and 16 GB of RAM. The hash function is SHA-512, and the signature technique is 2048 bits RSA (Table 3).

Table 3. Dataset.

Dataset	No. of objects	No. of distinct keywords	Avg no of keywords per object
LONDFLI	1,255,149	222,613	8

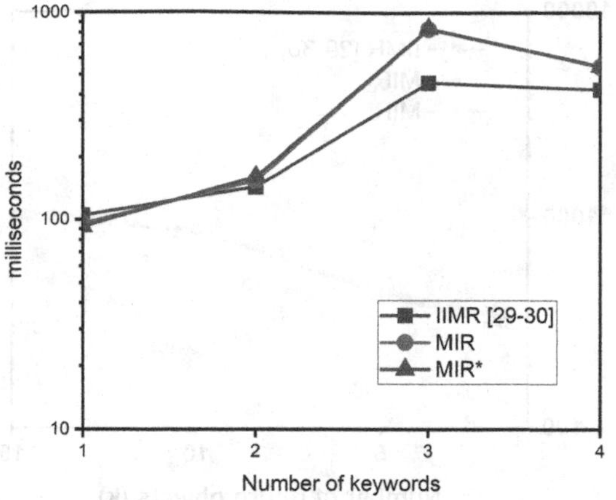

Fig. 5. Server elapsed time (varying the number of keywords).

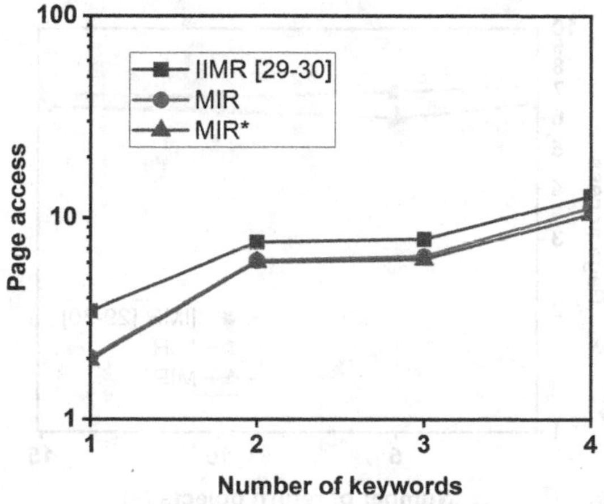

Fig. 6. Server I/O cost (varying the number of keywords).

We investigate our suggested approaches (MIR-tree and MIR*-tree) in various scenarios, including performance on a given dataset (LONDFLI), with different requested top-k results, varying numbers of query keywords and dataset sizes. We create an Inverted Index and MR-tree (IIMR) baseline method that integrates existing ideas [16,25]. This approach makes use of current techniques for CkSK query authentication. The object's text descriptions are indexed by an inverted index in IIMR, while an MR-tree indexes the object's spatial point coordinates. The verification sets VS_T and VS_S are used to generate a $\mathcal{VO}$. The inverted index is specifically utilized to authenticate the text relevancies of items while utilizing VS_T. MR-tree is used to authenticate the spatial distances of objects using VS_S, according to Pang and Mouratidis [16].

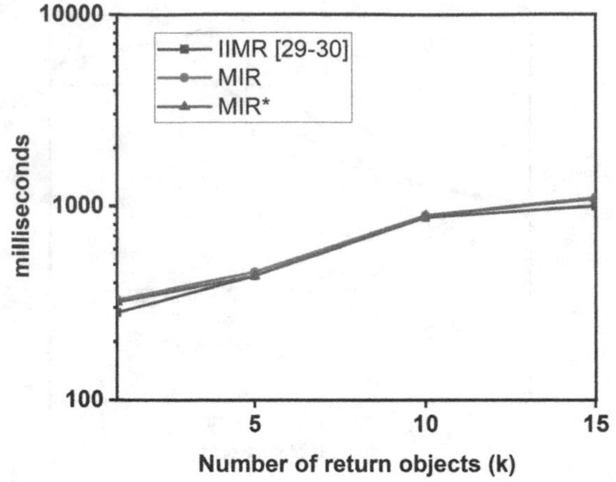

Fig. 7. Server elapsed time (performance by varying k).

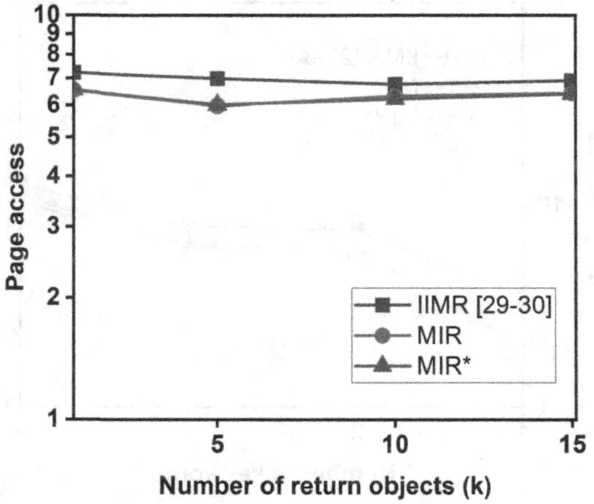

Fig. 8. Server I/O cost (performance by varying k).

The basic IIMR's server elapsed time and I/O cost are equivalent to MIR variations. However, MIR versions outperform IIMR in client elapsed time, the number of entries in $\mathcal{VO}$, and $\mathcal{VO}$ size by orders of magnitude.

Regarding server elapsed time shown in Fig. 5 and I/O cost as shown in Fig. 6, MIR-tree and MIR*-tree perform similarly. MIR-tree and MIR*-tree both have the same number of entries in $\mathcal{VO}$. The structures and processing methods of the two indexes are identical. In terms of digest computation, MIR-tree varies from MIR*-tree. MIR*-tree adds fewer digests to $\mathcal{VO}$, resulting in a substantially reduced client elapsed time and $\mathcal{VO}$ size than MIR-tree.

IIMR is the smallest index in terms of size. Because of the inverted files associated with non-leaf nodes, MIR-tree and MIR*-tree take considerably more space than IIMR. Except for IIMR, none of these indexes may be stored in the main memory.

Varying k. As the number k of necessary results on the dataset changes, the three approaches' performance also changes. In terms of cloud client elapsed time and $\mathcal{VO}$ size, MIR-tree variations consistently outperform the baseline. As we expected, when the k value rises, the elapsed server time, and size of $\mathcal{VO}$ increases, as shown in Fig. 7. On the other hand, when the value of k grows, server I/O costs (shown in Fig. 8) reduce modestly. Because more objects result in a smaller safe zone, allowing for more pruning. As a result, the number of index nodes (pages) fetched from the disk is reduced.

8 Conclusion

This paper investigates the authentication of the continuous moving objects top-k spatial keyword query problem. We also present MIR-tree, a novel authenticated data structure that ensures soundness and completeness of the top-k results. Each query sent to the cloud server has a safe zone built for it. We recommend that hyperbolas represent a safe zone. We design effective pruning algorithms and use indexing structures to increase the efficiency of the safe region calculation. The safe zones and the top-k results of CkSK searches are authenticated using a verification object. An algorithm for creating and manipulating verification objects is designed. MIR*-tree, an upgrade of MIR-tree, is proposed to minimize communication costs further. Extensive empirical experiments on real datasets show that our suggested strategies' effectiveness outperforms state-of-the-art methods by a wide margin. Moreover, this work may pave the way for some promising future avenues since it is worthwhile to investigate the authentication of top-k spatial keyword queries without losing location and keyword privacy.

References

1. Chen, L., Cong, G., Cao, X., Tan, K.L.: Temporal spatial-keyword top-k publish/subscribe. In: 2015 IEEE 31st International Conference on Data Engineering, pp. 255–266. IEEE (2015)
2. Chen, L., Cong, G., Jensen, C.S., Wu, D.: Spatial keyword query processing: an experimental evaluation. Proc. VLDB Endow. **6**(3), 217–228 (2013). https://doi.org/10.14778/2535569.2448955
3. Cong, G., Jensen, C.S., Wu, D.: Efficient retrieval of the top-k most relevant spatial web objects. Proc. VLDB Endow. **2**(1), 337–348 (2009)
4. De Felipe, I., Hristidis, V., Rishe, N.: Keyword search on spatial databases. In: 2008 IEEE 24th International Conference on Data Engineering, pp. 656–665. IEEE (2008)
5. Devanbu, P., Gertz, M., Martel, C., Stubblebine, S.G.: Authentic data publication over the internet 1. J. Comput. Secur. **11**(3), 291–314 (2003)
6. Dong, Y., et al.: Continuous top-k spatial-keyword search on dynamic objects. VLDB J. **30**(2), 141–161 (2021)

7. Guo, L., Shao, J., Aung, H.H., Tan, K.L.: Efficient continuous top-k spatial keyword queries on road networks. GeoInformatica **19**(1), 29–60 (2015)
8. Huang, W., Li, G., Tan, K.L., Feng, J.: Efficient safe-region construction for moving top-k spatial keyword queries. In: Proceedings of the 21st ACM International Conference on Information and Knowledge Management, pp. 932–941 (2012)
9. Li, F., Hadjieleftheriou, M., Kollios, G., Reyzin, L.: Dynamic authenticated index structures for outsourced databases. In: Proceedings of the 2006 ACM SIGMOD International Conference on Management of Data, pp. 121–132 (2006)
10. Mahmood, A., Aref, W.G.: Query processing techniques for big spatial-keyword data. In: Proceedings of the 2017 ACM International Conference on Management of Data, pp. 1777–1782 (2017)
11. Merkle, R.C.: A certified digital signature. In: Brassard, G. (ed.) CRYPTO 1989. LNCS, vol. 435, pp. 218–238. Springer, New York (1990). https://doi.org/10.1007/0-387-34805-0_21
12. Mouratidis, K., Bakiras, S., Papadias, D.: Continuous monitoring of top-k queries over sliding windows. In: Proceedings of the 2006 ACM SIGMOD International Conference on Management of Data, pp. 635–646 (2006)
13. Mouratidis, K., Papadias, D., Hadjieleftheriou, M.: Conceptual partitioning: an efficient method for continuous nearest neighbor monitoring. In: Proceedings of the 2005 ACM SIGMOD International Conference on Management of Data, pp. 634–645 (2005)
14. Okabe, A., Boots, B., Sugihara, K., Chiu, S.N.: Spatial Tessellations: Concepts and Applications of Voronoi Diagrams, vol. 501. Wiley, New York (2009)
15. Pang, H., Jain, A., Ramamritham, K., Tan, K.L.: Verifying completeness of relational query results in data publishing. In: Proceedings of the 2005 ACM SIGMOD International Conference on Management of Data, pp. 407–418 (2005)
16. Pang, H., Mouratidis, K.: Authenticating the query results of text search engines. Proc. VLDB Endow. **1**(1), 126–137 (2008)
17. Pang, H., Tan, K.L.: Authenticating query results in edge computing. In: Proceedings of the 20th International Conference on Data Engineering, pp. 560–571. IEEE (2004)
18. Rivest, R.L., Shamir, A., Adleman, L.: A method for obtaining digital signatures and public-key cryptosystems. Commun. ACM **21**(2), 120–126 (1978)
19. Wei, J., Tian, G., Shen, J., Chen, X., Susilo, W.: Optimal verifiable data streaming protocol with data auditing. In: Bertino, E., Shulman, H., Waidner, M. (eds.) ESORICS 2021. LNCS, vol. 12973, pp. 296–312. Springer, Cham (2021). https://doi.org/10.1007/978-3-030-88428-4_15
20. Wu, D., Choi, B., Xu, J., Jensen, C.S.: Authentication of moving top-k spatial keyword queries. IEEE Trans. Knowl. Data Eng. **27**(4), 922–935 (2014)
21. Wu, D., Cong, G., Jensen, C.S.: A framework for efficient spatial web object retrieval. VLDB J. **21**(6), 797–822 (2012)
22. Wu, D., Yiu, M.L., Cong, G., Jensen, C.S.: Joint top-k spatial keyword query processing. IEEE Trans. Knowl. Data Eng. **24**(10), 1889–1903 (2011)
23. Wu, D., Yiu, M.L., Jensen, C.S.: Moving spatial keyword queries: Formulation, methods, and analysis. ACM Trans. Database Syst. (TODS) **38**(1), 1–47 (2013)
24. Xiong, X., Mokbel, M.F., Aref, W.G.: SEA-CNN: scalable processing of continuous k-nearest neighbor queries in spatio-temporal databases. In: 21st International Conference on Data Engineering (ICDE 2005), pp. 643–654. IEEE (2005)
25. Yang, Y., Papadopoulos, S., Papadias, D., Kollios, G.: Authenticated indexing for outsourced spatial databases. VLDB J. **18**(3), 631–648 (2009)

26. Yao, B., Li, F., Xiao, X.: Secure nearest neighbor revisited. In: 2013 IEEE 29th International Conference on Data Engineering (ICDE), pp. 733–744. IEEE (2013)
27. Yetneberk, Z.: A survey on spatial keyword search over encrypted data. In: Xiong, J., Wu, S., Peng, C., Tian, Y. (eds.) MobiMedia 2021. LNICST, vol. 394, pp. 413–431. Springer, Cham (2021). https://doi.org/10.1007/978-3-030-89814-4_30
28. Yiu, M.L., Lin, Y., Mouratidis, K.: Efficient verification of shortest path search via authenticated hints. In: 2010 IEEE 26th International Conference on Data Engineering (ICDE 2010), pp. 237–248. IEEE (2010)
29. Yiu, M.L., Lo, E., Yung, D.: Authentication of moving kNN queries. In: 2011 IEEE 27th International Conference on Data Engineering, pp. 565–576. IEEE (2011)
30. Yu, X., Pu, K.Q., Koudas, N.: Monitoring k-nearest neighbor queries over moving objects. In: 21st International Conference on Data Engineering (ICDE 2005), pp. 631–642. IEEE (2005)
31. Yung, D., Lo, E., Yiu, M.L.: Authentication of moving range queries. In: Proceedings of the 21st ACM International Conference on Information and Knowledge Management, pp. 1372–1381 (2012)
32. Zheng, B., et al.: Keyword-aware continuous kNN query on road networks. In: 2016 IEEE 32nd International Conference on Data Engineering (ICDE), pp. 871–882. IEEE (2016)

Efficient Attribute-Based Proxy Re-encryption for Secure Deduplication

Tao Zhang(✉), Chen Wang, and Mulmediyage Imantha Udana Chandrasena

School of Computer Science, Nanjing University of Information Science and Technology, Nanjing, China
tzhang1704@126.com

Abstract. More and more data files are stored in cloud servers because of storage space. At the same time, many cryptographic techniques have been proposed to protect data privacy. However, a large amount of duplicate data is stored in the cloud server, resulting in a waste of resources. Most of the existing solutions rarely consider the problem of wasting storage resources. In this paper, we propose an attribute-based encryption (ABE) scheme that supports deduplication. What's more, we implemented the verification of data files using blockchain. Finally, experimental simulations show that the proposed mechanism can improve the efficiency of processing duplicate data and reduce latency.

Keywords: Blockchain · Verifiable · Deduplication

1 Introduction

With the popularization of smart devices such as mobile phones, computers, and tablets, people are exposed to a large amount of external data information every day, and at the same time, information containing users' private data will also be generated. Users will inevitably share some of this information with designated users. Therefore, in this era of rapid expansion of information, cloud storage services provided by third-party organizations are favored by more and more people. Through the cloud server, users can freely upload data to the cloud server or download the desired information from the cloud server. But obviously, it is not wise to directly transmit and store messages containing users' sensitive data to cloud servers. On the other hand, when the traditional public-key encryption method is applied in the one-to-many sharing environment, it will cause great computational overhead to the data encryptor, because each public key encryption method can only share the data with the designated individuals.

To ensure the security and privacy of data stored on cloud servers, attribute-based encryption (ABE) schemes [1,3,4,9] that can provide security and privacy protection and implement fine-grained access control are widely used, and after this, to deal with various other security risks, many schemes [7,10] have been proposed to protect secure data sharing in cloud computing environment. In

X. Chen et al. (Eds.): SocialSec 2022, CCIS 1663, pp. 52–64, 2022.
https://doi.org/10.1007/978-981-19-7242-3_4

addition, with the continuous growth of data volume, the storage burden of cloud servers is also rising, and a large part of these increased storage overheads can be avoided. Imagine this situation, as shown in Fig. 1, there are three different users User1, User2, and User3, they all have the same plaintext now and want to encrypt and upload it to the cloud server, but because everyone wants to share the ciphertext according to the ciphertext policy ABE scheme, where the access policy is bound to the ciphertext, and the ciphertexts generated by the three people will not be the same in the end. As a result, the cloud server will consider them to be three different messages to be stored separately when determining, resulting in a waste of storage space.

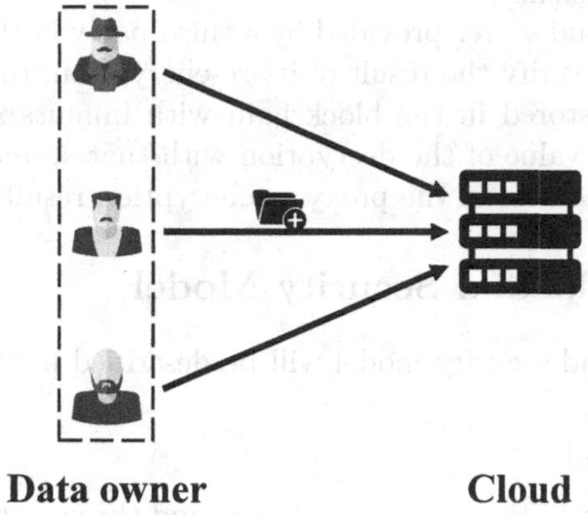

Fig. 1. Duplicate data

As a current research hotspot, blockchain has attracted the attention of various fields. This paper also fully considers the characteristics and advantages of blockchain and applies them to the scheme. In addition, there are many attribute-based encryption schemes on blockchain [2,5] proposed. Moreover, many schemes [8,11] have been proposed for secure deduplication using blockchain technology.

The blockchain is essentially a decentralized database with functions such as openness, transparency, traceability, and tamper resistance. Taking these into account and in combination with the cloud server that performs proxy re-encryption in the scheme of this paper is a semi-trusted organization, that is, it has the possibility to save computing resources and return random results, it is necessary to verify the results of the proxy re-encryption.

1.1 Contributions

In this paper, we propose a verifiable and efficient attribute-based proxy re-encryption scheme that supports data deduplication. The main contributions of this paper are as follows:

1. A cloud data sharing scheme that supports data deduplication is proposed. The scheme proposed in this paper supports the judgment of the ciphertext uploaded by the user and deletes the duplicated data of the plaintext. The cloud server will determine whether the original text contained in the ciphertext is the same through calculation. If they are the same, they will be merged. Finally, the cloud server only needs to store the unique ciphertext, which greatly reduces the storage overhead.
2. An efficient proxy re-encryption mechanism is proposed. The scheme proposed in this paper designs an efficient proxy re-encryption mechanism. The cloud server will merge and update the access policies in the ciphertext structure with the same plaintext, and update the ciphertext, which has higher computational efficiency.
3. Verifiable. The cloud server provided by a third party in this article is a semi-trusted entity. To verify the result of its re-encryption, the hash value of the plaintext will be stored in the blockchain with immutability. The user can compare the hash value of the decryption with that stored in the blockchain to verify the correctness of the proxy re-encryption result.

2 System Model and Security Model

The system model and security model will be described in this section.

2.1 System Model

There are five entities in the proposed scheme, and the specific definitions of the entities will be given below (Fig. 2).

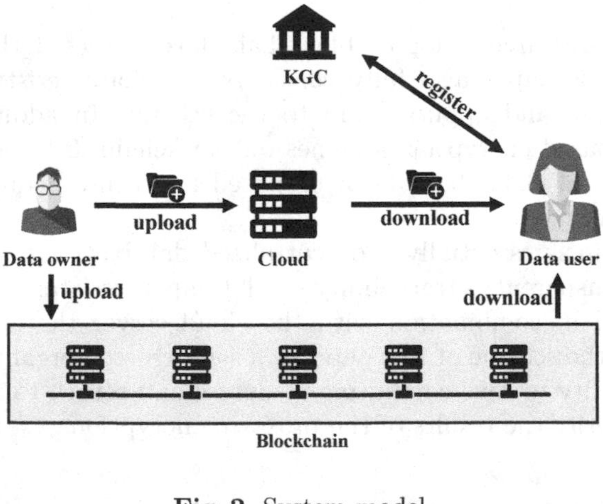

Fig. 2. System model

Key generation center (KGC): It is responsible for initializing the scheme. When a user submits a registration request, the secret key associated with the attribute set is generated by KGC. The secret key is sent to the user by KGC in an absolutely secure channel.

Blockchain: It is responsible for storing the verification value generated by the owner. When a data user wants to verify the correctness of the proxy re-encryption, the verification value will be downloaded by the user.

Cloud: Due to the large space of cloud storage, a large amount of data can be stored and data can be easily downloaded. However, a large number of ciphertexts from the same message are stored in the cloud, which will cause a waste of storage resources. In addition, the cloud has powerful computing power. Expensive computational operations (pairing operations) can be offloaded to the cloud.

Data owner (DO): DO owns the data and wants to outsource the data to the cloud for storage. To protect the privacy and security of the data, the data owner encrypts the data locally using the specified access structure. The ciphertext will be uploaded to the cloud for storage after the encryption is completed.

Data user (DU): DU will get the private key after submitting the registration request to KGC. The ciphertext stored in the cloud will be downloaded by DU when the user sends a download request. The user utilizes the key, then the data will be recovered from the ciphertext.

2.2 Security Model

The definition of selective security for the proposed scheme will be presented in this subsection. We will go through the description of the game between challenger C and adversary A. The specific definition of the game is as follows.

Initialization: An access structure A^* is picked by the adversary and sent to the challenger as a challenge target.

Setup: The challenger will generate the master public key MPK and send it to the adversary.

Query Phase 1: Secret keys queries with S_{DU} can be adaptively ask. The $KeyGen$ algorithm will be run by the challenger when the key query is issued by the adversary with the attribute set S_{DU}. The challenger will send the result to the adversary. The only restriction is $S_{DU} \notin A^*$.

Challenge: Two message M_0, M_1 with the same bit are carefully selected and send them to the challenger B. The *Encrypt* algorithm is run by the challenger to get the ciphertext CT^* under M_b, where M_b is randomly chosen between M_0 and M_1. The ciphertext CT^* is sent by the challenger B to the adversary A.

Query Phase 2: The secret key query can be adaptively ask as the same as query phase 1.

Guess: A guess b' is output by adversary A.

Definition 1. *Our scheme is selective CPA-secure if no adversary can win the above game by a non-negligible advantage.*

3 The Formal of Definition of the Basic Scheme

3.1 Algorithm Definition

There are six algorithms in the basic scheme. The specific definition as follows.

Setup$(1^K) \rightarrow (MPK, MSK)$: The *Setup* algorithm is executed by the KGC to deinitialize the system. The master public key MPK and the master key MSK will be output when the security parameter K is taken as input.

KeyGen$(S_{DU}, MSK) \rightarrow SK_{DU}$: The *KeyGen* algorithm is executed by the KGC to help DU complete registration. The DU's secret key will be output when the attribute set S_{DU} and the master key are taken as input.

Encrypt$(f, (M, \rho)) \rightarrow CT_{DO}$: The *Encrypt* algorithm is executed locally by the DU. The ciphertext CT_{DO} will be output when the data file f and the specified access structure (M, ρ) are taken as input.

Seek$(CT'_{DO}, CT''_{DO}) \rightarrow 1/0$: Cloud operates the *Seek* algorithm after the *Detect* algorithm output 1. On input the ciphertext CT'_{DO} and CT''_{DO}, Output 1 if two ciphertexts are from the same plaintext; otherwise, output 0.

ReE$((M', \rho'), CT_{DO}) \rightarrow RCT_{DO}$: Input the ciphertext CT_{DO} and a access structure (M', ρ') combined by private cloud. Output a re-encrypted ciphertext RCT.

Decrypt$(CT_{DO}/RCT_{DO}, SK_{DU}) \rightarrow f$: Input the ciphertext CT_{DO} or RCT_{DO} and the DU's secret key. Output the data file f.

3.2 The Constructions of the Basic Scheme

The constructions of the basic scheme will be shown. The specific constructions as follows.

Setup$(1^K) \rightarrow (MPK, MSK)$: The security parameter 1^K is taken as input. Firstly, the algorithm chooses a bilinear mapping $D = (p, G, G_T, e)$. Secondly, some terms g, u, h, w, v are chosen randomly in G. Moreover, a random α is chosen randomly in Z_p^*. Finally, a hash functions with collision-resistant $H : \{0,1\}* \rightarrow Z_p^*$ is chosen. The master public key and the master secret key are output as follows.

$$MPK = (D, g, h, w, v, u, e(g,g)^\alpha, H) \quad MSK = \alpha$$

KeyGen$(S_{DU}, MSK) \rightarrow SK_{DU}$: The DU's attribute set $S_{DU}((S_1, S_2, ..., S_t)$ and the master secret key are taken as input. First, $t+1$ randoms $r, r_1, r_2, ..., r_t$ are randomly chosen in Z_p^* by the *KeyGen* algorithm. The algorithm computes $SK_0 = g^\alpha w^r$, $SK_1 = g^r$. Second, the algorithm computes $SK_{j,2} = g^{r_j}$ and $SK_{j,3} = (u^{S_j} h)^{r_j} v^{-r}$, where j from 1 to t. Finally, the secret key associated with the user is obtained by KGC, where j from 1 to t.

$$SK_S = (SK_0 = g^\alpha w^r, SK_1 = g^r, \{SK_{j,2} = g^{r_j}, SK_{j,3} = (u^{S_j} h)^{r_j} v^{-r}\})$$

Encrypt$(f, (M, \rho)) \rightarrow (CT_{DO}, pf)$: DO calculates $H(f)$ and uploads it to blockchain before data file is encrypted. The encryption algorithm takes the data file f and the specific access structure (M, ρ). First, some randoms $s, y_2, y_3, ..., y_n$ are randomly chosen in Z_p^*. Then the algorithm will get the vector $\overrightarrow{y}$, where $\overrightarrow{y} = (s, y_2, y_3, ..., y_n)^T$. We assume that $\lambda_l = M\overrightarrow{y}$. Second, some randoms $t_1, t_2, ..., t_l$ are randomly chosen in Z_p^*. The algorithm computes $C_f = fe(g,g)^{\alpha s}$, $C_0 = g^s$, $C_1 = w^s$ and $C_N = {C_0}^{H(f)}$. For i from 1 to l, the algorithm computes as follows.

$$C_{i,1} = w^{\lambda_i} v^{t_i} \quad C_{i,2} = (u^{\rho(i)} h)^{-t_i} \quad C_{i,3} = g^{t_i}$$

Finally, the ciphertext $CT_{DO} = (C_f, C_N, C_0, C_1, \{C_{i,1}, C_{i,2}, C_{i,3}\}_{[1,l]})$ is output.

Seek$(CT'_{DO}, CT''_{DO}) \rightarrow 1/0$: The *Seek* algorithm is run by Cloud to deduplicate data and takes two ciphertexts as input as follow.

$$CT'_{DO} = (C'_f, C'_N, C'_0, C'_1, \{C'_{i,1}, C'_{i,2}, C'_{i,3}\}_{[1,l']})$$
$$CT''_{DO} = (C''_f, C''_N, C''_0, C''_1, \{C''_{i,1}, C''_{i,2}, C''_{i,3}\}_{[1,l'']})$$

Whether the equation $e(C'_N, C''_0) = e(C''_N, C'_0)$ is true by the cloud detection. If it holds, two ciphertext are equivalent and deduplicate data, which means that two ciphertext are generated by the same message; otherwise, two ciphertext are not equivalent.

ReE$((M', \rho'), CT_{DO}) \rightarrow RCT_{DO}$: Suppose there are some ciphertexts of the repeated data and the associated access structures as follows.

$$(CT_{DO1}, (M_1, \rho_1)), (CT_{DO2}, (M_2, \rho_2)), ..., (CT_{DOn}, (M_n, \rho_n))$$

Firstly, these access structures are combined by the cloud as (M', ρ'), where M' is a $l' \times n'$ matrix. The *ReE* algorithm is run by cloud. Set M'_i be the i-th row of M', and $M'_i = (M'_{i,1}, M'_{i,2}, ..., M'_{i,n'})$. Then n' randoms $s', y'_2, y'_3, ..., y'_{n'}$ are randomly chosen by the cloud in Z_p^* and the vector $\overrightarrow{y}' = (s', y'_2, y'_3, ..., y'_{n'})^T$ is set and computes a vector of shares of s' as $M'\overrightarrow{y}' = (\lambda'_1, \lambda'_2, ..., \lambda'_{l'})^T$. Firstly, the cloud computes $RCT_f = C_f \cdot e(g,g)^{\alpha s'} = fe(g,g)^{\alpha s} \cdot e(g,g)^{\alpha s'}$ and $RCT_0 = C_0 \cdot g^{s'} = g^s \cdot g^{s'}$. Secondly, the cloud computes that

$$RCT_{i,1} = w^{\lambda'_i} v^{t'_i} \quad RCT_{i,2} = (u^{\rho(i)'} h)^{-t'_i} \quad RCT_{i,3} = g^{t'_i} \quad RCT_{i,4} = C_1^{M'_{i,1}}$$

Finally, it sets the re-encrypted ciphertext as follows and store it in cloud.

$$RCT = (RCT_f, RCT_0, \{RCT_{i,1}, RCT_{i,2}, RCT_{i,3}, RCT_{i,4}\})$$

Decrypt$(RCT_{DO}, SK_{DU}) \rightarrow f$: The *Decrypt* algorithm is run by DU to recover the data file. The specific decryption of DO is as follows.

$$\begin{aligned} key &= \frac{e(RCT_0, SK_0)}{\prod_{i \in I}(e(RCT_{i,1}, SK_1)e(RCT_{i,2}, SK_{j,2})e(RCT_{i,3}, SK_{j,3})e(RCT_{i,4}, SK_1)^{\omega_i}} \\ &= \frac{e(g^{s+s'}, g^{\alpha} w^r)}{\prod_{i \in I}(e(w^{\lambda'_i} v^{t'_i}, g^r)e((u^{\rho(i)'} h)^{-t'_i}, g^{r_j})e(g^{t'_i}, (u^{S_j} h)^{r_j} v^{-r})e(C_1^{M'_{i,1}}, g^r))^{\omega_i}} \\ &= e(g,g)^{\alpha s} \end{aligned}$$

DU recovers the data file $f^* = C_f/key$ after the key is calculated. DO will download the verification value $H(f)$ from the blockchain when the user wants to verify the correctness of the cloud re-encryption. DU calculates $H(f^*)$ and judges whether $H(f) = H(f^*)$ holds. The result is correct if the equation holds.

4 The Formal of Definition of the Improved Scheme

Aiming at the problem of high computational overhead of proxy re-encryption and high computational cost of user decryption in the basic scheme, we propose an improved scheme. We use online/offline technology to reduce the computing overhead of cloud servers in improved scheme. Moreover, we use key blinding technology to generate a conversion key, which offloads complex computing operations during user decryption to cloud services.

4.1 System Model

Now, the system model of the improved scheme is given. It is the same as the basic scheme (Fig. 3).

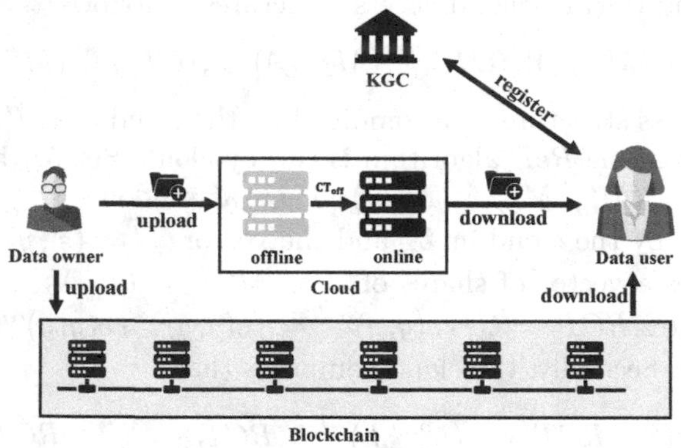

Fig. 3. Improved model

4.2 Algorithm Definition

There are nine algorithms in the improved scheme. Now, the specific definitions of the algorithms are as follows.

$Setup(1^K) \rightarrow (MPK, MSK)$: The $Setup$ algorithm is executed by the KGC to deinitialize the system. The master public key MPK and the master key MSK will be output when the security parameter K is taken as input.

$KeyGen(S_{DU}, MSK) \rightarrow SK_{DU}$: The $KeyGen$ algorithm is executed by the KGC to help DU complete registration. The DU's secret key will be output when the attribute set S_{DU} and the master key are taken as input.

$TKeyGen(SK_{DU}) \rightarrow (TK_{DU}, RK_{DU})$: The $TKeyGen$ algorithm is executed by the KGC to help DU generate conversion key. The DU's conversion key and the reclaiming key RK_{DU} will be output when the DU's secret key SK_{DU} is taken as input.

$Encrypt(f, (M, \rho)) \rightarrow (CT_{DO}, pf)$: The $Encrypt$ algorithm is executed locally by the DU. The ciphertext CT_{DO} will be output when the data file f and the specified access structure (M, ρ) are taken as input.

$Seek(CT'_{DO}, CT''_{DO}) \rightarrow 1/0$: Cloud operates the $Seek$ algorithm after the $Detect$ algorithm output 1. On input the ciphertext CT'_{DO} and CT''_{DO}, Output 1 if two ciphertexts are from the same plaintext; otherwise, output 0.

$Enc_{offline}(N) \rightarrow CT_{off}$: The $Enc_{offline}$ algorithm is executed by the cloud in the offline phase. Input a number N which must be larger than real attribute complexity. Output a offline ciphertext CT_{off}.

$ReE((M', \rho'), CT_{DO}, CT_{off}) \rightarrow RCT_{DO}$: Input the ciphertext CT_{DO}, the offline ciphertext CT_{off} and an access structure (M', ρ') combined by private cloud. Output a re-encrypted ciphertext RCT.

$Transform(RCT_{DO}, TK_{DU}) \rightarrow RCT'_{DO}$: Input the ciphertext RCT_{DO} and the conversion key TK_{DU}. Output a conversion ciphertext RCT'_{DO} if S satisfies (M, ρ); otherwise, output $\perp$.

$Decrypt(RCT'_{DO}, RK_{DU}) \rightarrow f$: Input the conversion ciphertext RCT'_{DO} and the reclaiming key RK_{DU}. Output the data file f.

5 The Constructions of the Improved Scheme

$Setup(1^K) \rightarrow (MPK, MSK)$: The security parameter 1^K is taken as input. First, the algorithm chooses a bilinear mapping $D = (p, G, G_T, e)$. Second, some elements g, u, h, w, v are chosen randomly in G. Moreover, a random α is chosen randomly in Z_p^*. Finally, a hash functions with collision-resistant $H : \{0,1\}* \rightarrow Z_p^*$ is chosen and the master public key and the master secret key are output as follows.

$$MPK = (D, g, h, w, v, u, e(g,g)^{\alpha}, H) \quad MSK = \alpha$$

$KeyGen(S_{DU}, MSK) \rightarrow SK_{DU}$: The DU's attribute set S_{DU} and the master secret key are taken as input. First, $t+1$ randoms $r, r_1, r_2, ..., r_t$ are randomly chosen in Z_p^* by the $KeyGen$ algorithm. The algorithm computes $SK_0 = g^{\alpha} w^r$, $SK_1 = g^r$. Second, the algorithm computes $SK_{j,2} = g^{r_j}$ and $SK_{j,3} = (u^{S_j} h)^{r_j} v^{-r}$, where j from 1 to t. Finally, the private key associated with the user is obtained by KGC, where j from 1 to t.

$$SK_S = (SK_0 = g^{\alpha} w^r, SK_1 = g^r, \{SK_{j,2} = g^{r_j}, SK_{j,3} = (u^{S_j} h)^{r_j} v^{-r}\})$$

$TKeyGen(SK_{DU}) \rightarrow (TK_{DU}, RK_{DU})$: First, a random δ is randomly chosen in Z_p^* by KGC. The algorithm computes $TK_0 = SK_0^{\delta}$ and $TK_1 = SK_1^{\delta}$. Second, for j from 1 to t, compute $TK_{j,1} = SK_{j,1}^{\delta}$, $TK_{j,2} = SK_{j,2}^{\delta}$ and $TK_{j,3} = SK_{j,3}^{\delta}$. Finally, $RK_{DU} = \delta$ is sent to data user.

$Enc_{offline}(N_{max}) \rightarrow CT_{off}$: Input a number N_{max} which must be larger than real attribute complexity. First, randoms s', a', b' are randomly chosen in Z_p^* by the Enc_{off} algorithm. The algorithm computes $C_f^{off} = e(g,g)^{\alpha s'}$, $C_0^{off} = g^{s'}$. Second, randoms $\lambda_i', t_i', x_i' \in Z_p^*$ are randomly chosen by the $Encrypt_{off}$ algorithm. The algorithm computes $C_{i,1}^{off} = \omega^{\lambda_i'} v^{t_i'}$, $C_{i,2}^{off} = (u^{x_i'} h)^{-t_i'}$, $c_{i,3}' = g^{t_i'}$, where $i = 1$ to N_{max}. Finally, the offline ciphertext is obtained by cloud, where i from 1 to N_{max}.

$$CT_{off} = (s', C_f^{off}, C_0^{off}, \{\lambda_i', t_i', x_i', CT_{i,1}^{off}, CT_{i,2}^{off}, CT_{i,3}^{off}\})$$

$ReE((M', \rho'), CT_{DO}, CT_{off}) \rightarrow RCT_{DO}$: Suppose there are some ciphertexts of the repeated data and the associated access structures as follows.

$$(CT_{DO1}, (M_1, \rho_1)), (CT_{DO2}, (M_2, \rho_2)), ..., (CT_{DOn}, (M_n, \rho_n))$$

Firstly, these access structures are combined by the cloud as (M', ρ'), where M' is a $l' \times n'$ matrix. The ReE algorithm is run by cloud. Set M_i' be the i-th row of M', and $M_i' = (M_{i,1}', M_{i,2}', ..., M_{i,n'}')$. It uses a offline ciphertext $CT_{off} = (s', C_f^{off}, C_0^{off}, \{\lambda_i', t_i', x_i', C_{i,1}^{off}, C_{i,2}^{off}, C_{i,3}^{off}\})$ generated by cloud, where i from 1 to n_{max}'. Then $n' - 1$ randoms $\overline{y}_2, \overline{y}_3, ..., \overline{y}_{n'}$ are randomly chosen by cloud in Z_p^* and the vector $\overrightarrow{y}' = (s', y_2', y_3', ..., y_{n'}')^T$ is set and computes a vector of shares of s' as $M'\overrightarrow{y}' = (\widetilde{\lambda}_1', \widetilde{\lambda}_2', ..., \widetilde{\lambda}_{l'}')^T$. Firstly, cloud computes $RCT_f = CT_f \cdot CT_f' = f \cdot e(g,g)^{\alpha s} \cdot e(g,g)^{\alpha s'}$ and $RCT_0 = C_0 \cdot C_0' = g^s \cdot g^{s'}$. Secondly, simple set

$$RCT_{i,1} = C_{i,1}', RCT_{i,2} = C_{i,2}', RCT_{i,3} = C_{i,3}'$$

where i from 1 to l'. Private cloud computes as follows.

$$RCT_{i,4} = \widetilde{\lambda}_i' - \lambda_i', RCT_{i,5} = t_i'(x_i' - \rho'(i)), RCT_{i,6} = c_1^{M_{i,1}'}$$

Finally, it sets the re-encrypted ciphertext as follows and store it in cloud.

$$RCT_{DO} = (RCT_0, \{RCT_{i,1}, RCT_{i,2}, RCT_{i,3}, RCT_{i,4}, RCT_{i,5}, RCT_{i,6}\})$$

$Transform(RCT_{DO}, TK_{DU}) \rightarrow RCT_{DO}'$: The $Transform$ algorithm is run by cloud when the user issues a decryption request. If S don't satisfy (M, ρ), output $\perp$. Cloud computes as follows when a decryption request and TK_{DU} are received.

$$A = \prod_{i \in I} (e(RCT_{i,1} \cdot RCT_{i,6}, TK_1) e(RCT_{i,2} \cdot u^{RCT_{i,5}}, TK_{j,2}) e(RCT_{i,3}, TK_{j,3}))^{\omega_i'}$$

$$RCT_{DO}' = \frac{e(RCT_0, TK_0)}{e(w^{\sum_{i \in I} RCT_{i,4} \omega_i'}, TK_1) \cdot A} = e(g,g)^{(s+s')\alpha\delta}$$

$Decrypt(RCT_{DO}', RK_{DU}) \rightarrow f$: After the user receives RCT_{DO}', the $Decrypt$ algorithm is run by the user to recover the data file. The specific decryption of DU is as follows. A transformed ciphertext RCT_{DO}' of a re-encrypted ciphertext and a reclaiming key RK_{DU} are used as input. It computes $key = RCT_{DO}'^{1/RK_{DU}}$ and $f = RCT_f / key$.

6 Secure Analysis

Theorem 1. *The proposed scheme is selective CPA-secure under the assumption that the CP-ABE scheme in [6] is selective CPA-secure.*

Proof. If there exists a polynomial adversary A that can break the proposed scheme, then we can build a simulator B. Simulator B can use the same method to break Rouselakis's scheme. It is easy to building simulator B because the proposed scheme has the same ciphertext distribution as Rouselakis's scheme. Therefore, we can conclude that the proposed scheme has the same probability as Rouselakis's scheme.

7 Performance Analysis and Evaluation

We will carry out theoretical analysis and experimental simulation of the proposed scheme respectively.

Table 1. Comparison cost comparison

Schemes	KeyGen	Encrypt	ReE	Decrypt
Basis	$(4S+3)T_e$	$(5S+4)T_e$	$(6S+2)T_e$	$(4S+1)T_p$
Improved	$(4S+3)T_e$	$(5S+4)T_e$	$(S+1)T_e$	$1T_e$

T_e: A modular exponential operation,
T_p: A pairing operation,
S: The number of attributes.

7.1 Performance Analysis

We analyze the algorithmic computational overhead of the proposed scheme. In the Table 1, we can easily compare the computational overhead of each stage. The computational overhead of key generation is $(4S+3)T_e$ in the basic scheme and it has the same overhead as the improved scheme, where T_e is a modular exponential operation and S is the number of attributes. In addition, the computational overhead of encryption $(5S+4)T_e$ is the same as the improved scheme. The computational cost of re-encryption in the base scheme is $(6S+2)T_e$. In the improved scheme, we greatly reduce the computational overhead $(S+1)T_e$, so that the proxy re-encryption time is reduced. What's more, we offload the expensive computing overhead in the DU's decryption process to the cloud server, so that DU can recover the data files in a lightweight manner. The computational overhead of decrypt is $(4S+1)T_p$ in the basic scheme. However, the computational overhead of decrypt is $1T_e$ in the improved scheme. With the improved scheme, DU can decrypt using resource-constrained devices (mobile phones, wireless sensors).

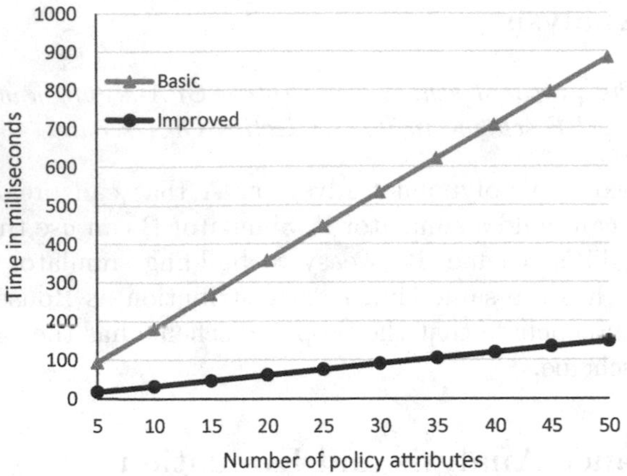

Fig. 4. Re-encryption time

7.2 Performance Evaluation

We conducted experimental simulations to further compare the effectiveness. Our experiments are simulated on a VMware Workstation with Intel Core i7-10510 at 2.30 GHz and 4G RAM. Based on the PBC and GMP library, we have implemented all algorithms of the scheme. The programming language is C.

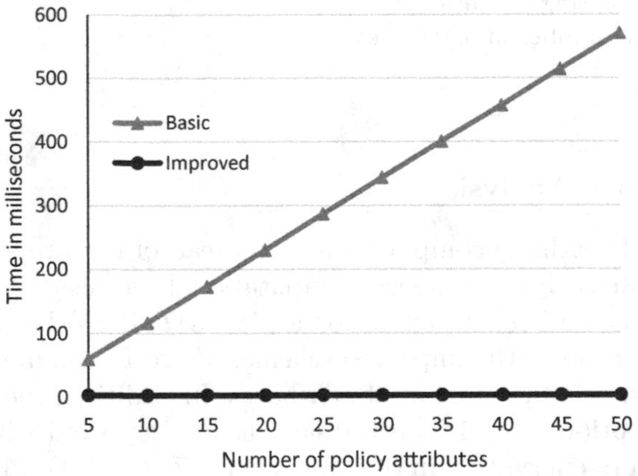

Fig. 5. Decryption time

Compared with the basic scheme, the improved scheme does not increase the computational overhead in the key generation and encryption phase, so we compare the overhead of the re-encryption and decryption phase. We can find that the computational overhead of re-encryption is proportional to the attribute complexity in Fig. 4. In the improved scheme, we use offline encryption technology, so that the cloud server generates offline ciphertext in the idle phase and stores it in the server. The cost of re-encryption for the improved scheme is lower than that of many existing schemes.

Compared with the basic scheme, the improved scheme achieves constant decryption computational overhead. In the basic scheme, the user decryption overhead is proportional to the attribute complexity. We use key blinding technology to offload expensive operations to the cloud server.

DU can recover data files through constant computational overhead. As shown in Fig. 5, we can find that the improved scheme is more suitable for resource-constrained devices.

8 Conclusion

In this paper, we propose an ABE scheme that supports deduplication in cloud computing environment. In addition, we implement the verification of cloud computing results based on blockchain. In order for the cloud server to complete the re-encryption quickly and efficiently, we propose an improvement scheme to reduce the delay. Through the improved scheme, users can achieve lightweight decryption.

References

1. Cui, H., Deng, R.H., Li, Y., Wu, G.: Attribute-based storage supporting secure deduplication of encrypted data in cloud. IEEE Trans. Big Data **5**(03), 330–342 (2019)
2. Gao, S., Piao, G., Zhu, J., Ma, X., Ma, J.: Trustaccess: a trustworthy secure ciphertext-policy and attribute hiding access control scheme based on blockchain. IEEE Trans. Veh. Technol. **69**(6), 5784–5798 (2020)
3. Li, J., Zhang, Y., Chen, X., Xiang, Y.: Secure attribute-based data sharing for resource-limited users in cloud computing. Comput. Secur. **72**, 1–12 (2018)
4. Qin, B., Deng, R.H., Liu, S., Ma, S.: Attribute-based encryption with efficient verifiable outsourced decryption. IEEE Trans. Inf. Forensics Secur. **10**(7), 1384–1393 (2015)
5. Rahulamathavan, Y., Phan, R.C.W., Rajarajan, M., Misra, S., Kondoz, A.: Privacy-preserving blockchain based IoT ecosystem using attribute-based encryption. In: 2017 IEEE International Conference on Advanced Networks and Telecommunications Systems (ANTS), pp. 1–6. IEEE (2017)
6. Rouselakis, Y., Waters, B.: Practical constructions and new proof methods for large universe attribute-based encryption. In: Proceedings of the 2013 ACM SIGSAC Conference on Computer & Communications Security, pp. 463–474 (2013)
7. Shen, J., Yang, H., Vijayakumar, P., Kumar, N.: A privacy-preserving and untraceable group data sharing scheme in cloud computing. IEEE Trans. Dependable Secure Comput. (2021). https://doi.org/10.1109/TDSC.2021.3050517
8. Tian, G., Hu, Y., Wei, J., Liu, Z., Huang, X., Chen, X., Susilo, W.: Blockchain-based secure deduplication and shared auditing in decentralized storage. IEEE Trans. Dependable Secure Comput. (2021)

9. Xu, R., Joshi, J., Krishnamurthy, P.: An integrated privacy preserving attribute-based access control framework supporting secure deduplication. IEEE Trans. Dependable Secure Comput. **18**(2), 706–721 (2019)
10. Yang, H., Shen, J., Zhou, T., Ji, S., Vijayakumar, P.: A flexible and privacy-preserving collaborative filtering scheme in cloud computing for VANETs. ACM Trans. Internet Technol. (TOIT) **22**(2), 1–19 (2021)
11. Yuan, H., Chen, X., Wang, J., Yuan, J., Yan, H., Susilo, W.: Blockchain-based public auditing and secure deduplication with fair arbitration. Inf. Sci. **541**, 409–425 (2020)

A Secure Word Vector Training Scheme Based on Inner-Product Functional Encryption

Mingwu Zhang[1,2](✉), Zhen-An Li[1], and Peihang Zhang[1]

[1] School of Computer Science and Information Security, Guilin University of Electronic Technology, Guilin, China
csmwzhang@gmail.com

[2] School of Computers, Hubei University of Technology, Wuhan, China

Abstract. Word vector training is usually deployed in machine learning to provide a model architecture and optimization, for example, to learn word embeddings from a large amount of datasets. Training word vector in machine learning needs a lot of datasets to train and output a model, however, some of which might contain private and sensitive information, and the training phase will lead to the exposure of the trained model and user datasets. In order to offer utilizable, plausible, and personalized alternatives to users, this process usually also entails a breach of their privacy. In this article, we investigate the problem of training high-quality word vectors on encrypted datasets by using privacy-preserving learning algorithms. Firstly, we use a pseudo-random function to generate a statistical token for each word to help build the vocabulary of the word vector. Then we employ functional inner-product encryption to calculate the activation function to obtain the inner product, securely. Finally, we use BGN cryptosystem to encrypt and hide the sensitive datasets, and complete the homomorphic operation over the ciphertexts to perform the training procedure. Compared with the existing solutions, it indicates that our scheme can provide a higher efficiency and less communication overhead.

Keywords: Word vector training · Privacy-preserving machine learning · Homomorphic encryption · Inner-product predicate

1 Introduction

As the training of word vectors requires a great mount of computational cost, especially in super large-scale word vector case. The rapid advancement of cloud computing technology has increased in data owners' willingness to outsource large amounts of big data to cloud-based servers [1–3], and numerous applications collect large amounts of data from a variety of data owners. Thus, users can be liberated from the complexities of data management. Machine learning methods are widely used to tap the rich value contained in big data outsourcing storage in the cloud [4], because machine learning methods typically improve efficiency

X. Chen et al. (Eds.): SocialSec 2022, CCIS 1663, pp. 65–82, 2022.
https://doi.org/10.1007/978-981-19-7242-3_5

and accuracy over time as the amount of data processed increases. In comparison to training with only local data sets, collaborative learning can improve the generative model's accuracy by incorporating more representative data.

While cloud computing has numerous advantages, privacy protection remains a significant challenge, since it will typically entail the disclosure of sensitive user word vector data, such as health status and economic data. With the dawn of the cloud era, privacy protection for big data in the cloud has garnered an increasing amount of attention. While collecting big data, it is possible that some sensitive or proprietary information will be included. Once exposed, it will have catastrophic consequences. As a result, cloud computing data must be encrypted. Machine learning algorithms, on the other hand, cannot directly access encrypted data. Data privacy cannot be guaranteed if the decryption key is provided to an honest but curious cloud service. Therefore, processing encrypted data via cloud-based machine learning algorithms is a difficult problem.

Related Works. The early research on privacy-preserving machine learning concentrated on k-means [5,6], KNN, SVM classification [7,8], and decision trees [9,10]. As neural networks become more widely used in practical applications, privacy protection has garnered considerable attention [11]. However, neural networks employ traditional methods, which suffer from low efficiency and accuracy.

Recently, differential privacy has been used to develop privacy-preserving machine learning algorithms [12]. In [13], it deals with the differential private approximation problem of principal component analysis, while [14] proposes a functional mechanism, which is a general differential private approximation designed for optimization-based large-scale analysis frame (such as linear regression and logistic regression). Shokri et al. [15], applied differential privacy to the updating of neural network parameters, thereby minimizing the privacy loss associated with collaborative deep learning. Abadi et al. [16] proposed two components for private neural network training: a differential private stochastic gradient descent algorithm, moment accounting, and hyperparameter tuning.

Homomorphic encryption on developing privacy-preserving machine learning algorithms is a useful tool. In [17,18], the authors gave a new encoding method to achieve negative encryption and designed several security build modules to provide security clinical diagnosis of multi-class SVM with privacy protection. [19] proposed a privacy-protecting matrix factorization protocol with fully homomorphic encryption that is more efficient than the protocol proposed in [20]. Bobst et al. [21] Constructed three widely used machine learning classification protocols, namely hyperplane decision-making, naive Bayes, and decision tree, and used homomorphic encryption to ensure privacy. In [22], Dowling et al. During the inference phase, a semi-homomorphic encryption scheme was used, and a method was proposed for converting the learned neural network to an encrypted network. Wang et al. [23], Create a secure multiplication protocol and train word vectors on encrypted data using homomorphic encryption. In [24], Zhang et al. gave a neighboring proposals that can provide a high efficiency method for privacy protection to find a meaningful-minded node to generate recommendations.

Our Contributions. In this paper, we focus on the use of machine learning technology in natural language processing, especially, for words treated as atomic units in various NLP applications or more complex tasks, and representing words in a vector space can help learning algorithms achieve better performance. We design a secure and privacy-preserving word vector training scheme that provides the privacy of input data during the learning and training procedures. Our most significant contributions are summarized below.

- We use a special functional encryption, i.e., inner product encryption, to protect the privacy of large-scale encrypted data collected from multiple participants for the purpose of training distributed word vectors, and it can also be used for other neural network learning algorithms, e.g., CNN. It also gives great significance to numerous NLP applications under the sensitive datasets.
- We employ inner product encryption and homomorphic encryption to perform the secure calculation of the activation function. These ciphertext-based algorithms are part of our custom structure.
- We conduct a thorough analysis of the privacy and efficiency of our proposed protocol. In order to further prove its practicability and effectiveness, we conduct an experimental evaluation on a representative real-world data set and compared the results obtained in the plain text domain.

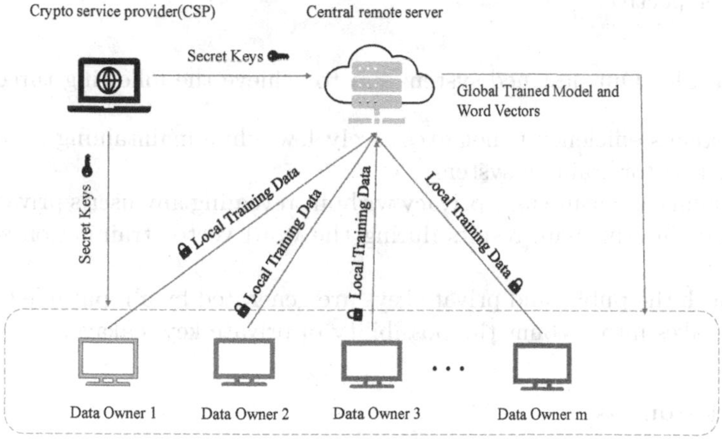

Fig. 1. System model

2 Problem Statement

Framework. As illustrated in Fig. 1, the system is composed of three entities: data owners, a crypto service provider CSP, and a central remote server S. More precisely, there are n data owners in total, denoted by $o_i(i = 1, \ldots, n)$. Each of these data owners owns a private data file f_i and wishes to perform collaborative neural network learning with the other participating data owners. More precisely, they will transmit their encrypted private data files to a central remote server. After receiving the encrypted data, the remote server trains the encrypted data and generates high-quality word vectors and models, which can be used for various natural language processing tasks in the future. The encryption service provider CSP is responsible for initializing the system and generating and issuing encryption/decryption keys to all data owners.

The privacy can be maintained in the above configuration as long as the remote server S and the crypto service provider CSP can not collude with each other. It is worth noting that this architecture of two non-colluding entities has been utilized frequently in previous works [25–27].

Threat Model. Our goal is to ensure that remote servers and encryption service providers $CSPs$ cannot deduce any information about user data other than what learning algorithms reveal. As mentioned previously, it is assumed that the remote server and the CSP is not colluding, that they are affiliated with two distinct organizations, such as Amazon EC2 and a government agency. As a result, collusion between them is highly improbable, as it would jeopardize their reputations. Additionally, we assume that the remote servers S and CSP are honest but curious entities [28,29], which means that they will run the protocol exactly as specified, but will attempt to deduce additional information from their protocol perspective.

Design Goals. Our designed system aim to achieve the following three goals:

1. The system's efficiency is not excessively low while maintaining accuracy of the word vector training system.
2. The system can ensure user privacy without revealing any user's private information or intermediate results during the word vector training on sensitive datasets.
3. Since both the public and private keys are generated by a reputable CSP, the system takes into account the possibility of private key leakage.

2.1 Backgrounds

Vector Representation of Words. The most intuitive and widely used method of word representation in natural language processing is One-hot Representation, which encodes each word as a very long vector. This vector has a dimension equal to the size of the vocabulary; the majority of the elements are zero, and only one dimension has a value of one. This dimension corresponds to the currently selected word. If words are represented using traditional sparse notation, it will result in dimensionality problems when attempting to solve certain tasks (such as building language models). There is no such issue when low-dimensional word vectors are used. Simultaneously, from a practical standpoint, if deep learning is applied to high-dimensional features, its complexity becomes almost unacceptably high, which is why low-dimensional word vectors are also highly desired in this context.

Nowadays, with the advancement of machine learning technology, it is possible to learn high-quality word vectors from massive amounts of data using neural networks. The word vectors are obtained incidentally during the language model's training. Word2Vec is a language model and a tool for creating word vectors. It is a model for unsupervised learning of semantic knowledge from a large number text predictions. Natural language processing makes extensive use of it.

We focus on two classic Word2vec models in this article: the Continuous Bag-of-Words Model (CBOW) and the Continuous Skip-Gram Model. The following is a brief introduction.

Continuous Bag-Of-Words Model (CBOW). The continuous bag of words model, abbreviated CBOW, is similar to the feedforward NNLM in that the non-linear hidden layer is eliminated and all words share the projection layer; thus, all words are projected to the same position (their vectors are averaged). The CBOW method uses the context to predict the central word, and the Gradient Desent method is used to continuously adjust the vectors of the surrounding words. After training is complete, each word is used as the central word, and the word vectors of the surrounding words are adjusted to obtain the word vectors for all the words in the text.

Functional Encryption for Inner Product. The inner product in finite field of two vectors $\vec{x} = (x_1, x_2, \cdots, x_l) \in Z_p^l$ and $\vec{y} = (y_1, y_2, \cdots, y_l) \in Z_p^l$ is defined as:

$$\vec{x} \cdot \vec{y} = x_1 y_1 + x_2 y_2 + \cdots + x_l y_l \bmod p \tag{1}$$

In the above inner product model, we assume that one party has the vector $\vec{x}$ and the other has the vector $\vec{y}$, the inner product value $< \vec{x}, \vec{y} >$ of the vector is calculated without revealing its own vector.

Traditional secure multi-party computation can calculate inner product, but secure multi-party computation has the disadvantages of high communication overhead and low computational efficiency, so we can use the method of inner product encryption [30] to solve the privacy calculation problem of inner product.

Let $\mathsf{PKE} = (\mathsf{Setup}, \mathsf{Enc}, \mathsf{Dec})$ be a public key encryption scheme that satisfies the conditions of *random number reuse, linear homomorphism of the key*, and *linear homomorphism of the ciphertext under the shared random number*. The general inner product function encryption $\mathsf{IPE} = (\mathsf{Setup}, \mathsf{KeyGen}, \mathsf{Enc}, \mathsf{Dec})$ scheme is constructed as follows:

- $\mathsf{IPE.Setup}(1^\lambda, l)$:
  1. Call the key generation algorithm $\mathsf{PKE.Setup}$ to generate l public/private key pairs $(\mathsf{pk}_1, \mathsf{sk}_1), \cdots, (\mathsf{pk}_l, \mathsf{sk}_l)$.

   2. Set system public parameters $\mathsf{pp} = \{\mathsf{pk}_i\}_{i\in[l]}\}$.
   3. Keep the master key $\mathsf{mk} = (\mathsf{sk}_1, \mathsf{sk}_2, \cdots, \mathsf{sk}_l)$.
- $\mathsf{IPE.KeyGen}(\mathsf{pp}, \mathsf{mk}, \vec{y})$:
  Taking system public parameters pp, master key $\mathsf{mk}$and vector $\vec{y} = (y_1, y_2, \cdots, y_l) \in \mathbb{Z}_p^l$ as inputs, this algorithm calculates the linear combination of master keys, that is:

$$\mathsf{sk}_y = y_1\mathsf{sk}_1 + y_2\mathsf{sk}_2 + \cdots + y_l\mathsf{sk}_l \bmod p \tag{2}$$

- $\mathsf{IPE.Enc}(\mathsf{pp}, \vec{x})$:
   1. Randomly select a shared random number $r \in \mathbb{Z}_p$ in PKE's randomness space.
   2. Caculate $\mathsf{ct}_0 = \mathsf{PKE.Commit}(r)$.
   3. Calculate $\mathsf{ct}_j = \mathsf{PKE.Enc}(\mathsf{pk}_j, x_j; r)$ for $i = 1, \cdots, l$.
   4. Output $\mathsf{ct}_x = (\mathsf{ct}_0, (\mathsf{ct}_1, \mathsf{ct}_2, \cdots, \mathsf{ct}_l))$.
- $\mathsf{IPE.Dec}(\mathsf{pp}, \mathsf{ct}_x, \mathsf{sk}_y)$:
  Output $\mathsf{PKE.Dec}((\mathsf{ct}_0, \prod_{i\in[l]} \mathsf{ct}_i^{y_i}), \mathsf{sk}_y)$

BGN Cryptosystem. BGN is a homomorphic public key encryption that is based on a composite order finite group capable of bilinear mapping [28], which combines the properties of Paillier [29] and Okamoto-Uchiyama [31] encryption schemes. The BGN cryptosystem employs the bilinear mapping to enable any number of additions and one multiplication on the ciphertext, whose cryptosystem is composed of three algorithms as follows.

$\mathsf{BGN.KeyGen}(1^\lambda)$: The key generation algorithm is used to generate the private key and public key for the user, which is described as follows.

1. On input a system security parameter $\lambda \in Z^+$, it generates composite order bilinear group $(p_1, p_2, \mathbb{G}, \mathbb{G}_T, e) \leftarrow \mathcal{G}(1^\lambda)$.
2. Compute $N = p_1 p_2$.
3. Randomly choose two generators $g, u \leftarrow \mathbb{G}$.
4. Compute $h = u^{p_2}$.
5. Set public key $\mathsf{pk} = (N, \mathbb{G}, \mathbb{G}_T, e, g, h)$ and secret key $\mathsf{sk} = p_1$.

$\mathsf{BGN.Enc}(\mathsf{pk}, m)$: Let the message space be $\mathbb{M} = \{0, 1, 2, ..., T\}$, where $T < p_2$. The encryption algorithm takes as the public key pk and a message m as inputs, and performs the encryption as follows:

1. At random choose a randnom number $r \in Z_n$.
2. Calculate $c = g^m h^r \in \mathbb{G}$.
3. Outputs the ciphertext c.

$\mathsf{BGN.Dec}(c, \mathsf{sk})$: The decryption algorithm does:

1. Compute $c^{p_1} = (g^m h^r)^{p_1} = (g^{p_1})^m$
2. Output $m \leftarrow \log_g c^{p_1}$, which is involved in solving the discrete logarithms of $(g^{p_1})^m modn$ with the base g^x using the Pollard's lambda algorithm and outputs the plaintext m.

3 Our Proposed Secure Word Training Protocol

In this section, we give the concrete construction of our privacy-preserving word vector training scheme, which is comprised of the procedure of two phases: *Initialization protocol* and *Privacy-preserving training protocol*.

3.1 Initialization

Our construction makes use of the BGN cryptosystem, Inner-product function encryption and a pseudo-random function P as the cryptographic primitives, where P is defined as: $\{0,1\}^{\lambda} \times \{0,1\}^{*} \rightarrow \{0,1\}^{\lambda}$. In the beginning, the CSP was responsible for setting up the environment. In particular, given a security parameter λ, CSP randomly and uniformly generates the following keys from their respective domains: a tuple $(\mathsf{pk}_u, \mathsf{sk}_u)$ for the BGN cryptosystem, Key pair $(\mathsf{mpk}, \mathsf{msk})$ for the inner product function encryption, and a PRF key $k_1 \xleftarrow{\$} \{0,1\}^{\lambda}$ for $P_{k_1}(\cdot)$. Then the CSP publishes the public keys $(\mathsf{pk}_u, \mathsf{mpk})$ and saved the msk , finally sends the private keys sk_u and k_1 to all users through a secure channel.

As we described in the system model above, each data owner has a private data file and hopes to train the model in collaboration with other data owners. Intuitively, data owners can protect their privacy by encrypting data before outsourcing their sensitive data to a remote server S. More specifically, for each data file f_i that contains a sequence of words $(w_1, w_2, ..., w_{T(f_i)})$, the data owner o_i calculates a token $\tau_j = P_{k_1}(w_j)$ for each word $w_j, \forall j \in [T(f_i)]$. In addition, for each deduplicated initial word vector $v(w_j)$, user o_i first converts each of its items $v(w_j)_k (k \in [d])$ to fixed-point representation, and then encrypt it under the BGN cryptosystem $[\![v(w_j)]\!]$. Therefore, each data owner o_i obtains the encrypted form c_i corresponding to their private file f_i, where c_i consists of a sequence of tokens τ_j and a set of encrypted word vectors $[\![v(w_j)]\!]$. Finally, each data owner o_i provides the encrypted data file c_i to the remote server S.

After the remote server S receives all the ciphertexts from the n data owners, it initializes a dictionary D, which is a data structure that stores key-value pairs. Subsequently, S traverses all the collected data and stores the tokens and their corresponding frequency count$(P_{k_1}(w))$ as the key-value pairs in the dictionary D. Finally, the dictionary D contains m key-value pairs extracted from the encrypted database. It should be noted that this type of statistical information is essential information in the process of neural network learning by remote servers, so we assume that this type of statistical information will not reveal any private information of the original data.

3.2 Privacy-Preserving Training Protocol

The model structures of the CBOW model (Continuous Bag-Of-Words Model) and the Skip-gram model (Continuous Skip-gram Model). CBOW is the context of the known current word to predict the current word, and Skip -gram is the opposite, predicting its context when the current word is known.

The objective function of the language model based on neural network is usually taken as the following log-likelihood function: $\mathcal{L} = \sum_{\omega \in C} \log p(\omega|context(\omega))$. Therefore, the key condition is to calculate the conditional probability of all words in the corpus of a given context: $p(\omega|context(\omega))$, where $context(\omega)$is a set of words surrounding ω.Obviously, it is impractical to perform such calculations for all words in each training sample in a large-scale training corpus. In order to optimize this problem, for the two models mentioned above, Word2vec respectively gives two sets of frameworks, which is designed based on Hierarchical Softmax and Negative Sampling respectively.Hierarchical softmax is to change the softmax of N classification to logN hierarchical binary classification, which solves the Huffman node weight matrix; negative sampling is to update only part of the hidden weight matrix for each training sample of each training sample.

WORD2VEC Based on Hierarchical Softmax. Hierarchical Softmax optimized the neural probability model's large-scale matrix operation and softmax normalization operation. To begin, we remove the hidden layer and convert the output layer to a Huffman tree. The fundamental idea behind hierarchical softmax is to represent all words in the dictionary D using a Huffman binary tree. In our protocol, the remote server obtains the exact frequency of the word using the dictionary D obtained during the initialization phase for the purpose of generating the Huffman tree, which means that words with a higher frequency have shorter binary codes. The Huffman tree that results has m leaf nodes and $m-1$ zero vector intermediate nodes, where m is the number of words in dictionary D.

The objective function of CBOW model optimization based on Hierarchical Softmax is defined as follows:

$$\mathcal{L} = \sum_{\omega \in C} \log p(\omega|context(\omega)) \tag{3}$$

and the training goal is to maximize the above function. As previously stated, the output layer is a Huffman binary tree. There is a unique path between each leaf node and the root, and this path is used to estimate the probability of the word represented by the leaf node. To be more precise, the conditional probability that a word is in the training sample is defined as follows:

$$p(\omega|context(\omega)) = \prod_{j=0}^{l^w-1} p(d_j^\omega|x_\omega, \theta_j^\omega) \tag{4}$$

where l^ω denotes the number of nodes in the path from the root to the leaf node w, θ_{j-1}^ω denotes the d-dimensional parameter vector associated with the jth internal node on the above path, and the probability $p(d_j^\omega|x_\omega, \theta_j^\omega)$ is defined as:

$$p(d_j^\omega|x_\omega, \theta_j^\omega) = \begin{cases} \sigma(x_\omega^T \theta_j^\omega), & d_j^\omega = 0 \\ 1 - \sigma(x_\omega^T \theta_j^\omega), & d_j^\omega = 1 \end{cases} \tag{5}$$

In the process from the root node to any leaf node, we will go through multiple branch judgments, and each branch is equivalent to a binary classification. Except for the root node, each node in the tree corresponds to a Huffman code with a value of 0 or 1. Therefore, in Word2vec, the node coded as 1 is defined as a negative class, and the point coded as 0 is defined as a positive class. In other words, when a node is classified, the left side is the negative class$(1 - \sigma(x_\omega^T \theta_j^\omega))$, and the right side is the positive class $(\sigma(x_\omega^T \theta_j^\omega))$.

Therefore, the likelihood function of the CBOW model based on Hierarchical Softmax is evaluated as:

$$\mathcal{L} = \sum_{\omega \in C} \sum_{j=1}^{l^\omega - 1} \{(1 - d_j^\omega) \cdot \log[\sigma(x_\omega^T \theta_j^\omega)] + d_j^\omega \cdot \log[1 - \sigma(x_\omega^T \theta_j^\omega)]\} \tag{6}$$

Next, we need to maximize the likelihood function above. The stochastic gradient ascent method is used in Word2vec. In order to simplify the process of finding the gradient, we will mark the part in the double brackets in the above formula as $\mathcal{L}(\omega, j)$, i.e.,

$$\mathcal{L}(\omega, j) = (1 - d_j^\omega) \cdot \log[\sigma(x_\omega^T \theta_j^\omega)] + d_j^\omega \cdot [1 - \sigma(x_\omega^T \theta_j^\omega)] \tag{7}$$

The method of stochastic gradient ascent is to update all parameters every time a sample is taken. The main parameters included in this function are: x_ω,θ_j^ω.

We first take the derivative of $\mathcal{L}(\omega, j)$; jth with regard to the parameter vector θ_j^ω of the j-th internal node and obtain:

$$\frac{\partial \mathcal{L}}{\partial \theta_j^\omega} = [1 - d_j^\omega - \sigma(x_\omega^T \theta_j^\omega)] x_\omega \tag{8}$$

The update is described as follows:

$$\theta_j^\omega = \theta_j^\omega + \eta [1 - d_j^\omega - \sigma(x_\omega^T \theta_j^\omega)] x_\omega \tag{9}$$

where η denotes a positive learning rate, and the update equation should be applied to $j = 0, 1, 2, \ldots, l^\omega - 1$. In the same way, we can obtain the partial derivative of $\mathcal{L}(\omega, j)$ with respect to x_ω by:

$$\frac{\partial \mathcal{L}}{\partial x_\omega} = [1 - d_j^\omega - \sigma(x_\omega^T \theta_j^\omega)] \theta_j^\omega \tag{10}$$

According to the above formula, the update equation of each word $context(\omega)_i (i \in [2c])$ can be obtained as follows:

$$v(context(\omega)_i) = v(context(\omega)_i) + \eta \sum_{j=1}^{l^\omega - 1} \frac{\partial \mathcal{L}}{\partial x_\omega} \tag{11}$$

In Algorithm 1, we summarize the details of how the remote server S can be trained in a safe manner. Given a training sample $(context(\omega), \omega)$ and an aggregation vector x_ω, the aggregation vector x_ω is jointly calculated by the data owner using the BGN additive homomorphism property. First,S applies to CSP to distribute the key SK_{x_ω} about x_ω, and then calls the IPE algorithm to calculate the inner product to obtain the sigmoid function value. Afterwards, for each parameter vector that needs to be updated on the path from the root to the target word ω, S can perform a privacy update according to Eq. 4, and similarly update the word vector according to Eq. 5.

Algorithm 1. CBOW with Hierarchical Softmax

Require: An aggregate vector x_ω , a training sample $(context(\omega), \omega)$ and ciphertext $CT_{\theta_j^\omega}$ and $[\![\theta_j^\omega]\!]$ of θ_j^ω.

Ensure: parameter vectors $[\![\theta_j^\omega]\!](j = 1, 2, \cdots, l^\omega - 1)$ and updated word vectors $[\![v(context(\omega)_i)]\!]$

1: Initialize a vector $e = 0$.
2: Applies for the key SK_{x_ω} to the CSP for x_ω.
3: **for** $j = 1, 2, \cdots, l^\omega - 1$ **do**
4: Use IPE to calculate $x_\omega^T \cdot \theta_j^\omega$ then calculate $q = \sigma(x_\omega^T \theta_j^\omega)$.
5: Compute $n = \eta(1 - d_j^\omega - q)$.
6: Compute $[\![e]\!] = [\![e]\!] \cdot [e([\![n]\!], [\![\theta_j^\omega]\!]) \cdot h_1^r] \cdot h^r$.
7: Update $[\![\theta_j^\omega]\!] = [\![\theta_j^\omega]\!] \cdot [\![nx_\omega]\!] \cdot h^r$.
8: **end for**
9: **for** $i = 1, 2, ..., 2c$ **do**
10: $[\![v(context(\omega)_i)]\!] = [\![v(context(\omega)_i)]\!] \cdot [\![e]\!] \cdot h^r$
11: **end for**

Different from the CBOW with hierarchical softmax, the objective function for the skip-gram model is given as:

$$\mathcal{L} = \sum_{\omega \in C} \log p(context(\omega)|\omega) \tag{12}$$

Similar to the derivation method of the CBOW model, we give the Skip-Gram privacy training method in Algorithm 2.

WORD2VEC Based on Negative Sampling Model. Word2vec proposes a CBOW model based on Negative Sampling, which uses random negative sampling to greatly improve computational performance. The fundamental calculation concept, however, remains unchanged. Negative Sampling is a simplified version of noise contrast estimation proposed by Gutmann et al. [26], which is an alternative to Hierarchical Softmax. Negative sampling is more intuitive than Hierarchical Softmax in that it requires only one sample of the output vector to be updated, rather than all vectors along the path from root to leaf.

In the CBOW model, the $context(\omega)$ of the word ω is known, and ω needs to be predicted. Therefore, for a given $context(\omega)$, the word ω is a positive sample, and other words are a negative sample. The number of occurrences of words in

Algorithm 2. Skip-Gram with Hierarchical Softmax

Require: A training sample($\omega, context(\omega)$),ciphertext $CT_{\theta_j^\omega}$ and $[\![\theta_j^u]\!]$ of θ_j^ω and $v(\omega)$.
Ensure: Parameter vectors $[\![\theta_j^u]\!](j = 1, 2, \cdots, l^u - 1)$ and updated word vectors $[\![v(\omega)]\!]$.

for $u \in context(\omega)$ **do**
  Initialize a vector $e = 0$.
  Applies for the key $SK_{v(\omega)}$ to the CSP for $v(\omega)$.
  for $j = 1, 2, \cdots, l^u - 1$ **do**
    Use IPE to calculate $v(\omega)^T \cdot \theta_j^\omega$
    Calculate $q = \sigma(v(\omega)^T \theta_j^\omega)$.
    Compute $n = \eta(1 - d_j^\omega - q)$.
    Compute $[\![e]\!] = [\![e]\!] \cdot [e([\![n]\!], [\![\theta_j^\omega]\!]) \cdot h_1^r] \cdot h^r$.
    Update $[\![\theta_j^\omega]\!] = [\![\theta_j^\omega]\!] \cdot [\![nv(\omega)]\!] \cdot h^r$.
  end for
end for
$[\![v(\omega)]\!] = [\![v(\omega)]\!] \cdot [\![e]\!] \cdot h^r$

dictionary D in corpus C is high or low. For those high-frequency words, we hope that the probability of being selected as a negative sample is relatively large, and for those low-frequency words, we hope that the probability of being selected is relatively small, we follow the idea in [22] and generate relative distributions based on the frequency of words stored in the dictionary D. The remote server can select negative samples with the following probability:

$$P_{NEG}(\omega_i) = \frac{[count(\omega_i)]^{\frac{3}{4}}}{\sum_{u \in D}[count(u_i)]^{\frac{3}{4}}} \tag{13}$$

where the label of positive samples is 1, and the label of negative samples is 0. Therefore, for a given $(\omega, contex(\omega))$, we hope to maximize the following objective function:

$$g(\omega) = \sum_{u \in \omega \cup NEG(\omega)} p(u|context(\omega)) \tag{14}$$

In this regard, we also update the parameters through the method of stochastic gradient ascent. First obtain the partial derivative of θ_u to get the update formula of θ^u.

$$\mathcal{L}(\omega, u) = L^\omega(u)\log(\sigma(x^\omega \theta^u)) + (1 - L^\omega(u))\log(1 - \sigma(x^\omega \theta^u)) \tag{15}$$

Which results in the following update equation:

$$\theta^u := \theta_u + \eta[L^\omega(u) - \sigma(\theta^u x_\omega)]x_\omega \tag{16}$$

In the same way, the update equation of $v(context(\omega)_i)$ can be obtained:

$$v(context(\omega)_i) = v(context(\omega)_i) + \frac{\partial \mathcal{L}}{\partial x_\omega} \tag{17}$$

where

$$\frac{\partial \mathcal{L}}{\partial x_\omega} = \eta \sum_{u \in \{\omega\} \cup NEG(\omega)} [L^\omega(u) - \sigma(\theta^u x_\omega)]\theta^u \tag{18}$$

Based on the update Eqs. (8) and (9), the details of how the remote server S trains CBOW under negative sampling in a safe manner are shown in Algorithm 3.

Algorithm 3. CBOW with Negative Sampling

Require: An aggregate vector x_ω, a training sample$(context(\omega), \omega)$ and ciphertext CT_{θ^u} and $[\![\theta^u]\!]$ of θ^u.
Ensure: parameter vectors $[\![\theta^u]\!](j = 1, 2, \cdots, l^\omega - 1)$ and updated word vectors $[\![v(context(\omega)_i)]\!]$

Initialize a vector $e = 0$.
Applies for the key SK_{x_ω} to the CSP for x_ω.
for $u = \{\omega\} \cup NEG(\omega)$ **do**
  Use IPE to calculate $x_\omega^T \cdot \theta^u$ then calculate $q = \sigma(x_\omega^T \theta^u)$.
  Compute $n = \eta(L^\omega(u) - q)$.
  Compute $[\![e]\!] = [\![e]\!] \cdot [e([\![n]\!], [\![\theta^u]\!]) \cdot h_1^r] \cdot h^r$.
  Update $[\![\theta^u]\!] = [\![\theta^u]\!] \cdot [\![nx_\omega]\!] \cdot h^r$.
end for
for $i = 1, 2, ..., 2c$ **do**
  $[\![v(context(\omega)_i)]\!] = [\![v(context(\omega)_i)]\!] \cdot [\![e]\!] \cdot h^r$
end for

The objective function for the Skip-gram model under negative sampling is defined as:

$$g(\omega) = \prod_{\widetilde{\omega} \in Context(\omega)} \prod_{u \in \{\omega\} \cup NEG^{\widetilde{\omega}}(\omega)} p(u|\widetilde{\omega}) \tag{19}$$

where $NEG^{\widetilde{\omega}}$ denotes the collection of negative samples with regard to ω handling with $\widetilde{\omega}$. In Algorithm 4, we give the details of the privacy protection training under negative sampling on the remote server S.

4 Theoretical Analysis

4.1 Security Analysis

In this section, we conduct a security analysis of the proposed protocol. From the process of computing the learning model, it is easily to see that no sensitive information of any user is leaked to the remote server or CSP, and the intermediate process part. Since it is assumed that there is no collusion between the remote server and the CSP, the security analysis is performed from the remote server side and the CSP side. We assume that the homomorphic encryption scheme adopted is secure.

Algorithm 4. Skip-Gram with Negative Sampling

Require: A training sample$(\omega, context(\omega))$,ciphertext CT_{θ^u} and $[\![\theta^u]\!]$ of θ^u and $v(\omega)$.
Ensure: Parameter vectors $[\![\theta^u]\!](j = 1, 2, \cdots, l^u - 1)$ and updated word vectors $[\![v(\omega)]\!]$.

Applies for the key $SK_{v(\omega)}$ to the CSP for $v(\omega)$.
for $\tilde{\omega} \in context(\omega)$ **do**
  Initialize a vector $e = 0$.
  for $u \in \{\omega\} \cup NEG^{\tilde{\omega}(\omega)}$ **do**
    Use IPE to calculate $v(\tilde{\omega})^T \cdot \theta_j^u$
    Calculate $q = \sigma(v(\tilde{\omega})^T \theta^u)$.
    Compute $n = \eta(L^\omega(u) - q)$.
    Compute $[\![e]\!] = [\![e]\!] \cdot [e([\![n]\!], [\![\theta_j^u]\!]) \cdot h_1^r] \cdot h^r$.
    Update $[\![\theta^u]\!] = [\![\theta^u]\!] \cdot [\![nv(\tilde{\omega})]\!] \cdot h^r$.
  end for
end for
$[\![v(\tilde{\omega})]\!] = [\![v(\tilde{\omega})]\!] \cdot [\![e]\!] \cdot h^r$

On the remote server side, an encrypted corpus is obtained after the initialization phase, which consists of a set of token sequences and a set of encrypted word vectors. [18] indicates that the output of PRF is computationally indistinguishable from random strings, so the token does not reveal any information about the corresponding plaintext word. Given a vector, the inner product of it and another vector is obtained through the inner product encryption algorithm, and the information of the other vector will not be obtained. The word vector is encrypted under the BGN cryptosystem. The BGN cryptosystem based on compound-order bilinear groups is proven to be semantically safe against selected plaintext attacks. In the subsequent training process, many homomorphic operations are also encrypted under the BGN cryptosystem, so it is impossible to deduce any meaningful content.

On the CSP side, it has the ability to decrypt ciphertexts. The data owner uses the public parameters released by him to encrypt private data without interacting with it. In the case of no collusion with the remote server, it cannot get any useful information. It is easily to see that our proposed construction scheme can well protect the privacy of user sensitive data.

4.2 Performance

Our efficiency analysis is mainly analyzed from hierarchical Softmax and negative sampling training algorithms. For simplicity, we only consider one training sample in these two cases. In the case of hierarchical softmax, the Huffman binary tree is used to represent the words of the entire dictionary. For each sample, the depth or number of iterations of the Huffman tree is about $\log m$, that is, the number of units that need to be updated is about $\log m$. During each iteration, the number of cryptographic arithmetic primitives that need to be called depends on the dimension d of the vector. Therefore, the complexity of each training sample is $\mathcal{O}(d \cdot \log m)$, whether it is computing or communicating.

Table 1. Arithmetic primitives invoked for a training sample

Model	Addition	Multiplication	IPE
CBOW_HS	$2c \cdot d + 2(\log m - 1) \cdot d$	$(\log m - 1) \cdot d$	$\log m - 1$
CBOW_NEG	$2c \cdot d + 2(\|NEG(\omega)\| + 1) \cdot d$	$(\|NEG(\omega)\| + 1) \cdot d$	$(\|NEG(\omega)\| + 1)$
Skip-Gram_HS	$4c \cdot d(\log m - 1) + d$	$2c \cdot d(\log m - 1)$	$2c \cdot (\log m - 1)$
Skip-Gram_NEG	$4c \cdot d(\|NEG(\omega)\| + 1) + d$	$2c \cdot d(\|NEG(\omega)\| + 1)$	$2c \cdot (\|NEG(\omega)\| + 1)$

The only difference between negative sampling and hierarchical softmax is that for each sample, the number of iterations is proportional to the number of negative samples. Then we can deduce that the computational and communication complexity of each training sample is $\mathcal{O}(d \cdot |NEG(\omega)|)$ (Table 1).

In addition, we analyze the number of times each cryptographic primitive is called during the training phase. Taking the CBOW model of hierarchical softmax as an example, each iteration starts to calculate the sigmoid function with an inner product as input, and the inner product is obtained by calling the inner product encryption algorithm once. In the process of updating e and θ_j^ω, two homomorphic addition and homomorphic multiplication operations are used respectively.Finally, to update the encrypted word vector in the training sample, 2c addition operations are required. Similarly, we can obtain the number of calls to each primitive in the remaining three cases, and summarize the results in Table 2.

Table 2. Parameters for accuracy evaluation

Windows size	Vector dimensions	Negative samples	Learning rate
2c = 4	100	8	0.0125

5 Experimental Analysis

Experiment Setup and Libraries. We conducted several experiments on real data sets from the IMDB movie review data set to illustrate the actual efficiency [32]. The protocol is compiled with Pycrypto crypto library and is running on Windows 10 with Intel(R) Core (TM) Realized on a PC with i7-8565U CPU @1.8 GHz processor and 8 GB RAM. We use BGN encryption technology to encrypt the 1024-bit coefficient version of the data, and use the mathematical library and random library from python to write the code of BGN encryption system.

5.1 Accuracy

We use $\mathcal{L}^*$ to represent the learning model obtained in plaintext, and $\mathcal{L}$ to represent the learning model obtained through our privacy protection scheme. Therefore, we define the error rate of the protocol as:

$$Err_{\mathcal{L}^*} = \left| \frac{F(\mathcal{L}) - F(\mathcal{L}^*)}{\mathcal{L}^*} \right| \tag{20}$$

The above formula can well reflect the loss of accuracy of our scheme. Among them, we use python to perform word vector training algorithm on plaintext. Table 2 gives the configuration of some extra default parameters needed in the accuracy evaluation.

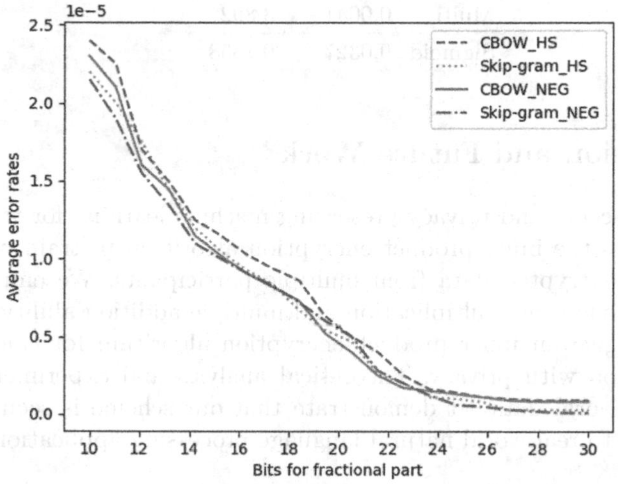

Fig. 2. Tradeoffs between error rates and the number of bits used for the fractional part

In Fig. 2, we illustrate the relationship between the number of bits in the decimal part of the fixed-point data type and the error rate generated.

5.2 Efficiency

Next, on the basis of the default parameters given in Table 3, we conduct the experiments on IMDB movie review dataset to evaluate the overall efficiency from the calculation time.

For clarity, we run each arithmetic primitive in the form of encryption and decryption to demonstrate their performance. The results are shown in Table 4. Among them, BGN solves the addition and subtraction operations and multiplication operations under the ciphertext, and the calculation result of the Sigmoid function under the ciphertext is calculated by the inner product encryption algorithm.

Table 3. Default parameters for efficiency evaluation

Window	Dimensions	Negative samples
2	100	8
Fractional bits	Learing rate	Terms
27	0.025	5

Table 4. Performance of each arithmetic primitive (ms)

	Plaintext	Ciphertext
Add	0.0007	0.0426
Sub	0.0008	0.764
Multi	0.0041	3.892
Sigmoid	0.0327	0.1358

6 Conclusion and Future Work

We propose a secure and privacy-preserving machine learning for training word vector that uses the inner product encryption algorithm to train word vectors on large-scale encrypted data from multiple participants. We employ a cryptossytem with one-time multiplication and multiple addition ability in our construction and give an inner product encryption algorithm for calculating the Sigmoid function with privacy. Theoretical analysis and experimental evaluation on a real-world data set demonstrate that our scheme is secure, efficient, and applicable to real-world natural language processing applications.

Acknowledgements. This work is partially supported by the National Natural Science Foundation of China under grants 62072134 and U2001205, and the Key projects of Guangxi Natural Science Foundation under grant 2019JJD170020, and the Key Research and Development Program of Hubei Province under Grant 2021BEA163..

References

1. Mikolov, T., Chen, K., Corrado, G. S., Dean, J.: Efficient estimation of word representations in vector space. arXiv preprint arXiv:1301.3781
2. Liu, F., Ng, WK., Zhang W.: Encrypted SVM for outsourced data mining. In: 2015 IEEE 8th International Conference on Cloud Computing, pp. 1085–1092 (2015)
3. Liu, F., Ng, WK., Zhang W.: Encrypted scalar product protocol for outsourced data mining. In: 2014 IEEE 7th International Conference on Cloud Computing, pp. 336–343 (2014)
4. Liu, F., Ng, WK., Zhang, W., Giang, D.H., Han, S.: Encrypted set intersection protocol for outsourced datasets. In: 2014 IEEE International Conference on Cloud Engineering, pp. 135–140 (2014)
5. Fan, Y., et al.: PPMCK: privacy-preserving multi-party computing for k-means clustering. J. Parallel Distrib. Comput. **154**, 54–63 (2021)

6. Mohassel, P., Rosulek, M., Trieu, N.: Practical privacy-preserving k-means clustering. Proc. Priv. Enhancing Technol. **2020**, 414–433 (2019)
7. Wang, J., Wu, L., Wang, H., Choo, K.K.R., He, D.: An efficient and privacy-preserving outsourced support vector machine training for internet of medical things. IEEE Internet Things J. **8**, 458–473 (2021)
8. Deng, G., Tang, M., Xi, Y., Zhang, M.: Privacy-preserving online medical prediagnosis training model based on soft-margin SVM. IEEE Trans. Serv. Comput. pp. 1–14 (2022)
9. Qi, Y., Atallah, M. J.: Efficient privacy-preserving K-nearest neighbor search. In: 2008 The 28th International Conference on Distributed Computing Systems, pp. 311–319 (2008)
10. Agrawal, R., Srikant, R.: Privacy-preserving data mining. In: SIGMOD 2000 (2000)
11. Zhang, M., Huang, S., Shen, G., Wang, Y.: PPNNP: a privacy-preserving neural network prediction with separated data providers using multi-client inner-product encryption. Comput. Stan. Interfaces **84**, 103678 (2023)
12. Dwork, C.: Differential privacy. In: Encyclopedia of Cryptography and Security (2006)
13. Chaudhuri, K., Sarwate, A. D., Sinha, K.: Near-optimal differentially private principal components. In: NIPS (2012)
14. Zhang, J., Zhang, Z., Xiao, X., Yang, Y., Winslett, M.: Functional mechanism: regression analysis under differential privacy. arXiv preprint arXiv:1208.0219 (2012)
15. Shokri, R., Shmatikov, V.: Privacy-preserving deep learning. In: 2015 53rd Annual Allerton Conference on Communication, Control, and Computing (Allerton), pp. 909–910 (2015)
16. Abadi, M., et al.: Deep learning with differential privacy. In: Proceedings of the 2016 ACM SIGSAC Conference on Computer and Communications Security (2016)
17. Zhang, M., Zhang, Y., Shen, G.: PPDDS: a privacy-preserving disease diagnosis scheme based on the secure mahalanobis distance evaluation model. IEEE Syst. J. **16**(3), 4552–4562 (2022)
18. Zhang, M., Song, W.-Y., Zhang, J.: A secure clinical diagnosis with privacy-preserving multiclass support vector machine in clouds. IEEE Syst. J. **16**, 67–78 (2022)
19. Kim, S., Kim, J., Koo, D., Kim, Y., Yoon, H., Shin, J.: Efficient privacy-preserving matrix factorization via fully homomorphic encryption: extended abstract. In: Proceedings of the 11th ACM on Asia Conference on Computer and Communications Security (2016)
20. Zhang, M., Chen, Y., Lin, J.: A privacy-preserving optimization of neighborhood-based recommendation for medical-aided diagnosis and treatment. IEEE Internet Things J. **8**, 10830–10842 (2021)
21. Bost, R., Popa, R.A., Stephen, T., Goldwasser, S.: Machine learning classification over encrypted data. IACR Cryptol. ePrint Arch. **2014**, 331 (2015)
22. Dowlin, N., Gilad-Bachrach, R., Laine, K., Lauter, K., Wernsing, J.: Cryptonets: applying neural networks to encrypted data with high throughput and accuracy. IEEE (2016)
23. Wang, Q., et al.: Privacy-preserving collaborative model learning: the case of word vector training. IEEE Trans. Knowl. Data Eng. **30**, 2381–2393 (2018)
24. Elmehdwi, Y., Samanthula, B.K., Jiang, W.: Secure K-nearest neighbor query over encrypted data in outsourced environments. In: 2014 IEEE 30th International Conference on Data Engineering, pp. 664–675 (2014)

25. Maas, A.L., Daly, R.E., Pham, P.T., Huang, D., Ng, A., Potts, c.: Learning word vectors for sentiment analysis. In: ACL (2011)
26. Goldreich, O.: The foundations of cryptography - volume 2: basic applications(2009)
27. Acar, A., Aksu, H., Uluagac, A.S., Conti, M.: A survey on homomorphic encryption schemes. ACM Comput. Surv. (CSUR) **51**, 1–35 (2018)
28. Boneh, D., Goh, E.-J., Nissim, K.: Evaluating 2-DNF formulas on ciphertexts. In: Kilian, J. (ed.) TCC 2005. LNCS, vol. 3378, pp. 325–341. Springer, Heidelberg (2005). https://doi.org/10.1007/978-3-540-30576-7_18
29. Paillier, P.: Public-key cryptosystems based on composite degree residuosity classes. In: Stern, J. (ed.) EUROCRYPT 1999. LNCS, vol. 1592, pp. 223–238. Springer, Heidelberg (1999). https://doi.org/10.1007/3-540-48910-X_16
30. Abdalla, M., Bourse, F., De Caro, A., Pointcheval, D.: Simple functional encryption schemes for inner products. In: Katz, J. (ed.) PKC 2015. LNCS, vol. 9020, pp. 733–751. Springer, Heidelberg (2015). https://doi.org/10.1007/978-3-662-46447-2_33
31. Okamoto, T., Uchiyama, S.: A new public-key cryptosystem as secure as factoring. In: Nyberg, K. (ed.) EUROCRYPT 1998. LNCS, vol. 1403, pp. 308–318. Springer, Heidelberg (1998). https://doi.org/10.1007/BFb0054135
32. Maas, A.L., Daly, R.E., Pham, P.T., Huang, D., Ng, A.Y., Potts, C.: Learning word vectors for sentiment analysis. In: The 49th Annual Meeting of the Association for Computational Linguistics (ACL 2011). (2011)

D2D Authentication Scheme for IoT-enabled Smart Home

Qingru Ma[1], Tianqi Zhou[2], and Haowen Tan[2](✉)

[1] School of Informatics Science and Technology, Zhejiang Sci-Tech University, Hangzhou 310018, China

[2] Department of Informatics, Kyushu University, Fukuoka 819-0395, Japan
tan_halloween@foxmail.com

Abstract. The rapid development of Internet of things (IoT) technology has created a good technical foundation for the establishment of the smart home. However, while a smart home brings convenience to people, it also has many hidden security issues. Smart home is related to the life and property safety of users in this environment. A large number of researchers have made research on the security issues in IoT-enabled smart home systems. With the in-depth development of intelligence, the independent authentication between devices is one of the trends of smart homes in the future. Therefore, device-to-device (D2D) authentication is particularly important for smart home systems. In this paper, a D2D authentication scheme is proposed. The proposed scheme can ensure that two intelligent devices can authenticate each other with the assistance of a home gateway. The security and performance analysis shows that the proposal is secure and efficient for the application in the smart home environment.

Keywords: Smart home · D2D authentication · IoT

1 Introduction

With the rapid development of emerging technologies such as the Internet of Things (IoT) [11] and 5G, the smart home industry has expanded rapidly and gradually entered people's daily life. The Internet of Things technology guarantees the networking of home devices and the ability to convey user instructions. The new generation of communication technologies such as 5G guarantees the rapid transmission of information in smart home networks. In addition, cloud and fog computing technologies ensure the storage and computing needs of smart home devices. With the support of these novel technologies, smart home has gradually become an alternative way of life for people. The purpose of smart home is to provide people with a convenient life through an intelligent living environment [12]. In a smart home environment, family members can remotely control various household devices in the home through mobile terminals such as smart phones. For example, people can control the connected lights, curtains,

X. Chen et al. (Eds.): SocialSec 2022, CCIS 1663, pp. 83–93, 2022.
https://doi.org/10.1007/978-981-19-7242-3_6

robot vacuums and other devices in the home by waking up smart speakers or sending commands through their mobile phones. In recent years, information security incidents caused by security breaches of smart homes have occurred from time to time [1]. Criminals may invade users' smart home systems to violate user privacy or maliciously manipulate smart devices. For example, some networked home monitoring systems were seized by criminals, which led to the exposure of users' private lives; in addition, some criminals carried out burglary by invading users' smart door locks [3].

As shown in Fig. 1, A smart home system is composed by a home gateway and some smart devices [15]. The home gateway takes responsibility to connect with all the smart devices on wireless channel, and connect with the service provider by wire. Users might use their personal terminals such as smart phone to send orders to the devices directly or indirectly.

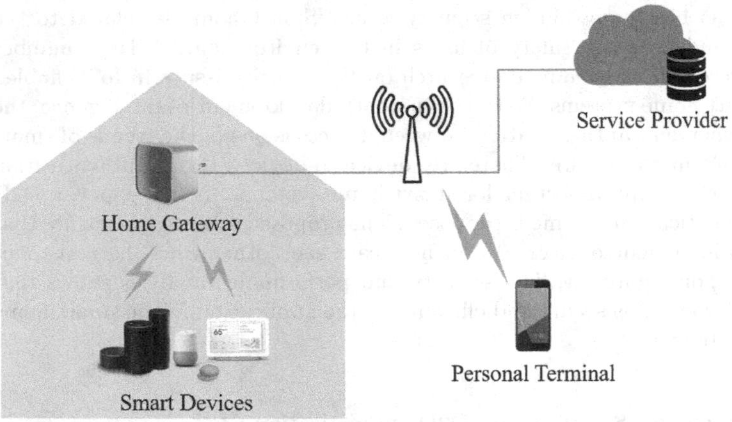

Fig. 1. A sample of smart home

Motivation of this paper: At present, much up-to-date work has carried out research on the security issues in smart home. Most of the schemes mainly focus on the authentication between devices and the gateway or the remote cloud servers, and rarely involve the authentication and data interaction between the smart home devices. Furthermore, home gateways, as available edge nodes, are rarely utilized to assist in the implementation of device-to-device (D2D) authentication.

1.1 Our Contributions

In this paper, an authentication scheme for devices in smart home is proposed. The contributions of this paper are listed as follows:

- **An IoT-enabled smart home system model is presented.** In this paper, a smart home system model enabled by IoT devices is presented. The smart devices in this scheme are able to authenticate any device they want to communicate within the smart home system.
- **A D2D authentication scheme is proposed for the smart home environment.** To ensure the secure interaction between smart devices in the system, a D2D authentication scheme is proposed. This scheme realizes effective D2D authentication and session key generation with the design of secret parameter pre-storage and synchronization calculation of authentication parameters.
- **The proposed scheme is analyzed to be secure and efficient.** The verification of the signatures in the proposed scheme is proved to be correct. In addition, the generation of the session key is also proved to be valid. The scheme is proved to be secure against a forged SD and an honest but curious HG. The simulation on the mobile node shows that the scheme is efficient.

1.2 Related Work

Researchers have been focus on the authentication in smart home systems [2,5]. Komninos *et al.* [8] survey the security issues in smart grid and smart home systems. They figure out that device authentication is one of the important issues for smart home systems to solve. Xiao *et al.* [14] provide an authentication framework without the need for sensitive credentials for smart home environment. A blockchain-based smart home mutual authentication scheme is proposed by Lin *et al.* [9]. Yang *et al.* [16] also present some ideas about solving the security issues in smart home by introducing blockchain technology. Shen *et al.* [13] present a data uploading scheme for smart home. Smart devices in their work are authenticated by the service provider. A biometric-based user identity authentication method is presented by Ji *et al.* [7]. They guarantee secure communication between other terminals with smart devices. Huang *et al.* [4] provide a solution to authenticate the devices with the home limited channel. Luo *et al.* [10] provide a method to authenticate the user with a hardware token. An anonymous authentication scheme is proposed by Iqbal *et al.* [6]. However, the D2D authentication scheme for smart homes has been rarely mentioned.

2 Preliminaries

Preliminaries such as bilinear pairing are mentioned in this section.

2.1 Bilinear Pairing

Choose two groups $\mathbb{G}_1$ and $\mathbb{G}_2$ with the same prime order q. Consider $\mathbb{G}_1$ as an additive group, and let $\mathbb{G}_2$ be a multiplicative group. A cryptographic bilinear map is a mapping e on $(\mathbb{G}_1, \mathbb{G}_2)$: $\mathbb{G}_1^2 \rightarrow \mathbb{G}_2$ and satisfies the following properties.

Bilinearity. $e(aP, bQ) = e(P, Q)^{ab}$ for all $P, Q \in \mathbb{G}_1$and $a, b \in Z_q^*$. This can be expressed in the following manner. For $P, Q, R \in \mathbb{G}_1$, $e(P + Q, R) = e(P, R)e(Q, R)$ and $e(P - Q, R) = e(P, R)e(Q, R)^{-1}$.

Non-degeneracy. If P is a generator of $\mathbb{G}_1$, then $e(P, P)$ is a generator of $\mathbb{G}_2$. In other words, $e(P, P) \neq 1$.

Computability. e is efficiently computable.

2.2 Complexity Assumption

Definition 1 (DL Assumption). *Discrete logarithm assumption (DL Assumption) is based on DL problem. The DL assumption can be defined as: Let* $\mathbb{G}$ *be a multiplicative group,* g *is a generator of* $\mathbb{G}$, *and* $g^a \in \mathbb{G}$, *where* $a \in \mathbb{Z}_p$. *It is difficult to compute* a. *The probability is negligible for an adversary* $\mathcal{A}$ *to calculate* a, *which can be demonstrated as Eq. (1).*

$$\mathrm{Adv}_{\mathcal{A}}^{\mathrm{DL}}(\mathcal{K}) = \Pr\left[\mathcal{A}(g, g^a) \to a\right] = \varepsilon_{\mathrm{DL}} \tag{1}$$

3 System and Security Models

In this section, the system model and the security model are described for the proposed scheme.

3.1 System Model

The system in this paper is composed of three different kinds of terminals: smart devices (SDs) and home gateway (HG).

The smart devices mentioned in this paper may refer to some smart speakers which have the ability to receive users' orders by sound. In addition, smart devices may also refer to devices that are responsible for receiving instructions and executing instructions to achieve a certain purpose. These devices are the main convenience providers in smart homes. For example, intelligent lighting, intelligent doors and windows, and intelligent curtains belong to this type of device.

The home gateway is mainly responsible for providing registration services for smart devices. Besides, HG also plays the role of parameter transfer and processing in the process of authentication between devices.

3.2 Security Model

In our security model, a smart device might be forged, and the HG might be honest but curious. To be specific, the detailed description is listed as follows:

A Forged Smart Device: In this paper, a smart device might be forged by an adversary. The adversary may disguise himself as a legitimate SD to send wrong instructions to achieve criminal purposes.

An Honest but Curious HG: An honest but curious HG can honestly perform various parameter calculations and transfer tasks set by the system. However, the HG may be interested in the session key generated between the two devices to obtain the user privacy data transmitted between them.

4 Main Idea

In this section, we first overview the main idea of the proposal. Then, according to the designed three phases of the scheme, the proposal is described detailedly.

4.1 Overview

To ensure the communication between devices in the smart home environment, a D2D authentication scheme is proposed. The scheme is composed of three phases: registration phase, authentication phase, and session key generation phase. All the devices involved in this communication process are registered in the registration phase. Some necessary parameters are written into the memories of these devices. When a device of the smart home is going to communicate with another one, an authentication phase is designed well for both sides of the communication. Finally, according to the parameters stored and received during the above two phases, a session key can be generated by the two devices in the third phase. These three phases are described in detail as follows (Fig. 2).

4.2 Registration Phase

In this phase, devices SD_A and SD_B send their identities ID_A and ID_B to the home gateway HG. HG generates two pseudo-identities for devices SD_A and SD_B:

$$PID_A = H_1\left(ID_A||f_1\right),$$

$$PID_B = H_1\left(ID_B||f_2\right).$$

The pseudo-identities are broadcast to all the devices in the smart home. Then, some secret values R_A and R_B are generated for SD_A and SD_B, respectively, as follows:

$$R_A = r \cdot PID_A,$$

$$R_B = r \cdot PID_B.$$

R_A and R_B are respectively written into SD_A and SD_B's memories. Device SD_A chooses a random number a from a nonzero integer group Z_p^*, and calculates $A = aP$. Similarly, a random number b is chosen by device SD_B from a nonzero integer group Z_p^*. SD_B also calculates $B = bP$.

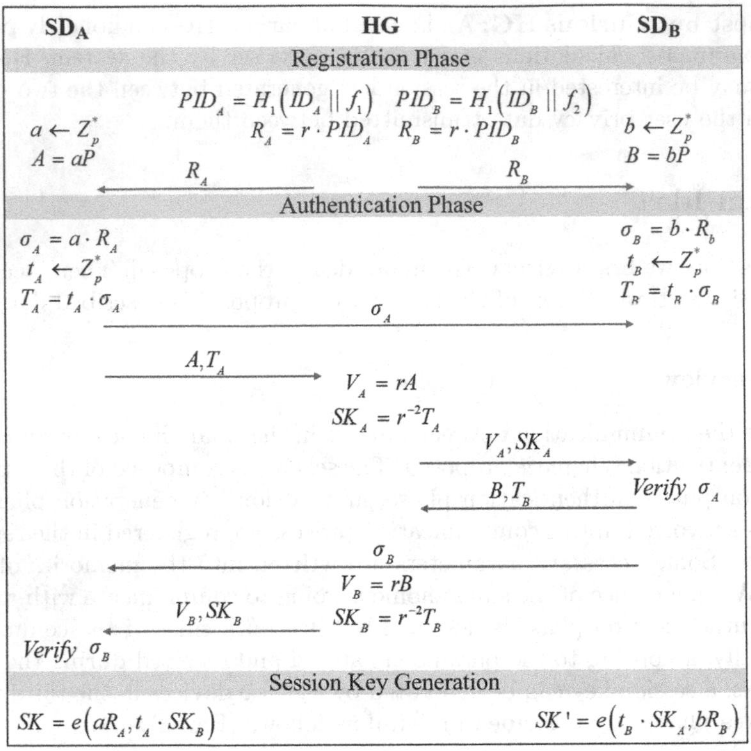

Fig. 2. The process of the proposed D2D authentication scheme

4.3 Authentication Phase

In the authentication phase, SD_A calculates a signature:

$$\sigma_A = a \cdot R_A,$$

where a is the random number chosen in the registration phase, and R_A is the secret value generated by the HG.

Then, SD_A chooses another random number $t_A \in Z_p^*$, and computes:

$$T_A = t_A \cdot \sigma_A.$$

A message contains A and T_A is sent to the HG and the signature σ_A is sent to SD_B. HG calculates V_A for SD_B to verify the signature of SD_A, and computes SK_A for the later generation of the session key:

$$V_A = rA,$$

$$SK_A = r^{-2}T_A.$$

After receiving V_A and SK_A, SD_B verifies the signature of SD_A by:

$$e(\sigma_A, P) \stackrel{?}{=} e(PID_A, V_A).$$

If the equation stands, SD_B sends its own signature and corresponding parameters generated by:

$$\sigma_B = b \cdot R_b,$$

$$T_B = t_B \cdot \sigma_B,$$

where t_B is a random number chosen by SD_B from a nonzero integer group Z_p^*. B and T_B are sent to the HG and σ_B is sent to SD_A.

HG also calculates V_B for SD_A to verify the signature of SD_B, and computes SK_B for the later generation of the session key:

$$V_B = rB,$$

$$SK_B = r^{-2} T_B.$$

After receiving V_B and SK_B, SD_A verifies the signature of SD_B by:

$$e(\sigma_B, P) \stackrel{?}{=} e(PID_B, V_B).$$

4.4 Session Key Generation Phase

If all the verification results in the authentication phase are acceptable, devices SD_A and SD_B will generate session keys respectively. SD_A generates the session key by:

$$SK = e(aR_A, t_A \cdot SK_B).$$

SD_B gets the session key by:

$$SK' = e(t_B \cdot SK_A, bR_B).$$

If $SK = SK'$, the two devices can communicate with each other.

5 Security Analysis

In this section, the correctness and the security against several kinds of adversaries defined in the security model are presented.

5.1 Correctness

Here, we give three theorems to prove the correctness of the proposal.

Theorem 1. *The verification of the signature of SD_A is correct.*

Proof. According to the definition of Bilinear pairing, the equation $e(\sigma_A, P) \stackrel{?}{=} e(PID_A, V_A)$ can be proved by:

$$\begin{aligned} & e(\sigma_A, P) \\ & = e(a \cdot R_A, P) \\ & = e(ar \cdot PID_A, P) \\ & = e(PID_A, ar \cdot P) \\ & = e(PID_A, r \cdot A) \\ & = e(PID_A, V_A) \end{aligned}$$

Theorem 2. *The verification of the signature of* SD_B *is correct.*

Proof. According to the proof of Theorem 1, the Theorem 2 can be easily proved.

Theorem 3. *The generation of the session key in the proposal is valid, in other words,* $SK = SK'$.

Proof. Firstly, according to the scheme, the session key SK generated by SD_A is calculated by:

$$SK = e(aR_A, t_A \cdot SK_B).$$

We can have the following equations:

$$\begin{aligned} SK & = e(aR_A, t_A \cdot SK_B) \\ & = e\left(ar \cdot PID_A, t_A \cdot r^{-2} T_B\right) \\ & = e\left(ar \cdot PID_A, t_A r^{-2} t_B \cdot \sigma_B\right) \\ & = e\left(ar \cdot PID_A, t_A r^{-2} t_B b \cdot R_b\right) \\ & = e\left(ar \cdot PID_A, t_A r^{-2} t_B br \cdot PID_B\right) \\ & = e(PID_A, PID_B)^{art_A r^{-2} t_B br} \\ & = e(PID_A, PID_B)^{abt_A t_B} \end{aligned}$$

Meanwhile, the session key SK' generated by SD_B is calculated by:

$$SK' = e(t_B \cdot SK_A, bR_B).$$

We can also have the following equations:

$$\begin{aligned} SK' & = e(t_B \cdot SK_A, bR_B) \\ & = e\left(t_B r^{-2} T_A, br \cdot PID_B\right) \\ & = e\left(t_B r^{-2} t_A \cdot \sigma_A, br \cdot PID_B\right) \\ & = e\left(t_B r^{-2} t_A a \cdot R_A, br \cdot PID_B\right) \\ & = e\left(t_B r^{-2} t_A ar \cdot PID_A, br \cdot PID_B\right) \\ & = e(PID_A, PID_B)^{t_B r^{-2} t_A arbr} \\ & = e(PID_A, PID_B)^{abt_A t_B} \end{aligned}$$

Since, $e(PID_A, PID_B)^{abt_A t_B} = e(PID_A, PID_B)^{abt_A t_B}$, $SK = SK'$ stands.

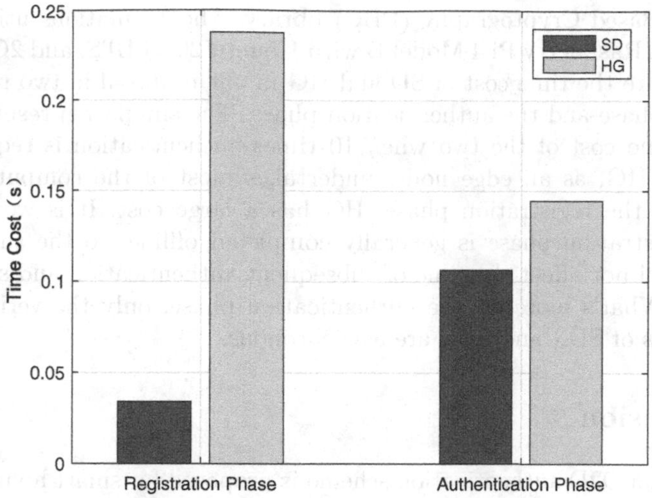

Fig. 3. The comparison between SD and HG when 10 times authentication is required

5.2 Security

The security of the proposed scheme can be analyzed from two aspects: security against a forged smart device and security against an honest but curious HG.

Security Against a Forged Smart Device. If an adversary wants to forge SD_A in the proposed scheme, he needs to know the secret parameter a generated by SD_A in the registration phase, and the secret value R_A generated by the HG in the registration phase. Without these two values, an adversary can hardly compute the signature of SD_A.

Security Against an Honest but Curious HG. If the HG wants to generate the session key between SD_A and SD_B, he needs to calculate the values of SK or SK', where $SK = e(aR_A, t_A \cdot SK_B)$ and $SK' = e(t_B \cdot SK_A, bR_B)$. HG has the values of R_A, R_B, SK_A, and SK_B. But the HG has no idea of the values of a, b, t_A, and t_B. So, the HG can hardly computes the values of SK or SK'. Although the HG knows $A = aP$ and P, according to DL problem, he cannot know the value of a. Although the HG knows $T_A = at_AR_A$ and R_A, according to DL problem, he cannot know the value of at_A.

6 Performance Analysis

The performance of the proposed scheme can be demonstrated by some simulations implemented with the GNU Multiple Precision Arithmetic (GMP) library and Pairing-Based Cryptography (PBC) library. The simulations utilize the C language on a Raspberry Pi 4 Model B with Ubuntu 20.04 LTS, and 2G of RAM.

We compare the time cost of SD and HG in our proposal in two phases: the registration phase and the authentication phase. The simulation result in Fig. 3 shows the time cost of the two when 10 times authentication is required. We can see that HG, as an edge node, undertakes most of the computing tasks. Especially in the registration phase, HG has a large cost. It is worth noting that the registration phase is generally completed offline, so the time cost of this phase will not affect the time of subsequent authentication and session key generation. What's more, in the authentication phase, only the verification of the signatures of SD_A and SD_B are asynchronous.

7 Conclusion

In this paper, a D2D authentication scheme is proposed for smart home systems. Devices can authenticate each other with the assistance of the home gateway. The correctness and security of the scheme against a forged smart device and an honest but curious home gateway are proved. The simulation result shows that the proposal is efficient since the gateway undertakes most of the computing tasks. In the future, the scheme is going to be improved to be more efficient for devices to generate session keys.

Acknowledgements. This work is supported by the National Natural Science Foundation of China under Grants No. 61922045, No. 61877034, No. U1836115, No. 61672290, the Natural Science Foundation of Jiangsu Province under Grant No. BK20181408, the Peng Cheng Laboratory Project of Guangdong Province PCL2018KP004, the CICAEET fund, and the PAPD fund.

References

1. Amraoui, N., Zouari, B.: Securing the operation of smart home systems: a literature review. J. Reliab. Intell. Environ. **8**(1), 67–74 (2022). https://doi.org/10.1007/s40860-021-00160-3
2. Goyal, G., Liu, P., Sural, S.: Securing smart home iot systems with attribute-based access control. In: Gupta, M., Khorsandroo, S., Abdelsalam, M. (eds.) Sat-CPS@CODASPY 2022: Proceedings of the 2022 ACM Workshop on Secure and Trustworthy Cyber-Physical Systems, Baltimore, MD, USA, 27 April 2022, pp. 37–46. ACM (2022). https://doi.org/10.1145/3510547.3517920
3. Guo, Y., Zhang, Z., Guo, Y.: Secfhome: secure remote authentication in fog-enabled smart home environment. Comput. Netw. **207**, 108818 (2022). https://doi.org/10.1016/j.comnet.2022.108818
4. Huang, Z., Zhang, L., Meng, X., Choo, K.R.: Key-free authentication protocol against subverted indoor smart devices for smart home. IEEE Internet Things J. **7**(2), 1039–1047 (2020). https://doi.org/10.1109/JIOT.2019.2948622
5. Huszti, A., Kovács, S., Oláh, N.: Scalable, password-based and threshold authentication for smart homes. Int. J. Inf. Sec. **21**(4), 707–723 (2022). https://doi.org/10.1007/s10207-022-00578-7

6. Iqbal, W., et al.: ALAM: anonymous lightweight authentication mechanism for SDN-enabled smart homes. IEEE Internet Things J. **8**(12), 9622–9633 (2021). https://doi.org/10.1109/JIOT.2020.3024058
7. Ji, S., Huang, R., Shen, J., Jin, X., Cho, Y.: A certificateless signcryption scheme for smart home networks. Concurr. Comput. Pract. Exp. **33**(7), 1 (2021). https://doi.org/10.1002/cpe.5081
8. Komninos, N., Philippou, E., Pitsillides, A.: Survey in smart grid and smart home security: issues, challenges and countermeasures. IEEE Commun. Surv. Tutorials **16**(4), 1933–1954 (2014). https://doi.org/10.1109/COMST.2014.2320093
9. Lin, C., He, D., Kumar, N., Huang, X., Vijayakumar, P., Choo, K.R.: Homechain: a blockchain-based secure mutual authentication system for smart homes. IEEE Internet Things J. **7**(2), 818–829 (2020). https://doi.org/10.1109/JIOT.2019.2944400
10. Luo, H., Wang, C., Luo, H., Zhang, F., Lin, F., Xu, G.: G2F: a secure user authentication for rapid smart home IoT management. IEEE Internet Things J. **8**(13), 10884–10895 (2021). https://doi.org/10.1109/JIOT.2021.3050710
11. Rizou, S., Egyptiadou, E.A., Ishibashi, Y., Psannis, K.E.: Preserving minors' data protection in IoT-based smart homes according to GDPR considering cross-border issues. J. Commun. **17**(3), 180–187 (2022). https://doi.org/10.12720/jcm.17.3.180-187
12. Samuel, S.S.I.: A review of connectivity challenges in IoT-smart home. In: 2016 3rd MEC International Conference on Big Data and Smart City (ICBDSC), pp. 1–4 (2016). https://doi.org/10.1109/ICBDSC.2016.7460395
13. Shen, J., Wang, C., Li, T., Chen, X., Huang, X., Zhan, Z.: Secure data uploading scheme for a smart home system. Inf. Sci. **453**, 186–197 (2018). https://doi.org/10.1016/j.ins.2018.04.048
14. Xiao, Y., Jia, Y., Liu, C., Alrawais, A., Rekik, M., Shan, Z.: Homeshield: a credential-less authentication framework for smart home systems. IEEE Internet Things J. **7**(9), 7903–7918 (2020). https://doi.org/10.1109/JIOT.2020.3003621
15. Yan, W., Wang, Z., Wang, H., Wang, W., Li, J., Gui, X.: Survey on recent smart gateways for smart home: systems, technologies, and challenges. Trans. Emerg. Telecommun. Technol. **33**(6), e4067 (2022). https://doi.org/10.1002/ett.4067
16. Yang, L., Liu, X., Gong, W.: Secure smart home systems: a blockchain perspective. In: 39th IEEE Conference on Computer Communications, INFOCOM Workshops 2020, Toronto, ON, Canada, July 6–9, 2020, pp. 1003–1008. IEEE (2020). https://doi.org/10.1109/INFOCOMWKSHPS50562.2020.9162648

Inner Product Encryption from Middle-Product Learning with Errors

Niao Yang[1,3], Shaojun Yang[2,4(✉)], Yong Zhao[1,3], and Wei Wu[2]

[1] College of Computer and Cyber Security, Fujian Normal University, Fuzhou 350117, China

[2] School of Mathematics and Statistics, Fujian Normal University, Fuzhou 350117, China
shaojunyang@fjnu.edu.cn

[3] Fujian Provincial Key Laboratory of Network Security and Cryptology, Fujian Normal University, Fuzhou 350007, China

[4] State Key Laboratory of Cryptology, Beijing 100878, China

Abstract. Inner product encryption (IPE) is an essential area of research for functional encryption systems. It has extensive applications in emerging fields such as cloud computing, where it can improve users' access control and fine-grained queries. Lattice-based inner product encryption has the advantages of resistance to quantum algorithm attack and relatively simple encryption algorithm, so it has a good application prospect. At present, the provable security of lattice-based public key cryptography algorithms is mostly based on Learning With Errors (LWE) and Polynomial Learning With Errors (PLWE) problems. However, the majority of encryption schemes based on the LWE problem have the issue of excessively large public keys and ciphertexts size. Although the encryption scheme based on the PLWE problem reduces the size even further, its hardness is limited by polynomials, and the security guarantee is diminished. Compared with LWE and PLWE problem, Middle-Product Learning With Errors (MP-LWE) problems loosen the restrictions on polynomials, and make full use of the polynomial characteristics to achieve a better balance between security and efficiency. Therefore, in this paper, we present the first MP-LWE based inner product encryption schemes with Indistinguishability against Selective Chosen Plaintext Attack secure (Sel-IND-CPA-secure), while keeping the algorithm structure simple and efficient.

Keywords: Middle-product learning with errors · Inner product encryption · Function encryption

1 Introduction

1.1 Background

Function encryption (FE) [9] is a new development in public key cryptography, which overcomes inherent "all or nothing" in public key encryption and data

X. Chen et al. (Eds.): SocialSec 2022, CCIS 1663, pp. 94–113, 2022.
https://doi.org/10.1007/978-981-19-7242-3_7

access for only one user. FE has strong advantages in many aspects, such as effective access control for ciphertext data and data privacy protection. Based on the above advantages, function encryption has good application prospects in cloud environments. In cloud computing platforms, the user could encrypt data and store it on the remote server. Then the user provides the server with keys associated with functions. At this time, the server is able to compute the function of underlying data without obtaining other content of the data, and realize "partial decryption" for ciphertexts.

Inner Product Encryption (IPE) is a special FE, and has been a hot research topic in recent years. In the encryption system, both the ciphertext and the key are associated with a vector, and decrypting the ciphertext with the key will obtain the inner product of the two vectors without revealing any information about the two vectors. Hence, IPE could be widely used in many practical scenarios, such as biometric recognition, statistical analysis and machine learning.

In 2015, Abdalla *et al.* [1] proposed the concept of IPE for the first time, and gave an inner product encryption scheme based on the Decisional Diffie-Hellman (DDH) and Learning With Errors (LWE) assumptions. However, this scheme is just Sel-IND-CPA-secure. In order to further improve the secure level, Abdalla et al. [2] proposedifficultd an IPE scheme with IND-CPA-secure. In 2016, Agrawal et al. [5] proposed an IND-CPA-secure IPE scheme using the "dual" LWE system to further shorten the length of the ciphertext and private key. In the follow-up work, Agrawal *et al.* [4] proved that the scheme in [5] is secure with adaptive simulation (AD-SIM). In 2016, Xu *et al.* [33] used an invertible matrix as the master private key, and constructed an IPE scheme with Indistinguishability against Chosen Ciphertext Attacks secure (IND-CCA-secure). However, the shortcoming of the scheme is that it does not rely on hardness problems such as discrete logarithms, and the security is weak. In 2017, Sun et al. [31] proposed a stateless IPE scheme based on the LWE assumption, which have improved the problem that the previous schemes could only ask linearly independent vectors in the key query stage, and relaxed the restrictions on the adversary's capabilities. In the same year, Benhamouda *et al.* [8] first constructed a general IND-CCA secure IPE scheme based on Decisional Composite Reminder (DCR), DDH and Matrix Diffie-Hellman (MDDH) assumptions by citing the hash proof system. In 2018, Castagnos *et al.* [11] constructed an unbounded IPE scheme with modulo p under the DDH assumption, which no longer limits the size of the generated inner product, and is more practical than previous work. Recently, Mera *et al.* [26] used Polynomial Learning With Errors (PLWE) as a problem hypothesis to construct an IND-CPA-secure inner product encryption scheme, which effectively reduces storage overhead.

In addition, researchers also extend many functions of IPE, including function-hiding [21,32], multi-input [3,15,22] and decentralized multi-client [12]. In 2020, Chotard *et al.* [13] constructed an IPE scheme that can be used to calculate the weighted sum of aggregated and encrypted data under the standard assumption of order groups and the random oracle model. In 2021, Deng *et al.* [16] proposed an identity-based verifiable key IPE scheme by using the bilinear mapping technology, which solved the problem that the general inner product encryption schemes could not specify the receiver and the key could be modified. This scheme is Sel-IND-CPA-secure.

With the in-depth study of quantum algorithm theory and the rapid development of quantum computers, traditional number theory problems are increasingly likely to be solved by quantum computers in polynomial time. Compared with the traditional number theory cryptosystem, lattice cryptography is resistant to quantum attacks, and have the following advantages: simple operations and easy to parallel. In fact, lattice-based construction could run faster through hardware acceleration. In addition, lattice cryptography has good reduction characteristics, that is, worst-case hardness problems can be reduced to average-case hardness problems, which provides more reliable and provable secure for public key cryptography. Furthermore, lattice-based hardness problems can realize a variety of cryptographic primitives. Hence, lattice cryptography is more suitable for real-world applications.

Now, in lattice-based public key cryptography, the provable secure is mostly based on Short Integer Solution problem (SIS), and LWE as well as their variants. Public key cryptography directly based on SIS and LWE problems, has reliable security guarantees. However, due to its large storage/communication overhead, including public key size, private key size, ciphertext length and signature length, the practicability of the cryptosystem is limited. Public key cryptography based on SIS and LWE variant problems, mainly refers to the Polynomial Short Integer Solution (PSIS) [24,27] and PLWE [29] problems on ideal lattices corresponding to polynomial rings. The public key cryptosystem based on the above two problems reduces space size, but its hardness is restricted by the polynomial f. Numerous research results [14,18,19] show that, under the condition of some polynomial f, PSIS^f, PLWE^f and standard hardness problems on ideal lattices are easier to be solved than the corresponding SIS and LWE problems. In 2016, Lyubashevsky [23] used ordinary polynomial multiplication to replace multiplication on polynomial rings and defined the problem. In 2017, Rosca *et al.* [28] gave the definition of the decisional MP-LWE problem, by making use of the Middle Product between polynomials modulo an integer q replacing the multiplication operation on polynomial rings, and proved that for any polynomial in the set, this problem can be reduced to the MP-LWE problem. By the reduction proof, the scheme based on the MP-LWE problem can better balance provable secure and space size, and has better practicability. In 2022, Yang and Huang [34] took the MP-LWE problem as a special example to define the UP-LWE problem using the idea of mathematical axiomatic, and further improved the hardness conclusion of the MP-LWE problem.

The goal of this work is to construct an inner product encryption scheme that takes into account both efficiency and security based on the MP-LWE assumption.

1.2 Our Contributions

We show a variant of public key encryption scheme [28] and [30] based on the MP-LWE problem. Then we prove that the scheme has linear homomorphism of the key and linear homomorphism of the ciphertext under shared randomness.

Based on the improved PKE scheme, we construct inner product encryption scheme with Sel-IND-CPA-secure. we take the ℓ public-private key pairs $(\mathsf{sk}_i, \mathsf{pk}_i)_{i\in[\ell]}$ in public key encryption scheme as the master public and private key in this scheme, and then linearly combine the column vector $\mathbf{w}$ and the master private key sk_i to generate the user private key $\mathsf{sk}_{\mathbf{w}}$, and then generate the ciphertext $\mathsf{ct}_{\mathbf{v}}$ containing the plaintext column vector $\mathbf{v}$ according to the encryption algorithm. Different from public key encryption scheme, this scheme needs to linearly combine the ciphertext $\mathsf{ct}_{\mathbf{v}}$ with the vector $\mathbf{w}$ before decryption. The purpose of this operation is to generate an item containing $\langle \mathbf{v}, \mathbf{w}\rangle$ in the formula, and then the decryption algorithm, subtract the redundant terms in the formula, when the infinity norm of the residual noise term is small, the inner product value $\langle \mathbf{v}, \mathbf{w}\rangle$ can be obtained.

Table 1 is the space complexity comparison between the IPE scheme of Sel-IND-CPA-secure in this paper and previous work. Compared with [26], the space complexity of the master public key in this paper is slightly larger. However, our scheme is based on MP-LWE assumption, which is more secure than scheme [26] (based on PWE assumption), because MP-LWE is not constrained by polynomial f compared to PLWE. Therefore, the advantage of this scheme is that the paper is mainly reflected in the balance between efficiency and security.

Table 1. Comparing space complexity and hard problems with prior works. The space complexity is given in $\mathbb{Z}_q$. The value ℓ is the length of the message vector, n and q are the hard problem parameters. However, the choice of other parameters (e.g. Gaussian parameters) is different. As for the security comparison, except [5] is IND-CPA-secure, others are Sel-IND-CPA-secure.

Scheme	$\lvert\mathsf{mpk}\rvert$	$\lvert\mathsf{msk}\rvert$	$\lvert\mathsf{ct}\rvert$	$\lvert\mathsf{sk}_f\rvert$	Hard problem
[1]	$O((n+\ell)n\log^2 q)$	$O(\ell n\log q)$	$O((\ell+n)\log q)$	$O(n\log^2 q)$	LWE
[5]	$O(n^2\log^2 q+\ell n\log q)$	$O(\ell n\log^2 q)$	$O(n\log q^2+\ell\log q)$	$O(n\log q)$	LWE
[26]	$O(\ell n\log q)$	$O(\ell n\log q)$	$O(\ell n\log q)$	$O(\ell n\log q)$	PLWE
Our work	$O(\ell n\log^2 q)$	$O(\ell n\log q)$	$O(\ell n\log q)$	$O(\ell n\log q)$	MP-LWE

2 Preliminaries

2.1 Notations

If no special note, we use black lowercase letters vector (such as $\mathbf{a}$), black capital letters matrix (such as $\mathbf{A}$), denote by $\mathbf{I}_n$ the $n \times n$ dimensional identity matrix. We shall denote with $\lfloor t \rfloor$ the rounding down of t, the notations $\|\mathbf{v}\|_\infty = \max_i \{|v_i|\}$ and $\|\mathbf{v}\| = \sqrt{\sum_i v_i^2}$ stand for the infinity and Euclidean norm of vector $\mathbf{v}$. For any positive integer ℓ, $[\ell]$ stands for the set $\{1, \ldots, \ell\}$. We use $1_R = 1 + x^2 + \cdots + x^d$ represents a polynomial with degree $d > 0$ and all coefficients 1, negl (κ) represents a negligible function with respect to parameter κ.

For a finite set S, we let $U(S)$ denote the uniform distribution over S, and use the notation $x \leftarrow U(S)$ to denote that x is sampled uniformly at random from S. Let R be a ring and $R[x]$ stands for a polynomial ring. For any integer $d > 0$ and any set $S \subseteq R$, we let $S^{<d}[x]$ denote the set polynomial in $R[x]$ of degree $< d$ whose coefficients are in S.

Given a polynomial $a(x) = \sum_{i=1}^{d} a_i x^{i-1} \in R^{<d}[x]$, define the coefficient vector of $a(x)$ as $\mathbf{a} = (a_1, \ldots, a_d) \in R^d$, the reversed coefficient vector of $a(x)$ as $\bar{\mathbf{a}} = (a_d, \ldots, a_1) \in R^d$. The $(d+1) \times 2d$ dimensional Toeplitz matrix generated by the coefficient vector of the polynomial $a(x)$ is denoted as $\mathrm{Toep}^{d+1,2d}(a(x))$, Without loss of generality, the above notations of polynomials can be extended to polynomial vectors. For a polynomial vector $\mathbf{a}(x) = (a_1(x), \ldots, a_m(x)) \in (R^{<d}[x])^m$ and any $j \in [m]$, let $\mathbf{a}_j = (a_{j,1}, \ldots, a_{j,d}) \in R^d$ denote the coefficient vector of the j-th polynomial of $\mathbf{a}(x)$.

Let $\mathbf{M}_f$ denote $m \times m$ dimensional matrix whose (i,j)-th element is the constant coefficient of the polynomial $x^{i+j-2} \mod f$, and let $\varrho_1(\mathbf{M}_f) \geq \varrho_2(\mathbf{M}_f) \geq \cdots \geq \varrho_m(\mathbf{M}_f)$ denote its singular values. The expansion factor of a polynomial $f \in \mathbb{Z}[x]$ of degree m is defined as $\mathrm{EF}(f) = \max\left(\frac{\|g \mod f\|_\infty}{\|g\|_\infty} : g \in \mathbb{Z}^{<2m-1}[x] \backslash \{0\}\right)$.

2.2 Discrete Gaussian Distribution

In this section, we give a definition of the discrete Gaussian distribution and present some results regarding it that will be used latter in the paper.

Lattice. A m dimension lattice Λ is a discrete additive subgroup of $\mathbb{R}^m$ (e.g., $\mathbb{Z}^m$). For integer $n < m$ and matrix $\mathbf{B} \in \mathbb{R}^{m \times n}$, $\Lambda(\mathbf{B}) = \{\mathbf{Bx} \in \mathbb{R}^m | \mathbf{x} \in \mathbb{Z}^n\}$ is the lattice generated by the columns of $\mathbf{B}$. If $n = m$, it is called full rank lattice.

Gaussian. For any $\mathbf{x} \in \mathbb{R}^n$, we call $\rho(\mathbf{x}) = \exp\left(-\pi \cdot \|\mathbf{x}\|^2\right)$ an n dimensional Gaussian function. In particular, for a matrix $\mathbf{B}$ composed of any n linearly independent column vectors, when $\mathrm{Span}(\mathbf{B}) = \mathrm{Span}(\Sigma)$ is satisfied, the linear transformation of matrix $\mathbf{B}$ on $\mathbf{x} \in \mathbb{R}^n$ produces a Gaussian function as $\rho_{\mathbf{B}}(\mathbf{x}) = \rho\left(\mathbf{B}^{-1}\mathbf{x}\right) = \exp(-\pi \mathbf{x}^{\mathrm{T}} \Sigma^{-\mathrm{T}} \mathbf{x})$. Where $\Sigma = \mathbf{B}\mathbf{B}^{\mathrm{T}} \geq 0$, we usually write the function as $\rho_{\sqrt{\Sigma}}$. Given a countable set $S \subset \mathbb{R}^n$, for any real number $\mathbf{c} \in \mathbb{R}^n$, $\sigma \in \mathbb{R}^+$, we define the discrete Gaussian distribution on S with center c and standard deviation σ as $D_{S,\sigma,c}(\mathbf{x}) = \frac{\rho_{\sigma,c}(\mathbf{x})}{\rho_{\sigma,c}(S)}$. If $c = 0$, it can be written as $D_{S,\sigma}$.

Definition 1 (The Smoothing Parameter, [25]). *For any ndimensional lattice Λ, real $\epsilon > 0$, the smoothing parameter $\eta_\epsilon(\Lambda)$ is defined as the smallest real number s such that $\rho_{1/s}(\Lambda^*/\{0\}) \leq \epsilon$ holds, where Λ^* is the dual lattice of lattice Λ.*

Lemma 1 ([20]). *Let $\Lambda = \mathbb{Z}^n$ be integer lattice, when the positive definite matrix Σ satisfies $\sqrt{\Sigma} \geq \eta_\epsilon(\Lambda)$, then for each $\mathbf{c} \in$ Span(Σ), there is an inequality $\rho_{\sqrt{\Sigma}}(\Lambda + \mathbf{c}) \leq \rho_{\sqrt{\Sigma}}(\Lambda)\varphi_c$, where $\varphi_c \in \left[\frac{1-\epsilon}{1+\epsilon}, 1\right]$.*

Lemma 2 **([20]).** *For any* $\sigma \geq \eta_\epsilon(\mathbb{Z})$ *and real numbers* $\iota > 0$*, the probability is satisfied* $\Pr_{x \leftarrow D_{\mathbb{Z},\sigma}}[|x| \geq \sigma\sqrt{\iota}] \leq 2^{-\Omega(\iota)} \cdot \frac{1+\epsilon}{1-\epsilon}$. *When* $0 < \epsilon < 1/2$ *and* $\iota \geq \omega(\sqrt{\log n})$*, its probability is negligible.*

Lemma 3 **([10]).** *Let real numbers* $\sigma' > 0$, $L(\mathbf{B}) \subseteq \mathbb{Z}^n$ *be a sublattice of dimension* ℓ *whose basis is given by the* $(n \times \ell)$*-matrix* $\mathbf{B}$*, column vector* $\alpha \in L(\mathbf{B})$*. Let positive definite matrix* $\Sigma \in \mathbb{R}^{\ell \times \ell}$ *and define* $\Sigma' = \sigma'^2 \alpha\alpha^T$*. Then sampling* $\mathbf{s}_1 \leftarrow D_{\sqrt{\Sigma}}$*, vectors* $\mathbf{s}$ *and* $\mathbf{s}_2$ *are sampling from the distributions* $D_{\sqrt{\Sigma+\Sigma'}}$ *and* $D_{\sqrt{\Sigma'}}$ *on lattice* $L(\mathbf{B})$*. When the inequality* $\sqrt{\sigma'^2 - \sigma'^4 \alpha^{\mathrm{T}} (\Sigma + \Sigma')^{-1} \alpha} > \eta_\epsilon(\mathbb{Z}^\ell)$ *established, then* $\mathbf{s}$ *is indistinguishable from* $\mathbf{s}' = \mathbf{s}_1 + \mathbf{s}_2$*.*

2.3 MP-LWE

Before defining the MP-LWE problem, we first introduce the operations and distributions on which its definition depends.

Definition 2 **(Middle-Product, [28]).** *Let* d_a, d_b, d, k *be integers such that* $d_a + d_b - 1 = d + 2k$*. The middle-product* $\odot_d : R^{<d_a}[x] \times R^{<d_b}[x] \rightarrow R^{<d}[x]$ *is the map:* $a(x) \odot_d b(x) = \left\lfloor \frac{a(x) \cdot b(x) \bmod x^{k+d}}{x^k} \right\rfloor$.

The reversed coefficient vector of the middle-product of two polynomials is in fact equal to the product of the Toeplitz matrix associated to one polynomial by the reversed coefficient vector of the second polynomial.

Lemma 4 **([28]).** *Let integers* $d, k > 0$*, polynomials* $r(x) \in R^{<k+1}[x]$*,* $a(x) \in R^{<k+d}[x]$ *and* $b(x) = r(x) \odot_d a(x)$*. Then* $\mathbf{b} = \overline{\mathrm{Toep}^{d,k+d}(r(x)) \cdot \bar{\mathbf{a}}}$*. In other words, we have* $\bar{\mathbf{b}} = \mathrm{Toep}^{d,k+d}(a(x)) \cdot \bar{\mathbf{r}}$.

Let integers $d, k, n, m > 0$, prime $q \geq 2$. For any polynomial row vector $\mathbf{a}(x) \in \left(\mathbb{Z}_q^{<n}[x]\right)^m$ and column vector $\mathbf{b}(x) \in \left(\mathbb{Z}_q^{<n+d-1}[x]\right)^m$, we denote $\mathbf{a}(x) \odot_d \mathbf{b}(x) = \sum_{j=1}^m (a_j(x) \odot_d b_j(x))$.

Lemma 5 **([28]).** *Let integer* $d, k, n, m > 0$*, prime* $q \geq 2$*. For any polynomial vector* $\mathbf{a}(x) \in \left(\mathbb{Z}_q^{<n}[x]\right)^m$*,* $\mathbf{r}(x) \in \left(\{0,1\}^{<k+1}[x]\right)^m$ *and polynomial* $s(x) \in \mathbb{Z}_q^{<n+d+k-1}[x]$*, we have* $\mathbf{r}(x) \odot_d (\mathbf{a}(x) \odot_{d+k} s(x)) = (\mathbf{r}(x) \cdot \mathbf{a}(x)) \odot_d s(x)$.

Definition 3 **(MP Distribution, [7,28]).** *Let integer* $n, d > 0$*, prime* $q \geq 2$*. Gaussian parameters* $\sigma_1, \sigma_2 > 0$*, distributions* $D_{\mathbb{Z},\sigma_1}$*,* $D_{\mathbb{Z},\sigma_2}$ *over* $\mathbb{Z}$ *and* $s(x) \in D_{\mathbb{Z},\sigma_2}^{<n+d-1}[x]$*. We define the distribution* $\mathrm{MP}_{q,n,d,\chi}(s(x))$ *over* $\mathbb{Z}_q^{<n}[x] \times \mathbb{Z}_q^{<d}[x]$ *as: Sampling* $a(x) \leftarrow U\left(\mathbb{Z}_q^{<d}[x]\right)$*,* $e(x) \leftarrow D_{\mathbb{Z},\sigma_2}^{<d}[x]$*, and returning* $(a(x), b(x) = a(x) \odot_d s(x) + e(x)) \in \mathbb{Z}_q^{<n}[x] \times \mathbb{Z}_q^{<d}[x]$*.*

Definition 4 **(MP-LWE, [7,28]).** *Let integer* $n, d > 0$*, prime* $q \geq 2$*, Gaussian parameters* $\sigma_1, \sigma_2 > 0$*, distributions* $D_{\mathbb{Z},\sigma_1}$ *and* $D_{\mathbb{Z},\sigma_2}$ *over* $\mathbb{Z}$*, respectively. The (Decision)* $\mathrm{MP\text{-}LWE}_{q,n,d,\sigma_1,\sigma_2}$ *problem consists in distinguishing between arbitrarily many samples from* $\mathrm{MP}_{q,n,d,\sigma_1,\sigma_2}(s(x))$ *and the same number of uniform samples in* $\mathbb{Z}_q^{<n}[x] \times \mathbb{Z}_q^{<d}[x]$*, with non-negligible probability over the choice of* $s(x) \leftarrow D_{\mathbb{Z},\sigma_1}^{<n+d-1}[x]$*.*

Theorem 1 (Hardness of MP-LWE, [7,28]**).** *Let prime $q \geq 2$, integer $n \geq d > 0$, and let $\Gamma(T,d,n)$ denote the set of all monic polynomials $g(x) \in \mathbb{Z}[x]$ with constant coefficient coprime to q, degree $m \in [d,n]$, and $\varrho_m(M_f) \geq T$. For any polynomial $f \in \Gamma(T,d,n)$ and $2\sqrt{n}/T \leq \sigma \leq q$, there exists a polynomial-time reduction from $\mathrm{PLWE}^{(f)}_{q,m,\sigma}$ to $\text{MP-LWE}_{q,n,d,\sigma_1,\sigma_2}$, where $\sigma_1 = n\sigma\sqrt{2n}\mathrm{EF}(f)^2$ and $\sigma_2 = n\sigma\sqrt{2d}\,\mathrm{EF}(f)$.*

2.4 Leftover Hash Lemma

In this section, we gives the relevant definitions about properties of entropy and leftover hash lemma [28], which will be used in the security analysis below.

For the hash function $h: Z \to Y$, any $z_1, z_2 \in Z$ $(z_1 \neq z_2)$, define $\delta_h(z_1,z_2) = 1$ if and only if $h(z_1) = h(z_2)$; Otherwise, $\delta_h(z_1,z_2) = 0$. Then define the sum of the number of hash function collisions in the finite hash function family as $\delta_{\mathcal{H}}(z_1,z_2) = \sum\limits_{h\in\mathcal{H}} \delta_h(z_1,z_2)$. If $\mathcal{H}$ satisfies the equation $\Pr_{h\leftarrow U(\mathcal{H})}[\delta_h(z_1,z_2) = 1] = 1/|Y|$, then the hash function family $\mathcal{H}$ is said to be universal.

Lemma 6 ([28])**.** *Let $m,q,n,d,k \geq 2$ and $k+d \leq n$. For the polynomial row vector $\mathbf{b}(x) \in (\mathbb{Z}_q^{<d+k})^m$ and column vector $\mathbf{r}(x) \in \left(\{0,1\}^{<k+1}[x]\right)^m$, define the function $\Phi_{\mathbf{b}(x)}: \left(\{0,1\}^{<k+1}[x]\right)^m \to \mathbb{Z}_q^{<d}[x]$ as $\mathbf{r}(x) \mapsto \mathbf{r}(x) \odot_d \mathbf{b}(x)$. Then the function family $\left\{\Phi_{\mathbf{b}(x)}\right\}$ is universal.*

For two random variables X and Y in a finite set Ω, the statistical distance is defined $\Delta(X,Y) = \sum\limits_{s\in\Omega} |\Pr[X=s] - \Pr[Y=s]|$. When $\Delta(X,Y)$ is negligible, then the random variables X and Y are said to be statistically indistinguishable and written $X \approx^s Y$. For a random variable X whose predictability is $\max_a \Pr[X=a]$, the minimum entropy $\mathbf{H}_\infty(X)$ of the variable is written as $-\log(\max_a \Pr[X=a])$. For two correlated random variables X and Y, if the adversary knows that the value of the variable Y is b, then the predictability is max, and the average expectation of the adversary successfully predicting X is $\mathbb{E}_{b\leftarrow Y}[\max_a \Pr[X=a\,|Y=b]]$. Therefore, the average minimum entropy of X given Y is expressed as $\widetilde{\mathbf{H}}_\infty(X|Y) = -\log(\mathbb{E}_{b\leftarrow Y}[\max_a \Pr[X=a\,|Y=b]]) = -\log\left(\mathbb{E}_{b\leftarrow Y}\left[2^{\mathbf{H}_\infty(X|Y=b)}\right]\right)$.

Lemma 7 ([10])**.** *Let W, I be random variables. If the variable I has at most q^ℓ possible values, then there is an inequality $\widetilde{\mathbf{H}}_\infty(W\,|I) \geq \mathbf{H}_\infty(W,I) - \ell\log q \geq \mathbf{H}_\infty(W) - \ell\log q$, where $\mathbf{H}_\infty(W,I)$ represents the joint entropy of random variables W and I.*

Lemma 8 (Generalized Leftover Hash Lemma, [10,17]**).** *Assume that the family of hash functions $\left\{H_x : \{0,1\}^n \to \{0,1\}^\ell\right\}_{x\in X}$ is universal. Then, for any random variables W and I, $\Delta((H_X(W),X,I),(U_\ell,X,I)) \leq \frac{1}{2}\sqrt{2^{-\widetilde{\mathbf{H}}_\infty(W|I)}2^\ell}$, where U_ℓ represents a uniform distribution over an ℓ-bit binary string.*

2.5 Inner Product Encryption

This section discusses the syntax of a FE scheme and its security notion.

Definition 5 (IPE Encryption scheme, [10]). *A IFE scheme is defined with regard to a some ring R, and consists of four probabilistic polynomial time algorithms:*

- *Setup*$(1^\kappa, 1^\ell) \mapsto$ *(pp, msk, mpk). On input security parameter κ and functionality parameter ℓ outputs public parameters pp, master secret key msk, and master public key mpk.*
- *KeyGen(pp, msk, y) $\mapsto$ sk_y. On input public parameter pp, master secret key msk, and key $y \in R^\ell$, outputs user secret key sk_y.*
- *Encrypt(pp, mpk, x) $\mapsto$ ct_x. On input public parameter pp, master public key mpk, and plaintext $x \in R^\ell$, outputs ciphertext ct_x.*
- *Decrypt(pp, sk_y, ct_x) $\mapsto$ m or $\perp$. On input public parameters pp, user secret key sk_y, and ciphertext ct_x, outputs a message $m \in R$ or an error symbol $\perp$.*

Definition 6 (Sel-IND-CPA-secure, [6]). *For an* IPE *scheme, we define Sel-IND-CPA-secure via the game Sel-IND$_{\mathcal{A}}^{b \leftarrow \{0,1\}}(1^\kappa)$ between the adversary $\mathcal{A}$ and challenger as follows:*

- *Initialize: The adversary selects challenge vectors $\mathbf{v}_0$,$\mathbf{v}_1$, the challenger runs* $(\mathsf{msk}, \mathsf{mpk}) \leftarrow \mathsf{Setup}(1^\kappa)$ *and send* mpk *to $\mathcal{A}$;*
- *Query: The adversary submits the query $\mathbf{w}$, if the query $\mathbf{w}$ satisfies the constraint $\langle \mathbf{v}_0, \mathbf{w}\rangle = \langle \mathbf{v}_1, \mathbf{w}\rangle$, then receives the response* $\mathsf{sk}_\mathbf{w} \leftarrow \mathsf{KeyGen}(\mathsf{msk}, \mathbf{w})$ *from the challenger; otherwise, returns the query failure;*
- *Challenge: The challenger runs* $\mathsf{ct}_\mathbf{v} \leftarrow \mathsf{Enc}(\mathsf{mpk}, \mathbf{v}_b)$ *and returns it to the adversary;*
- *Finalize: The adversary outputs b' as its guess for $b \leftarrow \{0,1\}$.*

We say the IFE *scheme is Sel-IND-CPA-secure, if for any PPT adversary $\mathcal{A}$, there is a negligible function* $\text{negl}(\kappa)$ *such that*

$$\text{Adv}_{\mathcal{A}}^{\text{IPE}}(\textit{Sel-IND}_{\mathcal{A}}^b) = \left|2 \cdot \Pr[\textit{Sel-IND}_{\mathcal{A}}^b(1^\kappa) = 1] - 1\right| \leq \text{negl}(\kappa).$$

3 Public-Key Encryption from MP-LWE

In this section, we present a variant (denoted as $\mathcal{E}$) of public key encryption scheme [28] and [30] based on the MP-LWE problem, and the relevant homomorphic properties of the scheme are proposed. The plaintext space of the scheme is $\mathbb{Z}_p$, and the ciphertext space is $\mathbb{Z}_q^{<n+k}[x] \times \mathbb{Z}_q^{<d}[x]$. The specific algorithm is described as follows (Fig. 1):

$\mathcal{E}$.Setup (1^{κ}) :

1. Set σ_1, σ_2
2. Choose $\mathbf{a}(x) \leftarrow U\left(\mathbb{Z}_q^{<n}[x]\right)^m$

Output : $\mathsf{pp} = (\mathbf{a}(x), \sigma_1, \sigma_2)$

$\mathcal{E}$.KeyGen (pp) :

1. Choose $s(x) \leftarrow D_{\mathbb{Z},\sigma_1}^{<n+k-1}[x]$,

   $\mathbf{e}(x) \leftarrow \left(D_{\mathbb{Z},\sigma_2}^{<d+k}[x]\right)^m$
2. Let $\mathbf{b}(x) = \mathbf{a}(x) \odot_{d+k} s(x) + \mathbf{e}(x)$

Output $\mathsf{sk} = s(x)$ and $\mathsf{pk} = \mathbf{b}(x)$

$\mathcal{E}$.Encrypt (pp, pk, v) :

1. Choose $\mathbf{r}(x) \leftarrow U\left(\{0,1\}^{<k+1}[x]\right)^m$
2. Let $\mathsf{ct}_0 = \mathbf{r}(x) \cdot \mathbf{a}(x)$,

   $\mathsf{ct}_1 = \mathbf{r}(x) \odot_d \mathbf{b}(x) + \lfloor q/p \rfloor v \cdot 1_R$

Output : $\mathsf{ct} = (\mathsf{ct}_0, \mathsf{ct}_1)$

$\mathcal{E}$.Decrypt (sk, ct) :

1. Let $\mu'(x) = \mathsf{ct} - \mathsf{ct}_0 \odot_d s(x) \bmod q$

Output : $\left\lfloor \lfloor q/p \rfloor^{-1} \mu'(x) \bmod x \right\rfloor$

Fig. 1. Public key encryption scheme $\mathcal{E}$

1. $n = n(q),\ q > p,\ \epsilon = 2^{-\kappa}$;
2. $m \geq \left((n+d+k)\log q + \log \frac{1}{4\epsilon^2}\right)(k+1)^{-1}$;
3. $\sigma_1 > \sigma n\sqrt{2n} \cdot \mathrm{EF}(f)^2,\ \sigma_2 > \sigma n\sqrt{2(d+k)} \cdot \mathrm{EF}(f)$,

   where $T > 0,\ 2q\sqrt{n}/T \leq \sigma \leq q$; (Theorem 1)
4. $\lfloor q/(2p) \rfloor > m\sigma_2\sqrt{\kappa}(k+1)$.

Fig. 2. Parameter settings of the scheme $\mathcal{E}$.

3.1 The Correctness and Security

To ensure the correctness and security of the public key encryption scheme , the relationship between the parameters is shown in Fig. 2.

Lemma 9 (Correctness). *Let the parameters satisfy* $m\sigma_2\sqrt{\kappa}(k+1) < \lfloor q/(2p) \rfloor$. *When the algorithm* $\mathcal{E}$.KeyGen *randomly generates a key, and the algorithm* $\mathcal{E}$.Encrypt *encrypts any plaintext* v *in the plaintext space with a probability of 1 to obtain a ciphertext, then* $\mathcal{E}$.Encrypt $= v$ *holds with an overwhelming probability.*

Proof. We mainly use the characteristics of the MP operation and the vector tail bounded lemma to prove the correctness of the scheme. The specific proof process is very similar to that in reference [28], and will not be repeated here.

Lemma 10 (Security). *Suppose that* $m \geq \left((n+d+k)\log q + \log \frac{1}{4\epsilon^2}\right)(k+1)^{-1}$, *where* $\epsilon = 2^{-\kappa}$. *Then under the* $\text{MP-LWE}_{q,n,d,k,\sigma_1,\sigma_2}$ *hardness assumption, scheme* $\mathcal{E}$ *is IND-CPA-secure.*

Proof. The proof is based on an adaptation of the leftover hash lemma based argument from [28] and [30], so the entire proof process is similar to the paper and will not be repeated here.

3.2 Linear Homomorphism

Next, we will give the concepts of key linear homomorphism and ciphertext linear homomorphism under shared randomness, and it is proved that the above scheme satisfies these two properties.

Definition 7 (Linear Key Homomorphism, [1]**).** *Let* $(\mathsf{sk}_1, \mathsf{pk}_1)$ *and* $(\mathsf{sk}_2, \mathsf{pk}_2)$ *be valid key pairs for a public key encryption scheme. For any* $y_1, y_2 \in \mathbb{Z}$, $\mathsf{pk}{=}y_1\mathsf{pk}_1 + y_2\mathsf{pk}_2$ *and* $\mathsf{sk} = y_1\mathsf{sk}_1 + y_2\mathsf{sk}_2$, $(\mathsf{sk}, \mathsf{pk})$ *is also a valid key pair of the scheme, then the public key encryption scheme is said to have linear key homomorphism.*

Definition 8 (Linear Ciphertext Homomorphism under Shared Randomness, [1]**).** *Let* $(\mathsf{sk}_1, \mathsf{pk}_1)$ *and* $(\mathsf{sk}_2, \mathsf{pk}_2)$ *be valid key pairs of a public key encryption scheme, encryption algorithm* E*:* $X \times Y \rightarrow S$*, where* X*,* Y *and are valid plaintext, key and ciphertext respectively space. For any randomness* r *and plaintext* $u_1, u_2 \in X$*, if the encryption algorithm satisfies the equation* $E(\mathsf{pk}_1, u_1; r) + E(\mathsf{pk}_2, u_1; r) = E(\mathsf{pk}_1 + \mathsf{pk}_2, u_1 + u_1; r)$*. Then the public key encryption scheme is said to have linear ciphertext homomorphism under shared randomness.*

Theorem 2. *Scheme* $\mathcal{E}$ *has the following properties:*

(a) Linear ciphertext homomorphism under shared randomness;
(b) Linear key homomorphism if and only if $\|\mathbf{r}(x) \odot_d (y_1\mathbf{e}_1(x) + y_2\mathbf{e}_2(x))\|_\infty < \lfloor q/(2p) \rfloor$.

Proof. The proof process of this theorem is shown in Appendix A.1.

4 Sel-IND-CPA-Secure Inner Product Encryption

In this section, we construct an inner product encryption scheme with Sel-IND-CPA security (denoted as IPE_1) based on the public key encryption scheme $\mathcal{E}$ described in Sect. 3. The basic idea of this construction is: take the ℓ public-private key pairs $(\mathsf{sk}_i, \mathsf{pk}_i)_{i\in[\ell]}$ in scheme $\mathcal{E}$ as the master public and private key in this scheme, and then linearly combine the column vector $\mathbf{w}$ and the master private key sk_i to generate the user private key $\mathsf{sk}_{\mathbf{w}}$, and then generate the ciphertext $\mathsf{ct}_{\mathbf{v}}$ containing the plaintext column vector $\mathbf{v}$ according to the encryption algorithm. Different from $\mathcal{E}$, this scheme needs to linearly combine the ciphertext $\mathsf{ct}_{\mathbf{v}}$ with the vector $\mathbf{w}$ before decryption.

$\mathsf{IPE_1.Setup}\left(1^\kappa, 1^\ell\right)$:	$\mathsf{IPE_1.Encrypt}\left(\mathsf{pp}, \mathsf{mpk}, \mathbf{v}\right)$:
1. Let $\mathsf{pp} = (\sigma_1, \sigma_2, \mathbf{a}(x)) \leftarrow \mathcal{E}.\mathsf{Setup}(1^\kappa)$	1. Choose $\mathbf{r}(x) \leftarrow U\left(\{0,1\}^{<k+1}[x]\right)^m$
2. **For** $i = 1, \ldots, \ell$ **do**	2. Let $\mathsf{ct}_0 = \mathbf{r}(x) \cdot \mathbf{a}(x)$
$\mathsf{sk}_i, \mathsf{pk}_i \leftarrow \mathcal{E}.\mathsf{KeyGen}(\mathsf{pp})$	3. **For** $i = 1, \ldots, \ell$ **do**
Output : pp, $\mathsf{msk} := \{\mathsf{sk}_i\}_{i\in[\ell]}$	$\mathsf{ct}_i = \mathbf{r}(x) \odot_d \mathsf{pk}_i + \lfloor q/p \rfloor v_i \cdot 1_R$
$\mathsf{mpk} := \{\mathsf{pk}_i\}_{i\in[\ell]}$	**Output** : $\mathsf{ct}_\mathbf{v} := (\mathsf{ct}_0, \{\mathsf{ct}_i\})_{i\in[\ell]}$
$\mathsf{IPE_1.KeyGen}(\mathsf{msk}, \mathbf{w})$:	
Output : $\mathsf{sk}_\mathbf{w} = \sum_{i=1}^{\ell} \mathsf{sk}_i \cdot w_i$	
$\mathsf{IPE_1.Decrypt}(\mathsf{sk}_\mathbf{w}, \mathsf{ct}_\mathbf{v})$:	
Output : $v' \leftarrow \mathcal{E}.\mathsf{Decrypt}\left(\mathsf{sk}_\mathbf{w}, \left(\mathsf{ct}_0, \sum_{i\in[\ell]} \mathsf{ct}_i \cdot w_i\right)\right)$	

Fig. 3. Formal description of the scheme IPE_1.

The Construction. In addition to the definition of scheme $\mathcal{E}$, the specific algorithm of the scheme also depends on the parameter $\ell, \mathcal{M}_\mathbf{v}, \mathcal{M}_\mathbf{w}$, where $\ell \in \mathbb{Z}^+$ represents the length of the vector, $\mathcal{M}_\mathbf{w}, \mathcal{M}_\mathbf{v} \in \mathbb{Z}_p$ be the bound of the infinity norms of the vector, i.e., $\mathbf{w} \in \mathcal{M}_\mathbf{w}^\ell, \mathbf{v} \in \mathcal{M}_\mathbf{v}^\ell$. The formal description of the Sel-IND-CPA-secure inner product encryption algorithm is shown in Fig. 3.

The Correctness and Security. The following are the specific proof process of the correctness and security of the scheme.

Lemma 11 (Correctness). *When the algorithm IPE_1.KeyGen randomly generates a private key, and the algorithm IPE_1.Encrypt encrypts all plaintext vectors* $\mathbf{v}$ *with a probability of 1 to obtain the ciphertexts, if the parameters satisfy the inequality $\ell m \mathcal{M}_\mathbf{w} \sigma_2 \sqrt{\kappa}(k+1) < \lfloor q/(2p) \rfloor$, then IPE_1.Decrypt$= \langle \mathbf{v}, \mathbf{w} \rangle$ established with overwhelming probability.*

Proof. From the decryption algorithm, we can obtain

$$
\begin{aligned}
&\sum_{i=1}^{\ell} \mathrm{ct}_i \cdot w_i - \mathrm{ct}_0 \odot_d \mathrm{sk}_\mathbf{w} \pmod q \\
=&\sum_{i=1}^{\ell} \sum_{j=1}^{m} r_j(x) \odot_d e_{ij}(x) \cdot w_i + \sum_{i=1}^{\ell} \lfloor q/p \rfloor v_i \cdot w_i \cdot 1_R \\
=&\,\mathrm{noise} + \lfloor q/p \rfloor \langle \mathbf{v}, \mathbf{w} \rangle \cdot 1_R.
\end{aligned}
$$

When $\|\mathrm{noise}\|_\infty < \lfloor q/(2p) \rfloor$, $v' = \left\lfloor \lfloor q/p \rfloor^{-1} \cdot (\mathrm{noise} + \lfloor p/q \rfloor \langle \mathbf{v}, \mathbf{w} \rangle \cdot 1_R) (\mathrm{mod} x) \right\rfloor = \left\lfloor \lfloor q/p \rfloor^{-1} \cdot \lfloor q/(2p) \rfloor + \langle \mathbf{v}, \mathbf{w} \rangle \right\rfloor = \langle \mathbf{v}, \mathbf{w} \rangle$. So v' is the inner product value $\langle \mathbf{v}, \mathbf{w} \rangle$.

Now prove that $\|\text{noise}\|_\infty < \ell m \mathcal{M}_{\mathbf{w}} \sigma_2 \sqrt{\kappa}(k+1) < \lfloor q/(2p) \rfloor$, set polynomial $c_{ij}(x) = r_j(x) \odot_d e_{ij}(x)$, each coefficient of polynomial $c_{ij}(x)$ can be regarded as a binary vector of at most $m(k+1)$ dimensions and ℓ vectors $\bar{\mathbf{e}}_i = (\bar{\mathbf{e}}_{i1}, \ldots, \bar{\mathbf{e}}_{im})$ for inner product in turn. From Lemma 2, for the security parameter κ, the inequality $\|\bar{\mathbf{e}}_{ij}\|_\infty \leq \sigma_2\sqrt{\kappa}$ holds with overwhelming probability. So $\|\text{noise}\|_\infty = \left\| \sum_{i=1}^{\ell} \sum_{j=1}^{m} r_j(x) \odot_d e_{ij}(x) \cdot y_i \right\|_\infty < \ell m \mathcal{M}_{\mathbf{w}} \sigma_2 \sqrt{\kappa}(k+1)$.

In summary, when $\|\text{noise}\|_\infty < \ell m \mathcal{M}_{\mathbf{w}} \sigma_2 \sqrt{\kappa}(k+1) < \lfloor q/(2p) \rfloor$, the correctness of the algorithm is satisfied.

Lemma 12 (Security). *Under the condition of choosing the correct parameters for the scheme IPE_1, if there is a polynomial-time adversary $\mathcal{B}$ to break the scheme IPE_1 and a polynomial-time adversary $\mathcal{G}$ to break the* MP-LWE *hardness assmuption, and the attack advantage between the adversaries satisfies the inequality*

$$\mathrm{Adv}_{\mathcal{B}}^{IPE_1}\left(Sel\text{-}IND_{\mathcal{B}}^{b}\right) \leq \mathrm{Adv}_{\mathcal{G},m,\ell}^{\text{MP-LWE}}(\kappa) + \mathrm{negl}(\kappa),$$

Then the scheme IPE_1 is said to be Sel-IND-CPA-secure, where $\mathrm{negl}(\kappa)$ *represents a negligible function.*

Proof. The following is a series of "game" jumps to prove that the real security model is indistinguishable from the last security model that can hide the challenge information bit b. Because the last security model hides the information of bit b, the advantage of adversary $\mathcal{B}$ can be ignored. The formal descriptions of games is given as follows.

Game$_1$: is a real game associated with bit b, and the description of real security model is shown in Definition 6.

Game$_2$: Game$_2$ and Game$_1$ are almost the same, except that the polynomial $s_i(x)$ and the polynomial vector $\mathbf{e}_i(x)$ in Game$_2$ are rewritten into the structures of $\alpha_i s^*(x) + s'_i(x)$ and $\alpha_i \mathbf{e}^*(x) + \mathbf{e}'_i(x)$, where $\mathbf{v}_1, \mathbf{v}_0$ are the challenge vectors selected by the adversary before the game starts, and α_i is the i-th element of $\alpha = \mathbf{v}_1 - \mathbf{v}_0$, the polynomials $s^*(x)$ and $s'_i(x)$ are sampled from the distributions $D_{\mathbb{Z},\sigma'_1}^{<n+d+k-1}[x]$ and $D_{\mathbb{Z},\tau_i}^{<n+d+k-1}[x]$, the polynomial vectors $\mathbf{e}^*(x)$ and $\mathbf{e}'_i(x)$ are sampled from the distributions $\left(D_{\sigma'_2}^{<d+k}[x]\right)^m$ and $\left(D_{\tau'_i}^{<d+k}[x]\right)^m$, the parameters τ_i, τ'_i satisfy $\tau_i = \sqrt{\sigma_1^2 - {\sigma_1'}^2 \alpha_i^2}$, $\tau'_i = \sqrt{\sigma_2^2 - {\sigma_2'}^2 \alpha_i^2}$.

Game$_3$: Game$_3$ and Game$_2$ are almost the same, except that the master key pair $(\mathsf{pk}_i, \mathsf{sk}_i)$ in Game$_3$ is rewritten to be generated by the linear combination of $(\mathsf{pk}^*, \mathsf{sk}^*)$ and $(\mathsf{pk}'_i, \mathsf{sk}'_i)$, that is, $\alpha_i(\mathsf{pk}^*, \mathsf{sk}^*) + (\mathsf{pk}'_i, \mathsf{sk}'_i)$, where $\mathsf{sk}^* = s^*(x)$, $\mathsf{pk}^* = \mathbf{a}(x) \odot_{d+k} s^*(x) + \mathbf{e}^*(x)$, $\mathsf{sk}'_i = s'_i(x)$, $\mathsf{pk}'_i = \mathbf{a}(x) \odot_{d+k} s'_i(x) + \mathbf{e}'_i(x)$.

Game$_4$: Game$_4$ and Game$_3$ are almost the same, except that in Game$_4$, the ciphertext ct_i is rewritten to be generated by a linear combination of ct^* and ct'_i, that is, $\alpha_i \mathsf{ct}^* + \mathsf{ct}'_i$, where $\mathsf{ct}^* = \mathbf{r}(x) \odot_d \mathsf{pk}^*$, $\mathsf{ct}'_i = \mathbf{r}(x) \odot_d \mathsf{pk}'_i + \lfloor q/p \rfloor v_{b,i} \cdot 1_R$.

Game$_5$: Game$_5$ and Game$_4$ are almost the same, except that in Game$_5$, the algorithm is no longer used to generate the public key pk^*, but is uniformly and randomly sampled from $\mathbb{Z}_q^{<d+k}[x]$, that is, $\mathsf{pk}^* \leftarrow U\left(\mathbb{Z}_q^{<d+k}[x]\right)^m$.

Game$_6$: Game$_6$ and Game$_5$ are almost the same, but Game$_6$ no longer uses pk_i' to generate ciphertext ct_i', but uses ct_0 to rewrite the ciphertext generation algorithm, namely, $\mathsf{ct}_i' = \mathsf{ct}_0 \odot_d s'_i(x) + \mathbf{r}(x) \odot_d \mathbf{e}_i'(x) + \lfloor q/p \rfloor v_{b,i} \cdot 1_R$.

Game$_7$: Game$_7$ and Game$_6$ are almost the same, except that Game$_7$ no longer uses the algorithm to generate ct_0 and ct^*, but sampled them uniformly and randomly from $\mathbb{Z}_q^{<n+k}[x]$ and $\mathbb{Z}_q^{<d}[x]$, namely, $\mathsf{ct}_0(x) \leftarrow U\left(\mathbb{Z}_q^{<n+k}[x]\right)$ and $\mathsf{ct}^*(x) \leftarrow U\left(\mathbb{Z}_q^{<d}[x]\right)$.

Game$_8$: Game$_8$ and Game$_7$ are almost the same, except that Game$_8$ uses the polynomial vector $\tilde{\mathbf{r}}(x) \leftarrow U\left(\{0,1\}^{<k+1}[x]\right)^m$ to generate the ciphertext ct_i', namely, $\mathsf{ct}_i' = \mathsf{ct}_0 \odot_d s_i'(x) + \tilde{\mathbf{r}}(x) \odot_d \mathbf{e}_i'(x) + \lfloor q/p \rfloor v_{b,i} \cdot 1_R$.

Game$_9$: Game$_9$ and Game$_8$ are almost the same, except that ct_0 and ct^* in Game$_9$ are no longer randomly selected from the distributions $\mathbb{Z}_q^{<n+k}[x]$ and $\mathbb{Z}_q^{<d}[x]$, but are generated according to the algorithm $\mathcal{E}.\mathsf{Encrypt}\left(\mathsf{pp}^*, \mathsf{pk}^*, 0\right)$, where $\mathsf{pp}^* = \left(\sigma_1', \sigma_2', \mathbf{a}(x) \leftarrow U\left(\mathbb{Z}_q^{<n}[x]\right)^m\right)$.

Game$_{10}$: Game$_{10}$ and Game$_9$ are almost the same, except that in Game$_{10}$, pk^* is no longer randomly selected from $\mathbb{Z}_q^{<d+k}[x]$, but is generated according to the algorithm $\mathcal{E}.\mathrm{KeyGen}\left(\mathsf{pp}^*\right)$, which is $s^*(x) \leftarrow D_{\mathbb{Z},\sigma_1'}^{<n+d+k-1}[x]$, $\mathbf{e}^*(x) \leftarrow \left(D_{\mathbb{Z},\sigma_2'}^{<d+k}[x]\right)^m$, $\mathsf{pk}^* = \mathbf{a}(x) \odot_{d+k} s^*(x) + \mathbf{e}^*(x)$. At this time, the challenge ciphertext is: $\mathsf{ct}_i = \alpha_i(\mathbf{r}(x) \odot_d \mathsf{pk}^*) + \mathsf{ct}_0 \odot_d s_i'(x) + \tilde{\mathbf{r}}(x) \odot_d \mathbf{e}_i'(x) + \lfloor q/p \rfloor v_{b,i} \cdot 1_R$
$= \alpha_i(\mathbf{r}(x) \odot_d \mathsf{pk}^*) + \mathsf{ct}_0 \odot_d s_i'(x) + \tilde{\mathbf{r}}(x) \odot_d \mathbf{e}_i'(x) + \lfloor q/p \rfloor (v_{0,i} + b(v_{1,i} - v_{0,i})) \cdot 1_R$
$= \alpha_i(\mathbf{r}(x) \odot_d \mathsf{pk}^* + \lfloor q/p \rfloor b \cdot 1_R) + \mathsf{ct}_0 \odot_d s_i'(x) + \tilde{\mathbf{r}}(x) \odot_d \mathbf{e}_i'(x) + \lfloor q/p \rfloor v_{0,i} \cdot 1_R$.

Obviously, the first half of the challenge ciphertext can be regarded as the ciphertext generated by encrypting b, namely, $\mathbf{r}(x) \odot_d \mathsf{pk}^* + \lfloor q/p \rfloor b \cdot 1_R$.

Game$_{11}$: Game$_{11}$ and Game$_{10}$ are almost the same, except that Game$_{11}$ no longer uses the key pair $(\mathsf{pk}^*, \mathsf{sk}^*)$ to encrypt b, but encrypts the plaintext M, where $M \leftarrow U(\mathbb{Z}_p)$.Then the challenge ciphertext is: $\mathsf{ct}_i = \alpha_i(\mathbf{r}(x) \odot_d \mathsf{pk}^* + \lfloor q/p \rfloor M \cdot 1_R) + \mathsf{ct}_0 \odot_d s_i'(x) + \tilde{\mathbf{r}}(x) \odot_d \mathbf{e}_i'(x) + \lfloor q/p \rfloor v_{0,i} \cdot 1_R$.

Advantage of Adversary $\mathcal{B}$: We now analyze the adversary advantage of the last game. In Game$_{11}$, because the distribution of challenge ciphertexts in this game is independent of b. Therefore, the adversary's advantage in this game is 0. Then according to the triangle inequality, there is $\left|\mathrm{Adv}_{\mathcal{B},\mathrm{G}_1}^{\mathrm{IPE}_1}(\kappa)\text{-}\mathrm{Adv}_{\mathcal{B},\mathrm{G}_{11}}^{\mathrm{IPE}_1}(\kappa)\right| \leq \sum_{1 \leq f < 11} \left|\mathrm{Adv}_{\mathcal{B},\mathrm{G}_f}^{\mathrm{IPE}_1}(\kappa)\text{-}\mathrm{Adv}_{\mathcal{B},\mathrm{G}_{f+1}}^{\mathrm{IPE}_1}(\kappa)\right|$.

From Lemma 13 to Lemma 19, the above equation be: $\mathrm{Adv}_{\mathcal{B}}^{\mathrm{IPE}_1}\left(\text{Sel-IND-CPA}_{\mathcal{B}}^{b}\right)$
$= \left|\mathrm{Adv}_{\mathcal{B},\mathrm{G}_1}^{\mathrm{IPE}_1}(\kappa)\right| = \left|\mathrm{Adv}_{\mathcal{B},\mathrm{G}_1}^{\mathrm{IPE}_1}(\kappa)\text{-}\mathrm{Adv}_{\mathcal{B},\mathrm{G}_{11}}^{\mathrm{IPE}_1}(\kappa)\right| \leq \mathrm{Adv}_{\mathcal{G},m,\ell}^{\mathrm{MP\text{-}LWE}}(\kappa) + \mathrm{negl}(\kappa)$.

The advantage of the adversary breaking MP-LWE problem can be ignored, that is, there is no effective adversary breaking the real security model, and the proof is completed.

Lemma 13. *Assume that* $\sigma_1 > 2\sigma_1'\sqrt{\ell}\mathcal{M}_{\mathbf{v}}$, $\sigma_2 > 2\sigma_2'\sqrt{\ell}\mathcal{M}_{\mathbf{v}}$, *and* $\sigma_1, \sigma_1', \sigma_2, \sigma_2'$ *satisfy* $\sigma_1'\sqrt{1-(\sigma_1'/\sigma_1)^{-2}\alpha^{\mathrm{T}}\alpha} \geq \eta_{\epsilon'}(\mathbb{Z}^\ell)$, $\sigma_2'\sqrt{1-(\sigma_2'/\sigma_2)^{-2}\alpha^{\mathrm{T}}\alpha} \geq \eta_{\epsilon''}(\mathbb{Z}^\ell)$, *where* $\epsilon' = 2^{-\kappa}/(\ell(n+d+k-1))$, $\epsilon'' = 2^{-\kappa}/(\ell m(d+k))$. *Then at the view of adversary* $\mathcal{B}$, Game_1 *and* Game_2 *are statistically indistinguishable.*

Proof. Let index $i \in [\ell]$, $j \in [n+d+k-1]$. Because the master private key is composed of polynomials $s_i(x) \leftarrow D_{\mathbb{Z},\sigma_1}^{<n+d+k-1}[x]$, it means that the corresponding ℓ coefficient row vectors $\mathbf{s}_i = (s_{i1}, \ldots, s_{i,n+d+k-1})$ can be represented by a matrix $\mathbf{S}$ of $\ell \times (n+d+k-1)$ dimension, that is, $\mathbf{S} = (\mathbf{s}_1 \ldots \mathbf{s}_\ell)^{\mathrm{T}}$, where s_{ij} represents The coefficient corresponding to the x^{j-1} degree item in the polynomial $s_i(x)$. Let $\tilde{\mathbf{s}}_j$ represent the j-th column of the matrix $\mathbf{S}$, the matrix $\mathbf{S}$ can also be written as $\mathbf{S} = (\tilde{\mathbf{s}}_1, \ldots, \tilde{\mathbf{s}}_{n+d+k-1})$. Let $\alpha = \mathbf{v}_1 - \mathbf{v}_0$, where $\mathbf{v}_1$, $\mathbf{v}_0$ denotes the challenge message vector preselected by the adversary before the experiment starts.

Select element $s_j^* \leftarrow D_{\sigma_1'}$ and column vector $\bar{\mathbf{s}}_j' \leftarrow D_{\Sigma}$, where $\sigma_1' > 0$, $\Sigma = \sigma_1^2\mathbf{I}_\ell - {\sigma_1'}^2\alpha\alpha^{\mathrm{T}}$. Because $\|\alpha\|_\infty \leq 2\mathcal{M}_x$, if $\sigma_1 > 2\sigma_1'\sqrt{\ell}\mathcal{M}_{\mathbf{v}}$, then Σ is a positive definite matrix. By Lemma 3, if $\sigma_1'\sqrt{1-(\sigma_1'/\sigma_1)^{-2}\alpha^{\mathrm{T}}\alpha} \geq \eta_\epsilon(\mathbb{Z}^\ell)$, $\alpha s_j^* + \bar{\mathbf{s}}_j'$ and $\tilde{\mathbf{s}}_j$ are statistically indistinguishable. So, the matrix $\mathbf{S}$ can be decomposed as $\mathbf{S} = (\tilde{\mathbf{s}}_1, \ldots, \tilde{\mathbf{s}}_{n+d+k-1}) \approx_s \alpha \cdot (s_1^*, \ldots, s_{n+d+k-1}^*) + (\bar{\mathbf{s}}_1', \ldots, \bar{\mathbf{s}}_{n+d+k-1}') = \alpha\mathbf{s}^* + (\bar{\mathbf{s}}_1', \ldots, \bar{\mathbf{s}}_{n+d+k-1}')$. Write the column vector group in the form of a row vector group, we have $\alpha\mathbf{s}^* + (\bar{\mathbf{s}}_1', \ldots, \bar{\mathbf{s}}_{n+d+k-1}') = (\alpha_1\mathbf{s}^*, \ldots, \alpha_\ell\mathbf{s}^*)^{\mathrm{T}} + (\mathbf{s}_1', \ldots, \mathbf{s}_\ell')^{\mathrm{T}} = (\alpha_1\mathbf{s}^* + \mathbf{s}_1', \ldots, \alpha_\ell\mathbf{s}^* + \mathbf{s}_\ell')^{\mathrm{T}} \approx_s (\mathbf{s}_1, \ldots, \mathbf{s}_\ell)^{\mathrm{T}}$, where $\mathbf{s}^* = (s_1^*, \ldots, s_{n+d+k-1}^*)$.

Then the vector $\alpha_i\mathbf{s}^* + \mathbf{s}_i'$ is statistically indistinguishable from $\mathbf{s}_i$, that is, the polynomial $s_i(x)$ corresponding to the vector is statistically indistinguishable from $\alpha_i s^*(x) + s_i'(x)$; similarly, it can be proved that if $\sigma_2'\sqrt{1-(\sigma_2'/\sigma_2)^{-2}\alpha^{\mathrm{T}}\alpha} \geq \eta_\epsilon(\mathbb{Z}^\ell)$, the polynomial vector $\mathbf{e}(x)$ is statistically indistinguishable from $\alpha_i\mathbf{e}^*(x) + \mathbf{e}_i'(x)$. It can be concluded that: Game_1 and Game_2 are statistically indistinguishable, so $\left|\mathrm{Adv}_{\mathcal{B},\mathrm{G}_2}^{\mathrm{IPE}_1}(\kappa)\text{-}\mathrm{Adv}_{\mathcal{B},\mathrm{G}_1}^{\mathrm{IPE}_1}(\kappa)\right| \leq 2(\epsilon'' m(d+k) + \epsilon'(d+k+n-1))$, where $\epsilon' = 2^{-\kappa}/(n+d+k-1)$ and $\epsilon'' = 2^{-\kappa}/(m(d+k))$.

Lemma 14. *At the view of adversary* $\mathcal{B}$, *the following conclusions hold:*

(a) $\mathit{Game}_2 = \mathit{Game}_3$;
(b) $\mathit{Game}_3 = \mathit{Game}_4$.

Proof. It suffices to prove (a): Let $\mathsf{sk}^* = s^*(x)$, $\mathsf{sk}_i' = s_i'(x)$, $\mathsf{pk}^* = \mathbf{a}(x) \odot_{d+k} s^*(x) + \mathbf{e}^*(x)$, $\mathsf{pk}_i' = \mathbf{a}(x) \odot_{d+k} s_i'(x) + \mathbf{e}_i'(x)$, $\left(\widetilde{\mathsf{pk}}_i, \widetilde{\mathsf{sk}}_i\right) = \alpha_i(\mathsf{pk}^*, \mathsf{sk}^*) + (\mathsf{pk}_i', \mathsf{sk}_i')$.

According to the linear key homomorphism (Theorem 2), $\left(\widetilde{\mathsf{pk}}_i, \widetilde{\mathsf{sk}}_i\right)$ can be calculated as: $\widetilde{\mathsf{sk}}_i = \alpha_i \cdot \mathsf{sk}^* + \mathsf{sk}_i' = \alpha_i \cdot s^*(x) + s_i'(x) = \mathsf{sk}_i$, $\widetilde{\mathsf{pk}}_i =$

$\alpha_i \cdot \mathsf{pk}^* + \mathsf{pk}'_i = \alpha_i \cdot (\mathbf{a}(x) \odot_{d+k} s^*(x) + \mathbf{e}^*(x)) + (\mathbf{a}(x) \odot_{d+k} s'_i(x) + \mathbf{e}'_i(x)) = (\alpha_i \cdot \mathbf{e}^*(x) + \mathbf{e}'_i(x)) + \mathbf{a}(x) \odot_{d+k} (\alpha_i \cdot s^*(x) + s'_i(x)) = \mathsf{pk}_i$.

So we draw the conclusion that Game$_2$ is equal to Game$_3$. Next, we can prove (b) holds in the same way: Let $\mathsf{ct}^* = \mathbf{r}(x) \odot_d \mathsf{pk}^*$, $\mathsf{ct}'_i = \mathbf{r}(x) \odot_d \mathsf{pk}'_i + \lfloor q/p \rfloor v_{b,i} \cdot 1_R$, $\widetilde{\mathsf{ct}}_i = \alpha_i \mathsf{ct}^* + \mathsf{ct}'_i$.

According to the linear ciphertext homomorphism under shared randomness (Theroem 2), the $\widetilde{\mathsf{ct}}_i$ can be calculated as follows, $\widetilde{\mathsf{ct}}_i = \alpha_i \mathsf{ct}^* + \mathsf{ct}'_i = \alpha_i (\mathbf{r}^{\mathrm{T}} \odot_d \mathsf{pk}^*) + (\mathbf{r}^{\mathrm{T}} \odot_d \mathsf{pk}'_i) + \lfloor p/q \rfloor v_{b,i} \cdot 1_R = \mathbf{r}^{\mathrm{T}} \odot_d (\alpha_i \cdot \mathsf{pk}^* + \mathsf{pk}'_i) + \lfloor p/q \rfloor v_{b,i} \cdot 1_R = \mathbf{r}^{\mathrm{T}} \odot_d \mathsf{pk}_i + \lfloor p/q \rfloor v_{b,i} \cdot 1_R = \mathsf{ct}_i$. Thus $\left|\mathrm{Adv}^{\mathrm{IPE}_1}_{\mathcal{B},\mathrm{G}_2}(\kappa)\right| = \left|\mathrm{Adv}^{\mathrm{IPE}_1}_{\mathcal{B},\mathrm{G}_3}(\kappa)\right| = \left|\mathrm{Adv}^{\mathrm{IPE}_1}_{\mathcal{B},\mathrm{G}_4}(\kappa)\right|$.

Lemma 15. *If the* MP-LWE *assumption is hard (Satisfy the condition of Theorem 1). Then for the adversary $\mathcal{G}$, the following conclusions are established:*

(a) the Game$_4$ is statistical indistinguishable with the Game$_5$;
(b) the Game$_9$ is statistical indistinguishable with the Game$_{10}$.

Proof. Due to space reasons, the proof process here will be given in the full version of the article. We can get $\left|\mathrm{Adv}^{\mathrm{IPE}_1}_{\mathcal{B},\mathrm{G}_5}(\kappa) \text{-} \mathrm{Adv}^{\mathrm{IPE}_1}_{\mathcal{B},\mathrm{G}_4}(\kappa)\right| \le \mathrm{Adv}^{\text{MP-LWE}}_{\mathcal{G},m,\ell}(\kappa)$ and $\left|\mathrm{Adv}^{\mathrm{IPE}_1}_{\mathcal{B},\mathrm{G}_{10}}(\kappa) \text{-} \mathrm{Adv}^{\mathrm{IPE}_1}_{\mathcal{B},\mathrm{G}_9}(\kappa)\right| \le \mathrm{Adv}^{\text{MP-LWE}}_{\mathcal{G},m,\ell}(\kappa)$.

Lemma 16. *At the view of adversary $\mathcal{B}$, Game$_5$ = Game$_6$.*

Proof. when ct_i computed using ct_0 (instead of pk'_i). Namely, $\mathsf{ct}'_i = \mathbf{r}(x) \odot_d \mathsf{pk}'_i + \lfloor q/p \rfloor v_{b,i} \cdot 1_R = \mathsf{ct}_0 \odot_d s'_i(x) + \mathbf{r}(x) \odot_d \mathbf{e}'_i(x) + \lfloor q/p \rfloor v_{b,i} \cdot 1_R$. Obviously, $\left|\mathrm{Adv}^{\mathrm{IPE}_1}_{\mathcal{B},\mathrm{G}_5}(\kappa)\right| = \left|\mathrm{Adv}^{\mathrm{IPE}_1}_{\mathcal{B},\mathrm{G}_6}(\kappa)\right|$.

Lemma 17. *Assume $m \ge \left(2d \log q + \log \frac{1}{4\epsilon^2}\right)(k+1)^{-1}$, where $\epsilon = 2^{-\kappa}$. Then at the view of adversary $\mathcal{B}$, the following conclusions are established:*

(a) Game$_6$ is statistical indistinguishable with the Game$_7$;
(b) Game$_8$ is statistical indistinguishable with the Game$_9$.

Proof. Firstly, we can prove that conclusion (a) holds: According to the definition of minimum entropy, we can get: $\mathbf{H}_\infty(\mathbf{r}(x)) = m(k+1)$. Which is $\mathbf{r}(x) \in U\left(\{0,1\}^{k+1}\right)^m$. Let W be a random variable of the form $\mathbf{r}(x) \odot_d \mathbf{e}^*(x) \in \mathbb{Z}_q^{<d}[x]$, where $\mathbf{e}^*(x) \in \left(D^{<d+k}_{\sigma_2'}[x]\right)^m$. The random variable W has at most q^d possible values, then it can be obtained from Lemma 7: $\tilde{\mathbf{H}}_\infty(\mathbf{r}(x)|W) \ge \mathbf{H}_\infty(\mathbf{r}(x)) - d \log q = m(k+1) - d \log q$.

So $2^{-\tilde{\mathbf{H}}_\infty(\mathbf{r}(x)|W)} \le 2^{-m(k+1)} \cdot q^d$. According to Lemma 6, it can be known that the function sequence $\{\Phi_{\mathsf{pk}^*}(\mathbf{r}(x)) = \mathbf{r}(x) \odot_d \mathsf{pk}^*\}$ is a general function family. Then according to Lemma 8 and $m \ge \left(2d \log q + \log \frac{1}{4\epsilon^2}\right)(k+1)^{-1}$, the following formula can be obtained: $\Delta\left(\left(\Phi_{\mathsf{pk}^*}(\mathbf{r}(x)), \mathsf{pk}^*, W\right), \left(U\left(\mathbb{Z}_q^{<d}[x]\right), \mathsf{pk}^*, W\right)\right) \le \frac{1}{2}\sqrt{2^{-\tilde{\mathbf{H}}_\infty(\mathbf{r}(x)|W)} q^d} \le \frac{1}{2}\sqrt{2^{-m(k+1)} \cdot q^{2d}} \le \epsilon$.

Therefore, the statistical distance between $\mathsf{ct}_i^* = \mathbf{r}(x) \odot_d \mathsf{pk}^*$ and $U\left(\mathbb{Z}_q^{n+k}\right)$ selected in the uniform distribution is less than ϵ. On the other hand, ct_0=$\mathbf{r}(x) \cdot \mathbf{a}(x)$ is uniformly distributed, so it can be concluded that Game$_7$ and Game$_6$ are statistically indistinguishable. Thus $\left|\mathrm{Adv}_{\mathcal{B},\mathrm{G}_7}^{\mathrm{IPE}_1}(\kappa)\text{-}\mathrm{Adv}_{\mathcal{B},\mathrm{G}_6}^{\mathrm{IPE}_1}(\kappa)\right| \leq \epsilon$.

Next, it is proved that the conclusion (b) holds: because the change from Game$_9$ to Game$_8$ is the same as that from Game$_6$ to Game$_7$, but the relevant information of the polynomial vector $\mathbf{r}(x)$ is not leaked during the change from to (because the identically distributed polynomial vector $\tilde{\mathbf{r}}(x)$ is used instead of $\mathbf{r}(x)$). The first half of the proof has proved that Game$_6$ to Game$_7$ are statistically indistinguishable, so it can be concluded that Game$_9$ and Game$_8$ are statistically indistinguishable. Thus $\left|\mathrm{Adv}_{\mathcal{B},\mathrm{G}_9}^{\mathrm{IPE}_1}(\kappa) - \mathrm{Adv}_{\mathcal{B},\mathrm{G}_8}^{\mathrm{IPE}_1}(\kappa)\right| \leq \epsilon$.

Lemma 18. *At the view of adversary $\mathcal{B}$, the Game$_7$ is statistical indistinguishable with the Game$_8$.*

Proof. Because the polynomial vector $\tilde{\mathbf{r}}(x)$ in Game$_8$ has the same distribution as $\mathbf{r}(x)$ in Game$_7$. At the same time, in Game$_8$, the polynomial vector $\tilde{\mathbf{r}}(x)$ has not been used in other places (except the challenge ciphertext), so the information of the polynomial vector will not be leaked, so the two games are statistically indistinguishable. Obviously, $\left|\mathrm{Adv}_{\mathcal{B},\mathrm{G}_8}^{\mathrm{IPE}_1}(\kappa)\right| = \left|\mathrm{Adv}_{\mathcal{B},\mathrm{G}_7}^{\mathrm{IPE}_1}(\kappa)\right|$.

Lemma 19. *If the public key encryption scheme $\mathcal{E}$ in Chap. 3 is IND-CPA-secure, then for the adversary $\mathcal{B}$, Game$_{10}$ is computational indistinguishable from Game$_{11}$.*

Proof. The only difference between Game$_{10}$ and Game$_{11}$ is the encrypted message. In Game$_{10}$, ct^* is the challenge ciphertext generated by encrypting bit b, while in Game$_{11}$, ct^* is the challenge ciphertext generated by encrypting $M \leftarrow U(\mathbb{Z}_p)$. Since sk^* does not appear (alone) anywhere else, it follows that under IND-CPA security of public key encryption scheme $\mathcal{E}$, Game$_{10}$ is computational indistinguishable from Game$_{11}$.

There, if the advantage that $\mathcal{B}$ can break the scheme $\mathcal{E}$ is ϵ, then it can distinguish Game$_{10}$ and Game$_{11}$ is also ϵ, so $\left|\mathrm{Adv}_{\mathcal{B},\mathrm{G}_{11}}^{\mathrm{IPE}_1}(\kappa) - \mathrm{Adv}_{\mathcal{B},\mathrm{G}_{10}}^{\mathrm{IPE}_1}(\kappa)\right| \leq \epsilon$.

5 Conclusion

Based on the public key encryption scheme based on MP-LWE problem, this paper constructs IPE schemes with Sel-IND-CPA-secure, and gives the security proofs of the scheme. It can be seen that the Sel-IND-CPA-secure scheme constructed in this paper has the advantages of efficiency and security balance, and is suitable for special application scenarios such as e-commerce.

Remark. By adding new elements, we change the Sel-IND-CPA inner product encryption scheme into the inner product encryption scheme with IND-CPA-secure. Then we can use the mechanism of Complexity Leverage (CL) [10] to prove the IND-CPA-secure of the scheme under the Sel-IND-CPA-secure. The specific construction of the IPE of IND-CPA-secure and its correctness and security proofs will be given in the full version of the paper.

Acknowledgements. The authors would like to thank anonymous reviewers for their helpful comments. This work is supported by National Natural Science Foundation of China (62032005, 62172096), Natural Science Foundation of Fujian Province (2019J01428, 2020J02016) and Open Fund of State Key Laboratory of Cryptology (MMKFKT202008).

A Appendix

A.1 Proof of Theorem 2

Proof. Let $y_1, y_2 \in \mathbb{Z}$, the polynomial vector $\mathbf{r}(x) \leftarrow U\left(\{0,1\}^{<k+1}[x]\right)^m$ and let the two key pairs in scheme $\mathcal{E}$ be:

$$(\mathsf{sk}_1, \mathsf{pk}_1),\ (\mathsf{sk}_2, \mathsf{pk}_2) \in D_{\mathbb{Z},\sigma_1}^{<n+k+d-1}[x] \times \left(\mathbb{Z}_q^{<d+k}[x]\right)^m,$$

$$\mathsf{pk}_1 = \mathbf{a}(x) \odot_{d+k} \mathsf{sk}_1 + \mathbf{e}_1(x),\ \mathsf{pk}_2 = \mathbf{a}(x) \odot_{d+k} \mathsf{sk}_2 + \mathbf{e}_2(x).$$

First prove that property (a) is established: encrypt the plaintext u_1 and u_2 with the public keys pk_1 and pk_2 respectively, then the following formula can be obtained according to the encryption algorithm (let E represents the encryption algorithm for generating the second part of the ciphertext):

$$\begin{aligned}
&\mathrm{E}(\mathsf{pk}_1, u_1; \mathbf{r}(x)) + \mathrm{E}(\mathsf{pk}_2, u_2; \mathbf{r}(x)) \\
&= \mathbf{r}(x) \odot_d \mathsf{pk}_1 + \mathbf{r}(x) \odot_d \mathsf{pk}_2 + \lfloor p/q \rfloor u_1 \cdot 1_R + \lfloor p/q \rfloor u_2 \cdot 1_R \\
&= \mathbf{r}(x) \odot_d (\mathsf{pk}_1 + \mathsf{pk}_2) + \lfloor p/q \rfloor (u_1 + u_2) \cdot 1_R \\
&= \mathrm{E}(\mathsf{pk}_1 + \mathsf{pk}_2, u_1 + u_2; \mathbf{r}(x)).
\end{aligned}$$

Next, prove that property (b) is established: encrypt the plaintext with the public key $\mathsf{pk} = y_1\mathsf{pk}_1 + y_2\mathsf{pk}_2$ to obtain the ciphertext $\mathsf{ct} = (\mathsf{ct}_0, \mathsf{ct}_1)$, and decrypt the ciphertext with the private key $\mathsf{sk} = y_1\mathsf{sk}_1 + y_2\mathsf{sk}_2$. Then according to the scheme $\mathcal{E}$ decryption algorithm, the following formula can be obtained:

$$\mathsf{ct}_1 - \mathsf{ct}_0 \odot_d \mathsf{sk} \mod q = \mathbf{r}(x) \odot_d (y_1\mathbf{e}_1(x) + y_2\mathbf{e}_2(x)) + \lfloor q/p \rfloor \mu \cdot 1_R \mod q.$$

It can be seen that if (sk, pk) can be successfully encrypted and decrypted, the constraint must be satisfied $\|\mathbf{r}(x) \odot_d (y_1\mathbf{e}_1(x) + y_2\mathbf{e}_2(x))\|_\infty < \lfloor q/(2p) \rfloor$.

That is to say, when the maximum norm of the linear sum of noise terms in scheme $\mathcal{E}$ is small, it has the key linear homomorphism.

References

1. Abdalla, M., Bourse, F., De Caro, A., Pointcheval, D.: Simple functional encryption schemes for inner products. In: Katz, J. (ed.) PKC 2015. LNCS, vol. 9020, pp. 733–751. Springer, Heidelberg (2015). https://doi.org/10.1007/978-3-662-46447-2_33
2. Abdalla M, Bourse F, De Caro A, et al.: Better security for functional encryption for inner product evaluations. Cryptology ePrint Archive, 2016/011 (2016)
3. Abdalla, M., Gay, R., Raykova, M., Wee, H.: Multi-input inner-product functional encryption from pairings. In: Coron, J.-S., Nielsen, J.B. (eds.) EUROCRYPT 2017. LNCS, vol. 10210, pp. 601–626. Springer, Cham (2017). https://doi.org/10.1007/978-3-319-56620-7_21
4. Agrawal, S., Libert, B., Maitra, M., Titiu, R.: Adaptive simulation security for inner product functional encryption. In: Kiayias, A., Kohlweiss, M., Wallden, P., Zikas, V. (eds.) PKC 2020. LNCS, vol. 12110, pp. 34–64. Springer, Cham (2020). https://doi.org/10.1007/978-3-030-45374-9_2
5. Agrawal, S., Libert, B., Stehlé, D.: Fully secure functional encryption for inner products, from standard assumptions. In: Robshaw, M., Katz, J. (eds.) CRYPTO 2016. LNCS, vol. 9816, pp. 333–362. Springer, Heidelberg (2016). https://doi.org/10.1007/978-3-662-53015-3_12
6. Ananth, P., Brakerski, Z., Segev, G., Vaikuntanathan, V.: From selective to adaptive security in functional encryption. In: Gennaro, R., Robshaw, M. (eds.) CRYPTO 2015. LNCS, vol. 9216, pp. 657–677. Springer, Heidelberg (2015). https://doi.org/10.1007/978-3-662-48000-7_32
7. Bai, S., et al.: MPSign: a signature from small-secret middle-product learning with errors. In: Kiayias, A., Kohlweiss, M., Wallden, P., Zikas, V. (eds.) PKC 2020. LNCS, vol. 12111, pp. 66–93. Springer, Cham (2020). https://doi.org/10.1007/978-3-030-45388-6_3
8. Benhamouda, F., Bourse, F., Lipmaa, H.: CCA-secure inner-product functional encryption from projective hash functions. In: Fehr, S. (ed.) PKC 2017. LNCS, vol. 10175, pp. 36–66. Springer, Heidelberg (2017). https://doi.org/10.1007/978-3-662-54388-7_2
9. Boneh, D., Sahai, A., Waters, B.: Functional encryption: definitions and challenges. In: Ishai, Y. (ed.) TCC 2011. LNCS, vol. 6597, pp. 253–273. Springer, Heidelberg (2011). https://doi.org/10.1007/978-3-642-19571-6_16
10. Bourse, F.: Functional encryption for inner-product evaluations (Doctoral dissertation). Université Paris sciences et lettres (2017)
11. Castagnos, G., Laguillaumie, F., Tucker, I.: Practical fully secure unrestricted inner product functional encryption modulo p. In: Peyrin, T., Galbraith, S. (eds.) ASIACRYPT 2018. LNCS, vol. 11273, pp. 733–764. Springer, Cham (2018). https://doi.org/10.1007/978-3-030-03329-3_25
12. Chotard, J., Dufour Sans, E., Gay, R., Phan, D.H., Pointcheval, D.: Decentralized multi-client functional encryption for inner product. In: Peyrin, T., Galbraith, S. (eds.) ASIACRYPT 2018. LNCS, vol. 11273, pp. 703–732. Springer, Cham (2018). https://doi.org/10.1007/978-3-030-03329-3_24
13. Chotard, J., Dufour-Sans, E., Gay, R., Phan, D.H., Pointcheval, D.: Dynamic decentralized functional encryption. In: Micciancio, D., Ristenpart, T. (eds.) CRYPTO 2020. LNCS, vol. 12170, pp. 747–775. Springer, Cham (2020). https://doi.org/10.1007/978-3-030-56784-2_25
14. Cramer, R., Ducas, L., Wesolowski, B.: Short stickelberger class relations and application to ideal-SVP. In: Coron, J.-S., Nielsen, J.B. (eds.) EUROCRYPT 2017.

LNCS, vol. 10210, pp. 324–348. Springer, Cham (2017). https://doi.org/10.1007/978-3-319-56620-7_12
15. Datta, P., Okamoto, T., Tomida, J.: Full-hiding (unbounded) multi-input inner product functional encryption from the k-linear assumption. In: Abdalla, M., Dahab, R. (eds.) PKC 2018. LNCS, vol. 10770, pp. 245–277. Springer, Cham (2018). https://doi.org/10.1007/978-3-319-76581-5_9
16. Deng, Q.Y., Song, G., Yang, B., et al.: Identity-based verifiable key-based public-key inner product function encryption algorithm (in Chinese). Chin. J. Comput. **44**(01), 209–221 (2021)
17. Dodis, Y., Reyzin, L., Smith, A.: Fuzzy extractors: how to generate strong keys from biometrics and other noisy data. In: Cachin, C., Camenisch, J.L. (eds.) EUROCRYPT 2004. LNCS, vol. 3027, pp. 523–540. Springer, Heidelberg (2004). https://doi.org/10.1007/978-3-540-24676-3_31
18. Eisenträger, K., Hallgren, S., Lauter, K.: Weak instances of PLWE. In: Joux, A., Youssef, A. (eds.) SAC 2014. LNCS, vol. 8781, pp. 183–194. Springer, Cham (2014). https://doi.org/10.1007/978-3-319-13051-4_11
19. Elias, Y., Lauter, K.E., Ozman, E., Stange, K.E.: Provably weak instances of ring-LWE. In: Gennaro, R., Robshaw, M. (eds.) CRYPTO 2015. LNCS, vol. 9215, pp. 63–92. Springer, Heidelberg (2015). https://doi.org/10.1007/978-3-662-47989-6_4
20. Gentry, C., Peikert, C., Vaikuntanathan, V.: Trapdoors for hard lattices and new cryptographic constructions. In: Proceedings of the Fortieth Annual ACM Symposium on Theory of Computing, pp. 197–206. ACM (2008)
21. Kim, S., Lewi, K., Mandal, A., Montgomery, H., Roy, A., Wu, D.J.: Function-hiding inner product encryption is practical. In: Catalano, D., De Prisco, R. (eds.) SCN 2018. LNCS, vol. 11035, pp. 544–562. Springer, Cham (2018). https://doi.org/10.1007/978-3-319-98113-0_29
22. Liang, Y., Cao, Z., Dong, X., Shen, J.: Efficient multi-keyword searchable encryption based on multi-input inner-product functional encryption. In: Naccache, D., et al. (eds.) ICICS 2018. LNCS, vol. 11149, pp. 377–392. Springer, Cham (2018). https://doi.org/10.1007/978-3-030-01950-1_22
23. Lyubashevsky, V.: Digital signatures based on the hardness of ideal lattice problems in all rings. In: Cheon, J.H., Takagi, T. (eds.) ASIACRYPT 2016. LNCS, vol. 10032, pp. 196–214. Springer, Heidelberg (2016). https://doi.org/10.1007/978-3-662-53890-6_7
24. Lyubashevsky, V., Micciancio, D.: Generalized compact knapsacks are collision resistant. In: Bugliesi, M., Preneel, B., Sassone, V., Wegener, I. (eds.) ICALP 2006. LNCS, vol. 4052, pp. 144–155. Springer, Heidelberg (2006). https://doi.org/10.1007/11787006_13
25. Micciancio, D., Regev, O.: Worst-case to average-case reductions based on Gaussian measures. SIAM J. Comput. **37**(1), 267–302 (2007)
26. Mera, J.M.B., Karmakar, A., Marc, T., et al.: Efficient lattice-based inner product functional encryption. In: Hanaoka, G., Shikata, J., Watanabe, Y. (eds.) PKC 2022. LNCS, vol. 13178, pp. 163–193. Springer, Cham (2022). https://doi.org/10.1007/978-3-030-97131-1_6
27. Peikert, C., Rosen, A.: Efficient collision-resistant hashing from worst-case assumptions on cyclic lattices. In: Halevi, S., Rabin, T. (eds.) TCC 2006. LNCS, vol. 3876, pp. 145–166. Springer, Heidelberg (2006). https://doi.org/10.1007/11681878_8
28. Roşca, M., Sakzad, A., Stehlé, D., Steinfeld, R.: Middle-product learning with errors. In: Katz, J., Shacham, H. (eds.) CRYPTO 2017. LNCS, vol. 10403, pp. 283–297. Springer, Cham (2017). https://doi.org/10.1007/978-3-319-63697-9_10

29. Stehlé, D., Steinfeld, R., Tanaka, K., Xagawa, K.: Efficient public key encryption based on ideal lattices. In: Matsui, M. (ed.) ASIACRYPT 2009. LNCS, vol. 5912, pp. 617–635. Springer, Heidelberg (2009). https://doi.org/10.1007/978-3-642-10366-7_36
30. Steinfeld, R., Sakzad, A., Zhao, R.K.: Practical MP-LWE-based encryption balancing security-risk versus efficiency. Des. Codes Crypt. **87**(12), 2847–2884 (2019)
31. Sun, Z., Zhang, L.: New perspectives on lattice-based functional encryption for analysis on encrypted data. ICIC Express Lett. **11**(4), 871–876 (2017)
32. Tomida, J., Abe, M., Okamoto, T.: Efficient functional encryption for inner-product values with full-hiding security. In: Bishop, M., Nascimento, A.C.A. (eds.) ISC 2016. LNCS, vol. 9866, pp. 408–425. Springer, Cham (2016). https://doi.org/10.1007/978-3-319-45871-7_24
33. Xu, Q., Tang, C.: Matrix-based inner product function encryption (in Chinese). J. Guangzhou Univ. (Nat. Sci. Edn.) **15**(2), 25–28 (2016)
34. Yang, S.J., Huang, X.Y.: Universal product learning with errors: a new variant of LWE for lattice-based cryptography. Theoret. Comput. Sci. **915**, 90–100 (2022)

Network Security and Privacy Protection

Publicly Verifiable Private Set Intersection from Homomorphic Encryption

Yuting Jiang[1(✉)], Jianghong Wei[2], and Jing Pan[3]

[1] State Key Laboratory of Integrated Service Networks (ISN), Xidian University, Xi'an 710071, China
jiangyuting@foxmail.com

[2] State Key Laboratory of Mathematical Engineering and Advanced Computing, PLA Strategic Support Force Information Engineering University, Zhengzhou 450001, China

[3] Guangzhou Institute of Technology, Xidian University, Guanzhou 510555, China
jinglap@aliyun.com

Abstract. Private Set Intersection (PSI) enables two mistrusting parties to securely evaluate the intersection of their private inputs, without revealing any additional information. With its wide application in privacy protection, it is required to ensure the correctness of the evaluation, especially in conventional client-server setting (also known as unbalanced PSI). Unfortunately, most existing work cannot verify the integrity of the data and the correctness of the evaluation. In this paper, we propose a new publicly verifiable private set intersection protocol in the malicious setting, based on oblivious pseudo-random function (OPRF), fully homomorphic encryption (FHE), and verifiable computation (VC). The key tool to obtain our new protocol is a new publicly verifiable inner product computation on encrypted data. The protocol supports public verification for computation correctness and integrity under preserving privacy with less round number (only requiring 2 rounds), allows batching technique under Residue Number System (RNS). That is used for enhancing the FHE. Also, we implement our protocol, and the result is close to the most effective unbalanced PSI.

Keywords: Private set intersection · Fully homomorphic encryption · Verifiable computation

1 Introduction

Private Set Intersection (PSI). As suggested by [16], PSI allows mutually mistrusting parties to jointly compute the intersection of their private sets without revealing any additional information. PSI is used for privacy-preserving scenarios such as remote diagnostics [7], DNA searching [38], social networks [29], private equality test [28], and privacy-preserving password checkup [26]. A canonical PSI with one-sided output is a protocol between two parties: a sender holds a set X, and a receiver holds a set Y. At the end of the protocol, the

X. Chen et al. (Eds.): SocialSec 2022, CCIS 1663, pp. 117–137, 2022.
https://doi.org/10.1007/978-981-19-7242-3_8

receiver learns only the output $X \cap Y$ and nothing else while the sender learns nothing. In terms of set sizes, PSI is categorized as balanced one and unbalanced variant. With the usage of the smart phone, unbalanced case is getting more and more attention.

Unbalanced PSI is a common form of PSI in conventional client-server setting. The sender's set from a high-end computing device may be substantially larger than the receiver's from a mobile device, such as Private Contact Discovery [12,27]. Chen et al. [11] first paid attention to unequal set sizes. They utilized a leveled fully homomorphic encryption and various optimizations to obtain the PSI with optimal communication complexity $O(|Y| \log |X|)$ in the semi-honest model, where $|Y| \ll |X|$. Later, the recent work [10] utilized a oblivious pseudo-random function (OPRF) preprocessing to achieve malicious security with one-sided simulation [21]. That is, it is secure against a malicious receiver, while providing privacy against a malicious sender.

Fully Homomorphic Encryption (FHE). Proposed by Gentry [17], FHE allows anyone to perform arbitrary computations on encrypted data without the secret decryption key. Over the past decade, researchers took pains to construct much more efficient protocols [4–6,14,19], bringing practical applications close to reality [9,18,20]. Residue Number System (RNS) decomposition is an important optimization technique for implements of FHE, which applies fast parallel arithmetic operations to ciphertexts with small moduli and is always used in practical FHE, such as SEAL [37] of the BFV scheme [5,14].

As suggested by [11] and [10], PSI protocols can efficiently reduce the number of rounds and communication complexity by FHE since the sender directly operates on encrypted data. However, these protocols cannot ensure the correctness of the outputs since the malicious sender can easily tamper with receivers encryption data or fiddle with computation results. Verifying the integrity of the data and the correctness of the computation of PSI while preserving the confidentiality of the senders data is a particular challenge. In other words, there is an essential need for verifiable PSI.

1.1 Our Contributions

In this paper, we deal with an important challenge posed in [10]: How to enforce the sender to perform correct computation? Based on fully homomorphic encryption (FHE), oblivious pseudo random function (OPRF) and verifiable computation (VC), we construct a *publicly verifiable PSI* to address the problem. The contributions are summarized in the following:

- We construct a publicly verifiable PSI with fully malicious security in the random oracle model. We achieve full simulation-based security against a malicious receiver and a malicious sender with 2 rounds of interaction and linear computation complexity for receiver as well as supporting batching and RNS techniques (used to enhancing the performance of FHE).
- We implement the proposed PSI, and compare it with previous protocols, and the results show that our protocol is nearly over those works.

1.2 Technical Overview

We construct a publicly verifiable PSI, in which the sender and receiver have sets X and Y respectively as input and the receiver gets $X \cap Y$ or $\perp$ as output. We achieve this goal by utilizing OPRF, FHE and VC, where OPRF against the malicious receiver, FHE for privacy-preserving and VC against malicious sender. Recall the strawman protocol in [11], the sender samples a uniformly random non-zero element r and defines a basic polynomial: $P(y) = r\prod_{x\in X}(y-x)$. At the start of the protocol, the sender contributes a PRF key s and locally computes the set $\mathrm{PRF}_X = \{\mathrm{PRF}_s(x) : x \in X\}$. The receiver updates its set to be $\mathrm{PRF}_Y = \{\mathrm{PRF}_s(y) : y \in Y\}$ by OPRF. In this way, the receiver and sender compute $S = \mathrm{PRF}_X \cap \mathrm{PRF}_Y$ instead of $X \cap Y$ to avoid the receiver learning something about $X \setminus Y$ since the items of $X \setminus Y$ are pseudo-random in receiver's perspective. Then, the receiver initially encrypts each of its elements $y \in \mathrm{PRF}_Y$ via FHE and sends to the sender. After that the sender performs polynomial computation at each of y homomorphically and returns back to receiver. The receiver decrypts the result by the secret decryption key. If the decryption result is zero, then y is in the intersection. Otherwise, the decryption result is a non-zero random number.

At the core of achieving verifiability is a new publicly verification inner product computation on encrypted data. Motivated by "hash-and-MAC", we start by introducing Fiore et al.'s collision-resistant homomorphic hash function $\mathtt{H}$ on bivariate polynomial [15]. Let the bivariate polynomial $m \in \mathbb{Z}_q[X][Y]$ in $m(x,y) = \sum_{i=0}^{n_1}\sum_{j=0}^{n_2} a_{i,j}X^iY^j$ be expressed as a univariate polynomial in X and Y of degrees n_1 and n_2, respectively. A bilinear group bg is described as $(q, \mathbb{G}_1, \mathbb{G}_2, \mathbb{G}_T, e, g_1, g_2)$ such that $\mathbb{G}_1, \mathbb{G}_2$ are cyclic groups of prime order q equipped with bilinear asymmetric map $e : \mathbb{G}_1 \times \mathbb{G}_2 \to \mathbb{G}_T$, $g \leftarrow \mathbb{G}_1, g_2 \leftarrow \mathbb{G}_2$ and $g_T = e(g, g_2) \in \mathbb{G}_T$. Sample two random numbers $\alpha, \beta \in \mathbb{Z}_q$ and calculate $g^{(i,j)} = g^{\alpha^i\beta^j}, g_2^{(i,j)} = g_2^{\alpha^i\beta^j}, g_T^{(i,j)} = g_T^{\alpha^i\beta^j}$ for all $i \in \{0, \cdots, n_1\}$ and $j \in \{0, \cdots, n_2\}$. Set public key $PK = (\mathsf{bg}, pk_g = \{g^{(i,j)}\}_{i,j=0}^{n_1,n_2}, pk_{g_2} = \{g_2^{(i,j)}\}_{i,j=0}^{n_1,n_2}, pk_{g_T} = \{g_T^{(i,j)}\}_{i,j=0}^{n_1,n_2})$. Set $\mathtt{H}(m) = (\prod_{i=0}^{n_1}\prod_{j=1}^{n_2} g^{a_{i,j}\alpha^i\beta^j}, \prod_{i=0}^{n_1}\prod_{j=1}^{n_2} g_2^{a_{i,j}\alpha^i\beta^j}) = (\sigma, \varsigma)$ as the hash value of m, which can be computed by using the group elements in the public key PK.

In our basic solution, the sender pre-computes coefficients $\{f_i\}_{i=0}^{|X|}$ of the polynomial $P(y)$ through Vieta's Theorem after OPRF, i.e., $P(y) = \sum_{\iota=0}^{|X|} f_\iota y^\iota$. Let $\mathcal{R}_q = \mathbb{Z}_q[X]/(X^n+1)$ with n power of 2 be a polynomial ring. The receiver encrypts y_ι using FHE to generate a ciphertext $c_\iota \in \mathcal{R}_q[Y]$ of degree-1. The sender then evaluates homomorphically the polynomial and returns the result c to the receiver. For $\iota \in \{0, \cdots, |X|\}$, the receiver sets the first half of the hash value $H(c_\iota) = (\sigma_\iota, \varsigma_\iota)$ as a tag, while the sender sets $\tau_\iota = g_2^{f_\iota}$ as a proof. Set the computation result as $ct(x,y) = \sum_{i=0}^{n}\sum_{j=0}^{1} c_{i,j}X^iY^j$. The verifier generates the verification value of the result $\sigma = \prod_{i=0}^{n}\prod_{j=0}^{1} g_T^{c_{i,j}\alpha^i\beta^j}$ and verifies whether $\prod_{\iota=0}^{|X|} e(\sigma_\iota, \tau_\iota) = \sigma$.

The parties always improve the performance through batching. In this case, the sender computes the inner product of two $|X|$-dimensional vectors over $\mathcal{R}_t$ (t is plaintext modulus), namely, $P(y) = \sum_{|X|} f_\iota x_\iota \in \mathcal{R}_t$, where $f_\iota, x_\iota \in \mathcal{R}_t$. We design a trick called *monomial hash* to this case. The receiver encrypts the polynomial x_ι with batching technique and generates a ciphertext $c_\iota \in \mathcal{R}_q[Y]$ of degree-1. The sender then computes the inner product homomorphically and returns the result $c \in \mathcal{R}_q[Y]$ to the receiver. Let $c_\iota = \sum_{i=0}^{n-1}(\sum_{j=0}^{1} a_{\iota,i,j} Y^j X^i)$. The receiver computes the homomorphic hash values of the monomials, i.e., $\sigma_{\iota,i} = \prod_{j=0}^{1} g^{a_{\iota,i,j}\beta^j \alpha^i}$. Set the monomial hash of c as $\tilde{\text{H}}_g(c_\iota) = (\sigma_{\iota,0}, \cdots, \sigma_{\iota,n-1})$, where $\sigma_{\iota,i}$ is the first half of the hash value of c_ι. For $f_\iota = (m_{\iota,0}, \cdots, m_{\iota,n-1}) \in \mathbb{Z}_t^n$, the sender computes the proof $\tau_{\iota,i} = g_2^{m_{\iota,i}}$. The verifier generates the verification value of the result σ by using the group elements in pk_{g_T} and verifies whether $\prod_{\iota=0}^{|X|}\prod_{i=0}^{n-1} e(\sigma_{\iota,i}, \tau_{\iota,i}) = \sigma$.

In RNS, the ciphertext module q is selected as a product of small pairwise primes $q_1, \cdots, q_\ell$. The FHE ciphertext $\texttt{ct}$ is expressed as $(|\texttt{ct}|_{q_1}, \cdots, |\texttt{ct}|_{q_\ell})$, where $|\texttt{ct}|_{q_i} \in \mathcal{R}_{q_i}$. Considering the independence principle and minimal collision of homomorphic hash function for any component of RNS representation of the ciphertext $\texttt{ct}$, verifier can randomly choose a branch $|\texttt{ct}|_{q_i}$ to verify its correctness.

1.3 Related Work

The first PSI protocol was proposed by Freedman et al. [16], by using polynomial representation of sets and additive homomorphic encryption. Over the last years, several main techniques have been put forward to realize efficient PSI protocols, such as hashing [32–34], oblivious pseudo-random function (OPRF) [21,22] and oblivious transfer (OT) [13,24,30]. These protocols started with hashing items into bins to build on a data structure. Then, they evaluated an OPRF for each bin, which is realized through an OT extension. However, OT-based PSI required multiple interactions between the receiver and sender. Besides, another disadvantage is that their communication complexity is linear in the sizes of both sets, which is not friendly for the resource-constrained receiver.

Chen et al. [11] first focus on the unbalanced PSI. They used a leveled FHE and various optimizations to reduce the communication complexity. Then the latter one [10] strengthen the security model via OPRF preprocessing. Several protocols have been proposed for unbalanced PSI that mainly focus on improving the communication complexity and applicability [25,35]. However, all of them cannot guarantee the output correctness.

Kamara et al. [23] first considered this verifiability issue. Concretely, they focused on delegated PSI evaluation on outsourced datasets to a untrusted server and used tags on bilinear maps for verification. But their verification procedure was set after decryption. Abadi et al. [1] extended outsourcing computation of PSI to multiple clients with verifiability. However, this protocol required that all parties shared partial set information and only supported private verifiability. Thus, to publicly verify the integrity of data and the correctness of PSI evaluation in the sense of preserving privacy is still a big challenge.

1.4 Roadmap

In Sect. 2, we describe some necessary preliminaries. In Sect. 3, we construct a publicly verifiable inner product computation on encrypted data. In Sect. 4, we present a publicly verifiable PSI protocol from homomorphic encryption and provide the security and efficiency analysis. We provide the performance evaluation in Sect. 5. In Sect. 6, our work is concluded.

2 Preliminaries

Throughout this paper, we abbreviate the set $\{0, \cdots, n-1\}$ to $[n]$. Let $\lambda_\sigma \in \mathbb{N}$ denote the statistical security parameter and λ_κ be the computational security parameter. We use $negl(\lambda)$ to denote the negligible function in λ. For $x, n \in \mathbb{N}$, we denote $|x|_n$ the result of x modulo n.

2.1 Fully Homomorphic Encryption

Let $\mathcal{R} = \mathbb{Z}[X]/(X^n + 1)$ be a polynomial ring with n power of two. In FHE cryptosystems, plaintexts will lie in $\mathcal{R}_t = \mathcal{R}/(t\mathcal{R})$ and ciphertexts are elements of $\mathcal{R}_q[Y]$. We state the FHE below, which satisfies correctness, semantic security and compactness [2].

Definition 1 (FHE [2]). *A (public-key) fully homomorphic encryption scheme $\mathcal{FHE}$ with plaintext space $\mathcal{R}_t$ and ciphertext space $\mathcal{R}_q[Y]$ is a 5-tuple of randomized algorithms as follows:*

- $\texttt{FHE.ParamGen}(\lambda)$*: Given a security parameter λ, generates the public parameters pp.*
- $\texttt{FHE.KeyGen}(pp)$*: Given pp, outputs a public key pk and an associated secret key sk. Also, this algorithm optionally products one or more evaluation keys evk.*
- $\texttt{FHE.Enc}(pk, m)$*: Encrypts a plaintext $m \in \mathcal{R}_t$ under public key pk, and outputs a ciphertext $c \in \mathcal{R}_q[Y]$.*
- $\texttt{FHE.Dec}(sk, c)$*: Decrypts the ciphertext $c \in \mathcal{R}_q[Y]$ using the secret key sk, and outputs m^*.*
- $\texttt{FHE.Eval}(f, (c_1, \cdots, c_k), evk)$*: Given the evaluation keys evk, an arithmetic circuit f with k input wires, and k ciphertexts $c_1, \cdots, c_k$, outputs a fresh ciphertext $c^* \in \mathcal{R}_q[Y]$.*

RNS Representation. For practical implementations, somewhat homomorphic encryption (SHE) is a more promising rationale that supports a limited number of arithmetic operations on ciphertexts, such as BFV [5,14]. In those work, the ciphertext modulus q can be selected as a ℓ-smooth number, s.t. $q = \prod_{i=1}^{\ell} q_i$, where $q_1, \cdots, q_\ell$ are several disparate prime moduli. We denote the RNS representation of a ciphertext $c \in \mathcal{R}_q[Y]$ relative to the RNS base $\{q_1, \cdots, q_\ell\}$ by $(c_1, \cdots, c_\ell)$ with $c_i = |c|_{q_i} \in \mathcal{R}_{q_i}[Y]$ [3]. This representation is due to a ring isomorphism $\mathcal{R}_q \simeq \mathcal{R}_{q_1} \times \cdots \times \mathcal{R}_{q_\ell}$ based on *the Chinese Remainder Theorem* (CRT). The RNS representation allows fast parallel arithmetic to be performed in the factors $\mathcal{R}_{q_i}$ at coefficient level to speed up the operations in $\mathcal{R}_q$.

2.2 Publicly Verifiable Computation

Definition 2 (Publicly Verifiable Computation [31]**).** *A publicly verifiable computation scheme $\mathcal{VC}$ is a 5-tuple of PPT algorithms as follows:*

- $\texttt{VC.KeyGen}(f, \lambda)$: *On input a function f and a security parameter λ, outputs a secret key sk_f and a public key pk_f.*
- $\texttt{VC.ProbGen}(pk_f, x)$: *Outputs an encoding σ_x of x that is sent to the computing party, and a public verification key τ_x which is sent to the verifier.*
- $\texttt{VC.Compute}(pk_f, \sigma_x)$: *Returns an encoded version σ_y of $y = f(x)$.*
- $\texttt{VC.Verify}(pk_f, \tau_x, \sigma_y)$: *Returns a bit acc, where acc $= 1$ denotes the verification algorithm acceptance and otherwise denotes the verification algorithm rejection.*
- $\texttt{VC.Decode}(sk_f, \sigma_y)$: *Returns a value y.*

Definition 3 (Correctness). *A publicly verifiable computation scheme $\mathcal{VC}$ is correct if for input x and any function f,*

$$\Pr\left[\begin{array}{l|l} \texttt{VC.Verify}(pk_f, \tau_x, \sigma_y) & (pk_f, sk_f) \leftarrow \texttt{VC.KeyGen}(f, \lambda) \\ = 1 \wedge \texttt{VC.Decode}(sk_f, \sigma_y) & (\sigma_x, \tau_x) \leftarrow \texttt{VC.ProbGen}(pk_f, x) \\ = f(x) & \sigma_y \leftarrow \texttt{VC.Compute}(pk_f, \sigma_x) \end{array}\right] = 1 - negl(\lambda).$$

The security experiment $\mathbf{Exp}_{\mathcal{A}}^{PVerif}[\mathcal{VC}, f, \lambda]$ and input privacy experiment are described below.

$\underline{\mathbf{Exp}_{\mathcal{A}}^{PVerif}[\mathcal{VC}, f, \lambda]}$
$(pk_f, sk_f) \leftarrow \texttt{VC.KeyGen}(f, \lambda)$;
$x \leftarrow \mathcal{A}(pk_f)$;
$(\sigma_x, \tau_x) \leftarrow \texttt{VC.ProbGen}(pk_f, x)$;
$\sigma_y^* \leftarrow \mathcal{A}(pk_f, \sigma_x, \tau_x)$;
$acc^* \leftarrow \texttt{VC.Verify}(pk_f, \tau_x, \sigma_y^*)$;
$y^* \leftarrow \texttt{VC.Decode}(sk_f, \sigma_y^*)$;
If $acc^* = 1$ and $y^* \neq f(x)$,
output 1, else 0.

$\underline{\mathbf{Exp}_{\mathcal{A}}^{IPriv}[\mathcal{VC}, f, \lambda]}$
$b \leftarrow \{0, 1\}$;
$(pk_f, sk_f) \leftarrow \texttt{VC.KeyGen}(f, \lambda)$;
$(x_0, x_1) \leftarrow \mathcal{A}(pk_f)$;
$(\sigma_b, \tau_b) \leftarrow \texttt{VC.ProGen}(pk_f, x_b)$;
$\hat{b} \leftarrow \mathcal{A}(pk_f, \sigma_b)$;
If $\hat{b} = b$, output 1, else 0.

Definition 4 (Security). *A publicly verifiable computation scheme $\mathcal{VC}$ is secure if for any function f and for any PPT adversary $\mathcal{A}$,*

$$\Pr\left[\mathbf{Exp}_{\mathcal{A}}^{PVerif}[\mathcal{VC}, f, \lambda] = 1\right] \leq negl(\lambda)$$

Definition 5 (Input Privacy). *A publicly verifiable computation scheme $\mathcal{VC}$ is input private if for any function f and for any PPT adversary $\mathcal{A}$,*

$$\Pr\left[\mathbf{Exp}_{\mathcal{A}}^{IPriv}[\mathcal{VC}, f, \lambda] = 1\right] = \frac{1}{2} + negl(\lambda)$$

.

2.3 Fiore et al.'s Homomorphic Hash Function

A family of keyed fahomomorphic hash function with domain $\mathcal{D}$ and range $\mathcal{R}$ is a triple (`H.KeyGen`, `H`, `H.Eval`) where:

- `H.KeyGen` generates the description of the hash functions.
- `H` computes the functions.
- `H.Eval` allows to compute over $\mathcal{R}$.

We say that `H` is collision resistant if for all $m, m' \in \mathcal{D}$ and $m \neq m'$ such that $\Pr[m \neq m' \wedge \mathtt{H}(m) = \mathtt{H}(m')] \leq negl(\lambda)$. In this section, we introduce the Fiore et al.'s [15] collision-resistant homomorphic hash function and prove it is still collision-resistant in RNS representation. This homomorphic hash function allows to "compress" a FHE ciphertext $c \in \mathbb{Z}_q[X][Y]$ into a single entry $v \in \mathbb{Z}_q$ such that $\mathtt{H.Eval}(f, \mathtt{H}(c_1), \cdots, \mathtt{H}(c_t)) = \mathtt{H}(f(c_1, \cdots, c_t))$. Let domain $\mathcal{D} = \{m \in \mathbb{Z}_q[X][Y] : \deg_X(m) \leq n_1, \deg_Y(m) \leq n_2\}$ and range $\mathcal{R} = \mathbb{Z}_q$ be defined in `H`. The construction is as follows:

- `H.KeyGen`: Given a security parameter λ, generates a bilinear group $\mathsf{bg} = (q, \mathbb{G}_1, \mathbb{G}_2, \mathbb{G}_T, e, g, h)$ from generator $\mathsf{bg}(1^\lambda)$ such that $\mathbb{G}_1, \mathbb{G}_2$ are cyclic groups of λ-bit prime order q equipped with bilinear asymmetric map $e : \mathbb{G}_1 \times \mathbb{G}_2 \rightarrow \mathbb{G}_T$, $g \in \mathbb{G}_1$ and $h \in \mathbb{G}_2$ are generators. Chooses random $\alpha, \beta \xleftarrow{\$} \mathbb{Z}_q$ and computes $g^{\alpha^i \beta^j}, h^{\alpha^i \beta^j}, e(g,h)^{\alpha^i \beta^j}$ for $i \in \{0, \cdots, n_1\}, j \in \{0, \cdots, n_2\}$. Output public key $pk = (\{g^{\alpha^i \beta^j}\}_{i,j=0}^{n_1,n_2}, \{h^{\alpha^i \beta^j}\}_{i,j=0}^{n_1,n_2}, \{e(g,h)^{\alpha^i \beta^j}\}_{i,j=0}^{n_1,n_2})$.
- `H`: On input $c \in \mathcal{D}$, the function $\hat{H}_{\alpha,\beta}$ evaluates c at $Y = \alpha$ over $\mathbb{Z}_q[X]$ and then evaluates $c(\alpha) \in \mathbb{Z}_q[X]$ at $X = \beta$ over $\mathbb{Z}_q$. If $\deg_Y(c) \leq 1$, then compute $(T, U) \leftarrow (g^{\hat{H}_{\alpha,\beta}(c)}, h^{\hat{H}_{\alpha,\beta}(c)}) \in \mathbb{G}_1 \times \mathbb{G}_2$. If $\deg_Y(c) = 2$, then compute $\hat{T} \leftarrow e(g,h)^{\hat{H}_{\alpha,\beta}(c)} \in \mathbb{G}_T$.
- `H.Eval`: Given two hash values (T_1, U_1), (T_2, U_2) (resp. $\hat{T}_1$, $\hat{T}_2$),
  - Addition (in the exponent): $T \leftarrow T_1 \cdot T_2, U \leftarrow U_1 \cdot U_2$ (resp. $\hat{T} \leftarrow \hat{T}_1 \cdot \hat{T}_2$).
  - Multiplication by constant $c \in \mathbb{Z}_q$: (T^c, U^c) (resp. $\hat{T}^c$).
  - Multiplication by two values: $\hat{T} \leftarrow e(T_1, U_2) \in \mathbb{G}_T$.

Theorem 1 ([15]). *The function H described above is homomorphic. Furthermore, if $\ell - BDHI$ assumption holds for* bg *and any $\ell \geq n_1, n_2$, then H is collision-resistant.*

2.4 Security in the Presence of Malicious Adversaries

Parameters: The sender holds a set of size N_X and the receiver holds a set of size N_Y. If the sender or receiver is corrupt, their set size is N_X^* or N_Y^*, respectively.
Functionality:

- The receiver inputs (SID, TAGs, Y). If it is honest, then $|Y| \leq N_Y$; otherwise $|Y| \leq N_Y^*$. Give output (RECEIVER-INPUT, SID) to the sender.
- The sender inputs (SID, PROOFs, X). If it is honest, then $|X| \leq N_X$; otherwise $|X| \leq N_X^*$.
- Provide output $X \cap Y$ or $\perp$ to the receiver.

Fig. 1. Ideal verifiable PSI functionality with one-sided output. TAGs and PROOFs are used in verifiability.

Definition 6 ([8]). *There is a simulation-based paradigm defined security with respect to real model and ideal model.*

- *Real model: A honest party attacked by a malicious adversary $\mathcal{A}$ runs the protocol π. A simulator* SIM *who can arbitrarily interact with $\mathcal{A}$ sends the honest party's input to the protocol π. The protocol π outputs the results to the* SIM.
- *Ideal model: A honest party and a malicious adversary $\mathcal{S}$ interact with the ideal PSI function of Fig. 1. The honest party sends the input provided by the simulator* SIM *to the PSI functionality and returns their output to* SIM.

If the output of the interaction in the real model cannot be distinguished from the output of the interaction between the honest party and the simulator SIM *of the ideal model, then the protocol π is said to securely compute the PSI functionality with abort in the presence of malicious adversaries.*

Definition 7 (Verifiability). *A PSI scheme is verifiable if for input x and the PSI functionality f,*

$$\Pr\left[\begin{array}{l|l}\texttt{VC.Verify}(PROOFs, TAGs, \sigma_y) & (PROOFs, sk_f) \leftarrow \texttt{VC.KeyGen}(f, \lambda)\\ = 1 \wedge \texttt{VC.Decode}(sk_f, \sigma_y) & (\sigma_x, TAGs) \leftarrow \texttt{VC.ProbGen}(pk_f, x)\\ = X \cap Y & \sigma_y \leftarrow \texttt{VC.Compute}(pk_f, \sigma_x)\end{array}\right]$$
$$= 1 - negl(\lambda). \tag{1}$$

3 Publicly Verifiable Inner Product Computation on Encrypted Data

Motivated by the sender's homomorphic evaluation of inner product in [11], we present a publicly verifiable inner computation scheme on encrypted data. The high-level idea is to apply a collision-resistant homomorphic hash function on the pre-image of the inner product computation process. The prover hashes the encrypted data to a tag using the collision-resistant hash function and verifier recomputes the result's tag by public key to verify the integrity and correctness of the inner product. Below, we prove Fiore et al.'s homomorphic hash function supporting RNS representation and construct a publicly verifiable inner product computation on encrypted data using the hash function.

3.1 Fiore et al.'s Hash Function for RNS Representation

The independence for exponentiation and minimal collision of Fiore et al.'s homomorphic hash function for any component of RNS will be shown below. With those mathematical background, verifier randomly chooses a branch $\mathtt{ct}_{q_i}$ to verify its correctness in stead of verifying the whole ciphertext. See Appendix A for specific proof.

Lemma 1. *Let $\mathcal{B} = \{q_1, \cdots, q_\ell\}$ be a RNS base of relatively prime moduli which size ℓ is its number of elements, $q = \prod_{i=1}^{\ell} q_i$. If x and g are given in their RNS form $(x_1, \cdots, x_\ell)$ and $(g_1, \cdots, g_\ell)$, then $|g^x|_q$ is in the RNS form $(|g_1^{x_1}|_{q_1}, \cdots, |g_\ell^{x_\ell}|_{q_\ell})$.*

Lemma 2. *Let n be positive integer and q be prime, $\mathcal{R}_q = \mathbb{Z}_q[X]/(X^n + 1)$. On $\mathcal{D} = \{c \in \mathcal{R}_q[Y] : \deg_X(c) < n, \deg_Y(c) \leq 1\}$, for all $c, c' \in \mathcal{D}$, the probability of a collision $\Pr[c \neq c' \wedge \mathtt{H}(c) = \mathtt{H}(c')] \leq (\frac{n^2+qn+2}{q^2} - \frac{(n-1)^3}{q^3})^2$.*

Note that $n \ll q$ in practical, the probability of a collision is very small.

3.2 Publicly Verifiable Inner Product Computation

We now construct a publicly verifiable inner product computation on encrypted data using the hash function. The inner product of two d-dimensional vectors over $\mathcal{R}_t$ is represented as

$$\begin{aligned} F(x_1, \cdots, x_d) : \quad & \mathcal{R}_t^d \quad \to \mathcal{R}_t \\ ((f_1, f_2, \cdots, f_d), (x_1, x_2, \cdots, x_d)) & \mapsto \sum_{\iota=1}^{d} f_\iota x_\iota, \end{aligned}$$

where $\boldsymbol{f} = (f_1, \cdots, f_d)$ and $\boldsymbol{x} = (x_1, \cdots, x_d) \in \mathcal{R}_t^d$.

In order to support batching of FHE, we start our work with a trick called *monomial hash.* A polynomial $x_\iota \in \mathcal{R}_t$ corresponding to the vector $(x_{\iota,0}, \cdots, x_{\iota,n-1})$ is encrypted together through batching technique. We can obtain a batching encryption $c_\iota \in \mathcal{R}_q[Y]$ of degree-1 by running $\mathtt{FHE.Enc}(pk, x_\iota)$. For each bivariate polynomial $c_\iota = \sum_{i=0}^{n-1}(\sum_{j=0}^{1} a_{\iota,i,j} Y^j X^i)$, the monomial $\sum_{j=0}^{1} a_{\iota,i,j} Y^j X^i$ is expressed as $c_\iota[i]$. The monomial $c_\iota[i]$ is hashes down to $(\sigma_{\iota,i}, \varsigma_{\iota,i}) = \mathtt{H}(c_\iota[i])$ by the collision-resistant homomorphic hash function described above, i.e., $\sigma_{\iota,i} = \prod_{j=0}^{1} g^{a_{\iota,i,j}\beta^j\alpha^i}$. The monomial hash of ciphertext c_ι is set as $\tilde{\text{H}}_g(c_\iota) = (\sigma_{\iota,0}, \cdots, \sigma_{\iota,n-1})$. we details the scheme $\mathcal{VC}_{inpro}$ through this trick below:

- $\texttt{VC.KeyGen}(\boldsymbol{f}, \lambda)$: Run $\texttt{FHE.ParamGen}(\lambda)$ to obtain the FHE parameters $pp = (n, q, t)$. Run $(pk_{HE}, sk_{HE}, evk) \leftarrow \texttt{FHE.KeyGen}(pp)$. In RNS, $q = \prod_{i=1}^{\ell} q_i$, where q_i is prime moduli for all i. For each $k \in \{1, \cdots, \ell\}$, suppose q_k of λ_k-bits is the ciphertext modulus representative. Set $pp_k = (n, q_k, t)$ and do the following: run $\texttt{H.KeyGen}(\lambda_k)$ to generate a bilinear group $\mathsf{bg} = (q_k, \mathbb{G}_1, \mathbb{G}_2, \mathbb{G}_T, e, g, g_2)$ equipped with $e : \mathbb{G}_1 \times \mathbb{G}_2 \rightarrow \mathbb{G}_T$ and pk_H. Let $g_T = e(g, g_2)$, $\boldsymbol{f} = (f_1, \cdots, f_d)$, where $f_\iota = (m_{\iota,0}, \cdots, m_{\iota,n-1}) \in \mathbb{Z}_t^n$ for all $\iota = \{1, \cdots, d\}$. Compute $\tau_{\iota,i} = g_2^{m_{\iota,i}}$ as a proof and set $pk_{g_2} = \{\tau_{\iota,i}\}_{\iota=1,i=0}^{d,n-1}$. Set $PK = (pk_{HE}, pp, \mathsf{bg}, pk_H, pk_{g_2}, evk)$, $SK = sk_{HE}$.
- $\texttt{VC.ProbGen}(PK, \boldsymbol{x} = (x_1, \cdots, x_d))$: Compute $c_\iota \leftarrow \texttt{FHE.Enc}(pk_{HE}, x_i)$ for $\iota \in \{1, \cdots, d\}$. For each branch $|c_\iota|_{q_k}$ of c_ι, compute the monomial hash $\sigma_\iota^{(q_k)} = \tilde{\text{H}}_g(|c_\iota|_{q_k})$ as a tag, i.e., $\sigma_\iota^{(q_k)} = (\sigma_{\iota,0}^{(q_k)}, \cdots, \sigma_{\iota,n-1}^{(q_k)})$, where $(\sigma_{\iota,i}^{(q_k)}, \varsigma_{\iota,i}^{(q_k)}) = \text{H}(c_\iota^{(q_k)}[i])$. Set $\sigma_{\boldsymbol{x}} = (c_1, \cdots, c_d, \{\sigma_1^{(q_k)}, \cdots, \sigma_d^{(q_k)}\}_{k=1}^{\ell})$, and $\tau_{\boldsymbol{x}} = pk_{g_2}$.
- $\texttt{VC.Compute}(PK, \sigma_{\boldsymbol{x}})$: Compute $c \leftarrow \texttt{FHE.Eval}(F, (c_1, \cdots, c_d), evk)$. Output $\sigma_y = (c, \{\sigma_1^{(q_k)}, \cdots, \sigma_d^{(q_k)}\}_{k=1}^{\ell})$,
- $\texttt{VC.Verify}(PK, \sigma_y, \tau_{\boldsymbol{x}})$: Choose a random $k \in \{1, \cdots, \ell\}$ and let $|c|_{q_k}$ be the representatively verifiable ciphertext of c. Compute the verification value $\sigma^{(q_k)} = g_T^{\hat{H}_{\alpha,\beta}(|c|_{q_k})}$ by using the group elements in public key pk_H.
  If $\prod_{\iota=1}^{d} \prod_{i=0}^{n-1} \texttt{H.Eval}(\sigma_{\iota,i}^{(q_k)}, \tau_{\iota,i}) \neq \sigma^{(q_k)}$, reject, else output c.
- $\texttt{VC.Decode}(SK, c)$: Run $y \leftarrow \texttt{FHE.Dec}(sk_{HE}, c)$ and output y.

Security Analysis. About the above construction, we can state the following security result.

Theorem 2. *In the presence of semantic secure full homomorphic encryption scheme and collision-resistant homomorphic hash function, then the protocol $\mathcal{VC}_{inpro}$ satisfies correctness, security, input privacy and function privacy.*

Proof. If verifier is honest, we show the verification equation are satisfied for correctness. Notice that

$$
\begin{aligned}
|c|_{q_k} &= \sum_{\iota=1}^{d} (m_{\iota,0} + \cdots + m_{\iota,n-1} X^{n-1}) \cdot \sum_{i=0}^{n-1} \sum_{j=0}^{1} a_{\iota,0,j} Y^j X^i \\
&= \sum_{\iota=1}^{d} [m_{\iota,0}(a_{\iota,0,0} + a_{\iota,0,1} Y) X^0 + \cdots + m_{\iota,n-1}(a_{\iota,n-1,0} + a_{\iota,n-1,1} Y) X^{n-1}],
\end{aligned}
$$

then, $\sigma^{(q_k)} = g_T^{\sum_{\iota=1}^{d} \sum_{i=0}^{n-1} m_{\iota,i}(a_{\iota,i,0} + a_{\iota,i,1}\beta)\alpha^i}$. We have

$$
\prod_{\iota=1}^{d} \prod_{i=0}^{n-1} e(\sigma_{\iota,i}^{(q_k)}, \tau_{\iota,i}) = \prod_{\iota=1}^{d} \prod_{i=0}^{n-1} e(g^{a_{\iota,i}\alpha^i + b_{\iota,i}\alpha^i\beta}, g_2^{m_{\iota,i}}) = e(g, g_2)^{acc},
$$

where $acc = \sum_{\iota=1}^{d}\sum_{i=0}^{n-1} m_{\iota,,i}(a_{\iota,i,0} + a_{\iota,i,1}\beta)\alpha^i$. Therefore, the verification equality $\prod_{\iota=1}^{d}\prod_{i=0}^{n-1} \texttt{H.Eval}(\sigma_{\iota,i}^{(q_k)}, \tau_{\iota,i}) = \sigma^{(q_k)}$ holds since $g_T = e(g, g_2)$.

To prove security, we give the following games:

- Game0: This is the experiment $\mathbf{Exp}_{\mathcal{A}}^{PVerif}[\mathcal{VC}, f, \lambda]$.
- Game1: As Game0, but replacing the value f_ι with a random $f_\iota^* \xleftarrow{\$} \mathbb{Z}_t^n$. The result $c^* \leftarrow \texttt{FHE.Eval}(F^*, (c_1, \cdots, c_d), evk)$, where $F^* = \sum_{\iota=1}^{d} f_\iota^* c_\iota$.
- Game2: As Game1, but replacing the value c_ι with a uniform $c_\iota^* \in \mathcal{R}_q[Y]$. The result $c^* \leftarrow \texttt{FHE.Eval}(F^*, (c_1^*, \cdots, c_d^*), evk)$. In this case, the verifier checks if $\prod_{\iota=1}^{d}\prod_{i=0}^{n-1} e(\sigma_{\iota,i}^{(q_k)}, \tau_{\iota,i}) = \sigma^{*(q_k)}$, which maintains correctness since $\sigma^{*(q_k)}$ is a homomorphic hash value of the representatively verifiable ciphertext of c^*.

The advantage of a cheating prover in Game2 is negligibly close to the one in Game1, since FHE is semantically secure, the ciphertext c_ι and the uniform c_ι^* are indistinguishable. Game1 is completely independent of the function, therefore cheating prover wins Game1 is negligibly close to the one in Game0. An adversary wins Game2 if it provides c^* that pass the verification check $\prod_{\iota=1}^{d}\prod_{i=0}^{n-1} e(\sigma_{\iota,i}^{(q_k)}, \tau_{\iota,i}) = \sigma^{*(q_k)}$, but such that $\texttt{FHE.Dec}(sk_f, c^*) \neq \texttt{FHE.Dec}(sk_f, c)$. The verification check passes means that $g_T^{\hat{H}_{\alpha,\beta}(|c|_{q_k})} \neq g_T^{\hat{H}_{\alpha,\beta}(|c^*|_{q_k})}$, which is incompatible with the collision resistance of H. So we get that any adversary wins the security Game2 with negligible probability.

Input privacy is guaranteed by a reduction to FHE semantic security. The ciphertext of FHE is indistinguishable from uniform and the verification check is independent of the encoded values. The adversary cannot distinguish $c_b \leftarrow \texttt{FHE.Enc}(pk, x_b)$ for $b \in \{0, 1\}$. So any adversary wins $\mathbf{Exp}_{\mathcal{A}}^{IPriv}[\mathcal{VC}, f, \lambda]$ with negligible probability. We conclude that the protocol $\mathcal{VC}_{inpro}$ satisfies input privacy. □

Efficiency Analysis. Regarding the computation complexity of the protocol, we main focus on the complexity of `VC.KeyGen`, `VC.ProbGen` and `VC.Verify` algorithms. We ignore the complexity of `VC.Compute` algorithm, since it is computed by the powerful server. Specially, we focus on the number of exponential operations which account for the main computational overhead. The `VC.KeyGen` algorithm run in time $6 \cdot d \cdot \ell$ to generate pk_g and pk_{g_T}, $d \cdot n \cdot \ell$ to generate pk_{g_2}. The `VC.ProGen` algorithm requires $4 \cdot d \cdot n \cdot \ell$ exponentiations to generate monomial hash $\{\sigma_1^{(q_k)}, \cdots, \sigma_d^{(q_k)}\}_{k=1}^{\ell}$. The `VC.Verify` algorithm runs in time $2 \cdot n$ to generate verification value $\sigma^{(q_k)}$. Since ℓ is a fixed constant, the final computation complexity of the $\mathcal{VC}_{inpro}$ protocol is $O(nd)$ exponentiations.

Note that $\mathcal{VC}_{inpro}$ scheme carries out the amortized model in which the parties in the protocol runs a one-time expensive phase in `VC.KeyGen` algorithm. After this stage, all the algorithms run efficiently. Additionally, the keypair (PK, SK) generated by `VC.KeyGen` can be reused many times.

4 Publicly Verifiable PSI from Homomorphic Encryption

In this section, we present a publicly verifiable PSI from homomorphic encryption in the full malicious security model, based on the publicly verifiable inner product evaluation on encrypted data aforementioned. Our work follows the paradigm in [10,11]. First, we describe a basic protocol as warm-up. Next, we detail the full protocol with several optimization methods.

4.1 The Full Construction

In the following detailed construction, we use the optimization methods provided by Chen et al. [11] to improve the efficiency, including batching, hashing, reducing the circuit depth by windowing and partitioning. The verifiable PSI can be divided into four phases: Sender-side Setup, Receiver-side Setup, Sender-side computation and Receiver-side Result Verification and Retrieval.

Sender-side Setup:

- **Pre-Process X**
  1. [OPRF] The parities perform a DH-OPRF pre-processing[1] [22]. The sender uses a oblivious pseudo-random function PRF with a sampling key s to amend its set to $X' = \{H(\mathtt{PRF}_s(x)) : x \in X\}$ [22]. Here H is a random hash function with short, fixed-length range.
  2. [Hashing] Let (h, m, B) be a set of hashing parameters, where h is the number of hash functions, m is the capacity of a Cuckoo hash table, and B is the bin capacity for the simple hashing. They are required that the success probability of Cuckoo hashing N_Y items into m bins is greater than $1 - 2^{-\lambda_\sigma}$. The max load of simple hashing hN_X items into m bins is B. Three random hash functions $h_1, h_2, h_3 : \{0,1\}^\sigma \to [m]$ are selected fairly by parties, where σ is the public length of bit strings of the sets. The sender performs simple hashing on X' into a table $\mathcal{C}_s$, which consists of m bins with load B.
  3. [Partitioning] To minimize the overall cost, the sender and receiver agree on the partitioning parameter $\alpha \in [1, B]$. For table $\mathcal{C}_s$, the sender partitions it vertically into α subtables $\mathcal{C}_s[1], \cdots, \mathcal{C}_s[\alpha]$ of size $B' = B/\alpha$.
  4. [Compute coefficients] The sender defines polynomials whose roots are elements of each row of the subtables. Formally, for each row v of r-th subtable, $1 \leq r \leq \alpha, 1 \leq v \leq m$, the sender replaces the row v with coefficients $f_{v,0}^{(r)}, \cdots, f_{v,B'}^{(r)}$ of the polynomial $\prod_{s \in [B']}(x - v_s)$.
  5. [Batching] For each refreshing subtable, the sender translates each of its column into a vector in $\mathbb{Z}_t^m$. Then the sender batches each vector into m/n plaintext polynomials. As a result, the r-the subtable is transformed

[1] Let H be a random oracle hash function with range $\mathbb{Z}_q$, H' be a map to a sufficiently long bit string. The receiver has an input $x \in \{0,1\}^*$ and the sender has a key $s \in \mathbb{Z}_q^*$. The receiver chooses $t \in \mathbb{Z}_q^*$ and sends $H(x)^t$ to the sender. The sender returns the $(H(x)^t)^s$. The receiver then outputs $H'(H(x)^s) = H'((H(x)^t)^s)^{1/t}$.

into $m/n \cdot B'$ polynomial $S_{i,j}^{(r)}$. The coefficients of polynomial $S_{i,j}^{(r)}$ is $f_{i,j,\iota}^{(r)}$ for $1 \le i \le m/n, 0 \le j \le B', 0 \le \iota \le n-1$ and $1 \le r \le \alpha$.

- **KeyGen**
  6. [Choose FHE parameters] The FHE parameters $pp = (n, q, t)$ are selected by the receiver for semantic secure FHE scheme, where n is the ring dimension of power of 2, q is the ciphertext modulus, and t is the plaintext modulus.
  7. [KeyGen] The parties run $\texttt{VC.Keygen}(\lambda)$ to generate a pair of keys $(PK = (pk_{HE}, pp, \mathsf{bg}, pk_H, pk_{g_2}), SK = sk_{HE})$, where the sender generates the proofs $pk_{g_2} = \{\tau_{i,j,\iota}^{(r)} = g_2^{f_{i,j,\iota}^{(r)}}\}$[2].

Receiver-side Setup:

- **Pre-Process Y**
  1. [OPRF] The receiver amends its set to $Y' = \{H(\texttt{PRF}_s(y)) : y \in Y\}$ by the interactive DH-OPRF pre-processing [22] with the sender.
  2. [Cuckoo Hashing] Three hash functions h_1, h_2, h_3 are used by the receiver to Cuckoo hashing on Y' into a table $\mathcal{C}_r$ with m bins.
  3. [Batching] The receiver first translates $\mathcal{C}_r$ into a vector in $\mathbb{Z}_t^m$. Then the vector is batched into m/n FHE plaintext polynomials $\bar{Y}_1, \cdots, \bar{Y}_{m/n}$.
  4. [Windowing] The windowing parameter $l \in [1, \log_2 B]$ is decided by the parties to reduce the circuit depth. For each batched plaintext polynomial $\bar{Y}_i$, the receiver computes the component-wise $\mu \cdot 2^\nu$-th powers $\bar{Y}_i^{\mu \cdot 2^\nu}$, for $1 \le i \le m/n, 1 \le \mu \le 2^l - 1$ and $0 \le \nu \le \lfloor \log_2(B')/l \rfloor$.
- **ProGen**
  5. [Encrypt and Tags] For each power $\bar{Y}_i^{\mu \cdot 2^\nu}$, the receiver runs procedure $\texttt{VC.ProGen}(PK, \bar{Y}_i^{\mu \cdot 2^\nu})$ to generate ciphertexts and monomial hash values $(c_i^{(\mu,\nu)}, (\sigma_{\iota,i}^{(\mu,\nu)})_{\iota=0}^{n-1})$. Set the tags of ciphertexts $\{c_i^{(\mu,\nu)}\}$ as $\{(\sigma_{\iota,i}^{(\mu,\nu)})_{\iota=0}^{n-1}\}$ and send them to the sender.

Sender-side computation:

1. [Homomorphically evaluate encryptions of all powers] The sender homomorphically evaluates all powers of ciphertexts $\{c_i^{(\mu,\nu)}\}$ and obtains a vector $\boldsymbol{c} = (c_0, \cdots, c_{B'})$, in which c_r is a homomorphic encryption of $\bar{Y}^j$. At last, the sender achieves m/n vectors $\boldsymbol{c}_1, \cdots, \boldsymbol{c}_{m/n}$.
2. [Compute tags of all powers] For each ciphertext c_j that not provided by the receiver, the sender uses the group elements in pk_H to generate its tag $\{(\sigma_{i,j,\iota})_{\iota=0}^{n-1}\}$ and sends to the receiver.
3. [Homomorphically compute the inner product] The sender computes homomorphically $\boldsymbol{d}_{i,r} = \sum_{j=0}^{B'} \boldsymbol{c}_i[B' - j] \cdot S_{i,j}^{(r)}$, for all $1 \le i \le m/n, 0 \le j \le B', 1 \le r \le \alpha$, and returns them back.

[2] The proofs can be used repeatedly by different people, so it is difficult for the sender to provide false proofs.

Receiver-Side Result Verification and Retrieval:

1. [Verification] The receiver (or trusted third party) uses the group elements in pk_H to generate the verification value $\sigma_T^{(d_{i,r})}$ of ciphertext $\boldsymbol{d}_{i,r}$. The receiver (or trusted third part) verifies whether $\prod_{j=0}^{B'} \prod_{\iota=0}^{n-1} e(\sigma_{i,B'-j,\iota}, \tau_{i,j,\iota}^{(r)}) = \sigma_T^{(d_{i,r})}$ for each i and r. If the answer is no, rejects; otherwise, accepts.
2. [Retrieval] The receiver decrypts all ciphertexts. It outputs the corresponding y if the ciphertext decryption corresponding to the position that y occupies in $\mathcal{C}_r$ is zero.

4.2 Security Analysis

The verifiability is obvious since the correctness of the publicly verifiable inner product computation. We state the claims of security for our publicly verifiable PSI protocol in malicious adversary model. The ideal verifiable PSI functionality with one-sided output is described in Fig. 1.

Theorem 3. *The full publicly verifiable PSI protocol is secure for the verifiable PSI functionality in the malicious setting.*

Proof. We consider two cases where the receiver or the sender is corrupt.

Case 1: the receiver is corrupt. For every adversary $\mathcal{A}$ that operates in the real model, there is a simulator SIM_r in the ideal model that controls the corrupted receiver. We demonstrate that the transcript for the protocol execution generated by the simulator SIM_r and the sender in the ideal model is indistinguishable from interaction with the receiver and the sender in the real model. Detailed description follows.

1. SIM_r is given hashing parameters (h, m, B), partition parameter α, FHE parameters (n, q, t) and bilinear group $(q, \mathbb{G}_1, \mathbb{G}_2, \mathbb{G}_T, e, g, g_2)$.
2. SIM_r gets the proofs relative to the sender's input from the receiver. Note that SIM_r does not distinguish the proof of x from the uniform since the unpredictability of OPRF and discrete logarithm (DL) assumption.
3. SIM_r uses the random oracle to obtain the input Y^* from Y' and forwards to ideal verifiable PSI functionality.
4. Ideal verifiable PSI functionality response with $X^* = X \cap Y^*$ or $\perp$. SIM_r wants learn some additional information from X^*.
5. If ideal PSI functionality response X^*, SIM_r uses random values which not in Y^* to pad X^* to size of N_X since OPRF is an unpredictable function.
6. SIM_r replaces honest sender's X with X^* and performs the whole publicly verifiable PSI protocol.

Since all OPRF values apart from $X \cap Y^*$ are uniformly distributed from the view of receiver, which also maintain uniform distribution of proofs under DL assumption. Padding X^* with random values not in Y^* produces the same uniform distribution. Hence, the output of the interaction between the receiver and the sender of the real world cannot be distinguished from the output of the interaction between the sender and the simulator SIM_r of the ideal world.

Case 2: the sender is corrupt. For every adversary $\mathcal{A}$ that operations in the real model, there is simulator SIM_s in the ideal model that controls the corrupted sender. We demonstrate that the transcript for the protocol execution generated by the simulator SIM_s and the receiver in the ideal model is indistinguishable from interaction with the receiver and the sender in the real model. Detailed description follows.

1. SIM_s is given hashing parameters (h, m, B), partition parameter α, FHE parameters (n, q, t), bilinear group $(q, \mathbb{G}_1, \mathbb{G}_2, \mathbb{G}_T, e, g, g_2)$ and proofs.
2. SIM_s uses the random oracle to obtain the input X^* from X' and forwards to ideal verifiable PSI functionality.
3. Ideal verifiable PSI functionality response with $Y^* = X^* \cap Y$ or $\perp$.
4. If ideal verifiable PSI functionality response Y^*, SIM_s uses random values which not in X^* to pad Y^* to size of N_Y since OPRF is an unpredictable function.
5. SIM_s encrypts items of Y^* to generate new ciphertexts in place of the receiver's encryptions and performs the whole protocol.

First, by the semantic security of FHE, the new ciphertexts generated by the SIM_s is indistinguishable from the sender's perspective in the real world, which ensure the receiver privacy from malicious sender. Next, by the security of $\mathcal{VC}_{inpro}$, new encryption's hash value cannot pass the verification check, the ideal verifiable PSI functionality response with abort. Hence, the output of the interaction between the sender and the receiver of the real world cannot be distinguished from the output of the interaction between the receiver and the simulator SIM_s of the ideal world. □

4.3 Efficiency Analysis

In this section, we present the efficiency analysis of the proposed protocol and give a comparison with protocols [1,10,36]. Table 1 summarises the results.

We have 2 rounds in the protocol: 1 round for the execution of OPRF; 1 round for the receiver sending part of the public key $(pk_{HE}, pp, \mathsf{bg}, pk_H)$, ciphertexts $\{c_y\}_{y \in Y}$ and tags of $\{PRF_s(y) : y \in Y\}$ to the sender; the sender sending proofs pk_{g_2} and the ciphertext c, which is homomorphically evaluated from $\{c_y\}_{y \in Y}$.

Our protocol has the initial overhead of a PSI protocol from homomorphic encryption plus the overhead of a verifiable computation scheme for inner product. The overhead of PSI protocol from homomorphic encryption was already given in [10], the communication complexity is $O(|Y| \log |X|)$ and the computation complexity is $O(|X|^2 + |X||Y|)$. The communication complexity of verifiable computation scheme is $O(|X|)$ for sender's proofs. The computation complexity is $O(|Y|)$ for generating sender's proofs and $O(|X|)$ for generating receiver' tags. In summary, our protocol increases communication complexity $O(|X|)$ and computation complexity $O(|Y| + |X|)$ compared with [10]. To the best of our knowledge, [36] is state-of-the-art two-party PSI protocol with fully malicious security. However, [36] requires multiple interactions between sender and receiver, and the parties' sets need to be populated to the same size. It is inefficient for unbalanced PSI and unfriendly for resource-constrained receiver. We evaluate verifiable PSI by comparing its properties to the protocol [1] that supports verification. In [1], the receiver can securely delegate PSI evaluation to the cloud. However the parties must share partial set information. Therefore, the protocol cannot support public verification and prevent the malicious receiver.

Table 1. Comparison to related protocols.

Property	This work	[10]	[36]	[1][b]
Integrity verification	✓	×	×	✓
Correctness verification	✓	×	✓	✓
Security against receiver	✓	✓	✓	×
Security against sender	✓	pp[a]	✓	✓
Number of rounds	2	2	$O(\|X\|+\|Y\|)$	2
Classification	Unbalanced	Unbalanced	Balanced	Balanced
Cryptography techniques	FHE, OPRF, VC	FHE, OPRF	OT, PRF	Paillier, PRF
Computation of receiver	$O(\|Y\|)$	$O(1)$	$O(\|X\|)$	O(Y)
Computation of sender	$O(\|X\|^2)$	$O(\|X\|^2)$	$O(\|X\|)$	O(X)
Communication complexity	$O(\|X\|)$[c]	$O(\|Y\| \log \|X\|)$	$O(\|X\| \log \|X\|)$	$O(\|X\|+\|Y\|)$

[a] Privacy-persevering.

[b] The parties need to share partial information, so the protocol do not support public verifiability.

[c] For verifiers, there is no need to transmit all sender proofs. Verifiers can randomly choose part of the evaluation results and proofs to verify, effectively reduce the communication complexity.

5 Performance Evaluation

In this section, we provide a thorough experimental evaluation of the proposed publicly verifiable PSI protocol. All experiments were using a standard desktop computer (Lenovo Intel® Core™ i7-4710MQ CPU @2.5 GHZ) on Ubuntu. Our implementations are single threaded. For our tools, we made use of the following libraries in C/C++:

- For fully homomorphic encryption (FHE), SEAL [37] implements BFV scheme in a full RNS variant without KeySwitch and ModulusSwitch.
- For oblivious pseudo-random function (OPRF) [22], Openssl implements DH of [22]. Also, Openssl implements Cuckoo hashing and simple hashing.
- For verifiable computation (VC), PBC implements group and pairing operations with Type A1 pairing.

We choose a string length $\sigma = 32$ bits, a statistical security level $\lambda_\sigma = 40$, a computational security level $\lambda_\kappa = 128$ and windowing parameter $l = 1$. In unbalanced case, the receiver has a substantially smaller set than the sender.

We performs the protocols for $|X| \in \{2^{16}, 2^{18}, 2^{20}\}$ and $|Y| \in \{5535, 11041\}$. If $|X| = 2^{16}$, then the partitioning parameter $\alpha = 20$; If $|X| = 2^{18}$, then $\alpha = 64$; If $|X| = 2^{20}$, then $\alpha = 128$. FHE parameters and hashing parameters selection we summarized in Table 2.

In experiments, we compare with [10], which is state-of-the art unbalanced PSI protocol in malicious setting. It provides security against a malicious receiver, while keeping privacy against a malicious sender. Our protocol is in the full malicious security. Both of the protocols are on the random oracle model. The detailed computational performance results, communication cost and comparision to Chen et al. [10] is given in Table 3. Running time is in seconds and communication cost is in MB. S and R are short for the sender and receiver, Com. is short for computation, respectively. Receiver-side Retrieval phase includes verification in our protocol.

Table 2. Sample parameters for PSI.

Receiver's set size	$\|Y\|$	5535	11041
FHE parameters	n	8192	16384
	t	8519681	8519681
	q	218-bit	438-bit
Hashing parameters	h	3	3
	m	8192	16384
	B	20	128

As shown in Table 3, the computation overhead center on phase of sender-side setup due to the amortized model. We see that our computation overhead is more than 9% compared to [10] in sender-side setup since the sender needs to generate proofs in our protocol. There is little difference in the computational overhead of sender-side computation and receiver-side retrieval. However, the computational overhead for generating proofs in our Sender-side setup can be used repeatedly multiple times. The communication overhead of sender-side setup is improved significantly due to the transmission of proofs and tags. But the additional communication overhead is necessary to ensure the correctness and integrity of the PSI computation. After expensive pre-processing phase, the cost of sender-side computation phase is same as [10].

Table 3. Comparing the running time and the communication cost with [10]

|X|	|Y|	Protocol	Computing Phase (in seconds)				Communication Phase (in MB)		
			S's Setup	R's Setup	S's Com.	R's Com	S's Setup (S→R)	R's Setup (R→S)	S's Com. (S→R)
2^{16}	5535	[10]	1.04	0.98	0.006	0.003	4.3	4.72	8.6
		Ours	1.12	0.98	0.006	0.003	9.8	17	8.6
	11041	[10]	1.16	1.95	0.014	0.008	8.5	10.3	36.5
		Ours	1.31	1.95	0.014	0.011	19.5	34.88	36.5
2^{18}	5535	[10]	3.90	0.98	0.015	0.006	4.3	4.72	27.7
		Ours	4.43	0.98	0.015	0.020	39.5	17	27.7
	11041	[10]	4.07	1.95	0.038	0.025	8.5	10.3	116.9
		Ours	4.53	1.95	0.038	0.026	48.9	34.88	116.9
2^{20}	5535	[10]	14.07	0.98	0.029	0.011	4.3	4.72	55.4
		Ours	15.42	0.98	0.029	0.034	43.6	17	55.4
	11041	[10]	15.34	1.95	0.070	0.038	8.5	10.3	233.7
		Ours	16.24	1.95	0.070	0.041	88.9	34.88	233.7

6 Conclusions

Although there has been a fast unbalanced PSI from homomorphic encryption, it is still unpractical since the sender can provide wrong results to receiver easily. In this work, we mainly present a publicly verifiable private set intersection from homomorphic encryption with malicious security. Motivated by "hash-and-MAC" paradigm, we construct a publicly verifiable inner product computation scheme on encrypted data based on a homomorphic hash function with collision resistance, which also supports RNS. Our work supports public verification under the preserving privacy, batching and RNS used to enhancing the performance of FHE, with only 2 rounds. We also leave an interesting challenge from a practical perspective: How to design of a verifiable PSI with lower communication complexity?

Acknowledgements. This work was supported by the National Nature Science Foundation of China (No. 62172434).

A Fiore et al.'s Hash Function for RNS Representation

Lemma 3. *Let $\mathcal{B} = \{q_1, \cdots, q_\ell\}$ be a RNS base of relatively prime moduli which size ℓ is its number of elements, $q = \prod_{i=1}^{\ell} q_i$. If x and g are given in their RNS form $(x_1, \cdots, x_\ell)$ and $(g_1, \cdots, g_\ell)$, then $|g^x|_q$ is in the RNS form $(|g_1^{x_1}|_{q_1}, \cdots, |g_\ell^{x_\ell}|_{q_\ell})$.*

Proof. The Chinese Remainder Theorem (CRT) ensures the uniqueness of this representation $|g^x|_q = |g^{|\sum_{i=1}^{\ell} |x_i \frac{q_i}{q}|_{q_i} \times \frac{q}{q_i}|_q}|_q = \prod_{i=1}^{n} |g^{||x_i \frac{q_i}{q}|_{q_i} \times \frac{q}{q_i}|_q}|_q$, where $\frac{q_i}{q}$ is the multiplicative inverse of $\frac{q}{q_i}$ on q_i. Due to $\frac{q}{q_i} \cdot \frac{q_i}{q} = 1 \bmod q_i$, $\frac{q}{q_i} \cdot \frac{q_j}{q} = 0 \bmod q_i, i \neq j$,

$$|g^x|_q \bmod q_i = |g^{||x_i \frac{q_i}{q}|_{q_i} \times \frac{q}{q_i}|_q}|_q = g^{x_i} \bmod q_i = g_i^{x_i} \bmod q_i.$$

Therefore, the RNS form of g^x is $(|g_1^{x_1}|_{q_1}, \cdots, |g_\ell^{x_\ell}|_{q_\ell})$. □

Lemma 4. *Let n be positive integer and q be prime, $\mathcal{R}_q = \mathbb{Z}_q[X]/(X^n + 1)$. On $\mathcal{D} = \{c \in \mathcal{R}_q[Y] : \deg_X(c) < n, \deg_Y(c) \leq 1\}$, for all $c, c' \in \mathcal{D}$, the probability of a collision $\Pr[c \neq c' \wedge \mathtt{H}(c) = \mathtt{H}(c')] \leq (\frac{n^2+qn+2}{q^2} - \frac{(n-1)^3}{q^3})^2$.*

Proof. If $\mathtt{H}(c) = \mathtt{H}(c')$, then $g^{\hat{H}_{\alpha,\beta}(c)} = g^{\hat{H}_{\alpha,\beta}(c)} \wedge h^{\hat{H}_{\alpha,\beta}(c')} = h^{\hat{H}_{\alpha,\beta}(c')}$. Let $\Delta = c - c' \in \mathcal{R}_q[Y]$. Then, Δ is a non-zero polynomial of degree less than n in X and degree at most 1 in Y. Let α, β be random in $\mathbb{Z}_q$. Every collison is either $\Delta(x, \beta) = 0$ or $\Delta(x, \beta) \neq 0 \wedge \Delta(\alpha, \beta) = 0$. In the first case, assuming $\Delta(x, \beta) = a_1(x)\beta + a_0(x) = 0$. If $a_1(x) = 0 \wedge a_0(x) = 0$, then we have $\Delta(x, \beta)$ must be equal to zero for all $\beta \in \mathbb{Z}_q$. The probability is at most $\frac{n-1}{q} \times \frac{n-1}{q}$. If $a_1(x) \neq 0$, then we have $\beta = -\frac{a_0(x)}{a_1(x)} \in \mathbb{Z}_q$. The probability that β has a solution is at most $(1 - \frac{n-1}{q}) \times \frac{1}{q}$. In the second case, the probability that $\Delta(x, \beta)$ is not equal to zero is at most $1 - \frac{n-1}{q} \times \frac{n-1}{q} - (1 - \frac{n-1}{q} \times \frac{1}{q}) \times \frac{1}{q}$ and the probability that α has a solution is at most $\frac{n-1}{q}$. So we conclude that the the probability

$$\begin{aligned}\Pr[\mathtt{H}(c) = \mathtt{H}(c') \wedge \Delta \neq 0] &= \Pr[\Delta(x, \beta) = 0] + \Pr[\Delta(\alpha, \beta) = 0 | \Delta(x, \beta) \neq 0] \\ &\leq (\frac{n^2 + qn + 2}{q^2} - \frac{(n-1)^3}{q^3})^2.\end{aligned}$$

□

References

1. Abadi, A., Terzis, S., Dong, C.: VD-PSI: verifiable delegated private set intersection on outsourced private datasets. In: Grossklags, J., Preneel, B. (eds.) FC 2016. LNCS, vol. 9603, pp. 149–168. Springer, Heidelberg (2017). https://doi.org/10.1007/978-3-662-54970-4_9
2. Armknecht, F., et al.: A guide to fully homomorphic encryption. IACR Cryptology ePrint Archive, p. 1192 (2015)
3. Bajard, J.-C., Eynard, J., Hasan, M.A., Zucca, V.: A full RNS variant of FV like somewhat homomorphic encryption schemes. In: Avanzi, R., Heys, H. (eds.) SAC 2016. LNCS, vol. 10532, pp. 423–442. Springer, Cham (2017). https://doi.org/10.1007/978-3-319-69453-5_23
4. Bos, J.W., Lauter, K., Loftus, J., Naehrig, M.: Improved security for a ring-based fully homomorphic encryption scheme. In: Stam, M. (ed.) IMACC 2013. LNCS, vol. 8308, pp. 45–64. Springer, Heidelberg (2013). https://doi.org/10.1007/978-3-642-45239-0_4
5. Brakerski, Z., Gentry, C., Vaikuntanathan, V.: (Leveled) fully homomorphic encryption without bootstrapping. ACM Trans. Comput. Theory **6**(3), 13:1–13:36 (2014)
6. Brakerski, Z., Vaikuntanathan, V.: Efficient fully homomorphic encryption from (standard) LWE. SIAM J. Comput. **43**(2), 831–871 (2014)
7. Brickell, J., Porter, D.E., Shmatikov, V., Witchel, E.: Privacy-preserving remote diagnostics. In: CCS 2007, pp. 498–507. ACM (2007)
8. Canetti, R.: Universally composable security: a new paradigm for cryptographic protocols. In: FOCS 2001, pp. 136–145. IEEE Computer Society (2001)
9. Chen, H., Dai, W., Kim, M., Song, Y.: Efficient multi-key homomorphic encryption with packed ciphertexts with application to oblivious neural network inference. In: CCS 2019, pp. 395–412. ACM (2019)
10. Chen, H., Huang, Z., Laine, K., Rindal, P.: Labeled PSI from fully homomorphic encryption with malicious security. In: CCS 2018, pp. 1223–1237. ACM (2018)
11. Chen, H., Laine, K., Rindal, P.: Fast private set intersection from homomorphic encryption. In: CCS 2017, pp. 1243–1255. ACM (2017)
12. Demmler, D., Rindal, P., Rosulek, M., Trieu, N.: PIR-PSI: scaling private contact discovery. Proc. Priv. Enhancing Technol. **2018**(4), 159–178 (2018)
13. Dong, C., Chen, L., Wen, Z.: When private set intersection meets big data: an efficient and scalable protocol. In: CCS 2013, pp. 789–800. ACM (2013)
14. Fan, J., Vercauteren, F.: Somewhat practical fully homomorphic encryption. Cryptology ePrint Archive, p. 144 (2012)

15. Fiore, D., Gennaro, R., Pastro, V.: Efficiently verifiable computation on encrypted data. In: Proceedings of the 2014 ACM SIGSAC Conference on Computer and Communications Security, pp. 844–855. ACM (2014)
16. Freedman, M.J., Nissim, K., Pinkas, B.: Efficient private matching and set intersection. In: Cachin, C., Camenisch, J.L. (eds.) EUROCRYPT 2004. LNCS, vol. 3027, pp. 1–19. Springer, Heidelberg (2004). https://doi.org/10.1007/978-3-540-24676-3_1
17. Gentry, C.: Fully homomorphic encryption using ideal lattices. In: STOC 2009, pp. 169–178. ACM (2009)
18. Gentry, C., Halevi, S., Smart, N.P.: Homomorphic evaluation of the AES circuit. In: Safavi-Naini, R., Canetti, R. (eds.) CRYPTO 2012. LNCS, vol. 7417, pp. 850–867. Springer, Heidelberg (2012). https://doi.org/10.1007/978-3-642-32009-5_49
19. Gentry, C., Sahai, A., Waters, B.: Homomorphic encryption from learning with errors: conceptually-simpler, asymptotically-faster, attribute-based. In: Canetti, R., Garay, J.A. (eds.) CRYPTO 2013. LNCS, vol. 8042, pp. 75–92. Springer, Heidelberg (2013). https://doi.org/10.1007/978-3-642-40041-4_5
20. Gilad-Bachrach, R., Dowlin, N., Laine, K., Lauter, K.E., Naehrig, M., Wernsing, J.: CryptoNets: applying neural networks to encrypted data with high throughput and accuracy. In: ICML 2016, pp. 201–210. JMLR.org (2016)
21. Hazay, C., Lindell, Y.: Efficient protocols for set intersection and pattern matching with security against malicious and covert adversaries. In: Canetti, R. (ed.) TCC 2008. LNCS, vol. 4948, pp. 155–175. Springer, Heidelberg (2008). https://doi.org/10.1007/978-3-540-78524-8_10
22. Jarecki, S., Liu, X.: Fast secure computation of set intersection. In: Garay, J.A., De Prisco, R. (eds.) SCN 2010. LNCS, vol. 6280, pp. 418–435. Springer, Heidelberg (2010). https://doi.org/10.1007/978-3-642-15317-4_26
23. Kamara, S., Mohassel, P., Raykova, M., Sadeghian, S.: Scaling private set intersection to billion-element sets. In: Christin, N., Safavi-Naini, R. (eds.) FC 2014. LNCS, vol. 8437, pp. 195–215. Springer, Heidelberg (2014). https://doi.org/10.1007/978-3-662-45472-5_13
24. Kerschbaum, F.: Outsourced private set intersection using homomorphic encryption. In: ASIACCS 2012, pp. 85–86. ACM (2012)
25. Kiss, Á., Liu, J., Schneider, T., Asokan, N., Pinkas, B.: Private set intersection for unequal set sizes with mobile applications. Proc. Priv. Enhancing Technol. **2017**(4), 177–197 (2017)
26. Li, J., Liu, Y., Wu, S.: Pipa: privacy-preserving password checkup via homomorphic encryption. In: ASIA CCS 2021, pp. 242–251. ACM (2021)
27. Marlinspike, M.: The difficulty of private contact discovery (2014). https://whispersystems.org/blog/contact-discovery. A company sponsored blog post
28. Mayer, D.A., Wetzel, S.: Verifiable private equality test: enabling unbiased 2-party reconciliation on ordered sets in the malicious model. In: ASIACCS 2012, pp. 46–47. ACM (2012)
29. Mezzour, G., Perrig, A., Gligor, V., Papadimitratos, P.: Privacy-preserving relationship path discovery in social networks. In: Garay, J.A., Miyaji, A., Otsuka, A. (eds.) CANS 2009. LNCS, vol. 5888, pp. 189–208. Springer, Heidelberg (2009). https://doi.org/10.1007/978-3-642-10433-6_13
30. Orrù, M., Orsini, E., Scholl, P.: Actively secure 1-out-of-N OT extension with application to private set intersection. In: Handschuh, H. (ed.) CT-RSA 2017. LNCS, vol. 10159, pp. 381–396. Springer, Cham (2017). https://doi.org/10.1007/978-3-319-52153-4_22

31. Parno, B., Raykova, M., Vaikuntanathan, V.: How to delegate and verify in public: verifiable computation from attribute-based encryption. In: Cramer, R. (ed.) TCC 2012. LNCS, vol. 7194, pp. 422–439. Springer, Heidelberg (2012). https://doi.org/10.1007/978-3-642-28914-9_24
32. Pinkas, B., Schneider, T., Segev, G., Zohner, M.: Phasing: private set intersection using permutation-based hashing. In: USENIX Security Symposium 2015, pp. 515–530. USENIX Association (2015)
33. Pinkas, B., Schneider, T., Weinert, C., Wieder, U.: Efficient circuit-based PSI via cuckoo hashing. In: Nielsen, J.B., Rijmen, V. (eds.) EUROCRYPT 2018. LNCS, vol. 10822, pp. 125–157. Springer, Cham (2018). https://doi.org/10.1007/978-3-319-78372-7_5
34. Pinkas, B., Schneider, T., Zohner, M.: Faster private set intersection based on OT extension. In: USENIX Security Symposium 2014, pp. 797–812. USENIX Association (2014)
35. Resende, A.C.D., Aranha, D.F.: Faster unbalanced private set intersection. In: Meiklejohn, S., Sako, K. (eds.) FC 2018. LNCS, vol. 10957, pp. 203–221. Springer, Heidelberg (2018). https://doi.org/10.1007/978-3-662-58387-6_11
36. Rindal, P., Rosulek, M.: Malicious-secure private set intersection via dual execution. In: CCS 2017, pp. 1229–1242. ACM (2017)
37. Microsoft SEAL (release 3.6) (2020). https://github.com/Microsoft/SEAL. Microsoft Research, Redmond, WA
38. Troncoso-Pastoriza, J.R., Katzenbeisser, S., Celik, M.U.: Privacy preserving error resilient DNA searching through oblivious automata. In: CCS 2007, pp. 519–528. ACM (2007)

Secure Asynchronous Federated Learning for Edge Computing Devices

Dayu Cao[1,2](✉), Yinghui Zhang[1,2], Wei Liu[1,2], and Xuanni Wei[1,2]

[1] School of Cyberspace Security, Xi'an University of Posts and Telecommunications, Xi'an 710121, China
c17509999962@163.com

[2] National Engineering Laboratory for Wireless Security, Xi'an University of Posts and Telecommunications, Xi'an 710121, China

Abstract. Federated learning (FL) solves the problem of isolated data islands and improves machine learning models by training on large amounts of data collected from multiple parties. However, the traditional synchronous FL training method will lead to the problem of laggards due to the insufficient computing power of some edge computing devices, which in turn affects the accuracy of training and increases communication overhead. Asynchronous federated learning solves the training problem of traditional FL very well. However, traditional privacy-preserving methods for FL are not suitable for asynchronous federated learning, existing asynchronous training schemes cannot guarantee the privacy of data. Faced with this challenge, this paper proposes a weighted secure asynchronous federated learning scheme, WASecAgg, which can ensure training accuracy and data privacy on the premise of guaranteeing the training efficiency of federated learning. The final experiments show that WASecAgg performs better in terms of training efficiency, training accuracy and privacy-preserving of federated learning.

Keywords: Federated learning · Privacy preserving · Edge computing · Asynchronous algorithms

1 Introduction

Federated machine learning, also known as federated learning, is a machine learning framework that can support multiple institutions conducting data usage and machine learning modeling effectively while ensuring clients' privacy, data security, and government regulations. Different from traditional deep learning, federated learning mainly emphasizes the concept of "federation", that is, data can be exchanged and processed jointly between various parties, so as to improve learning efficiency and data flexibility.

The training of federated learning requires massive data obtained from clients, but clients may be reluctant to share their own data, because this data

X. Chen et al. (Eds.): SocialSec 2022, CCIS 1663, pp. 138–147, 2022.
https://doi.org/10.1007/978-981-19-7242-3_9

may contain personal privacy or sensitive information. Although the later federated learning can be trained without collecting the clients' original information, [1] pointed out that the training method in which the clients only upload the gradients to achieve the model update may still reveal private information. Therefore, privacy preservation is still an important part of federated learning.

In addition, an important parameter in federated learning is concurrency: the number of concurrently trained clients (sometimes referred to as clients per round). In synchronous federated learning, the optimal learning rate tends to increase with concurrency because higher concurrency reduces the number of epochs required to reach the target accuracy. However, in order to obtain stable and convergent training dynamics, the learning rate cannot be increased indefinitely, because the final model will saturate, resulting in a sub-linear acceleration of the learning rate, so traditional synchronous federated learning cannot achieve high concurrency.

Although most work in federated learning has focused on synchronous training because this training method is easier to analyze and debug, and more suitable for privacy, this method is easy to lead to the problem of laggards due to insufficient computing power of laggard clients. The laggards participate in the training at the slowest speed, and a round of aggregation in synchronous training must wait for all participating clients to complete local updates, which is the laggard problem of synchronous training.

On the contrary, in asynchronous federated learning, in each iteration as long as the client sends input to the server, the server performs the update, so it can be updated directly without waiting for the laggards, which greatly improves the efficiency and concurrency of learning [2]. However, due to the characteristics of asynchronous learning, it is not compatible with secure aggregation protocol, so it is difficult to ensure data privacy and data security in asynchronous training as that in synchronous training.

In this paper, we try to solve the above problems. We propose a scheme suitable for asynchronous federated learning, which can also ensure the privacy of clients' data and improve the concurrency of learning. We demonstrate the feasibility of the scheme through simulation experiments.

Our Contribution. An asynchronous federated training scheme with weights is proposed to improve the training efficiency, and we attach the number of samples and the staleness of each client as a weight in the training process so that the training can reach the required accuracy faster; An asynchronous federated learning scheme compatible with secure aggregation is proposed, which not only ensures that the training can continue after the participants are disconnected but also ensures the privacy of the training data and the privacy of the dropped clients.

2 Framework

In this section, we first describe the details of asynchronous federated learning. Then we give a framework of our system model.

2.1 System Environment

Mobile terminals and edge computing devices are equipped with multi-core CPUs, graphics processing units (GPUs), and more hardwares. These devices vary in computing power, storage and memory capacity, so clients with these devices typically do not perform synchronously when updating locally. Most of the current local updates are performed when the device is in an idle state (such as when the client is charging the device). In this scenario, the problem of laggards in synchronous training will be particularly prominent, because the clients cannot guarantee that they are all at the same time, which is not realistic.The best way to achieve this asynchrony is to send clients' local model to a cluster of queues and then wait for the server to aggregate and update.

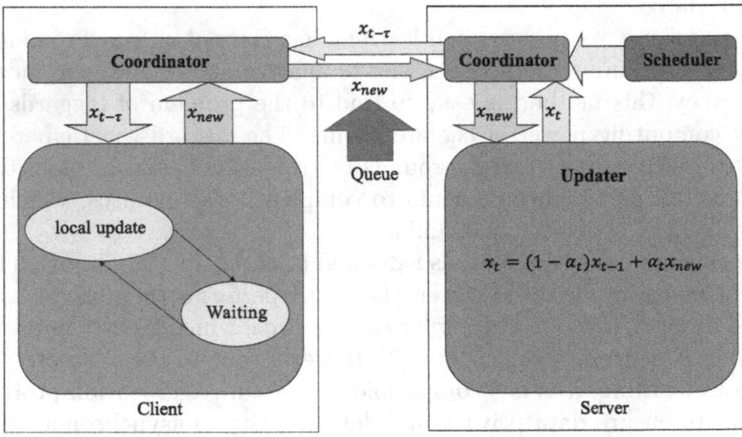

Fig. 1. Details of asynchronous federated learning

As shown in Fig. 1, on the server side, asynchronous federated learning has two threads running asynchronously in parallel: the scheduler and the updater. In the $t - \tau$ global epoch, the server receives the client's local updated model and then updates the global model as $x_t = (1 - \alpha_t)x_{t-1} + \alpha_t x_{new}$. Since greater staleness leads to greater errors in updating the global model, α is reduced to mitigate the error caused by staleness and $\alpha_t = \alpha \times \sigma(t - \tau)$. The staleness coefficient $\sigma(t - \tau)$ is a monotonically decreasing function that accounts for the staleness of the global model. The stale candidate functions (parameterized by a,b>0) proposed in [2] are as follows:

$$\text{Liner: } \sigma_a(t-\tau) = \frac{1}{a(t-\tau)+1} \quad (1)$$

$$\text{Polynomial: } \sigma_a(t-\tau) = (t-\tau+1)^{-a} \quad (2)$$

$$\text{Exponential: } \sigma_a(t-\tau) = \exp(-a(t-\tau)) \quad (3)$$

$$\text{Hinge: } \sigma_{a,b}(t-\tau) = \begin{cases} 1 & \text{if } t-\tau \leq b \\ \frac{1}{a(t-\tau-b)+1} & \text{otherwise} \end{cases} \quad (4)$$

The simulation experiment in this paper uses a polynomial decay function as [2].

2.2 Aggregation

To further improve the efficiency of each round of training, our system model introduces a **weighting system** during the training process. The weights are determined by the number of samples held by clients participating in the training and how stale their local models are. The more samples clients held, the lower the staleness degree of the local model, the more influence its local model has on the global model, and the more proportion it finally takes in the global model. Besides, although the dropout problem in asynchronous federation learning has little influence on its training effect, in our scheme, in order to ensure the correct output of the server in secure aggregation, we still need to use the mask to encrypt the data, but the data here is the original data multiplied by the weight. Each client exposes the number of samples held, which is used to update the global model when the server evaluates the weighted average model as the sum of all the samples needed.

In asynchronous training, we aggregate the clients in the sequence like [3], [4], as long as the number of clients in the sequence reaches the limit, the server perform aggregation on these clients and refresh the sequence. During this process, we use the scheduler to update the operations of the clients and server, and the coordinator to tell clients whether to wait for the server to perform aggregations or to do local updates.

To facilitate understanding of the aggregation, we introduce some cryptographic primitives used in our WASecAgg.

Pseudorandom Generator. We need a secure Pseudorandom Generator [5], [6] that takes a uniform random seed of fixed length to generate a string of fixed length, and as long as the seed is hidden from the discriminator, the random seed cannot be distinguished from the evenly sampled elements in the output space in computation, that is, the adversary cannot distinguish the output characters from other random strings.

Secret Sharing. We adopt Shamir's t-out-of-n Secret Sharing [7], which allows clients to divide a secret s into n sub-secrets, such that any t sub-secrets can recover s, but any sub-secrets with less than t parts cannot recover s. Secret generation is defined as $\boldsymbol{S.share}\,(s,t,\mathcal{U}) \rightarrow (n, S_n)_{n\in\mathcal{U}}$, it will divide the secret s into n sub-secrets corresponding to n clients, where $\mathcal{U}$ represents the set of clients' IDs and $t \leq |\mathcal{U}|$. Secret recovery is defined as $\boldsymbol{S.recon}\left((n, S_n)_{n\in M}, t\right) \rightarrow s$, it will recover the secret s, where $n \in M \subseteq \mathcal{U}$ and $t \leq |M|$.

Key Agreement. We use Diffie-Hellman key agreement [8] to create a session key between any two clients. Specifically, the parameters are first generated as $\boldsymbol{KA.param}(k) \rightarrow (G, g, q, H)$, where G is the q-order prime number group, g is the generator of G, and H is the hash function. Then the private key and public key of each client a are defined as $\boldsymbol{KA.gen}\,(G, g, q, H) \rightarrow \left(SK_a, g^{SK_a}\right)$, SK_a is randomly selected from Z_q, SK_a and g^{SK_a} are its private key and public key, respectively. Finally, for a given client b's public key g^{SK_b}, the session key between client a and client b is defined as $\boldsymbol{KA.agree}\left(SK_a, g^{SK_b}\right) \rightarrow s_{a,b}$. In practical application, we take $S_{a,b} = H\left(g^{SK_b^{SK_a}}\right)$.

Authenticated Encryption. We use symmetric encryption for authenticated encryption and the negotiated key as the session key, which can ensure confidentiality and integrity in the process of message transmission between two parties. It includes three algorithms: key generation algorithm, encryption algorithm and decryption algorithm. The key generation algorithm is to generate the *key* for key negotiation; Encryption algorithm is defined as $\boldsymbol{AE.enc}\,(key, x) \rightarrow ciphertext$. And the decryption algorithm is defined as $\boldsymbol{AE.dec}\,(key, ciphertext) \rightarrow x$ or $\perp$. If decrypted correctly, there is $\boldsymbol{AE.dec}\,(key, \boldsymbol{AE.enc}(key, x)) = x$.

Signature. The signature scheme consists of three algorithms: $\boldsymbol{SIG.gen}(k) \rightarrow (d^{PK}, d^{SK})$, used to generate a public-private key pair; $\boldsymbol{SIG.sign}\left(d^{SK}, m\right) \rightarrow \sigma$, indicating that the message m is signed with the private key; $\boldsymbol{SIG.ver}\left(d^{PK}, m, \sigma\right) \rightarrow 0, 1$, verifies the signature through the public key, and compares it with the original message m to determine whether the verification passes.

Double-Masking Protocol. We adopt the double-mask mechanism of [9] to ensure privacy while solving the problem of clients' dropout. Each client a randomly samples a seed β_a in the same round of generating the session key $S_{a,b}$. During secret sharing, the client also generates a sub-secret of β_a and distributes it to every other clients. When finally uploading data to the server, the client adds a mask in the following way to ensure data privacy:

$$y_a = n_a \cdot \alpha_t^{(a)} \cdot x_a + \mathbf{PRG}(\beta_a) + \sum_{b\in\mathcal{U}:a<b} \mathbf{PRG}(s_{a,b}) - \sum_{b\in\mathcal{U}:a>b} \mathbf{PRG}(s_{b,a})(\bmod R)$$

, where n_a is the number of samples of client a, $\alpha_t^{(a)}$ is the staleness coefficient of client a at time t. It should be noted that the staleness coefficient here is based on time that the client participated in the aggregation, while the staleness coefficient used for server global updates is based on the number of epoch rounds.

In this protocol, all clients share the key by secret sharing, and use authentication encryption to ensure that only clients can decrypt each other. When one client drops, the rest of the clients can recover the privacy vector to offset the server's double mask during aggregation. The output of this protocol is a weighted aggregation model. Note that when the output is obtained, the server does not know the real information uploaded by the client, but only the aggregated data.

If the server receives a model that is too lagging, it can choose to discard the model, because the model that is too lagging has little effect on the global model. The clients participate in secure aggregation and perform local updates asynchronously to the server performing global model updates. As long as the number of clients in the queue reaches the upper limit, the aggregation will be performed. And the coordinator can still continue to arrange the clients for the next update.

After the server outputs the aggregation results, the total number of samples is obtained according to the final clients participating in the aggregation. According to the federated average algorithm [10], divide the aggregated data by the total number of samples, the server completes the update and gets a new model, which realizes the weighted average. Then the server perform the global update as shown in Fig. 1. The server then broadcasts the global model. Each client updates their own model after receiving the new global model, and then sends the model to the server according to the above aggregation scheme, and iterates this process until the model converges and the training is completed.

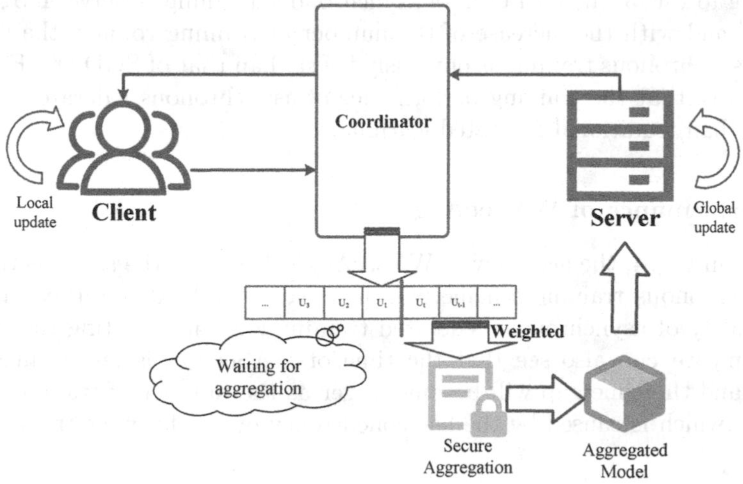

Fig. 2. WASecAgg system model

As shown in Fig. 2, the server and the clients have their own coordinators to coordinate the operations of the two parties during the training process. If some clients are slow to update locally and upload data correspondingly because the device was heterogeneous with other clients, the next client who has completed the local update can directly join this training. At this time, the server can perform aggregation. These heterogeneous clients can join a new round of aggregation at any time after completing the local update. In the case that the heterogeneous client is behind, the whole training will not fall into the waiting state, because the aggregation and the local update of the clients are asynchronous.

3 Performance Evaluation

We conduct experiments following the settings in the [11] benchmark. In our experiment, there are 1000 clients with non-IID data distribution by default, and the MNIST data set is used for training and test. Due to the distributed nature of federated learning, the newly generated model is used to evaluate the accuracy of the scheme after each round of aggregation.

We also compare the computational load under synchronous and asynchronous training scenarios. As in [12], in order to evaluate the computational load, we compare the number of GigaFLOPS(GFLOPS) performed in the entire client system under different conditions.

In our experiment, we default batch size to 10, polynomial discount function $\alpha = 0.5$, and learning rate $\eta = 0.01$.

3.1 Performance of Asynchronous Training

According to Fig. 3, the GFLOPS of asynchronous training is between SGD and FedAVG, and with the increase of the number of training rounds, the training time of asynchronous training is obviously lower than that of SGD and FedAVG, which proves that the training performance of asynchronous federated learning is better than traditional federated learning.

3.2 Performance of WASecAgg

As shown in Fig. 4, the accuracy of WASecAgg is basically the same as the original asynchronous training scheme, which proves that WASecAgg can guarantee the safety of asynchronous federated training without affecting the training effect. And we can also see that the time of WASecAgg is less than that in SecAgg, and the time gap will become larger as the number of training rounds increases, which is caused by the low concurrency of synchronous training.

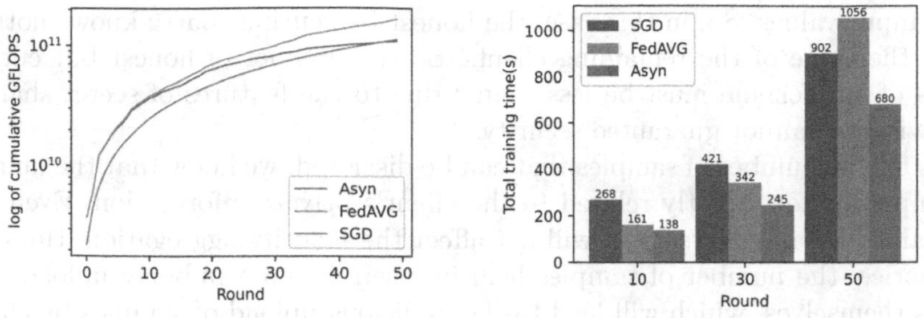

(a) (b)

Fig. 3. Performance comparison between synchronous and asynchronous training.

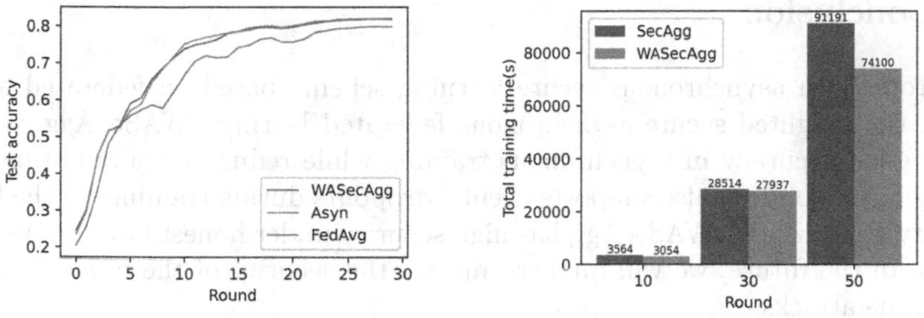

(a) (b)

Fig. 4. Performance comparison between WASecAgg and traditional federated training.

4 Security Analysis

The security of WASecAgg under honest-but-curious conditions, where the server can collude with up to t-1 clients but can't get any information rather than the aggregated values and the number of samples in our threat model. In this paper, the view of any party is defined as its private messages (including its input and nonce) and all messages received from other parties. Note that when a party drops at some point, that party will immediately stop receiving messages.

According to [9], a joint view of a subset of any (excluding servers) honest clients can be modeled with the input of these clients, which means that these clients cannot know anything other than their own input. In addition, for a probabilistic polynomial-time simulator, given clients' input, the simulator can simulate any honest but curious clients and sever, and can only simulate the sum of the input values of the remaining clients, which means that these clients and the server are only aware of their own input and the sum of the input of other clients.

Furthermore, if too many clients dropped before decoding, then we can simulate the view of an honest but curious party without providing the remaining client input values. So, in this case, the honest but curious party knows nothing about the value of the remaining clients. So the number of honest but curious clients of our scheme must be less than t due to the features of secret sharing, otherwise we cannot guarantee security.

As for the number of samples that can be disclosed, we know that the number of samples is not directly related to the client's private information. Even if it is obtained by an adversary, it will not affect the security aggregation. However, in practice, the number of samples held by users is often publicly uploaded by clients themselves, which will lead to the malicious upload of samples by clients with active attacks, thus changing their weight value, and thus interfering with the training process. We will solve this problem in the future.

5 Conclusion

We propose an asynchronous secure learning scheme based on federated averaging, the weighted secure asynchronous federated learning WASecAgg, which shows good accuracy in asynchronous training while reducing training time. In addition, the solution also supports clients' dropouts during training. In the final security analysis, our WASecAgg has high security under honest but curious scenarios. In the future, we will further improve the security of the model against Byzantine attacks.

Acknowledgement. This work is supported by the National Natural Science Foundation of China (No. 62072369, 62072371) and the Graduate Innovation Foundation of Xi'an University of Posts and Telecommunications(No.CXJJZL2021025).

References

1. Chai, D., Wang, L., Chen, K., Yang, Q.: Secure federated matrix factorization. IEEE Intell. Syst. **36**(5), 11–20 (2020)
2. Xie, C., Koyejo, S., Gupta, I.: Asynchronous federated optimization. arXiv preprint arXiv:1903.03934 (2019)
3. Nguyen, J., et al.: Federated learning with buffered asynchronous aggregation. arXiv preprint arXiv:2106.06639 (2021)
4. So, J., Ali, R.E., Güler, B., Avestimehr, A.S.: Secure aggregation for buffered asynchronous federated learning. arXiv preprint arXiv:2110.02177 (2021)
5. Blum, M., Micali, S.: How to generate cryptographically strong sequences of pseudorandom bits. SIAM J. Comput. **13**(4), 850–864 (1984)
6. Yao, A.C.: Theory and application of trapdoor functions. In: 23rd Annual Symposium on Foundations of Computer Science (SFCS 1982), pp. 80–91. IEEE (1982)
7. Shamir, A.: How to share a secret. Commun. ACM **22**(11), 612–613 (1979)
8. Diffie, W., Hellman, M.E.: New directions in cryptography. In: Secure Communications and Asymmetric Cryptosystems, pp. 143–180. Routledge (2019)
9. Bonawitz, K., et al.: Practical secure aggregation for privacy-preserving machine learning. In: Proceedings of the 2017 ACM SIGSAC Conference on Computer and Communications Security, pp. 1175–1191 (2017)

10. McMahan, B., Moore, E., Ramage, D., Hampson, S., y Arcas, B.A.: Communication-efficient learning of deep networks from decentralized data. In: Artificial intelligence and statistics, pp. 1273–1282. PMLR (2017)
11. Caldas, S., et al.: Leaf: a benchmark for federated settings. arXiv preprint arXiv:1812.01097 (2018)
12. Jin, H., Yan, N., Mortazavi, M.: Simulating aggregation algorithms for empirical verification of resilient and adaptive federated learning. In: 2020 IEEE/ACM International Conference on Big Data Computing, Applications and Technologies (BDCAT), pp. 124–133. IEEE (2020)

FedBC: An Efficient and Privacy-Preserving Federated Consensus Scheme

Mengfan Xu[1(✉)] and Xinghua Li[2]

[1] School of Computer Science, Shaanxi Normal University, Xi'an, China
cybersecurityxu@snnu.edu.cn

[2] School of Cyber Engineering, Xidian University, Xi'an, China
xhli1@mail.xidian.edu.cn

Abstract. The capacity of federated learning (FL) to tackle the issue of "Data Island" while maintaining data privacy has garnered significant attention. Nonetheless, semi-trusted cloud platforms can infer the actual data distribution of local users via intermediate characteristics such as gradients. The blockchain proposal has resolved the challenge of consistency in decentralized data sharing. It is difficult to guarantee the accuracy of the block's data based on the existing study. To address this issue, we present a federated consensus mechanism that is both efficient and protective of privacy (FedBC). This approach can effectively limit the impact of Byzantine nodes on consistency and accuracy. During this procedure, crucial intermediate parameters, such as the gradient of the data owner, will not leak. Specifically, we proposed a gradient-similarity-based secure consensus technique (*Sec*PBFT) to minimize Byzantine gradients. All nodes transmit the DO sub-gradients during each consensus round and cluster and partition the sub-gradients in the consensus with care. Then, the dynamic elimination of Byzantine gradients in each round of the consensus procedure is accomplished. Theoretically, we demonstrated the scheme's security and confirmed the scheme's efficacy. FedBC's attack success rate is at least 50% lower than if no defense mechanisms were in place.

Keywords: Blockchain · Federated learning · Privacy-preserving · Poisoning attacks

1 Introduction

Simply transmitting data for traditional distributed machine learning to train models would be viewed as illegal with the repeated proclamation and implementation of legislation and regulations relating to personal privacy protection in recent years [7]. Fortunately, Google prospectively proposed the federated learning (FL) framework in 2016 [1]. Under the presumption of legal compliance, the FL can safeguard personal data privacy while facilitating effective machine learning across numerous participants. Particularly, a single user can only fit a

X. Chen et al. (Eds.): SocialSec 2022, CCIS 1663, pp. 148–162, 2022.
https://doi.org/10.1007/978-981-19-7242-3_10

small portion of the real data distribution because they have a finite amount of data. The global model's performance will be significantly better than the model trained by a single user, which is learned by combining various local data. As a result, the "Data Island" issue, which is brought on by the challenges associated with data sharing (such as building user trust and facilitating communication), can be resolved. Local users just need to submit intermediate parameters, like gradients, to the cloud platform for aggregation throughout this process instead of raw data. FL can thus also realize the preservation of local data's privacy. However, it's typically challenging to obtain a truly reliable cloud platform. An honest aggregation of the global model by a semi-trusted cloud platform has been demonstrated by current research, but it has also been demonstrated that a semi-trusted cloud platform may be inferred from intermediate parameters like gradients. Even the final global model will be modified by malicious cloud platforms to target a single user [5,22,23]. For instance, semi-trusted nucleic acid testing companies can use salivary data to further examine a user's health state during the COVID-19 pandemic. Additionally, unscrupulous testing companies may alter with nucleic acid results to stir up fear or postpone the prevention of epidemics.

A concept for a decentralized trust architecture is provided by the blockchain technology that Satoshi Nakamoto suggested in 2008 [9,12]. Many nations have labeled the blockchain industry as a "Sunset Industry" due to the resource waste associated with the physical resource proof (PoW, PoC, PoSt) [3,13,18] consensus protocol. Only virtual currencies like BTC and ETH 1.0 continue to use this type of consensus process as of right now [19–21]. The blockchain technology has advanced quickly, making Casper [2], PBFT [15], Raft [11], and consensus protocol more energy-efficient. Compared to Casper, which needs equity support, the Raft consensus protocol is more flexible. In contrast to Raft, the PBFT consensus algorithm can withstand Byzantine node attacks even when its communication complexity rises to $O(n^2)$.

The consistency issue of on-chain data in the blockchain system can be successfully resolved by the aforementioned consensus protocols. They do not, however, take into account the accuracy of the data that is on-chain. The block contains errors or intentionally contaminated data. The current consensus protocols, in particular, ignore the accuracy of the on-chain data itself in favor of conducting efficient and regular research on it. For instance, after the consensus process has been completed, the client submits a bill to a blockchain network with the message "$1 + 1 = 3$". The master node (leader) of the current consensus mechanism only concerns if there are more secondary nodes (followers) than the required number to confirm receipt of the message "$1 + 1 = 3$". The truth of the statement "$1 + 1 = 3$" is disregarded. Lower weights may be given to parameters with less resemblance in the centralized FL architecture when they are compared to the benign benchmark parameters offered by the cloud platform. In decentralized FL, it might be challenging to find neutral benchmark criteria for comparison. By comparing parameters with poor resemblance to the benignbench-mark parameters, as seen in Fig. 1, the current FL study on anti-poisoning attacks always provides lower weights to those parameters. However, it is challenging to find neutral benchmark criteria for comparison in decentralized FL. Additionally, recent research has revealed that intermediary parameters like gradients allow attackers to further deduce the true distribution of local data. Therefore, the two key issues facing contemporary decentralized FL research are how to maintain the veracity of on-chain data and how to ensure that the privacy of on-chain data is not compromised.

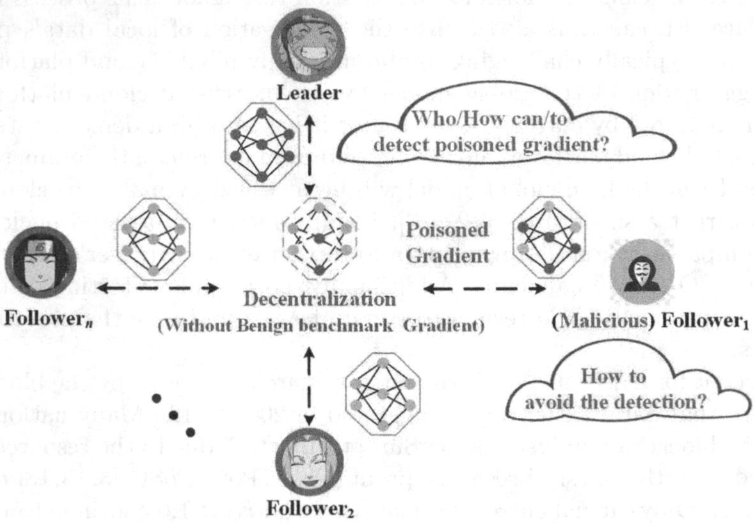

Fig. 1. The challenge arise with decentralization.

To address the above issues, we propose an efficient and privacy-preserving federated consensus approach. This method provides aggregation services without a trusted third party. The correctness of the on-chain gradient are ensured while the gradient privacy of each node is not leaked. The main contributions of our work are as follows.

- We propose FedBC, a federal consensus framework for protecting privacy based on additive homomorphic encryption. Using three rounds of broadcast interaction on ciphertext gradients, the system eliminates the effect of malicious gradients on global model performance. Intermediate critical parameters such as gradients will not leak during this procedure.
- We also present *Sec*PBFT, a secure consensus approach based on gradient similarity. Specifically, gradients in each node are communicated during each consensus round. The gradients are then divided using a safe clustering technique based on DBSCAN to achieve the dynamic eradication of malicious gradients in each round of consensus.
- We demonstrate that the proposed system is secure. In addition, testing on real-world datasets demonstrate that FedBC can effectively withstand Byzantine attacks without benchmarking benign gradients, and its performance is at least 80% better than the scheme without anti-poisoning features.

The remainder of the paper is organized as follows. In Sect. 2, we introduce the related works and compared them with our scheme. Then, we introduce the system and threat model and design goals of this paper in Sect. 3. We introduce the mathematical notation and preliminary material used in this paper in Sect. 4. The design details of our scheme are presented in Sect. 5. Section 6 and Sect. 7 discuss the security and performance analysis. Finally, we conclude the paper in Sect. 8.

2 Related Works

To defense the poisoning attacks, Yin et al. [25] proposed a distributed gradient descent algorithm based on median and coordinate clipped mean, established statistical error rates of strongly convex, non-strongly convex, and non-convex total loss functions, and realized synchronous optimization of gradient statistics and communication efficiency in a distributed environment for the first time. Mhamdi et al. Research [10] proposed a general Byzantine aggregation rule, Bulyan, which can be Brute, Krum, Medoid, geometric median, or any other norm-based or infinite norm-based Byzantine elasticity rule, ensuring that the global gradient is determined by Byzantine Most local gradients selected by elastic aggregation rules are aggregated. Xie et al. [24] proposed a provably robust federated learning framework (CRFL) against backdoor attacks. Aiming at the problem that local users easily resist disturbance in the field during training, the model parameters are clipped and smoothed to control the smoothness of the global model. The model parameters are clipped and interference during training and smoothed during testing to realize the accurate detection of backdoor attacks. However, it has been proved that the attacker can infer the distribution of the original data through gradient information.

Currently, some studies have aimed to protect the privacy of shared gradients while resisting poisoning attacks in federated learning. [16] proposed a privacy-enhanced FL (PEFL) framework that employs homomorphic encryption as the underlying technology to ensure the integrity and availability of the global model and utilizes the Pearson coefficient to measure the similarity between gradients to eliminate abnormal angles. However, if the server in the framework is breached, the key used for encryption will be directly leaked, resulting in the privacy of all intermediate parameters. The ShieldFL [17] framework designs a federated privacy protection scheme based on dual trapdoor servers. It proposes a secure cosine similarity calculation method to measure the distance between two encrypted gradients to eliminate malicious angles during aggregation. This method provides a feasible solution for detecting encrypted harmful tips. This scheme assumes that the two trapdoor servers cannot collude. Once the servers collude, the privacy of local users will be leaked. To reduce the risk of the server due to a breach of privacy issues, Feng et al. [8] propose a decentralized FL framework based on blockchain; it realizes nodes cross-domain authentication through multiple signatures and uses intelligent contract model blockchain polymerization to avoid a centralized server failure problem in the process of polymerization. This scheme can only ensure the credibility of an initial gradient of nodes through signature authentication. Still, it cannot eliminate the local angle shared by malicious nodes during the model update.

In summary, the current research on federated learning privacy protection based on anti-poisoning attacks has made some progress. However, how to ensure the authenticity of on-chain data and ensure that the privacy of on-chain data is not leaked are two main challenge of current decentralized FL researches. The Comparison of the existing works and FedBC in coarse-grained pairs are shown in Table 1.

Table 1. Comparison of the existing works and FedBC

Scheme	PGP	WBG
FL against poisoning attacks [10,25] [26]	✘	✘
PEFL [16]	✔	✘
ShieldFL [17]	✔	✘
BE-DHFL [8]	✔	✘
FedBC	✔	✔

Note: **PGP**: Protect gradient privacy; **WBG**: Without benign gradient. ✘indicates that the challenge was not considered or could not be addressed by the solution.✔ indicates that the solution can not fully address the challenge. ✔means that the solution completely solves the challenge.

3 Problem Formulation

3.1 System Model

In this research, we offer an effective federated consensus system that protects privacy. As depicted in Fig. 2, our proposed system model comprises four (class) entities, including the key generation center (KGC), the Leader, the Follower, and the Data Owner (DO). The function of each (class) entity is outlined below.

- KGC: The KGC is an independent and reputable body that manages and distributes all public and private keys. In this approach, public and private key pairs (pk_c, sk_c) and (pk_d, sk_d) are generated and distributed to the leaders and followers who execute the consensus process and the data source data owners, respectively.
- Leader: The master node gets the aggregate request from the data owner, communicates with the follower to validate the request's consistency via the consensus protocol, and stores the request in the block.
- Follower: The secondary node receives the Leader node's broadcast information, aggregates the obtained gradient data, and eliminates harmful gradients. The final encrypted gradient average output for client verification.
- Data Owner (DO): Different DOs upload the sub-gradients used in the machine learning model training process, the consensus mechanism identifies fraudulent gradients, and multiple iterations of aggregation yield the best overall model.

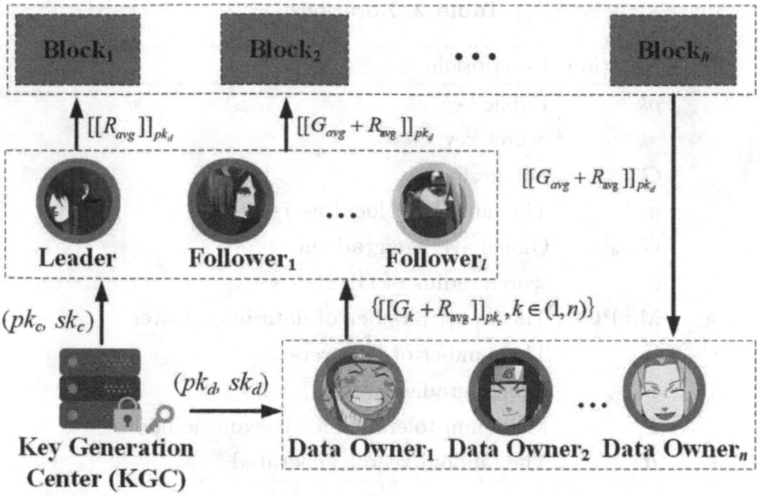

Fig. 2. System model.

3.2 Threat Model

In this approach, the owner of the data achieves the ideal global model by updating the shared sub-gradient iteratively. During this procedure, the data owner does not want any other party to receive the whole sub-gradient. Leaders and followers are viewed as Byzantine nodes, and they engage in malevolent activities such as tampering with gradients that must be aggregated. By uploading fraudulent gradients, the aforementioned Byzantine nodes can affect or even control the global model if they exist in the data owner.

3.3 Design Goals

FedBC has the following two design goals.

- Correctness: This paper must make sure that the accuracy of the global model is within a tolerable range because the byzantine nodes' tampering behavior will cause the global model to be misclassified.
- Security: To prevent byzantine nodes from using gradients to create a complete global model and derive the true distribution of users. Therefore, this paper must make sure that the global model and intermediate parameters, such as gradients uploaded by DO, are kept a secret.

4 Preliminaries

4.1 Notations

All the symbol definitions covered in this article are described in Table 2.

Table 2. Notations.

Notation	Description
pk	Public key
sk	Secret key
G_k	Sub-gradient
n	The number of local users
G_{avg}	Global average gradient
ε	search radius of DBSCAN
MinPts	The lowest number of data in a cluster
l	The number of followers
C_{max}	Benign gradient set
F	Maximum tolerance for Byzantine nodes
R	The random vector generated

4.2 Practical Byzantine Fault Tolerance (PBFT)

This approach prevents harmful behavior from the PBFT consensus protocol-based consensus procedure. Based on the Byzantine Generals dilemma, as depicted in Fig. 3, the consistency assurance of the PBFT algorithm is mostly comprised of the five steps listed below.

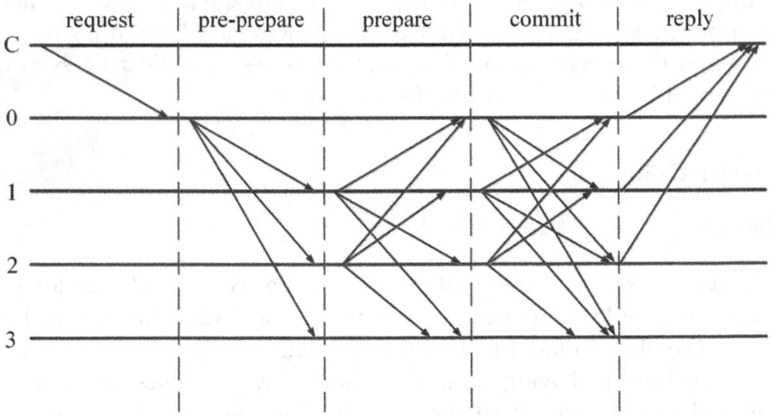

Fig. 3. The process of PBFT.

1. **Request**: The requester C sends a request to the master node 0;
2. **Pre-Prepare**: Node 0 broadcasts request from C and spreads to 123;
3. **Prepare**: Nodes 123 receive it, record it, and then broadcast it again; nodes 1 through 023, 2 through 013, and 3 are unable to transmit owing to downtime;

(this step is to prevent the master node from sending different requests to different slave nodes);
4. **Commit**: Nodes 0123 in the Prepare stage will join the Commit stage and broadcast the Commit request if they get the same request more than a specified number of times ($2F$ in real use, where F is the maximum number of Byzantine nodes that may be tolerated);
5. **Reply**: Node 0123 will provide feedback to C if one of them receives the same request more than a specific number $(2F+1)$ during the commit stage.

The consistency is solvable in the situation of $N \geq 3F+1$, where N is the total number of nodes and F is the number of byzantine nodes, according to the technique described above.

4.3 DBSCAN Algorithm

To get rid of fraudulent gradients uploaded by DO and guarantee the performance of the overall model, this technique develops a safe aggregated gradient consensus process based on the DBSCAN algorithm. The maximum-density connected sample set produced from the density reachability relationship is clustered using the DBSCAN method. This is the precise procedure.

1. Randomly select a data object point p from the data set;
2. If for the parameters ε and MinPts, the selected data object point p is the core point, then find all the data object points density reachable from p to form a cluster;
3. If the selected data object point p is an edge point, select another data object point;
4. Repeat steps (2) and (3) until all points are processed.

Each cluster can have one or more core points [4]. If there is only one core point, other non-core point samples in the cluster are in the ε neighborhood of this core point. If there are multiple core points, there must be one other core point in the ε neighborhood of any core point in the cluster, otherwise the two core points cannot be density reachable. The set of all samples in the ε neighborhood of these core points forms a DBSCAN cluster.

5 Proposed Scheme

In this section, we will introduce FedBC in detail, as shown in Fig. 4, it is mainly divided into two stages: system initialization and model secure consensus. Different from the existing server-based schemes, the proposed scheme needs to use the broadcast process of blockchain consensus mechanism to share gradients. Without benign benchmark gradients, the average gradient is aggregated through multiple iterations of consensus. The consensus mechanism can aggregate the average gradient with the Byzantine nodes.

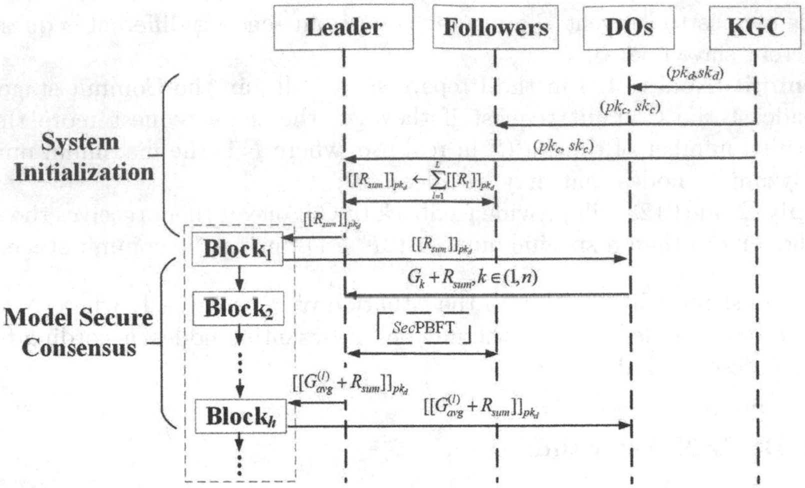

Fig. 4. The process of FedBC.

5.1 System Initialization

KGC uses the Paillier encryption algorithm to generate and issue public/private key pairs (pk_d, sk_d) and (pk_c, sk_c) for data owners, leaders, and followers, respectively. First, Leader and Followers generate random vectors R_L and $\{R_j, j \in [1, l]\}$, respectively, which are encrypted by DO's public key pk_d, and broadcast to each other. Then, each node sums their recived vectors to obtain $[[R_{sum}]]_{pk_d}$ using Paillier's additive homomorphism property. Finally, the consistency is confirmed based on the PBFT protocol, and the leader records it to the new block after confirmation.

5.2 Model Security Consensus

DO first downloads the random vector $[[R_{sum}]]_{pk_d}$ of the ciphertext from the block and decrypts it. After training sub-gradient with local data, it adds the random vector and uploads it to the Leader node, interacts with Followers to eliminate malicious gradients. Specifically,leader node performs the first round broadcast after receiving $\{G_k + R_{sum}, k \in [1, n]\}$ (Pre-Prepare). Then, the Followers who receive $\{G_k + R_{sum}, k \in [1, n]\}$ broadcast the second round to confirm whether the received information is consistent (Prepare). If the received requests exceed a certain number of identical requests, the commit stage is entered. In this stage, in order to further propose malicious gradients, we design the *Sec*PBFT algorithm, whose formalization process is shown as Fig. 5.

First, all sub-gradients are marked as unvisited states, and one gradient is randomly selected as a visited state and classified into cluster C_1. Find the adjacent gradients of $G_k + R_{sum}$ within the ε radius to get the set N. And further select the gradient $G_j + R_{sum}$ in the set N to iterate the above search. Then,

Input: $G_k + R_{sum}, k \in (1, n)$

Output: $[[G_{avg}^{(l)} + R_{sum}]]_{pk_d}$.

Mark all sub-gradients as unvisited

Do

Randomly select an unvisited $G_k + R_{sum}$, and mark $G_k + R_{sum}$ as visited

If the ε neighborhood of $G_k + R_{sum}$ has at least MinPts gradients

  Create a new cluster C_i and add $G_k + R_{sum}$ to C_i

  Let N be the gradients set of ε neighborhood of $G_k + R_{sum}$

  For $(G_j + R_{sum}) \in N$

    If $State_{(G_j + R_{sum})} = unvisited$

      $State_{(G_j + R_{sum})} = visited$

      If the ε neighborhood of $G_j + R_{sum}$ has at least MinPts gradie--nts, add these gradients to N

      If $G_j + R_{sum}$ do not belong to any cluster, then $G_j + R_{sum} \in C_i$

  End for

Else $Label_{G_k + Rsum} = abnormal$

Until $\mathbf{max}|C_i| > \frac{n}{2}$ $i \in (1, I)$ and $|State_{G_k + R_{sum}}| = 0$

Return $C_{\max}^{(l)}$

Calculate $G_{avg}^{(l)} + R_{sum} \xleftarrow{Fedavg} C_{\max}$.

Return $[[G_{avg}^{(l)} + R_{sum}]]_{pk_d}$

Fig. 5. *Sec*PBFT: Malicious model elimination without disclosing DO's privacy.

the potential of all clusters is calculated, the cluster with the largest potential is determined as a benign gradient set, and the average gradient $G_{avg}^{(l)} + R_{sum}C_{\max}$ is calculated, and encrypted to recorded on the block using the public key pk_d. Finally, DO decrypts and eliminates random vectors, and uses $G_{avg}^{(l)}$ to update the global model.

6 Security Analysis

We will prove the security rigorously using a simulation example. We construct a simulator using the inputs and outputs of relevant parties to prove that the information sequence obtained during simulation is computationally indistinguishable from the information sequence obtained during real execution.

Case 1. We will build a simulator Sim_{Leader}, that generate computationally indistinguishable sequences of information. In the real execution process, the *View* of the Leader is $View_{\text{Leader}}(\wedge, \wedge) = \{\wedge, R, G_k + R_{sum}(k \in [1, n])\}$,where $\wedge$ indicates that the input of the Leader is an empty set, and R is a set of random numbers (vectors). The simulator Sim_{Leader} performs the following process. It randomly selects the gradient vector$\{G_k^{'} + R_{sum}^{'}, k \in [1, n]\}$.

Then, the subsequent process is performed based on$\{G_k^{'} + R_{sum}^{'}, k \in [1, n]\}$, that is, the information sequence generated by the Leader during the simulation process is $Sim_{\text{Leader}}(\wedge, \lambda) = \{\wedge, R^{'}, G_k^{'} + R_{sum}^{'}, (k \in [1, n])\}$.

In $View_{Leader}$ and Sim_{Leader}, $\{G_k^{'}+R_{sum}^{'}, (k \in [1, n])\}$ and $\{G_k+R_{sum}, (k \in [1, n])\}$ are computationally indistinguishable from the randomness of random vectors $R^{'}$ and R, $R_{sum}^{'}$ and R_{sum}. That is $View_{Leader}(\wedge, \wedge) \overset{c}{\equiv} Sim_{Leader}(\wedge, \lambda)$.

Case 2. We will build a simulator $Sim_{Follower}$, that generate computationally indistinguishable sequences of information. In the real execution process, the *View* of the Leader is $View_{Follower}(\wedge, \wedge) = \{\wedge, G_k+R_{sum}, (k \in [1, n])\}$,where $\wedge$ indicates that the input of the Leader is an empty set. The simulator $Sim_{Follower}$ performs the following process. It randomly selects the gradient vector $\{G_k^{'} + R_{sum}^{'}, k \in [1, n]\}$.

Then, the subsequent process is performed based on $G_k^{'} + R_{sum}^{'} k \in [1, n]$, that is, the information sequence generated by the Leader during the simulation process is $Sim_{Follower}(\wedge, \lambda) = \wedge, G_k^{'} + R_{sum}^{'}(k \in [1, n])$.

In $View_{Follower}$ and $Sim_{Follower}$, $\{G_k^{'} + R_{sum}^{'}(k \in [1, n])\}$ and $\{G_k + R_{sum}$ $(k \in [1, n])\}$ are computationally indistinguishable from the randomness of random vectors $R_{sum}^{'}$ and R_{sum}. That is $View_{Follower}(\wedge, \wedge) \overset{c}{\equiv} Sim_{Follower}(\wedge, \lambda)$.

7 Performance Evaluation

7.1 Experiment Setup

In this paper, the global model of this scheme's classification performance is assessed using the MNIST and EMNIST datasets. The National Institute of Standards and Technology (NIST) of the United States has released the MNIST dataset, which includes ten categories of black and white image data ranging from 0 to 9. It is the machine learning industry's de facto standard benchmark dataset [14]. EMNIST is an expanded dataset of MNIST that contains handwritten letters, numbers, and other symbols in addition to handwritten digits [6]. Additionally, each DO is configured to update the local model using stochastic gradient descent (SGD), and the learning rate is further adjusted using the StepLR approach.

A dual-channel Zhikee5 2680 CPU, 256 GB of 1333 MHz DDR3 memory, an NVIDIA GeForce GTX 3090 GPU, and a 1TB SSD make up the experimental gadget, which is a desktop computer. Windows 10 is used as the OS. Python 3.7 is the programming language, while PyTorch is one of the programming libraries used.

7.2 Experiment Results

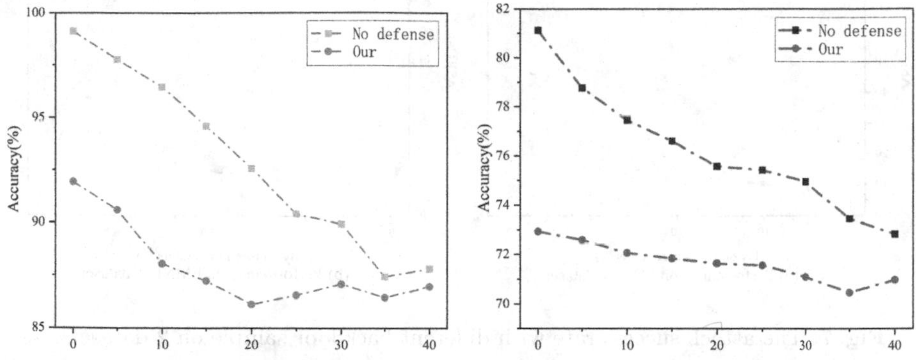

(a) Performance on MNIST dataset
(b) Performance on EMNIST dataset

Fig. 6. The effectiveness of FedBC on 2 datasets.

Effectiveness Analysis. First, the proposed scheme is compared with the global model before and after poisoning, and tested on MNIST and EMNIST datasets, respectively. As shown in Fig. 6(a), with the increase of Byzantine nodes, the accuracy of the model without defense measures is at least 15% lower than that without the attacker. After using this scheme, the accuracy of the model does not fluctuate by more than 5% when Byzantine nodes are existed. This is owing to the security aggregation algorithm's design, which minimizes the impact of the poisoned model on the overall model by calculating the gradient center and dividing the benign and poisonous gradient sets over a number of iterations. The optimization of the clustering approach, which will also be the subject of our further study, is the fundamental reason why the detection performance of our scheme is less than that of the model without poisoning. Additionally, the scheme's overall accuracy on the EMNIST data set is less than 80%, which is due to the choice of the benchmark model, and the performance optimization issue of various algorithms on datasets is also outside the purview of this research.

The Influence of Different Byzantine Nodes on the Attack Success Rate. With the increasing Byzantine nodes, the attack success rate is greatly improved. As shown in Fig. 7, under the premise of no defense measures, when the percentage of Byzantine nodes is higher than 5%, the success rate of the attacker on the two datasets reaches 98% and 90%, respectively. In this scheme, when the percentage of Byzantine nodes is higher than 20%, the attack success rate can only be improved to a certain extent. Even when the percentage of Byzantine nodes is equal to 40%, the attack success rate is less than 50%. It indicates that the SecPBFT protocol designed by this scheme can effectively eliminate malicious gradients from the gradient set, and iteratively select the optimal benign

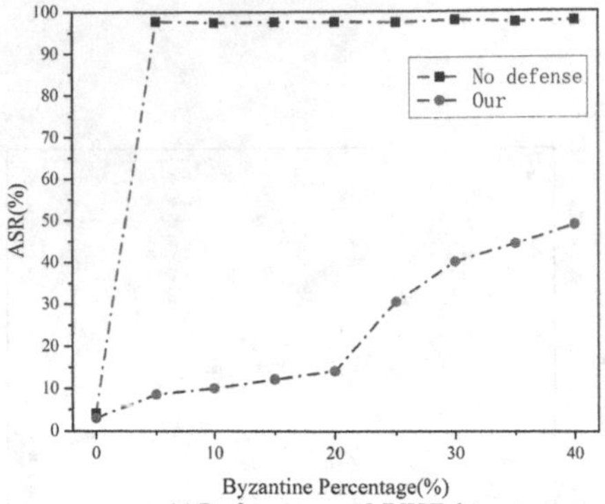

(a) Performance on MNIST dataset

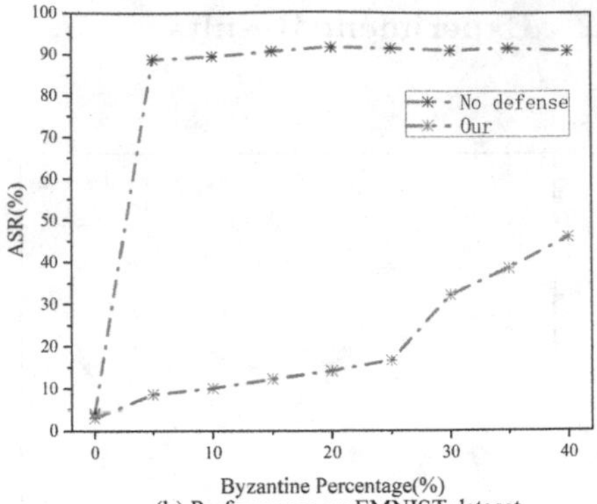

(b) Performance on EMNIST dataset

Fig. 7. The attack success rate with different backdoor sample on 2 datasets.

gradients and aggregate them. Therefore, in this paper, the Byzantine node percentages of 20% and 25% are selected for experiments which can ensure the robustness of the global model.

Efficiency Analysis. The gradient vector is assumed to be γ dimensional in this paper. The commit phase of the protocol SecPBFT generates the computational overhead. Leader and Followers encrypt the final vector$G_{avg}^{(l)} + R_{sum}$, all of which need to perform γ encryption operations. Therefore, it can be seen that Paillier encryption and decryption require running two modular exponential operations once, and the protocol *Sec*PBFT needs to perform $(l+1)\ \gamma$ modular exponentiation with a computational complexity $O(l\gamma)$. Since the four phases of the protocol *Sec*PBFT are consistent with PBFT, their communication complexity is $O(l^2)$. Among them, l is the total number of Follower nodes.

8 Conclusion

In this paper, we propose an efficient and privacy-preserving federated consensus scheme (FedBC). It can ensure that Byzantine nodes cannot upload poisoned gradients to affect the accuracy of the global model. Theoretical analysis demonstrates the security of FedBC. Additionally, the experimental results demonstrate that when FedBC has no protection measures, the assault success rate is decreased by at least 50%, significantly enhancing the global model's defense capacity.

Acknowledgment. This work was supported by the National Natural Science Foundation of China (62125205), the Natural Science Basic Research Plan in Shaanxi Province (2022JQ-594).

References

1. Achituve, I., Shamsian, A., Navon, A., Chechik, G., Fetaya, E.: Personalized federated learning with gaussian processes. Adv. Neural Inf. Process. Syst. **34** (2021)
2. Buterin, V., Reijsbergen, D., Leonardos, S., Piliouras, G.: Incentives in Ethereum's hybrid Casper protocol. Int. J. Netw. Manag. **30**(5), e2098 (2020)
3. Büyüközkan, G., Tüfekçi, G.: A decision-making framework for evaluating appropriate business blockchain platforms using multiple preference formats and VIKOR. Inf. Sci. **571**, 337–357 (2021)
4. Chen, H., Liang, M., Liu, W., Wang, W., Liu, P.X.: An approach to boundary detection for 3D point clouds based on DBSCAN clustering. Pattern Recogn. **124**, 108431 (2022)
5. Chen, J., Zhang, X., Zhang, R., Wang, C., Liu, L.: De-Pois: an attack-agnostic defense against data poisoning attacks. IEEE Trans. Inf. Forensics Secur. **16**, 3412–3425 (2021)
6. Cohen, G., Afshar, S., Tapson, J., Van Schaik, A.: EMNIST: extending MNIST to handwritten letters. In: 2017 International Joint Conference on Neural Networks (IJCNN), pp. 2921–2926. IEEE (2017)
7. Consulting, I.: General data protection regulation-official (2016). https://gdpr-info.eu/
8. Feng, C., Liu, B., Yu, K., Goudos, S.K., Wan, S.: Blockchain-empowered decentralized horizontal federated learning for 5G-enabled UAVs. IEEE Trans. Ind. Inf. **18**(5), 3582–3592 (2021)
9. Feng, Y., Zhang, W., Luo, X., Zhang, B.: A consortium blockchain-based access control framework with dynamic orderer node selection for 5G-enabled industrial IoT. IEEE Trans. Ind. Inf. **18**(4), 2840–2848 (2021)
10. Guerraoui, R., Rouault, S., et al.: The hidden vulnerability of distributed learning in Byzantium. In: International Conference on Machine Learning, pp. 3521–3530. PMLR (2018)
11. Hou, L., Xu, X., Zheng, K., Wang, X.: An intelligent transaction migration scheme for raft-based private blockchain in internet of things applications. IEEE Commun. Lett. **25**(8), 2753–2757 (2021)
12. Jia, B., Zhang, X., Liu, J., Zhang, Y., Huang, K., Liang, Y.: Blockchain-enabled federated learning data protection aggregation scheme with differential privacy and homomorphic encryption in IIoT. IEEE Trans. Ind. Inform. (2021)
13. Lax, G., Russo, A., Fascì, L.S.: A blockchain-based approach for matching desired and real privacy settings of social network users. Inf. Sci. **557**, 220–235 (2021)
14. LeCun, Y., Bottou, L., Bengio, Y., Haffner, P.: Gradient-based learning applied to document recognition. Proc. IEEE **86**(11), 2278–2324 (1998)
15. Li, W., Feng, C., Zhang, L., Xu, H., Cao, B., Imran, M.A.: A scalable multi-layer PBFT consensus for blockchain. IEEE Trans. Parallel Distrib. Syst. **32**(5), 1146–1160 (2020)
16. Liu, X., Li, H., Xu, G., Chen, Z., Huang, X., Lu, R.: Privacy-enhanced federated learning against poisoning adversaries. IEEE Trans. Inf. Forensics Secur. **16**, 4574–4588 (2021)
17. Ma, Z., Ma, J., Miao, Y., Li, Y., Deng, R.H.: ShieldFL: mitigating model poisoning attacks in privacy-preserving federated learning. IEEE Trans. Inf. Forensics Secur. **17**, 1639–1654 (2022)
18. Ouyang, L., Yuan, Y., Cao, Y., Wang, F.Y.: A novel framework of collaborative early warning for COVID-19 based on blockchain and smart contracts. Inf. Sci. **570**, 124–143 (2021)

19. Rodler, M., Li, W., Karame, G.O., Davi, L.: {EVMPatch}: timely and automated patching of Ethereum smart contracts. In: 30th USENIX Security Symposium (USENIX Security 2021), pp. 1289–1306 (2021)
20. Su, L., et al.: Evil under the sun: understanding and discovering attacks on Ethereum decentralized applications. In: 30th USENIX Security Symposium (USENIX Security 2021), pp. 1307–1324 (2021)
21. Torres, C.F., Camino, R., et al.: Frontrunner jones and the raiders of the dark forest: an empirical study of frontrunning on the Ethereum blockchain. In: 30th USENIX Security Symposium (USENIX Security 21), pp. 1343–1359 (2021)
22. Weerasinghe, S., Alpcan, T., Erfani, S.M., Leckie, C.: Defending support vector machines against data poisoning attacks. IEEE Trans. Inf. Forensics Secur. **16**, 2566–2578 (2021)
23. Wen, J., Zhao, B.Z.H., Xue, M., Oprea, A., Qian, H.: With great dispersion comes greater resilience: efficient poisoning attacks and defenses for linear regression models. IEEE Trans. Inf. Forensics Secur. **16**, 3709–3723 (2021)
24. Xie, C., Chen, M., Chen, P.Y., Li, B.: CRFL: certifiably robust federated learning against backdoor attacks. In: International Conference on Machine Learning, pp. 11372–11382. PMLR (2021)
25. Yin, D., Chen, Y., Kannan, R., Bartlett, P.: Byzantine-robust distributed learning: towards optimal statistical rates. In: International Conference on Machine Learning, pp. 5650–5659. PMLR (2018)

A Secure and Privacy-Preserving Authentication Scheme in IoMT

Yuxiang Zhou[1(✉)], Haowen Tan[2], and Karunarathina Chandrathilaka Appuhamilage Asiria Iroshan[1]

[1] School of Computer Science, Nanjing University of Information Science and Technology, Nanjing 210044, China
zyx_nuist@126.com

[2] Cyber Security Center, Kyushu University, Fukuoka, Japan

Abstract. The development of 5G communication and cloud computing and big data technology has promoted the rapid rise of the Internet of medical things (IoMT). IoMT is gradually entering all aspects of people's lives and providing more intelligent services for people. Similarly, this brings many opportunities to the field of health care. However, in open and complex scenarios, IoMT, is still in its infancy. Before popularization and application, it must stand the test of clinical verification, data security, and privacy protection. In order to meet the challenges of data security and privacy protection faced by IoMT and ensure secure communication in open and complex scenarios, based on the principle of challenge authentication handshake protocol, we propose a new security authentication scheme suitable for IoMT. The scheme meets the security authentication, negotiates the session key for the communication between the intelligent sensor and the medical server embedded in the environment, ensures the session security, and supports dynamic management. Security and performance analysis show that the protocol is safe and efficient.

Keywords: IoMT · Security · Authentication

1 Introduction

With the rapid development of Internet of things technology in recent years, the continuous iterative updating of intelligent devices and the popularity of a large number of low-cost, convenient, and efficient sensing devices provide important support conditions for IoMT. In addition, with the rapid development of the Internet, big data technology, and cloud computing technology, the ability of terminal equipment to store and process data is continuously enhanced, and the ability to analyze and process the massive data continuously collected from the surrounding environment, so as to provide decision-making information for all fields of society. IoMT has gradually become an indispensable part of real life. For

Supported by organization x.

X. Chen et al. (Eds.): SocialSec 2022, CCIS 1663, pp. 163–174, 2022.
https://doi.org/10.1007/978-981-19-7242-3_11

example, the number of wearable smart devices is rising in a straight line on the scale of hundreds of millions, which is the key thrust to promoting IoMT into real life. As mentioned earlier, human-computer interaction will become more intuitive and efficient. With the processing of technology, the dialogue between people and intelligent devices will become more direct, greatly reducing people's cognitive burden and better helping people process and make decisions on various data and information. When the concept of IoMT was just put forward, its development was restricted by the computing power and storage capacity of software and hardware. Most of it only existed at the level of conception and did not develop rapidly or even realize on the ground. Now, with the rapid rise of artificial intelligence and big data and the popularity of non-contact sensor hardware, IoMT is gradually entering all aspects of our work and life. And providing more intelligent services for people. Through non-contact sensors for data acquisition, data authentication, and data analysis, combined with the current hot artificial intelligence technology to judge personal behavior, IoMT supports but is not limited to multiple scenarios such as medical data monitoring and data analysis.

Although IoMT supports the collection, transmission, and analysis of health data of the elderly or patients, so that children or doctors can understand the health status of the elderly and patients, and can provide people with convenient and accurate access to information and services, IoMT faces the challenges of data security and user privacy. In IoMT, various health index data and daily behavior data of the human body can be continuously collected and analyzed through a variety of sensors, and these data are often the most important and sensitive privacy of a person [1]. If these privacy data are leaked, it may lead to unimaginable consequences, and the user's personal privacy and data security can not be ignored. The increasingly iterative and updated technology can indeed bring convenience to people's work and life, but people's privacy will be easily exposed to malicious attackers in the network. Attention should be paid to identity privacy and communication security. At the same time, the communication efficiency between intelligent devices and medical servers should not be ignored.

Therefore, in order to eliminate the above security threats, researchers have proposed various solutions. Generally, authentication and message signature technologies are used to deal with the above threats. Identity authentication technology can play a vital role in the field of communication security and personal privacy protection in an intelligent environment. Signature technology can be used to ensure the authenticity and integrity of communication data sources, prevent attackers from tampering with data, and ensure the authenticity and effectiveness of data. The introduction of secure identity authentication can prevent potential malicious attackers in the network from launching active or passive attacks to steal and tamper with data. Data security and personal privacy data protection have become important restrictive factors in the promotion of IoMT. Under these security requirements, authentication can provide a safe and powerful secure communication guarantee for IoMT. Therefore, in order to ensure the communication security and privacy protection of IoMT and ensure that the personal privacy of user data security is not leaked, only legitimate users can access data, and legitimate networks can serve intelligent sensors. It is of great significance to introduce a safe and reliable authentication scheme. At present, a large number of research scholars have put forward valuable suggestions and formed schemes and architectures, but the existing research architecture is not mature, systematic, and complete [2]. There are still some problems to be solved, such as data monitoring, user privacy disclosure, lack of effective data management, insufficient security, and so on.

The contribution of this paper is as follows:

In this paper, we design a provably secure authentication scheme for privacy-preserving in IoMT. In addition, the scheme also has a variety of security features, such as realizing identity anonymity to protect users' privacy, realizing dynamic management function to restrict users' or sensors' abnormal behavior, and resisting common network attacks.

Security and performance analysis shows that compared with other schemes, our scheme provides better security without sacrificing efficiency.

2 Related Work

In recent years, researchers have proposed a series of authentication schemes in order to protect the communication data security and user privacy in IoMT. Amin et al. [3], based on bilinear pairing technology, proposed a three-factor authentication scheme for multi-server environment. Unfortunately, chandrakar [4] et al. analyzed the security of Amin's scheme and pointed out that this scheme can not resist offline dictionary guessing attacks. Based on this problem, chandrakar et al. redesigned a remote user authentication scheme based on biometric technology. The security analysis of the scheme shows that it can resist offline dictionary guessing attacks and key simulation attacks. Based on elliptic curve encryption technology, he et al. [5] used a fuzzy extractor to extract user biometrics and constructed an authentication scheme. However, some researchers pointed out that the scheme proposed by he et al. can't resist the attack of secret information disclosure. Wang et al. [6] designed an identity authentication scheme suitable for a multi-server environment based on three factors of authentication. However, Yang et al. [7] found that Wang et al.'s scheme could not resist privileged internal attacks, and the security was worrying. Li et al. [8] proposed a new authentication and key establishment protocol for an electronic medical environment based on chaotic mapping technology. Subsequently, Madhusudhan et al. [9] analyzed the scheme proposed by Li et al. And found that the protocol could not resist password guessing attacks. Qiu et al. [10] designed a robust authentication scheme for an electronic medical environment based on Elliptic Curve Cryptography (ECC) protocol. Unfortunately, Kumari [11] proved that the scheme proposed by Qiu et al. does not have anonymity and is not resistant to camouflage and guessing attacks. Therefore, Kumari et al. Proposed an improved password authentication and key agreement scheme based on biometrics, which made up for the defects of Fan et al. [12] designed a lightweight authentication protocol supporting privacy protection and suitable for RFID scenarios from the two aspects of efficiency and security, so as to achieve the purpose of protecting telemedicine data. However, Chen et al. [13] evaluated the security of the protocol proposed by fan et al. and pointed out that the scheme can not resist security attacks such as denial of service attacks and replay attacks. Ravambakhsh [14] designed an efficient mutual authentication protocol for the privacy protection of the telemedicine system. Later, Sharif et al. [15] analyzed and evaluated the scheme proposed by ravambakhsh et al. and found that its scheme could not resist the attack of temporary secret information disclosure. It is not difficult to see that data communication security and personal privacy protection are the "stumbling block" to the popularization of Internet of medical things (IoMT).

3 System and Security

3.1 System Architecture

Let's briefly introduce the system model. In IoMT, the collected health data can be uploaded to the medical server for processing and analysis by embedding heart rate sensors, blood oxygen sensors, gravity accelerometers, communication modules and other sensing devices in intelligent wearable devices, so as to select doctors and give the best medical suggestions, and finally give the most real and accurate electronic feedback to users, This environmental intelligence embedded in the medical field can realize the close monitoring of the elderly living alone or the health status of patients, so that professional medical staff or children can understand the physical conditions of patients and the elderly. The details of each entity in the system are as follows.

CA. It is completely trustworthy. In real life, it mainly refers to the authoritative department of the health committee. It has powerful computing and storage capabilities, and can generate system parameters, register users and update keys. Only it can dynamically manage and track users or sensors.

User. It refers to that patients or caregivers can collect human voice, infrared image,s and other data in a specific scene through a large number of passive and intelligent sensing devices embedded in the environment. In addition, the intelligent wearable device integrating a heart rate sensor, blood oxygen sensor, 5G communication module, and other sensing devices can transmit the health status and action track data of the elderly living alone or patients to the remote server.

Sensor. It refers to a large number of non-active and contactless sensors embedded in the environment, which are used to collect the user's voice, infrared image, health status, and other data, and send them to the server for fusion mining and specific processing of the data, so as to perceive the user's health status and behavior, call the data resources commonly existing in the environment, collect, analyze and feedback the user's activity information to the information space, Then respond to the needs of users.

Server. It is a trusted entity with strong data storage and computing power. It is responsible for collecting the health data of patients, analyzing and processing the data, and forwarding it to the corresponding doctors for diagnosis, so as to provide the best nursing guidance and medical suggestions for caregivers or patients.

4 Our Proposed Scheme

4.1 Initialization Phase

The CA will complete the following operations.

Step 1. Generates a group $\mathbb{G}$. Here, q is its prime order and $g$is its generator.

Step 2. Generates a nonce $s \in \mathbb{Z}_q^*$, compute $g_p = g^s$.

Step 3. Generates hash functions: $h : \{0,1\}^* \rightarrow \{0,1\}^l$, $H_1 : \{0,1\}^* \rightarrow \mathbb{Z}_q^*$, $H_2 : \{0,1\}^* \times \mathbb{G} \rightarrow \mathbb{Z}_q^*$, $H_3 : \mathbb{Z}_q^* \rightarrow \mathbb{Z}_q^*$. The public parameters $\{\mathbb{G}, q, g, g_{pub}, H_1, H_2, H_3\}$. Here, h is only saved in sensors.

4.2 Registration Phase

Next, the user needs to register with the server.

Step 1. U_i input personal information ID_i, PW_i, and BIO_i into AS_i.

Step 2. After AS_i receiving a user personal information, AS_j chooses $a_i \in \mathbb{Z}_q^*$ and computes $Gen(BIO_i)$, PID_i, P_i, B_i, and A_i. AS_j submits request to CA.

Step 3. After CA getting a request from AS_j, CA generates an identifier $A_i \in \mathbb{Z}_q^*$ indicates AS_j identity and calculates E_i. Then, CA sends it to AS_j. AS_j store it. CA generates a database table to record the corresponding relationship parameters between them. For more details, see Fig. 1.

Note 1. AF_i indicates the number of authentication failures. *status* indicates whether the sensor AS_j is credible. Set an upper limit on AF_i to prevent malicious users or sensors from attempting single sign on attacks.

4.3 Update Key Phase

CA can dynamically manage users or sensors by observing the performance of users or sensors and regularly and quantitatively updating the time key of registered sensors according to their honesty, so as to restrict the behavior of users or sensors. The details are shown in Fig. 2.

Step 1. CA first checks the status of AS_j.

Step 2. If the status of AS_j is No, stop updating key. Otherwise, CA chooses a reasonable time T and updating key AS_j.

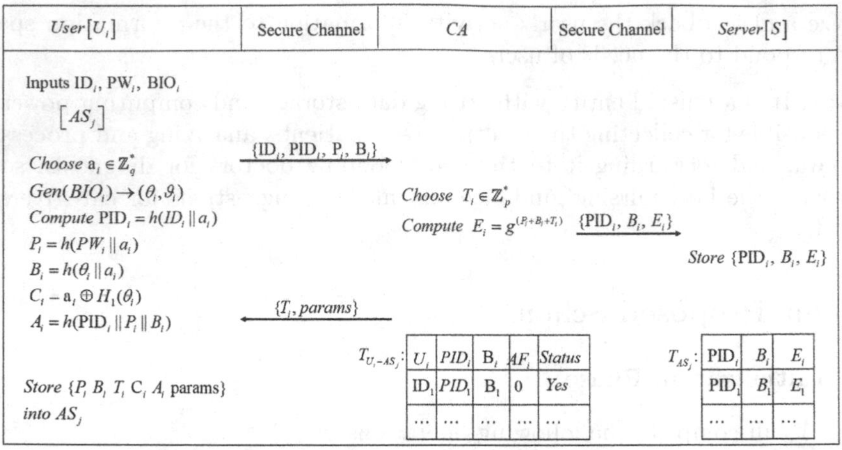

Fig. 1. Registration phase

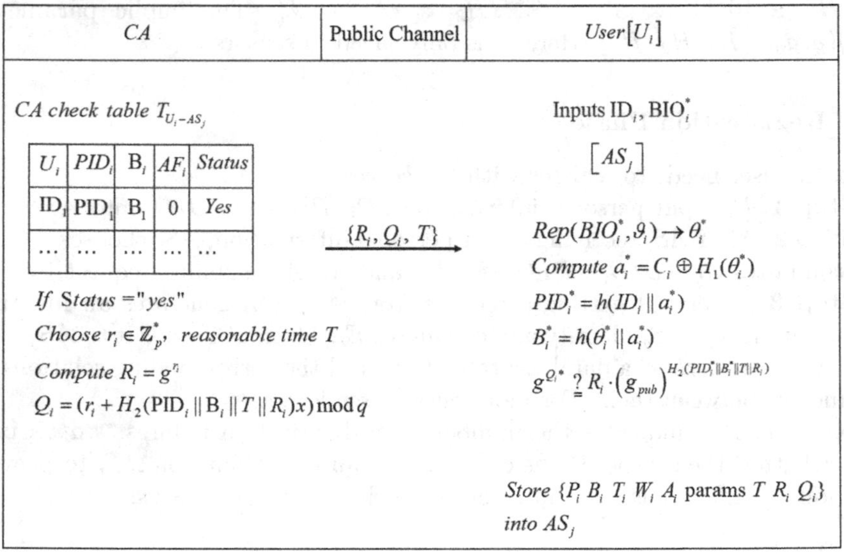

Fig. 2. Time key constraint phase

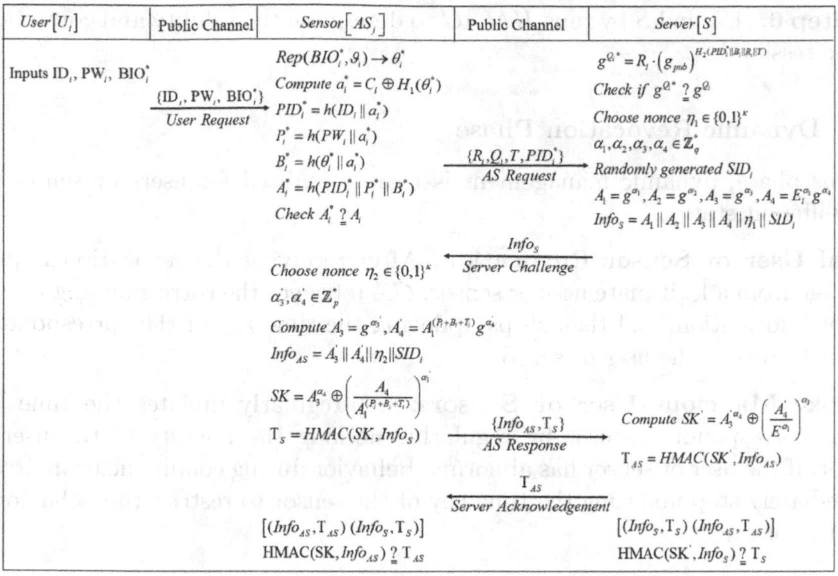

Fig. 3. Sensors-to-server authentication phase

4.4 User-to-Sensors Authentication Phase

As shown in Fig. 3, the following interactions shall be conducted between the sensor and the server.

Step 1. U_i sends *User Login Request* to AS_j.

Step 2. AS_j calculates some parameters.

Step 3. Check whether the equation is true. If not, the authentication will be terminated immediately, and the authentication record will be added automatically.

4.5 Sensors-to-Server Authentication Phase

As shown in Fig. 3, the interaction between the sensor and the server is as follows. *Rep*() is part of fuzzy extraction Algorithm [18].

Step 1. First, AS_j sends the parameters to the S as an *AS Request*.

Step 2. S will check the PID_i^* and calculate g^{Q_i} to check whether the equation is true. If not, S rejects this request.

Step 3. S chooses a series of random numbers. Here, SID_i ,mark this unique session. S calculates some parameters sends *Server Challenge* to AS_j.

Step 4. AS_j chooses a series of random numbers and computes $A_3^{'}$, $A_4^{'}$, $Info_{AS}$. Now, it can get SK. AS_j then get a tag T_S. Finally, it sends AS *Response* to S.

Step 5. S calculates $SK^{'}$, T_{AS}, $Info_{AS}$. S sends Server *Acknowledgement* to AS_j.

Step 6. AS_j and S by runs $HMAC$ to determine the validity and correctness of the session key.

4.6 Dynamic Revocation Phase

In this phase, dynamic management is mainly realized for users or sensors in two different states.

Legal User or Sensor Revocation. After receiving the revocation request message from a legitimate user or sensor, CA retrieves the corresponding user or sensor information, and then stops updating the time key of the corresponding sensor to revoke the user or sensor.

Revoke Malicious User or Sensors. CA regularly updates the time key of the corresponding sensor by regularly checking the honesty of the user or sensor. If the user or sensor has abnormal behavior during communication, it will immediately stop updating the time key of the sensor to restrict the behavior of the user or sensor.

5 Security Analysis

Mutual Authentication. To ensure the secure communication in iomt, the communication parties must authenticate each other before establishing the secure channel. Our protocol realizes the mutual authentication between the user and the server, which is good news for the subsequent secure communication between the two parties.

Anonymity and Traceability. Since some personal privacy information is stored in the sensor SA_j, in order to prevent the disclosure of biological information, password and other personal information, the sensor should not use the real ID_i during authentication. In our protocol, random function and hash function are used to encrypt the user's real identity, so as to generate a pseudo identity identifier corresponding to the user. If $\mathcal{A}$ in the network plans to extract the user's real ID_i from the anonymous PID_i. However, random numbers and hash functions participate in the calculation of the user's pseudo identity. Due to the randomness, unidirectionality and irreversibility of hash function, the purpose of anonymous user's real identity is finally realized. CA can query the corresponding relationship between the user's real identity and pseudo identity, so that CA can track malicious users and sensors when necessary.

Dynamic Management. In our protocol, CA can observe the credibility of users or sensors according to the scenarios of users and sensors, so as to set a reasonable time threshold of T. This approach will undoubtedly make CA more flexible in managing users or sensors, rather than rigid. In addition, we can also observe the honesty of users and give appropriate time rewards and punishments. CA can judge whether the state of the sensor is abnormal according to the state values of users and sensors in the database table, so it can give some punishment or reward. Therefore, the scheme can support flexible dynamic revocation function.

Forward Security. Therefore, with the participation of random numbers, even if $\mathcal{A}$ steals the long-term key E_i, the session key previously negotiated by the current instance will not be damaged, ensuring the forward security, so as to ensure the communication security of the protocol.

Resistant Replay Attack. In our protocol, some random numbers η_1, η_2 and temporary session identifiers are involved in the generation of each round of session secret key, because each random number and temporary session identifier are temporarily selected, and the session key for each round is fresh. Therefore, our protocol can be protected from replay attacks.

Resistant Man-in-the-Middle Attack. The adversary $\mathcal{A}$ in the network may eavesdrop on the interactive information generated during the operation of the protocol through the passive attack, so as to fabricate some other information, so as to fake the legitimate participation (SA_j or S) in some destructive activities in the protocol. However, in our protocol, each authentication not only carefully verifies the personal identity of the participants (SA_j or S), but also needs to verify the time key regularly updated by the independent third-party CA. Therefore, this attack method has no effect on our scheme.

6 Performance Analysis

6.1 Security Features

As shown in Table 1, we compare the security features of our scheme with Sahoo's scheme [16], Jia's scheme [17]. SF1: mutual authentication, SF2: dynamic management, SF3: anonymous traceability of users or sensors, SF4: resistance to replay attacks, SF5: forward security. Obviously, our scheme has advantages in terms of security features.

Table 1. Security features comparison

	$SF1$	$SF2$	$SF3$	$SF4$	$SF5$
Sahoo's [16]	√	×	×	√	√
Jia's [17]	√	×	√	√	√
Our	√	√	√	√	√

6.2 Computation Cost

In this subsection, we analyze the computational costs of the login and authentication phases of our scheme and compare [16,17].

Our hardware equipment composes of an Intel (R) Core (TM) i5-9500 CPU with a 3.00 GHz clock frequency, 8G running memory, and Windows 10 operating

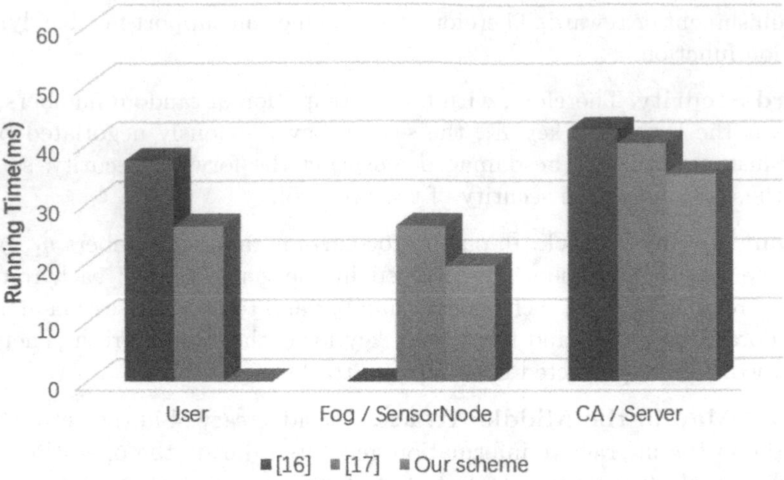

Fig. 4. Comparison of computational overhead

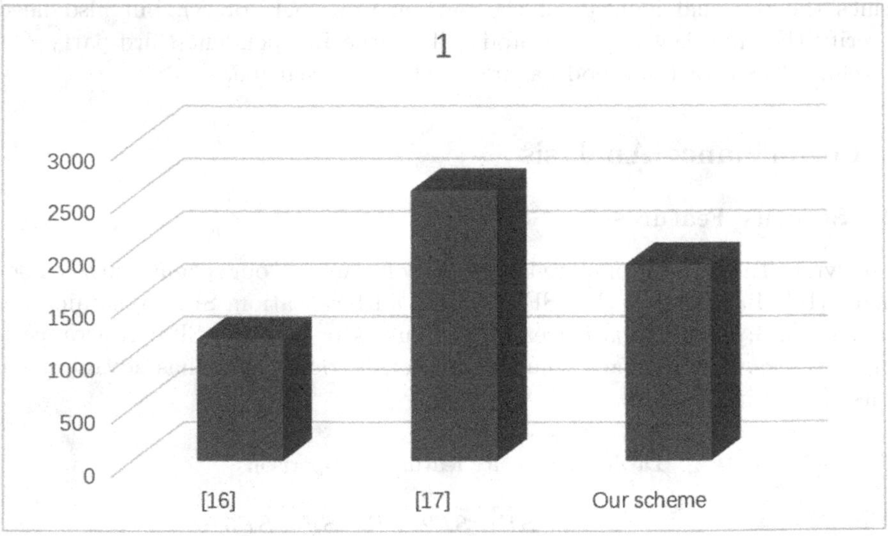

Fig. 5. Comparison of communication overhead

system based on an x64 processor. The experiment used a 160-bit standard elliptic curve, and are selected as two 32-bit random numbers. The execution time of the cryptographic operations in our protocol is completed with a pairing-based cryptography (PBC) library.

As shown in Fig. 4, the computational overhead of our scheme for the sensor end and server-end is significantly better than the other schemes. In addition, our scheme has better security features.

6.3 Communication Cost

To make it easier to compare communication costs between schemes, it is assumed that the lengths of the identifiers, passwords, biometrics, timestamps, and random numbers are all 32 bits. It is assumed that the length of the hash function output, and the length of the value in G are 160 bits, the length of encryption or decryption is 128 bits.

As shown in Fig. 5, communication cost experiments show that the user end and sensor end are significantly better than the other schemes. Although the communication overhead of this scheme is higher than other schemes, the cost of our communication scheme is also acceptable and has better security features.

7 Conclusion

Based on fuzzy decimator and schnorr signature technology, we design a provably secure authentication scheme for privacy-preserving in IoMT. The scheme can achieve secure and reliable authentication key agreement, so that iomt can ensure secure communication and avoid the intrusion of privacy disclosure. In addition, it can also realize dynamic user or sensor management. Security and performance analysis show that the scheme is safe and effective.

References

1. Shen, J., Zhou, T., Cao, Z.: Protection methods for cloud data security. J. Comput. Res. Dev. **58**(10), 2079–2098 (2021)
2. Shen, J., Zhou, T., He, D., Zhang, Y., Sun, X., Xiang, Y.: Block design-based key agreement for group data sharing in cloud computing. IEEE Trans. Dependable Secure Comput. **16**(6), 996–1010 (2017)
3. Amin, R., Biswas, G.: Design and analysis of bilinear pairing based mutual authentication and key agreement protocol usable in multi-server environment. Wirel. Pers. Commun. **84**(1), 439–462 (2015). https://doi.org/10.1007/s11277-015-2616-7
4. Chandrakar, P., Om, H.: Cryptanalysis and improvement of a biometric based remote user authentication protocol usable in a multiserver environment. Trans. Emerg. Telecommun. Technol. **28**(12), e3200 (2017)
5. He, D., Wang, D.: Robust biometrics-based authentication scheme for multiserver environment. IEEE Syst. J. **9**(3), 816–823 (2014)
6. Wang, C., Zhang, X., Zheng, Z.: Cryptanalysis and improvement of a biometric-based multi-server authentication and key agreement scheme. Plos One, **11**(2) (2016)
7. Yang, Li., Zheng, Z.: Cryptanalysis and improvement of a biometrics-based authentication and key agreement scheme for multi-server environments. Plos One, **13**(3) (2018)
8. Li, C., Lee, C., Weng, C., Chen, S.: A secure dynamic identity and chaotic maps based user authentication and key agreement scheme for e-healthcare systems. J. Med. Syst. **40**(11), 1–10 (2016). https://doi.org/10.1007/s10916-016-0586-2

9. Madhusudhan, R., Nayak, C.S.: A robust authentication scheme for telecare medical information systems. Multimedia Tools Appl. **78**(11), 15255–15273 (2018). https://doi.org/10.1007/s11042-018-6884-6
10. Qiu, S., Xu, G., Ahmad, H., Wang, L.: A robust mutual authentication scheme based on elliptic curve cryptography for telecare medical information systems. IEEE Access **6**, 7452–7463 (2017)
11. Kumari, S., Renuka, K.: Design of a password authentication and key agreement scheme to access e-healthcare services. Wireless Pers. Commun. **117**(1), 27–45 (2021). https://doi.org/10.1007/s11277-019-06755-7
12. Fan, K., Jiang, W., Li, H., Yang, Y.: Lightweight RFID protocol for medical privacy protection in IoT. IEEE Trans. Industr. Inf. **14**(4), 1656–1665 (2018)
13. Chen, X., Geng, D., Zhai, J., Liu, W., Zhang, H., Zhu, T.: Security analysis and enhancement of the most recent RFID protocol for telecare medicine information system. Wireless Pers. Commun. **114**(2), 1371–1387 (2020). https://doi.org/10.1007/s11277-020-07424-w
14. Ravanbakhsh, N., Nazari, M.: An efficient improvement remote user mutual authentication and session key agreement scheme for e-health care systems. Multimedia Tools Appl. **77**(1), 55–88 (2018). https://doi.org/10.1007/s11042-016-4208-2
15. Ostad-Sharif, A., Abbasinezhad-Mood, D., Nikooghadam, M.: An enhanced anonymous and unlinkable user authentication and key agreement protocol for tmis by utilization of ECC. Int. J. Commun. Syst. **32**(5) (2019)
16. Sahoo, S.S., Mohanty, S., Majhi, B.: A secure three factor based authentication scheme for health care systems using IoT enabled devices. J. Ambient. Intell. Humaniz. Comput. **12**(1), 1419–1434 (2020). https://doi.org/10.1007/s12652-020-02213-6
17. Jia, X., He, D., Kumar, N., Choo, K.-K.R.: Authenticated key agreement scheme for fog-driven IoT healthcare system. Wireless Netw. **25**(8), 4737–4750 (2018). https://doi.org/10.1007/s11276-018-1759-3
18. Wang, C., Huang, R., Shen, J., et al.: A novel lightweight authentication protocol for emergency vehicle avoidance in VANETs. IEEE Internet Things J. **8**(18), 14248–14257 (2021)

Secure and Efficient *k*-Nearest Neighbor Query with Privacy-Preserving Authentication

Zehao Li, Guohua Tian(✉), and Shichong Tan

State Key Laboratory of Integrated Service Networks (ISN), Xidian University, Xi'an 710071, China

gh_tian0621@163.com, sctan@mail.xidian.edu.cn

Abstract. Dealing with k-nearest neighbor (kNN) on untrusted cloud servers without revealing private information is an existing challenge. Although a large number of encryption and authentication techniques have been studied to guarantee data privacy and the integrity of results, there are defective in efficiency and security. This paper focuses on finding k-nearest neighbor (kNN) on encrypted data and verifying the query results. Firstly, this paper designs a novel index structure to support sub-linear computation. Based on it, we further propose a batch reading protocol for a faster read operator, by way of batch reading it is more suitable for large-scale kNN search. Secondly, all calculations are performed under ciphertext without clouds learning anything about the dataset, query and result, other indirect information such as access pattern privacy and intermediate result privacy also are guaranteed to resist the latest data recovery attacks. Moreover, this paper designs a verifiable strategy for secure kNN. Our verification process considers the privacy of authentication, which hides the confidential or unnecessary data in Verification Object using Paillier. This work integrates the index structure, verifiable structure and Paillier encryption to build secure and verifiable kNN scheme that gains strong privacy and low latency. Detailed experiments and analysis also are performed in this paper, and our schemes S-kQ and SV-kQ are an order of magnitude faster than the state-of-the-art work on real-world datasets.

Keywords: Secure k-nearest neighbor query · Paillier encryption · Location-based services · Authenticated data structure

1 Introduction

With the boom of cloud computing, location-based services (LBSs) are proliferating and being widely deployed. LBS providers rely on commercial clouds to store and process large amounts of geospatial data, providing convenient and efficient services to users while reducing costs. However, such a service model brings data security issues. Firstly, cloud servers are often untrusted. Given outsourced data

X. Chen et al. (Eds.): SocialSec 2022, CCIS 1663, pp. 175–198, 2022.
https://doi.org/10.1007/978-981-19-7242-3_12

and query requests, they tend to capture or infer confidential spatial data and inquirer privacy information (e.g., name, location, behavioral preferences). Secondly, cloud servers may even be malicious. They return tampered or incorrect results for profit incentives (e.g., bidding on rankings or saving computational costs). Moreover, vulnerable cloud servers can be hacked and leak all sensitive information to hackers.

Thus, we focus on carrying out location-based k nearest neighbor on encrypted geodata and verifying the integrity of results. For instance, user issues 5NN query for nearby hospitals, clouds calculate and return the top-5 nearest hospitals to user. As for secure kNN (SkNN), basic privacy such as the hospitals' location database, inquirer's information and query results are kept secret from clouds. As for verifiable kNN (VkNN), user can be convinced the returned hospitals are real and correct to avoid cloud faking. More importantly, the verification process cannot expose additional Points of Interests (POIs) to user (e.g., user pay 5NN query can infer more than five nearest POIs in fact.), for LBSs are generally on a pay-as-you-go basis and additional POIs should also be charged.

This paper design **S**ecure ***k***NN **Q**uery (S-kQ) scheme and **S**ecure and **V**erifiable ***k***NN **Q**uery (SV-kQ) scheme to solve above problems. Different from the traditional related works, there are three key challenges we shall deal with:

- *How to design an efficient read protocol while maintaining access pattern privacy*? Most existing SkNN schemes [2–6] discuss only basic privacy but ignore access pattern privacy, and such indirect information can be applied to infer confidential information as described in [9–11]. To this end, Elmehdwi et al. [12] adopt two non-colluding clouds to provide strong security through secure interaction. Likewise, the idea of secure two-party computation is adopted by Chen et al. [19] to build secure kNN, it provides access pattern privacy and acceptable efficiency by sacrificing accuracy. However, previous twin-cloud base schemes [9,12,13] adopt a naive read approach that involves the calculation for the entire database. It is not suitable for large-scale databases and the computation of multiple nearest neighbors. To this end, we propose Pre-Read protocol to obtain a batch of nearest neighbor POIs at once while guaranteeing access pattern privacy. More trickily, we aim to design a search mechanism enabling Pre-Read to support accurate kNN query.
- *How to design Authenticated Data Structure (ADS) and support privacy-preserving authentication*? The traditional verification process [4,14] exposed additional POIs to user. To solve this problem other works [16–18] discuss the privacy-preserving authentication on the query of plaintext, but how to extend the above work into ciphertext is a challenging work. Besides, The ADS of two-dimensional kNN is more complicated than that of range query [16]. Meanwhile, privacy-preserving authentication is a tough problem and only has a few related works. We attempt to design a novel ADS based on Voronoi Diagram and integrate it with the index structure. Then, we propose a verification protocol based on the properties of Paillier and the twin-cloud model. User can verify results using encrypted POIs and enjoy high efficiency.

- *How to further optimize S-kQ and SV-kQ schemes*? Secure index structures are widely discussed in [4,5,13,17] to fast kNN. In [13,17] propose a two-level partitioning index, those works adopt a square grid to partition the space, which is not adaptive to the data distribution and incurs a large amount of padding, especially in non-uniformly distributed datasets. Moreover, points at the boundary of each grid generate multiple copies of redundant storage. An optimized strategy that splits database dynamically is mentioned in [17], but it is only a greedy algorithm. To pursue higher efficiency and security, we adopted an optimized two-level partition structure to fast kNN which is influenced by [13,17] but significantly different, we emphasize that our index structure is more concise and supports an efficient reading approach. In the real-world geospatial dataset, the SV-kQ scheme is almost $\times 10$ faster than the state-of-the-art scheme in [13] (perform 10NN queries on 6,000 POIs). Besides, we also discuss secure strategies such as indistinguishable read and bidirectional verification while giving corresponding security analyses.

1.1 Contributions

The contributions of this paper are organized as follows:

1) We point out the error of verification protocol in [13] and propose SV-kQ scheme. To the best of our knowledge, this is the first SkNN work that ensures access pattern privacy and privacy-preserving authentication.
2) We design a verifiable and secure index structure to build our computation and verification protocols of kNN. Meanwhile, Pre-Read protocol is proposed to speed up the read operation on the index structure.
3) We propose optimization strategies for security and efficiency while performing detailed complexity and security analyses on our schemes.
4) We perform elaborate experiments using real-world data. The efficiency of our schemes is an order of magnitude faster than the state-of-the-art scheme [13] on average.

1.2 Related Works

Over the past few decades, SkNN is discussed to ensure data privacy. Fang et al. [2] reduce high-dimensional data to one dimension and combine Order Preserving Encryption (OPE) to solve kNN problem, it guarantees data privacy and efficiency while providing weak security. To reduce leakage of comparison information, Lei et al. [3] use Location-Sensitive Hash (LSH) to simplify the kNN problem, and Boldyreva et al. [7] even consider access pattern further using Oblivious Random Access Machine (ORAM), this kind of solution is efficient for approximate kNN. Moreover, software Guard Extensions (SGX) provides an concise idea to implement SkNN in [2], and SGX relies on trust in hardware vendors. Recent works [9–11] present data recovery attacks against the SkNN scheme, the adversary can recover the entire distribution of POIs with high accuracy from access pattern or comparison leakage. Thus twin-cloud base schemes

[12,13] are widely studied to resist above attacks, they carry out secure computing based on two non-colluding clouds and Paillier cryptosystem. Such a model is also adopted by us. Note that secure two-party computation model adopted in [19] is different from ours. It is based on data sharing between two parties, while ours relies on separating ciphertext and key on two clouds. Other work based on Private Information Retrieval (PIR) [1] focus on private retrievals on dataset, it pays no attention to dataset privacy so does not apply to our scenario.

VkNN, especially built on SkNN, has only a few related works [4,13,14] because of its difficulty. Recent work [14] proposes an efficient verification scheme exploiting Voronoi Diagram. However, a vast number of non-essential location information is exposed to user. Pang et al. [16] first discuss privacy-preserving authentication in range query, which adopts multiple hash to hide sensitive data. Other works such as [17,18] future extend authentication for range query to kNN query on the plaintext, however, corresponding ADS is complex when dealing with two-dimensional data. Other ADS for VkNN such as VR-tree is studied in [26], nevertheless, it only supports approximate kNN. Cui et al. in [13] consider privacy-preserving authentication on SkNN using Linearity-based Transformation approach, but we argue that the verification scheme of Cui et al. has a fatal flaw that cannot guarantee the correctness of results.

1.3 Paper Organization

The remainder of this paper is organized as follows. Section 2 formally describes the preliminaries and Sect. 3 gives system framework. Then, Sect. 4 proposes a two-level index structure to speed up kNN computation while Sect. 5 proposes Pre-Read protocol to fast kNN reading. Section 6 build S-kQ and SV-kQ schemes. At last, comprehensive experiments and comparisons are performed in Sect. 7 to test our schemes. Besides, the analysis of security and complexity is presented in the appendix.

2 Preliminaries

Paillier Cryptosystem. Paillier is a probabilistic asymmetric cryptosystem enjoying additive homomorphism [20]. Paillier randomly generate two large prime numbers p and q, let $N = p * q$. There are public key $pk = N$ and privacy key $sk = (p, q)$; Given pk, a message $m \in \mathbb{Z}_N$ can be encrypted as Eq. 1, Here random number $r \in \mathbb{Z}_N^*$ which brings randomness to encryption. The encrypted message $E(m, r)$ or $E(m)$ can be decrypted by $D_{sk}(\cdot)$ function. Paillier bulit on decisional composite residuosity assumption (DCRA) which is considered intractable. Moreover, Paillier provides semantic security against chosen-plaintext attacks (IND-CPA), namely, given arbitrary ciphertexts, an attacks infer nothing about the plaintext. The additive homomorphism of Paillier can be described as Eq. 2 and Eq. 3.

$$E(m, r) = (1 + N)^m * r^N \mod N^2 \tag{1}$$

$$E(m_1, r_1) * E(m_2, r_2) = E(m_1 + m_2, r_1 r_2) \mod N^2 \tag{2}$$

$$E(m_1, r_1)^{m_2} = E(m_1 * m_2, r_1^{m_2}) \mod N^2 \tag{3}$$

Data Packing. Data Packing (DP) can make full use of the message space of Paillier and reduce the number of decryptions. Under the plaintext, given λ σ-bits integers $x_1, ..., x_\lambda$ we can pack them into one value $\langle x_1 | ... | x_\lambda \rangle = \sum_{i=1}^{\lambda} x_i 2^{\sigma(\lambda - i)}$. Similar to the ciphertext, we store only one ciphertext $E(x_1|...|x_\lambda)$ instead of λ ciphertexts $E(x_1), ..., E(x_\lambda)$. Note that the packed value must meet $\sigma\lambda < \|N\|$ to avoid overflow ($\|N\|$ denotes the bit length of N). Only need $\lceil \frac{\sigma\lambda}{\|N\|} \rceil$ times decryptions can restore $x_1, ..., x_\lambda$. The data packing operation in ciphertext is shown as Eq. 4.

$$E(x_1|...|x_\lambda) = \prod_{i=1}^{\lambda} E(x_i)^{2^{\sigma(\lambda-i)}} \tag{4}$$

Voronoi Diagram. Given geospatial database $\mathcal{D} = \{p_0, p_1, ..., p_{n-1}\}$, Voronoi Diagram divides $\mathcal{D}$ into n disjoint Voronoi Cells $\mathcal{VC}$, and every p_i $(0 \leq i \leq n-1)$ corresponds to a unique $\mathcal{VC}$ denoted as $\mathcal{VC}(p_i)$. In addition, every $\mathcal{VC}(p_i)$ has several adjacent $\mathcal{VC}$, corresponding adjacent points of $\mathcal{VC}(p_i)$ are denoted as $L(p_i)$ (e.g., $L(p_0) = \{p_4, p_8, p_7\}$ in Fig. 2). Given query point q, Voronoi Diagram has the following well-known properties:

Property 1: If p is 1^{th}NN to q, then q must fall into $\mathcal{VC}(p)$;
Property 2: If $t_1, t_2, ..., t_k$ are the top-k nearest points to q in order $(k \geq 1)$, there must be $(k+1)^{th}$NN $t_{k+1} \in L(t_1) \cup L(t_2) \cup ... \cup L(t_k)$;
Property 3: For every $p \in \mathcal{D}$, the average size of $L(p)$ is no more than six;

3 System Framework

3.1 System Model

We adopt two non-colluding clouds model [4,12–15] to build SV-kQ scheme. As shown in Fig. 1, suppose LBS provider owns a geospatial database $\mathcal{D}$ of n POIs, C_1 and C_2 are not colluding servers and user request location services from servers. The system model works as follows:

- **LBS Provider:** LBS provider generates key pair $\langle pk, sk \rangle$ and $\langle pk_s, sk_s \rangle$ for encryption and signature, respectively. More precisely, LBS provider builds verifiable index structure $\mathcal{I}$ on $\mathcal{D}$ and outsources $E(\mathcal{I})$ (encrypt $\mathcal{I}$ using pk) to C_1. Besides, LBS provider allocates pk to cloud C_1, $\{pk, sk\}$ to cloud C_2 and $\{pk, pk_s\}$ to authorized users;
- **Cloud Servers:** Cloud servers include two parts C_1 and C_2. C_1 is responsible for storing and computing $E(\mathcal{I})$ while C_2 keeps the secret key sk to jointly run secure sub-protocols with C_1. Because $E(\mathcal{I})$ and sk are stored separately, C_1 and C_2 cannot obtain any confidential information but securely return kNN results $\mathcal{R}$ and corresponding Verification Object ($\mathcal{VO}$) to users.
- **Users:** The authorized user submits token $E(q)$ (encrypt using pk) to C_1. After that, C_1 and C_2 return two secret shares of kNN result $\mathcal{R}$ and $\mathcal{VO}$. User can restore $\langle \mathcal{R}, \mathcal{VO} \rangle$ and verifies $\mathcal{R}$ using $\mathcal{VO}$ and pk_s.

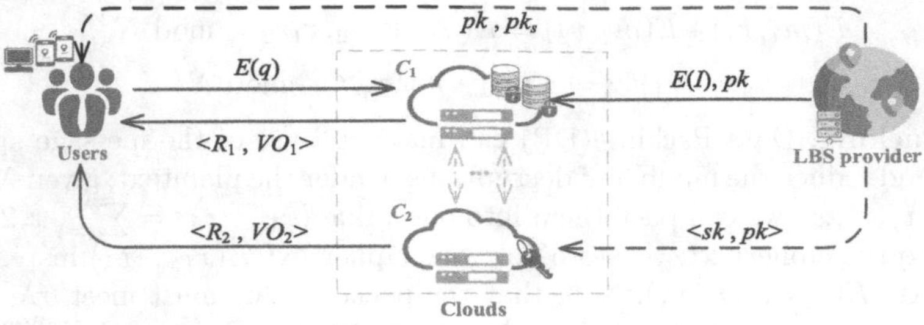

Fig. 1. Twin-cloud server model

In this model, users and LBS provider are a low burden for not being involved in computation; However, there is a heavy operation burden between C_1 and C_2. To address the dilemma, we design a concise secure index and employ a batch read protocol on it to obtain reasonable query latency;

3.2 Security Assumptions and Security Goals

There are some security assumptions in our model. 1) Clouds are malicious but not a conspiracy. We stress that one can purchase cloud services from two different suppliers, because business competition conspiracy is a low probability. Moreover, some anti-conspiracy techniques [27,28] can applied to keep it; 2) User is authorized, but he/she attempts to infer POIs more than $\mathcal{R}$ and avoids paying; 3) LBS provider performs index construction, data encryption and key distribution operations honestly. Besides, we assume that all channels adopt secure transport protocols such as TLS or SSL. Based on the above assumptions, we define the security goals of S-kQ as follows:

- **Dataset/Query/Result privacy:** C_1 and C_2 know nothing about the contents of database $\mathcal{D}$, query q, and kNN results $\mathcal{R}$.
- **Access pattern privacy:** C_1 and C_2 cannot learn which encrypted records are queried in index $E(\mathcal{I})$.
- **Intermediate result privacy:** C_1 and C_2 know nothing about the intermediate result in the computation process, e.g., which POIs are closer than the other.

The above security goals are insufficient because clouds may tamper with $\mathcal{R}$ motivated by profit. To extend S-kQ to the verifiable scheme SV-kQ while hiding no-essential POIs, we define the following two more goals:

- **Result integrity:** For every point $p \in \mathcal{R}$, user can verify p belongs to database $\mathcal{D}$ (correctness), and future verify p is correctly computed (completeness).
- **Privacy-preserving authentication:** In the verification process, user cannot obtain or infer extra information about database $\mathcal{D}$ except results $\mathcal{R}$.

3.3 Secure Sub-protocols

Sub-protocols are applied to implement critical sub-operations on the ciphertext, such as distance compute and top-k select. In sub-protocols C_2 uses sk to assist C_1's calculation, and C_1 only obtains encrypted data while C_2 only obtains noised data so no available data is leaked. The following are some definitions for sub-protocols that have been widely discussed in [5,9,12,13,21,22].

- ***Secure Multiplication*(SM)** [21]: This protocol supposes C_1 with input $E(a)$ and $E(b)$. After computing with C_2, SM protocol outputs $E(a * b)$ to C_1 without a and b leaked to C_1 or C_2.
- ***Secure Squared Euclidean Distance*(SSED)** [21]: Suppose that C_1 with input encrypted points $E(p) = \langle E(x_p), E(y_p)\rangle$ and $E(q) = \langle E(x_q), E(y_q)\rangle$, C_2 with input sk. SSED protocol outputs squared Euclidean distance $E(d) = E(|x_p - x_q|^2 + |y_p - y_q|^2)$ to C_1 securely.
- ***Secure Comparsion*(SCP)** [22]: C_1 with input $E(d_0)$, $E(d_1)$ and C_2 with input sk, SCP protocol outputs $E(1)$ to C_1 if $d_0 \leq d_1$, otherwise outputs $E(0)$. Meanwhile, C_1 and C_2 know nothing about d_0 and d_1.
- ***Secure Minimum*(SMIN):** C_1 with input $\langle E(d_0), E(id_0)\rangle, \langle E(d_1), E(id_1)\rangle$ and C_2 with input sk, SMIN outputs tuple $\langle E(d_{min}), E(id_{min})\rangle$ corresponding $min(d_0, d_1)$ to C_1 securely;

SCP protocol in [22] adopts an efficient idea to achieve comparison. Specifically, C_1 computes $E(\alpha) = E(2 * d_0) * E(2 * d_1 + 1)^{N-1}$ or $E(\alpha) = E(2 * d_1 + 1) * E(2 * d_0)^{N-1}$ randomly. Then, C_2 determines $\alpha > 0$ or not through the magnitude of α. Combined with the judgment result, C_1 restores the actual result locally. Note that SCP inputs $(2*d_0, 2*d_1+1)$ instead of (d_0, d_1) to avoid equivalence leakage. Namely, C_2 can infer two inputs are equal from $\alpha = 0$.

SMIN protocol [13] suffers from equivalence leakage as discussed above. Thus we build SMIN protocol based on SCP. Assume that $\epsilon = bool(d_0 \leq d_1)$, then $d_{min} = d_0{*}\epsilon{+}d_1{*}\neg\epsilon$ and $id_{min} = id_0{*}\epsilon{+}id_1{*}\neg\epsilon$. Therefore, C_1 calculates $E(\epsilon) = \text{SCP}(E(d_0), E(d_1))$. Next $E(d_{min}) = \text{SM}(E(d_0), E(\epsilon)) * \text{SM}(E(d_1), E(1 - \epsilon))$; $E(id_{min}) = \text{SM}(E(id_0), E(\epsilon)) * \text{SM}(E(id_1), E(1 - \epsilon))$;

SMIN out of n Numbers: We organize n times SMIN in a bottom-up tree structure to securely compute the minimum in multi-input. For each layer of execution, C_1 packs all interaction data into one and send to C_2, by few times decryption C_2 can obtain corresponding data. Not only SMIN_n, we stress that other sub-protocols are also suitable for such DP optimization.

3.4 The Main Idea of kNN Query

We briefly describe the main idea of our kNN query in plaintext on index $\mathcal{I}$. First of all, cloud C_1 determines which subspace q falls in and reads all points contained in it at once, and we add these points into candidate set $\mathcal{C}$. Then the read and computation of kNN are executed on $\mathcal{C}$ instead of the entire dataset $\mathcal{I}$. To support accurate kNN, when the search area of kNN crosses into a new subspace, C_1 reads another group of points and appends it to $\mathcal{C}$.

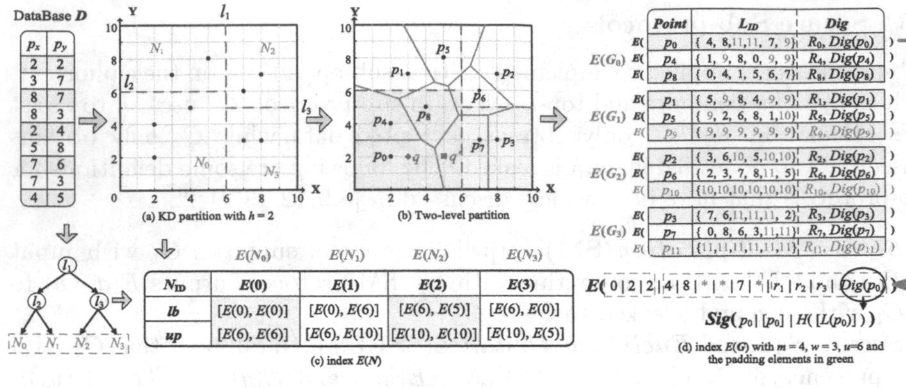

Fig. 2. Secure two-level partition index

4 Secure Index Structure

In this section, we design a secure two-level partition index structure $E(\mathcal{I})$ that adapts to data distribution dynamically. We emphasize that our index structures can achieve the fewest padding and no storage redundancy compared with [13, 17]. To be specific, the first level of $E(\mathcal{I})$ is encrypted K-D partition index $E(\mathcal{N})$. It divides data space $E(\mathcal{D})$ into smaller subspaces, then kNN will be performed on a subspace rather than the entire $E(\mathcal{D})$. However, this approach only supports appropriate kNN as [5], so we further create the second level index $E(\mathcal{G})$ using Voronoi partition. From $E(\mathcal{G})$ one can easily retrieve neighbors at a given point. Using this property, we can realize 1) rectify approximate kNN results to accurate kNN results; 2) extend 1NN problem to kNN problem.

4.1 Secure Two-Level Partition Index

Encrypted K-D Partition Index $E(\mathcal{N})$. To realize kNN computation in sublinear time, LBS provider utilizes K-D tree iteratively splitting the rectangular data space $\mathcal{D}$ into smaller ones along either horizontal or vertical lines. After this process, LBS provider gets $m = 2^{h-1}$(where h is the height of the K-D tree) nodes. We assume all points do not fall on the split line, thus every node contains almost the same number of points. Then index structure $\mathcal{N}$ is created to describe all nodes. As shown in Fig. 2(a), the first column $\boldsymbol{N_{ID}}$ is the identity of every node which from 0 to $m-1$, the lower bound($\boldsymbol{lb}$) and upper bound($\boldsymbol{up}$) record the lower left and upper right vertices of every nodes. At last, LBS provider encrypts $\boldsymbol{N_{ID}}$ and sharp information respectively using pk getting $E(\mathcal{N})$. In fact, $\mathcal{N}$ utilizes only the leaf nodes information in the K-D tree, because the tree structure is not suitable for our read operator.

Encrypted Voronoi Partition Index $E(\mathcal{G})$. LBS provider further builds Voronoi partition index on $\mathcal{N}$. As shown in Fig. 2(b) and Fig. 2(d), $\mathcal{G}$ first divides all points into m groups. For every POI points p in $\mathcal{D}$, p is put in the i-th group $\mathcal{G}_i$

if p falls in the region of $\mathcal{N}_i (0 \leq i \leq m-1)$. Next, LBS provider pads each group to the same size w ensuring groups cannot be distinguished by their sizes. The padding points with coordinates far enough away to not affect the kNN result. Note that the amount of padding is negligible for every group has almost the same size already. After that, LBS provider allocates id for points. Specifically, Given the j-th $(0 \leq j \leq w-1)$ point in $\mathcal{G}_i$, its id (denoted as $\mathcal{G}_{ij}.id$) is computed as Eq. 5; The ***Point*** part consists of point id and its coordinate. As for $\boldsymbol{L_{ID}}$ part, LBS provider splits $\mathcal{D}$ into n disjoint $\mathcal{VC}$ using Voronoi Diagram as Fig. 2(b). Given points p, $\boldsymbol{L_{ID}}$ records the id of $L(p)$. Similarly, LBS provider pads $\boldsymbol{L_{ID}}$ part to same size u to ensure every point has the same number of neighbors while not affecting the correctness of kNN. ***Dig*** part is used to extend S-kQ to SV-kQ which is discussed in Sect. 6. To reduce storage and facilitate our read operations, LBS provider packs every record element together and encrypts packed record getting $E(\mathcal{G})$.

$$\mathcal{G}_{ij}.id = i * m + j \tag{5}$$

5 Pre-read Protocol

Before describing the S-kQ scheme, we present read protocol that guarantees access pattern privacy. Unlike [12,13,15] adopt a read-by-read approach, our protocol adopts a pre-read strategy to obtain a group of records at once. We discuss three types of reading methods, all of which consists of locate and extract two-step, the detail is as follow:

5.1 Type-1: Secure Group Read Based on $E(\mathcal{N})$

Remember the main idea of S-kQ. C_1 needs to read the node where q is contained. So Type-1 group read method has two goals: 1) How to securely locate the $E(\mathcal{N}_z)$ $(0 \leq z \leq m-1)$ where the $E(q)$ falls into; 2) How to "blindly" extract all records contained in group $E(\mathcal{G}_z)$.

1) For every $\mathcal{N}_i$ $(0 \leq i \leq m-1)$, it is necessary to check whether the conditions $\boldsymbol{lb}_i.x < q.x$, $q.x < \boldsymbol{up}_i.x$, $\boldsymbol{lb}_i.y < q.y$ and $q.y < \boldsymbol{up}_i.y$ hold in ciphertext simultaneously. Thus, C_1 first adopts four times SCP protocols to get the corresponding comparison results $E(o_1)$, $E(o_2)$, $E(o_3)$, $E(o_4)$ in sequence. Then, using SM protocols C_1 compute $E(o_1 * o_2 * o_3 * o_4)$ securely, and only $E(1)$ indicates $E(q)$ falls into. In this process, C_1 gets a selection vector $E(\boldsymbol{\eta})$ with length m while reveal nothing to C_1 or C_2. As example in Fig. 2, the $E(\boldsymbol{\eta})$ corresponding to $E(q)$ is $\{E(1), E(0), E(0), E(0)\}$;
2) After getting $E(\boldsymbol{\eta})$ C_1 aims to extract the relevant group $E(\boldsymbol{g})$ in $E(\mathcal{G})$ securely. Therefore we propose SGR protocol as shown in Algorithm 1:

***Secure Group Read* (SGR):** C_1 adds random noise Φ_{ij} to record $E(\mathcal{G}_{ij})$ and lets $\|\mathcal{G}_{ij}\| \leq \|\Phi_{ij}\|$ to completely mask the bit of $\mathcal{G}_{ij}$ (Lines 1–4). Then two

Algorithm 1: Secure Group Read (SGR)

Input: C_1 has $E(\boldsymbol{\eta}), E(\mathcal{G})$; C_2 has sk;
Output: C_1 gets chosen group $E(\boldsymbol{g})$;
/* Calculate on C_1: */
1 **for** $i = 0$ *to* $m-1$ **do**
2   **for** $j = 0$ *to* $w-1$ **do**
3   Generate random number $\Phi_{ij} \in \mathbb{Z}_N$; // $\|\mathcal{G}_{ij}\| \leq \|\Phi_{ij}\|$
4     $E(\mathcal{G}'_{ij}) \leftarrow E(\mathcal{G}_{ij}) * E(\Phi_{ij})$;
5 $E(\Gamma) \leftarrow \pi_2(\pi_1(E(\mathcal{G}')))$; $E(\widetilde{\boldsymbol{\eta}}) \leftarrow \pi_1(E(\boldsymbol{\eta}))$;
6 Send $E(\widetilde{\boldsymbol{\eta}}), E(\Gamma)$ to C_2;
/* Calculate on C_2: */
7 $\widetilde{\boldsymbol{\eta}} \leftarrow D_{sk}(E(\widetilde{\boldsymbol{\eta}}))$;
8 **for** $j = 0$ *to* $m-1$ **do**
9   **if** $\widetilde{\eta}_j == 1$ **then** $E(\boldsymbol{\mu}) \leftarrow E(\Gamma_j) * E(\mathbf{0})$; // Re-encrypt $E(\Gamma_j)$
10 Send $E(\boldsymbol{\mu})$ to C_1;
/* Calculate on C_1: */
11 $E(\boldsymbol{g}') \leftarrow \pi_2^{-1}(E(\boldsymbol{\mu}))$;
12 **for** $j = 0$ *to* $w-1$ **do**
13   $E(\phi_j) \leftarrow \prod_{i=0}^{m-1} E(\boldsymbol{\eta}_j)^{\Phi_{ij}}$;
14   $E(g_j) \leftarrow E(g'_j) * E(\phi_j)^{-1}$;
15 Return $E(\boldsymbol{g})$;

random permutation functions π_1 and π_2 permute $E(\mathcal{G})$ in intra-group and out-group two dimensions, $E(\boldsymbol{\eta})$ also is permuted with π_1 (line 5). Subsequently, C_1 sends $E(\Gamma)$ and $E(\widetilde{\boldsymbol{\eta}})$ to C_2 (Line 6);

Upon receiving encryped data, C_2 gets $\widetilde{\boldsymbol{\eta}}$ and then retrieves the chosen group $E(\Gamma_j)$ corresponding to $\widetilde{\boldsymbol{\eta}}_j = 1$ (Lines 7–9). Note that C_2 returns $E(\Gamma_j) * E(\mathbf{0})$ instead of $E(\Gamma_j)$ to prevents C_1 from referring which group is chosen (Line 10).

After receiving $E(\boldsymbol{\mu})$, C_1 computes the inverse permutation getting $E(\boldsymbol{g}')$ and extracts the noise $E(\boldsymbol{\phi}_j)$ (Lines 11–13). For the semantic security of Paillier, C_1 speculate nothing from $E(\boldsymbol{\phi}_j)$. At last, $E(\boldsymbol{g})$ can remove noise as $E(\boldsymbol{g}'_j) * E(\boldsymbol{\phi}_j)^{-1}$ (Line 14). Note that $E(\boldsymbol{\phi}_j)^{-1} \equiv E(-\boldsymbol{\phi}_j) \mod N^2$;

Discussion 1: SGR in line 3 needs to generate n encrypted random numbers, in line 7 performs $\lceil \frac{m}{\|N\|} \rceil$ times decryptions and in line 13 computes n times modulo powers on big integers. We only discuss above time-consuming cryptographic operations, thus the complexity of SGR is $O(n)$ where n is database size.

5.2 Type-2: Secure Group Read Based on $E(id)$

Type-1 method can read the first group based on $E(\mathcal{N})$. However Type-2 method aims to read subsequent groups securely. Given $E(id)$ (which is contained in L_{ID}), there are two goals have to achieve: 1) How to judge whether the target record is already in $E(g)$; 2) If not, how to locate and extract another group containing $E(id)$. To solve it, we propose SIC protocol as follows:

***Secure ID Compution* (SIC):** As shown in Algorithm 2. We assume that $E(T)$ includes l groups has been read in by SGR. After SIC C_1 gets choose vector $E(\eta)$ if $E(id)$ outside $E(T)$. Otherwise gets $\varnothing$ (codes in pink). We show an example in accordance with Fig. 2. Suppose that $E(\mathcal{G}_0)$ has been read into $E(T)$ using Type-1 method, C_1 aims to read p_7. After SIC, a new group $E(\mathcal{G}_3)$ can be marked by $E(\eta)$, then $E(\mathcal{G}_3)$ is extracted using SGR protocol and added into $E(T)$.

Discussion 2: The running time of SIC is $O(l)$. Generally, a small l can handle a considerable number of NN in kNN query (e.g., on average, four groups can deal with 40NN in ours experiments), and the larger the k, the greater the advantage in read. Because when q is near the K-D split line, even a small k may incur several times of SGR.

Algorithm 2: Secure ID Compution (SIC)

Input: C_1 has $E(id)$, $E(T)$; C_2 has sk;
Output: C_1 gets $E(\eta)$ or $\varnothing$;
`/* Calculate on` C_1: `*/`
$E(T) \leftarrow \pi_1(E(T))$; $E(\alpha) \leftarrow E(id + r)$; //$\pi_1(E(T))$ permutes all groups in $E(T)$
Initialize random numbers vector ϕ with length l;
for $k = 0$ *to* $l - 1$ **do**
  $E(\delta_k) \leftarrow E(id) * E(m * \phi_k - T_{k0}.id)$; //$T_{k0}.id$ denotes the first record's id in group in T_k
Send $E(\delta), E(\alpha)$ to C_2;
`/* Calculate on` C_2: `*/`
$\delta \leftarrow D_{sk}(E(\delta))$; $\alpha \leftarrow D_{sk}(E(\alpha))$
for $k = 0$ *to* $l - 1$ **do**
  if $\delta_k \equiv 0 \mod m$ **then**
    Send *tag* to C_2 and terminate; // $\delta_k \equiv 0 \mod m$ means desired record in $E(T_k)$
Initialize $E(\widetilde{\eta}) \leftarrow \varnothing$; $j \leftarrow \alpha \mod m$; // j marks the position of group containing desired record
for $i = 0$ *to* $m - 1$ **do**
  if $i == j$ **then** $E(\widetilde{\eta})$ append $E(1)$;
  otherwise $E(\widetilde{\eta})$ append $E(0)$;
Send $E(\widetilde{\eta})$ to C_1;
`/* Calculate on` C_1: `*/`
if receive *tag* **then** return $\varnothing$ and terminate;
else $E(\eta) \leftarrow CL(E(\widetilde{\eta}), r \mod m)$; //Cyclic right shift $r \mod m$ units to remove offset caused by r
Return $E(\eta)$;

5.3 Type-3: Secure Record Read Based on $E(id)$

Using the judgment approach in SIC, C_1 determine $E(id)$ in group $E(T_k)$ where $0 \leq k \leq l-1$. Then, type-3 read method aim to "blindly" read the record from $E(T_k)$ as follow:

Location: To generate record selection vector $E(\boldsymbol{\eta})$, a natural idea is to match $E(id)$ with all records using homomorphic subtraction property, just as [12,13,15]. This approach is clearly secure but leads to $O(w)$ computational overhead. To improve, we leverage the same idea in SIC protocol that only $O(1)$ running time. The critical steps are simplified as follows: C_1 noises $E(id)$ as step 1. Next, C_2 computes index value j in step 2, j is used to generate vector $E(\widetilde{\boldsymbol{\eta}})$ (length is w), which only j-th element is $E(1)$ and the others are $E(0)$. At last, using $CL(\cdot)$ function C_1 eliminates the offsets caused by r, such that $E(\boldsymbol{\eta})$ indicates the position of target record;

① $\boldsymbol{C_1}$: $E(\alpha) \leftarrow E(id + m * r - T_{k0})$;
② $\boldsymbol{C_2}$: $j \leftarrow \alpha/m \mod w$;
③ $\boldsymbol{C_1}$: $E(\boldsymbol{\eta}) \leftarrow CL(E(\widetilde{\boldsymbol{\eta}}), r \mod m)$;

Extraction: SGR protocol is also adopt to the extraction of record. In particular, C_1 sets the group size w to one. with inputs $E(T_k)$ and $E(\boldsymbol{\eta})$, the amended SGR outputs the encrypted record corresponding to $E(id)$.

6 Secure *k*NN Schemes S-*k*Q and SV-*k*Q

This section describes how to build encrypted *k*NN scheme S-*k*Q based on sub-protocols and Pre-Read protocol. Then we design ADS and corresponding authentication protocol extending S-*k*Q to SV-*k*Q. At last, an optimization strategy is proposed to speed up the ciphertext generation. Following the model of simulation paradigm in [25], we present security proofs for S-*k*Q and SV-*k*Q in the appendix, and it shows our schemes achieve strong security.

6.1 Secure *k*NN Scheme S-*k*Q

we discuss S-kQ scheme which consists of the following three steps: Step of secure 1st NN rectification aims to find the first nearest point, and secure *k*NN computation extends 1NN query to *k*NN query. Then results are returned to user by the secure return step.

Step1: Secure 1^{st}NN Rectification(@S-*k*Q). Given index $E(\mathcal{I})$ and query $E(q)$, C_1 invokes Type-1 read method to get the first group containing q. Because all records are stored using DP, it is essential to unpack ***Point*** part by interacting with C_2. Then, C_1 computes the distance $E(d)$ between each record in $E(T)$ and $E(q)$ using SSED protocol, and the minimum distance $E(d'_{min})$ with its $E(id'_{min})$ can be filtered by SMIN_n protocol. To hide access pattern, C_1 uses Type-3 read method getting record corresponding to $E(id'_{min})$ (denoted as

1^{st}NN$'$). We stress that 1^{st}NN$'$ is possibly not the nearest point in $\mathcal{D}$. As shown in Fig. 2(b), the query $E(q')$ falls into $E(\mathcal{N}_0)$, in the way above C_1 gets 1^{st}NN$'$ $E(p_0)$. Nevertheless, the nearest point is $E(p_8)$. Given this observation, we propose the following theorem which can be proved by the *property 2* of Voronoi Diagram.

Theorem 1. *When the split line of kd-tree passes through* $\mathcal{VC}(1^{st}NN')$ *may lead to the inaccuracy of the first NN, but* $\mathcal{VC}(1^{st}NN')$ *and* $\mathcal{VC}(1^{st}NN)$ *must be adjacent.*

Based on Theorem 1, we do 1^{st}NN$'$ rectification, that is, retrieving 1^{st}NN from neighbors of 1^{st}NN$'$. Specifically, C_1 obtains the encrypted neighbors' *id* from the $\boldsymbol{N_{ID}}$ part, and then retrieves neighbor records through Type-3 read method. Note that this process may require reading a new group into $E(T)$ using Type-2 read method. Similar to the computation of 1^{st}NN$'$, C_1 filters out the nearest record to $E(q)$ from 1^{st}NN$'$ and its neighbors. At last, 1^{st}NN is inserted into $\mathcal{R}$.

Step2: Secure kNN Computation(@S-kQ). The main idea of kNN computation is finding the successor in the nearest points' neighbors. To query 2^{nd}NN, C_1 "blindly" reads $L(1^{st}$NN) in $E(T)$ combining Type-2 and Type-3 read methods. Note that C_1 only needs to read ***Point*** part instead of the entire record, which can significantly reduce the time spent on Type-3 read method for the shorter the message bit length, the more efficient SGR in lines 12–14. Then C_1 adds $L(1^{st}$NN) into candidate set $E(\mathcal{C})$. Based on *property 2* of Voronoi Diagram, C_1 can rapidly find 2^{nd}NN in set $E(\mathcal{C})$ using SEED and SMIN$_n$ protocols. To benefit the next round search, C_1 appends $L(2^{nd}$NN) to $E(\mathcal{C})$ and then finds 3^{th}NN in it. Repeat the above process until the top-k results are added to $E(\mathcal{R})$. Crucially, $E(\mathcal{C})$ may contain the records already inserted into $E(\mathcal{R})$, it is essential to delete them to avoid being revisited. Considering the access pattern privacy, we adopt delete protocol in [12] to hide which records are "deleted", its main idea is to set the already visited points' distance to the maximum value.

Step3: Secure Result Return(@S-kQ). After getting $\mathcal{R}$, C_1 and C_2 securely return result to user as follows: C_1 generates random number set $\mathcal{R}_1$ with size k, for every record belong to $E(\mathcal{R})$, a corresponding noise in $\mathcal{R}_1$ is added on it. Then C_1 returns noise $\mathcal{R}_1$ to user, while C_2 decrypts and returns noised results $\mathcal{R}_2$ to user. User can restore $\mathcal{R}$ by removing noise in plaintext as step3.

① $\boldsymbol{C_1}$: $E(\mathcal{R}_2) \leftarrow E(\mathcal{R}+\mathcal{R}_1)$; Send $\mathcal{R}_1$ to user;
② $\boldsymbol{C_2}$: $\mathcal{R}_2 \leftarrow D_{sk}(E(\mathcal{R}_2))$; Send $\mathcal{R}_2$ to user;
③ **User**: Get $\mathcal{R} \leftarrow \mathcal{R}_1 - \mathcal{R}_2$;

6.2 Verifiable Scheme Based on *LT*

Nevertheless, a malicious server may return tempered or false results to user in S-kQ. Thus we aim to verify the S-kQ result further. This part first discusses the verification scheme in [13] and points out its shortcomings; To improve it, the next part shows clouds how to generate $\mathcal{VO}$ by secure sharing and user how to verify results with comparison privacy and privacy-preserving authentication.

To verify that $\mathcal{R} = \{t_1, t_2, ..., t_k\}$ contains the top-k nearest neighbors in $\mathcal{D}$, Cui et al. based on the Voronoi properties to proof the distance relation for user. Given the neighbors information in $L(t_i)$, the main idea is as follows:

- If $i \geq 2$, verify $t_i \in L(t_1) \cup L(t_2) \cup ... \cup L(t_{i-1})$.
- For $\forall p \in L(t_1) \cup L(t_2) \cup ... \cup L(t_i) - t_1 \cup t_2 \cup ... \cup t_{i-1}$, verify $d(t_i, q) \leq d(p, q)$.

The running time of above idea is only related to k, however $L(t_i)$ exposes extra POIs to user incurring the risk of leakage. Thus, Cui et al. utilizes linearity-based transformation (LT) to transform $L(t_i)$ and q. For each p belonging to $L(t_i)$, LT does rotate and translate on p and q simultaneously getting p' and q' while maintaining $d(p,q) = d(p',q')$. They define tuple of $\mathcal{VO}$ as $\langle L(t_i)', \{q'\}, H(L(t_i)), Dig(t_i)\rangle$. Given $H(L(t_i))$ user can prove correctness by verifying $Dig(t_i)$. Then, due to the property of LT user can verify completeness.

However, the distance-preserving property is insufficient to hide $L(t_i)$ as discussed in [6]. A more fatal flaw is that the $Dig(t_i)$ binds the t_i and $L(t_i)$ together instead of t_i and $L(t_i)'$, which means $Dig(t_i)$ cannot guarantee the correctness of $L(t_i)'$. Therefore, Clouds can bypasses the geometric verification by forging $\{L(t_i)'\}$ as *Example* 1.

Example 1: In Fig. 2(b), we give an example under plaintext. User query 1NN p_0 at location q. $L(p_4)' = \{p_1', p_9', p_8', p_0', p_9', p_9'\}$, Clouds forge it as $L(\hat{p_4})' = \{p_9', p_9', p_9', p_9', p_9', p_9'\}$. then return $\hat{\mathcal{R}} = \{p_4\}$ and $\hat{\mathcal{VO}} = \langle L(\hat{p_4})', \{q'\}, H(L(p_4)), Dig(p_4)\rangle$ to user. User first verifies $Dig(p_4)$ using $H(L(p_4))$ and p_4. Next, for $d(q', p_9')$ bigger than $d(q', p_4')$, user is convinced by the wrong result.

6.3 Secure and Verifiable *k*NN Scheme SV-*k*Q

To address this problem in [13], we employ Paillier to hide $L(p)$ and extend S-kQ to SV-kQ. Noted that Paillier achieves semantic security so no distance is exposed. All operations about reading and computation of kNN are just like that of S-kQ, thus, this part focus on how to build ADS and how to carry out privacy-preserving authentication.

ADS Structure(@SV-*k*Q). Assuming $p_1 = (x_1, y_1), p_2 = (x_2, y_2), q = (q_x, q_y)$, ADS structure needs to support the comparison of Euclidean distances on ciphertexts. By simplifying $d(p_1, q)$ and $d(p_2, q)$, it is equivalent to comparing $E(a)$ and $E(b)$ as follows.

$$\begin{aligned} E(a) &= E(x_1^2 + y_1^2) * E(-2x_1)^{q_x} * E(-2y_1)^{q_y}; \\ E(b) &= E(x_2^2 + y_2^2) * E(-2x_2)^{q_x} * E(-2y_2)^{q_y}; \end{aligned} \tag{6}$$

All entries except q_x and q_y can be precomputed and signed by LBS provider. For each p_i belonging to $\mathcal{D}$, we define $[p_i] = \{E(x_i^2 +$

$y_i^2, r_1), E(-2x_i, r_2), E(-2y_i, r_3)\}$. LBS provider first computes $H([p_i])$ as Eq. 7. For the probabilistic property of Paillier, r_1, r_2 and r_3 must be discussed to ensure that user can reproduce $H([p_i])$. Then, LBS provider computes $H([L(p_i)]) = H([L_1(p_i)]||...|[L_u(p_i)])$. At last, p_i, $[p_i]$ and $H([L(p_i)])$ are bound together getting $Dig(p_i)$ as Eq. 8.

$$H([p_i]) = H(E(x_i^2 + y_i^2, r_1)|E(-2x_i, r_2)|E(-2y_i, r_3)); \tag{7}$$

$$Dig(p_i) = Sig(p_i|H([p_i])|H([L(p_i)])); \tag{8}$$

In summary, we extend ***Dig*** part on $E(\mathcal{G})$ as shown in Fig. 2(d), where R_i includes three random numbers r_1, r_2, r_3 corresponding to $E(x_i^2 + y_i^2)$, $E(-2x_i)$ and $E(-2y_i)$, respectively. We emphasize that encrypting R_i is necessary, for user can restore the plaintext m as Eq. 9 if knows the adopted random number r.

$$m = \frac{(E(m, r) * r^{-N}) \mod N^2 - 1}{N}; \tag{9}$$

$\mathcal{VO}$ Generation(@SV-kQ). We defind $\mathcal{VO}$ of SV-kQ as $\langle[\mathcal{R}], [L(\mathcal{R})], Dig(\mathcal{R})\rangle$ and its *i-th* tuple as $\langle[t_i], [L(t_i)], Dig(t_i)\rangle$ $(1 \leq i \leq k)$, here $[\mathcal{R}] = \{[t_1] \cup ... \cup [t_k]\}$ and $[L(\mathcal{R})] = \{[L(t_1)] \cup ... \cup [L(t_k)]\}$. Given ***Point*** part, C_1 calculates $E(x^2 + y^2)$,$E(-2x)$,$E(-2y)$ by the homomorphism property and SM protocol. As mentioned above, the r provides randomness and security to Paillier. Thus, $\mathcal{VO}$ generation contains two challenges: 1) In order to reproduce $H([L(p_i)])$ on user, how to eliminate the randomness of Paillier; 2) How to guarantee the security of r. To this end, we design SCG protocol to generate $\mathcal{VO}$ securely.

Shared Ciphertext Generation **(SCG):** $E(x^2 + y^2)$ or $E(-2x)$ or $E(-2y)$ is uniformly denoted as $E(e)$, $E(r_s)$ is the corresponding Paillier random. r_a, r_b are random noise generated by C_1. The crucial steps of SCG are as follows: C_1 adds noise to $E(e)$ and $E(r_s)$ getting $E(e')$ and $E(r')$ (step 1). Then, C_1 returns one share $E(e_1)$ to user (step 2). After C_2 receiving $E(e')$ and $E(r_s')$, C_2 returns another share $E(e_2)$ to user (step 3). Noting that user can compute $E(e_1) * E(e_2) = E(x' - r_a, r_s' * r_b^{-1}) = E(e, r)$.

① $\boldsymbol{C_1}$: $E(e') \leftarrow E(e) * E(r_a)$; $E(r_s') \leftarrow E(r_s)^{r_b}$;
② $\boldsymbol{C_1}$: $E(e_1) \leftarrow E(r_a, r_b)^{-1}$; Send $E(e_1)$ to user;
③ $\boldsymbol{C_2}$: $E(e_2) \leftarrow E(e', r_s')$; Send $E(e_2)$ to user;

For all ciphertext involved in $[L(\mathcal{R})]$ and $[\mathcal{R}]$, C_1 and C_2 apply SCG protocol to deal with. Then, $\mathcal{VO}$ can be split into $\mathcal{VO}_1$ and $\mathcal{VO}_2$. User can restore $\mathcal{VO}$ to verify $\mathcal{R}$.

Verification Process(@SV-kQ). For signature verification, user verifies every $t_i \in \mathcal{R}$ $(1 \leq i \leq k)$ using *i-th* tuple of $\mathcal{VO}$. Specifically, user computes $H([L(t_i)])$ and verifies $Dig(t_i)$ using pk_s to guarantee correctness. After that, user is convinced: 1)t_i belongs to $\mathcal{D}$ while $[t_i]$ and $[L(t_i)]$ not be tempered; 2) $[L(t_i)]$ indeed about the neighbors of t_i or $[t_i]$; For geometric verification, we optimize the verification conditions in [13] by eliminating redundant comparisons and present Theorem 2.

Algorithm 3: Secure Distance Verification (SDV)

Input: User has $\mathcal{VO}$; C_2 has sk;
Output: User and C_2 verify each other;
/* Calculate on user: */
Remove $[\mathcal{R}]$ from $[L(\mathcal{R})]$ get $[L(\mathcal{R})-\mathcal{R}]$; // Deletes all points contained in $[\mathcal{R}]$ from $[L(\mathcal{R})]$
Remove duplicate points from $[L(\mathcal{R})-\mathcal{R}]$ get $[\mathcal{V}]$ with size s; // Avoid redundant comparison
$E(a_k) \leftarrow [t_k]_1 * ([t_k]_2)^{q_x} * ([t_k]_3)^{q_y}$; // $[t_k]_i$ denotes the i-th elements in set $[t_k]$
for $i = 0$ *to* $s-1$ **do**
  Get $i\text{-}th$ point $[p_i]$ from $[\mathcal{V}]$;
  $E(b_i) \leftarrow [p_i]_1 * ([p_i]_2)^{q_x} * ([p_i]_3)^{q_y}$; //$E(b_i)$ or $E(a_k)$ is bulid as Eq.2
  $\phi_i \xleftarrow{\$} \mathbb{Z}_N$; $\rho_i \xleftarrow{\$} \{0,1\}$; //$\phi_i$ serves as random noise and ρ_i is used to swap a_k and b_i randomly
  if $\rho_i = 0$ **then** $E(\delta_i) \leftarrow E(a_k - b_i)^{\phi_i}$;
  otherwise $E(\delta_i) \leftarrow E(b_i - a_k)^{\phi_i}$;
$c \leftarrow H(H(\rho))$; Send $E(\delta)$ and c to C_2;
/* Verify on C_2: */
$\delta \leftarrow D(E(\delta))$;
for $i = 0$ *to* $s-1$ **do**
  if $\delta_i > 0$ **then** $\hat{\rho}_i \leftarrow 1$; **otherwise** $\hat{\rho}_i \leftarrow 0$;
Verify $H(H(\hat{\rho})) \stackrel{?}{=} c$; //$\hat{\rho} = \rho$ means protocols are executed honestly with high probability
$\hat{c} = H(\hat{\rho})$; Send $\hat{c}$ to user;
/* Verify on user: */
Verify $H(\rho) \stackrel{?}{=} \hat{c}$;

Theorem 2. *kNN result $\mathcal{R}$ satisfies the following conditions: 1) For $\forall p_{in} \in \mathcal{R}$, let $t_k \in \mathcal{R}$ meets $d(t_k, q) \geq d(p_{in}, q)$. 2) For $\forall p_{out} \in \{L(\mathcal{R}) - \mathcal{R}\}$, let $d(t_k, q) \leq d(p_{out}, q)$;*

User first verifies 1) in Theorem 2 and obtains the $k\text{-}th$ nearest neighbor t_k. As for *2)*, it is equivalent to verify condition *2′): For* $\forall[p_{out}] \in [L(\mathcal{R}) - \mathcal{R}]$, *let* $d([p_k], q) \leq d([p_{out}], q)$. Thus we present protocol in Algorithm 3 and give corresponding *Example* 2 as follow.

Example 2: As shown in Fig. 2(b), user query 2NN = $\{p_0, p_4\}$ at location q, Clouds return tuples of $\mathcal{VO}$ as $\langle [p_0], \{[p_4], [p_8], [p_{11}], [p_{11}], [p_7], [p_9]\}, Dig(p_0)\rangle$ and $\langle [p_4], \{[p_1], [p_9], [p_8], [p_0], [p_9], [p_9]\}, Dig(p_4)\rangle$. User generates $[\mathcal{V}] = \{[p_8], [p_{11}], [p_7], [p_9], [p_1]\}$. Suppose $\rho = \{0,1,0,0,1\}$, for $d(q,[p_4]) < d(q,[p_8]), d(q,[p_{11}]) > d(q,[p_4]), d(q,[p_4]) < d(q,[p_7]), d(q,[p_4]) < d(q,[p_9]), d(q,[p_1]) > d(q,[p_4])$. C_2 generates $\hat{\rho}_i = \{0,1,0,0,1\}$; $\rho = \hat{\rho}$ means the completeness is authenticated with high probability.

Discussion 3: The average size of $[\mathcal{V}]$ is less than $6k$ for *property 3* of Voronoi Diagram, so the complexity of SDV is $O(6k)$. SDV is a bidirectional verification protocol between user and C_2. For a malicious user may compute on other sets he/she concerns instead of $[\mathcal{V}]$. In this way, user can speculate the comparison results between any ciphertext. Although hash is a one-way function, it is possible to infer $\hat{\boldsymbol{\rho}}$ given c. Specifically, by controlling the valid length s, user may recover $\hat{\boldsymbol{\rho}}$ with at most 2^s times hash. Similarly, if C_2 operates as an adversary hoping to bypass distance verification by faking, the adversary can only guess the vector $\boldsymbol{\rho}$ with a probability of $1/(2^s)$. To ensure this probability is negligible, user padding $E(\boldsymbol{\delta})$ with the encrypted random number and $\boldsymbol{\rho}$ with the corresponding bool value if s is too short.

6.4 The Optimized Ciphertext Generation

Our schemes need to generate a large number of random numbers in ciphertext, and this is a time consuming operation. Therefore, we show the optimized Paillier ciphertext generation scheme to improve schemes efficiency. In Eq. 1, the part of $(1+N)^m \mod N^2$ can be optimized as $(mN+1) \mod N^2$ as [24]. As for the computation of $r^N \mod N^2$, C_1 generate a pool that stores a large number of N powers of random. When performing encryption, C_1 randomly picks several values to produce new r^N by modular multiplication. We set pool size as 2000 and ten values are selected to generate r^N, for new r^N is pseudo-random and $C_{2000}^{10} > 2^{70}$, it is impossible for an adversary to guess adopted r^N. In this way, one-time encryption requires only 11 times modular multiplication.

7 Performance Evaluation

Implementation: We implement all codes in Java and carry out all experiments on Windows 10 machine equipped with 16 GB RAM and 3.2 GHz 16-core AMD R7-5800H CPU. Besides, we adopt SHA-256 as hash algorithm and 160bit ECDSA as signature algorithm.

Dataset: (1) **CA** contains 21,047 real-world POIs non-uniformly distributed in California, which is publicly available on [23]. (2) **SYN** is a synthetic dataset containing 10,000 same format spatial data with uniform distribution.

Parameter Setting: We adopt different parameter setting to measure the performance of all schemes. For instance, the number of POIs n varies from 2,000 to 10,000, the query parameter k from 1 to 40, the key length K from 1024 to 3072. At last, by adjusting the height of K-D tree h, let the group size w vary in four intervals $[16,32)$, $[32,64)$, $[64,128)$, $[128,256)$ (note that $w = \lceil n/2^h \rceil$). $[64,128)$ is the default interval in experiments unless otherwise stated.

7.1 Evaluation of Different SkNN Schemes

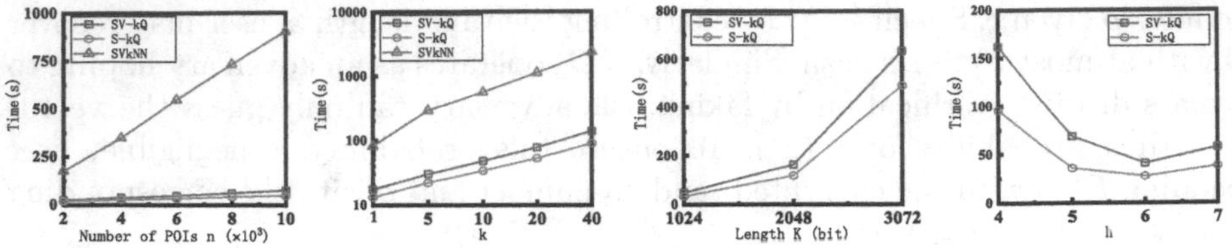

(a) vary n with k=10 (b) vary k with n=6000 (c) vary K (d) vary h

Fig. 3. Impact of varying parameters on SYN

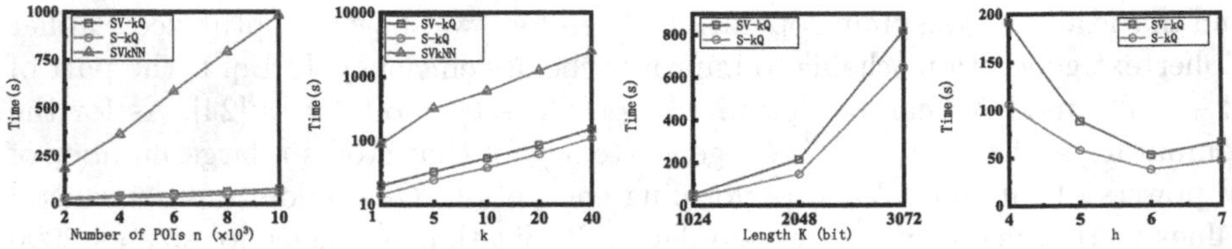

(a) vary n with k=10 (b) vary k with n=6000 (c) vary K (d) vary h

Fig. 4. Impact of varying parameters on CA

We compare SV-kQ, S-kQ, and SVkNN schemes in different datasets. Note that we remove SVkNN verification process for its error but remain query process, and query latency in experiments is tested as the average of fifteen sets of data under different q.

Impact of varying n: Analyzing Fig. 3(a) and Fig. 4(a), the time cost is approximately linearly related to n for all schemes. **CA** dataset is slightly more efficient than **SYN** for random spatial data leading to smaller u and l. Our schemes have significant advantages over SVkNN. Specifically, in $n = 2000$ and $k = 10$, the query latency of S-kQ, SV-kQ and SVkNN are 23 s, 28 s and 182 s under **CA** dataset respectively, and when n is expanded to 10, 000, the corresponding times are 60 s, 78 s and 982 s, respectively.

Impact of varying k: Fig. 3(b) and Fig. 4(a) depict the performance of all schemes with the varied k on different datasets. The time cost of S-kQ and SV-kQ increase linear with k, for the case of $k = 1$, $n = 6,000$, and in **CA** dataset, the time taken by S-kQ, SV-kQ and SVkNN are 14 s, 19 s, and 88 s respectively. When k is expanded to 40, the corresponding times are 108 s, 151 s and 2488 s respectively. The average growth rate of SV-kQ is about 5.5% of SVkNN, this is affect by Pre-Read protocol, optimized Paillier encryption and index structure. The time consumption of S-kQ is about 2/3 of SV-kQ. Because S-kQ reads fewer data elements and does not need to generate $\mathcal{VO}$.

Impact of varying K: The time cost by S-kQ and SV-kQ increases exponentially with the varying key length K in. As shown in Fig. 3(c) and Fig. 4(c), for

$k = 10, n = 6,000, K = 2048$, the time cost of S-$k$Q and SV-$k$Q in **CA** dataset are 148 s and 215 s, respectively. While in **SYN** dataset, the corresponding time are 118 s and 163 s, respectively.

Impact of varying h: Fig. 3(d) and Fig. 4(d) show the effect of k-d tree height h on the efficiency of S-kQ and SV-kQ for $n = 6000$ and $k = 10$. It can be seen that schemes have the best efficiency when $h = 6$, which is a balance between group read time, intra-group read time and secure computation time. The optimal h value is affected by both k and n, in fact, additional experimental data shows the optimal efficiency is generally achieved when $\lceil n/2^h \rceil \in [64, 128)$.

7.2 Evaluation of Verification Process

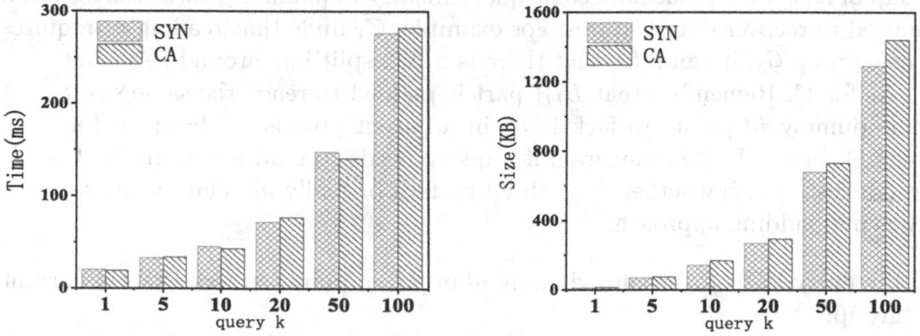

(a) Verification time on User (b) VO size on User

Fig. 5. Evaluation of verification process

We evaluate the performance of the verification operation under different datasets. As shown in Fig. 5(a). For k from 1 to 100, the user-side verification time under **SYN** and **CA** increases from 20 ms to 276 ms and from 19 ms to 282 ms, respectively. There is no significant difference under different datasets. Figure 5(b) shows the effect of k on $\mathcal{VO}$ size. Specifically, when k increases from 1 to 100, the $\mathcal{VO}$ size under **SYN** increases from 13 KB to 1390 KB while increases from 14 KB to 1441 KB under **CA**. The $\mathcal{VO}$ size of **CA** is larger than that of **SYN** on average, because the number of neighbors under real dataset is bigger than that of random dataset after padding.

8 Conclusion

This paper focuses on the secure and verifiable kNN problem in cloud computing. We design a novel partition-based index structure and employ an efficient read (Pre-Read) protocols to deal with kNN, this novelties also can be employed by other service models. We then show the error of existing solution, and present the verifiable scheme by Paillier to solve it. Besides, extensive experiments and detailed analyses demonstrate the strong security and high efficiency of our schemes. Future work aim to extend our work to dynamic datasets, and our index structure supports efficient dynamic operation for the impact of update cannot spread in Voronoi diagram. However, our read method is difficult to apply to this scenario, one possible solution is to combine technology ORAM. Higher dimensions is also our focus, and more efficient computation sub-protocols and index structure in high dimensions have important research significance.

A Indistinguishable Read Operation

There are two leakages in our read methods: 1) C_1 and C_2 know whether the target record is in $E(T)$ or not; 2) Further, C_1 knows the target record in which group of $E(T)$. If Clouds have some query history in plaintext, these leakages can be used to recover data features. For example, C_1 finds that reading p_7 requires a new group $\mathcal{G}_3$, it can infer that there is a KD split line around p_7.

As for 1): Remember that $\boldsymbol{L_{ID}}$ part is padded to reach the same size u. Let some dummy id points to fack POIs in adjacent groups as shown in Fig. 2(d) green elements. In this way, even if a query needs to read a new group, Clouds cannot distinguish whether it is caused by fack or really id. Thus we present the following padding approach:

① For every POIs p, initialize dummy id in $p.L_{ID}$ points to fack POIs in current group;
② For every POIs p_e approaching the K-D split line, make a circle A with p_e as the center and a as the radius;
③ If A crosses to node $\mathcal{N}_i$, with probability 1/2 modify a dummy id in $p_e.L_{ID}$ points to fack POI in group $\mathcal{G}_i$;

As for 2): When the target record is not in a group of $E(T)$, C_2 returns a selection vector with full $E(0)$ instead a tag in SIC protocol, so that all groups are indistinguishable for C_1. The full $E(0)$ selection vector extracts data $E(0)$, by multiplying the extraction together, C_1 gets the target record.

B Complexity Analysis

We gives the complexity analysis for read methods and SkNN schemes. We only discuss the encryption, decryption and modular-exponentiation operations, for the time consumption of other operations can be ignored.

The Pre-Read protocol requires the execution of 1 time Type-1 methods. $l-1$ times Type-2 method and $uk+k$ times Type-3 methods. Combining *discuss* 1-3, the running time for generating selection vector is $O(m+(l-1)l+(ku+k)l) = O(lku+m)$, and the complexity for extraction is $O(ln+(uk+k)w) = O(ln+kuw)$. Note that the uk times Type-3 method can be optimized by extracting only the essential elements. We set w as a constant, when n is large enough (e.g., $n >$

1, 0000), the time taken for Type-3 is almost negligible. As for kNN computation, 1NN involves SEED and SMIN_n protocols on $E(\boldsymbol{g})$, and the subsequent kNN incurs SEED and SMIN_n protocols on set $E(\mathcal{C})$. Other operations such as delete, $\mathcal{VO}$ generating can be ignored. Thus the complexity is $O(w + u + 2u + ... + ku) = O(w + k^2u)$. In summary, the complexity of S-kQ and SV-kQ is $O(ln + kuw) + O(w + k^2u)$, which can be simplified as $O(ln) + O(k^2u)$. Using the same analysis we get the running time of Bucket-Read protocol and SVkNN scheme are $O(k\sqrt{n}) + O(kn)$ and $O(kn) + O(\sqrt{n} + k^2u)$ respectively.

C Security Analysis

In this subsection, we describe acceptable leakage in our secure model and adopt simulation paradigm framework [25] to perform security proof for S-kQ and SV-kQ.

Leakage Functions $\mathcal{L}$: We define two leakage functions. (1) $\mathcal{L}_{setup}(\mathcal{I}) = (m, w, u)$: Given index $\mathcal{I}$, $\mathcal{L}_{setup}$ outputs the number of group m, the group size w and the number of neighbors u. (2) $\mathcal{L}_{query}(\mathcal{I}, q) = \mathcal{L}_{read}$: Given index $\mathcal{I}$ and query q, $\mathcal{L}_{query}$ outputs the reading behavior $\mathcal{L}_{read}$ which includes how many groups are read and when they are read.

Theorem 3. *All sub-protocols between Clouds are secure on* $(\mathcal{L}_{setup}, \mathcal{L}_{query})$.

Proof. Suppose there is a simulator $\mathcal{S}$ and a probabilistic polynomial-time (PPT) adversary $\mathcal{A}$. (1) For sub-protocols except SIC: From C_2's view, C_2 only obtains the masked data which cannot be distinguished with the random data, and the data magnitude (in SCP) is also indistinguishable for C_2. Besides, the permutation function π makes C_2 obtain the random record or group position. Thus, $\mathcal{S}$ can simulate all interactions with C_2 using $\mathcal{L}_{setup}$. From C_1's view, C_1 receives the encrypted data from C_2. Because IND-CPA security of Paillier C_1 cannot distinguish the ciphertexts while $\mathcal{S}$ can simulate all interactions with C_1. To sum up, the real-world view $Real^{\mathcal{A}}$ and the ideal-world view $Sim^{\mathcal{A}}$ cannot be distinguished by $\mathcal{A}$. (2) For sub-protocol SIC: $\mathcal{S}$ determines the execution of SIC based on $\mathcal{L}_{read}$. Following the above ideas, $Sim^{\mathcal{A}}_{SIC}$ and $Real^{\mathcal{A}}_{SIC}$ cannot be distinguished. (3) The verification protocol: Our verification is on encrypted $\mathcal{VO}$, and probability that $\mathcal{A}$ distinguishes $Real^{\mathcal{A}}_{SDV}$ from $Sim^{\mathcal{A}}_{SDV}$ is $1/(2^s)$ which can be ignored. Thus $\mathcal{A}$ obtains nothing except $\mathcal{L}_{setup}$. In summary, Theorem 3 can be proved.

Theorem 4. *S-kQ scheme and SV-kQ scheme are secure on leakage functions* $(\mathcal{L}_{setup}, \mathcal{L}_{query})$.

Proof. The function π, Paillier encryption and random noise guarantee that all intermediate results are random or pseudorandom on Clouds. Besides, $\mathcal{VO}$ and $\mathcal{R}$ are returned to user in a secure manner. Based on Theorem 3 and composition theorem in [25], we concluded that S-kQ is secure. Further, signature algorithm and SDV protocol make all forgery impossible because Theorem 2, so SV-kQ is also secure.

D Evaluation of Read Protocol and Other Data Setting

We compare Pre-Read protocol with the Bucket-Read protocol by Cui et al. [13]. As shown in Fig. 6(a) and Fig. 6(b). Under different n and k, Pre-Read protocol takes significantly less time than the Bucket-Read protocol. Specifically, for $n = 2000$ and $k = 10$, the Pre-Read takes 19 s while the Bucket-Read takes 143 s. When n increases to $10,000$, the Pre-Read (use 47 s) takes 5.5% time of Bucket-Read (use 854 s). When $k = 40, n = 6,000$, the Pre-Read (use 112 s) takes 4.8% time of bucket reading (use 2400 s); The value in red indicates the number of groups to be read which is denoted as $\bar{l}$, it can be seen that reading four groups can handle 40NN on average. Moreover, the location time of Pre-Read is independent of n and more efficient. For $n = 6000, k = 10$, it takes about 1.8 s to generate selection vectors while Bucket-Read takes 26 s. The time cost of read methods grows approximately linear with k, but the average growth rate of Pre-Read is only 4% of Bucket-Read method. Combined with Fig. 4(b), SV-kQ spends about 80% of its time on reading operations on average.

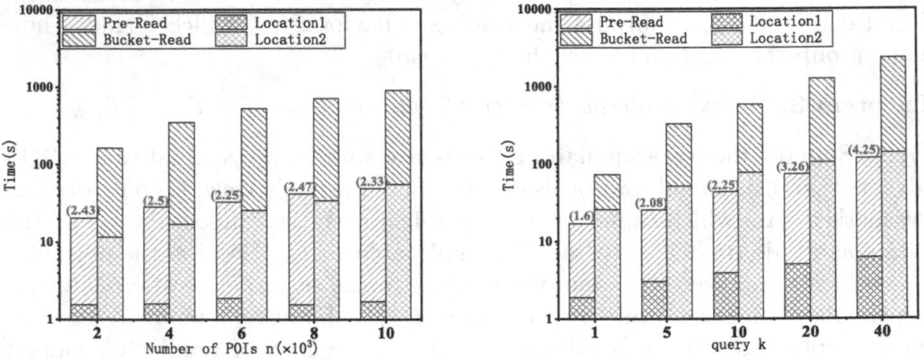

(a) vary n (k=10, K=1024) (b) vary k(n=6000, K=1024)

Fig. 6. Time consumption of read protocols on CA

Data Setting: Note that all of our experiments have the following data settings, (1) Before encrypting, all latitude and longitude coordinates in datasets are scaled to integers with length of 18 bits. (2) To store records with DP, we allocate 20 bits for coordinates data and record id, allocate 80 bits for Paillier random, allocate $(320 + 1)$ bit for signature. With above data setting, one record can be packed into one ciphertext. (3) The statistical security parameter $\kappa = 18$ for the noise is at least 18 bit.

References

1. Papadopoulos, S., Bakiras, S., Papadias, D.: Nearest neighbor search with strong location privacy. Proc. VLDB Endowment **3**(1–2), 619–629 (2010)

2. Fang, S., Kennedy, S., Wang, C., et al.: Sparser: secure nearest neighbor search with space-filling curves. In: IEEE INFOCOM 2020-IEEE Conference on Computer Communications Workshops (INFOCOM WKSHPS), pp. 370–375. IEEE (2020)
3. Lei, X., Liu, A.X., Li, R., et al.: SecEQP: a secure and efficient scheme for SkNN query problem over encrypted geodata on cloud. In: 2019 IEEE 35th International Conference on Data Engineering (ICDE), pp. 662–673. IEEE (2019)
4. Liu, Q., Hao, Z., Peng, Y., et al.: SecVKQ: Secure and verifiable kNN queries in sensor-cloud systems. J. Syst. Architect. **120**, 102300 (2021)
5. Kim, H.I., Kim, H.J., Chang, J.W.: A secure kNN query processing algorithm using homomorphic encryption on outsourced database. Data Knowl. Eng. **123**, 101602 (2019)
6. Wong, W.K., Cheung, D.W., Kao, B., et al.: Secure kNN computation on encrypted databases. In: Proceedings of the 2009 ACM SIGMOD International Conference on Management of data, pp. 139–152 (2009)
7. Boldyreva, A., Tang, T.: Privacy-preserving approximate k-nearest-neighbors search that hides access, query and volume patterns. Proc. Priv. Enhancing Technol. **4**, 549–574 (2021)
8. Wang, J., Du, M., Chow, S.S.M.: Stargazing in the dark: secure skyline queries with SGX. In: Nah, Y., Cui, B., Lee, S.-W., Yu, J.X., Moon, Y.-S., Whang, S.E. (eds.) DASFAA 2020. LNCS, vol. 12114, pp. 322–338. Springer, Cham (2020). https://doi.org/10.1007/978-3-030-59419-0_20
9. Yao, B., Li, F., Xiao, X.: Secure nearest neighbor revisited. In: 2013 IEEE 29th International Conference on Data Engineering (ICDE), pp. 733–744. IEEE (2013)
10. Kornaropoulos, E.M., Papamanthou, C., Tamassia, R.: Data recovery on encrypted databases with k-nearest neighbor query leakage. In: 2019 IEEE Symposium on Security and Privacy (SP), pp. 1033–1050. IEEE (2019)
11. Markatou, E.A., Falzon, F., Tamassia, R., et al.: Reconstructing with less: leakage abuse attacks in two dimensions. In: Proceedings of the 2021 ACM SIGSAC Conference on Computer and Communications Security, pp. 2243–2261 (2021)
12. Elmehdwi, Y., Samanthula, B.K., Jiang, W.: Secure k-nearest neighbor query over encrypted data in outsourced environments. In: 2014 IEEE 30th International Conference on Data Engineering, pp. 664–675. IEEE (2014)
13. Cui, N., Yang, X., Wang, B., et al.: SVkNN: efficient secure and verifiable k-nearest neighbor query on the cloud platform. In: 2020 IEEE 36th International Conference on Data Engineering (ICDE), pp. 253–264. IEEE (2020)
14. Yang, S., Tang, S., Zhang, X.: Privacy-preserving k nearest neighbor query with authentication on road networks. J. Parallel Distrib. Comput. **134**, 25–36 (2019)
15. Liu, J., Yang, J., Xiong, L., et al.: Secure skyline queries on cloud platform. In: 2017 IEEE 33rd International Conference on Data Engineering (ICDE), pp. 633–644. IEEE (2017)
16. Pang, H.H., Jain, A., Ramamritham, K., et al.: Verifying completeness of relational query results in data publishing. In: Proceedings of the 2005 ACM SIGMOD International Conference on Management of Data, pp. 407–418 (2005)
17. Chen, Q., Hu, H., Xu, J.: Authenticating top-k queries in location-based services with confidentiality. Proc. VLDB Endowment **7**(1), 49–60 (2013)
18. Hu, H., Xu, J., Chen, Q., et al.: Authenticating location-based services without compromising location privacy. Proc. ACM SIGMOD Int. Conf. Manage. Data **2012**, 301–312 (2012)
19. Chen, H., Chillotti, I., Dong, Y., et al.: SANNS: scaling up secure approximate k-nearest neighbors search. In: 29th USENIX Security Symposium (USENIX Security 20), pp. 2111–2128 (2020)

20. Paillier, P.: Public-key cryptosystems based on composite degree residuosity classes. In: Stern, J. (ed.) EUROCRYPT 1999. LNCS, vol. 1592, pp. 223–238. Springer, Heidelberg (1999). https://doi.org/10.1007/3-540-48910-X_16
21. Liu, A., Zhengy, K., Liz, L., et al.: Efficient secure similarity computation on encrypted trajectory data. In: 2015 IEEE 31st International Conference on Data Engineering, pp. 66–77. IEEE (2015)
22. Ding, X., Wang, Z., Zhou, P., et al.: Efficient and privacy-preserving multi-party skyline queries over encrypted data. IEEE Trans. Inf. Forensics Secur. **16**, 4589–4604 (2021)
23. F. Li, Real datasets for spatial databases. https://www.cs.utah.edu/~lifeifei/SpatialDataset.htm
24. Damgård, I., Jurik, M., Nielsen, J.B.: A generalization of Paillier's public-key system with applications to electronic voting. Int. J. Inf. Secur. **9**(6), 371–385 (2010)
25. Canetti, R.: Universally composable security: a new paradigm for cryptographic protocols. In: Proceedings 42nd IEEE Symposium on Foundations of Computer Science, pp. 136–145. IEEE (2001)
26. Cheng, W., Pang, H.H., Tan, K.-L.: Authenticating multi-dimensional query results in data publishing. In: Damiani, E., Liu, P. (eds.) DBSec 2006. LNCS, vol. 4127, pp. 60–73. Springer, Heidelberg (2006). https://doi.org/10.1007/11805588_5
27. Rezvani, M., Ignjatovic, A., Bertino, E., et al.: Secure data aggregation technique for wireless sensor networks in the presence of collusion attacks. IEEE Trans. Dependable Secure Comput. **12**(1), 98–110 (2014)
28. Yaseen, Q., Aldwairi, M., Jararweh, Y., et al.: Collusion attacks mitigation in internet of things: a fog based model. Multimedia Tools Appl. **77**(14), 18249–18268 (2018)

A Network Security Situation Assessment Method Based on Multi-attention Mechanism and HHO-ResNeXt

Dongmei Zhao[1,2,3](✉), Guoqing Ji[1], and Shuiguang Zeng[1]

[1] School of College of Computer and Cyber Security, Hebei Normal University, Shijiazhuang 050024, China
zhaodongmei666@126.com

[2] Hebei Provincial Key Laboratory of Network and Information Security, Hebei Normal University, Shijiazhuang 050024, China

[3] Hebei Provincial Engineering Research Center for Supply Chain Big Data Analytics and Data Security, Hebei Normal University, Shijiazhuang 050024, China

Abstract. Because the traditional convolutional neural network (CNN) cannot obtain the importance of each channel and its receptive field is limited, it is difficult to deal with the increasingly complex network environment. Aiming at the shortcomings, this paper combines the Contextual Transformer (COT) block and the Efficient Channel Attention (ECA) module with ResNeXt and uses Harris Hawks Optimization (HHO) algorithm to choose the most suitable hyperparameters to improve the model performance. This model enables the rich contexts among neighbor keys to be fully exploited and can obtain the importance of each channel to improve the weight of the useful channel and suppress the less useful channel, effectively making up for the shortcomings of the traditional convolutional neural network. The experiments on a network security dataset show that the model is superior to other models in the network security situation assessment effect and its comprehensive performance in accuracy, precision and F-score.

Keywords: Convolutional neural network · ResNeXt · Contextual transformer block · Efficient channel attention module · Harris Hawks Optimization · Network security situation assessment

1 Introduction

With the continuous enrichment of Internet functions, network security issues have become more and more complex. The increasingly complex network security needs cannot be met by traditional network security defense measures. Therefore, adopting more advanced technologies and methods to prevent network accidents is necessary. Under this background, network security situation awareness (NSSA) technology came into being.

In 1988, Endsley et al. [1] put forward the new notion of situation awareness. Bass et al. [2] first applied the notion of situation awareness to the field of cybersecurity in

X. Chen et al. (Eds.): SocialSec 2022, CCIS 1663, pp. 199–211, 2022.
https://doi.org/10.1007/978-981-19-7242-3_13

1999 and proposed the concept of situation awareness of intrusion detection framework after multi-sensor integration [3]. Gong et al. [4] systematically elaborated the definition and fundamental concepts of NSSA.

CNN play a pivotal role in many fields because of its mighty learning ability and adaptability. Recently, network attacks have become more frequent, and it has become more and more meaningful to apply CNNs to the field of cybersecurity. However, the traditional CNN cannot cope with the increasingly complex network environment due to the inability to obtain the importance of each channel and the limited receptive field. Therefore, this paper combines the CoT block [5] and the ECA module [6] with ResNext [7] and use HHO [8] to optimize the hyperparameters, which enables the rich contexts among neighbor keys to be fully exploited and can obtain the importance of each channel. This model effectively makes up for the shortcomings of the traditional CNN, and makes the CNN perform better in the field of NSSA.

The contributions of this paper are summarized as follow:

(1) Combining the multi-attention mechanism with ResNeXt effectively makes up for the defects of the traditional CNN that cannot obtain the importance of each channel and the limited receptive field. Therefore, the performance of the model is improved, and the effect of the model to assess the network situation is enhanced.
(2) Experiments on UNSW-NB15 dataset show that compared with other models, the model proposed in this paper can more accurately identify the types of attacks and better evaluate the network conditions.

2 Related Work

Network security situation assessment can evaluate the network condition by analyzing the information of the whole network environment, which is very valuable research in the field of cybersecurity. A situation assessment method based on Dempster–Shafer theory to solve the uncertainty of network situation was put forward by Zheng et al. [9]. The model does not require a lot of prior knowledge, but the computational complexity may be higher due to reasoning.

More and more experts have applied machine learning and deep learning to the field of cybersecurity recently. Cheng et al. [10] applied radial basis function (RBF) neural network to NSSA and optimized the model using hybrid hierarchy genetic algorithm and simulated annealing algorithm. Samuel et al. [11] applied a model combining artificial neural network (ANN) and DT to the field of NSSA. The model extracts the features through the decision tree and takes the extracted features as the input of ANN. However, because the effect of the decision tree extracting features is not very good, the effect of this model is relatively general. Zhang et al. [12] applied the improved CNN to the field of situation awareness, which combines the strengths of depth-wise separable convolution and translating into several smaller convolutions. However, due to the limited depth of the model, the feature information obtained is not comprehensive enough, so the optimization of the model is limited.

3 Convolutional Neural Network (CNN)

3.1 The Structure of the ResNeXt Block

ResNeXt combines the strengths of ResNet [13] and Inception. It not only avoids the degradation problem caused by the deep network, but also does not need to manually design the complicated Inception structure because each branch selects the same topology structure. The output of the ResNeXt block is expressed by the coming formula:

$$y = x + \sum_{i=1}^{G} L_i(x) \tag{1}$$

where x denotes the input, y refers to the output, L denotes the topology structure, and G denotes the number of branches. Figure 1 is an equivalent transformation of the ResNeXt block.

The parameters of each layer in Fig. 1 represent the number of input channels, kernel size and the number of output channels from left to right. After HHO optimization, the group is set to 4 in this paper.

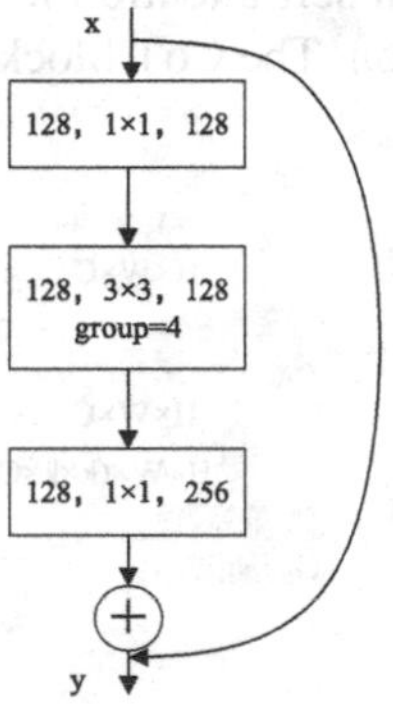

Fig. 1. An equivalent transformation of the ResNeXt block

3.2 Efficient Channel Attention (ECA) Module

Compared with the SE module [14], The ECA module avoids dimension reduction and dimension increase and makes the model less complex, which effectively improves the performance of the channel attention mechanism. The specific detail of ECA module is shown in Fig. 2.

Fast $1D$ convolution of size k can implement the ECA module. To avoid manual resizing of k, the ECA module can adaptively determine k, and the formula for calculating k is as follows:

$$k = \psi(C) = \left| \frac{\log_2 C}{\gamma} + \frac{b}{\gamma} \right|_{odd} \tag{2}$$

where $|t|_{odd}$ represents the nearest odd number of t and C indicates channel dimension. b and γ are usually set to 1 and 2, respectively.

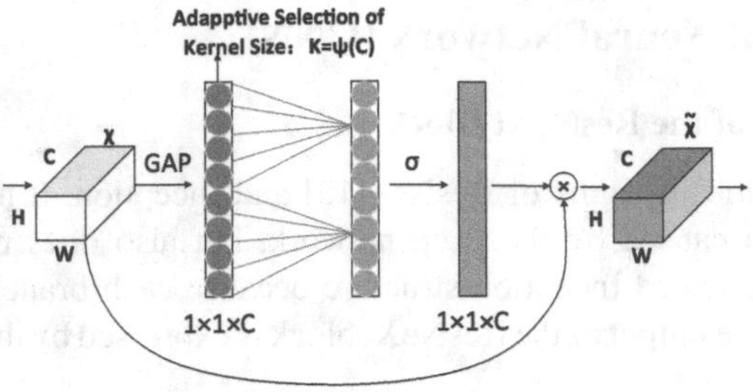

Fig. 2. The efficient channel attention module

3.3 Contextual Transformer (CoT) Block

With the appearance of architecture design based on Transformer, Transformers are widely used in long-distance modeling. But most existing Transformer-based architectures are designed to act directly on *2D* feature maps, and the rich contexts among neighbor keys can't be fully exploited. The CoT block can alleviate this problem. It integrates contextual information mining with self-attention learning into a unified architecture, which enhances visual representation. The CoT block is shown in Fig. 3.

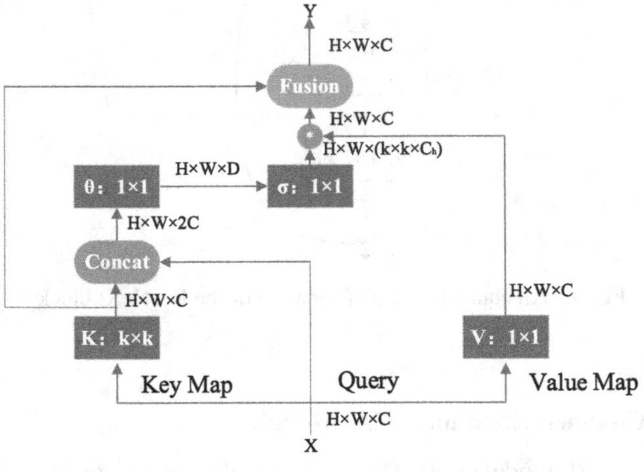

Fig. 3. Contextual Transformer (CoT) block

The size of the input feature map in the figure is $H \times W \times C$. The values, keys and queries are defined as $V = XW_v$, $K = X$ and $Q = X$, respectively. First, CoT module uses $k \times k$ group convolution to obtain the contextualized keys $K^1 \in \mathbb{R}^{H \times W \times C}$. After that, the K^1 and Q is concatenated, and the attention matrix is obtained by two consecutive 1×1 convolutions:

$$A = \left[K^1, Q\right] W_\theta W_\delta \tag{3}$$

Next, the module obtains the attended feature map K^2 by aggregating the contextualized attention matrix A:

$$K^2 = V \circledast A \tag{4}$$

K^2 is called the dynamic context. The CoT module finally fuses the static context K^1 and the dynamic context K^2 to output.

4 Harris Hawks Optimization (HHO)

HHO is a good swarm intelligence algorithm. The entire optimization process of the algorithm includes the exploration phase, the transition from exploration to exploitation and the exploitation phase.

4.1 Eploration Phase

At this stage, all individuals of Harris' hawk randomly inhabit certain positions and search for prey according to the following two strategies:

a: When q < 0.5, the hawks perching position are determined by the location of other family members and the rabbit.

b: When q ≥ 0.5, the hawk's habitat position is any location within the group's home range.

$$X(\mathrm{t}+1) = \begin{cases} X_{rand}(t) - r_1|X_{rand}(t) - 2r_2X(t)| & q \geq 0.5 \\ (X_{rabbit}(t) - X_m(t)) - r_3(lb + r_4(ub - lb)) & q < 0.5 \end{cases} \tag{5}$$

where $X_{rand}(t)$ represents the position of random individuals, ub and lb represent the upper and lower bounds of the search space, $X_{rabbit}(t)$ indicates the location of the prey, $X_m(t)$ indicates the average location of all members in the population, r_1, r_2, r_3, q and r_4 are random numbers within (0,1), $X(\mathrm{t}+1)$ denotes the location of hawks in the next iteration, and t indicates the number of iterations.

4.2 Transition from Exploration to Exploitation

When the rabbit escapes, the escape energy will be greatly reduced:

$$E = 2E_0(1 - t/T) \tag{6}$$

where E indicates the escape energy of the prey, E_0 represent the initial value of the escaping energy of the rabbit which varies randomly in the interval (−1, 1) for each iteration, and T refers to the maximum of iterations.

4.3 Exploitation Phase

Harris' hawks have four attack strategies. Suppose r is the escaping probability of a rabbit. When $r \geq 0.5$, it indicates that the hawks have caught the prey, and when $r < 0.5$, it indicates that the life of the rabbit is kept. Depending on the escape energy, the hawks will surround the rabbit softly or hard When $|E| \geq 0.5$, the soft attack is performed, and when $|E| < 0.5$, the hard attack happens.

Soft Besiege
Harris' hawks surround the rabbit softly when r ≥ 0.5 and |E| ≥ 0.5, and this behavior can be expressed by the coming formula:

$$X(t+1) = \Delta X(t) - E|J \cdot X_{rabbit}(t) - X(t)| \tag{7}$$

$$\Delta X(t) = X_{rabbit}(t) - X(t) \tag{8}$$

where $J = 2 * (1 - r_5)$ indicates the jumping distance of the prey throughout the escaping procedure, r_5 refers to a random number within (0, 1) and $\Delta X(t)$ represents the distance between the location of the prey and the current location in iteration t.

Hard Besiege
The hawks hardly surround the prey when $r \geq 0.5$ and $|E| < 0.5$. In this situation, renewal the current location by the following formula:

$$X(t+1) = X_{rabbit}(t) - E|\Delta X(t)| \tag{9}$$

Soft Besiege with Progressive Rapid Dives
The hawks choose the soft besiege with progressive rapid dives when $r < 0.5$ and $|E| \geq 0.5$, and the following formula can model this behavior:

$$Y = X_{rabbit}(t) - E|JX_{rabbit}(t) - X(t)| \tag{10}$$

After updating the location, if the possible result of such a movement is not better than before, perform another strategy:

$$Z = Y + S \times LF(D) \tag{11}$$

where D denotes the dimension of problem and S is a random vector by size $1 \times D$ and LF denotes the levy flight function. The formula for calculating LF is as follows:

$$LF(x) = 0.01 \times \frac{u \times \sigma}{|v|^{\frac{1}{\beta}}} \tag{12}$$

$$\sigma = \left[\frac{\Gamma(1+\beta) \times \sin\left(\frac{\pi\beta}{2}\right)}{\Gamma\left(\frac{1+\beta}{2}\right) \times \beta \times 2^{\frac{\beta-1}{2}}}\right]^{\frac{1}{\beta}} \tag{13}$$

where β is set to 1.5 and u, v are random numbers within (0,1).

Hence, the final strategy can be performed by the following formula:

$$X(t+1) = \begin{cases} Y \text{ if } fitness(Y) < fitness(X(t)) \\ Z \text{ if } fitness(Z) < fitness(X(t)) \end{cases} \tag{14}$$

Hard Besiege with Progressive Rapid Dives

Harris' hawks choose the hard besiege with progressive rapid dives when $r < 0.5$ and $|E| \geq 0.5$, and the hawks choose their next attack behavior according to the following formula:

$$X(t+1) = \begin{cases} Y \text{ if } fitness(Y) < fitness(X(t)) \\ Z \text{ if } fitness(Z) < fitness(X(t)) \end{cases} \tag{15}$$

where Y and Z are obtained by the following formulas (16) and (17).

$$Y = X_{rabbit}(t) - E|JX_{rabbit}(t) - X_m(t)| \tag{16}$$

$$Z = Y + S \times LF(D) \tag{17}$$

5 Construction of Network Model Based on Multi-attention Mechanism and HHO-ResNeXt

5.1 The ECA-ResNeXt Block

The ECA-ResNeXt block is formed by embedding the ECA module into the ResNeXt block and the detail of this block is shown in Fig. 4. The input in the figure is X, and the output is $\tilde{X}$.

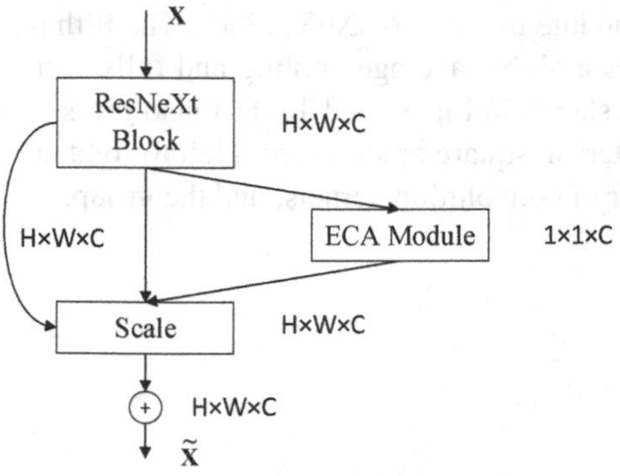

Fig. 4. The ECA-ResNeXt block

5.2 The CoTNeXt Block

The advantage of the CoT block is that it can replace the 3 × 3 convolution in the ResNeXt block to form the CoTNeXt block and the detail of the block is shown in Fig. 5. In the figure, X is the input and Y is the output. The parameters of each layer represent the number of input channels, kernel size or the CoT block, and the number of output channels from left to right.

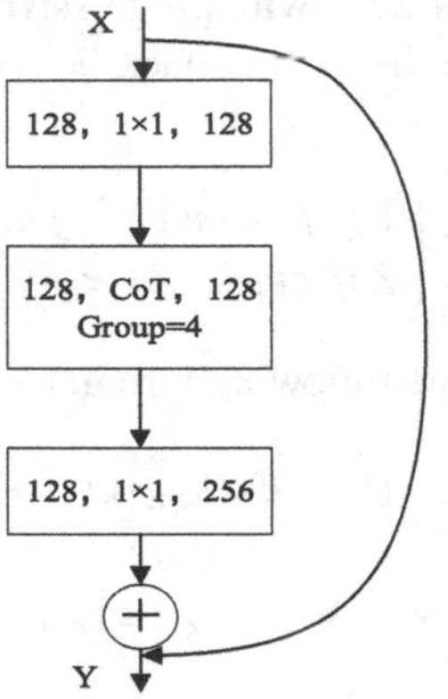

Fig. 5. The CoTNeXt block

5.3 The Complete Structure of the Model in This Paper

The model in this paper mainly consists of six parts. After the hyperparameters are optimized by HHO, the information of each part is as follows. The first part is a 3 × 3 convolution. The second part consists of one CotNeXt block and two CoT blocks. The third part consists of a ResNeXt block, and two convolutional layers and the convolution kernel size is 3 × 3. The fourth part is the ECA-ResNeXt block, which is formed by embedding the ECA module into the ResNeXt block. The fifth part is a ResNext block, and the sixth part takes a global average pooling and fully connected layer as output. The model structure is shown in Fig. 6, and Table 1 also gives the details of the model. In Table 1, the parameters in square brackets from left to right are the convolution type, kernel size, the number of convolution kernels, and the group.

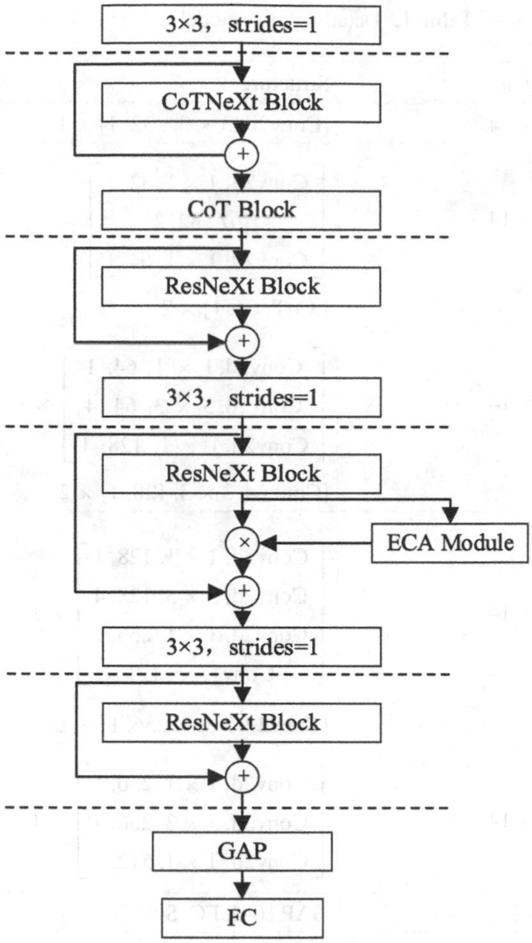

Fig. 6. The complete structure of the model

6 Experiments

6.1 Dataset Description

The UNSW-NB15 dataset [15] is a relatively novel and authoritative dataset. There are 9 attack types in this dataset, and each data contains 49 features. The parts selected as the test dataset and the train dataset in this paper are UNSW_NB15_testing-set.csv and UNSW_NB15_training-set.csv respectively.

6.2 UNSW-NB15 Dataset Preprocessing

In the dataset, the features of each data contain 3 categorical features, namely proto, service and state. These three features are not numerical values. One-Hot Encoding can be used to digitize these three features. After one-hot encoding, the number of features

Table 1. Details of this model

Stage	Output	Structure
res1	14 × 14	[Conv2d, 3 × 3, , 32, 1] × 1
res2	14 × 14	$\begin{bmatrix} \text{Conv2d, } 1 \times 1, 32, 1 \\ CoT, 32, 2 \\ \text{Conv2d, } 1 \times 1, 64, 1 \end{bmatrix} \times 1$ [CoT, 64, 1] × 2
res3	14 × 14	$\begin{bmatrix} \text{Conv2d, } 1 \times 1, 64, 1 \\ \text{Conv2d, } 3 \times 3, 64, 4 \\ \text{Conv2d, } 1 \times 1, 128, 1 \end{bmatrix} \times 1$ [Conv2d, 3 × 3, 128, 1] × 2
res4	14 × 14	$\begin{bmatrix} \text{Conv2d, } 1 \times 1, 128, 1 \\ \text{Conv2d, } 3 \times 3, 128, 4 \\ \text{Conv2d, } 1 \times 1, 256, 1 \\ \text{Conv1d, } 5, 1, 1 \end{bmatrix} \times 1$ [Conv2d, 3 × 3, 256, 1] × 2
res5	14 × 14	$\begin{bmatrix} \text{Conv2d, } 1 \times 1, 256, 1 \\ \text{Conv2d, } 3 \times 3, 256, 4 \\ \text{Conv2d, } 1 \times 1, 512, 1 \end{bmatrix} \times 1$
	1 × 1	GAP,10-d, FC, Softmax

becomes 196, and we convert each data into a 14 × 14 feature map when inputting the data into the model. In the dataset, the data values of different features vary widely. To reduce the influence of this difference on the experiment, the following formula is used to normalize the features:

$$x_{norm} = \frac{x - x_{min}}{x_{max} - x_{min}} \tag{18}$$

where x_{max} and x_{min} indicates the maximum and minimum of each feature, respectively. Because the ratio of the number of each attack type to the total number of samples in the train dataset is larger than that in the test dataset, which affects the model performance, this paper redistributes the train dataset and the test dataset.

6.3 Selected Hyperparameters

This experiment uses tensorflow-gpu-2.4.0 to build the model. When HHO is used to optimize the hyperparameters, the population number is set to 5, the maximum of iterations is 10, and the evaluation function for finding the optimal parameters is the Mean Square Error (MSE). In order to prevent the Harris' hawks from searching for preys aimlessly and affecting the optimization efficiency, a limit is set for the hyperparameters that need to be optimized.

HHO minimizes the MSE through the exploration phase, the transition from exploration to exploitation and the exploitation phase, and outputs the hyperparameters when MSE reaches the minimum value. The final optimized hyperparameters are shown in Table 1.

6.4 Experiment Results

Multi-class Classification Results

To verify the effectiveness of the model, this paper will conduct comparative experiments. The algorithms compared with the model in this paper are the decision tree and artificial neural network proposed in literature [11], The improved CNN proposed in literature [12], ResNet proposed by literature [13] and ResNeXt proposed by [7]. Taking accuracy, precision and F-scores as evaluation indicators, Table 2 shows the experimental results on the dataset.

From the evaluation results of each indicator in Table 2, it can be observed that the accuracy, precision and F-scores of the model in this paper have achieved the best results on the datasets, which means that the model studied in this paper has the best situation assessment effect. Therefore, compared with other methods, the model studied in this paper has the best comprehensive performance.

Table 2. Experiment results for different models

Model	UNSW-NB15 dataset		
	Accuracy%	Precision%	F-scores%
Improved CNN	80.15	78.52	76.80
DT-ANN	79.29	73.44	75.66
ResNet	82.44	82.08	80.09
ResNeXt	82.35	81.98	80.38
The model in this paper	82.77	82.40	80.83

7 Conclusion

This paper proposes a network security situation assessment model based on multi-attention mechanism and HHO-ResNeXt. The model combines the COT block and the

ECA module with ResNeXt and uses HHO to optimize the hyperparameters of the model, which makes up for the defects that the traditional convolutional neural network cannot obtain the importance of each channel and its receptive field is limited. Experiments on UNSW-NB15 dataset show that this method has the best comprehensive performance and outperforms some existing algorithms.

The next step will be carried out from the following directions:

(1) The experiments are only done on the UNSW-NB15 dataset, and the selected datasets are not enough. To verify the effectiveness of the model in this paper, it is necessary to conduct experiments on more datasets.
(2) Although this paper presents the effect of network security situation assessment, the presentation method still adopts a more traditional method. In the future, we will try various methods of situation presentation to present the network status to readers more intuitively.

Acknowledgements. This work was supported by the National Natural Science Foundation of China under Grant (No.61672206), the Central Government Guides Local Science and Technology Development Fund Project Under Grant (No.216Z0701G), the Key Research and Development Program of Hebei Under Grant (No.20310701D).

References

1. Endsley, M.R.: Design and evaluation for situation awareness enhancement. In: Proceedings of the Human Factors Society Annual Meeting, vol. 32, pp. 97–101. SAGE Publications, Los Angeles (1988)
2. Bass, T., Gruber, D.: A glimpse into the future of id. Mag. USENIX & SAGE **24**(4), 40–45 (1999)
3. Bass, T., Robichaux, R.: Defense-in-depth revisited: qualitative risk analysis methodology for complex network-centric operations. In: 2001 MILCOM Proceedings Communications for Network-Centric Operations: Creating the Information Force (Cat. No. 01CH37277), vol. 1, pp. 64–70. IEEE (2001)
4. Gong, J., Zang, X., Su, Q., et al.: Survey of network security situation awareness. J. Softw. **28**(04), 1010–1026 (2017)
5. Li, Y., Yao, T., Pan, Y., et al.: Contextual transformer networks for visual recognition. IEEE Trans. Pattern Anal. Mach. Intell. (2022)
6. Qi, L., Wang, B., Wu, P., et al.: ECA-NET: efficient channel attention for deep convolutional neural networks. In: 2020 IEEE/CVF Conference on Computer Vision and Pattern Recognition, CVPR 2020, Seattle, WA, USA, 13–19 June 2020, pp. 11531–11539. IEEE (2020)
7. Xie, S., Girshick, R., Dollár, P., et al.: Aggregated residual transformations for deep neural networks. In: Proceedings of the IEEE Conference on Computer Vision and Pattern Recognition, pp. 1492–1500 (2017)
8. Heidari, A.A., Mirjalili, S., Faris, H., et al.: Harris Hawks optimization: algorithm and applications. Futur. Gener. Comput. Syst. **97**, 849–872 (2019)
9. Zheng, W.: Research on situation awareness of network security assessment based on Dempster-Shafer. In: MATEC Web of Conferences, vol. 309, p. 02004. EDP Sciences (2020)

10. Cheng, J., Qi, Z., Cheng, T.: Network security situation awareness based on RBF neural networks. J. Nanjing Univ. Posts Telecommun. (Nat. Sci.) **39**(04), 88–95 (2019). https://doi.org/10.14132/j.cnki.1673-5439.2019.04.012
11. Samuel, O.S.: Cyber situation awareness perception model for computer network. Int. J. Adv. Comput. Sci. Appl. **12**(1), 1–6 (2021)
12. Zhang, R., Zhang, Y., Liu, J., et al.: Network security situation prediction method using improved convolution neural network. Comput. Eng. Appl. **55**(6), 86–93 (2019)
13. He, K., Zhang, X., Ren, S., et al.: Deep residual learning for image recognition. In: Proceedings of the IEEE Conference on Computer Vision and Pattern Recognition, pp. 770–778 (2016)
14. Hu, J., Shen, L., Sun, G.: Squeeze-and-excitation networks. In: Proceedings of the IEEE Conference on Computer Vision and Pattern Recognition, pp. 7132–7141 (2018)
15. Moustafa, N.,Slay, J.: UNSW-NB15: a comprehensive data set for network intrusion detection systems (UNSW-NB15 network data set). In: Proceedings of the 2015 Military Communications and Information Systems Conference (MilCIS), pp. 1–6. IEEE, Canberra (2015)

A Privacy-Preserving Federated Learning with Mutual Verification on Vector Spaces

Mingwu Zhang[1,2(✉)], Chenmei Cui[1], Gang Shen[1], and Yudi Zhang[1,3]

[1] School of Computer Science, Hubei University of Technology, Wuhan, China
csmwzhang@gmail.com

[2] School of Computer Science and Information Security, Guilin University of Electronic Technology, Guilin, China

[3] School of Computing and Information Technology, University of Wollongong, Wollongong, Australia

Abstract. Federated learning has received widespread attention in recent years, since it trains a model by only sharing gradients without accessing training sets. In this paper, we consider two security issues in the training process of federated learning, i.e., privacy preservation and message verification, which mainly consider the security of the local gradients uploaded by clients and the aggregation result. We give the detail design about the privacy preserving federated learning with mutual authentication, which provides the privacy-preserving and mutually verifiable federated learning framework on the vector space. To extend the numerical operations to the vector space, we modify the secret sharing of numbers to that of vectors, and advance the commitment to numbers to a commitment to polynomials.

Keywords: Federated learning · Privacy preserving · Mutual verification · Polynomial commitment

1 Introduction

Federated learning is proposed to solve the problem of *data island* [1,2]. As a special case of distributed machine learning, it is getting increasing attention, and plays a significant role in many applications, such as intelligent medical diagnosis [3], smart city [4], and credit investigation [5]. Those applications based on federated learning have penetrated into many aspects of our society, and have gradually influenced our lifestyle [6].

In the traditional federated learning, the system usually consists of a server for gradients aggregation and several clients with their private datasets [1,7]. During the training process of federated learning, each client trains a local model on its private datasets, calculates the local gradient, and then uploads it to the aggregation server to obtain a global model. And the performance of the global model can be improved after several rounds of iterations [8]. Since the datasets

X. Chen et al. (Eds.): SocialSec 2022, CCIS 1663, pp. 212–226, 2022.
https://doi.org/10.1007/978-981-19-7242-3_14

of clients are not exposed to the aggregation server or other entities, the privacy of datasets can be protected [9].

However, federated learning is in the early stage of development, and some recently proposed researches show that it is confronted with potential security issues, such as privacy leakage and data integrity [10]. In a federated learning system, the aggregation server and clients are usually semi-honest, in which case they execute the protocol properly, but attempt to derive additional information from the received messages [11]. Therefore, the local gradients of clients are likely to be initiated member inference attacks by the semi-honest aggregation server, or be eavesdropped by adversaries [12]. And the aggregation result may also be leaked. Besides, the messages transmitted in the training process may be tampered with by adversaries [13].

In this paper, we propose a privacy-preserving federated learning with mutual verification scheme on vector spaces, namely PPFL-MVVS, which adopts blinding technology and Blakley Secret Sharing to protect the data privacy and Polynomial Commitment to guarantee the data integrity. Compared with the existing schemes based on homomorphism encryption or differential privacy, secret sharing leads to less computational cost and higher model accuracy [14], through which other problems such as clients dropping out can also be solved. In addition, the local gradients uploaded by clients and the aggregation result returned from the server are usually feature vectors in the real scene [15,16], so we extend the numerical operations to the vector space. At the same time, most of the existing commitment schemes are based on Pedersen Homomorphic Commitment, which only make commitments to numbers [17]. Considering that all messages transmitted in the training process are expressed as vectors, we advance the commitment to numbers to a commitment to polynomials.

The main contribution of this work is described as follows:

- *W*e adopts blinding technology to protect the local gradients uploaded by clients, and exploit Blakley Secret Sharing to protect the aggregation result returned from the server. In addition, we make commitments to the messages transmitted in the training process to guarantee the data integrity.
- *S*ince the local gradients uploaded by clients and the aggregation result returned from the server are usually feature vectors in the real scene, we extend all operations in our scheme to the vector space. Concretely, we modify the secret sharing of numbers to that of vectors, and advance the commitment to numbers to a commitment to polynomials.
- *W*e give a comprehensive security analysis for our PPFL-MVVS. We claim that the aggregation server or other entities will not obtain any useful information of local gradients, and the aggregation result will not be leaked to adversaries.

2 Related Work

Privacy-Preserving Federated Learning. During the training process of federated learning, adversaries can conduct member inference attacks on the gradients to derive the private datasets [18]. The existing privacy preserving technologies of federated learning mainly consists of the following three: 1) differential privacy; 2) homomorphic encryption; 3) secure multi-party computation.

Differential privacy perturbs the parameters by adding noise to them, so that adversaries could not obtain any valid information of the trained model. Wu X et al. [19] added Gaussian noise to the gradient data, and Luca M et al. [20] adopted Laplace noise. However, the schemes with differential privacy usually have lower model accuracy.

In the schemes with homomorphic encryption, messages are protected by encryption techniques such as Paillier. Ho Q R [21] adopted homomorphic encryption to implement a privacy preserving protocol for horizontal linear regression, and Hardy S et al. [22] applied homomorphic encryption and entity resolution to perform privacy-preserving federated learning of vertical distributed datasets. However, the computation overhead of those schemes is usually very high.

Secure multi-party computation is usually used to realize the secure aggregation, which is the key stage in federated learning. The existing schemes have made great progress in different aspects. Bell et al. [23] and Payman [24] protected the privacy of training data by using secret sharing, which is representative technology to implement SMC. Fereidooni et al. [25] introduced a generic design called SAFELearn for secure aggregation of federated learning. It is adaptable to various security requirements and multiple aggregation mechanisms.

Secret Sharing. Secret sharing is one of the secure multi-party computation technologies. It is an important building block for various cryptographic protocols, such as distributed key generation, threshold cryptosystems, attribute-based encryptions, secure multi-party computation, etc. The earliest two secret sharing schemes were proposed by Shamir and Blakley respectively. However, Shamir's scheme [26] is based on polynomial interpolation, which only operates on numerical values, while Blakley's scheme [27] is based on hyperplane geometry, which can operate on vectors.

Shamir's secret sharing has gained wide acceptance and has been employed in most of the existing cryptographic protocols where threshold secret sharing is needed. Anmin Fu et al. [28] proposed the VFL, a verifiable federated learning with privacy-preserving for big data in industrial IoT, which uses Lagrange interpolation to elaborately set interpolation points for verifying the correctness of the aggregated gradients. Bonawitz et al. [29] put forward a practical and secure architecture for federated learning by exploiting the secret sharing and key agreement protocol, which allows users to be offline during the execution while still guaranteeing high accuracy [30]. Although Blakley's secret sharing has been introduced for decades, not many applications of it can be found in the literature. Since our scheme aims to realize the privacy protection for the data represented in the form of vectors, the Blakley secret sharing is selected.

3 System Model and Design Goal

3.1 System Model

As shown in Fig. 1, our system model is composed of three types of entities: an aggregation server (AS), n clients (C_i, $i \in n$), and a trusted third party (TTP).

And messages are transmitted through security channels by the trusted third party. We assume that the aggregation server and clients are semi-honest, which means they will execute the protocol correctly but attempt to infer additional information of the messages from the other members.

- *Aggregation Server (AS)*: The aggregation server is responsible for the verification and aggregation of the blinded gradients, as well as making a commitment to the aggregation result. In addition, the AS distributes a subkey for each client, which can be used to recover the aggregation result. The subkeys will not leak the aggregation result and are therefore semantically secure.
- *Clients* (C_i, $i \in N$): Each client trains a model on the private datasets, blinds the gradient with a random vector, and then makes a commitment to the blinded gradient. When one of the iterations is completed, all the online clients could cooperate to recover the aggregation result.
- *Trusted Third Party (TTP)*: The main job of the trusted third party is to set the public parameters for commitments, and to restore the random vectors which are used to blind the local gradients. Then the TTP calculates the sum of all the random vectors, and sends it to the AS for decryption.

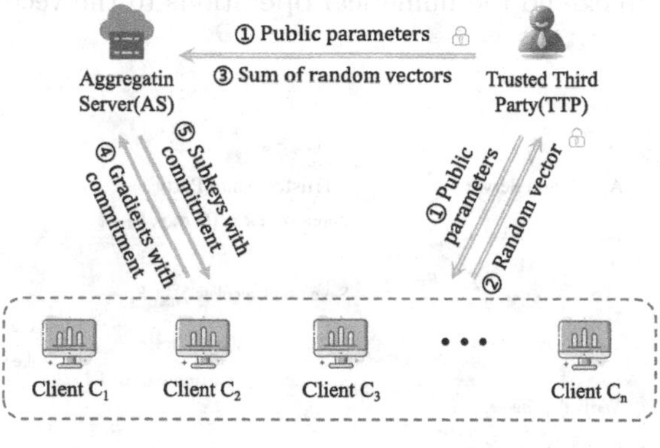

Fig. 1. System model

3.2 Design Goal

We aim to develop an efficient, privacy-preserving, and mutual verifiable federated learning scheme, which mainly protects the confidentiality and integrity of the gradients uploaded by clients and the aggregation result returned from the server. In particular, the following five desirable objectives need to be considered:

- *Confidentiality*: In this work, the gradients uploaded by clients and the aggregation result returned from the server need to be protected.

1. Local Gradients: Local gradients should be protected to resist the member inference attacks initiated by the semi-honest server and eavesdropping of adversaries.
2. Aggregation Result: the aggregation result needs to be distributed to each client as a subkey, which will not reveal any information about the aggregation result and is therefore semantically secure.

- *Integrity*: To prevent the messages transmitted in the training process from being tampered with by adversaries, commitments should be made to protect the data integrity. Considering that local gradients and the aggregation result are expressed as feature vectors in the real scene, the commitments should be extended to the vector space.
- *Efficiency*: In our scheme, secret sharing is applied to protect the privacy of the aggregation result. It is less computationally expensive than the schemes with homomorphic encryption, and has higher model accuracy compared to the schemes with differential privacy.
- *Tolerance of clients dropping out*: Our scheme also tolerates clients dropping out during the recovery stage since secret sharing is adopted to protect the aggregation result.
- *Extend the numerical operations to the vector space*: In the real scene of federated learning, local gradients and the aggregation result are vectors, so it is necessary to extend the numerical operations to the vector space.

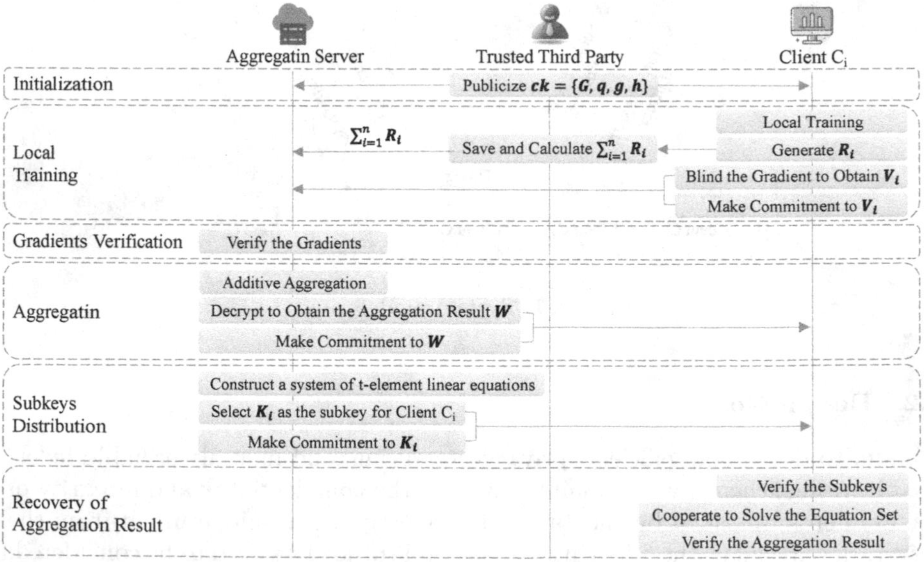

Fig. 2. *Overview*

4 Our Scheme

As is shown in Fig. 2, our proposed scheme consists of six stages: **System Initialization, Local Training, Gradients Verification, Gradients Aggregation, Subkeys Distribution**, and **Recovery of the Aggregation Result**.

4.1 System Initialization

TTP generates the public parameters $ck = \{\mathbb{G}, q, g, h\}$ for commitments, among which g is the generator of the q-order finite cyclic group $\mathbb{G}$, and $h = g^x \bmod q$ is an element in $\mathbb{G}$. It is difficult to calculate x, the discrete logarithm of h.

4.2 Local Training

The local training process of federated learning is comprised of the following steps.

1. Each client C_i trains on its private datasets to obtain a local model, and then calculate the gradient: $\mathbf{G_i} = (\mathbf{g_{i1}}, \mathbf{g_{i2}}, ..., \mathbf{g_{it}})$.
2. C_i generates a t-dimensional random vector $\mathbf{R_i} = (\mathbf{r_{i1}}, \mathbf{r_{i2}}, ..., \mathbf{r_{it}})$, which is used to blind the gradient. And the blinded gradient is expressed as $\mathbf{V_i} = \mathbf{G_i} + \mathbf{R_i} = (\mathbf{g_{i1}} + \mathbf{r_{i1}}, \mathbf{g_{i2}} + \mathbf{r_{i2}}, ..., \mathbf{g_{it}} + \mathbf{r_{it}})$, take $g_{ij} + r_{ij}$ as v_{ij}, $j = 1, 2, ..., t$, then $\mathbf{V_i} = (\mathbf{v_{i1}}, \mathbf{v_{i2}}, ..., \mathbf{v_{it}})$.
3. C_i makes a commitment to the blinded gradient $\mathbf{V_i}$, which consists of the following sub-steps:
   (a) C_i constructs a polynomial of degree $t-1$:

$$fv_i(x) = v_{i1} + v_{i2}x + ... + v_{it}x^{t-1} = \sum_{j=0}^{t-1} v_{i,j+1}x^j \tag{1}$$

   with $v_{i1}, v_{i2}, ..., v_{it}$ in the blinded gradient $\mathbf{V_i}$ as coefficients, and then constructs the other polynomial:

$$hv_i(x) = \rho_{i1} + \rho_{i2}x + ... + \rho_{it}x^{t-1} = \sum_{j=0}^{t-1} \rho_{i,j+1}x^j \tag{2}$$

   with random numbers $\rho_{i1}, \rho_{i2}, ..., \rho_{it}$ from the finite field $\mathbb{Z}_q^*$ as coefficients. Obviously, a polynomial can be represented by its coefficient vector, therefore, $fv_i(x)$ can be represented as $\mathbf{V_i} = (\mathbf{v_{i1}}, \mathbf{v_{i2}}, ..., \mathbf{v_{it}})$, and $hv_i(x)$ can be represented as $\mathbf{P_i} = (\boldsymbol{\rho_{i1}}, \boldsymbol{\rho_{i2}}, ..., \boldsymbol{\rho_{it}})$.

   (b) C_i makes a commitment to each coefficient of $fv_i(x)$, which means to calculate:

$$cv_{ij} = PolyCom_{ck}(v_{ij}, \rho_{ij}) = g^{v_{ij}}h^{\rho_{ij}}, j = 1, 2, \ldots, t \tag{3}$$

   then the commitment can be expressed as $\mathbf{CV_i} = (\mathbf{cv_{i1}}, \mathbf{cv_{i2}}, \ldots, \mathbf{cv_{it}})$.

(c) C_i substitutes i into $fv_i(x)$ and $hv_i(x)$ respectively to compute $\alpha_i = fv_i(i)$ and $\beta_i = hv_i(i)$, which are the parameters required for verification.
4. Each client C_i sends $\mathbf{V_i} \parallel \mathbf{CV_i} \parallel \alpha_i \parallel \beta_i$ to the AS.
5. Each client C_i sends the random vector $\mathbf{R_i}$ to the TTP through a security channel.

The encryption and commitment of gradients are described in Algorithm 1.

Algorithm 1. Encryption and Commitment of Gradients

Input: Each C_i has a gradient $\mathbf{G_i}$, a random vector $\mathbf{R_i}$, and public parameters $\{\mathbb{G}, q, g, h\}$ for commitments;
Output: The AS obtains all the blinded gradients: $\mathbf{V_1}, \mathbf{V_2}, ..., \mathbf{V_n}$, and the commitments of them: $\mathbf{CV_1}, \mathbf{CV_2}, ..., \mathbf{CV_n}$;
The TTP obtains all the random vectors: $\mathbf{R_1}, \mathbf{R_2}, ..., \mathbf{R_n}$.
for $i = 1, 2, ..., n$ **do**
  C_i computes $\mathbf{V_i} = \mathbf{G_i} + \mathbf{R_i} = (\mathbf{g_{i1}} + \mathbf{r_{i1}}, \mathbf{g_{i2}} + \mathbf{r_{i2}}, ..., \mathbf{g_{it}} + \mathbf{r_{it}}) = (\mathbf{v_{i1}}, \mathbf{v_{i2}}, ..., \mathbf{v_{it}})$;
  C_i constructs a polynomial $fv_i(x) = v_{i1} + v_{i2}x + ... + v_{it}x^{t-1} = \sum_{j=0}^{t-1} v_{i,j+1}x^j$;
  C_i constructs the other polynomial $hv_i(x) = \rho_{i1} + \rho_{i2}x + ... + \rho_{it}x^{t-1} = \sum_{j=0}^{t-1} \rho_{i,j+1}x^j$;
  C_i computes $cv_{ij} = g^{v_{ij}}h^{\rho_{ij}}, j = 1, 2, ..., t$ and $\mathbf{CV_i} = (\mathbf{cv_{i1}}, \mathbf{cv_{i2}}, ..., \mathbf{cv_{it}})$;
  C_i computes $\alpha_i = fv_i(i)$ and $\beta_i = hv_i(i)$;
  C_i sends $\mathbf{V_i} \parallel \mathbf{CV_i} \parallel \alpha_i \parallel \beta_i$ to AS;
  C_i sends $\mathbf{R_i}$ to TTP.
end for

4.3 Gradients Verification

The AS verifies the integrity of the gradients they received according to a verification equation:

$$PolyCom_{ck}(\alpha_i, \beta_i) = \prod_{j=1}^{t} cv_{ij}^{i^j} \tag{4}$$

4.4 Gradients Aggregation

Gradients aggregation is composed of the following steps:

1. The AS calculates the sum of all the blinded gradients which have been verified:

$$\sum_{i=1}^{n} \mathbf{V_i} = \sum_{i=1}^{n} (\mathbf{G_i} + \mathbf{R_i}) = \sum_{i=1}^{n} \mathbf{G_i} + \sum_{i=1}^{n} \mathbf{R_i} \tag{5}$$

2. The TTP calculates the sum of all the random vectors: $\sum_{i=1}^{n} \mathbf{R_i}$, and sends it to the AS through a security channel.

3. The AS calculates:

$$\sum_{i=1}^{n} \mathbf{G_i} = \sum_{i=1}^{n} \mathbf{V_i} - \sum_{i=1}^{n} \mathbf{R_i} = \sum_{i=1}^{n} (\mathbf{G_i} + \mathbf{R_i}) - \sum_{i=1}^{n} \mathbf{R_i} \tag{6}$$

to obtain the aggregation result, which is expressed as a vector $\mathbf{W} = \sum_{i=1}^{n} \mathbf{G_i} = (\omega_1, \omega_2, ..., \omega_t)$.

4. The AS makes a commitment to the aggregation result $\mathbf{W}$, which consists of the following sub-steps.
   (a) The AS constructs a polynomial of degree $t-1$:

$$fw(x) = \omega_1 + \omega_2 x + ... + \omega_t x^{t-1} = \sum_{j=0}^{t-1} \omega_{j+1} x^j \tag{7}$$

   with $\omega_1, \omega_2, ..., \omega_t$ in the aggregation result $\mathbf{W}$ as coefficients, and then constructs the other polynomial:

$$hw(x) = \delta_1 + \delta_2 x + ... + \delta_t x^{t-1} = \sum_{j=0}^{t-1} \delta_{j+1} x^j \tag{8}$$

   with random numbers $\delta_1, \delta_2, ..., \delta_t$ from the finite field $\mathbb{Z}_q^*$ as coefficients. As described in Sect. 4.2, $fw(x)$ can be represented as $\mathbf{W} = (\omega_1, \omega_2, ..., \omega_t)$, and $hw(x)$ can be represented as $\mathbf{D} = (\delta_1, \delta_2, ..., \delta_t)$.
   (b) The AS makes a commitment to each coefficient of $fw(x)$, which means to calculate:

$$cw_j = PolyCom_{ck}(\omega_j, \delta_j) = g^{\omega_j} h^{\delta_j}, j = 1, 2, ..., t \tag{9}$$

   then the commitment can be expressed as $\mathbf{CW} = (\mathbf{cw_1}, \mathbf{cw_2}, ..., \mathbf{cw_t})$.
   (c) The AS substitutes i into $fw(x)$ and $hw(x)$ respectively to compute $\gamma = fw(i)$ and $\lambda = hw(i)$, which are the parameters required for verification.

Gradients aggregation and the commitment of the aggregation result are described in Algorithm 2.

4.5 Subkeys Distribution

Subkeys distribution is comprised of the following steps.

1. The AS constructs an equation set consisting of n t-element linear equations (a system of t-element linear equations):

$$\begin{cases} a_{11}\omega_1 + a_{12}\omega_2 + \cdots + a_{1t}\omega_t = b_1 \\ a_{21}\omega_1 + a_{22}\omega_2 + \cdots + a_{2t}\omega_t = b_2 \\ \cdots \\ a_{n1}\omega_1 + a_{n2}\omega_2 + \cdots + a_{nt}\omega_t = b_n \end{cases} \tag{10}$$

Algorithm 2. Gradients Aggregation and Commitment of Aggregation Result

Input: The AS has all the blinded gradients: $\mathbf{V_1}, \mathbf{V_2}, ..., \mathbf{V_n}$, the commitments of them: $\mathbf{CV_1}, \mathbf{CV_2}, ..., \mathbf{CV_n}$, and public parameters $\{\mathbb{G}, q, g, h\}$ for commitments; The TTP has the sum of all the random vectors: $\sum_{i=1}^{n} \mathbf{R_i}$;

Output: The AS has the aggregation result: $\mathbf{W} = (\omega_1, \omega_2, ..., \omega_t)$ and the commitment of it: $\mathbf{CW}$.

```
The AS computes Σ_{i=1}^n V_i = Σ_{i=1}^n (G_i + R_i) = Σ_{i=1}^n G_i + Σ_{i=1}^n R_i;
TTP:
    1) Computes Σ_{i=1}^n R_i;
    2) Sends it to the AS;
AS:
    1) Computes Σ_{i=1}^n G_i = Σ_{i=1}^n V_i − Σ_{i=1}^n R_i = Σ_{i=1}^n (G_i + R_i) − Σ_{i=1}^n R_i, and
       takes it as W = Σ_{i=1}^n G_i = (ω_1, ω_2, ..., ω_t);
    2) Constructs a polynomial fw(x) = ω_1 + ω_2 x + ... + ω_t x^{t−1} = Σ_{j=0}^{t−1} ω_{j+1} x^j;
    3) Constructs the other polynomial hw(x) = δ_1 + δ_2 x + ... + δ_t x^{t−1} =
       Σ_{j=0}^{t−1} δ_{j+1} x^j;
    4) Computes cw_j = PolyCom_ck(ω_j, δ_j) = g^{ω_j} h^{δ_j}, j = 1, 2, ..., t, and CW =
       (cw_1, cw_2, ..., cw_t);
    5) Computes γ = fw(i) and λ = hw(i).
```

with $\omega_1, \omega_2, ..., \omega_t$ in the aggregation result $\mathbf{W}$ as variables. Take

$$\mathbf{A} = \begin{bmatrix} a_{11} & a_{12} & \cdots & a_{1t} \\ a_{21} & a_{22} & \cdots & a_{2t} \\ \vdots & \vdots & \ddots & \vdots \\ a_{n1} & a_{n2} & \cdots & a_{nt} \end{bmatrix}, \mathbf{B} = \begin{bmatrix} b_1 \\ b_2 \\ \vdots \\ b_n \end{bmatrix}, \mathbf{W} = \begin{bmatrix} \omega_1 \\ \omega_2 \\ \vdots \\ \omega_t \end{bmatrix} \tag{11}$$

then $\mathbf{AW} = \mathbf{B}$, and $\widetilde{\mathbf{A}} = (\mathbf{A}, \mathbf{B})$. Obviously, we have $Rank(\mathbf{A}) = \mathbf{Rank}(\widetilde{\mathbf{A}}) = \mathbf{t}$, and for a matrix composed of any t rows in $\mathbf{A}$, the rank is t. Therefore, the equation set only has one solution, the aggregation result $\mathbf{W}$.

2. The AS selects a vector $(a_{i1}, a_{i2}, ..., a_{it}, b_i)$ in the augmented matrix $\widetilde{\mathbf{A}}$ for each client C_i as a subkey, which is defined as $\mathbf{K_i} = (\mathbf{k_{i1}}, \mathbf{k_{i2}}, ..., \mathbf{k_{i,t+1}})$. If t clients cooperate to obtain an equation set containing t t-element linear equations, the aggregation result can be solved.
3. The AS makes a commitment to each subkey $\mathbf{K_i}$, which consists of the following sub-steps:
   (1) The AS constructs a polynomial of degree t:

$$fk_i(x) = k_{i1} + k_{i2}x + ... + k_{i,t+1}x^t = \sum_{j=0}^{t} k_{i,j+1}x^j \tag{12}$$

with $k_{i1}, k_{i2}, ..., k_{i,t+1}$ in the subkey $\mathbf{K_i}$ as coefficients, and then constructs the other polynomial:

$$hk_i(x) = \tau_{i1} + \tau_{i2}x + ... + \tau_{i,t+1}x^t = \sum_{j=0}^{t} \tau_{i,j+1}x^j \tag{13}$$

with random numbers $\tau_{i1}, \tau_{i2}, ..., \tau_{i,t+1}$ from the finite field $\mathbb{Z}_q^*$ as coefficients. As described in Sect. 4.2, $fk_i(x)$ can be represented as $\mathbf{K_i} = (\mathbf{k_{i1}}, \mathbf{k_{i2}}, \ldots, \mathbf{k_{i,t+1}})$, and $hk_i(x)$ can be represented as $\mathbf{T_i} = (\tau_{i1}, \tau_{i2}, ..., \tau_{i,t+1})$.

(2) The AS makes a commitment to each coefficient of $fk_i(x)$, which means to calculate:

$$ck_{ij} = PolyCom_{ck}(k_{ij}, \tau_{ij}) = g^{k_{ij}} h^{\tau_{ij}}, j = 1, 2, \ldots, t+1 \quad (14)$$

then the commitment can be expressed as a vector $\mathbf{CK_i} = (\mathbf{ck_{i1}}, \mathbf{ck_{i2}}, \ldots, \mathbf{ck_{i,t+1}})$.

(3) The AS substitutes i into $fk_i(x)$ and $hk_i(x)$ respectively to compute $\mu_i = fk_i(i)$ and $\eta_i = hk_i(i)$, which are the parameters required for verification.

4. The AS sends $\mathbf{K_i} \parallel \mathbf{CK_i} \parallel \mu_i \parallel \eta_i$ to the corresponding client C_i.
5. The AS sends $\mathbf{CW} \parallel \gamma \parallel \lambda$ to all clients.

The commitment of subkeys are described in Algorithm 3.

Algorithm 3. The Distribution and Commitment of Subkeys

Input: AS has the aggregation result: $\mathbf{W} = (\omega_1, \omega_2, ..., \omega_t)$, the commitment of it: $\mathbf{CW}$, and public parameters $\{\mathbb{G}, q, g, h\}$ for commitments;

Output: Each C_i has the corresponding subkey: $\mathbf{K_i} = (\mathbf{k_{i1}}, \mathbf{k_{i2}}, ..., \mathbf{k_{i,t+1}})$, the commitment of it: $\mathbf{CK_i} = (\mathbf{ck_{i1}}, \mathbf{ck_{i2}}, ..., \mathbf{ck_{i,t+1}})$, and the commitment of the aggregation result $\mathbf{CW}$.

for $i = 1, 2, ..., n$ **do**
  AS constructs an equation set $\mathbf{AW} = \mathbf{B}$;
  AS selects $\mathbf{K_i} = (\mathbf{a_{i1}}, \mathbf{a_{i2}}, ..., \mathbf{a_{it}}, \mathbf{b_i})$ as a subkey, and takes it as $\mathbf{K_i} = (\mathbf{k_{i1}}, \mathbf{k_{i2}}, ..., \mathbf{k_{i,t+1}})$;
  AS constructs a polynomial $fk_i(x) = k_{i1} + k_{i2}x + ... + k_{i,t+1}x^t = \sum_{j=0}^{t} k_{i,j+1}x^j$;
  AS constructs the other polynomial $hk_i(x) = \tau_{i1} + \tau_{i2}x + ... + \tau_{i,t+1}x^t = \sum_{j=0}^{t} \tau_{i,j+1}x^j$;
  AS computes $ck_{ij} = g^{k_{ij}} h^{\tau_{ij}}, j = 1, 2, ..., t+1$, and $\mathbf{CK_i} = (\mathbf{ck_{i1}}, \mathbf{ck_{i2}}, ..., \mathbf{ck_{i,t+1}})$;
  AS computes $\mu_i = fk_i(i)$ and $\eta_i = hk_i(i)$;
  AS sends $\mathbf{K_i} \parallel \mathbf{CK_i} \parallel \mu_i \parallel \eta_i$ to the corresponding C_i;
  AS sends $\mathbf{CW} \parallel \gamma \parallel \lambda$ to all of C_is.
end for

4.6 Recovery of the Aggregation Result

In the recovery of the aggregation result, the following steps are proposed.

1. Each client C_i verifies the validity of the subkeys they received according to a verification equation:

$$PolyCom_{ck}(\mu_i, \eta_i) = \prod_{j=1}^{t+1} ck_{ij}^{i^j} \quad (15)$$

2. If t clients cooperate to obtain an equation set containing t t-element linear equations, the aggregation result $\mathbf{W} = (\omega_1, \omega_2, ..., \omega_t)$ can be solved.
3. No less than t clients who participated in the recovery verify the correctness of the aggregation result they obtained according to a verification equation:

$$PolyCom_{ck}(\gamma, \lambda) = \prod_{j=1}^{t} cw_j^{i^j} \tag{16}$$

5 Security Analysis

In this section, we give the security of our proposed scheme. We consider the confidentiality and verifiability of the scheme, which means the private datasets and local gradients of clients should not be leaked to the AS or any other entities, and the aggregation result should also be protected. Moreover, the messages transmitted in the training process should not be tampered with by adversaries.

5.1 Privacy

1) *Confidentiality of Local Gradients*: In federated learning, all clients can jointly train a global model without sharing their private datasets. In our proposed PPFL-MVVS, the local gradient of each client is represented in the form of a vector: $\mathbf{G_i} = (\mathbf{g_{i1}}, \mathbf{g_{i2}}, ..., \mathbf{g_{it}})$, and it is blinded before being uploaded to the AS, which is expressed as $\mathbf{V_i} = \mathbf{G_i} + \mathbf{R_i} = (\mathbf{g_{i1}} + \mathbf{r_{i1}}, \mathbf{g_{i2}} + \mathbf{r_{i2}}, ..., \mathbf{g_{it}} + \mathbf{r_{it}})$. So our scheme can resist the member inference attacks initiated by a semi-honest aggregation server. If someone intercepts the blinded gradients $\mathbf{V_i}$, he could not obtain any valid information because of the random vectors $\mathbf{R_i} = (\mathbf{r_{i1}}, \mathbf{r_{i2}}, ..., \mathbf{r_{it}})$ used for blindness, so eavesdropping of adversaries can also be resisted.
2) *Confidentiality of the Aggregation Result*: The elements in the aggregation result $\mathbf{W} = (\omega_1, \omega_2, ..., \omega_t)$ is used as variables to construct an equation set:

$$\begin{cases} a_{11}\omega_1 + a_{12}\omega_2 + \cdots + a_{1t}\omega_t = b_1 \\ a_{21}\omega_1 + a_{22}\omega_2 + \cdots + a_{2t}\omega_t = b_2 \\ \qquad \cdots \\ a_{n1}\omega_1 + a_{n2}\omega_2 + \cdots + a_{nt}\omega_t = b_n \end{cases} \tag{17}$$

And each equation is distributed to each client as a subkey:

$$\mathbf{K_i} = (\mathbf{a_{i1}}, \mathbf{a_{i2}}, ..., \mathbf{a_{it}}, \mathbf{b_i}) = (\mathbf{k_{i1}}, \mathbf{k_{i2}}, ..., \mathbf{k_{i,t+1}}) \tag{18}$$

which would not disclose any valid information of the aggregation result and is therefore semantically secure. The aggregation result can be cooperatively solved only if the number of online clients reaches the threshold (i.e. not less than t). So this scheme is robust to the collusion of c ($2 \leq c \leq t-1$, and $t \leq \frac{n+1}{2}$) clients in the training process, and is supportive of clients dropping out during the recovery of the aggregation result.

5.2 Verification

In order to prevent the messages transmitted in the training process from being tampered with by adversaries, commitments need to be made to ensure that they are verifiable. Since the local gradients uploaded by clients and the subkeys distributed by the AS are represented in the form of feature vectors, it is necessary to extend the commitment to the vector space. And the integrity of the messages will be guaranteed.

1) *Verifiability of the Blinded Gradients*: The blinded gradient of client C_i is expressed as a vector: $\mathbf{V_i} = (\mathbf{v_{i1}}, \mathbf{v_{i2}}, ..., \mathbf{v_{it}})$, which is likely to be tampered with by adversaries while being uploaded to the AS. Therefore, the blinded gradients should be verified by the AS before being aggregated. In our scheme, the verifiability of the blinded gradients is guaranteed by making commitments to them. Client C_i makes a commitment to each element $v_{i1}, v_{i2}, ..., v_{it}$ of the blinded gradient $\mathbf{V_i}$, which means to calculate: $cv_{ij} = PolyCom_{ck}(v_{ij}, \rho_{ij}) = g^{v_{ij}} h^{\rho_{ij}}, j = 1, 2, ..., t$, then the commitment of $\mathbf{V_i}$ can be expressed as a vector $\mathbf{CV_i} = (\mathbf{cv_{i1}}, \mathbf{cv_{i2}}, ..., \mathbf{cv_{it}})$. To verify the integrity of the blinded gradients, the AS calculates the verification equation:

$$\begin{aligned} PolyCom_{ck}(\alpha_i, \beta_i) &= g^{\alpha_i} h^{\beta_i} = g^{fv_i(i)} h^{hv_i(i)} = g^{\sum_{j=0}^{t-1} v_{i,j+1} i^j} h^{\sum_{j=0}^{t-1} \rho_{i,j+1} i^j} \\ &= \prod_{j=1}^{t} (g^{v_{ij}} h^{\rho_{ij}})^{i^j} = \prod_{j=1}^{t} cv_{ij}^{i^j} \end{aligned} \tag{19}$$

Then the gradient received from client C_i is proved to be correct.

2) *Verifiability of Subkeys*: The subkey of client C_i is expressed as a vector: $\mathbf{K_i} = (\mathbf{k_{i1}}, \mathbf{k_{i2}}, ..., \mathbf{k_{i,t+1}})$, which is likely to be tampered with by adversaries while being distributed to clients. Therefore, each client should verify the subkeys they received before jointly solving the aggregation result. In our scheme, the verifiability of the subkeys is guaranteed by making commitments to them. The AS makes a commitment to each element $k_{i1}, k_{i2}, ..., k_{i,t+1}$ of the subkey $\mathbf{K_i}$, which means to calculate: $ck_{ij} = PolyCom_{ck}(k_{ij}, \tau_{ij}) = g^{k_{ij}} h^{\tau_{ij}}, j = 1, 2, ..., t+1$, then the commitment of $\mathbf{K_i}$ can be expressed as a vector $\mathbf{CK_i} = (\mathbf{ck_{i1}}, \mathbf{ck_{i2}}, ..., \mathbf{ck_{i,t+1}})$. To verify the validity of the subkeys, each client C_i calculates the verification equation:

$$\begin{aligned} PolyCom_{ck}(\mu_i, \eta_i) &= g^{\mu_i} h^{\eta_i} = g^{fk_i(i)} h^{hk_i(i)} = g^{\sum_{j=0}^{t} k_{i,j+1} i^j} h^{\sum_{j=0}^{t} \tau_{i,j+1} i^j} \\ &= \prod_{j=1}^{t+1} (g^{k_{ij}} h^{\tau_{ij}})^{i^j} = \prod_{j=1}^{t+1} ck_{ij}^{i^j} \end{aligned} \tag{20}$$

Then the subkeys received from the AS are proved to be valid.

3) *Verifiability of the Aggregation Result*: The aggregation result is expressed as a vector: $\mathbf{W} = (\omega_1, \omega_2, ..., \omega_t)$. To ensure that the aggregation result obtained by clients are consistent with that returned from the AS, it should be verified

by clients after jointly solving the equation set. In our scheme, the verifiability of the aggregation result is guaranteed by making commitments to it. The AS makes a commitment to each element $\omega_1, \omega_2, ..., \omega_t$ of the aggregation result $\mathbf{W}$, which means to calculate: $cw_j = PolyCom_{ck}(\omega_j, \delta_j) = g^{\omega_j} h^{\delta_j}, j = 1, 2, ..., t$, then the commitment of $\mathbf{W}$ can be expressed as a vector $\mathbf{CW} = (\mathbf{cw_1}, \mathbf{cw_2}, ..., \mathbf{cw_t})$. To verify the correctness of the aggregation result they obtained, clients calculates the verification equation:

$$
\begin{aligned}
PolyCom_{ck}(\gamma, \lambda) = g^{\gamma} h^{\lambda} = g^{fw(i)} h^{hw(i)} &= g^{\sum_{j=0}^{t-1} \omega_{j+1} i^j} h^{\sum_{j=0}^{t-1} \delta_{j+1} i^j} \\
&= \prod_{j=1}^{t} (g^{\omega_j} h^{\delta_j})^{i^j} = \prod_{j=1}^{t} cw_j^{i^j}
\end{aligned} \tag{21}
$$

Then the aggregation result obtained by clients is proved to be correct.

As the security analysis above, in the PPFL-MVVS scheme, neither the AS nor any other entities would obtain the valid information of the private datasets or local gradients, and only the AS holds the aggregation result before clients recover it. In addition, the local gradients uploaded by clients are verifiable for the AS, and the subkeys distributed by the AS are also verifiable for clients. Therefore, our proposed scheme is both privacy-preserving and mutually verifiable for the AS and clients, which has achieved the design goal.

6 Conclusion

In this paper, we have proposed a privacy-preserving and mutually verifiable federated learning framework on the vector spaces. The privacy of both local gradients and aggregation result is fully protected, and mutual verification between clients and aggregation server is realized. Also, we modify the secret sharing of numbers to that of vectors, and advance the number for a commitment to polynomials. Moreover, our scheme can also tolerant of clients dropping out during the training process. Security analysis demonstrates the high security of our scheme under the semi-honest security setting.

Acknowledgement. This work is partially supported by the National Natural Science Foundation of China under grants 62072134, 62102137 and U2001205, and the Key projects of Guangxi Natural Science Foundation under grant 2019JJD170020, and he Key Research and Development Program of Hubei Province under Grant 2021BEA163.

References

1. Zhang, C., Xie, Y., Bai, H., Yu, B., Li, W., Gao, Y.: A survey on federated learning. Knowl.-Based Syst. **216**, 106775 (2021)
2. Wang, J., et al.: Research review of federated learning algorithms. Big Data Res. **6**(6), 70–88 (2020)

3. Połap, D., Srivastava, G., Yu, K.: Agent architecture of an intelligent medical system based on federated learning and blockchain technology. J. Inf. Secur. Appl. **58**, 102748 (2021)
4. Qolomany, B., Ahmad, K., Al-Fuqaha, A., Qadir, J.: Particle swarm optimized federated learning for industrial IoT and smart city services. In: 2020 IEEE Global Communications Conference, GLOBECOM 2020, pp. 1–6. IEEE (2020)
5. Kawa, D., Punyani, S., Nayak, P., Karkera, A., Jyotinagar, V.: Credit risk assessment from combined bank records using federated learning. Int. Res. J. Eng. Technol. (IRJET) **6**(4), 1355–1358 (2019)
6. Li, L., Fan, Y., Tse, M., Lin, K.Y.: A review of applications in federated learning. Comput. Ind. Eng. **149**, 106854 (2020)
7. Mothukuri, V., Parizi, R.M., Pouriyeh, S., Huang, Y., Dehghantanha, A., Srivastava, G.: A survey on security and privacy of federated learning. Futur. Gener. Comput. Syst. **115**, 619–640 (2021)
8. Briggs, C., Fan, Z., Andras, P.: A review of privacy-preserving federated learning for the internet-of-things. In: Rehman, M.H., Gaber, M.M. (eds.) Federated Learning Systems. SCI, vol. 965, pp. 21–50. Springer, Cham (2021). https://doi.org/10.1007/978-3-030-70604-3_2
9. Hao, M., Li, H., Luo, X., Xu, G., Yang, H., Liu, S.: Efficient and privacy-enhanced federated learning for industrial artificial intelligence. IEEE Trans. Industr. Inf. **16**(10), 6532–6542 (2019)
10. Kairouz, P., et al.: Advances and open problems in federated learning. Found. Trends Mach. Learn. **14**(1–2), 1–210 (2021)
11. Bouacida, N., Mohapatra, P.: Vulnerabilities in federated learning. IEEE Access **9**, 63229–63249 (2021)
12. Lee, H., Kim, J., Ahn, S., Hussain, R., Cho, S., Son, J.: Digestive neural networks: a novel defense strategy against inference attacks in federated learning. Comput. Secur. **109**, 102378 (2021)
13. Chen, Y., Luo, F., Li, T., Xiang, T., Liu, Z., Li, J.: A training-integrity privacy-preserving federated learning scheme with trusted execution environment. Inf. Sci. **522**, 69–79 (2020)
14. Yin, X., Zhu, Y., Hu, J.: A comprehensive survey of privacy-preserving federated learning: a taxonomy, review, and future directions. ACM Comput. Surv. (CSUR) **54**(6), 1–36 (2021)
15. Brisimi, T.S., Chen, R., Mela, T., Olshevsky, A., Paschalidis, I.C., Shi, W.: Federated learning of predictive models from federated electronic health records. Int. J. Med. Inform. **112**, 59–67 (2018)
16. Zhang, M., Song, W., Zhang, J.: A secure clinical diagnosis with privacy-preserving multiclass support vector machine in clouds. IEEE Syst. J. **16**, 67–78 (2020)
17. Nguyen, T., Thai, M.T.: Preserving privacy and security in federated learning. arXiv preprint arXiv:2202.03402 (2022)
18. Hu, H., Salcic, Z., Sun, L., Dobbie, G., Zhang, X.: Source inference attacks in federated learning. In: 2021 IEEE International Conference on Data Mining (ICDM), pp. 1102–1107. IEEE (2021)
19. Wu, X., Li, F., Kumar, A., Chaudhuri, K., Jha, S., Naughton, J.: Bolt-on differential privacy for scalable stochastic gradient descent-based analytics. In: Proceedings of the 2017 ACM International Conference on Management of Data, pp. 1307–1322 (2017)
20. Melis, L., Danezis, G., De Cristofaro, E.: Efficient private statistics with succinct sketches. arXiv preprint arXiv:1508.06110 (2015)

21. Ho, Q., et al.: More effective distributed ml via a stale synchronous parallel parameter server. In: Advances in Neural Information Processing Systems 26 (2013)
22. Hardy, S., et al.: Private federated learning on vertically partitioned data via entity resolution and additively homomorphic encryption. arXiv preprint arXiv:1711.10677 (2017)
23. Bell, J.H., Bonawitz, K.A., Gascón, A., Lepoint, T., Raykova, M.: Secure single-server aggregation with (poly) logarithmic overhead. In: Proceedings of the 2020 ACM SIGSAC Conference on Computer and Communications Security, pp. 1253–1269 (2020)
24. Mohassel, P., Zhang, Y.: SecureML: a system for scalable privacy-preserving machine learning. In: 2017 IEEE Symposium on Security and Privacy (SP), pp. 19–38. IEEE (2017)
25. Fereidooni, H., et al.: SAFELearn: secure aggregation for private federated learning. In: 2021 IEEE Security and Privacy Workshops (SPW), pp. 56–62. IEEE (2021)
26. Shamir, A.: How to share a secret. Commun. ACM **22**(11), 612–613 (1979)
27. Blakley, G.R.: Safeguarding cryptographic keys. In: International Workshop on Managing Requirements Knowledge, p. 313. IEEE Computer Society (1979)
28. Fu, A., Zhang, X., Xiong, N., Gao, Y., Wang, H., Zhang, J.: VFL: a verifiable federated learning with privacy-preserving for big data in industrial IoT. IEEE Trans. Industr. Inf. **8**, 3316–3326 (2020)
29. Bonawitz, K., et al.: Practical secure aggregation for privacy-preserving machine learning. In: Proceedings of the 2017 ACM SIGSAC Conference on Computer and Communications Security, pp. 1175–1191 (2017)
30. So, J., Güler, B., Avestimehr, A.S.: Byzantine-resilient secure federated learning. IEEE J. Sel. Areas Commun. **39**(7), 2168–2181 (2020)

Data Detection

Patch-Based Backdoors Detection and Mitigation with Feature Masking

Tao Wang[1], Xiaoyu Zhang[1(✉)], Yulin Jin[1], Chenyang Chen[1], and Fei Zhu[2]

[1] State Key Laboratory of Integrated Service Networks (ISN), Xidian University, Xi'an 710071, People's Republic of China
{twang19151213465,cychen_1}@stu.xidian.edu.cn, xiaoyuzhang@xidian.edu.cn

[2] School of Computing Technologies, RMIT University, Melbourne, VIC 3000, Australia

Abstract. Pre-trained models have been employed by substantial downstream tasks, achieving remarkable achievements in transfer learning scenarios. However, poisoning the training samples guides the target model to make misclassification in the inference phase, backdoor attacks against pre-trained models represents a new security threat. In this paper, we propose two patch-based backdoors detection and mitigation methods via feature masking. Our approaches are motivated by the observation that, patch-based triggers induce abnormal feature distribution at the intermediate layer. By exploiting the feature importance extraction method and gradient-based threshold method, the backdoored samples can be detected and the abnormal feature values can be backward linked to the trigger position. Hence, masking the features within the trigger posed achieves the correct labels for those backdoored samples. Finally, we employ the unlearning technique to dramatically mitigate the negative effect of the backdoor attacks. The extensive experimental results show that our approaches perform better in defense effectiveness and model inference accuracy on clean examples than the state-of-the-art method.

Keywords: Backdoor attack · Backdoor detection and defense · Feature masking · Unlearning

1 Introduction

Deep neural networks (DNNs) have demonstrated their powerful capabilities to solve complex real-world missions [1,2]. They are increasingly applied to numerous security-critical applications, such as autonomous driving [3], medical diagnosis [4,5], industrial internet of things [6], and photo-realistic image generation [7]. Meanwhile, with the rapid growth of data, the pre-trained models (PTMs), which require knowledgeable training sets to construct general-purpose models and they are employed by various types of downstream tasks, have been

X. Chen et al. (Eds.): SocialSec 2022, CCIS 1663, pp. 229–246, 2022.
https://doi.org/10.1007/978-981-19-7242-3_15

made remarkable achievements in transfer learning. Instead of training a complex model from scratch, the open-source PTMs (e.g., BERT [8] and XLNet [9] from Google) provide the Internet users a shortcut by allowing to be downloaded and fine-tuned for particular downstream tasks. At this point, the PTMs offer a tremendous alternative for model initialization, where its security concerns arise.

Due to the complexity and opacity of DNNs and big data, the PTMs created by one model developer naturally provide a tremendous opportunity for backdoor attacks [10,11], *i.e.*, a new type of data poisoning attack. The backdoor attack is an active attack that happens during training time, which adds small perturbations (or specific patterns) on clean samples and then poisons them into training data to manipulate the inference labels of the target model. As a result, backdoor attacks can fool the target model to make incorrect predictions by forcing it to learn the strong corrections between the triggers and corresponding specific labels while remaining normal behaviors on clean samples.

Most defense methods against backdoor attacks are dedicated to mitigating adversarial effects by utilizing standard fine-tuning [12] or fine-pruning [13] strategies. Even though the above-mentioned approaches have been performing reasonably well on defending against backdoors, Zhao et al. [14] demonstrated that the proposed MCR (mode connectivity repair) method significantly outperforms these several baselines. MCR shows that path connections trained by a small proportion of clean samples can successfully purify backdoored or poisoned models. Recently, Li et al. proposed a backdoor erasing approach NAD motivated by knowledge distillation [15], and ABL to automatically resist backdoor attacks during training time [16]. While these approaches, to some extent, achieve defense effects, it is still not well understood whether the activation pattern (or distribution) induced by the backdoored sample is similar to that of one clean example.

In this paper, we empirically observe that solid connections between specific characteristics of intermediate activation and input triggers can be constructed if studied from an intermediate layer activation perspective. We find that the triggers activate abnormal feature distribution, reflecting in the activation magnitudes of triggers are higher than normal input features. It means that triggers carry out the signal-boosting impact on the intermediate layer activation. In this paper, we focus on designing feature masking backdoors detection and mitigation methods that are customized for patch-based backdoors, including Trojan and Badnets. The contributions can be summarized as follows.

- We design a backdoor detection method based on the feature importance extraction function. We can identify the trigger position and mask the positions of the trigger to acquire its correct label. Then, the negative effect of triggers can be mitigated by leveraging unlearning techniques.
- We propose a backdoor detection approach based on the intermediate gradient threshold method. By calculating the derivative of the final label regarding the ith layer's output, we can backward link the abnormal feature distribution to the trigger position on the input. Hence, we can detect the backdoored

samples and refine the backdoored models by utilizing the same techniques with the first method.

- We empirically demonstrate that our schemes, evaluated on CIFAR10 dataset and MNIST dataset, are resilient to the same types of backdoor attacks. Compared to the state-of-the-art backdoor defense method, our schemes have a preferable performance in defense effect and model inference accuracy on clean samples.

2 Related Work

2.1 Backdoor Attack

Gu et al. [10] made the first attempt to propose a backdoor attack (Badnets), *i.e.*, a malicious model provider creates an outsourced and pre-trained network that normally performs on user's training and validation examples while misbehaving on attack-specified triggers. At the same time, Liu et al. [17] proposed to launch backdoor attack (Trojan) without training set, which improved the reality of backdoor attack. The recent backdoor target to make the input triggers more stealthy, such as invisible perturbation [18], clean-label backdoor [19], reflection backdoor [20], and dynamic patterns [21]. Regarding the attack on pre-trained networks in transfer learning, Yao et al. [12] presented latent backdoors that are some potential backdoors injected into a "Teacher" model, and automatically inherited by "Student" models (*i.e.*, downstream tasks) through transfer learning. However, the latent backdoor attack requires that the downstream tasks have to contain the target class, which dramatically limits its universality.

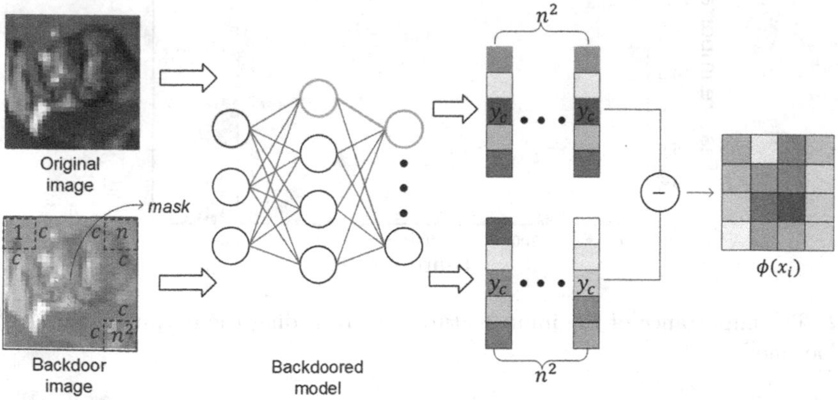

Fig. 1. The architecture of scheme I.

2.2 Backdoor Defense

Most defense methods against backdoor attacks are dedicated to mitigating negative effects by utilizing standard fine-tuning [12] or fine-pruning [13] strategies. Even though these methods, to some extent, achieve defense effects, Zhao et al. [14] demonstrate that the proposed MCR (mode connectivity repair) the method significantly outperforms these several baselines. MCR shows that path connections trained by a small proportion of clean samples can successfully purify backdoored or poisoned models. Recently, Li et al. proposed a backdoor erasing approach NAD motivated by knowledge distillation [15], and ABL to automatically resist backdoor attacks during training time [16]. While these approaches perform reasonably well in defending against backdoors, it is still not well understood whether the activation pattern (or distribution) induced by the backdoored sample is similar to that of one clean example.

3 Abnormal Feature Distribution and Detection and Defense

In this section, we present the observations on the feature distributions of backdoor samples with or without feature masking. By observing the differences between before and after feature masking on the backdoor samples, we propose two threshold-based backdoor samples detection and defense approaches.

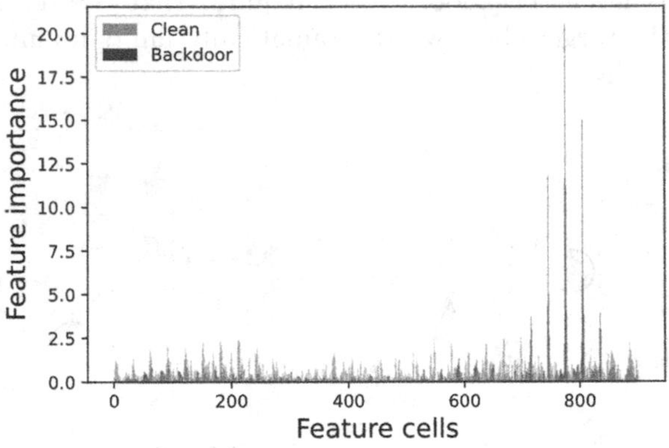

Fig. 2. The importance of the input feature cells regarding the output of the Trojan backdoor model.

3.1 Backdoors Detection and Defense Based on Feature Cells Importance

The target model f: $x \rightarrow f(x)$ maps the input image x to a confidence vector $f(x)$, where $x \in \mathbb{R}^{l \times w \times h}$, $f(x) \in \mathbb{R}^{C}$. In this paper, we focus on patch-based backdoor samples detection. As shown in Fig. 1, we divide the input image x

into $n \times n$ cells, where the size of each cell is $c * c$. Figure 2 shows the importance of each feature cell in the input image to the output of the backdoor model. We can see that only a few feature cells (trigger regions) in the backdoor samples have large feature attribution values, and feature cells in other regions attract less attention or are even ignored by the model. The feature attribution value of the 775th feature cell is the largest because the feature cell just contains the whole trigger region, and the feature importance values of other feature cells containing the trigger region will be greater than that of feature cells without trigger region. The results show that the backdoor model can classify only by the features in the trigger region, and will not pay attention to other normal features. Based on these observations and inspired by Leave-One-Out (LOO) method [22] and ML-LOO method [23], we design the following backdoor detection and defense methods based on feature importance.

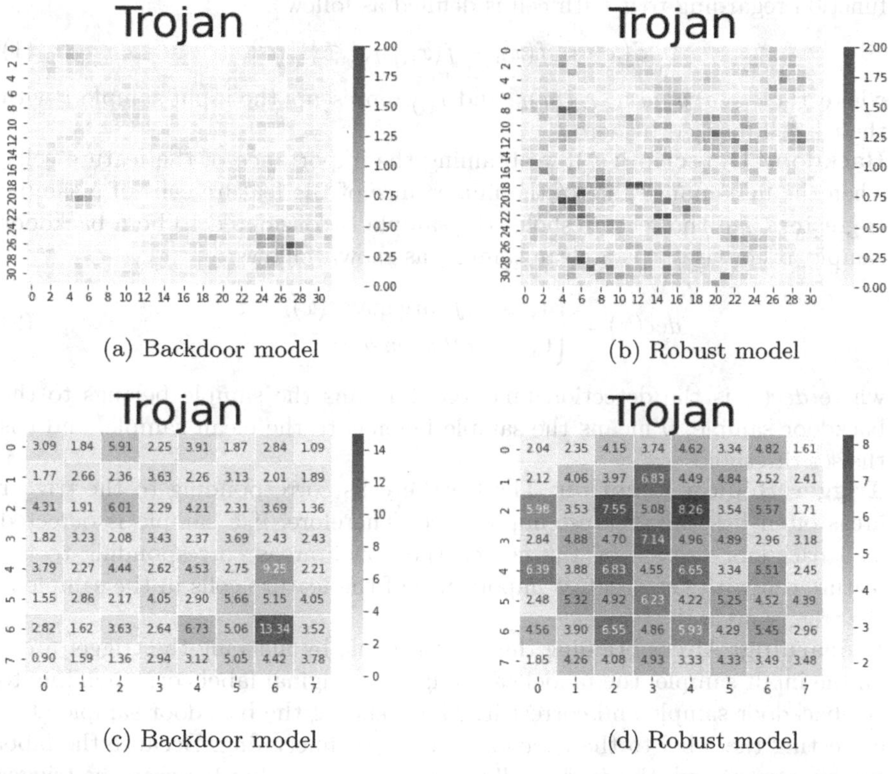

Fig. 3. The first row is the gradients of the outputs of the backdoor model (a) and robust model (b) on the backdoor sample on CIFAR10 to the input. The second row is the gradients of outputs of the backdoor model (c) and robust model (d) on the backdoor sample on CIFAR10 to the neurons in the penultimate layer.

The whole scheme is mainly divided into four steps: **Feature Importance Extraction, Backdoor Detection, Trigger Region Location and Unlearning.**

- **Feature Importance Extraction:** Feature importance extraction calculates the importance of different features relative to the target label, and carries out backdoor detection by comparing the relationship between the maximum value of the extracted feature importance and the threshold. A feature importance extraction function $\mathcal{E}(\cdot)$ is defined as mapping a modified cell (maybe only one pixel) of the input sample to a vector of the same size with the input image x, indicating the ith specific cell of x dominates the contribution in the model prediction, where $i \in [1, n^2]$. That is to say, we modify the input sample x's ith cell by masking it with zero, and the changes in the prediction of the model on the input image x tells the contribution of x's ith cell in the classification task. The feature importance extraction function regarding to x's ith cell is defined as follows,

$$\mathcal{E}(x)_i = f(x)_t - f(x_{(i)})_t, i \in [1, n^2], \tag{1}$$

  where $f(x)_t = argmax_{k \in C} f(x)_k$, and $x_{(i)}$ represents the input sample x with the ith cell masked by zero.
- **Backdoor Detection:** After obtaining the importance of the feature cells, when the maximum value of the importance of the feature cells of a sample is greater than the set threshold, the sample is considered to be a backdoor sample, otherwise, it is a clean sample; as shown follows.

$$dec(x) = \begin{cases} 1, & if \ \arg\max \varepsilon(x)_i > t \\ 0, & otherwise, \end{cases} \tag{2}$$

  where $dec(\cdot)$ is the detection function, 1 means the sample belongs to the backdoor sample, 0 means the sample belongs to the clean sample, and l is the set threshold.
- **Trigger Region Location:** The feature cells corresponding to the trigger areas often has the greatest importance. Therefore, if a sample is detected as a backdoor sample by the model, the image areas corresponding to the feature cell with the greatest importance of the feature cells in the sample is the trigger areas.
- **Unlearning:** After obtaining the trigger areas, by masking the trigger areas on the input sample, the model can judge the original label corresponding to the backdoor sample and correct it. Then sending the backdoor sample after correcting the label to the backdoor model for finetuning. Because the label has been corrected, the model will forget the relationship between the trigger and the target label, and the performance of the model on the clean sample does not decline sharply.

3.2 Backdoors Detection Based on Gradient Method

As demonstrated in [24], the saliency map depicts the dominating role of the input feature in classification results. More concretely, the saliency map is achieved by taking the derivative of the gradient on the final label, *i.e.*, the maximum of softmax layer's output $f_y(x)$. Figure 3 shows the gradients of the outputs of the backdoor model (a) and clean model (b) to the backdoor sample. As we can see from Fig. 3, the gradient of the trigger on the backdoor model (a) is abnormally large, while the trigger is not being paid more attention than other features on the robust model (b). Due to the extra noise introduced by taking the derivative of the final label $f_y(x)$ concerning the input pixel, we find that the abnormal feature distribution is not exactly linked to the trigger patterns. That is to say, taking the derivative of the output label $f_y(x)$ with respect to the input pixel is difficult to identify the abnormal feature distribution which is induced by the triggers. Hence, we observe how the abnormal feature distribution performs in the gradient of the intermediate layer's output, as shown in Fig. 3(c) and Fig. 3(d). The gradient method is also divided into four steps, which is basically the same as the method based on feature cells importance, the difference lies in the feature importance extraction and backdoor detection.

- **Feature Importance Extraction:** If the gradient value of a neuron in the *ith* layer is greater than 50% of the maximum gradient value of neurons in this layer, the neuron is considered to be an important neuron; Otherwise, it is an unimportant neuron. The extraction process is defined as follows,

$$I(f_i^k) = \begin{cases} 1, & if\ \frac{\partial f_y(x)}{\partial f_i^k(x)} > 0.5 \times \arg\max \frac{\partial f_y(x)}{\partial f^k(x)} \\ 0, & otherwise, \end{cases} \tag{3}$$

  where $I(\cdot)$ represents the importance measurement function, 1 represents important, 0 represents unimportant, and f_i^k indicates the *ith*neuron in the *kth* layer.
- **Backdoor Detection:** After obtaining the importance of neurons, that is, when the number of important neurons in an intermediate layer corresponding to a sample is less than the set threshold, the sample is considered to be a backdoor sample; otherwise, it is a clean sample. The detection process is defined as follows,

$$dec(x) = \begin{cases} 1, & if\ \#\{I(f^k = 1)\} > t \\ 0, & otherwise, \end{cases} \tag{4}$$

  where $dec(x)$ is detection function, # represents the number of neurons. The trigger region location and unlearning are the same as the method based on feature cells importance.

4 Experimental Evaluations

Attack Configuration. In this section, we evaluate the defense effect on Trojan and Badnets backdoor attacks. We train a classical model architecture, *i.e.*, ResNet-18 for 150 epochs on CIFAR10 and MNIST using SGD with momentum

Table 1. Results in DPC and DPB on CIFAR10 of our schemes.

Attack	Scheme I		Scheme II	
	DPC	DPB	DPC	DPB
Trojan	99.34%	99.31%	98.76%	95.91%
Badnets	97.77%	94.16%	99.17%	99.22%

Table 2. Results in DPC and DPB on MNIST of our schemes.

Attack	Scheme I		Scheme II	
	DPC	DPB	DPC	DPB
Trojan	99.60%	99.29%	98.12%	99.05%
Badnets	99.99%	99.98%	98.27%	92.85%

0.9, weight decay 10^{-4}, and the initial learning rate 0.1 which is divided by 10 at 70th and 120th epoch. To evaluate fairness, we follow the previous methods' configurations, including trigger pattern, size, and target label. For backdoor attacks, we use 10% of the clean samples in the training set for poisoning and train the backdoored model using poison samples and the remaining 90% of the clean training set.

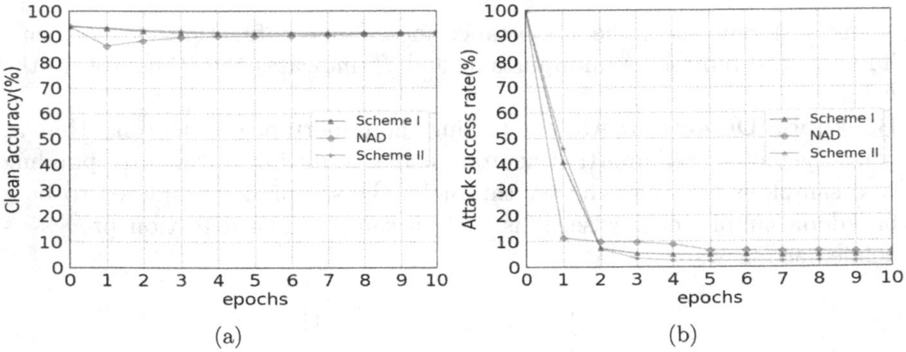

Fig. 4. Performance of three defense methods against Trojan attack on CIFAR10.

Defense Configuration. For defense, we first detect the backdoor samples, when the feature attribution value of a sample is greater than the threshold value or the number of backdoor neurons in the penultimate layer is greater than a certain threshold, we think that the sample is a backdoor sample; otherwise, it is a clean sample. Since the datasets encountered in real life are unknown, we conduct the experiments on the test set for practical consideration. We poisoned half of the data in the test set, and then send the test set with poisoned samples to the detector. When the number of detected backdoor samples is larger than 100, we stop the detection operations. For each backdoor sample, we mask the regions where the trigger is located and feed the masked sample into the target model, generating the correct classification label. Finally, the modified 100 backdoor samples are used as the training set to fine-tune the target model. It only needs to fine-tune 10 rounds. The learning rate starts from 0.002 and is divided by 10 every five rounds.

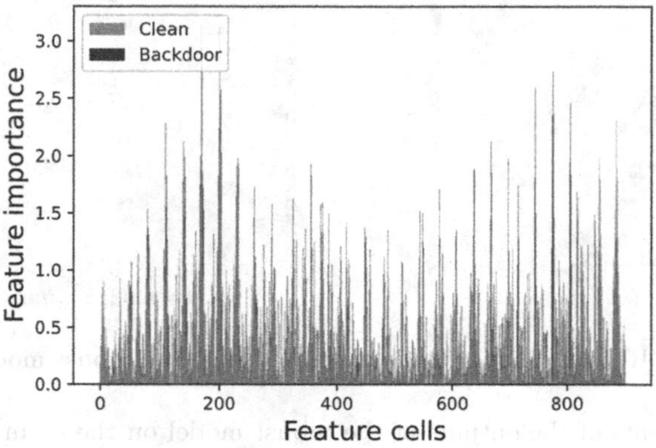

Fig. 5. The importance of the input feature cells regarding the output of the robust model.

Defense Metrics. To evaluate the effectiveness of our proposed backdoor detection and defense methods, we evaluate its performance on two backdoor attack methods using four metrics, detection probability of clean samples (DPC), detection probability of backdoor samples (DPB), model's accuracy on clean samples (ACC), and attack success rate (ASR), which is the proportion of the backdoor samples misclassified as target label. We compare our defense algorithm with NAD [15], which utilizes 100 samples in clean training data to fine-tune ten rounds at a learning rate of 0.01. We does not compare our defense algorithm with ABL [16], because ABL [16] trains a clean model on poisoned samples, rather than training a backdoor model first and then finetune to get a clean model.

Datasets. We perform our experiments on CIFAR10 and MNIST, which are popular image classification datasets. CIFAR10 has 60000 image samples in total, the size of these samples is 32×32. These samples are divided into 10 categories, with 6000 samples in each category. Among these samples, 50000 samples are used for training, forming five training batches, with 10000 samples in each batch. The remaining 10000 samples are used for testing. The test data is taken from each of the 10 categories, and 1000 samples are taken at random for each category. The remaining samples are randomly picked out to constitute a training batch. Note that the number of samples in each category in a training batch is not required to be the same, in general, there are 5000 samples in each category in the training batch. MNIST is initiated by the National Institute of Standards and Technology. It counted handwritten digital images from 250 different people, of which 50% were high school students and 50% were staff of the Census Bureau. The data set contains 10 categories, 60000 images in the training set and 10000 images in the test set. The size of each image is 28 × 28.

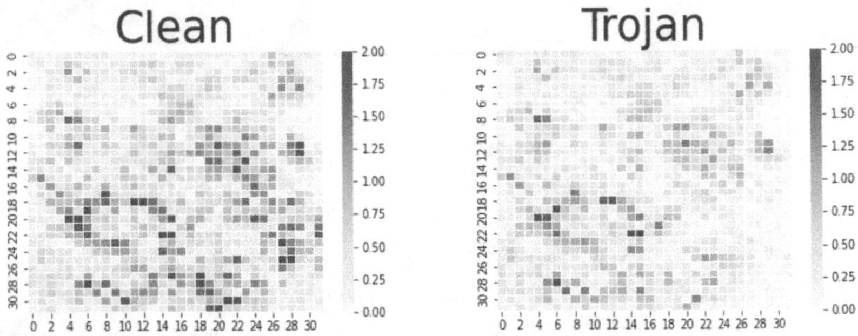

(a) Robust model (b) Robust model

Fig. 6. The gradients of the outputs of the robust model on the clean sample (a) and the backdoor sample (b) on CIFAR10 to the input.

Table 3. Comparison on ASR and ACC on CIFAR10 among several methods.

Attack	Baseline		NAD		Scheme I		Scheme II	
	ACC	ASR	ACC	ASR	ACC	ASR	ACC	ASR
Trojan	93.93%	100.00%	91.61%	4.78%	91.58%	2.77%	91.34%	2.38%
Badnets	93.78%	100.00%	91.73%	31.3%	–	–	90.72%	2.84%

4.1 Backdoors Detection and Mitigation Against Trojan Attack

As we can see from the experimental results of the Trojan attack on CIFAR10 in the first row of Table 1, the DPC and DPB of scheme I and scheme II are more than 98% and 95% respectively. the results of the Trojan attack on MNIST in the first row of Table 2 shows that the DPC and DPB of scheme I and scheme II are more than 98% and 99% respectively. Both experiments reveal that the detection algorithms in our schemes are pretty effective. Moreover, the proposed scheme I can successfully distinguish clean samples and backdoor samples on CIFAR10 and MNIST with a probability of close to 100%. The effects of the defense algorithms against Trojan attack in our schemes are shown in the first row of Table 3 and Table 4. Experimental results show that both scheme I and scheme II can significantly reduce the attack success rate on CIFAR10 from 100% to less than 3%, and the attack success rate of MNIST from 99.96% to less than 1%, and both have little negative impact on ACC. In contrast, the state-of-the-art work NAD [15] can only reduce the attack success rate to 4.78% on

Table 4. Comparison on ASR and ACC on MNIST among several methods.

Attack	Baseline		NAD		Scheme I		Scheme II	
	ACC	ASR	ACC	ASR	ACC	ASR	ACC	ASR
Trojan	99.57%	99.96%	98.18%	5.62%	99.35%	0.27%	99.26%	0.95%
Badnets	99.63%	100.00%	99.26%	0.90%	99.30%	0.19%	99.31%	1.56%

CIFAR10 and reduce the attack success rate to 5.62% on MNIST. The detailed performance of our schemes and NAD under different training epochs against Trojan attack on CIFAR10 is recorded in Fig. 4. As we can see from Fig. 4, our methods can significantly reduce the ASR of the backdoor in only one round. After two or three rounds, the backdoor effect can be dramatically erased, which proves that our methods are very efficient. Although the reduction effect of NAD on ASR is obvious after one round, we deduce that this phenomenon might be put down to its lower values of ACC. When the ACC of the model is fixed, the effect of our methods in removing the backdoor is more obvious.

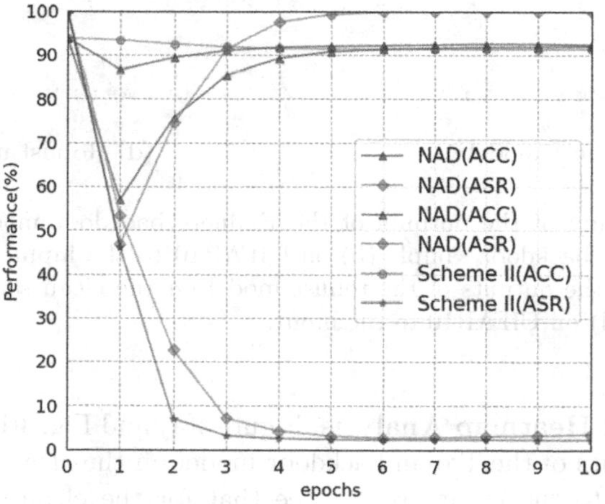

Fig. 7. Performance of two defense methods against Badnets attack on CIFAR10.

Feature Importance Analysis. As we can see from Fig. 2, when the Trojan backdoor model identifies a certain clean sample, it will pay attention to the key features in the sample, but when it identifies a certain backdoor sample, it will only pay attention to the trigger features in the sample, thus ignoring other features in the samples. Interestingly, as shown in Fig. 5, the robust model (after unlearning) obtained by our method is very different from this, regardless of identifying a clean sample or a backdoor sample, the model will focus on key features in the sample, rather than being attracted only by trigger features, which also illustrates that our method is very effective. The experimental results of our scheme II are the same.

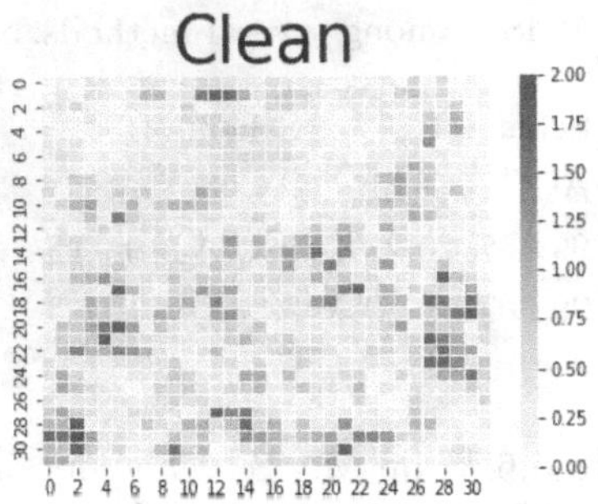

(a) Backdoor model

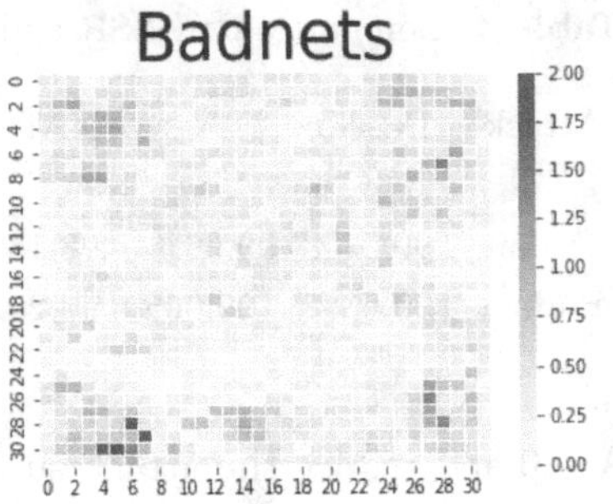

(b) Backdoor model

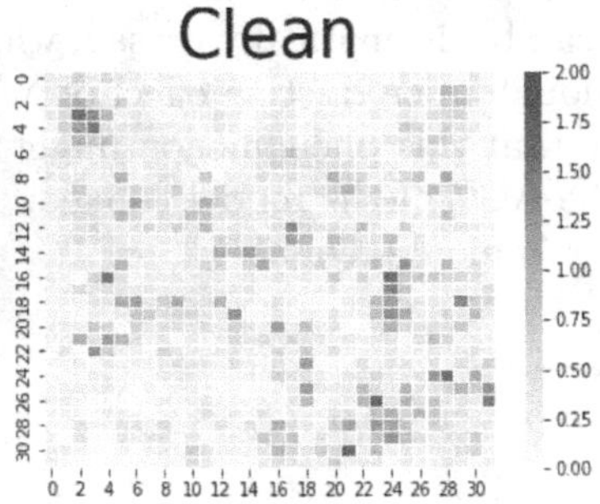

(c) Robust model

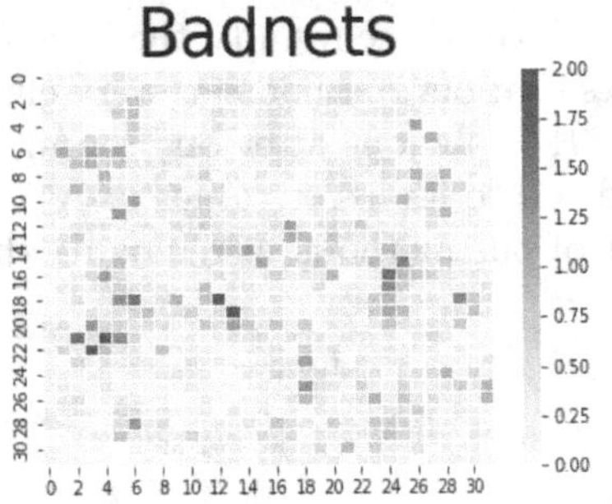

(d) Robust model

Fig. 8. The gradients of the outputs of the Badnets backdoor model on the clean sample (a) and the backdoor sample (b) on CIFAR10 to the input. The second row is the gradients of the outputs of the robust model on the clean sample (c) and the backdoor sample (d) on CIFAR10 to the input.

Gradient-Based Heatmap Analysis. Figure 3(a) and Fig. 3(b) show the gradient of the outputs of the Trojan backdoor model on the clean sample and the backdoor sample to the input, we can see that for the clean sample, the key features on the input image are significantly highlighted. That is, where the gradient value is large, while for the backdoor sample, only the gradient value in the lower right corner is large, which is the area where the trigger is located. After the effect of the proposed scheme II, the key features in the backdoor samples will be recognized by the model, and the importance of trigger features to model prediction will be significantly weakened, as shown in Fig. 6(b), which proves that our scheme is very effective.

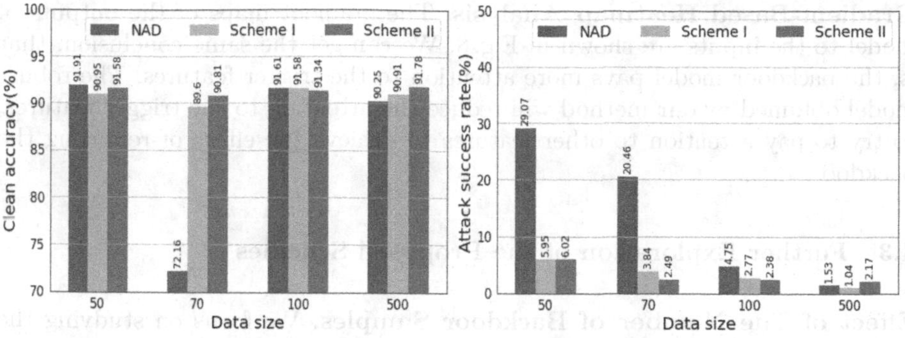

(a) Performance of clean accurcay (b) Performance of attack success rate

Fig. 9. Performance of three defense methods under different available samples against Trojan attack on CIFAR10.

4.2 Backdoors Mitigation and Defense Against Badnets Attack

We also extensively evaluate our schemes on Badnets attacks , and the experimental results show that our methods are also very effective. The DPC and DPB of the scheme I and scheme II on CIFAR10 are more than 97% and 94% and on MNIST are more than 98% and 92% respectively. Moreover, the proposed scheme II can successfully distinguish clean samples and backdoor samples on CIFAR10 with a probability of 99.17% and 99.22% and the proposed scheme I can successfully distinguish clean samples and backdoor samples on MNIST with a probability of 99.99% and 99.98% respectively. As can be seen from the second row of Table 3 and Table 4, the scheme II significantly reduces the ASR on CIFAR10 from 100.0% to 2.84% and the scheme I can reduces the ASR on MNIST from 100.0% to 0.19%, which are slightly better than that of NAD. In addition, we speculate that the reason why the scheme I cannot defend against Badnets attack on CIFAR10 may be that for CIFAR10, when there are more than one trigger region, the detection algorithm of the scheme I can only distinguish between clean samples and backdoor samples, but can not accurately judge the exact positions of triggers. Therefore, when we mask the trigger features according to the detection algorithm of the scheme I, we may mask the features including trigger features and key features, resulting in poor performance of the model. However, when we use the scheme I to defend against Badnets attack with only one trigger in the lower right corner, our scheme is very effective. The performance of our scheme and NAD over Badnets attack is recorded in Fig. 7. We can see that when the number of samples used for fine-tuning is only 100, the effect of NAD is very unstable. As shown in Fig. 7, NAD can reduce the ASR to a lower value, and sometimes it has no effect at all. In contrast, our scheme can significantly reduce ASR, and the decline rate of ASR is significantly faster than that of NAD.

Gradient-Based Heatmap Analysis. The gradient maps of the outputs of model to the inputs are shown in Fig. 8. We can get the same conclusion, that is, the backdoor model pays more attention to the trigger features. The robust model obtained by our method will reduce the attention to the trigger features, to try to pay attention to other features to achieve the effect of removing the backdoor.

4.3 Further Exploration of the Proposed Schemes

Effect of The Number of Backdoor Samples. We focus on studying the correlation between the performance of our schemes and NAD and the number of available backdoor samples. Intuitively, when we have more backdoor training samples, we expect our schemes to be more effectiveness. The performance of our schemes and NAD with various amounts of "training dataset" for Trojan is recorded in Fig. 9, and the performance for Badnets is recorded in Fig. 10. Here, we only consider that the maximum amount of samples is 500, because the detection time will arise with the number of samples increasing. In addition, our method only needs a small number of backdoor samples to achieve preferable performances. As we expected, when the number of samples used for fine-tuning increases, the ASR will drop. For Trojan attack, no matter how many samples are used for fine-tuning, our method is better than NAD. Moreover, when the number of samples used for fine-tuning is only 50, the scheme I is still effective, reducing the ASR to less than 10%, which is much better than NAD. When the number of samples used for fine-tuning is 500, the proposed scheme I can even reduce the ASR to less than 1%. For Badnets attack, we also achieve the same experimental results.

Effect of The Combination of Clean Samples and Backdoor Examples Similarly, we are also interested in the impact of mixed fine-tuning of detected clean samples and backdoor samples on the performance of the target model. We set up comparative experiments with 50, 70, 100, and 500 samples, respectively, in which the number of clean samples and the backdoor samples account for half. Empirically, we believe that when the number of backdoor samples used for fine-tuning is reduced, the effect of removing the backdoor of the robust model will be weakened, and we believe that due to the existence of clean samples, the performance of the robust model on the clean samples should be slightly improved. The performance of our schemes with the mixing of clean samples and backdoor samples is recorded in Fig. 11.

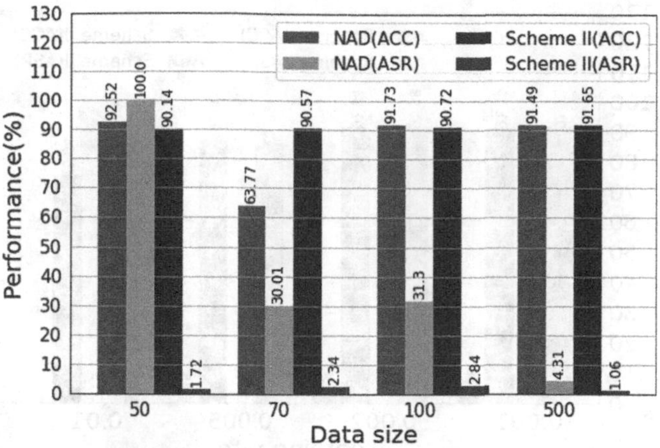

Fig. 10. Performance of two defense methods under different available samples against Badnets attack on CIFAR10.

The experimental results show that we can still remove the backdoor effect by using the mixed clean samples and backdoor samples to fine-tune the backdoor model, and the more samples, the better effect we can achieve in removing the backdoor. Compared with using only backdoor samples for fine-tuning, we can see that the performance of the model obtained by using mixed samples for fine-tuning on clean samples is also relatively poor.

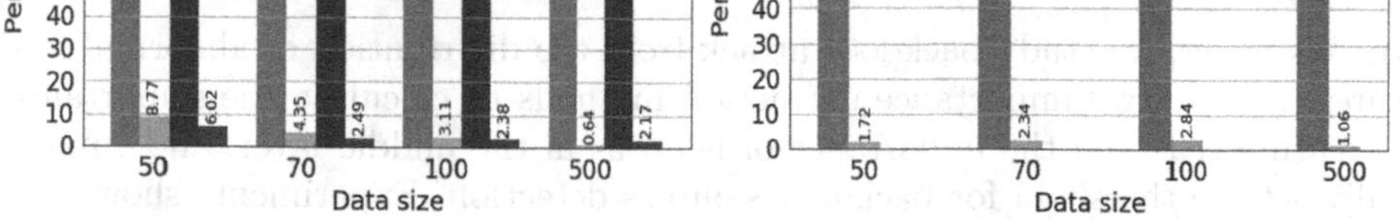

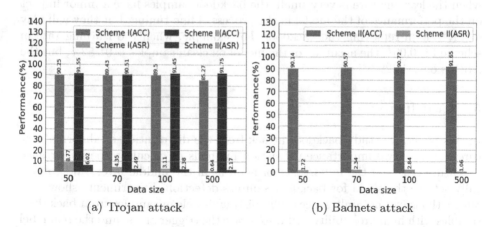

(a) Trojan attack (b) Badnets attack

Fig. 11. Performance of our schemes under different available mixed samples against backdoor attacks on CIFAR10.

Effects of Different Learning Rates. Here, we perform the proposed schemes for different learning rates to evaluate the effect of learning rate on model performance. This experiment is conducted on CIFAR10 against Trojan attack, and

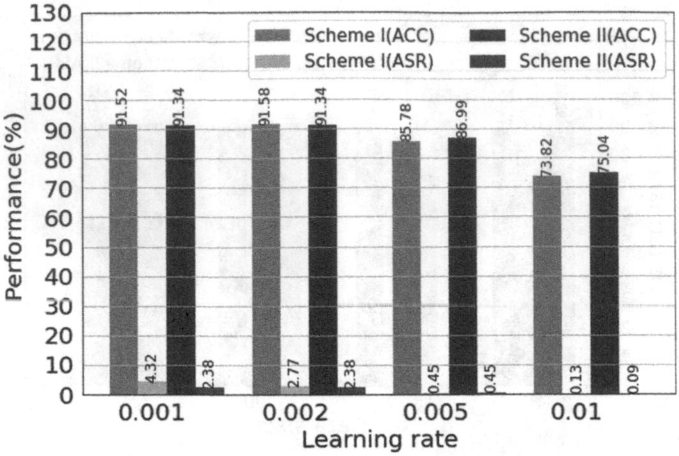

Fig. 12. Performance of our schemes under different learning rates against Trojan attack on CIFAR10.

the number of backdoor samples used for fine-tuning is 100. As shown in Fig. 12, when the learning rate is very large, the backdoor samples will play a significant role in removing the backdoor in the fine-tuning procedure, but it will also seriously affect the performance of the model on clean samples. For example, when the learning rate in the scheme I is 0.01, the ASR is 0.14%, which is close to 0, but the accuracy of the model on clean samples is only 75.91%. On the contrary, when the learning rate is very small, the backdoor samples have a minor impact on the performance of the model in the process of fine-tuning, but they will play a tiny role in removing the backdoor. For example, when the learning rate in scheme I is 0.001, the accuracy of the model on clean samples is 91.52%, but the ASR is only 4.32%.

5 Conclusion

In this paper, we study backdoor attack from the distribution of abnormal features. We use two importance extraction methods to calculate the importance of feature cells and the importance of neurons in the middle layer, and empirically set the threshold for backdoor samples detection. Experiments show that our methods can not only successfully distinguish clean samples from back door samples with high probability, but also locate the trigger areas, and the real label corresponding to the backdoor sample can be obtained by masking the trigger areas. The extensive experimental results on CIFAR10 and MNIST demonstrate that by using the corrected backdoor samples to finetune the backdoor model, the negative impact of backdoor attack can be significantly mitigated.

Acknowledgment. This work is supported by the National Natural Science Foundation of China (No. 62102300).

References

1. Kai, W., Wang, C., Liu, J.: Evolutionary multitasking multi-layer network reconstruction. IEEE Trans. Cybern. (2021). https://doi.org/10.1109/TCYB.2021.3090769
2. Kai, W., Hao, X., Liu, J., Liu, P., Shen, F.: Online reconstruction of complex networks from streaming data. IEEE Trans. Cybern. **52**(6), 5136–5147 (2022)
3. Bojarski, M., et al.: End to end learning for self-driving cars. arXiv preprint arXiv:1604.07316 (2016)
4. Esteva, A., et al.: Dermatologist-level classification of skin cancer with deep neural networks. Nature **542**(7639), 115–118 (2017)
5. Ma, X., Chen, X., Zhang, X.: Non-interactive privacy-preserving neural network prediction. Inf. Sci. **481**, 507–519 (2019)
6. Zhang, X., Chen, X., Liu, J.K., Xiang, Y.: DeepPAR and DeepDPA: privacy preserving and asynchronous deep learning for industrial IoT. IEEE Trans. Ind. Inf. **16**(3), 2081–2090 (2019)
7. Zhang, H., et al.: Stackgan: text to photo-realistic image synthesis with stacked generative adversarial networks. In: Proceedings of the IEEE International Conference on Computer Vision, pp. 5907–5915 (2017)
8. Devlin, J., Chang, M.W., Lee, K., Toutanova, K.: Bert: pre-training of deep bidirectional transformers for language understanding. arXiv preprint arXiv:1810.04805 (2018)
9. Yang, Z., Dai, Z., Yang, Y., Carbonell, J., Salakhutdinov, R.R., Le, Q.V.: Xlnet: Generalized autoregressive pretraining for language understanding. Advances in Neural Information Processing Systems 32 (2019)
10. Gu, T., Dolan-Gavitt, B., Garg, S.: Badnets: identifying vulnerabilities in the machine learning model supply chain. arXiv preprint arXiv:1708.06733 (2017)
11. Xi, Z., Pang, R., Ji, S., Wang, T.: Graph backdoor. In: 30th USENIX Security Symposium, pp. 1523–1540 (2021)
12. Yao, Y., Li, H., Zheng, H., Zhao, B.Y.: Latent backdoor attacks on deep neural networks. In: Proceedings of the 2019 ACM SIGSAC Conference on Computer and Communications Security, pp. 2041–2055 (2019)
13. Liu, K., Dolan-Gavitt, B., Garg, S.: Fine-pruning: defending against backdooring attacks on deep neural networks. In: Bailey, M., Holz, T., Stamatogiannakis, M., Ioannidis, S. (eds.) RAID 2018. LNCS, vol. 11050, pp. 273–294. Springer, Cham (2018). https://doi.org/10.1007/978-3-030-00470-5_13
14. Zhao, P., Chen, P.Y., Das, P., Ramamurthy, K.N., Lin, X.: Bridging mode connectivity in loss landscapes and adversarial robustness. arXiv preprint arXiv:2005.00060 (2020)
15. Li, Y., Lyu, X., Koren, N., Lyu, L., Li, B., Ma, X.: Neural attention distillation: Erasing backdoor triggers from deep neural networks. arXiv preprint arXiv:2101.05930 (2021)
16. Li, Y., Lyu, X., Koren, N., Lyu, L., Li, B., Ma, X.: Anti-backdoor learning: training clean models on poisoned data. Advances in Neural Information Processing Systems 34 (2021)
17. Liu, Y., Ma, S., Aafer, Y., et al.: Trojaning attack on neural networks (2017)
18. Liao, C., Zhong, H., Squicciarini, A., Zhu, S., Miller, D.: Backdoor embedding in convolutional neural network models via invisible perturbation. arXiv preprint arXiv:1808.10307 (2018)
19. Turner, A., Tsipras, D., Madry, A.: Clean-label backdoor attacks (2018)

20. Liu, Y., Ma, X., Bailey, J., Lu, F.: Reflection backdoor: a natural backdoor attack on deep neural networks. In: Vedaldi, A., Bischof, H., Brox, T., Frahm, J.-M. (eds.) ECCV 2020. LNCS, vol. 12355, pp. 182–199. Springer, Cham (2020). https://doi.org/10.1007/978-3-030-58607-2_11
21. Salem, A., Wen, R., Backes, M., Ma, S., Zhang, Y.: Dynamic backdoor attacks against machine learning models. arXiv preprint arXiv:2003.03675 (2020)
22. Li, J., Monroe, W., Jurafsky, D.: Understanding neural networks through representation erasure. arXiv preprint arXiv:1612.08220 (2016)
23. Yang, P., Chen, J., Hsieh, C.J., Wang, J.L., Jordan, M.: Ml-loo: detecting adversarial examples with feature attribution. In: Proceedings of the AAAI Conference on Artificial Intelligence, vol. 34, no. 4, pp. 6639–6647 (2020)
24. Zhou, B., Khosla, A., Lapedriza, A., Oliva, A., Torralba, A.: Learning deep features for discriminative localization. In: Proceedings of the IEEE Conference on Computer Vision and Pattern Recognition, pp. 2921–2929 (2016)

Detection and Defense Against DDoS Attack on SDN Controller Based on Feature Selection

Yan Xu(✉), Yongming Liu, and JinXing Ma

School of Computer Science and Technology, Anhui University, Hefei, China
xuyan@ahu.edu.cn

Abstract. Software-defined networking (SDN) can provide flexible traffic control and is an important part of the next-generation computer network. Distributed Denial of Service (DDoS) attack targeting the controller can seriously affect the performance of SDN. Although there are many schemes to detect and defend against this type of attack, the detection accuracy and efficiency of these schemes are severely limited due to the large scale and high dimension of traffic in SDN. According to the characteristics of SDN, this paper presents a new feature selection method to detect and defend against DDoS attacks targeting the controller. Firstly, Spearman's rank correlation coefficient and Gini impurity were used to extract the optimal feature subset. Then the attack detection module will detect the DDoS attack. Finally, attack defense module is introduced to filter attack packets and protect controller computing resources. We used the NSL-KDD dataset for evaluation and comparison with other schemes. Experimental results show that our scheme can detect and defend against DDoS attacks accurately.

Keywords: SDN · DDoS attack · GRU · Feature selection · Network defense mechanisms

1 Introduction

In 2009, Nike et al. proposed the concept of SDN architecture, aiming at simplifying the increasingly bloated network equipment and improving the processing speed of network traffic [1]. The introduction of phase separation technology between the control plane and forwarding plane enables SDN to flexibly control network traffic, while the centralization of logic control functions solves the problem that traffic processing speed increases with the expansion of network size in traditional networks [2,3]. However, while these features provide convenience for SDN, new attacks that can threaten the performance of SDN, such as DDoS attacks targeting the controller and OpenFlow (OF) switch attacks, are also generated [4]. DDoS attack targeting the controller will have a serious impact on the network performance and has been widely concerned.

DDoS attack targeting the controller aims to consume the computing resources of the controller, and then paralyze the controller, thus weakening the

X. Chen et al. (Eds.): SocialSec 2022, CCIS 1663, pp. 247–263, 2022.
https://doi.org/10.1007/978-981-19-7242-3_16

performance of the whole network [5]. At present, there are many schemes to detect and defend against this type of attack, most of which need to obtain network traffic features to realize attack detection. However, with the development of technology, the traffic of DDoS attack presents the trend of high complexity [6]. A study conducted by Reddy et al. shows that as the complexity of network attack traffic increases, some of the original features may not be able to represent the network attack traffic [7]. Therefore, many schemes for detecting DDoS attack targeting the controller have the defects of low detection accuracy and increased training time [8–10]. Using the feature selection method to select the optimal feature subset that can represent the network attack traffic is one of the available methods to solve these defects [11].

This paper designs and implements a scheme to detect and defend against DDoS attacks targeting the controller. Firstly, a new feature selection method is used to process the network traffic, and the optimal feature subset is selected to form the data sample. Then the deep neural network built by Gated Recurrent Unit (GRU) will conduct attack detection on the generated data samples. Finally, an intermediate module is introduced to filter the network traffic, so as to protect the controller resources and reduce the impact on normal services. Experimental results show that the proposed scheme can accurately detect various types of DDoS attacks. The introduction of the intermediate module can effectively filter out the attack traffic, so that the controller resources always maintain normal state and then maintain the overall performance of the whole network. The contribution points of this paper are summarized as follows:

- We propose a new feature selection method. In this method, Spearman's rank correlation coefficient and Gini impurity are used to select the optimal feature subset. The data samples processed by this feature selection method can more accurately reflect the change trend of network traffic.
- We propose to use intermediate module for DDoS attack defense. The intermediate module mainly filters Packet_IN messages. The processing based on unknown packet protocol makes the intermediate module capable of defending against various types of DDoS attacks. It can not only improve the processing efficiency of attack traffic, but also ensure the processing of legitimate requests from normal users.
- We construct a deep neural network model for attack detection. The model is composed of GRU algorithm, because GRU algorithm can achieve the same detection accuracy as Long Short-Term Memory (LSTM) algorithm while reducing the training time of the whole model.

The rest of this paper is organized as follows. Section 2 introduces the background knowledge of the scheme, and Sect. 3 mainly describes the related work. As for Sect. 4, it illustrates the details of the scheme. The evaluation result is provided in Sect. 5. Finally, in Sect. 6, this paper will be concluded.

2 Background

In this section, we will introduce the SDN architecture and OpenFlow [12] protocol.

2.1 Software Defined Network

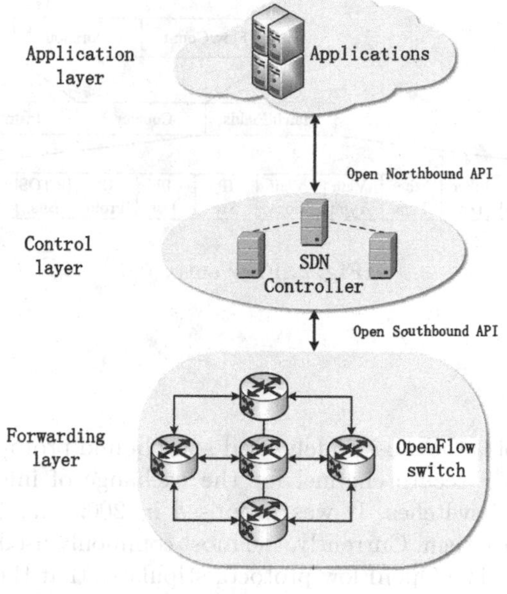

Fig. 1. SDN architecture

SDN has a layered structure as shown in Fig. 1. It mainly includes the following parts.

- Application layer: The application layer of SDN consists of all kinds of SDN applications [13]. Common applications include Load Balancing, Quality of Service, etc. Through manual programming, the user can call the controller with the help of the special part of the northward interface to realize various complex network functions conveniently.
- Control layer: The main object of the Control layer is the SDN controller. The entire layer integrates all logic processing capabilities and is responsible for formulating data forwarding policies, monitoring network link status, and managing network equipment on the Forwarding layer. The idea of SDN numerical control separation makes the device configuration get rid of the limitation of the application manufacturer, so controllers applied in different scenarios are born, such as OpenDayLight [14], Floodlight [15], etc.

- Forwarding layer: The forwarding layer consists of OF switches. Traffic flow is forwarded, modified, and discarded in this layer. Any action the OF switch does on the packet is directed by the flow table it contains internally. The flow table is issued and modified by the controller of the Control layer. The forwarding devices do not need to interact with each other to determine the forwarding strategy, so compared with the traditional network, SDN solves the defect that the processing efficiency decreases with the expansion of the network scale.

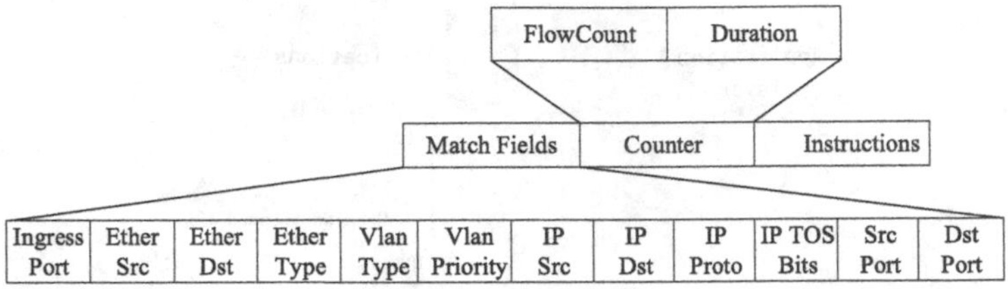

Fig. 2. Flow entry

2.2 OpenFlow

OpenFlow protocol is the most widely used southbound protocol in the industry so far. It provides a secure channel for the exchange of information between controllers and OF switches. It was proposed in 2009 and has gone through several versions since then. Currently, the most commonly used protocol versions are V1.0 and V1.3. The OpenFlow protocol stipulates that the flow table in OF switch is responsible for processing data packets. The flow table is composed of several flow entries. The components of a flow entry are shown in Fig. 2. It mainly composed of *Match Fields*, *Counters* and *Instructions*. Each time a packet matches *Match Fields* content of a flow entry, the packet performs the actions contained in *instructions*. The function of the *Counters* is to count the number of packets that match the current flow entry and other statistics.

Due to the characteristics of SDN, OF switch will package the packet which does not match any flow entry send it to the controller for waiting for processing as a Packet_IN message [16]. The controller will also constantly consume computing resources to process these messages. Therefore, an attacker only needs to send a large number of unknown packets to multiple forwarding devices to generate a large number of Packet_IN messages and consume controller resources. This is the principle of DDoS attack targeting the controller.

3 Related Work

This section mainly introduces and analyzes the DDoS attack detection scheme based on feature extraction.

Feature extraction is an important and outstanding task in machine learning. It is the goal of feature extraction to reduce the feature dimension and ensure the accuracy of model performance. In [17], authors point out that the feature extraction task should select feature subsets with low redundancy among each other and strong correlation with tags. Generally speaking, feature extraction methods can be divided into the following categories: filter-based method and wrapper-based method [18,19].

Filter-based methods do not pay attention to classification or learning algorithms, but use evaluation criteria to measure the correlation and redundancy between different features, and ultimately select the optimal feature subset. In 2020, Wei et al. [20] proposed a new feature selection algorithm: M-DFIFS. The algorithm uses the dynamic feature importance as the measurement parameter and selects the optimal feature subset according to this parameter to reduce the number of features. The author has done comparative experiments on fourteen kinds of high-dimensional data sets, and achieved good detection results while obviously reducing the number of features. However, the calculation cost of this scheme is high, which will increase the computing burden of the equipment.

Kavitha et al. [21] proposed an intrusion detection scheme based on the GRRF-FWSVM feature selection algorithm in 2020. The algorithm used in the scheme builds the guided regularization random forest, computing the feature weights and finally getting the optimal feature subset. The comparative experiment proves that the GRRF-FWSVM feature selection method can effectively reduce the number of features. At the same time, compared with the experimental group, the method achieved the best detection effect. However, the effectiveness of this scheme in detecting unknown attacks has not been verified.

The Wrapper based method divides the features into several subsets [22], uses different feature subsets for the classification task, and uses the classification accuracy as the feedback to select the optimal feature subset. Feature selection algorithms based on encapsulated classes usually achieve the best results, but they need to consume more computing resources. In 2019, Wang et al. [23] proposed a dynamic multilayer perceptron scheme based on feature selection algorithm to detect DDoS attacks. In this scheme, sequential feature selection and multilayer perceptron are combined to select the optimal feature. When feature subset is selected continuously, the multi-layer perceptron also modifies the structural parameters continuously. In this scheme, the feature subset with the best detection effect is selected as the optimal feature subset. Experimental results show the effectiveness of the proposed scheme. However, the calculation cost of this scheme is high, which will affect the normal operation of the equipment.

WFEU-FEDNN [24] is an anomaly detection scheme. In this scheme, the extra tree algorithm is used first, and a simplified subset of the optimal features is generated after updating the algorithm several times. Then the scheme uses the feature subset to train the feedforward deep neural network, and each update of the feedforward deep neural network will affect the selection of the optimal feature subset. The scheme was verified by using UNSW-NB15 and other data sets, and good detection results were obtained. However, the algorithm does not consider the influence of the algorithm that generates the optimal feature subset on the original feature set.

When a DDoS attack occurs in SDN, a lot of computing resources of the controller will be consumed [25]. Using feature extraction algorithms with high computational overhead will speed up the breakdown of the entire network. Therefore, lightweight computing scheme can be used for feature extraction to improve the accuracy of DDoS attack detection.

4 The Designed Scheme

This section describes the details of the proposed scheme. The scheme consists of three modules: data process module, attack detection module and attack defense module. The schema diagram is shown in Fig. 3.

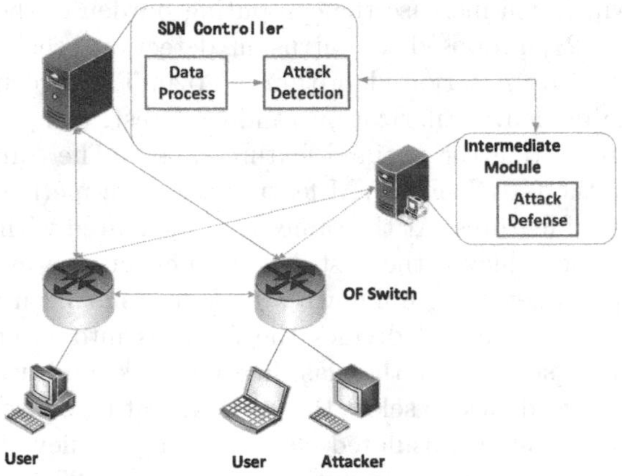

Fig. 3. System architecture of our scheme

- *Data Process Module*: This module includes two parts: Data Collection and Feature Extraction. Data Collection part collects the Packet_IN message received by the controller, sends the corresponding request to the OF switch, and obtains the various attributes and flow table information for creating the connection in unit time, which together set F_{total}. The function of Feature Extraction part is to select the optimal feature from the set F_{total} and form the optimal feature subset F_{best}.
- *Attack Detection Module*: This module mainly includes the model composed of the GRU algorithm. The model takes the data sample from Data Process module as input to detect whether a DDoS attack targeting the controller has occurred. The detection result of the model will be sent to Attack Defense Module to take corresponding measures.

- *Attack Defense Module*: After receiving the attack result, Attack Defense Module will activate the intermediate component to filter the Packet_IN message and protect the controller resources. At the same time, based on the information received, a defense flow entry is generated to further protect the device resources.

4.1 Data Process Module

Data Process Module is embedded in the controller. Because the controller can not only receive the Packet_IN message corresponding to the unknown packet, but also obtain the flow table information inside OF switch, which is more conducive to data processing.

Data Collection: Data Collection is designed to capture features that reflect traffic changes from the flow table and Packet_IN messages in OF switch. These features include packet content features and data flow features, so the collection period needs to be set. The paper [26] compares the period determination schemes based on time and data packet, and concludes that the scheme based on data packet is more efficient. So this module sets the collection period for F_{total} to the time it takes to generate a hundred connections.

Feature Extraction: The feature selection method used in this module is based on Spearman's rank correlation coefficient and Gini impurity. Spearman's rank correlation coefficient is commonly used in statistics to measure the dependence between two variables. In feature selection task, it can be used to describe the correlation between two features. Its calculation formula is as follows:

$$p = \frac{\sum_{i=1}^{N}(R_i - \overline{R})(S_i - \overline{S})}{\sum_{i=1}^{N}(R_i - \overline{R})\sum_{i=1}^{N}(S_i - \overline{S})} \tag{1}$$

In the formula, R and S represent two features, while R_i and S_i represent the feature of the ith sample in the set and the corresponding value of the feature. $\overline{R}$ and $\overline{S}$ represent the average of feature R and feature S. The value of Spearman's rank correlation coefficient is between -1 and 1, and the closer it is to 0, the lower the correlation between the two features corresponding to the coefficient will be.

Gini Impurity is the probability of misclassifying randomly selected features in a data set after labeling them according to the class distribution in the data set. Its calculation formula is as follows:

$$Gini(A) = \sum_{i=1}^{C} p(i)(1 - p(i)) \tag{2}$$

A represents any feature in the feature set of the dataset, C represents the number of sample types, and $P(i)$ represents the probability of correct classification using the feature. Gini Impurity can reflect how well a dataset is classified using either feature. The higher its value is, the worse the effect of using this feature to classify the sample is.

Algorithm 1. Feature extraction algorithm.

Require: Collection F_{total}; Spearman's rank correlation coefficient thresold β; The number of features of the optimal subset F_{best};
Ensure: Optimal subset F_{best}
Initialize optimal subset F_{best}; Intermediate feature set F_{middle}; Gini impurity score table $Gini_{score}$
for Each f_i,f_j in F_{total} **do** Calculate the Spearman's rank correlation coefficient $P(f_i, f_j)$ between feature f_i and feature f_j;
end for
for f_i in F_{total} **do**
    for f_j in F_{total} **do**
        if $|p(f_i, f_j)| \geq \beta$ **then**
            return line 4;
        end if
    end for F_{middle}.add(f_i);
end for
for f_i in F_{middle} **do**
    Calculate the Gini impurity $Gini(f_i)$ corresponding to feature f_i
    $Gini_{score}$.add($Gini(f_i)$)
end for
$Gini_{score}$ was sorted in reverse order, and the first γ features were selected to form the optimal feature subset F_{best}
return F_{best}

The description of feature selection algorithm is shown in Algorithm 1. The algorithm will first calculate the Spearman's rank correlation coefficient P corresponding to each feature in the collection F_{total}. According to the threshold β, features with little correlation with each other are selected to form the middle subset F_{middle}. Then, the Gini impurity of each feature in F_{middle} is calculated. The lower the Gini impurity fraction corresponding to the feature, the more favorable the feature is for attack detection. The γ features with the lowest score will constitute the optimal feature subset F_{best}. The threshold value β and the number of feature subsets γ can be selected according to different network conditions. The values of two parameters are given in the experimental evaluation.

4.2 Attack Detection Module

The attack detection module contains an attack detection model composed of GRU, a variant of LSTM algorithm. The reason for using GRU algorithm is that it combines input gate and forgetting gate into update gate, simplifying the complexity of algorithm update. Under the premise of achieving the same performance as LSTM, the time required for model training is reduced. The attack detection model uses cross entropy as the loss function of the model, because the DDoS attack detection task can be regarded as a binary classification task.

In the binary classification task, the cross entropy loss function can accelerate the optimization of the model and further save the training time compared with other loss functions. At the same time, the scheme uses Adam optimizer to optimize the model, which can quickly converge the model and make the model reach the optimal state as soon as possible.

After the samples obtained by Data Process Module are input into the attack detection model, the GRU algorithm after training will carry out attack detection on the samples according to the temporal characteristics between the samples. If DDoS attack is detected, this module will collect the flow table information of the OF switch and notify Attack Defense Module to start the defense against DDoS attack.

4.3 Attack Defense Module

After receiving the attack detection result sent by Attack Detection Module, Attack Defense Module will start to work. It will first activate the intermediate component, after which all Packet_IN messages sent by OF switch will be sent to the intermediate component for caching. The role of the intermediate component is not only to temporarily save the Packet_IN message, but also to take different measures according to the protocol type of the unknown packet after parsing out some properties of the unknown packet corresponding to the Packet_IN message. Algorithm 2 shows the concrete implementation of the attack detection algorithm.

Algorithm 2. Attack Defense algorithm

Require: The Packet_IN message set PAN; Minimum TCP packet threshold T_{min}; Maximum TCP packet threshold T_{max}; Other protocol packet number threshold F_n; Other protocol packet average packet size threshold A_p

Ensure: Suspicious IP tables S_{table}

Initialize Suspicious IP tables S_{table}; The IP address table of the TCP packet T_{table}; List of IP addresses for other protocol packets F_{table}

for Each Pan in PAN **do** Parse the corresponding packet protocol type PRT, source IP address Src, destination IP address Dst, packet size PKT

    if PRT = "TCP" **then**

        if Src in T_{table} **then**

            T_{table}[Src] += 1

            if $T_{table}[Src] \geq T_{max}$ **then**

                S_{table}.add(Src)

            end if

        end if

        if Src not in T_{table} **then**

            T_{table}.add(Src,1)

        end if

    end if

    if $PRT \neq$ "TCP" **then**

        if Src in F_{table} **then**

```
                $F_{table}[Src]$ += 1
                if $F_{table}[Src] > F_n \& PKT > A_p$ then
                    $S_{table}$.add($Src$)
                end if
            end if
        end if
end for
for Each $t$ in $T_{table}$ do
    if $T_{table}[t] < T_{min}$ then
        $S_{table}$.add($t$)
    end if
end for
return $S_{table}$
```

Since the establishment of a TCP connection requires multiple packets to be sent to each other and the process has retransmission characteristics, if the unknown TCP packet that produces the Packet_IN message comes from a normal user, the intermediate component should receive several packets from the same IP address in a short time. Therefore, if the intermediate component receives fewer TCP packets from an IP per unit time than the set threshold, that IP may be a forged IP created by the attacker and will be added to the suspect IP table S_{table}. In addition, if a host suddenly sends many TCP packets to other hosts under the same network in a unit time, the host may be controlled by an attacker, aiming to establish the maximum number of TCP connections in the shortest time, in order to occupy the victim server's TCP connection cache. Therefore, the IP address corresponding to the host will also be added to the suspect IP table S_{table}.

In addition to the relatively special TCP protocol, unknown packets of other protocols may also be generated by the attacker. Therefore, for unknown packets of other types except TCP protocol, the intermediate component will measure whether these packets are normal according to the size and number of packets received within the cycle. If there is an exception, the corresponding IP address of these packets will also be added to the suspect IP table S_{table}.

After obtaining the suspect IP table S_{table}, the controller can choose whether to issue the filter flow entry according to the current usage of the flow table in each OF switch, so as to discard the attack packet before generating the PACKET_IN message. The controller issues a filter flow entry when OF switch flow table space satisfies the following formula:

$$\frac{ST_{use}}{ST_{total}} < \delta \tag{3}$$

ST_{use} represents the number of flow entries in OF switch, and ST_{total} represents the maximum number of table entries that OF switch can accommodate. The filter flow entry is shown in Table 1. S_{ip} is the IP address recorded in the S_{table}.

Table 1. Filter flow entry

Priority	Match fields	Counter	Instructions
Minimal	$Source = S_{ip}$		Actions = Drop

5 Experiments and Evaluation

5.1 Experiment

The relevant parameters of the scheme are shown in Table 2. After many experiments, we found that setting the sample time period to be calculated once for every 100 connections produces the best effect, and the choice of parameter δ is obtained by counting the flow table utilization rate of each OF switches.

Table 2. Scheme related parameters

Parameter	Explanation	Value
α	The time period of each sample is generated. The basic unit is the time taken for a connection to be established	100
β	The threshold of Spearman's rank correlation coefficient	0.5
γ	The number of features contained in the optimal feature subset	20
δ	Generates thresholds for filter flow entry	0.4

Table 3. NSL-KDD dataset composition

Name	NSL-KDD
Normal sample	58361
Attack sample	67343
Proportion	0.87:1
Normal reduction rate	16.44%
Attack reduction rate	93.32%

In order to verify the effectiveness of this scheme in processing high-dimensional data, the experiment uses the NSL-KDD dataset as the training set. NSL-KDD dataset solves the problems of data redundancy and classifier bias in the KDD'99 [27] dataset. In addition, the number of attack samples is greatly optimized in this dataset, so that the remaining attack samples are highly representative. At the same time, the NSL-KDD dataset has a total of 41 features, and the data of the training set and the test set are reasonable and highly comparable. The specific composition of this data set is shown in Table 3.

We use Mininet [28] as the network simulator, which can help us build a network topology similar to the real environment. The experimental topology is shown in Fig. 4. We use FloodLight, a traditional controller, as SDN controller. And for the southbound interface protocol, we chose OpenFlow1.3, since it is the most commonly used protocol in the industry. The simulation runs on an 8 GRAM, Intel Core i5-4590 3.30 GHz CPU with Ubuntu 14.04OS.

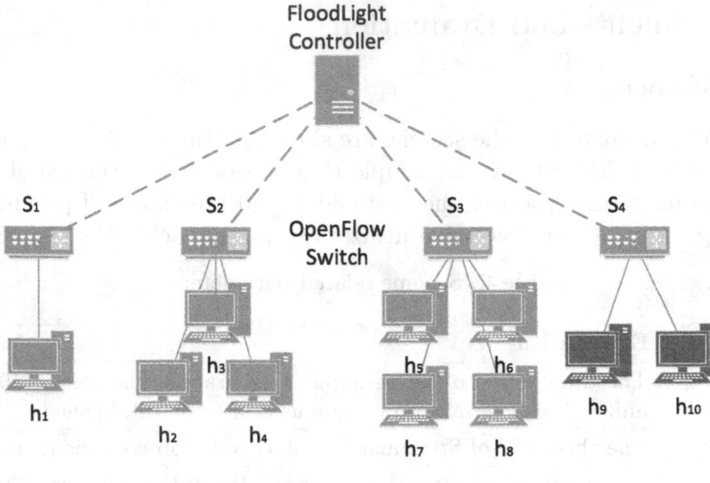

Fig. 4. Network topology used.

$S_1 - S_4$ in the Fig. 4 represents OF switch, and the normal clients in the figure are $h_1 - h_8$. In order to simulate the normal state of network communication, different numbers of hosts are set under different switches. h_9 and h_{10} are set as the clients controlled by the attacker. After being taken over by an attacker, the two clients send a large number of attack packets across the network. As for verifying that the scheme can effectively block the traffic of DDoS attack, we simulated several DDoS attacks. The types and duration of simulated DDoS attacks are shown in Table 4.

Table 4. Attack description

Attack type	Protocol	Start time (s)	Duration (s)
Neptune	TCP	240	30
Smurf	ICMP	480	30
DNS flood	DNS	360	60
Http slow header	Http	120	360

5.2 Performance Metrics

We set up several experimental groups for control. The attack detection models of the other several experimental groups respectively used the CNN+LSTM detection model proposed by the scheme [29] and the detection model using the traditional machine learning algorithm SVM and BPNN. The reason why we choose these algorithms is that SVM and BPNN, as classical machine learning algorithms, are often used in the field of attack detection and can be recognized.

Since DDoS attack detection can be regarded as a classification problem, We use the ACC (Accuracy), P (Precision), R (Recall), TPR (True Positive Rate) and FPR (False Positive Rate) as the criteria to evaluate detection efficiency. These criteria are calculated from the following four parameters:

- *True Position (TP)*: The number of attack samples that were correctly detected
- *True Negative (TN)*: The number of normal samples that were correctly identified
- *False Position (FP)*: The number of attack samples detected as normal samples.
- *False Negative (FN)*: The number of normal samples detected as attack samples.

To compute the five criteria mentioned above, the following equations are applied.

$$ACC = \frac{TP + TN}{TP + TN + FP + FN}$$

$$P = \frac{TP}{TP + TN}$$

$$R = \frac{TP}{TP + FN}$$

$$TPR = \frac{TP}{TP + FN}$$

$$FPR = \frac{FP}{FP + TN}$$

Table 5. Accuracy, Precision and Recall

Algorithm	Accuracy	Precision	Recall
SVM	0.883	0.912	0.877
BPNN	0.842	0.867	0.910
CNN+LSTM (Proposed by [29])	0.917	0.902	0.890
Our Proposed	0.964	0.974	0.982

The experimental results are shown in Table 5. It can be seen from the table that the attack detection model of scheme [29] can extract spatial-temporal features of data, so its detection accuracy and accuracy are still higher than that of the attack detection model using classical machine learning algorithm. However, the data samples in the NSL-KDD dataset all have high-dimensional features, so when the detection model of scheme [29] uses these data to train the model, the accuracy of the model is affected because the redundant features in the samples cannot be eliminated. In our scheme, 20 features with the highest importance score were selected as samples for model training. The order of importance of these features is shown in Fig. 5. These features not only have low information redundancy among each other, but also are closely related to sample labels. The experimental results show that the performance of the detection model proposed in this paper is the best among all the contrast experimental groups.

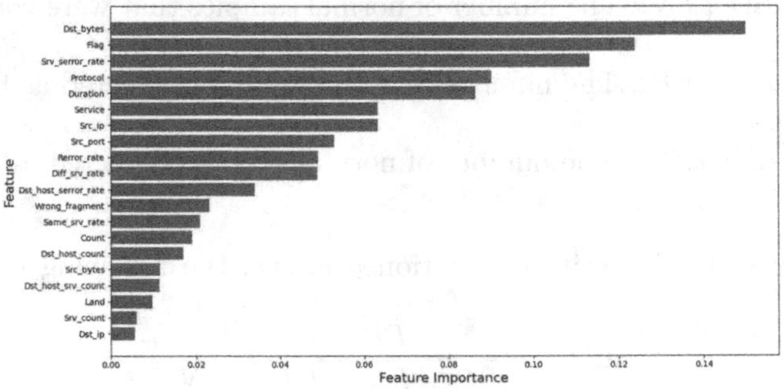

Fig. 5. Feature importance score

In order to further demonstrate the performance of different attack detection models, the ROC curve is drawn in this scheme, which can more intuitively show the relationship between model detection rate and misjudgment rate. The larger the area of the closed graph formed by the curve and the FPR axis, the higher the performance of the model is generally indicated. The performance of the four test models of the comparative experimental groups can be intuitively shown in Fig. 6. The performance of the attack detection model in this scheme is better than that of other schemes because it selects the most appropriate feature subset.

Since the computing resources of the controller are the target of the DDoS attack targeting the controller, the change of the CPU utilization of the controller can be used as the standard to measure the performance of the defense against DDoS attack. Figure 7 shows the CPU utilization of the controller with different defense schemes. It can be seen from the figure that the slow DDoS attack does not have a great impact on the controller, while the Flood type attack will seriously consume the controller CPU resources because it will generate a large number of Packet_IN messages in a short time. Both the control group

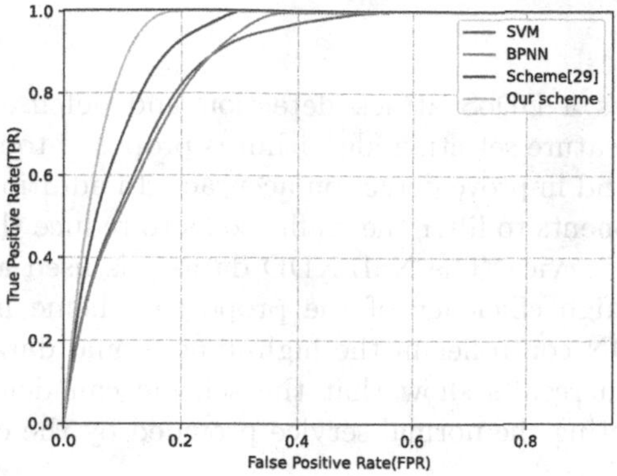

Fig. 6. ROC curve comparison for different algorithms

based on scheme [29] and the experimental group based on filtering defense method can realize the defense against DDoS attack. Compared with the two experimental groups, the experimental group based on scheme [29] needs to generate defense flow entries according to the flow table to block attack traffic, so it may affect normal users and consume additional CPU resources to generate defense flow entries. The experimental group based on filtering defense method uses the intermediate component to filter attack packets, so that the controller will only receive and process unknown packets judged to be sent by normal users, which further reduces the data that the controller needs to process. Therefore, the CPU utilization of the experimental group using the filtering defense method can always be kept within the normal level.

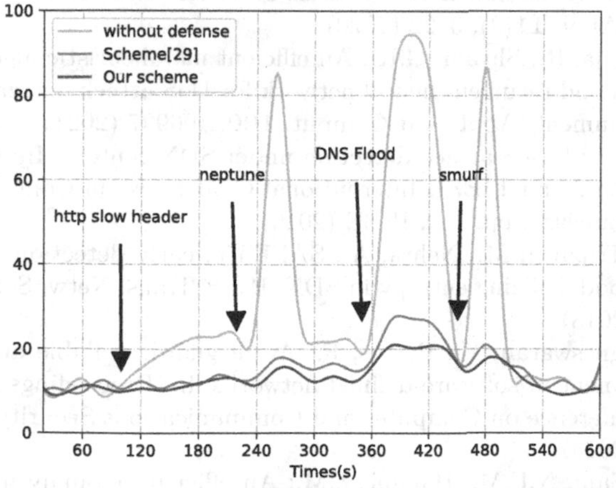

Fig. 7. System CPU utilization

6 Conclusion

This paper proposes a DDoS attack detection and defense scheme targeting SDN controller. A feature selection algorithm is proposed to reduce the number of sample features and improve detection accuracy. In addition, the scheme uses intermediate components to filter the traffic so as to reduce the impact of traffic blocking on normal service. The NSL-KDD dataset is used as the training set, which verifies the high efficiency of the proposed scheme in detecting DDoS attack targeting SDN controller in the high-dimensional data set. At the same time, the simulation results show that the scheme can defend against DDoS attack without affecting the normal service provided by the controller.

References

1. Lopes, F.A., Santos, M., Fidalgo, R.: A software engineering perspective on SDN programmability. IEEE Commun. Surv. Tutorials **18**(2), 1255–1272 (2015)
2. Sarmiento, D.E., Lebre, A., Nussbaum, L.: Decentralized SDN control plane for a distributed cloud-edge infrastructure: a survey. IEEE Commun. Surv. Tutorials **23**, 256–281 (2021)
3. Das, T., Sridharan, V., Gurusamy, M.: A survey on controller placement in SDN. IEEE Commun. Surv. Tutorials **22**(1), 472–503 (2019)
4. Yurekten, O., Demirci, M.: SDN-based cyber defense: a survey. Futur. Gener. Comput. Syst. **115**, 126–149 (2021)
5. Yan, Q., Yu, F.R., Gong, Q.: Software-defined networking (SDN) and distributed denial of service (DDoS) attacks in cloud computing environments: a survey, some research issues, and challenges. IEEE Commun. Surv. Tutorials **18**(1), 602–622 (2015)
6. Abhishta, A., Heeswijk, W., Junger, M.: Why would we get attacked? An analysis of attacker's aims behind DDoS attacks. J. Wirel. Mob. Netw. Ubiquit. Comput. Dependable Appl. **11**(2), 3–22 (2020)
7. SaiSindhuTheja, R., Shyam, G.K.: An efficient metaheuristic algorithm based feature selection and recurrent neural network for DoS attack detection in cloud computing environment. Appl. Soft Comput. **100**, 106997 (2021)
8. Xu, Y., Liu, Y.: DDoS attack detection under SDN context. In: IEEE INFOCOM 2016-The 35th Annual IEEE International Conference on Computer Communications, San Francisco, pp. 1–9. IEEE (2016)
9. Kumar, P., Tripathi, M., Nehra, A.: SAFETY: early detection and mitigation of TCP SYN flood utilizing entropy in SDN. IEEE Trans. Netw. Serv. Manag. **15**(4), 1545–1559 (2018)
10. Shin, S., Yegneswaran, V., Porras, P.: Avant-guard: scalable and vigilant switch flow management in software-defined networks. In: Proceedings of the 2013 ACM SIGSAC Conference on Computer and Communications Security, Berlin, pp. 413–424. ACM (2013)
11. Sarvari, S., Sani, N.F.M., Hanapi, Z.M.: An efficient anomaly intrusion detection method with feature selection and evolutionary neural network. IEEE Access **8**, 70651–70663 (2020)
12. McKeown, N., Anderson, T., Balakrishnan, H.: OpenFlow: enabling innovation in campus networks. ACM SIGCOMM Comput. Commun. Rev. **38**(2), 69–74 (2008)

13. Rawas, S.: Energy, network, and application-aware virtual machine placement model in SDN-enabled large scale cloud data centers. Multimed. Tools Appl. **80**(10), 15541–15562 (2021). https://doi.org/10.1007/s11042-021-10616-6
14. Medved, J., Varga, R., Tkacik, A.: OpenDaylight: towards a model-driven SDN controller architecture. In: Proceeding of IEEE International Symposium on a World of Wireless. Mobile and Multimedia Networks, Sydney, pp. 1–6. IEEE (2014)
15. Floodligh[EB/OL]. http://www.projectfloodlight.org/. Accessed 4 Oct 2021
16. Dayal, N., Maity, P., Srivastava, S.: Research trends in security and DDoS in SDN. Secur. Commun. Netw. **9**(18), 6386–6411 (2016)
17. Hancer, E., Xue, B., Zhang, M.: A survey on feature selection approaches for clustering. Artif. Intell. Rev. **53**(6), 4519–4545 (2020). https://doi.org/10.1007/s10462-019-09800-w
18. Agrawal, P., Abutarboush, H.F., Ganesh, T.: Metaheuristic algorithms on feature selection: a survey of one decade of research (2009–2019). IEEE Access **9**, 26766–26791 (2021)
19. Qin, J., Zhang, X., Li, P.: Anomaly detection based on feature correlation and influence degree in SDN. In: 2020 International Conferences on Internet of Things (iThings) and IEEE Green Computing and Communications (GreenCom) and IEEE Cyber. Physical and Social Computing (CPSCom) and IEEE Smart Data (SmartData) and IEEE Congress on Cybermatics (Cybermatics), Rhodes Island, pp. 186–192. IEEE (2020)
20. Wei, G., Zhao, J., Feng, Y.: A novel hybrid feature selection method based on dynamic feature importance. Appl. Soft Comput. **93**, 106337 (2020)
21. Kavitha, G., Elango, N.M.: An approach to feature selection in intrusion detection systems using machine learning algorithms. Int. J. e-Collaboration (IJeC) **16**(4), 48–58 (2020)
22. Jiang, L., Kong, G., Li, C.: Wrapper framework for test-cost-sensitive feature selection. IEEE Trans. Syst. Man Cybern.: Syst. **51**(3), 1747–1756 (2019)
23. Wang, M., Lu, Y., Qin, J.: A dynamic MLP-based DDoS attack detection method using feature selection and feedback. Comput. Secur. **88**, 101645 (2020)
24. Kasongo, S.M., Sun, Y.: A deep learning method with wrapper based feature extraction for wireless intrusion detection system. Comput. Secur. **92**, 101752 (2020)
25. Sebbar, A., Karim, Z., Baadi, Y.: Using advanced detection and prevention technique to mitigate threats in SDN architecture. In: 2019 15th International Wireless Communications and Mobile Computing Conference (IWCMC), Morocco, pp. 90–95. IEEE (2019)
26. Kim, Y., Lau, W.C., Chuah, M.C.: PacketScore: statistics-based overload control against distributed denial-of-service attacks. In: IEEE INFOCOM 2004, Toronto, pp. 2594–2604. IEEE (2004)
27. NSL-KDD Data Set[EB/OL]. http://nsl.cs.unb.ca/NSL-KDD. Accessed 23 June 2021
28. Mininet. http://mininet.org/. Accessed 20 Oct 2021
29. Xu, Y., Ma, J., Zhong, S.: Detection and defense against DDoS attack on SDN controller based on spatiotemporal feature. In: Yu, S., Mueller, P., Qian, J. (eds.) SPDE 2020. CCIS, vol. 1268, pp. 3–18. Springer, Singapore (2020). https://doi.org/10.1007/978-981-15-9129-7_1

Commodity-Tra: A Traceable Transaction Scheme Based on FISCO BCOS

Chunmei Li[1], Lei Shang[2], Zheng Wei[1], Jun Ge[1], Mingyue Zhang[1], and Yun Fang[1](✉)

[1] School of Computer Science, Qufu Normal University, Jining, China
ylwangqfnu@163.com

[2] School of Cyberspace Security, Shandong University of Political Science and Law, Jinan, China

Abstract. In recent years, because online shopping has the advantages of abundant products, easy selection, fast door-to-door delivery, and timely information feedback, people are more and more fond of online shopping compared to physical store shopping. With the wave of online shopping, the use of commodity transaction systems has become more and more widespread. However, the traditional commodity transaction system generally adopts centralized management and cannot be traced, which cannot guarantee the openness and transparency of commodity source information, and cannot well meet the commodity purchasing needs of consumers. In order to solve the above problems, we use blockchain technology to propose Commodity-Tra: a traceable transaction scheme based on FISCO BCOS platform. The system Commodity-Tra is suitable for the scene of commodity traceability, and can provide consumers with true and accurate commodity traceability information, which can better meet consumers' purchasing needs. In addition, we analyze the impact of the traceability on page response time from the aspects of network bandwidth and virtual machine memory, respectively. The experimental results show that the page response time only increases by 2.8 s on average. Therefore, Commodity-Tra is capable of providing the traceability function without affecting users' experience.

Keywords: Commodity transaction · Blockchain · Traceability query · Trust guarantee

1 Introduction

E-commerce is booming today, and network security online transactions are widely used. The commodity transaction system is based on the actual needs of the current business network and speed to achieve convenient, fast, and door-to-door services for commodity purchases. The commodity transaction system is based on the actual needs of current business networking and speed. It mainly has functions such as order transaction, wholesale management, order management, and return management. It can realize convenient, fast, and door-to-door commodity purchase services, which has been widely used. However, the traditional commodity transaction system is often limited by the following conditions in the operation process: (1) Centralized management is generally

X. Chen et al. (Eds.): SocialSec 2022, CCIS 1663, pp. 264–280, 2022.
https://doi.org/10.1007/978-981-19-7242-3_17

adopted, it has absolute initiative, and it naturally lacks credibility. At the same time, there are also central node security risks, including central nodes stop working, central nodes are stolen, etc. In the process of data transmission, the data itself may be illegally tampered with or lost, resulting in a decrease in system reliability. (2) Generally, only relational database management systems such as MySQL are used to store commodity source information, and it is easy to tamper with data in such database management systems. In order to maximize their own interests, many unscrupulous businesses disregard the interests of consumers and arbitrarily tamper with commodity source information. From this point of view, the traditional commodity transaction system lacks the traceability function, and the source information of commodity is not transparent enough for consumers to guarantee the authenticity and reliability of the information.

The above problems show that the current situation of the traditional commodity transaction system is really worrying, and how to improve the existing commodity transaction system for better commodity transaction has become the focus of our attention. Therefore, it is urgent to develop a reliable and traceable transaction scheme, and to promote the improvement and development of the traceability system.

1.1 Related Works

In order to make the transaction process widely used in the world, Amin MB et al. (2012) [1] proposed a process system such that the system is applied to the transaction and has different functions applied to the transaction. To further ensure transaction security, Repin M et al. (2017) [2] implemented a complete transaction monitoring system that includes several different algorithmic modules that perform hierarchical checks on the payments made. To improve resilience to new types of fraud, the system architecture includes a model correction module that allows one to detect new threat patterns and adjust appropriate responses, while keeping false alarms low. With the development of science and technology, emerging technologies have begun to be widely used. Afrianto I et al. (2021) [3] utilized digital payment mechanism and QR code technology to develop a transaction system that can accelerate and facilitate the buying and selling transaction process in traditional market environment. However, these traditional transaction systems generally adopted centralized management, and the source information of commodities was not transparent enough to guarantee users' trust in the system.

Traceability technology is of great significance and has been widely used in food [4–7], pharmaceuticals [8–11], clothing [12], electronics [13–30] and other industries. In order for consumers to experience the connection between the products they are consuming and the origin of the products, while at the same time guaranteeing the validity of this connection and thus the origin attribute of the product, a traceability system is required. Chen et al. (2013) [4] proposed a vegetable quality and safety traceability model by analyzing the restrictive factors affecting the quality and safety of vegetable products. For more practical implementation, Dong et al. (2016) [5] proposed a quality and safety traceability system from the perspective of the agricultural product supply chain. The system could be divided into 5 subsystems, including registration, production, enterprise management, government supervision and traceability, which realized the whole process tracking and traceability of the agricultural product supply chain from planting, harvesting and processing to sales.

With the development and progress of network technology, some researchers gradually began to use real-time technology to achieve traceability. Li et al. (2019) [6] developed a real-time monitoring traceability system using emerging IoT technologies. The system had the function of monitoring the environmental parameters of pine mushroom cold chain logistics, and could track and monitor the fluctuations of temperature, humidity, oxygen and carbon dioxide in the cold chain in real time. It was significant to meet the deeper needs of traceability systems. However, these traditional traceability systems generally had shortcomings such as inability to guarantee the authenticity of traceability information, low traceability efficiency, and high traceability costs.

In response to the above problems, Wang et al. (2022) [7] developed a supply chain traceability system framework based on blockchain and radio frequency identification (RFID) technology. The system used Hyperledger Fabric 2.0 as the development platform, and creatively designed a blockchain data structure in the RFID tag to ensure data security and reliability. Nevertheless, the study did not evaluate the system. Considering that joining blockchain based on the traditional traceability system may increase the time delay, if the delay is too long, it will mean poor system performance and ruin users' experience. Consequently, it is essential to evaluate the system.

1.2 Motivation

In view of the above reasons, we have fully integrated blockchain technology into the traditional commodity transaction system. While realizing the basic functions of the system, the data on the blockchain can be stored according to the time of occurrence, traceable and verifiable, and can ensure the traceability of commodity source information. Additionally, we evaluate Commodity-Tra according to the response time of the page, and the main factors considered are network bandwidth and virtual machine memory.

Our contributions are as follows:

(1) We propose a system Commodity-Tra, a traceable commodity scheme based on FISCO BCOS. It realizes the functions of transaction system, including order transaction, wholesale management, order management, return management, etc., which can well meet the needs of consumers.
(2) We combine the traditional commodity transaction system and blockchain technology to realize the traceability function of commodity sources, that is, the corresponding commodity source information can be queried according to the name of the commodity. Since the blockchain has the characteristics of non-tampering, openness and transparency, it can ensure the authenticity and reliability of commodity traceability information, thereby ensuring the basis of trust between users and the system.
(3) In order to verify the impact of the traceability function on Commodity-Tra, we evaluate the response time of the page. We mainly consider the impact of network bandwidth and virtual machine memory factors on page response time. The experimental results show that after the introduction of the traceability function, the page response time increases by 2.8 s on average, which has little impact on the user experience.

1.3 Roadmap

Section 2 presents some preliminaries used in this paper, like Django Framework, MTV Mode, FISCO BCOS etc. Section 3 describes the framework of Commodity-Tra including the system architecture design and FISCO BCOS design. More details on the implementation of traceability is presented in Sect. 4. For example, it lists the system development environment, the codes of solidity smart contract, and the calling of API interface etc. Some experiments are designed to verify the performance of Commodity-Tra in Sect. 5. More specifically, we mainly evaluate the page response time considering the effect of network bandwidth and virtual machine memory. Section 6 concludes this paper and prospect some future works.

2 Preliminaries

This chapter provides a brief overview of the key technologies used during Commodity-Tra development. In Commodity-Tra, Python is the server development language, html is the client development language, Pycharm is the development environment, MySQL is the database, and FISCO BCOS framework is the underlying blockchain environment of the system. The architectural pattern used in the overall development is the Django framework based on the MTV (Model Template View) software design pattern.

2.1 Django Framework and MTV Mode

Django is an open-source web application framework written in Python. Commodity-Tra is developed based on the Django framework. By configuring the system Python SDK, the code in the Django framework can interact with the functions in the solidity smart contract.

Django itself is based on the MVC (Model View Controller) model. The MVC pattern divides the framework into three modules, reducing the coupling between each module. Django's MTV mode is essentially the same as MVC, and it is also to maintain a loosely coupled relationship between components, but the definition is slightly different. Django's MTV refers to:

(1) M represents the model (Model): the function that the program should have, and is responsible for the mapping (ORM) between the business object and the database.
(2) T represents the template (Template): responsible for how to display the page (html) to the user.
(3) V represents the view (View): responsible for business logic, and calls Model and Template when appropriate.

In addition to the above three layers, a URL distributor is also required. Its function is to distribute page requests of each URL to different Views for processing, and then the Views call the corresponding Model and Template. The response pattern of MTV is shown in Fig. 1.

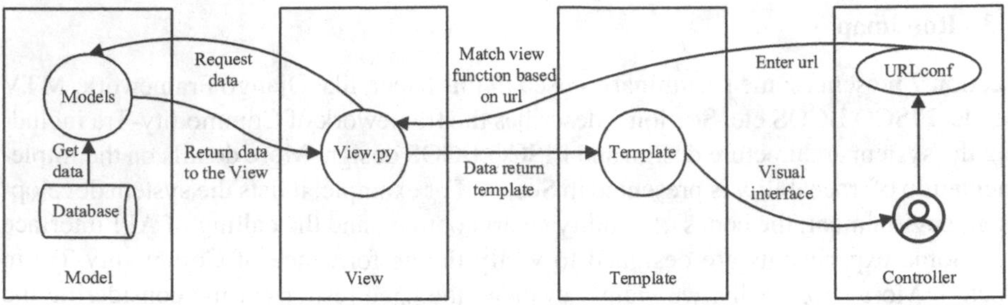

Fig. 1. The response pattern of MTV.

2.2 FISCO BCOS Blockchain Framework

FISCO BCOS applies the alliance link line. The main difference from the public link line is that it does not issue coins, and the alliance members are few and certified. The underlying platform has superior performance. Hundreds of application projects are developed based on the underlying platform of FISCO BCOS, and have been widely used in cultural copyright, judicial services, finance, smart communities and other fields.

Multilingual SDK makes the FISCO BCOS platform more widely used. The FISCO BCOS blockchain exposes interfaces. Through the corresponding SDK, external programs can call these interfaces to realize the interaction between the program and the blockchain. Developers can choose the SDK (Java SDK, Python SDK, Go SDK, etc.) corresponding to the project, deploy the SDK into the project, and realize data uploading on the blockchain by calling the API interface provided by the SDK. The FISCO BCOS architecture diagram is shown in Fig. 2.

Wang et al. [31] pointed out that FISCO BCOS has excellent performance by comparing with several current mainstream blockchain platforms based on transaction throughput and transaction delay. We can detect that in general settings, Ethereum's TPS is clearly lower than the other three systems by comparing the four blockchain systems. The performance of Fabric is far better than that of Ethereum, but under the same test conditions, the theoretical value of the performance of Ethereum and Fabric is far away. Furthermore, the TPS of Sawtooth and FISCO BCOS is higher than Fabric. In terms of time delay, the average time delay of Ethereum and Fabric is slightly longer, that of Sawtooth will be shorter, and that of FISCO BCOS is the shortest, as shown in Table 1.

3 Commodity-Tra Overall Design

3.1 The Architecture of Commodity-Tra

The architecture of Commodity-Tra is mainly composed of users, servers, administrators, and blockchain. Specifically, after successful registration and login in Commodity-Tra, users will have the authority to use the system, and can send requests to the servers through the browser, then the servers will respond according to the received request. The administrators are the managers of the system, mainly responsible for user management, order management, data uploading, etc., and can provide technical support for the servers.

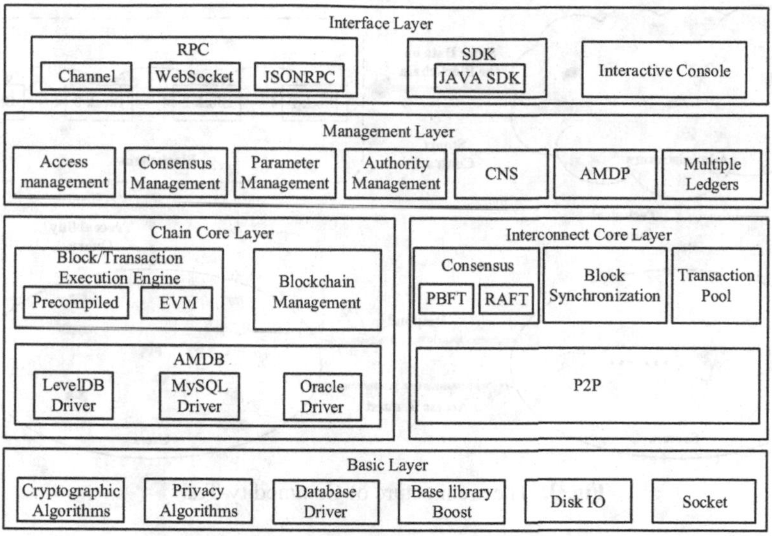

Fig. 2. FISCO BCOS architecture diagram.

Table 1. Performance comparison of four blockchain systems.

	TPS	Time delay(s)
Ethereum	10–30	5.0
Fabric	100–200	1.0–10.0
Sawtooth	500–2000	0.5–5.0
FISCO BCOS	1500–3000	0.5

Among them, the data on-chain relies on the Solidity smart contract. After the data is uploaded to the blockchain, users can trace the source of the information on the blockchain. The architecture of Commodity-Tra is shown in Fig. 3.

3.2 The Design of FISCO BCOS

To improve the computing speed with limited memory, only the wholesale information is uploaded to the blockchain. After submitting the upload request through the browser, the server will call the function in the Solidity smart contract to realize the information upload through the Python SDK. It will be explained in detail below.

First of all, it is necessary to build a single-group FISCO BCOS alliance chain. In the Ubuntu system, we use the build_chain.sh script to build a FISCO BCOS chain with four nodes locally. After creating, we start the FISCO BCOS chain and check the progress and log output. The main contents of the check log output include checking the number of nodes linked by node node0 as well as whether the consensus is in progress. If the

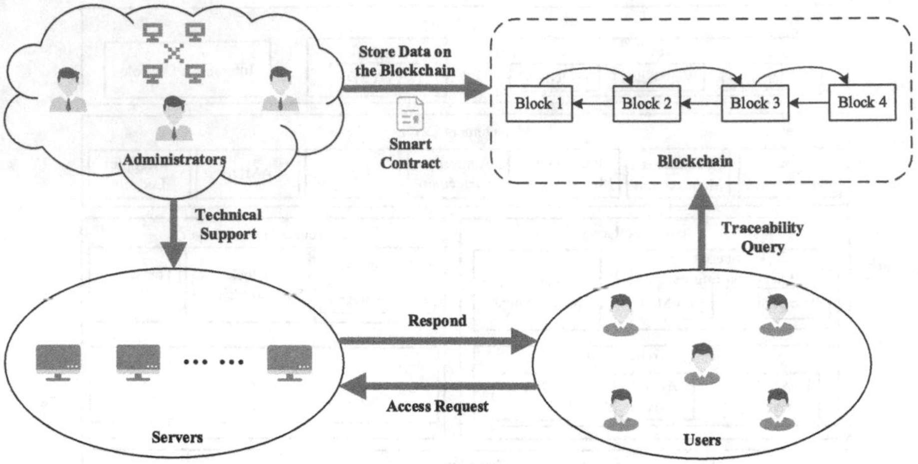

Fig. 3. The architecture of Commodity-Tra.

number of nodes linked by node0 is 3 and the consensus is normal, it will mean the establishment of the FISCO BCOS alliance chain is successful.

Second, we get the console source code, copy the console configuration file and certificate to start and use the console. In the console, we can get the client version, node information, block height and other information. Additionally, contracts can be deployed and invoked in the console. Among them, the premise of deploying and invoking contracts is to use the contract compilation tool to compile Solidity contract files into abi and binary files. In the Python SDK used in this project, we can use the solc compiler to compile, or use the remix compiler to manually compile the code in the Solidity contract file into abi and binary files. What's more, they are supposed to be placed in the contracts directory.

After the contract is deployed, the contract is created and published, and then the contract can be invoked. A contract call refers to a function that calls a deployed contract and can be divided into transaction and query. Between them, the query does not need to be synchronized and sent to other nodes for consensus on the entire network, while the transaction needs to be sent to the entire network for consensus on the blockchain. The more detailed difference between transaction and query is shown in Table 2.

Table 2. Detailed difference between transaction and query.

	Contract performance	rpc type	Execution node	Whether to consume gas	Whether to change the storage state
Transaction	No view modification	sendTransaction	Executive level	Yes	Yes
Query	View modification	call	All consensus nodes	No	No

4 Traceability Implementation of Commodity-Tra

4.1 The Development Environment

This section mainly describes Commodity-Tra development environment, including Windows system environment information, FISCO BCOS blockchain environment information, Channel communication protocol configuration information, etc., as shown in Table 3.

Table 3. Commodity-Tra development environment.

	Windows	Virtual machine
CPU	Intel(R) Core(TM) i5-8250U CPU @ 1.60 GHz	Not applicable
Memory	8 GB	2 GB
Operating system	Windows 10 Pro	Ubuntu 21.10
Python	Python 3.7.3	Not applicable
Development IDE	Pycharm Professional 2020.3	Not applicable
Database	MySQL 5.7.17	Not applicable
FISCO BCOS	Not applicable	FISCO BCOS 2.8.0
Alliance chain node	Not applicable	node0, node1, node2, node3
Node channel IP	Not applicable	192.168.218.133
Node channel port	Not applicable	20200

4.2 Solidity Smart Contracts in Details

Solidity smart contracts are implemented with Solidity syntax, support various basic or complex data type operations, logical operations, and provide high-level language-related features such as inheritance and overloading.

In the development process of this system, the writing of smart contracts is the key to realizing data on-chain. The main functions and related descriptions in the Solidity contract used in Commodity-Tra are shown in Table 4.

Table 4. Solidity contract main functions and related descriptions.

Function name	Parameter type	Return value	Function
getname	string	Traceability query conditions	Passed as a parameter to call
getid	uint256	Traceability query results	Passed as a parameter to call
getaddress	address	Contract address	Output contract address
getall	string, uint256, address	All results of the query	Passed as a parameter to call
Set	string, uint256, address	0	Passed as a parameter to sendRawTransactionGetReceipt

4.3 Design of Python SDK Calling API Interface

The Python SDK needs to call the related API to implement contract deployment and contract transactions. The API interfaces and related descriptions that need to be called in Commodity-Tra are shown in Table 5.

4.4 Implementation of Information On-Chain and Traceability

This section will specifically describe the detailed implementation of the information on-chain and traceability functions. First, load the abi definition from the file, and instantiate a client object through client = BcosClient(). The relevant code is shown in Fig. 4. Second, deploy the Solidity smart contract MaterialInfo.sol used in Commodity-Tra, and store the deployment results in a file for future reference. Among them, MaterialInfo.sol must be stored in the folder called contracts under the Python package named sdk to be deployed. And the relevant code is shown in Fig. 5. Next, call the set function in the smart contract MaterialInfo.sol to upload the information to the blockchain. The relevant code is shown in Fig. 6. After the information is successfully uploaded to the blockchain, an example record of the data structure of a single wholesale commodity can be obtained. It is shown in detail in Table 6. Finally, calling the call interface can realize traceability query, and the relevant code is shown in Fig. 7.

Table 5. API interfaces and related descriptions.

Python API	Parameter	Descriptions
Deploy	Contract binary code	Deploy contract
sendRawTransactionGetReceipt	Contract address, contract abi interface name, parameter list, contract binary code	Send transaction and get transaction execution result
getTransactionByHash	Transaction hash	Get transaction information based on transaction hash
Call	Contract address, contract abi, calling interface name, parameter list	Call contract
getNodeVersion	None	Get blockchain node version information
getBlockNumber	None	Get the latest block height
getPeers	None	Get the connection information of the blockchain node

Table 6. An example record of a single wholesale commodity data structure.

Serial number	Data structure	Deploy contract	Send transaction
1	Material name	Milk	Milk
2	Factory ID	200011	20011
3	Place of origin	Rizhao City, Shandong Province	Rizhao City, Shandong Province
4	Quantity	10L	10L
5	Unit price	3r/L	3r/L
6	Previous hash	Not applicable	0xc4058129ef09e79ffa77b04dfe73844 4b3caa49fd9e2cb234603a7c17af068e4
7	Hash value	0xc4058129ef09e79ffa77b04dfe73844 4b3caa49fd9e2cb234603a7c17af068e4	0x71941e67ab24c49d03f406bd1217a1a 3a32b2427c146bb72889d66bc9872a40f

5 The Evaluation on Response Time

Compared with the traditional commodity transaction system, Commodity-Tra adds data uploading steps, which mainly include deploying the contract, storing the deployment result in a file for future reference, sending the transaction, calling the contract interface, and calling the call interface to obtain data, etc. These steps can ensure the traceability of commodity source information, but may increase the time delay to a certain extent. If the delay on the blockchain is too long, it will ruin users' experience. In view of the increased time delay in the blockchain in this scheme, Commodity-Tra is evaluated in

```
if os.path.isfile(client_config.solc_path) or os.path.isfile(client_config.solcjs_path):
  Compil-
er.compile_file("D:\\djangocode\\djangoProject\\app\\views\\sdk\\contracts\\MaterialInfo
.sol")
abi_file = "D:\\djangocode\\djangoProject\\app\\views\\sdk\\contracts\\MaterialInfo.abi"
data_parser = DatatypeParser()
data_parser.load_abi_file(abi_file)
contract_abi = data_parser.contract_abi
try:
  client = BcosClient()
```

Fig. 4. Instantiate client object related code.

```
print("\n>>Deploy:----------------------------------------------------------")
with
open("D:\\djangocode\\djangoProject\\app\\views\\sdk\\contracts\\MaterialInfo.bin", 'r')
as load_f:
  contract_bin = load_f.read()
  load_f.close()
result = client.deploy(contract_bin)
print("deploy", result)
print("new address : ", result["contractAddress"])
contract_name = os.path.splitext(os.path.basename(abi_file))[0]
memo = "tx:" + result["transactionHash"]
ContractNote.save_address_to_contract_note(contract_name, result["contractAddress"])
```

Fig. 5. Deployment contract related code.

```
print("\n>>sendRawTransaction:----------------------------------------------------")
to_address = result['contractAddress']
args = [materlainame, int(factoryid),
to_checksum_address('0x7029c502b4F824d19Bd7921E9cb74Ef92392FB1c')]
receipt = client.sendRawTransactionGetReceipt(to_address, contract_abi, "set", args)
print("receipt:", receipt)
```

Fig. 6. Code related to information uploading.

```
print("\n>>Call:-----------------------------------------------------------------------")
res = client.call(to_address, contract_abi, "getname")
print("call materialname:", res)
res = client.call(to_address, contract_abi, "getid")
print("call factoryid result:", res)
res = client.call(to_address, contract_abi, "getall")
print("call getall result:", res)
print("done,demo_tx,total req {}".format(client.request_counter))
```

Fig. 7. Calling the call interface for traceability query related code.

terms of page response time. The evaluation mainly considers network bandwidth and virtual machine memory factors.

In this section, we evaluate Commodity-Tra in terms of page response time, mainly considering network bandwidth and virtual machine memory factors. During the evaluation, the default computer configuration is shown in Table 3 in Sect. 4.

5.1 The Effect of Network Bandwidth

Since the data uploading process relies on the network, changes in the network environment may lead to changes in the uploading time, which in turn lead to changes in page response time. As a consequence, under the condition that the virtual machine memory is constant at 2 GB and the computer environment configuration is unchanged, we study the impact of network bandwidth on page response time before and after the blockchain. Specifically, in Fig. 8, we test the page response time before and after joining blockchain under the network bandwidth of 10 Mbps, 12 Mbps, 14 Mbps, 16 Mbps, and 18 Mbps, respectively. The relevant experimental data obtained is shown in detail in Table 7.

The experimental results show that when the network bandwidth is 10 Mbps, the page response time before joining blockchain is 0.19 s, and the page response time after joining blockchain is 4.93 s, the difference between the two is 4.74 s; when the network bandwidth is 18 Mbps, the page response time before joining blockchain is 0.06 s, and the page response time after joining blockchain is 1.99 s, the difference between the two is 1.93 s. The results show that, within a certain range, with the increase of network bandwidth, the page response time before and after joining blockchain decreases. At the same time, the larger the network bandwidth, the smaller the difference in page response time before and after joining blockchain under the same network bandwidth. It can be seen from the above descriptions that the time delay is indeed increased after joining blockchain.

After analysis, the main reason for the increase in time delay is the addition of steps such as deploying contracts and sending transactions. However, joining blockchain has the advantages of decentralization, ensuring the authenticity and reliability of the information on the blockchain, and traceable query, which is incomparable to the traditional commodity transaction system that has not joined blockchain. If users can use the system in an environment with large network bandwidth, the time delay caused by the chaining can be reduced, and users' experience can be basically guaranteed. Moreover, changes in network bandwidth have little effect on the page response time before joining blockchain, but have a significant impact on the page response time after joining blockchain. This shows that it is necessary to consider the network bandwidth factor when using the commodity transaction scheme after joining blockchain.

5.2 The Effect of Virtual Machine Memory

The memory size of the virtual machine has an impact on the speed at which the virtual machine processes data, which in turn affects the link-up time, which in turn affects the page response time. As a result, under the condition of constant network bandwidth and computer configuration, we study the impact of virtual machine memory before and after joining blockchain on page response time. Specifically, in Fig. 9, we conduct

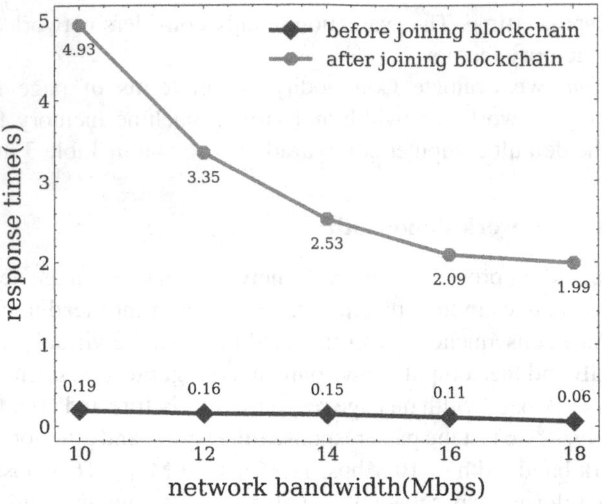

Fig. 8. The impact of network bandwidth on page response time before and after joining blockchain.

Table 7. Experimental results of network bandwidth.

Network bandwidth(Mbps)	Before joining blockchain(s)	After joining blockchain(s)	The page response time difference before and after joining blockchain(s)
10	0.19	4.93	4.74
12	0.16	3.35	3.19
14	0.15	2.53	2.38
16	0.11	2.09	1.98
18	0.06	1.99	1.93

experiments with a network bandwidth of 12 Mbps, and set the virtual machine memory to 1.0 GB, 1.2 GB, 1.4 GB, 1.6 GB, 1.8 GB, and 2.0 GB, respectively. Page response times before and after blockchain were tested. The relevant experimental data obtained is shown in Table 8.

The experimental results show that when the virtual machine memory is 1.0 GB, the page response time before joining blockchain is 0.16 s, and the page response time after joining blockchain is 4.07 s, the difference between the two is 3.91 s; When the virtual machine memory is 2.0 GB, the page response time before joining blockchain is 0.16 s, and the page response time after joining blockchain is 3.35 s, the difference between the two is 3.19 s. The results show that, within a certain range, with the increase of virtual machine memory, the page response time after joining blockchain keeps decreasing. At the same time, the larger the virtual machine memory, the smaller the difference in page response time before and after joining blockchain to the same virtual machine memory.

It can be seen from the above descriptions that within a certain range, the larger the virtual machine memory, the faster the linking speed.

After analysis, the main reason is that the increase in the memory of the virtual machine will increase the speed of the virtual machine to process data. As a result, during the data uploading process, the uploading speed will increase, resulting in a decrease in page response time. If users can use a virtual machine with a larger memory, it will reduce the delay caused by the blockchain and not ruin users' experience. Moreover, changes in virtual machine memory have little effect on page response times before joining blockchain. After analysis, before joining blockchain, this system only runs on the Windows system and does not use the virtual machine, so the page response time does not change much. As can be seen from the above descriptions, the virtual machine memory factor must be considered when using the commodity transaction scheme after joining blockchain.

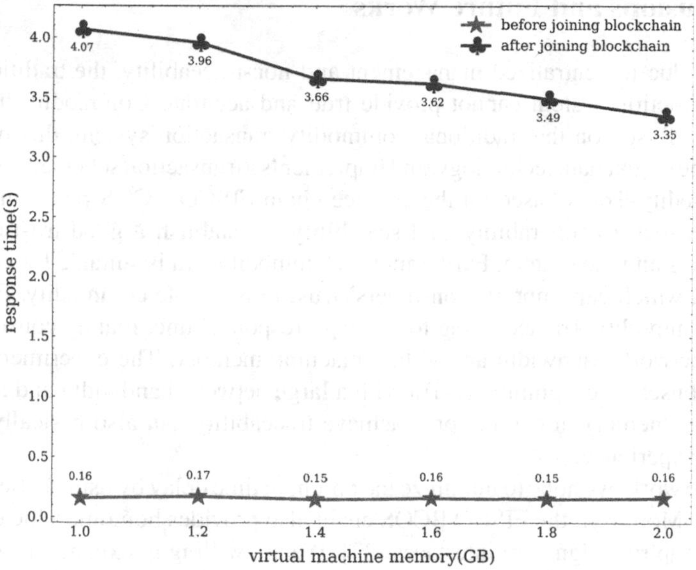

Fig. 9. The impact of virtual machine memory on page response time before and after joining blockchain.

Table 8. Experimental results of virtual machine memory.

Virtual machine memory(GB)	Before joining blockchain(s)	After joining blockchain(s)	The page response time difference before and after joining blockchain(s)
1.0	0.16	4.07	3.91
1.2	0.17	3.96	3.79
1.4	0.15	3.66	3.51
1.6	0.16	3.62	3.46
1.8	0.15	3.49	3.34
2.0	0.16	3.35	3.19

6 Conclusions and Future Works

To sum up, due to centralized management and non-traceability, the traditional commodity transaction system cannot provide true and accurate Commodity traceability information. Based on the traditional commodity transaction system, this paper fully integrates the blockchain technology, and implements a transaction scheme: Commodity-Tra. Commodity-Tra is based on the alliance chain FISCO BCOS platform, using its ease of use, security, operability, and scalability to establish a good trust ecosystem between users and the system. Furthermore, Commodity-Tra is suitable for commodity traceability, which can improve consumers' trust in traceable commodity. Finally, we evaluate Commodity-Tra according to the page response time, mainly considering the factors of network bandwidth and virtual machine memory. The experimental results show that if users use Commodity-Tra with a large network bandwidth and a large virtual machine memory, it can not only achieve traceability, but also basically does not ruin users' experience.

In future work, we hope to minimize the on-chain time delay by using better performing devices. Moreover, the FISCO BCOS chain also provides homomorphic encryption [32] and group ring signature interfaces [33]. We are willing to expand the application in the future, apply cryptography-related knowledge, and meet more business needs.

References

1. Amin, M.B., Alauddin, M.D., Azad, M.M.: Business transaction processing system. Int. J. Comput. Inf. Syst. **4**(5), 11–60 (2012)
2. Repin, M., Mikhalsky, O., Pshehotskaya, E.: Architecture of transaction monitoring system of Central banks. In: International Conference on Actual Issues of Mechanical Engineering 2017 (AIME 2017), pp. 654–658. Atlantis Press, Russia (2017)
3. Afrianto, I., Sasmita, M.H.H., Atin, S.: Prototype mobile contactless transaction system in traditional markets to support the covid-19 physical distancing program. Bull. Electr. Eng. Inform. **10**(6), 3303–3312 (2021)
4. Ma, C., Li, J., Liu, L.H., Guo, M.R.: The vegetable quality and safety traceability model research in China. Adv. Mater. Res. **787**, 1034–1037 (2013)

5. Dong, Y., Ding, B., Zhang, G., Jin, G., Zhao, X.: Quality and safety traceability system based on agricultural product supply chain. Editor. Off. Trans. Chin. Soc. Agric. Eng. **32**(1), 280–285 (2016)
6. Li, X., Yang, L., Duan, Y., Wu, Z., Zhang, X.: Developing a real-time monitoring traceability system for cold chain of tricholoma matsutake. Electronics **8**(4), 423–441 (2019)
7. Wang, L., He, Y., Wu, Z.: Design of a blockchain-enabled traceability system framework for food supply chains. Foods **11**(5), 744 (2022)
8. Chaudhari, R., Deshmukh, R., Bari, V., Rajput, S., Rode, K.: Medicine traceability system using blockchain. J. Trend in Sci. Res. Dev. **3**(4), 346–349 (2019)
9. Wang, Z., Wang, L., Xiao, F., Chen, Q., Lu, L., Hong, J.: A traditional Chinese medicine traceability system based on lightweight blockchain. J. Med. Internet Res. **23**(6), e25946 (2021)
10. Mueen, U.: Blockchain medledger: hyperledger fabric enabled drug traceability system for counterfeit drugs in pharmaceutical industry. Int. J. Pharm. **597**, 120235 (2021)
11. He, M., Shi, J.: Circulation traceability system of Chinese herbal medicine supply chain based on Internet of Things agricultural sensor. Sustain. Comput.: Inform. Syst. **30**(10), 100518 (2021)
12. Hader, M., Tchoffa, D., El Mhamedi, A., Ghodous, P., Dolgui, A., Abouabdellah, A.: Applying integrated blockchain and big data technologies to improve supply chain traceability and information sharing in the textile sector. J. Ind. Inf. Integr. **28**, 100345 (2022)
13. Wessel, J., Turetskyy, A., Wojahn, O., Herrmann, C., Thiede, S.: Tracking and tracing for data mining application in the lithium-ion battery production. Procedia CIRP **93**, 162–167 (2020)
14. Jiang, N., Jie, W., Li, J., Liu, X., Jin, D.: GATrust: a multi-aspect graph attention network model for trust assessment in OSNs. IEEE Trans. Knowl. Data Eng. (2022)
15. Zhu, T., Zhou, W., Ye, D., Cheng, Z., Li, J.: Resource allocation in IoT edge computing via concurrent federated reinforcement learning. IEEE Internet Things J. **9**(2), 1414–1426 (2022)
16. Zhu, T., Li, J., Xiangyu, H., Xiong, P., Zhou, W.: The dynamic privacy-preserving mechanisms for online dynamic social networks. IEEE Trans. Knowl. Data Eng. **34**(6), 2962–2974 (2022)
17. Li, J., et al.: Efficient and secure outsourcing of differentially private data publishing with multiple evaluators. IEEE Trans. Dependable Secure Comput. **19**(1), 67–76 (2022)
18. Li, J., Huang, Y., Wei, Y., Lv, S., Liu, Z., Dong, C., Lou, W.: Searchable symmetric encryption with forward search privacy. IEEE Trans. Dependable Secure Comput. **18**(1), 460–474 (2021)
19. Li, T., Li, J., Chen, X., Liu, Z., Lou, W., Hou, Y.T.: NPMML: a framework for non-interactive privacy-preserving multi-party machine learning. IEEE Trans. Dependable and Secure Comput. **18**(6), 2969–2982 (2021)
20. Gao, C.Z., Li, J., Xia, S.B., Choo, K.K.R., Lou, W., Dong, C.: MAS-encryption and its applications in privacy-preserving classifiers. IEEE Trans. Knowl. Data Eng. **34**(5), 2306–2323 (2022)
21. Mo, K., Tang, W., Li, J., Yuan, X.: Attacking deep reinforcement learning with decoupled adversarial policy. IEEE Trans. Dependable Secure Comput. (2022)
22. Ai, S., Hong, S., Zheng, X., Wang, Y., Liu, X.: CSRT rumor spreading model based on complex network. Int. J. Intell. Syst. **36**(5), 1903–1913 (2021)
23. Yan, H., Hu, L., Xiang, X., Liu, Z., Yuan, X.: PPCL: privacy-preserving collaborative learning for mitigating indirect information leakage. Inf. Sci. **548**, 423–437 (2021)
24. Hu, L., Yan, H., Li, L., Pan, Z., Liu, X., Zhang, Z.: MHAT: an efficient model-heterogenous aggregation training scheme for federated learning. Inf. Sci. **560**, 493–503 (2021)
25. Yan, H., Chen, M., Li, H., Jia, C.: Secure video retrieval using image query on an untrusted cloud. Appl. Soft Comput. **97**, 106782 (2020)
26. Kuang, X., et al.: DeepWAF: detecting web attacks based on CNN and LSTM models. In: Vaidya, J., Zhang, X., Li, J. (eds.) CSS 2019. LNCS, vol. 11983, pp. 121–136. Springer, Cham (2019). https://doi.org/10.1007/978-3-030-37352-8_11

27. Chen, C., Huang, T.: Camdar-adv: Generating adversarial patches on 3D object. Int. J. Intell. Syst. **36**(3), 1441–1453 (2021)
28. Ren, H., Huang, T., Yan, H.: Adversarial examples: attacks and defenses in the physical world. Int. J. Mach. Learn. Cybern. **12**(11), 3325–3336 (2021). https://doi.org/10.1007/s13042-020-01242-z
29. Mo, K., Liu, X., Huang, T., Yan, A.: Querying little is enough: model inversion attack via latent information. Int. J. Intell. Syst. **36**(2), 681–690 (2021)
30. Alfian, G.: Integration of RFID, wireless sensor networks, and data mining in an e-pedigree food traceability system. J. Food Eng. **212**, 65–75 (2017)
31. Wang, R., Ye, K., Meng, T., Xu, C.Z.: Performance evaluation on blockchain systems: a case study on Ethereum, Fabric, Sawtooth and Fisco-Bcos. In: Wang, Q., Xia, Y., Seshadri, S., Zhang, L.J. (eds.) Services Computing, vol. 12409, pp. 120–134. Springer, Cham (2020). https://doi.org/10.1007/978-3-030-59592-0_8
32. Chen, J., You, F.: Application of homomorphic encryption in blockchain data security. In: Proceedings of the 2020 4th International Conference on Electronic Information Technology and Computer Engineering, pp. 205–209. Association for Computing Machinery, Xiamen (2020)
33. Mohit, M., Kaur, S., Singh, M.: Design and implementation of transaction privacy by virtue of ownership and traceability in blockchain based supply chain. Clust. Comput. **25**(3), 2223–2240 (2021). https://doi.org/10.1007/s10586-021-03425-x

A Defect Heterogeneous Risk Assessment Method with Misclassification Cost

Lixia Xie[1], Siyu Liu[1], Hongyu Yang[2,1(✉)], and Liang Zhang[3]

[1] School of Computer Science and Technology, Civil Aviation University of China, Tianjin 300300, China

[2] School of Safety Science and Engineering, Civil Aviation University of China, Tianjin 300300, China

yhyxlx@hotmail.com

[3] School of Information, The University of Arizona, Tucson, AZ 85721, USA

Abstract. Existing software defect prediction techniques do not pay enough attention to the different cost impacts caused by misclassification and cannot prioritize modules with high defect risk. To address these problems, a defect heterogeneity risk assessment method with misclassification cost (DHRA) is proposed. Firstly, noise samples, discrete samples, and high-dimensional features are processed. Secondly, the imbalance ratio and the ratio of misclassification of different categories are calculated to obtain the overall misclassification cost (MC). The heterogeneous classifiers are selected based on the evaluation metric and MC. Then, the defective assessment value is calculated by multiplying the voting weight matrix based on misclassification cost and the base probability matrix. Finally, the defect risk grade of the module is assessed based on the defect risk table. The experimental results show that DHRA outperforms other methods in terms of accuracy, *F*-score, and Matthews correlation coefficient. The defect risk grade obtained by this method can accurately reflect the potential defects of the samples.

Keywords: Defect heterogeneous risk assessment · Misclassification cost · Voting weight · Defect risk table

1 Introduction

With the gradual expansion of the scope of computer applications and the booming development of cyber-attacks, a series of security problems have emerged in the development and maintenance of computer software [1]. Software defects [2], security vulnerabilities [3], and malware [4] have become important concerns in both the software industry and the field of cybersecurity.

X. Chen et al. (Eds.): SocialSec 2022, CCIS 1663, pp. 281–293, 2022.
https://doi.org/10.1007/978-981-19-7242-3_18

In recent years, software defect prediction techniques have been developed by mining, analyzing, and building a suitable classification model on the premise of the selection of features. The defect module is processed according to the predicted defect propensity or the number of defects [5].

Due to the limited testing resources, and the inability of regression algorithms to accurately predict the number of defects [6], it takes time and effort to predict and process the defective modules one by one. Therefore, it is important to assess the defect grades according to the probability in the software module by assigning different testing resources for different defect risk grades.

2 Related Work

Researchers began to use software defect prediction methods based on deep learning and machine learning to solve the security problems caused by software defects.

WANG et al. [7] proposed a software defect prediction method based on deep belief network (DBN), which could obtain semantic features automatically. ZHOU et al. [8] proposed a multi-grained cascade forest (gcForest). ISSAM et al. [9] proposed an average probability ensemble (APE) method and verified that the feature selection of samples is of great significance to the accurate classification of defects. An enhanced APE method was proposed by integrating the feature selection into the APE. CHEN et al. [10] proved that cost-sensitive learning can effectively improve the prediction performance by analyzing the assessment metrics of heterogeneous defect prediction methods in different project databases.

Among the above methods, the results of the defect prediction methods cannot sort the potential risk grade of defect modules The defect number prediction method cannot accurately predict the number of defects. Aiming at the weaknesses, a defect heterogeneous risk assessment method with misclassification cost (DHRA) is proposed.

3 A Defect Heterogeneous Risk Assessment Method

The defect heterogeneous risk assessment method based on misclassification cost is consist of three parts: sample processing, misclassification cost quantization, and defect heterogeneous risk assessment. The architecture is shown in Fig. 1.

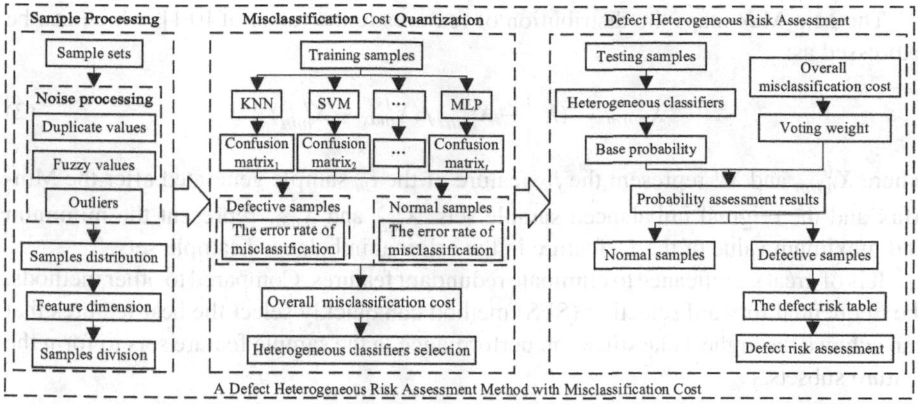

Fig. 1. Defect heterogeneous risk assessment architecture.

4 Sample Processing

This section deals with the samples comprehensively from the aspects of noise samples, discrete distribution, and high-dimensional features.

Authoritative sample sets in the field of software defect prediction are collected. Among them, noise samples have a great impact on the accuracy of defect prediction, so noise sample processing is of great significance. Noise samples include duplicate values, fuzzy values, and outliers.

The duplicate values are deleted directly, which can effectively reduce the redundancy of samples on the premise of ensuring the integrity of samples. Then the basic information such as sample mean and features mean is calculated. The fuzzy value and outliers are substituted by these mean values to avoid the problems of false deletion of important samples and excessive temporal and spatial complexity.

Most of the sample's features belong to the numerical features of discrete distribution [11]. Therefore, it is of great significance to reduce the features of defect samples to a unified distribution range in proportion.

Common sample distribution methods include the Z-Score standardization (Z-Score) method and the Min-Max normalization (Min-Max) method [12]. The Z-Score maps the distribution to the standard normal distribution, which can be expressed as:

$$X_{stad}^{ij} = (X^{ij} - \mu^j)/\sigma^j \tag{1}$$

where X_{stad}^{ij} represents the j_{th} feature of the corresponding i_{th} sample after Z-Score, μ^j represents the expectation value of the j_{th} feature in the original imbalanced sample sets, and σ^j represents the variance value of the j_{th} feature.

The Min-Max maps the distribution of features to the range of [0,1], which can be expressed as:

$$X_{norm}^{ij} = (X^{ij} - X_{min}^{j})/(X_{max}^{j} - X_{min}^{j}) \tag{2}$$

where X_{norm}^{ij} and X^{ij} represent the j_{th} feature of the i_{th} sample generated after the Min-Max and the original imbalanced sample sets. X_{min}^{j} and X_{max}^{j} represent the minimum and maximum value of the j_{th} feature in the original imbalanced sample sets.

It is of great significance to eliminate redundant features. Compared to other methods, the Sequential forward selection (SFS) method can quickly select the best features that can achieve the highest classification performance in the sample feature sets to form the feature subsets.

5 Misclassification Cost Quantization

In this section, an overall misclassification cost quantification algorithm based on different categories of misclassification is proposed using the processed samples in Sect. 3. The heterogeneous classifiers are determined based on the value of cross-validation accuracy and misclassification cost (MC).

5.1 Overall Misclassification Cost Quantization Algorithm

Misclassification of defective samples keeps researchers from performing the necessary code review, and misclassification of normal samples makes researchers perform a meaningless review. Therefore, misclassification of defective samples is more costly, and it is important to adjust the training target for defective samples.

The imbalance ratio (IR) was used to measure the proportion of defective and normal samples, which is expressed as:

$$IR = N^{-}/N^{+} \tag{3}$$

where N^{+}, and $N^{-}$is the number of the defective and normal samples.

The training objective of the classifiers is transformed from minimizing the overall sample error to minimizing the overall misclassification cost. The classifiers include *k*-Nearest Neighbor (KNN), Naïve Bayes (NB), Logistic Regression (LR), Support Vector Machine (SVM), Decision Tree (DT), Multi-layer Perceptron (MLP), Random Forest (RF), Stochastic Gradient Descent (SGD), Gradient Boosting (GB) and Adaptive Boost (AdaBoost). The overall misclassification cost quantification algorithm is shown in Algorithm 1. In the confusion matrix, positive or negative is used to describe the defective or non-defective category, and true or false is used to describe whether the result is correct, as shown in Fig. 2.

Algorithm 1 Overall misclassification cost quantization algorithm

Input: Sample set: $S = \{(x_i, y_i), i = 1, 2, \ldots, N, y_i \in \{0, 1\}\}$.

Output: Overall misclassification cost: σ_c.

S_{train}, S_{test} ← train_test_split(pd.read_csv(S), test_size=0.3)
clfs ← [KNN, NB, LR, SVM, DT, MLP, RF, SGD, GB, AdaBoost]
σ_*list* ← [] //Overall misclassification cost list
for *c* **in** *clfs*:
  $D_c \leftrightarrow$ *clf* //Confusion matrix ***D*** of the *clf*
  $\lambda_c, \zeta_c \leftarrow D_c$ //The error rate of the defective and normal samples
  $\Phi_{\lambda c} \leftarrow \lambda_c / (IR_c+1)$ // The misclassification cost of the normal category
  $\Phi_{\zeta c} \leftarrow IR_c \zeta_c / (IR_c+1)$ //The misclassification cost of the defective category
  $\sigma_c \leftarrow (\Phi_{\lambda c}+\Phi_{\zeta c})^2/2$ //The misclassification cost
  σ_*list*.append(σ_c)
end for

		Actual Category	
		Positive	Negative
Actual Result	True	True Positive(TP)	True Negative (TN)
	False	False Positive(FP)	False Negative (FN)

Fig. 2. Confusion matrix.

5.2 Heterogeneous Classifiers Selection

From Algorithm 1, the smaller λ_c and ζ_c, the smaller σ_c, and the better performance of the heterogeneous classifiers. Compared to homogeneous classifiers, heterogeneous classifiers can effectively reconcile the performance of different base classifiers. Therefore, the performance of each base classifier is obtained by comparing the evaluation metric and the σ_c.

According to different feature distributions, NB classifiers are divided into Gaussian NB (GNB), Multinomial NB (MNB), and Bernoulli NB (BNB). The cross-validation accuracy of GNB, MNB, and BNB is compared by a function named cross_val_score in the same samples' environment, and then determines the kind of NB, as shown in Table 1.

It can be seen from Table 1 that the accuracy of GNB is better in NASA MDP, PROMISE, AEEEM, and ReLink databases. Therefore, GNB is selected as the candidate base classifier.

Table 1. Cross-validation accuracy of GNB, MNB, and BNB.

Project databases	Sample sets	GNB	MNB	BNB
NASA MDP	CM1	0.671	0.730	**0.766**
	MC2	**0.726**	0.622	0.696
	PC1	**0.902**	0.753	0.762
	PC2	**0.708**	0.646	0.649
	PC3	**0.863**	0.765	0.836
PROMISE	Ant v1.7	0.660	0.638	**0.804**
	Camel v1.6	**0.897**	0.865	0.792
	Jedit v4.3	**0.907**	0.862	0.853
AEEEM	EQ	**0.637**	0.629	0.635
	Mylyn	0.646	**0.725**	0.629
ReLink	Apache	**0.573**	0.551	0.534
	Safe	**0.624**	0.579	0.618

The complexity of MLP is higher than KNN, GNB, LR, SVM, and DT, and the σ_c is higher than RF, AdaBoost, and GB. According to the fact that the σ_c of DT is higher than RF and the σ_c of AdaBoost is higher than GB. To ensure the difference of each base classifier. Therefore, the heterogeneous classifiers include KNN, GNB, LR, SVM, RF, and GB.

6 Defect Heterogeneous Risk Assessment

In the section, the voting weights of the heterogeneous classifiers are calculated according to the σ_c calculated in Sect. 4. According to the high voting weights of RF and GB, so the classification performance of GNB, KNN, LR, and SVM can be balanced effectively. The defect assessment results by comparing probability assessment values, which can assess the defect grade based on the defect risk table.

The voting weight V_{1c} of each base classifier is calculated according to the complementary of σ_c in the range of [0, 1] to construct the voting weight matrix $\boldsymbol{V}$. V_{1c} can be expressed as:

$$V_{1c} = (\sum_{c}^{6} \sigma_c - \sigma_c) / \sum_{c}^{6} \sigma_c \quad (4)$$

$$\boldsymbol{V} = \begin{bmatrix} V_{11} \; V_{12} \cdots V_{1c} \cdots V_{16} \end{bmatrix}$$

The testing samples are input into the heterogeneous classifiers, and the base probability matrix $\boldsymbol{P}$ is output.

$$\boldsymbol{P} = \begin{bmatrix} P_{1(non)} & P_{2(non)} & \dots & P_{i(non)} & \dots & P_{6(non)} \\ P_{1(def)} & P_{2(def)} & \dots & P_{i(def)} & \dots & P_{6(def)} \end{bmatrix}^T$$

where $P_{i(non)}$ and $P_{i(def)}$ represent the normal and defective probability of i_{th} base classifier.

Referring to the asset importance grade and risk assessment specification [13] and the value range of $P_{i(def)}$, the base probability table is produced, as shown in Table 2.

Table 2. The base probability table.

$P_{i(def)}$	Grade	Definition
(0.8, 1]	Higher	Defects have a higher impact on the module
(0.6, 0.8]	High	Defects have a high impact on the module
(0.4, 0.6]	Medium	Defects have a medium impact on the module
(0.2, 0.4]	Low	Defects have a low impact on the module
(0, 0.2]	Lower	Defects have a lower impact on the module
0	Non-defective	Defects have no impact on the module

The probability assessment matrix $\boldsymbol{A}$ is obtained by multiplying $\boldsymbol{V}$ and $\boldsymbol{P}$.

$$\boldsymbol{A} = \left[V_{ass(non)} \ V_{ass(def)} \right]^T$$

where $V_{ass(non)}$ and $V_{ass(def)}$ represent the normal and defective assessment results.

By comparing the values of $V_{ass(non)}$ and $V_{ass(def)}$, the sample is assessed. Based on the theoretically derived analysis, the $V_{ass(def)}$ can be expressed as:

$$V_{ass(def)} = \sum_{c}^{6} V_{1c}P_{i(def)} = \sum_{c}^{6} P_{i(def)} - \sum_{c}^{6} (\sigma_c P_{i(def)} / \sum_{c}^{6} \sigma_c) \tag{5}$$

It can be seen that $\sigma_c \in [0, 1]$, $\sigma_c / \sum_c^6 \sigma_c \in [0, 1]$, and $\sum_c^6 P_{i(def)} \geq \sum_c^6 (\sigma_c P_{i(def)} / \sum_c^6 \sigma_c)$, so $V_{ass(def)} \geq 0$. Besides, it can be known that the maximum value of $P_{i(def)}$ is 1 to obtain $max\{\sum_k^6 P_{i(def)}\} = 6$, and $\sum_c^6 \sigma_c P_{i(def)} = \sum_k^6 \sigma_c$ in this situation, so $V_{ass(def)} \leq 5$. Therefore, the value range of the defective assessment result $V_{ass(def)}$ is [0, 5].

To give priority to the defect modules with higher criticality in time, referring to the asset importance grade and risk assessment specification [13] and the value range of $V_{ass(def)}$ to generate the defect risk table, as shown in Table 3.

Table 3. The defect risk table.

$V_{ass(def)}$	Grade	Definition
(4, 5]	Higher	If there is a defect, it will cause complete damage to the assets
(3, 4]	High	If there is a defect, it will cause significant damage to the assets
(2, 3]	Medium	If there is a defect, it will cause general damage to the assets
(1, 2]	Low	If there is a defect, it will cause less damage to the assets
(0, 1]	Lower	If there is a defect, the damage to the assets can be ignored
0	Non-defective	This module has no impact on assets

7 Experiments and Results

7.1 Experimental Samples

Four public project databases are collected, which include NASA MDP [14], PROMISE [15], AEEEM [16], and Relink [17]. The basic information of the original samples and noise processing samples is shown in Table 4.

7.2 Evaluation Metrics

Different evaluation metrics to measure the prediction results. The area under curve (AUC), accuracy, *F*-score, and Matthews Correlation Coefficient (MCC) are used, which can be expressed as:

$$\text{Accuracy} = \frac{\text{TP} + \text{TN}}{\text{TP} + \text{FP} + \text{TN} + \text{FN}} \tag{6}$$

$$F\text{ - score} = \frac{2\text{TP}}{2\text{TP} + \text{FN} + \text{FP}} \tag{7}$$

$$\text{MCC} = \frac{\text{TP} \times \text{TN} - \text{FP} \times \text{FN}}{\sqrt{(\text{TP} + \text{FP})(\text{TP} + \text{FN})(\text{TN} + \text{FP})(\text{TN} + \text{FN})}} \tag{8}$$

7.3 Samples Distribution Experiment

In the experiment, the noise samples are processed using the Min-Max and Z-Score to calculate the AUC of different sample distribution methods in different *k*-value of the KNN classifier, as shown in Fig. 3.

Experiments show that the Z-Score has the most stable and the best performance. Due to the different influence grades of nearest neighbor samples, *k* fluctuates greatly between 1 and 5. When $k = 5$, the AUC can reach a higher score. After $k = 10$, the performance is gradually stable. Therefore, considering that the larger the value of *k*, the higher the complexity and the longer the running time, the nearest neighbor number *k* of the KNN classifier is set to 10.

Table 4. The basic information of the original samples and noise processing samples.

Project databases	Sample sets	Original samples			Noise processing samples			
		Instances	Defects	Features	Instances	Defects	% of defects	IR
NASA MDP	MC2	161	52	39	158	52	32.91%	2.04
	CM1	505	48	37	505	48	9.50%	9.52
	JM1	10878	2102	21	8905	2003	22.49%	3.45
	PC1	1107	76	37	961	69	7.18%	12.93
	PC2	5589	23	40	1406	23	1.64%	60.13
	PC3	1563	160	40	1439	153	10.63%	8.41
PROMISE	Ant v1.7	745	166	20	724	166	22.93%	3.36
	Camel v1.6	965	188	20	884	184	20.81%	3.80
	Jedit v4.3	492	11	20	476	8	1.68%	58.50
AEEEM	Mylyn	1862	245	61	1804	237	13.14%	6.61
	EQ	324	129	60	265	129	48.68%	1.05
	Lucene	691	64	58	685	61	8.91%	10.23
ReLink	Apache	194	98	26	194	98	50.52%	0.98
	Safe	56	22	26	56	22	39.29%	1.55
	Zxing	399	118	26	399	118	29.57%	2.38

7.4 Defect Risk Assessment Experiment

The evaluation metrics can effectively reflect the software defect assessment ability. To prove the superiority of DHRA, the *F*-score, and MCC are calculated to compare DHRA with three traditional methods and two ensemble methods of different sample sets, as shown in Table 5 and Table 6. The accuracy and *F*-score are calculated to compare DHRA with four advanced methods of different sample sets, as shown in Fig. 4.

Experiments show that DHRA gets the highest *F*-score and MCC in the CM1, JM1, PC1, and Ant v1.7 sample sets. The corresponding MCC is 0.874 and 0.627 respectively, which are 68.7% and 63.7% higher than AdaBoost respectively. The DHRA obtains the highest accuracy and *F*-score, as shown in Fig. 4. The accuracy and *F*-score of DHRA are higher than the other four methods, as shown in Fig. 4(a).

DHRA can clean noisy samples, normalize discrete distributions and quickly reduce feature dimensionality in the sample processing stage. In the heterogeneous classifiers stage, it can assign different costs to different classes of misclassification, thus enabling weighted voting on different base classifiers to obtain defect risk results.

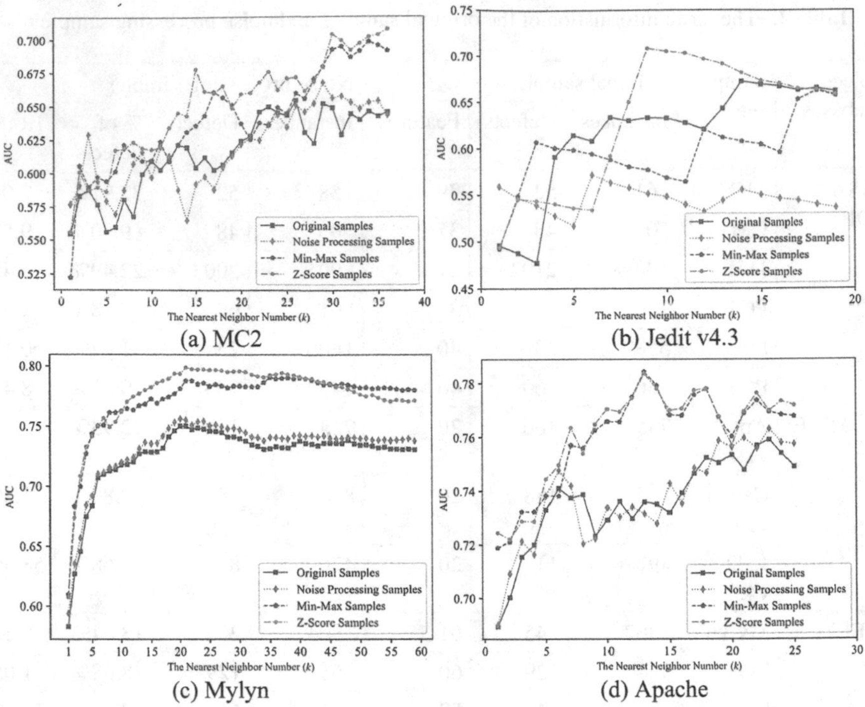

Fig. 3. AUC of different sample distribution methods in different *k*-value of KNN classifier.

Table 5. *F*-score with traditional and ensemble methods.

Methods	CM1	JM1	PC1	Ant v1.7	EQ	Lucene
DHRA	**0.558**	**0.874**	**0.643**	**0.619**	0.657	0.460
KNN	0.507	0.497	0.476	0.542	0.575	0.483
LR	0.443	0.483	0.476	0.494	**0.658**	**0.650**
MLP	0.499	0.604	0.438	0.341	0.625	0.424
AdaBoost	0.530	0.541	0.414	0.495	0.649	0.500
SGD	0.442	0.438	0.294	0.521	0.431	0.353

To further prove the advantages of the defect risk assessment method, $V_{ass(def)}$ is analyzed and divided defect grades with reference to Table 3. The $V_{ass(def)}$ in the JM1, PC1, and Ant v1.7 sample set to obtain the defect risk assessment results.

Taking one sample in the JM1 sample set as an example, firstly, the error rates of the defective and normal samples are calculated according to the confusion matrix of six base classifiers. Secondly, the corresponding σ_c is calculated, which are 0.453, 0.519, 0.522, 0.513, 0.342 and 0.331 respectively. Then W_{1c} of each base classifier according to the σ_c, which are 0.831, 0.806, 0.805, 0.809, 0.872 and 0.876 respectively. Finally,

Table 6. MCC with traditional and ensemble methods.

Methods	CM1	JM1	PC1	Ant v1.7	EQ	Lucene
DHRA	**0.557**	**0.847**	**0.627**	**0.514**	0.590	0.418
KNN	0.443	0.470	0.513	0.418	0.603	0.420
LR	0.440	0.441	0.513	0.399	**0.692**	**0.617**
MLP	0.448	0.515	0.436	0.189	0.615	0.407
AdaBoost	0.154	0.518	0.383	0.367	0.654	0.469
SGD	0.442	0.436	0.253	0.334	0.526	0.377

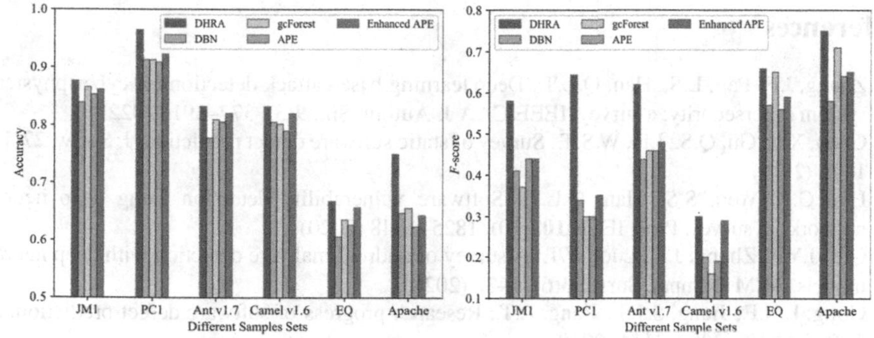

(a) Accuracy (b) *F*-score

Fig. 4. Accuracy and *F*-score with advanced methods.

the $V_{ass(def)}$ is obtained by multiplying ***V*** and ***P*** which is 3.269. Referring to Table 3, the defect risk grade of the sample is high, showing that if there is a defect, it will cause significant damage to the asset. In the actual situation of the sample classification label, the sample label value is 1 showing that there is a defect. The $P_{i(def)}$ of RF and GB are 0.798 and 0.785 respectively. Referring to Table 2, it can be judged that the defect grade is high. The $P_{i(def)}$ of GNB and LR are 0.489 and 0.465 respectively. Referring to Table 2, it can be judged that the defect grade is medium. DHRA method weights and enhances the prediction results of RF and GB. Therefore, the actual situation of the sample label is consistent with the assessment results.

The experimental results show that the allocation of software resources can be effective according to the proportion of software defect grade.

8 Conclusion

A defect heterogeneous risk assessment method with misclassification cost is proposed, which can effectively divide the potential risk grade of defect modules and reasonably allocate limited testing resources. Based on the machine learning method, the base probability of heterogeneous classifiers with different performances is used for voting weight considering the different cost effects caused by misclassification. The defective assessment value is calculated to obtain the software defect risk grade.

The feasibility and effectiveness of this method are verified by the verification experiments of traditional methods, ensemble methods, and advanced methods under the same sample environment. Compared with other methods, the method can give higher weights to the base classifiers with good performance. The ranking of module defect risk grades according to the defect risk table can reflect the safety status of modules comprehensively and accurately.

Acknowledgment. This work was supported by the National Natural Science Foundation of China (No. U1833107).

References

1. Zhang, J.F., Pan, L.S., Han, Q.L.T.: Deep learning based attack detection for cyber-physical system cybersecurity: a survey. IEEE/CAA J. Autom. Sin. **9**(3), 377–391 (2022)
2. Chen, X.F., Gu, Q.S., Liu, W.S.T.: Survey of static software defect prediction. J. Softw. **27**(1), 1–25 (2016)
3. Lin, G.F., Wen, S.S., Han, Q.L.T.: Software vulnerability detection using deep neural networks: a survey. Proc. IEEE **108**(10), 1825–1848 (2020)
4. Qiu, J.Y.F., Zhang, J.S., Luo, W.T.: A survey of android malware detection with deep neural models. ACM Comput. Surv. **53**(6), 1–36 (2020)
5. Gong, L.N.F., Jiang, S.J.S., Jiang, L.T.: Research progress of software defect prediction. J. Softw. **30**(10), 3090–3114 (2019)
6. Yu, X.F., Jacky, K.S., Xiao, Y.T.: Predicting the precise number of software defects are we there yet. Inf. Softw. Technol. **146**(1), 106847–106863 (2022)
7. Wang, S.F., Liu, T.Y.S., Tan, L.T.: Automatically learning semantic features for defect prediction. In: Dillon, L.F., Visser, W.S. (eds.) IEEE/ACM 38th International Conference on Software Engineering 2016, ICSE, vol. 38, pp. 297–308. Association for Computing Machinery, New York (2016)
8. Zhou, Z.H.F., Feng, J.S.: Deep forest: towards an alternative to deep neural networks.In: Sierra, C.F. (ed.) Twenty-Sixth International Joint Conference on Artificial Intelligence 2017, IJCAI, vol. 26, pp. 3553–3559. Morgan Kaufmann, San Francisco (2017)
9. Issam, H.L.F., Mohammad, A.S., Lahouari, G.T.: Software defect prediction using ensemble learning on selected features. Inf. Softw. Technol. **58**(1), 388–402 (2015)
10. Chen, H.W.F., Jing, X.Y.S., Li, Z.Q.T.: An empirical study on heterogeneous defect prediction approaches. IEEE Trans. Softw. Eng. **47**(12), 2803–2822 (2020)
11. Amal, A.F., Hamoud, A.S.: Code smell detection using feature selection and stacking ensemble: an empirical investigation. Inf. Softw. Technol. **138**(1), 106648–106661 (2021)
12. Yang, H.Y.F., Zhang, Z.X.S., Xie, L.X.T.: Network security situation assessment with network attack behavior classification. Int. J. Intell. Syst. **37**(3), 1–19 (2022)
13. GB/T 20984, Information security technology-risk assessment specification for information security. National Standard of the People's Republic of China (2007)
14. Shepperd, M.F., Song, Q.S., Sun, Z.T.: Data quality: some comments on the NASA software defect datasets. IEEE Trans. Softw. Eng. **39**(9), 1208–1215 (2013)
15. Jurecako, M.F., Mmadeyski, L.S.: Towards identifying software project clusters with regard to defect prediction. In: Proceedings of the 6th International Conference on Predictive Models in Software Engineering 2010, ICSE, pp. 1–10. Association for Computing Machinery, New York (2010)

16. D'Ameros, M.F., Lanza, M.S., Robbes, R.T.: Evaluating defect prediction approaches: a benchmark and an extensive comparison. Empirical Softw. Eng. **17**(4), 531–577 (2012). https://doi.org/10.1007/s10664-011-9173-9
17. Wu, R.F., Zhang, H.S., Kim, S.T.: Relink: recovering links between bugs and changes. In: Proceedings of the 19th ACM SIGSOFT Symposium and the 13th European Conference on Foundations of Software Engineering 2011, ICSE, pp. 15–25. Association for Computing Machinery, New York (2011)

Squeeze-Loss: A Utility-Free Defense Against Membership Inference Attacks

Yingying Zhang, Hongyang Yan(✉), Guanbiao Lin, Shiyu Peng, Zhenxin Zhang, and Yufeng Wang

Institute of Artificial Intelligence and Blockchain, Guangzhou University, Guangdong 510006, China
zhangyingying@e.gzhu.edu.cn, hyang.yan@foxmail.com

Abstract. Membership inference attacks can infer whether a data sample exists in the training set of the target model based on limited adversary knowledge, which results in serious leakage of privacy. A large number of recent studies have shown that model overfitting is one of the main reasons why membership inference attacks can be executed successfully. Therefore, some classic methods to solve model overfitting are used to defend against membership inference attacks, such as dropout, spatial dropout, and differential privacy. However, it is difficult for these defense methods to achieve an available trade-off in defense success rate and model utility. In this paper, we focus on the impact of model training loss on model overfitting, and we design a Squeeze-Loss strategy to dynamically find the training loss that achieves the best balance between model utility and privacy. Extensive experimental results show that our strategy can limit the success rate of membership inference attacks to the level of random guesses with almost no loss of model utility, which always outperforms other defense methods.

Keywords: Membership inference attack · Squeeze training loss · Deep learning · Data privacy · Defense strategy

1 Introduction

Machine learning has been widely used in both industry and academia over the past few decades. It has achieved great success in image recognition [2,27,32,33], speech recognition [3,26,31,36], face recognition [28,29], natural language processing [4,30] and other fields. This success is due to the fact that today's devices can process huge amounts of data. In general, machine learning models usually need a large amount of training data to achieve a feasible model utility, which include some user privacy data, such as face data, medical data and so on. Therefore, it has raised concerns about whether deep learning models could reveal sensitive personal data. Recently, some studies [34,35,37–40] have exposed the inevitability of this concern, they show that deep learning models will remember or leak their training set information, and the adversary can infer whether a sample exists in the training set of the model with few operations, which causes great privacy security problems.

X. Chen et al. (Eds.): SocialSec 2022, CCIS 1663, pp. 294–306, 2022.
https://doi.org/10.1007/978-981-19-7242-3_19

Membership inference attacks (MIA) are gaining attention, where the goal is to infer whether a given piece of data is part of the training set of an ML model. Recently, many defensive methods on membership inference attacks have been proposed. These defense methods can be broadly classified into confidence masking [5], regularization [6–8], and provable defense against differential privacy [9,10].

In this paper, we propose an approach to defend against membership inference attacks while maximizing the utility of the model. Our basic idea is to defend against MIA by reducing the accuracy of the ML model on the training data so that it becomes indistinguishable between the training and test data. As we all know, when the model starts to overfit, the knowledge learned from model training is no longer helpful to increase the utility of the model. For this reason, we introduced a validation dataset for determining model overfitting during model training. Our main contributions are summarized as follows:

- We propose a new approach, called Squeeze-Loss, which defends against membership inference attacks by modifying the model training process. It also has excellent privacy and utility tradeoff.
- We performed experimental analysis using several datasets, including MNIST, CIFAR10 and CIFAR100. to demonstrate the effectiveness of our defense, we compared four membership inference attacks and conducted comparative experiments with several commonly used defense methods.

2 Preliminaries

2.1 Membership Inference Attack

Membership inference attack (MIA) are used to infer whether a given piece of data is part of the target model's training set. MIA can pose serious privacy risks, especially for models involving medical data. An attacker can infer whether that patient's data is part of the training set of the target model through a membership inference attack, and thus know whether that patient has a certain disease. The National Institute of Standards and Technology (NIST) in [11] refers to MIA to determine whether the target model's training The inclusion of a defined data in the set is a breach of confidentiality.

Membership inference attacks on machine learning models were first proposed by Shokri et al. [1], who trained attack models using the output confidence of shadow models by training multiple shadow models with the same structure as the target model, and their experiments showed that the attack models could distinguish the affiliation of data by the output confidence distribution of the target ML model. Google, Amazon and other large Internet companies use machine learning as a service (MLaaS), where users can only upload data to train a model through an API interface, and finally the service returns a trained model. That means the target model is only accessible in most cases, and is agnostic about its internal structure. Salem et al. [1] show that training a single shadow model is also capable of implementing membership inference attacks, and they also show experimentally that membership inference attacks can be successful even if the shadow model has a different distribution of training data than the target model.

2.2 Overfitting

The situation where the features learned by a model in the training dataset do not generalize well to the test dataset is called overfitting. Shokri et al. [12] showed that overfitting is a common, but not the only, cause of different performance of machine learning models on training and test data. Samuel Yeom et al. [13] showed that as the degree of model overfitting increases, the more vulnerable the model is to membership inference attacks, but overfitting is not the only factor contributing to the success of membership inference attacks. To reduce the effects of overfitting, weight decay and early stopping [14] methods have been gradually proposed.

3 Related Work

3.1 Scheme of Membership Inference Attack

Hu et al. [15] classified membership inference attack into binary classifier-based membership inference attack and metric-based membership inference attacks according to their attacks. Membership inference attack based on binary classifiers were first proposed by Shokri et al. [12], who trained a model that mimics the behavior of the target model, called a shadow model, and used the output of this shadow model to train a binary classifier for distinguishing whether a given data is a member or a non-member. Metric-based membership inference attacks, where the metric can be prediction correctness, prediction loss, prediction confidence, and prediction entropy. Samuel Yeom et al. [13] proposed membership inference attacks based on the prediction loss metric and prediction correctness, where prediction loss-based MIA is a membership inference attack using the difference between the prediction loss of the training data and the prediction loss of the test data, inferring that a given data is a non-member if its prediction loss is greater than the average training loss of the model, and a member otherwise.

3.2 Methods for Defense Against MIAs

Existing defense methods for membership inference attacks can be broadly classified into confidence score masking, regularization, and privacy-preserving methods commonly used in machine learning, i.e., differential privacy.

Confidence-Score Masking. In 2019 Jia et al. [5] proposed a defense method called Memguard, which is the first defense method for membership inference attacks with utility guarantees.

Regularization. Regularization methods commonly used to defend against MIA are Dropout, earlyStopping, and model stacking. Kaya et al. [16] show that existing regularization methods do not achieve a nice privacy-utility tradeoff.

Differential Privacy. Differential privacy was proposed by Dwork et al. [17] in 2006. Samuel Yeom et al. [13] showed that the membership advantage of a membership inference attacker is limited by the privacy budget ϵ of differential privacy. Bargav et al. [18] showed that the current differential privacy mechanism does not provide a good utility-privacy tradeoff.

4 Method

We propose the squeeze-loss method, where we set a variable threshold T as the gradient ascent criterion, and we introduce a validation set for determining model overfitting. In this section, we describe the specific procedure of our method in detail.

4.1 Gradient Ascent

Overfitting is the process of making assumptions too stringent in order to obtain a consistent hypothesis. The criterion for judging overfitting is that the model performs well on the training set and poorly on the test set. We introduce a correction set to determine model overfitting. Our proposed defense method is similar to the early stopping method in regularization techniques, which mainly defends against MIA by reducing the overfitting of the model. The difference is that we use the gradient ascent method to adjust the training loss of the model.

Chen et al. [19] proposed a defense method called Relax-loss, which uses a gradient ascent step to adjust the loss distribution. Our proposed method also employs the gradient ascent method. However, the Relax-loss method requires setting a fixed T-value as the threshold for gradient ascent, and the choice of T-value affects its defense effectiveness. Our method uses a variable T. We will expand to describe the details of the variation of T in Sect. 4.2.

Optimizers are tools for guiding the updating of neural network model parameters in machine learning. The common optimizers are SGD(stochastic gradient descent) [20], SGDM (stochastic gradient descent with momentum) [21], Adagrad (Adaptive Gradient) [22], Adam (Adaptive moment estimation) [23], RMSProp (root mean square prop) [24].

Adam algorithm is a combination of AdaGrad, RMSprop and momentum method. The step direction is determined by the average value of the gradient shift. Adam has a small amount of hyperparameter tuning but it can also obtain good performance. Parameter update algorithm for Adam optimizer:

$$\theta_t = \theta_{t-1} - \alpha * \hat{m}_t / (\sqrt{\hat{v}_t} + \epsilon) \tag{1}$$

The purpose of applying gradient ascent is to find more precisely the point where the model starts to overfit, and the magnitude of the gradient ascent should be controlled to be small. Therefore, the parameter update algorithm we use to perform the gradient ascent is as follows:

$$\theta_t = \theta_{t-1} + [\alpha * \hat{m}_t / (\sqrt{\hat{v}_t} + \epsilon)] / \gamma \tag{2}$$

where θ_t denotes the parameter vector updated in round t, γ controls the gradient rise, $\hat{m}_t$ denotes the first moment vector, and $\hat{v}_t$ denotes the second moment vector. $\hat{m}_t$ and $\hat{v}_t$ updates are controlled by the exponential decay rates β_1 and β_2.

4.2 Squeeze-Loss Framework

We propose a defense method that preserves the utility of the model. Here we describe the details of the squeeze loss method in detail. We introduce a correction set to determine overfitting of the model and a variable threshold T as a marker to determine overfitting, and if the model is overfitted, we use a gradient ascent method on the model to mitigate the overfitting. We train a model by the training method shown in Fig. 1 so that it performs as consistently as possible in both training and test data.

(1) Overfitting judgment: We introduce a correction set for determining whether the model is overfitting, and we determine that the model starts to overfit when the loss in the correction set is no longer decreasing.

(2) Adaptive threshold T: The loss of the correction set of a neural network model fluctuates during training, which simply means that the loss of the correction set of the model during training will rise at some point and then continue to fall. This phenomenon can affect our judgment of model overfitting. Therefore, we mitigate this situation by introducing a threshold value T, and we operate the judgment when the training loss of the model is less than T. If the training loss is less than T, but the model is not overfitting at this point we lower T and vice versa. T is adjusted as follows:

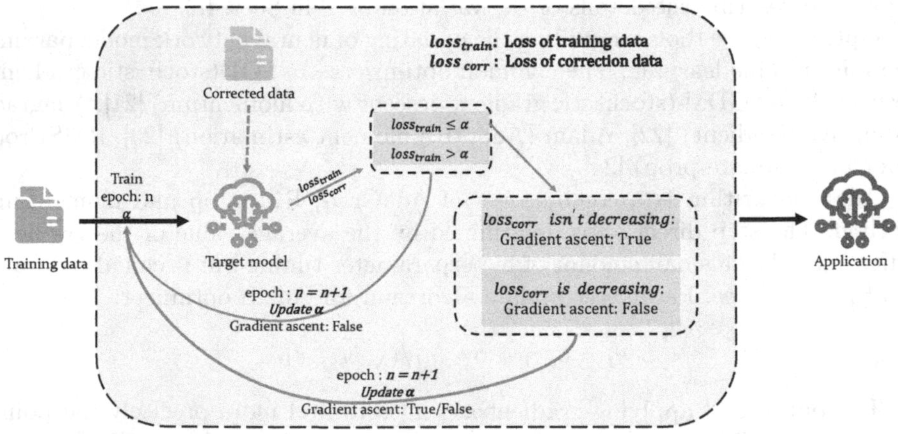

Fig. 1. The framework of Squeeze-Loss.

No overfitting:

$$T_t = \begin{cases} T_0/1.15, & \text{if t} = 0 \\ (5 * T_{t-1} + T_{t-2})/6, & \text{if t} \neq 0 \end{cases} \tag{3}$$

Overfitting:

$$T_t = \begin{cases} T_0/1.1, & \text{if t} = 0 \\ (5 * T_{t-2} + T_{t-1})/6, & \text{if t} \neq 0 \end{cases} \tag{4}$$

where t denotes the t-th round of updating T values and T_0 is where we set the initial value. Equation 3 is the update T_t method to determine that the classifier is not overfitted, and Eq. 4 is the update T_t method for overfitting.

Table 1. Data partitioning of the target model, shadow model and attack model trained by the membership inference attack is performed for each dataset.

Dataset	Training dataset					Test dataset		
	D^{train}_{Target}	D^{train}_{Shadow}	D^{train}_{Attack}	D^{corr}_{Target}	D^{corr}_{Shadow}	D^{test}_{Target}	D^{test}_{Shadow}	D^{test}_{Attack}
Mnist	10000	10000	1000	1000	20000	10000	10000	20000
Cifar10	10000	10000	1000	1000	20000	10000	10000	20000
Cifar100	10000	10000	1000	1000	20000	10000	10000	20000

5 Evaluation

We present the evaluation of Squeeze-Loss in this section. We first describe the dataset used, and then describe our experimental setup and model. We evaluate several membership inference attacks to verify the while effectiveness of our defense methods, and we also compare several methods commonly used to defend against membership inference attacks, i.e., regularization, DP (differential privacy), and MemGuard.

5.1 Experiment Setup

In this paper, experiments were conducted using three different datasets, namely MNIST, CIFAR10, and CIFAR100. We briefly describe these three datasets below.

A. Datasets

MNIST. This is a dataset containing 70,000 handwritten digits for computer vision. The dataset is divided into a training set of 60,000 images and labels, and a test set of 10,000 images and labels. Each image contains 28 * 28 pixel points.

CIFAR-10. The classification problem for this dataset is an open benchmark test problem in machine learning. It consists of 60,000 32 * 32 RGB color images, which contain 10 classes with 6,000 images each. The training set has 50,000 images and the test set has 10,000 images.

Table 2. Attack 1. Where "gap" is the difference between the training accuracy and test accuracy of the target model, "trainacc" and "testacc" are the training accuracy and test accuracy of the target model, and "attackacc" is the attack accuracy. (a) is the undefended attack. (b) is the attack with our defense method applied.

(a) Defense

$Dataset$	gap	$train_{acc}$	$test_{acc}$	$attack_{acc}$
Mnist	0.0144	0.9852	0.9808	0.5053
Cifar10	0.2258	0.7863	0.5655	0.5067
Cifar100	0.259	0.4820	0.223	0.5042

(b) No defense

$Dataset$	gap	$train_{acc}$	$test_{acc}$	$attack_{acc}$
Mnist	0.0157	1.00	0.9843	0.54085
Cifar10	0.4286	1.00	0.5714	0.84485
Cifar100	0.7880	0.9998	0.21	0.9519

CIFAR-100. This dataset is similar to the CIFAR-10 dataset in that it has 60,000 images, 100 classes, and 600 images per class. It has 50,000 training set and 10,000 test set like CIFAR-10.

Splitting of the dataset. Table 1 shows the split of our dataset in the experiment.

B. Architecture of the model

Target model. Our model uses a convolutional neural network with two convolutional layers and one hidden layer as the target classifier. We use the popular Relu function for the convolutional layer and Tanh for the hidden layer. The activation function of the output layer is softmax. The settings of the shadow and attack models follow those of Salem et al. [1].

C. Evaluation Metrics

The metrics for our experimental results are as follows.

Classification Accuracy. This metric is measured over both the training and test datasets of the model. The classification accuracy on the test dataset reflects the performance of the classifier on the classification task, and the classification accuracy gap between the training and test data reflects the generalization performance of the model.

Attack Accuracy: Like classification accuracy, this metric is measured with the attack model. It is the classification accuracy of the classifier's member and non-member data on the attack model, and this metric reflects the effectiveness of the member inference attack. We consider this data to be 50% when the membership inference attack is completely ineffective.

5.2 Evaluation with Membership Inference Attack

In this section, we use our defense method to defend against existing membership inference attacks, and to show the effectiveness of our defense, we compare the accuracy of the attacks before and after the defense.

Table 3. Attack 2. Vertically represents the data for training the target model and horizontally represents the data for training the shadow model. (a) is the attack accuracy without the defense method, and (b) is the attack accuracy using our defense method.

(a) Defense

Dataset	$test_{acc}$	*Mnist*	*Cifar*10	*Cifar*100
Mnist	0.9824	0.54085	0.53195	0.5186
Cifar10	0.5587	0.70605	0.84485	0.772
Cifar100	0.2158	0.51865	0.72155	0.9519

(b) No defense

Dataset	$test_{acc}$	*Mnist*	*Cifar*10	*Cifar*100
Mnist	0.9708	0.5053	0.5096	0.5011
Cifar10	0.5551	0.52405	0.53	0.503
Cifar100	0.221	0.4818	0.51735	0.52425

Attack 1: The first membership inference attack method proposed by Salem et al. [1] is used here, where the attacker trains a model, called a shadow model, using the same distribution of data as the target model training data. The output confidence distribution of the shadow model's membership and non-membership data is used to train a binary classifier as an attack model. By applying the output confidence distribution of the given data on the target model, the attacker attack model can determine the affiliation of that data.
Attack 2: The second attack proposed by Salem et al. [1] is similar to the strategy of attack one. The difference is that the distribution of the training

Table 4. Performance comparison of not using defense and using different defense methods for different datasets.

Dataset	*Defense*	$train_{acc}$	$test_{acc}$	adv_1	adv_3
Cifar10	No defense	1.0	0.5714	0.84485	0.852
	Ours	**0.7863**	**0.5655**	**0.5067**	**0.513**
	Dropout	0.888	0.5545	0.5709	0.574
	DP-SGD ($\epsilon = 3.85$)	0.489	0.4408	0.5	0.51
Cifar100	No defense	0.99	0.21	0.9519	0.947
	Ours	**0.4820**	**0.223**	**0.50425**	**0.52**
	Dropout	0.5802	0.2109	0.5669	0.578
	DP-SGD ($\epsilon = 17.32$)	0.1792	0.1178	0.5	0.504
Mnist	No defense	1.0	0.9843	0.5408	0.541
	Ours	**0.9852**	**0.9808**	**0.5053**	**0.5**
	Dropout	0.9987	0.9786	0.5172	0.516
	DP-SGD ($\epsilon = 3.85$)	0.9548	0.9449	0.5023	0.505

data of the shadow model is different from the training data of the target model. That is, the training data of the shadow model is $Mnist$, while the training data of the target model is $Cifar10$ or $Cifar100$.

Attack 3: Based on the attack strategy of Yeom et al. [13] and Song et al. [25] using thresholds for prediction confidence, Song et al. proposed that the adversary infers that the input sample is a member if the adversary's prediction confidence is greater than a predetermined threshold, and a nonmember otherwise.

We use our defense scheme against these three membership inference attack methods to proof the effectiveness of our defense method. In our experiments, for these three attacks we use the same training data and test data to train the target model and the shadow model. Next, we present the defense effectiveness of each of these three attack methods.

First we conducted experiments on attack method 1 using different data. As shown in Table 2, the attack accuracy of $Cifar10$ decreases from 84.485% to 50.67% after applying our defense method, a reduction of about 30% points. $Cifar100$ decreases by about 40% points, and $Mnist$ decreases by about 4% points. This proves the effectiveness of our defense method.

For the $Cifar100$ dataset, its attack accuracy is reduced by a higher percentage point after applying our defense method, which is mainly because the gap of the accuracy of the model trained with $Cifar100$ data is larger. That is, the generalization performance of the model trained with $Cifar100$ is poor, and therefore the behavior of the training data and the test data on the classifier will be more different, so the membership inference attack is successful. After applying our defense method, the gap of the $Cifar100$-trained classifier is reduced from 78.8% to 25.9%, which is a reduction of 52 percentage points. The change in classifier training accuracy is acceptable, which also demonstrates the effectiveness of our defense method in retaining model utility.

For the $Mnist$ dataset. After applying our defense method, its attack accuracy is reduced by about 4% points. Since its dataset has a simple structure and the classifier trained with it already has good generalization performance, the attack accuracy is not high. Therefore, even after applying our defense method, its attack accuracy does not decrease much.

For attack 2, as shown in Table 3, our experiments also show the effectiveness of our defense method. For attack 3, our defense scheme is equally effective. As shown in Tables 4, our defense approach achieves almost the same defense effect on the cifar10 and cifar100 datasets with almost no loss of classifier utility.

5.3 Comparison with Different Defense Methods

In this section we compare different defense methods with our defense method. We compare the attacks of Attack1, Attack2, Attack3 and Attack4 with different data. Due to the specificity of Attack2, we will illustrate it separately from the other three attack methods.

Comparison with Regularization. We compare our defense method with this regularization method, Dropout. For this regularization method, we set the random deactivation rate to 0.5. dropout is a simple technique provided by hinton et al. [24]. The method is to dropout the neurons in the network with probability p (random deactivation rate) in each iteration of the training neural network.

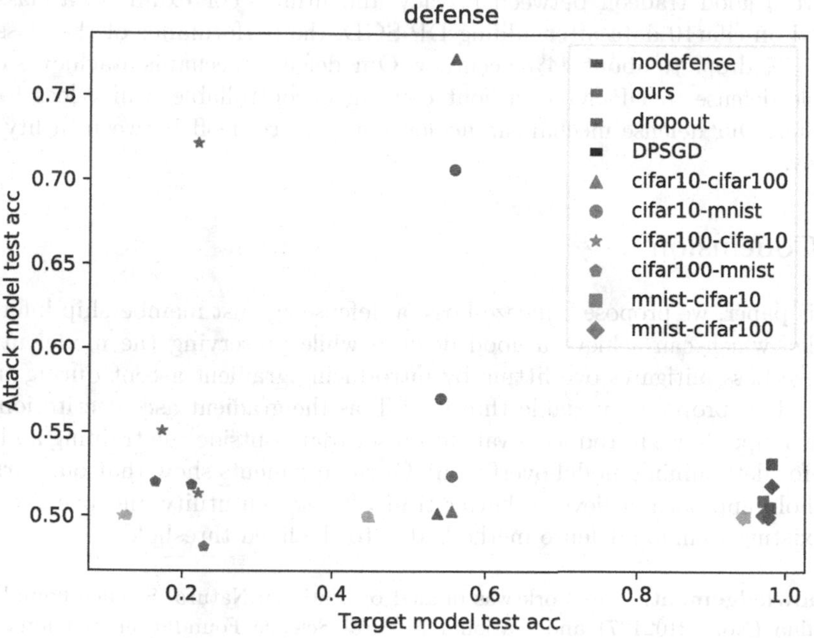

Fig. 2. The results obtained with different defense methods for different datasets of Attack2. The X-axis indicates the testing accuracy of the target model and the Y-axis indicates the training accuracy of the attack model. Different colors indicate different defense methods, and different shapes indicate different datasets. For example, $cifar10 - cifar100$ indicates that $cifar10$ trains the target model and $cifar100$ trains the shadow model.

The experimental results of applying the dropout defense in attacks 1 and 3 are shown in Table 4, and the results of attack 2 are shown in Fig. 2. From the data in the table, it can be seen that the gap between the training accuracy and testing accuracy of the classifier decreases after applying dropout. Although dropout reduces the risk of membership inference attacks, its attack accuracy is still high. For example, the attack accuracy of the classifier trained by cifar10 is still around 57% for attacks 1 and 3 after adding dropout. And our defenses can reduce the accuracy of these three attacks to about 51%. This proves that our defenses are better than this regularization technique.

Comparison with DP-SGD. Differential privacy (DP) is a protection mechanism that keeps publicly visible information from revealing personal privacy through the use of random noise. Based on differential privacy, Abadi et al. [9]

proposed a general training strategy DP-SGD. For cifar10 and mnist we use a privacy budget of $\epsilon = 3.85$ and for cifar100 we use $\epsilon = 17.32$.

The experimental results of DP-SGD are shown in Table 4 and Fig. 2. From the experimental results, we can see that DP-SGD can reduce the accuracy rate of the member inference attack to about 50%. However, this defense does not achieve a good tradeoff between privacy and utility. For example, a classifier trained on cifar10 data after adding DP-SGD, the performance of the classifier from 57% drops to about 44% accuracy. Our defense mechanism achieves comparable defense to DP-SGD without causing uncontrollable utility loss to the classifier. Our defense mechanism achieves a good tradeoff between utility and privacy.

6 Conclusion

In this paper, we propose Squeeze-Loss, a defense against membership inference attacks, which can achieve a good defense while preserving the model utility. Squeeze-Loss mitigates overfitting by introducing gradient ascent during training, and we propose a variable threshold T as the gradient ascent criterion, for which T update we introduce a validation set (data outside the training and test sets) for determining model overfitting. Our experiments show that our variable threshold approach achieves a better tradeoff between utility and privacy than the existing common defense methods due to the fixed threshold.

Acknowledgement. This work was funded by National Natural Science Foundation of China (No. 62102107) and National Natural Science Foundation of China (No. 62072132).

References

1. Salem, A., Zhang, Y., Humbert, M., Berrang, P., Fritz, M., Backes, M.: ML-Leaks: model and data independent membership inference attacks and defenses on machine learning models. arXiv preprint arXiv:1806.01246 (2018)
2. He, K., Zhang, X., Ren, S., Sun, J.: Delving deep into rectifiers: surpassing human-level performance on ImageNet classification. In: Proceedings of the IEEE International Conference on Computer Vision, pp. 1026–1034 (2015)
3. Deng, L., Hinton, G., Kingsbury, B.: New types of deep neural network learning for speech recognition and related applications: an overview. In: 2013 IEEE International Conference on Acoustics, Speech and Signal Processing, pp. 8599–8603. IEEE (2013)
4. Mikolov, T., Karafiat, M., Burget, L., Cernock'y, J., Khudanpur, S.: Recurrent neural network based language model. In: Interspeech, Makuhari, vol. 2, no. 3, pp. 1045–1048 (2010)
5. Jia, J., Salem, A., Backes, M., Zhang, Y., Gong, N.Z.: MemGuard: defending against black-box membership inference attacks via adversarial examples. In: Proceedings of the 2019 ACM SIGSAC Conference on Computer and Communications Security, pp. 259–274 (2019)

6. Zhang, C., Bengio, S., Hardt, M., Recht, B., Vinyals, O.: Understanding deep learning (still) requires rethinking generalization. Commun. ACM **64**(3), 107–115 (2021)
7. Srivastava, N., Hinton, G., Krizhevsky, A., Sutskever, I., Salakhutdinov, R.: Dropout: a simple way to prevent neural networks from overfitting. J. Mach. Learn. Res. **15**(1), 1929–1958 (2014)
8. Labach, A., Salehinejad, H., Valaee, S.: Survey of dropout methods for deep neural networks. arXiv preprint arXiv:1904.13310 (2019)
9. Abadi, M., et al.: Deep learning with differential privacy. In: Proceedings of the 2016 ACM SIGSAC Conference on Computer and Communications Security, pp. 308–318 (2016)
10. Dwork, C.: Differential privacy: a survey of results. In: Agrawal, M., Du, D., Duan, Z., Li, A. (eds.) TAMC 2008. LNCS, vol. 4978, pp. 1–19. Springer, Heidelberg (2008). https://doi.org/10.1007/978-3-540-79228-4_1
11. Tabassi, E., Burns, K.J., Hadjimichael, M., Molina-Markham, A.D., Sexton, J.T.: A taxonomy and terminology of adversarial machine learning. NIST IR, pp. 1–29 (2019)
12. Shokri, R., Stronati, M., Song, C., Shmatikov, V.: Membership inference attacks against machine learning models. In: 2017 IEEE Symposium on Security and Privacy (SP), pp. 3–18. IEEE (2017)
13. Yeom, S., Giacomelli, I., Fredrikson, M., Jha, S.: Privacy risk in machine learning: analyzing the connection to overfitting. In: 2018 IEEE 31st Computer Security Foundations Symposium (CSF), pp. 268–282. IEEE (2018)
14. Raskutti, G., Wainwright, M.J., Yu, B.: Early stopping and nonparametric regression: an optimal data-dependent stopping rule. J. Mach. Learn. Res. **15**(1), 335–366 (2014)
15. Hu, H., Salcic, Z., Sun, L., Dobbie, G., Yu, P.S., Zhang, X.: Membership inference attacks on machine learning: a survey. ACM Comput. Surv. (CSUR) (2021)
16. Kaya, Y., Dumitras, T.: When does data augmentation help with membership inference attacks? In: International Conference on Machine Learning, pp. 5345–5355. PMLR (2021)
17. Dwork, C., McSherry, F., Nissim, K., Smith, A.: Calibrating noise to sensitivity in private data analysis. In: Halevi, S., Rabin, T. (eds.) TCC 2006. LNCS, vol. 3876, pp. 265–284. Springer, Heidelberg (2006). https://doi.org/10.1007/11681878_14
18. Jayaraman, B., Evans, D.: Evaluating differentially private machine learning in practice. In: 28th USENIX Security Symposium (USENIX Security 2019), pp. 1895–1912 (2019)
19. Chen, D., Yu, N., Fritz, M.: RelaxLoss: defending membership inference attacks without losing utility. In: International Conference on Learning Representations (2021)
20. Bottou, L.: Large-scale machine learning with stochastic gradient descent. In: Lechevallier, Y., Saporta, G. (eds.) Proceedings of COMPSTAT 2010, pp. 177–186. Springer, Heidelberg (2010). https://doi.org/10.1007/978-3-7908-2604-3_16
21. Sutskever, I., Martens, J., Dahl, G., Hinton, G.: On the importance of initialization and momentum in deep learning. In: International Conference on Machine Learning, pp. 1139–1147. PMLR (2013)
22. Luo, L., Xiong, Y., Liu, Y., Sun, X.: Adaptive gradient methods with dynamic bound of learning rate. arXiv preprint arXiv:1902.09843 (2019)
23. Kingma, D.P., Ba, J.: Adam: a method for stochastic optimization. arXiv preprint arXiv:1412.6980 (2014)

24. Hinton, G., Srivastava, N., Swersky, K.: Neural networks for machine learning lecture 6a overview of mini-batch gradient descent. Cited on **14**(8), 2 (2012)
25. Song, L., Mittal, P.: Systematic evaluation of privacy risks of machine learning models. In: 30th USENIX Security Symposium (USENIX Security 2021), pp. 2615–2632 (2021)
26. Reddy, D.R.: Speech recognition by machine: a review. Proc. IEEE **64**(4), 501–531 (1976)
27. Dosovitskiy, A., et al.: An image is worth 16 × 16 words: transformers for image recognition at scale. arXiv preprint arXiv:2010.11929 (2020)
28. Zhao, W., Chellappa, R., Phillips, P.J., Rosenfeld, A.: Face recognition: a literature survey. ACM Comput. Surv. (CSUR) **35**(4), 399–458 (2003)
29. He, X., Yan, S., Hu, Y., Niyogi, P., Zhang, H.-J.: Face recognition using laplacianfaces. IEEE Trans. Pattern Anal. Mach. Intell. **27**(3), 328–340 (2005)
30. Nadkarni, P.M., Ohno-Machado, L., Chapman, W.W.: Natural language processing: an introduction. J. Am. Med. Inform. Assoc. **18**(5), 544–551 (2011)
31. Ai, S., Hong, S., Zheng, X., Wang, Y., Liu, X.: CSRT rumor spreading model based on complex network. Int. J. Intell. Syst. **36**(5), 1903–1913 (2021)
32. Yan, H., Chen, M., Hu, L., Jia, C.: Secure video retrieval using image query on an untrusted cloud. Appl. Soft Comput. **97**, 106782 (2020)
33. Chen, C., Huang, T.: Camdar-adv: generating adversarial patches on 3D object. Int. J. Intell. Syst. **36**(3), 1441–1453 (2021)
34. Ren, H., Huang, T., Yan, H.: Adversarial examples: attacks and defenses in the physical world. Int. J. Mach. Learn. Cybern. **12**(11), 3325–3336 (2021). https://doi.org/10.1007/s13042-020-01242-z
35. Mo, K., Huang, T., Xiang, X.: Querying little is enough: model inversion attack via latent information. In: Chen, X., Yan, H., Yan, Q., Zhang, X. (eds.) ML4CS 2020. LNCS, vol. 12487, pp. 583–591. Springer, Cham (2020). https://doi.org/10.1007/978-3-030-62460-6_52
36. Jiang, N., Jie, W., Li, J., Liu, X., Jin, D.: GATrust: a multi-aspect graph attention network model for trust assessment in OSNs. IEEE Trans. Knowl. Data Eng. (2022)
37. Li, J., Hu, X., Xiong, P., Zhou, W., et al.: The dynamic privacy-preserving mechanisms for online dynamic social networks. IEEE Trans. Knowl. Data Eng. (2020)
38. Li, J., et al.: Efficient and secure outsourcing of differentially private data publishing with multiple evaluators. IEEE Trans. Dependable Secure Comput. (2020)
39. Li, T., Li, J., Chen, X., Liu, Z., Lou, W., Hou, Y.T.: NPMML: a framework for non-interactive privacy-preserving multi-party machine learning. IEEE Trans. Dependable Secure Comput. **18**(6), 2969–2982 (2020)
40. Mo, K., Tang, W., Li, J., Yuan, X.: Attacking deep reinforcement learning with decoupled adversarial policy. IEEE Trans. Dependable Secure Comput. (2022)

Blockchain and its Applications

Improved WAVE Signature and Apply to Post-quantum Blockchain

Zhuoran Zhang[1,2], Haibo Tian[1,2], and Fangguo Zhang[1,2](✉)

[1] School of Computer Science and Engineering, Sun Yat-sen University, Guangzhou 510006, China
isszhfg@mail.sysu.edu.cn

[2] Guangdong Key Laboratory of Information Security Technology, Guangzhou 510006, China

Abstract. Blockchain has raised public concern due to its public, distributed, and decentration characteristics. This technique has been applied not only in the financial area, but also in e-government, e-health and many other digital systems. However, the security of the most widely used blockchain technique was built on the elliptic curve cryptography, which will be insecure in the will-coming quantum computing era. In this paper, we propose to use a quantum-resisted digital signature scheme from coding theory instead of ECDSA. More precisely, we modified the well-known WAVE signature scheme from $(U, U+V)$ code into $(U, U+V, U+V+W)$ code, and achieve better performance. With this post-quantum signature scheme, we build a post-quantum blockchain system.

Keywords: Blockchain · Post-quantum · Code-based cryptography

1 Introduction

Blockchain was firstly proposed by [17] and it is the basic technique of the Bitcoin system. Because of its public, distributed, and decentration characteristics, blockchain technology has shown promising application prospects. Since blockchain is one of the core technology in the financial technology industry, users are very concerned about its security.

In the design of blockchain, many cryptographic techniques are used to protect the integrity and privacy of data, especially to authenticate transactions. For example, hash functions allow for generating digital signatures and for linking the blocks of a blockchain. Another significant cryptographic tool used in the blockchain is the digital signature scheme. Digital signature schemes allow a public verification of one information signed by a specific user. When using blockchain, the user will generate a pair of public key and secret key. The public key (or its hash value) will be regarded as a pseudonym and serves as the user's address. The user will sign on a transaction with his secret key, and only when this signature passed the verification, this transaction will be counted and recorded.

X. Chen et al. (Eds.): SocialSec 2022, CCIS 1663, pp. 309–323, 2022.
https://doi.org/10.1007/978-981-19-7242-3_20

Digital signature schemes also play an important role in the modern information society. However, many signature schemes in use today, such as ECDSA which is used in the Bitcoin system, are facing the threat of quantum computing. The reason is that the security of ECDSA is based on the intractability of certain mathematical problems, say discrete logarithms over elliptic curves for ECDSA, and these problems can be efficiently solved by quantum algorithms. Therefore, how to build signature schemes that can resist attacks from quantum computers raises the researcher's concern.

There are several kinds of post-quantum cryptography, and the principal available techniques are code-based cryptography, lattice-based cryptography, multivariate cryptography, hash-based cryptography, etc. There has several works suggest build post-quantum blockchain, namely from lattice [16,25], multivariate [21], and hash [6]. Among them, the proposal from multivariate-based signature Rainbow [11] is unsafe now since the signature has been broken [5]. In order to get a long-term security promise blockchain, it is necessary to select a signature scheme whose security is truly trustworthy.

The code-based McEliece system [15], whose security relies on the hardness of decoding a random linear code, is one of the best-known public-key cryptosystems, and has already resisted 40 years of cryptanalysis since its proposition in 1978. Niederreiter [18] gave a variant of the McEliece system, and a significant amount of research went into analyzing and improving them. Their security is based on the conjectured intractability of problems in coding theory, such as the syndrome decoding problem, which has been proven to be NP-complete by Berlekamp, McEliece, and van Tilborg [4].

Unlike the rapid development of code-based public-key encryption schemes, since the McEliece encryption scheme is not invertible, how to construct signature schemes based on coding theory has been an open problem for a long time. During the last two decades of years, several attempts were made to propose code-based signature schemes. The first trial was done by Wang [23], then Harn *et al.* [13] and Alabbadi *et al.* [2]. However, these constructions are all broken [1,24]. Another attempt to construct code-based signature schemes is turning the Stern zero-knowledge authentication scheme [22] into a signature scheme by the Fiat-Shamir heuristic. The third way to build code-based signature schemes was presented by [14]. However, the KKS scheme [14] and its variants [3,12], although performing well on signing speed, are considered to be one-time signature schemes.

In 2001, Courtois, Finiasz, and Sendrier [7] (CFS) showed how to achieve a code-based signature scheme whose security is based on the syndrome decoding problem. In [8], Dallot proposed a modified CFS (mCFS) and gave a security proof in the random oracle model (ROM). In 2019, Debris-Alazard et al. presented a signature scheme called WAVE [9], which can also be considered as a variant of CFS scheme. They use $(U, U+V)$ code instead of Goppa code, and choose large weight error rather than small weight error as a part of the signature. These changes bring a better performance than the original CFS signature. Roughly speaking, the WAVE signature scheme has a very small signature size (about 2 KB for 128 security level), and tolerable running time (hundreds of milliseconds).

Our Contributions: We show a post-quantum blockchain from coding theory. The most significant contribution is to transform the WAVE signature scheme into a more efficient version such that it is adapted for blockchain.

1. We substitute the $(U, U+V)$ code used in the WAVE signature with the $(U, U+V, U+W)$ code, thus the signing step can be departed into three decode sub-routines and achieves better performance.
2. We present how to execute the decode sub-routine in the WAVE scheme by solving linear systems.
3. We proved that distinguishing an $[n, k]$ $(U, U+V, U+W)$ code from a random linear code is not easier than distinguishing an $[2/3n, k]$ $(U, U+V)$ code from a random one. Thus the security of the new signature is the same as the original WAVE scheme.
4. We describe how to apply our signature scheme to constructing a post-quantum blockchain.

Organization: The rest of the paper is organized as follows. In Sect. 2, we review some preliminaries that will be used later. Section 3 shows our improved WAVE signature scheme and the detailed decoding sub-routine. In Sect. 4, we present the security of the improved signature scheme. Section 5 shows the post-quantum blockchain established from our improved signature scheme. Lastly, Sect. 6 concludes this paper.

2 Preliminaries

In this section, we present the notions of blockchain and coding theory that are prerequisite for the following chapters.

2.1 Blockchain

The concept of blockchain has evolved significantly since its original definition for Bitcoin [17]. The most common definition of blockchain is considered as a public ledger that stores data that are shared among multiple entities that do not necessarily trust each other. The structure of a blockchain is shown in Fig. 1.

Every transaction on the blockchain is verified and stored by following a consensus protocol. The main features of this technique include

- Decentralization. If one node of the blockchain is attacked or shut down, its information keeps on being available from the other blockchain nodes.
- Data privacy and integrity. Blockchain uses public-key cryptography and hash functions for providing data privacy, integrity, and authentication.
- Data immutability. Once a transaction is stored on the blockchain, it is not possible to make further modifications to it.

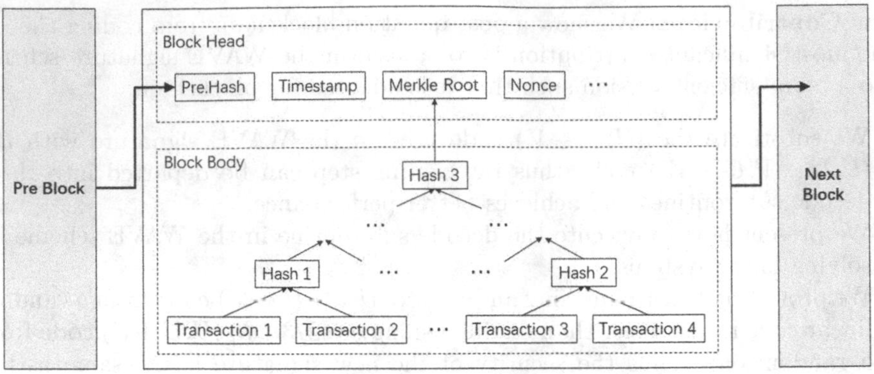

Fig. 1. The structure of blockchain

An important concept for blockchain is the nodes. Blockchain nodes can be classified into three types. The regular blockchain nodes only interact with the blockchain, and the full nodes have a copy of the blockchain and contribute to it by validating transactions. The blockchain miner is the third type of node. Their contribution is essential during blockchain transaction validations: to carry out the validation, they perform certain actions following a consensus protocol. There are many consensus protocols. And the most popular protocols are Proof-of-Work (PoW), Byzantine Fault Tolerance (BFT) methods, and Proof-of-Stake (PoS).

2.2 Linear Codes and Code-Based Signature Schemes

An $[n, k]_q$ linear error-correcting code $\mathcal{C}$ is a linear subspace of a vector space $\mathbb{F}_q^n$, where $\mathbb{F}_q$ denotes the finite field of q elements, and k denotes the dimension of the subspace. The generator matrix for a linear code is a $k \times n$ matrix with rank k which defines a linear mapping from $\mathbb{F}_q^k$ (called the message space) to $\mathbb{F}_q^n$. Namely, the code $\mathcal{C}$ is

$$\mathcal{C} = \mathcal{C}(\mathbf{G}) = \{\mathbf{xG} \mid \mathbf{x} \in \mathbb{F}_q^k\}.$$

If $\mathcal{C}$ is the kernel of a matrix $\mathbf{H} \in \mathbb{F}_q^{(n-k)\times k}$, we call $\mathbf{H}$ a parity check matrix of $\mathcal{C}$, i.e.

$$\mathcal{C} = \mathcal{C}^{\perp}(\mathbf{H}) = \mathrm{Ker}(\mathbf{H}) = \{\mathbf{y} \in \mathbb{F}_q^n | \mathbf{Hy} = \mathbf{0}\}$$

We call a vector in $\mathcal{C}$ a codeword.

Given a codeword $\mathbf{c} = (c_1, c_2, \ldots, c_n) \in \mathbb{F}_q^n$, its Hamming weight $\mathrm{wt}(\mathbf{c})$ is defined to be the number of non-zero coordinates, i.e. $\mathrm{wt}(\mathbf{c}) = |\{i \mid c_i \neq 0, 1 \leq i \leq n\}|$. The distance of two codewords $\mathbf{c}_1, \mathbf{c}_2$, denoted by $d(\mathbf{c}_1, \mathbf{c}_2)$ counts the number of coordinates in which they differ. The minimum distance $d(\mathcal{C})$ of code $\mathcal{C}$ is the minimal value of the distance between any two different codewords. By the linearity of $\mathcal{C}$, we know that $d(\mathcal{C})$ is determined by the minimum Hamming weight among all non-zero codewords in $\mathcal{C}$, i.e.

$$d(\mathcal{C}) = \min\{\text{wt}(\mathbf{c}) \mid \mathbf{c} \in \mathcal{C} \setminus \{0\}\}.$$

If a linear $[n,k]_q$ code has d as the minimum distance, then $\mathcal{C}$ is called a $[n,k,d]_q$ linear code.

If $\mathbf{c}$ is a codeword and $\mathbf{c}+\mathbf{e}$ is the received word, then we call $\mathbf{e}$ the error vector and $\{i|e_i \neq 0\}$ the set of error positions and $\text{wt}(\mathbf{e})$ is the number of errors of the received word. If $\mathbf{r}$ is the received word and the distance from $\mathbf{r}$ to the code $\mathcal{C}$ is t', then there exists a codeword $\mathbf{c}'$ and an error vector $\mathbf{e}'$ such that $\mathbf{r} = \mathbf{c}' + \mathbf{e}'$ and $\text{wt}(\mathbf{e}') = t'$. If the number of errors is at most $(d-1)/2$, then it is sure that $\mathbf{c} = \mathbf{c}'$ and $\mathbf{e} = \mathbf{e}'$. In other words, the nearest codeword to $\mathbf{r}$ is unique when $\mathbf{r}$ has distance at most $(d-1)/2$ to $\mathcal{C}$.

The CFS signature scheme adapted the full domain hash approach to Niederreiter's encryption scheme. The original CFS signature scheme was considered to be impractical due to its inefficient sign step. In order to get a decodable syndrome hash value, the CFS sign algorithm has to try $t!$ random paddings on average, where t is the design distance of the Goppa code. The reason is that for a given $[n,k,2t]$ binary Goppa code, there are 2^{n-k} syndromes and only $\binom{n}{t}2^t$ are decodable. As a consequence, this gap leads to a $t!$ trail in the signing algorithm. Although the CFS signature scheme does not perform well in running time, its signature size is really small. The WAVE signature scheme retains the advantage of the CFS scheme, and achieves a better performance. In this signature scheme, a linear code called $(U, U+V)$ code is used. If the generator matrix of code U is $\mathbf{G}_u$ and the generator matrix of code V is $\mathbf{G}_v$, then the generator matrix of a $(U, U+V)$ code is defined as

$$\begin{bmatrix} \mathbf{G}_u & \mathbf{G}_u \\ \mathbf{0} & \mathbf{G}_v \end{bmatrix}.$$

The WAVE signature scheme also chooses to use a large weight error instead of a small weight error as the signature. This modification leads to a less rejection rate and thus a better performance. Their large weight syndrome decoding algorithm is adjusted from the information set decoding algorithm [19].

The WAVE Signature Scheme

- **Setup:** Input the security level λ, and output the public parameters $params = (n,k,w,k_u,k_v)$ and a hash function $\mathsf{Hash}: \{0,1\}^* \to \mathbb{F}_3^{n-k}$. Here n is an odd integer, $k = k_u + k_v < n$, $w < n$ are integers.
- **KeyGen:** Input the pubic parameters, and output the key pair (sk, pk).
  1. Randomly choose two full rank matrix $\mathbf{H}_u \in \mathbb{F}_3^{(n/2-k_u)\times n/2}$ and $\mathbf{H}_v \in \mathbb{F}_3^{(n/2-k_v)\times n/2}$;
  2. Randomly choose an inverse matrix $\mathbf{S} \in \text{GL}(k,3)$ and an n-order permutation matrix $\mathbf{P}$;
  3. Set

$$\mathbf{H}_{sk} = \begin{bmatrix} \mathbf{H}_u & \mathbf{0} \\ -\mathbf{H}_v & \mathbf{H}_v \end{bmatrix};$$

4. Set $\mathbf{H}_{pk} = \mathbf{S}\mathbf{H}_{sk}\mathbf{P}$;
5. $sk = (\mathbf{H}_{sk}, \mathbf{S}, \mathbf{P})$, $pk = \mathbf{H}_{pk}$.

- **Sign:** Input the secret key $sk = (\mathbf{H}_{sk}, \mathbf{S}, \mathbf{P})$ and a message m, and output the signature σ.
  1. $r \leftarrow_\$ \{0,1\}^\lambda$;
  2. $\mathbf{s} = \mathsf{Hash}(m||r)$;
  3. $\mathbf{e} = \mathsf{Decode}(\mathbf{S}^{-1}\mathbf{s})$;
  4. $\sigma = (\mathbf{e}\mathbf{P}, r) := (\tilde{\mathbf{e}}, r)$.
- **Vrfy:** Input the public key $pk = \mathbf{H}_{pk}$ and a signature σ, and output a bit $b \in \{0,1\}$.
  1. Check whether $\mathrm{wt}(\tilde{\mathbf{e}}) = w$. If not, return $b = 0$;
  2. Check whether $\mathbf{H}_{pk}\tilde{\mathbf{e}}^T = \mathsf{Hash}(m||r)$. If true, return $b = 1$, else return $b = 0$.

Based on the decoding one out of many problem, the following theorem is also proved under random oracle model (ROM) in [9].

Theorem 1 (Theorem 2, [9]). *The WAVE signature is secure under existential unforgeability under an adaptive chosen message attack (EUF-CMA).*

More details about the WAVE signature and its security analysis please refer to [9].

3 The Improved Wave Signature

In this section, we will propose how to modify the WAVE signature to achieve a better performance.

3.1 Our Signature Scheme

We change the WAVE signature from using $(U, U+V)$ code to $(U, U+V, U+W)$ code. The scheme is proposed as follows:

- **Setup:** Input the security level λ, and output the public parameters $params = (n, k, w, k_u, k_v)$ and a hash function $\mathsf{Hash} : \{0,1\}^* \rightarrow \mathbb{F}_3^{n-k}$. Here $n = 0 \mod 3$, $k = k_u + k_v < n$, $w < n$ are integers.
- **KeyGen:** Input the pubic parameters, and output the key pair (sk, pk).
  1. Randomly choose three full rank matrix $\mathbf{H}_u \in \mathbb{F}_3^{(n/3-k_u)\times n/3}$, $\mathbf{H}_v \in \mathbb{F}_3^{(n/3-k_v)\times n/3}$ and $\mathbf{H}_w \in \mathbb{F}_3^{(n/3-k_v)\times n/3}$;
  2. Randomly choose an inverse matrix $\mathbf{S} \in \mathrm{GL}(k, 3)$ and an n-order permutation matrix $\mathbf{P}$;
  3. Set

$$\mathbf{H}_{sk} = \begin{bmatrix} \mathbf{H}_u & \mathbf{0} & \mathbf{0} \\ -\mathbf{H}_v & \mathbf{H}_v & \mathbf{0} \\ -\mathbf{H}_w & \mathbf{0} & \mathbf{H}_w \end{bmatrix};$$

4. Set $\mathbf{H}_{pk} = \mathbf{S}\mathbf{H}_{sk}\mathbf{P}$;
5. $sk = (\mathbf{H}_{sk}, \mathbf{S}, \mathbf{P})$, $pk = \mathbf{H}_{pk}$.

- **Sign:** Input the secret key $sk = (\mathbf{H}_{sk}, \mathbf{S}, \mathbf{P})$ and a message m, and output the signature σ.
  1. $r \leftarrow_{\$} \{0,1\}^{\lambda}$;
  2. $\mathbf{s} = \mathsf{Hash}(m\|r)$;
  3. $\mathbf{e} = \text{DecodeUVW}(\mathbf{H}_{sk}, \mathbf{S}^{-1}\mathbf{s})$;
  4. $\sigma = (\mathbf{eP}, r) := (\tilde{\mathbf{e}}, r)$.
- **Vrfy:** Input the public key $pk = \mathbf{H}_{pk}$ and a signature σ, and output a bit $b \in \{0,1\}$.
  1. Check whether $\text{wt}(\tilde{\mathbf{e}}) = w$. If not, return $b = 0$;
  2. Check whether $\mathbf{H}_{pk}\tilde{\mathbf{e}}^T = \mathsf{Hash}(m\|r)$. If true, return $b = 1$, else return $b = 0$.

Completeness. If $\sigma = (\tilde{\mathbf{e}}, r)$ is a signature generated by a honest user with secret key sk, then we have

$$\mathbf{H}_{pk}\tilde{\mathbf{e}}^T = (\mathbf{SHP})(\tilde{\mathbf{e}}\mathbf{P})^T = \mathbf{SH}(\mathbf{PP}^T)\tilde{\mathbf{e}}^T) = \mathbf{S}(\mathbf{H}\tilde{\mathbf{e}}^T) = \mathbf{S}(\mathbf{S}^{-1}\mathbf{s}) = \mathbf{s} = \mathsf{Hash}(m\|r).$$

Namely, when input an honest signature and corresponding public key into the **Vrfy** algorithm, it will definitely output $b = 1$ to indicate this is a legal signature.

3.2 The Decoding Sub-routine

Now we describe how the decoding sub-routine DecodeUVW works. In the original WAVE signature scheme, the authors tweak the information set decoding algorithm for reaching a large weight decoder. In fact, we find it is more convenient to explain this process by solving the linear system. In the following part, we will show how to get a such large weight error vector.

For a given syndrome $\mathbf{s} = [\mathbf{s}_1, \mathbf{s}_2, \mathbf{s}_3]$, we have

$$\mathbf{H}_{sk}\mathbf{e}^T = \begin{bmatrix} \mathbf{H}_u & \mathbf{0} & \mathbf{0} \\ -\mathbf{H}_v & \mathbf{H}_v & \mathbf{0} \\ -\mathbf{H}_w & \mathbf{0} & \mathbf{H}_w \end{bmatrix} \begin{bmatrix} \mathbf{e}_1^T \\ \mathbf{e}_2^T \\ \mathbf{e}_3^T \end{bmatrix} = \begin{bmatrix} \mathbf{H}_u\mathbf{e}_1^T \\ \mathbf{H}_v(\mathbf{e}_2 - \mathbf{e}_1)^T \\ \mathbf{H}_w(\mathbf{e}_3 - \mathbf{e}_1)^T \end{bmatrix} = \begin{bmatrix} \mathbf{s}_1^T \\ \mathbf{s}_2^T \\ \mathbf{s}_3^T \end{bmatrix}.$$

That is to say, we can depart the syndrome $\mathbf{s}$ into three parts and then solve the decoding problem respectively. Namely, if we have

$$\begin{cases} \mathbf{H}_u\mathbf{e}_u^T = \mathbf{s}_1, \\ \mathbf{H}_v\mathbf{e}_v^T = \mathbf{s}_2, \\ \mathbf{H}_w\mathbf{e}_w^T = \mathbf{s}_3, \end{cases}$$

then

$$\mathbf{H}_{sk}[\mathbf{e}_u, \mathbf{e}_u + \mathbf{e}_v, \mathbf{e}_u + \mathbf{e}_w]^T = \mathbf{s}^T.$$

The main signature build block is DecodeUVW in Algorithm 1.

Algorithm 1: DecodeUVW($\mathbf{H}, \mathbf{s}$)

Input: params $= (n, k, w, k_u, k_v, k_w), \mathbf{H}_u, \mathbf{H}_v, \mathbf{H}_w, \mathbf{s}$.
Output: $\mathbf{e} \in \mathbb{F}_3^n$ such that $\mathbf{He}^T = \mathbf{s}$.

$\mathbf{e}_v \leftarrow$ DecodeV$(\mathbf{H}_v, \mathbf{s}_v)$;
repeat
  $\mathbf{e}_u =$ DecodeU$(\mathbf{H}_u, \mathbf{s}_u, \mathbf{e}_v, \mathbf{e}_w)$;
  $\mathbf{e}_w \leftarrow$ DecodeW$(\mathbf{H}_w, \mathbf{s}_w)$;
  $\mathbf{e} = (\mathbf{e}_u, \mathbf{e}_u + \mathbf{e}_v, \mathbf{e}_u + \mathbf{e}_w)$;
until wt$(\mathbf{e}) = w$;
Return $\mathbf{e}$;

This decoder has three sub-routines, namely DecodeV, DecodeU, and DecodeW. Without the matrices $\mathbf{H}_u, \mathbf{H}_v$ and $\mathbf{H}_w$ as trapdoor, anyone can use $\mathbf{H}_{pk}$ to decode a syndrome into an error vector whose weight between $2/3(n-k)$ and $k + 2/3(n-k)$. That is to say, we have to ensure the output vector of DecodeUVW has a weight larger than $k + 2/3(n-k)$. The main idea of our DecodeUVW algorithm is inspired by [9], and we illustrate it in Fig. 2.

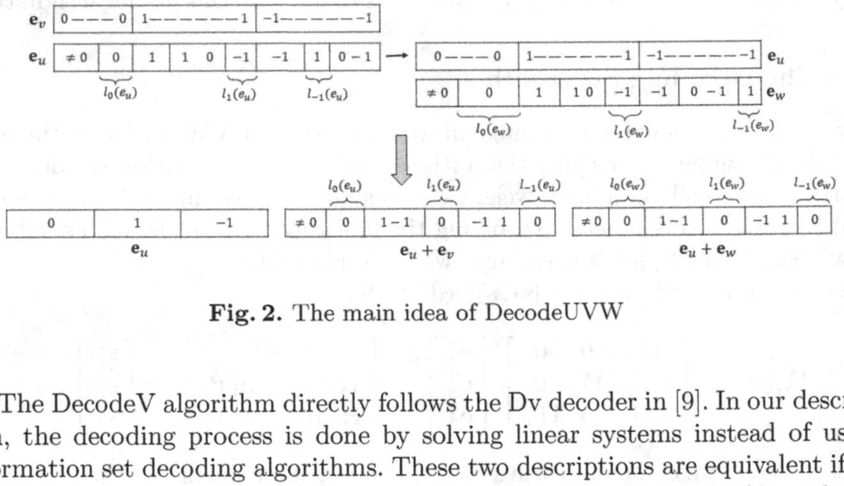

Fig. 2. The main idea of DecodeUVW

The DecodeV algorithm directly follows the Dv decoder in [9]. In our description, the decoding process is done by solving linear systems instead of using information set decoding algorithms. These two descriptions are equivalent if we view the information set as the set of free variables. We show it in Algorithm 2.

The main idea of the design of DecodeU is trying to keep $\mathbf{e}_u + \mathbf{e}_v$ has as many non-zero coordinates as possible with the knowledge of $\mathbf{e}_v$. We present it in Algorithm 3.

Then we decode $\mathbf{e}_w$ with the knowledge of $\mathbf{e}_u$. As above, we hope the output $\mathbf{e}_w$ satisfies wt$(\mathbf{e}_u + \mathbf{e}_w) \geq$ wt$(\mathbf{e}_u)$. In fact, this procedure can be viewed as an inverse of decode $\mathbf{e}_u$ from $\mathbf{e}_v$.

Without the secret key $\mathbf{H}_u, \mathbf{H}_v, \mathbf{H}_w$, anyone can get an error vector $\mathbf{e}'$ with its weight wt$(\mathbf{e}') \in [2/3(n-k); k + 2/3(n-k)]$ by solving $\mathbf{H}_{pk}\mathbf{e}^T = \mathbf{s}$. However, with the secret trapdoor, we can get an error vector $\mathbf{e}$ whose weight is about

Algorithm 2: DecodeV($\mathbf{H}_v, \mathbf{s}_2$)

Input: params $= (n, k_v), \mathbf{H}_v, \mathbf{s}_2$.
Output: $\mathbf{e}_v \in \mathbb{F}_3^{n/3}$ such that $\mathbf{H}_v \mathbf{e}_v^T = \mathbf{s}_2$.

Solve $\mathbf{H}_v \mathbf{e}_v^T = \mathbf{s}_2$ and get its solution space;
Randomly choose a set of variables as the free variables, and denote them as $\mathcal{I} = \{e_{i_1}, e_{i_2}, \dots, e_{i_{k_v}}\}$;
Select $t \leftarrow \mathcal{D}_v$, where $\mathcal{D}_v$ is a distribution over $[0; k_v]$ as in [9];
Evaluate $\mathbf{e}_v = (e_1, e_2, \dots, e_{n/3})$ by randomly choose $\{e_{i_1}, e_{i_2}, \dots, e_{i_{k_v}}\}$ such that there are t non-zero elements in $\mathcal{I}$;
$t_1 = |\{i : \mathbf{e}_v = (e_1, e_2, \dots, e_{n/3}), e_i = 1\}|$ and $t_2 = |\{i : \mathbf{e}_v = (e_1, e_2, \dots, e_{n/3}), e_i = 2\}|$;
Return $\mathbf{e}_v$;

Algorithm 3: DecodeU($\mathbf{H}, \mathbf{s}$)

Input: params $= (n, k, k_u), \mathbf{H}_u, \mathbf{s}_1, \mathbf{e}_v$.
Output: $\mathbf{e}_u \in \mathbb{F}_3^{n/3}$ such that $\mathbf{H}_u \mathbf{e}_u^T = \mathbf{s}_1$.

Solve $\mathbf{H}_u \mathbf{e}_u^T = \mathbf{s}_1$ and get its solution space;
repeat
    Select $j_1, j_2 \leftarrow \mathcal{D}_u$, where $\mathcal{D}_u$ is a distribution over $[0; t_1] \times [0; t_2]$ and $j_1 + j_2 \leq k_u$ as in [9];
    Randomly choose a set of variables as the free variables, and denote them as $\mathcal{I} = \{e_{i_1}, e_{i_2}, \dots, e_{i_{k_u}}\}$;
    Evaluate $\mathbf{e}_u = (e_1, e_2, \dots, e_{n/3})$ by randomly choose $\{e_{i_1}, e_{i_2}, \dots, e_{i_{k_u}}\}$ such that there are j_1 elements in $\mathcal{I}$ are equal to 1 and j_2 elements in $\mathcal{I}$ are equal to 2;
    $m_1 = |\{i : \mathbf{e}_u = (e_1, e_2, \dots, e_{n/3}), e_i = 1\}|$ and $m_2 = |\{i : \mathbf{e}_u = (e_1, e_2, \dots, e_{n/3}), e_i = 2\}|$;
until wt$(\mathbf{e}_u + \mathbf{e}_v) \geq w/3$;
Return $\mathbf{e}_u$;

Algorithm 4: DecodeW($\mathbf{H}, \mathbf{s}$)

Input: params $= (n, k, w, k_w), \mathbf{H}_w, \mathbf{s}_3$.
Output: $\mathbf{e}_w \in \mathbb{F}_3^{n/3}$ such that $\mathbf{H}_w \mathbf{e}_w^T = \mathbf{s}_3$.

Solve $\mathbf{H}_w \mathbf{e}_w^T = \mathbf{s}_3$ and get its solution space;
repeat
    Select $l_1, l_2 \leftarrow \mathcal{D}_w$, where $\mathcal{D}_w$ is a distribution over $[0; m_1] \times [0; m_2]$ and $j_1 + j + 2 = k_w$;
    Randomly choose a set of variables as the free variables, and denote them as $\mathcal{I} = \{e_{i_1}, e_{i_2}, \dots, e_{i_{k_w}}\}$;
    Evaluate $\mathbf{e}_w = (e_1, e_2, \dots, e_{n/3})$ by randomly choose $\{e_{i_1}, e_{i_2}, \dots, e_{i_{k_w}}\}$ such that there are l_1 elements in $\mathcal{I}$ are equal to 1 and l_2 elements in $\mathcal{I}$ are equal to 2;
until wt$(\mathbf{e}_u + \mathbf{e}_w) \geq w/3$;
Return $\mathbf{e}_w$;

$3(k_u + 2/3(n/3 - k_u))$. Since $k_u > k/3$, we have $\mathrm{wt}(\mathbf{e}) > \mathrm{wt}(\mathbf{e}')$. By carefully choosing parameters, especially the parameters k_u, k_v, k_w and w, we can always ensure that $\mathrm{wt}(\mathbf{e}') = w$ is impossible but $\mathrm{wt}(\mathbf{e}) = w$ is easy.

4 Security

In this section, we will show the security of the improved WAVE signature scheme.

4.1 Distinguish $(U, U+V, U+W)$ Code

In this subsection, we will show that the distinguishability between the $(U, U+V, U+W)$ code and a random linear code with code length n is not easier than that between the $(U, U+V)$ code and a random linear code with code length $2/3n$. We are going to do this by reducing the distinguishing $(U, U+V, U+W)$ code from a random one to distinguishing $(U, U+V)$ code from a random one.

Theorem 2. *If there exists an algorithm $\mathcal{A}$ who can distinguish $(U, U+V, U+W)$ code from a random one, then we can build an algorithm $\mathcal{B}$ to distinguish $(U, U+V)$ code from a random one.*

Proof. Suppose algorithm $\mathcal{A}$ can distinguish $(U, U+V, U+W)$ code from a random one, then we can build an algorithm $\mathcal{B}$. When given an $[n, k]$ code $\mathcal{C}$ with parity check matrix $\mathbf{H}_c$, $\mathcal{B}$ invoke $\mathcal{A}$ as follows (Fig. 3):

1. Calculate a generator matrix $\mathbf{G}_c$ corresponds to $\mathbf{H}_c$. If $\mathcal{C}$ is a $(U, U+V)$ code, then there must exists an permutation matrix $\mathbf{P}_1$ such that $\mathbf{P}_1\mathbf{G}_c = [\mathbf{G}_u \,|\, \mathbf{G}_u + \mathbf{G}_v]$.
2. Randomly choose a full rank matrix $\mathbf{G}' \in \mathbb{F}_3^{k_w \times n/2}$.
3. Randomly choose $n/2$ columns from $\mathbf{G}_c$ and denote the sub-matrix consisted by them as $\mathbf{G}_b$, and set $\mathbf{G}_a = [\mathbf{G}_c \,|\, \mathbf{G}_b + \mathbf{G}']$. If $\mathcal{C}$ is a $(U, U+V)$ code, then there must exists an permutation matrix $\mathbf{P}_2$ such that $\mathbf{P}_2\mathbf{G}_a = [\mathbf{G}_u \,|\, \mathbf{G}_u + \mathbf{G}_v \,|\, \mathbf{G}_u + \mathbf{G}_v' + \mathbf{G}'] = [\mathbf{G}_u \,|\, \mathbf{G}u + \mathbf{G}_v \,|\, \mathbf{G}_u + \mathbf{G}_w]$.
4. Invoke $\mathcal{A}$ with $\mathbf{G}_a$ as input. If $\mathcal{A}$ determines $\mathbf{G}_a$ is the generator matrix of a random linear code, then $\mathcal{B}$ determines $\mathcal{C}$ is a random linear code. Otherwise $\mathcal{B}$ determines $\mathcal{C}$ is a $(U, U+V)$ code. □

4.2 Security Proof

In [9], it has been proved that the advantage for any probability polynomial time (PPT) adversary, the advantage of break the EUF-CMA-secure of WAVE is less than that of solve the DOOM problem. In our improved WAVE signature scheme, we only change the construction of the public parity check matrix. Since distinguishing an $[n, k]$ $(U, U+V, U+W)$ codes from random codes is not easier

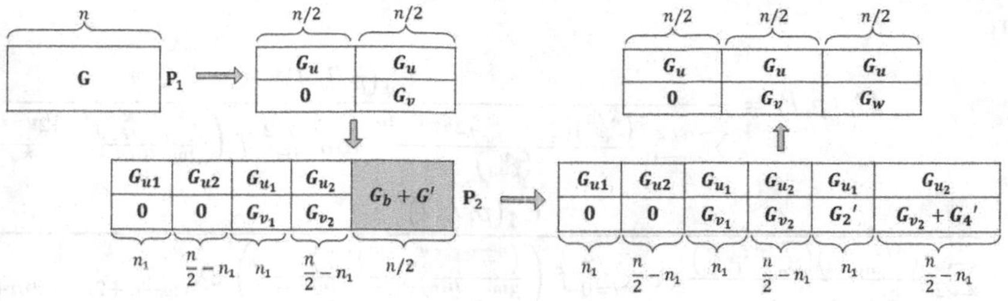

Fig. 3. A Sketch of the reduction

than distinguishing a $[2/3n, k]$ $(U, U+V)$ codes from random codes, then from the view of any PPT adversary, the public key of the improved WAVE signature scheme is indistinguishable from the public key of the original WAVE signature scheme. As a result, we have the following theorem.

Theorem 3. *If there exists an algorithm $\mathcal{A}$ who can break our improved WAVE signature scheme, then we can build an algorithm $\mathcal{B}$ to break the original WAVE signature scheme. And thus the improved WAVE signature is EUF-CMA secure.*

4.3 Known Attacks

As it is shown in the original WAVE signature scheme, the main attacks toward this kind of signature scheme includes decoding one out of many (DOOM) attack [20] and distinguish $(U, U+V)$ code from a random one. The computational complexity of DOOM attack is

$$\mathrm{WF}_{p,l,L} = \max\left(1, \frac{q^l}{P_{p,l}L^2}\right) \max\left(L, \frac{L^2}{q^l}\right), \tag{1}$$

where

$$P_{p,l} = \frac{q^L \binom{n-k-l}{w-k-l+p} (q-1)^{w-k-l+p}}{\min\left(q^{n-k}, \binom{n}{w}(q-1)^w\right)},$$

and $0 \le p \le n-w, 0 \le w-k+p, 1 \le L \le \binom{(k+l)/2}{p/2}(q-1)^{(k+l-p)/2}$ are additional optimal parameters.

Distinguishing a permuted $(U, U+V)$ code from a random linear code has been proved to be NP-completeness [10]. As is analysed in [9], there is only a very slight difference between the weight distribution of a random linear code and that of a random admissible generalized $(U, U+V)$ code of the same length and dimension. The computational complexity of the distinguishing attack is given by

$$\min\left(O(\min_{p,l} C_u(p,l)), O(\min_{p,l} C_v(p,l))\right),$$

where

$$C_u(p,l) = \frac{C_1(p,k,l)}{\sum_{w=0}^{n/2} \frac{\binom{n/2}{w}\binom{n/2-w}{k+l-2w}2^{k+l-2w}}{\binom{n}{k+l}} \max_{i=0}^{p/2} f\left(\frac{\binom{k+l-2w}{p-2i}\binom{w}{i}2^{p-i}}{3^{\max(0,k+l-w-k_u)}}\right)},$$

$$C_v = \frac{C_1(p,k,l)}{\sum_{\mathcal{I}} \frac{\binom{n/2-n_I}{m}\binom{n_I}{n-k-l-w}}{\binom{n}{n-k-l}} \max_{i=0}^{p/2} f\left(\frac{\binom{n-n_I-w-2m}{p-2i}\binom{m}{i}2^{p-i}}{3^{\max(0,n-n_I-w-m-k_v)}}\right) 2^j \binom{n_I}{w-n+2n_I+2m+j}}.$$

Here $C_1(p,k,l)$ is the complexity of computing a constant fraction of the codewords of weight p in a $[k+l,k]$ code, function $f(x) = \max(x(1-x/2), 1-1/x)$, and $\mathcal{I} = \{(w,m,j) \mid 0 \leq \min(n-k-l, n-n_I), 0 \leq m \leq n/2 - n_I, 0 \leq j \leq n/2 - n_I - m\}$.

The complexity of distinguishing $(U, U+V)$ codes is far more lager than that of the DOOM attack. As a result, we can use the same parameters as [9] to reach the aimed security level. For example, to reach the 128-bit secure, the WAVE signature scheme recommend $(n,k,w,k_u,k_v) = (5172, 3908, 4980, 2299, 1609)$ and our scheme will enquire $(n,k,w,k_u,k_v,k_w) = (5172, 3908, 4980, 2299, 1609, 1609)$. The public key size and the signature length of these two schemes are both the same, i.e. 0.98 MB for public key size and 8326 bits for signature length. Our scheme will cost a larger secret key size, but this does not matter because $\mathbf{H}_u, \mathbf{H}_v$ and $\mathbf{H}_w$ are parity check matrices of random linear codes, and thus they can be stored by some random seeds, and will not cost a large storage size. These features of the improved WAVE signature scheme are suitable for being applied in blockchain systems.

5 The Construction of Post-quantum Blockchain

Now we instead the ECDSA signature used in signing the transaction by the improved WAVE signature scheme (Fig. 4).

- **Blockchain System Setup:** The system public the parameters. In particular, the public parameters should include (n,k,w,k_u,k_v,k_w) as described in Sect. 3.1.
- **Transaction Preparation:** The users set a random seed and run the **KeyGen** algorithm as described in Sect. 3.1. Then they calculate the hash value of their public key as their transaction address. The complete public key will be publicized on some public-known websites. In order to resist the statistical attack, a new public key and corresponding address should be generated for any new transaction. That is to say, every user in the blockchain network should store numerous secret keys for new transactions, and the wallet will become more and more burdensome. However, as the improved WAVE signature has a tight secret key, a lightweight wallet can be designed to solve this problem. By decreasing the wallet redundancy, it is more suitable for the transaction implementation in the blockchain system.

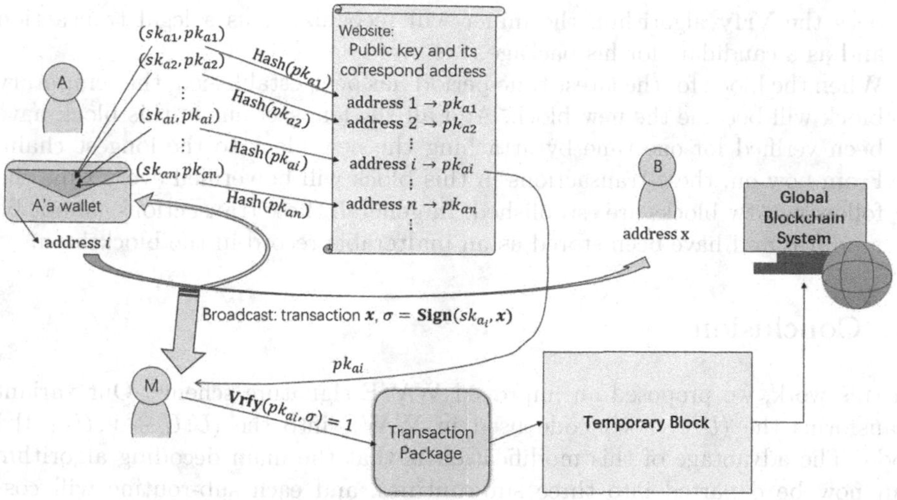

Fig. 4. Post-quantum blockchain system

- **Transaction Implementation:** As the general user, if the user A wants to send some bitcoins through a transaction to a user B, they will execute the following three steps to accomplish this transaction.
  1. The user A initiates a transfer request.
  2. The user B selects one public and secret keys pair, generates his address and sends it to user A for transaction implementation.
  3. The user A creates this transaction and broadcasts it to the whole network. A will run **Sign** as described in Sect. 3.1 to sign this transaction signed by her secret key corresponding to the output amount. This signature will be broadcast together with the transaction itself.

  Notice that the total input amount of the transaction must be equal to the total output amount. And if the user A's output amount is bigger than the required amount, he should create a new address to receive surplus bitcoins. Moreover, the miner's reward for establishing a new block will also be recorded as a transaction in the blockchain. In the mining process, every miner will create a special reward transaction in the temporary block. This The transactions that has been broadcasted in the whole blockchain network in the latest time period will also be recorded in the block. Once one miner obtains the rights for establishing the new block, his reward transaction will be confirmed as well.
- **Transaction Confirmation:** As the transactions were broadcasted to the network and verified by the miner, they will be collected and packaged into the temporary block.

  The miner will verify each transaction by executing the **Vrfy** as described in Sect. 3.1. The verify algorithm takes the public key which is corresponded to the output amount address as input. Once the transaction and its signature

pass the **Vrfy** algorithm, the miner will recognize it as a legal transaction and as a candidate for his package.
When the block for the latest time period has been established, the temporary block will become the new block. And all the transactions in this block have been verified for one time by attaching the new block to the longest chain. From now on, these transactions in this block will be verified every time the following new blocks are established. In general, these transactions cannot be modified and have been stored as an inalterable record in the blockchain.

6 Conclusion

In this work, we proposed an improved WAVE signature scheme. Our variant transforms the $(U, U+V)$ code used in WAVE into the $(U, U+V, U+W)$ code. The advantage of this modification is that the main decoding algorithm can now be departed into three sub-routines, and each sub-routine will cost less complexity due to smaller parameters. We proved that distinguishing an $[n, k]$ $(U, U+V, U+W)$ code from a random linear code is not easier than distinguishing a $[2/3n, k]$ $(U, U+V)$ code from a random linear code. That is to say, our modification will not affect the security property of the original WAVE signature scheme. The improved signature scheme has a short signature length and its signing step and verifying step can both be executed efficiently, and thus can be applied in the blockchain system to build a post-quantum blockchain system.

acknowledgements. This work is supported by Guangdong Major Project of Basic and Applied Basic Research (2019B030302008) and the National Natural Science Foundation of China (No. 61972429).

References

1. Alabbadi, M., Wicker, S.B.: Security of Xinmei digital signature scheme. Electron. Lett. **28**(9), 890–891 (1992)
2. Alabbadi, M., Wicker, S.B.: Digital signature scheme based on error-correcting codes. In: ISIT 1993, Piscataway, pp. 19–29. IEEE (1993)
3. Barreto, P.S., Misoczki, R., Simplicio, M.A.J.: One-time signature scheme from syndrome decoding over generic error-correcting codes. J. Syst. Softw. **84**(2), 198–204 (2011)
4. Berlekamp, E.R., Mceliece, R.J., van Tilborg, H.C.A.: On the inherent intractability of certain coding problems. IEEE Trans. Inf. Theor. **24**(3), 384–386 (1978)
5. Beullens, W.: Breaking rainbow takes a weekend on a laptop. IACR Cryptology ePrint Archive, Report 2022/214 (2022)
6. Chalkias, K., Brown, J., Hearn, M., Lillehagen, T., Nitto, I., Schroeter, T.: Blockchained post-quantum signatures. In: 2018 IEEE International Conference on Internet of Things (iThings) and IEEE Green Computing and Communications (GreenCom) and IEEE Cyber, Physical and Social Computing (CPSCom) and IEEE Smart Data (SmartData), Piscataway, pp. 1196–1203. IEEE (2018)

7. Courtois, N.T., Finiasz, M., Sendrier, N.: How to achieve a McEliece-based digital signature scheme. In: Boyd, C. (ed.) ASIACRYPT 2001. LNCS, vol. 2248, pp. 157–174. Springer, Heidelberg (2001). https://doi.org/10.1007/3-540-45682-1_10
8. Dallot, L.: Towards a concrete security proof of Courtois, Finiasz and Sendrier signature scheme. In: Lucks, S., Sadeghi, A.-R., Wolf, C. (eds.) WEWoRC 2007. LNCS, vol. 4945, pp. 65–77. Springer, Heidelberg (2008). https://doi.org/10.1007/978-3-540-88353-1_6
9. Debris-Alazard, T., Sendrier, N., Tillich, J.-P.: Wave: a new family of trapdoor one-way preimage sampleable functions based on codes. In: Galbraith, S.D., Moriai, S. (eds.) ASIACRYPT 2019. LNCS, vol. 11921, pp. 21–51. Springer, Cham (2019). https://doi.org/10.1007/978-3-030-34578-5_2
10. Debris-Alazard, T., Sendrier, N., Tillich, J.P.: The problem with the surf scheme. Preprint (2017). arXiv:1706.08065
11. Ding, J., Schmidt, D.: Rainbow, a new multivariable polynomial signature scheme. In: Ioannidis, J., Keromytis, A., Yung, M. (eds.) ACNS 2005. LNCS, vol. 3531, pp. 164–175. Springer, Heidelberg (2005). https://doi.org/10.1007/11496137_12
12. Gaborit, P., Schrek, J.: Efficient code-based one-time signature from automorphism groups with syndrome compatibility. In: ISIT 2012, Piscataway, pp. 1982–1986. IEEE (2012)
13. Harn, L., Wang, D.C.: Cryptoanalysis and modification of digital signature scheme based on error-correcting codes. Electron. Lett. **28**(2), 157–159 (1992)
14. Kabatianskii, G., Krouk, E., Smeets, B.: A digital signature scheme based on random error-correcting codes. In: Darnell, M. (ed.) Cryptography and Coding 1997. LNCS, vol. 1355, pp. 161–167. Springer, Heidelberg (1997). https://doi.org/10.1007/BFb0024461
15. Mceliece, R.J.: A public-key cryptosystem based on algebraic. JPL DSN Prog. Rep. **44**, 114–116 (1978)
16. Li, C., Chen, X., Chen, Y., Hou, Y., Li, J.: A new lattice-based signature scheme in post-quantum blockchain network. IEEE Access **7**, 2026–2033 (2019)
17. Nakamoto, S.: Bitcoin: a peer-to-peer electronic cash system. https://bitco.in/pdf/bitcoin.pdf
18. Niederreiter, H.: Knapsack-type cryptosystems and algebraic coding theory. Probl. Control Inf. Theor. **15**(2), 159–166 (1986)
19. Prange, E.: The use of information sets in decoding cyclic codes. Ire Trans. Inf. Theor. **8**(5), 5–9 (1962)
20. Sendrier, N.: Decoding one out of many. In: Yang, B.-Y. (ed.) PQCrypto 2011. LNCS, vol. 7071, pp. 51–67. Springer, Heidelberg (2011). https://doi.org/10.1007/978-3-642-25405-5_4
21. Shen, R., Xiang, H., Zhang, X., Cai, B., Xiang, T.: Application and implementation of multivariate public key cryptosystem in blockchain (short paper). In: Wang, X., Gao, H., Iqbal, M., Min, G. (eds.) CollaborateCom 2019. LNICST, vol. 292, pp. 419–428. Springer, Cham (2019). https://doi.org/10.1007/978-3-030-30146-0_29
22. Stern, J.: A new identification scheme based on syndrome decoding. In: Stinson, D.R. (ed.) CRYPTO 1993. LNCS, vol. 773, pp. 13–21. Springer, Heidelberg (1994). https://doi.org/10.1007/3-540-48329-2_2
23. Wang, X.: Digital signature scheme based on error-correcting codes. Electron. Lett. **13**, 898–899 (1990)
24. Xu, S., Doumen, J., van Tilborg, H.: On the security of digital signature schemes based on error-correcting codes. Des. Codes Crypt. **28**, 187–199 (2003)
25. Zhang, X., Wu, F., Yao, W., Wang, W., Zheng, Z.: Post-quantum blockchain over lattice. Comput. Mater. Continua **63**(2), 845–859 (2020)

Secure Government Data Sharing Based on Blockchain and Attribute-Based Encryption

Daling Shi[1,2], Chunjie Cao[1,2], and Jun Ye[1,2](✉)

[1] School of Cyberspace Security, Hainan University, Haikou 570228, China
yejun@hainanu.edu.cn

[2] Key Laboratory of Internet Information Retrieval of Hainan Province, Haikou, China

Abstract. In the social informatization, more and more government data are interacted in it. With the development of information technologies, traditional government data sharing systems may not be suitable for modern social inforatization. In this paper, a secure data sharing scheme based on the revocable attribute CP-ABE and blockchain is proposed, with which fine-grained access control and flexible updating can be achieved through the attribute revocation. In the proposed scheme, a combined on-chain and off-chain storage model is used, and the computational cost of encryption and decryption is reduced through smart contract technology, where the cryptographic hash is uploaded to the blockchain and the access control is implemented by smart contracts. With the identity verification and access management technologies in blockchain, the security of government data is enhanced on chain. Furthermore, it also enables decentralised, transparent and traceable access processes.

Keywords: Ciphertext policy attribute based encryption · Bolckchain · Cryptography · IPFS

1 Introduction

In the process of building digital government, sharing of government affairs data is a basic and key issue. Data sharing and business collaboration of E-government in different provinces are key nodes to implement "Internet plus government services" and promote modernization of national governance. However, there are still some problems and challenges in government data sharing: (1) The government data grows exponentially; (2) The contradiction between personal privacy

This work is supported in part by the Hainan Province Science and Technology Special Fund (ZDYF2021GXJS216), the National Natural Science Foundation of China (62162020). This work is supported by the Science Project of Hainan University (KYQD(ZR)20021).

X. Chen et al. (Eds.): SocialSec 2022, CCIS 1663, pp. 324–338, 2022.
https://doi.org/10.1007/978-981-19-7242-3_21

protection and data sharing in government data is prominent; (3) Most government data are stored independently by the databases of various units, which is easy to form a "data island", resulting in poor sharing and can not meet the data sharing needs of relevant industries. Attribute based encryption (ABE) provides technical support for data sharing because it can realize one to many access control and can be encrypted. For example, document [1] proposes an attribute encryption scheme supporting any state to realize data sharing in cloud computing. However, in today's large data age, the generation of massive data will lead to huge consumption of cloud storage space, and centralized cloud storage has its own limitations, that is, the collapse of the central server will lead to the downtime of the whole system, resulting in data leakage and loss in the process of storage and sharing [2–5]. Blockchain has attracted wide attention due to the de-centralization and tamper-proof features. It can prevent the problem of single point of failure and improve the problem of trust between "information islands". Therefore, the combination of blockchain and attribute encryption technology can better provide new ideas for the safe and reliable large-scale sharing of massive data. Document [6] proposed a multi-attribute authority attribute based encrypted access control system based on blockchain. They put the authorization center and attribute authority into the smart contract of Ethereum, and then realized a decentralized data sharing scheme. Document [7,8] combines block chain with attribute encryption to achieve fine-grained access control for data. All operations of users can not be tampered with and permanently retained after being chained. Wang et al. [9] proposed a decentralized storage system and data sharing framework for fine-grained access control based on blockchain, but did not consider the protection of user privacy. Xia et al. As personal electronic health records (EHRs) can easily disclose patient privacy when shared externally and in order to control access rights, the literature [10] proposes a hierarchical attribute-based encryption (RS-HABE) scheme for revocable storage by adding user revocation, key delegation and ciphertext update to the original ABE. The literature [11] presents a concept of identity-based revocable storage encryption (RS-IBE) that can provide forward/backward security of ciphertexts by introducing user revocation and ciphertext update functions. This scheme can be used to build real-time data sharing systems with cryptographically enhanced access control to shared data. Although both schemes achieve fine-grained access control, neither addresses the problem of untrustworthy or semi-trustworthy authorisation centres, while failing to achieve traceability of historical operations and meet the security requirements of open and transparent data access.

The contribution points contributed in this article are as follows: A support of revoked attribute base (CP-ABE) encryption scheme is proposed in this paper. By using subset coverage technology, fine-grained access control and secure secret key updating is achieved, so that the revoked user cannot do further implement. The traceability characteristics of the blockchain, track the access or use of data. This scheme uses the linear secret sharing (LSSS) to achieve the complete concealment of access policies, and access policy will not be revealed. In addition, the scheme adopts the hybrid encryption method: AES algorithm is used to encrypt data, and CP-ABE algorithm is used to encrypt data Hash path. In this way, it is not only protects data confidentiality, but also realizes flexible data management. When the attribute or the user is revoked, the subset coverage technology is used to generate a new attribute group for the valid members in the group. The key and ciphertext will be updated timely and effectively, so that the revoked user can be prevent from continuing to access the data, thus, the system data security is improved. On the other hand, in order to solve the problems of data abuse and responsibility identification, we use blockchain and smart contracts to realize information tracking and traceability in the process of data encryption and sharing, and realize the behavior accountability of all participants, and improve the process management of the whole life cycle of data.

2 Preliminaries

2.1 Bilinear Mapping

Let p be a large prime, G_0 and G_1 be two multiplicative cycle groups of order p, g be the group G generator element, and define the bilinear map e: $G_0 \times G_0 \rightarrow G_1$. Meet the following properties:

1. bilinearity, for any g $\in G_0$, a, b $\in Z_p$, have $e(g^a, g^b) = e(g^b, g^a) = e(g, g)^{ab}$.
2. non-degeneracy, exist $g \in G_0$, $e(g, g) \neq 1$.
3. computability, there is an effective calculation $e(g, g)$.

2.2 Linear Secret-Sharing Scheme (LSSS)

Secret sharing scheme Γ on the participant set p. If the following conditions are met, it is called a linear secret sharing scheme on the Z_p.

1. Each share of the shared secret constitutes a vector on the Z_p.
2. For the secret sharing scheme, there exists a $l \times n$ matrix M, the mapping function specifies the for of M, for $i = 1, ..., l$, ρ(i) is the participant associated with line i. Consider a column vector $v = (s, y_2, \ldots\ldots, y_n)$, s is the secret of being shared, r_i was chosen randomly ($i = 2, \ldots\ldots,$ n). According to the plan Γ, Mv is the I secret shares where secret s are shared, $\lambda_i = v_i \cdot M_i (i = 1, 2, \ldots\ldots l)$ Represents a secret shared key share;
3. Linear secret sharing scheme has the property of linear reconstruction, If $s \in A$ is an access authorization collection, then there is a constant $w_i \in Z_p$, Make the $\sum w_i \cdot \lambda_i = s$, $i \in I$ hold, λ_i is a valid share of the secret s, $I = \{i : \rho(\mathrm{i}) \in s\}$.

2.3 Subcoverage Technology

Suppose $\boldsymbol{T}$ is a fully binary tree with n nodes and n represents the size of the user set. The depth(μ) represents the depth of the node. Path(μ) $= \{\mu_{\mathrm{i}_0} = \mathrm{root}, \ldots,$ $\mu_{\mathrm{i}_{\mathrm{depth}(\mu)}} = \mu\}$, represents the path from the root node to the node μ. The given leaf node set The given leaf node set R_{list} represents the undo user set represents the undo user set, cover R_{list} Calculates the unrevoked users. Tree $\boldsymbol{T}$ has 8 leaf nodes L $= \{h, i, j, k, l, m, n, o\}$, Suppose that you need to undo the users h and k, so $R_{list} = \{h, k\}$. The paths going down from the root node to the user h and k are respectively path (h) $= \{a, b, d, h\}$, path (k) $= \{a, b, e, k\}$. Cover R_{list} represents a minimum subset of nodes not unrevoked after the tree $\boldsymbol{T}$, therefore, cover $R_{list} = \{i, j, c\}$.

3 System Model

The proposed system architecture of the union chain government data sharing system based on revocation able attribute based encryption is shown in Fig. 1, and consists of 5 entities: data provider (DP), IPFS distributed cluster, data requestor (DR), key generating node, and smart contract.

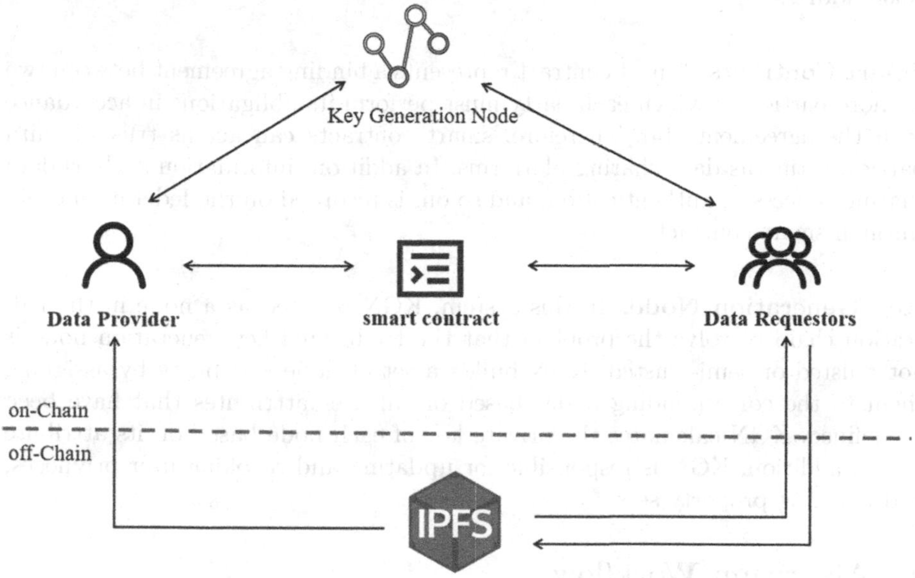

Fig. 1. Diagram of the system model

Data Provider. DP is the provider of the data sharing platform. When DP wants to share data with the outside world, it needs to call the smart contract to generate a summary information description file of the data. Then there are two tasks to be performed: (1) DP formulates the corresponding scope and control strategy, and only data requesters that meet the access policy can access the data; (2) Then encrypt the data, get the ciphertext data, and upload it to the IPFS distributed cluster. IPFS distributed clusters generate unique Hash identities based on content and send them to DP. DP publishes the Hash identity to Hyperledger Fabric.

Data Requestor. Data requester DR is the data user of the data sharing platform. DR uses the summary information description file uploaded by DP to determine if the data is what it needs. DR obtains the master key from the key generation node, then generates the user attribute private key using its own set of attributes, downloads the cryptographic data from the IPFS distributed cluster, and decrypts it.

IPFS Distributed Cluster. IPFS provides a point-to-point distributed storage structure in which a large number of data files can be stored [12]. IPFS stores content addressing hashes in a distributed hash list, uses version control history, and deletes duplicate data files [13]. Data providers use attribute bases to encrypt data that is shared externally, and then upload the ciphertext data to the IPFS network, which returns a unique Hash identity based on the content of the ciphertext data. The data request downloads the data file based on the Hash address.

Smart Contracts. Smart contract represents a binding agreement between two or more parties, in which each party must perform its obligations in accordance with the agreement [14]. Therefore, smart contracts can act as trusted third parties, acting as data-sharing platforms. In addition, information such as data sharing processes, authentication, and so on, is recorded on the federation chain through smart contracts.

Key Generation Node. In this system, KGN is acted as a node in the federation chain to solve the problem that the traditional key generation node is not trusted or semi-trusted. KGN builds a set of node attributes by assigning them to the corresponding nodes based on all user attributes that have been predefined. KGN calculates the private key of each node based on its attribute set. In addition, KGN is responsible for updating and revoking user privileges, and revoking property sets.

4 Algorithm Workflow

This scheme involves five types of entities: a key generation center (KGC), data owners, data users, smart contracts and the IPFS distributed cluster, and consists of eight algorithms given below. The experimental results are shown in Fig. 2.

1. Setup(λ, U, v, T) $\rightarrow$ {$\mathrm{P_k}, \mathrm{M_k}$}: Given a security parameter λ, number of system users U, attribute range V, set the space for version number ver = {0, 1, ..., T}.
2. OriKeyGen ($\mathrm{P_k}, \mathrm{M}_k$, UID, $\mathrm{S_{UID}}$) $\rightarrow$ {$\mathrm{Osk_{UID}}$}: The original key generation algorithm takes the attribute set of the public parameter $\mathrm{P_k}$, the master key M_k, the user's unique identifier UID, and the attribute set of UID($\mathrm{S_{UID}}$) as input. Finally, return to the user $Osk_{UID} = \{Key_{1,\sigma}, Key_{1,\sigma}\}$.

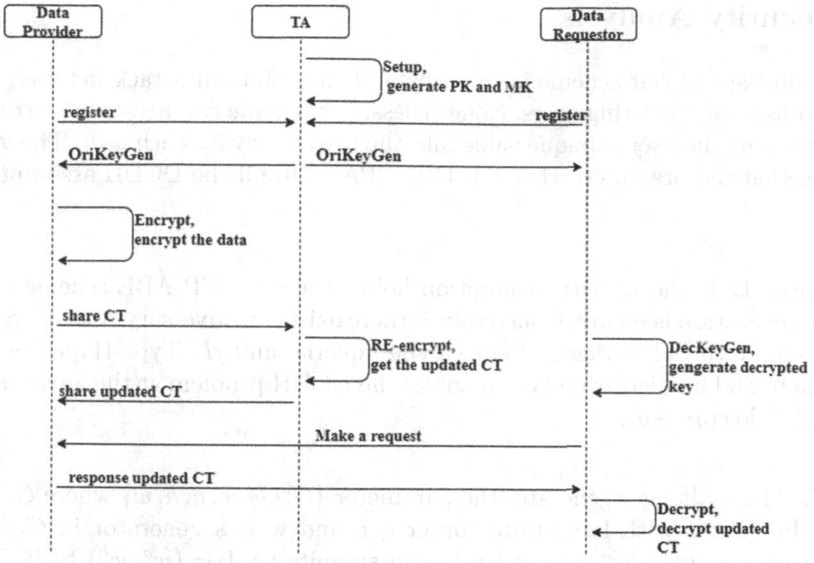

Fig. 2. Algorithm workflow

3. UMGen(P, P_k, M_k, Arls, Url, ver): Updating the material generation algorithm requires input of common parameters P_k, primary keys M_k, attribute revocation lists Arls, user revocation lists Url, and the next version number, ver.Once the updated material is generated, It packages the material as UMver = {VUMver, AUMver,UUMver} and broadcasts it through public channels.
4. Encrypt(P, P_k, m, (M, ρ)): The data encryption algorithm outputs the original ciphertext using the common parameters P_k , message M and LSSS access structure (M, ρ) as input.
5. Re−encrypt (P_k, CT, VUM_{ver}) $\rightarrow$ {CT_{ver}}: The ciphertext re-encryption algorithm takes the public key P_k , the original ciphertext CT, and the latest version of the update material VUM_{ver} as input, and outputs the updated ciphertext.
6. DecKeyGen (Osk_{UID}, AUM_{ver}) $\rightarrow$ {Dsk_{UID}}: The decryption key generation algorithm takes the user's original key Osk_{UID} and attribute update material AUM_{UID} as input and outputs the decryption key Dsk_{UID}.
7. Decrypt (P_k, CT_{ver}, Dsk_{UID}, UUM_{ver}, VUM_{ver}) $\rightarrow$ {$m/\perp$}: Cipher key decryption algorithm takes public key P_k , updated cipher CT_{ver}, user decryption key Dsk_{UID}, user update material UUM_{ver} and version update material VUM_{ver} as input; If the user's key is satisfied, clear m is output. If not, it will output $\perp$.
8. Vertify (P_k, CT_{ver}, VUM_{ver}) $\rightarrow$ {1/0}: The validation algorithm can be executed by either party. It takes public keys P_k , update ciphertext CT_{ver}, and version update materials VUM_{ver} as input. If the update is correct, output 1, or output 0, indicates that it is not updated to the latest version.

5 Security Analysis

The main issue in our scheme is to withstand the collusion attack between the revoked users and existing users. Nonetheless, our scheme can resist such attacks by embedding the user's unique value into the private key for each user. Theorem 1 states that the presented scheme is IND-CPA secure if the DCDH assumption holds.

Theorem 1. If the DCDH assumption holds, then our CP-ABE scheme with flexible revocation is secure. Concretely, if there exists an adversary A that breaks our scheme at the advantage ε after qI Type-I queries and qII Type-II queries, we are able to find an algorithm B that solves the DCDH problem at the advantage: $Adv_A \leq \varepsilon / \log(q_I + q_{II})$.

Proof. The challenger generates the parameter $\{G, G_T, e, g, h, w\}$ where G, G_T are cyclic groups with large prime order g, h and w is a generator in G. The challenger chooses $a, b \in Z_p^*$ randomly and submits (A, B)=(w^a, w^b) to B. The goal of algorithm B is to output $w^{a/b}$ through interacting with A as follows.

Init. The adversary A selects the challenge LSSS access structure (M^*, ρ^*), the challenge attribute att^* and the challenge version number ver^* and sends them to B.

Setup. Algorithm B sets the maximum version number

$$\mathrm{T} = ver^* \left(2^{t^*-1} \leq ver^* \leq 2^{t^*} - 1\right)$$

and runs Setup() to generate the public key and master key:

$$\mathrm{PK} = \left\{g, h, w, e(g, h)^{\alpha}, \{\mathrm{T_i} = g^{-r_i}\}_{1 \leq i \leq |v|}, \{e_j\}_{\mathrm{j} \in [0, \ldots \mathrm{t^*}+1]}\right\}$$

$$\mathrm{MK} = \left\{\alpha, \{r_i\}_{1 \leq i \leq |v|}, st\right\}$$

Algorithm B then sends the public parameter PK to A.

Phase 1. A queries the oracle in polynomial many times, B maintains an attribute revocation list Arl^* of challenge attribute att^* and initializes it to empty.

Osk(UID, S): A makes the secret key query with the identity UID and an attribute set S.B answers the query (UID, S) as follows:

Type-I secret key query $O_{sk}(UID_I, S_I)$:

If S_I is an attribute set that satisfies (M^*, ρ^*), UID_I is considered as a revoked user that the challenge attribute att^* of UID_I has been revoked. B computes secret key as: B chooses a random element $u_I \in Z_p$ for UID_I, and picks an unassigned leaf node σ from the binary tree ST and stores $<u_I, S_I>$ in node σ.

For each attribute $att_i \in S_I - \{att^*\}(1 \le i \le |S_I|)$, S_I denotes the size of S_I, B fetches each node $\theta \in \text{Path}(\sigma)$ and recalls the secret value ρ_θ. If ρ_θ has not been defined before, B chooses a random exponent $\rho_\theta \in Z_p$ and stores it in the node θ. The original secret key is $key_{1,I} = g^{u1}$, $key_{2,I} = \{\forall att_i \in \{S_I - \{att^*\}\} : \{w^{\rho\theta \cdot r_i} \cdot h^{u_1}\}$. For att^*, B picks a random number $\beta^* \in Z_p$ and computes the original key as $key_{2,I} = \{att^* : \{A^{\rho\theta \cdot \beta^*} \cdot h^{u1}\}, \theta \in \text{Path}(\sigma)\}$.

Algorithm B sends $Osk_{UID_{II}} = \{key_{1,II}, key_{2,II}\}$ to A.

Oct(ver): A makes the re-encryption query with a version number ver. If $ver < ver^*$, B runs Re-encrypt() to generate a new ciphertext CT_{ver} and responds to adversary A. Otherwise, B returns $\perp$ indicating that cannot be queried. $y_{2,II}$ to A.

Oku (UID, ver): A makes the updating materials query with the identity UID and a version number ver. B finds $UIDs$ in ST and answers the query (UID, ver) as follows:

1. If UID has been queried as UID_I and $ver < ver^*$, B recalls $<u_I, S_I>$ from node σ and computes AUM $= \{\omega^{-\rho\,\text{root}\cdot r_i} \cdot F(\ell, ver)^{r_i}\}$, $\forall att_i \ne att^* \cup \{A^{-\rho\,\text{root}} \cdot \beta^* \cdot F(\ell, ver)^{r^*}$. Then B chooses a random element $\xi \in Z$p and calculates $U_0 = h^{\alpha - u_1} \cdot F(\ell, ver)^\xi$, $U_1 = g^\xi$.
2. If UID has been queried as UID_{II} and $ver < ver^*$, B recalls $<u_{II}, S_{II}>$ from node σ and computes

$$AUM = \{\omega^{-\rho\,\text{root}\, r_i} \cdot F(\ell, ver)^{r_i}\}, \forall att_i \ne att^* \cup \left\{B^{-\rho\,\text{root}\,r^*} \cdot F(\ell, ver)^{r^*}\right\}$$

   Then B chooses a random element $\xi \in Z_R$ and calculates $U_0 = h^{\alpha - u_{II}} \cdot F(\ell, ver)^\xi$, $U_1 = g^\xi$.
3. Otherwise, B returns$\perp$as an invalid query.

Algorithm B sends AUM, U_0, U_1 to adversary A.

Challenge. Once Phase 1 ends, A submits two messages of equal length m_0 and m_1 to B. B flips a random coin to obtain a bit $\bar{b} \in \{0, 1\}$ and then runs Encrypt() algorithm to generate the challenge updated ciphertext as $CT_{\bar{b}} = \{C_0' = m_{\bar{b}} \cdot e(g, h)^{\alpha.s}, C_1' = g^s, C_i' = h^{\lambda_i - s}, C_{ver^*} = F(\ell, ver^*)^s\}$

We assume that the original encryption phase and the ciphertext update phase are at the same time(ver^*), so we omitted the re-encryption and directly encoded the time parameters to C_{ver^*}.

Algorithm B sends CT_b^- to the adversary A.

Phase 2. A proceeds to launch queries as Phase 1 and B replies as in Phase 1.

Guess. Finally, B ignores A's output and performs the updating materials generation algorithm.

1. For each attribute $att_i \in v - \{att^*\}(1 \leq i \leq |v|)$, B picks the root node value ρ_{root} and computes the attribute-updating material as $AUM_i = \{\omega^{-\rho\ \text{root}\ \cdot r_i} \cdot F(\ell, ver^{r_i}\}$
2. For the challenge attribute att^*, B takes the revocation list Arl^* as the input to algorithm KUNode, and calculates non-revoked user set as $N^* = \text{KUNode}(\text{Arl}^*)$.
3. For the user-updating material, B computes $U_0 = h^{\alpha - u_{II\sigma}} \cdot F(\ell, ver^*)^{\xi}$, $U_1 = g^{\xi}$.

B sends $\{AUM_i, AUM^*, U_0, U_1\}$ to adversary A. The theoretical evidence is that if A is able to decrypt the challenge ciphertext CT_b^-, he must have get the secret key D_i of the challenge attribute att^*. Therefore, $key_{2,1} = A^{\rho_\theta \cdot \beta^*} \cdot h^{u_I}$ and $AUM^* = B^{-\rho_{\theta'} \cdot r^*} \cdot F(\ell, ver)^{r^*}$ must can be combined. We formulate above theory evidence as $A^{\rho_\theta \cdot \beta^*} \cdot B^{-\rho_{\theta'} \cdot r^*} = 1$. So, B finally outputs $w^{a/b} = w^{\rho_{\theta'} \cdot r^* / \rho_\theta \cdot \beta^*}$ as his answer.

If B does not return⊥during the game, then A's view is the same as its view in the real attack. To complete the proof, it remains to calculate the probability that B succeeds during the simulation. Suppose A makes qI Type-I queries and qII Type-II queries. Then the number of nodes in AUM^* is n $\in [1, q_{II}]$, and the number of nodes owned by each UID_I is $n' = \log \mu\, (q_I + q_{II} \leq \mu)$. The probability that B picks out the correct ρ_θ and $\rho_{\theta'}$ is at most $1/log(q_I + q_{II}) \cdot q_I$. This shows that B's advantage is at most $\varepsilon / log(q_I + q_{II}) \cdot q_I$.

6 Experimental Analysis

Based on nodejs and python language, this paper implements an alliance chain government data sharing system based on revocable attribute base encryption. The experimental environment is mainly based on the blockchain environment of hyperledger fabric. Fabric node SDK is used to realize the communication with the alliance chain, and the intelligent contract records the processes of data sharing, data encryption and decryption. There are two organizations in the alliance chain environment, including one sorting node and two peer nodes. In the experiment, the block time of the alliance chain is designed to be 2 s, and each block has an average of 10 transactions. The server configuration and fabric network configuration are exploded in Table 1:

Table 1. Server configuration and fabric network configuration

Quota	Config
Operating system (OS)	**Ubuntu 20.04 LTS**
Processor	**Intel@Core i5-10400U**
Memory	**32G**
Hard drive	**1.2 TB**
Fabric-version	**V 2.2**
Consensus algorithm	**Raft**

6.1 Revocation Mechanism Performance

As shown in Fig. 3, the time cost of user revocation and attribute revocation is tested when the number of user attributes in the system is different. We set the number of users in the system to 10 and the maximum version number to 2^{11}. The experimental results show that the user revocation is independent of the number of user attributes, and the computational cost is 23 ms. The computational cost of attribute revocation is 140–180 ms. It shows that the proposed scheme is practical and efficient.

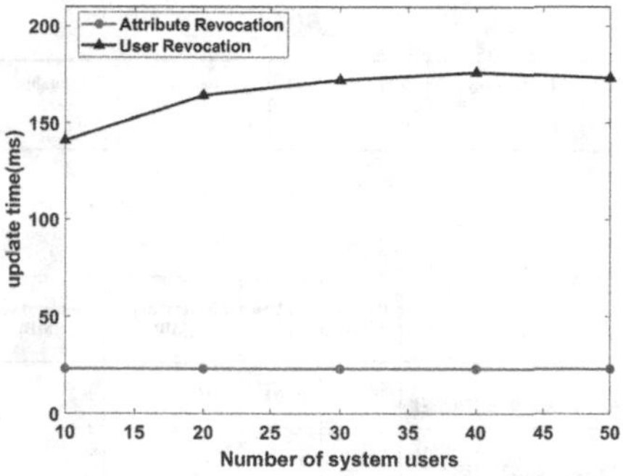

Fig. 3. The time cost of user revocation and attribute revocation

6.2 Encryption and Decryption Performance

In order to test the computational overhead of encryption and decryption in each stage of the algorithm. In this experiment, the amount of users and attributes are fixed, and the depth of cp-abe binary tree is changed, ranging from 4 to 11. The experimental results are shown in Fig. 4.

As shown in Fig. 4, the computational cost of oskgen algorithm is directly proportional to the depth of binary tree, while other algorithms are not affected by the depth of binary tree. The maximum upper limit is 32 ms. On the whole, it is relatively effective and practical.

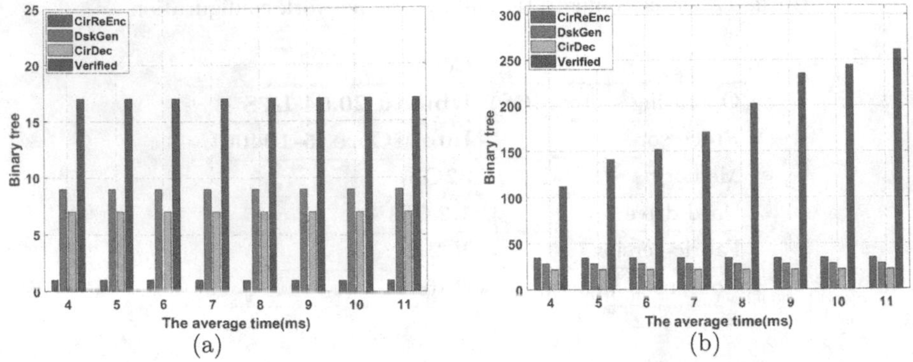

Fig. 4. Calculation overhead of different binary tree depth algorithms

6.3 System Performance Evaluation

In this experiment, the hyperledger caliper tool is used to test the government system with attribute base and the government system without attribute base. The experimental results are shown in Fig. 5 and Fig. 6.

Performance metrics for Non_ABE

Name	Succ	Fail	Send Rate (TPS)	Max Latency (s)	Min Latency (s)	Avg Latency (s)	Throughput (TPS)
Non_ABE	18020	0	609.0	0.02	0.00	0.01	609.0

Resource utilization for Non_ABE

Resource monitor: docker

Name	CPU% (max)	CPU% (avg)	Memory(max) [MB]	Memory(avg) [MB]	Traffic In [MB]	Traffic Out [MB]	Disc Write [KB]	Disc Read [B]
dev-peer0.org1.example.com-basic_1.0-3cfcf67978d6b3f7c5e0375660c995b21db19c4330946079afc3925ad7306881	38.55	18.00	9.04	8.22	33.7	14.4	0.00	0.00
dev-peer0.org2.example.com-basic_1.0-3cfcf67978d6b3f7c5e0375660c995b21db19c4330946079afc3925ad7306881	2.09	0.19	7.64	7.43	0.0442	0.0173	0.00	0.00
cli	0.00	0.00	14.6	14.6	0.000562	0.00	0.00	0.00
peer0.org1.example.com	69.83	34.16	97.8	92.2	40.5	59.9	288	0.00
orderer.example.com	1.26	0.31	36.4	35.8	0.104	0.197	284	0.00
peer0.org2.example.com	5.09	2.05	49.3	41.0	0.200	0.136	288	0.00

Fig. 5. Government system without attribute base

As shown in Fig. 6, the performance evaluation results of the government sharing system without attribute base are shown. Within 60 s, the government system has successfully executed 18020 transactions, the maximum transaction delay is 20 ms, the minimum transaction delay is 10 ms, the average transaction delay is 10 ms, and the system throughput is 609 tps; As shown in the figure, the mean transaction delay was 30 ms for the system and 30 ms for the system

Performance metrics for CP_ABE

Name	Succ	Fail	Send Rate (TPS)	Max Latency (s)	Min Latency (s)	Avg Latency (s)	Throughput (TPS)
CP_ABE	16879	0	563.0	0.04	0.02	0.03	563.0

Resource utilization for CP_ABE

Resource monitor: docker

Name	CPU% (max)	CPU% (avg)	Memory(max) [MB]	Memory(avg) [MB]	Traffic In [MB]	Traffic Out [MB]	Disc Write [KB]	Disc Read [B]
dev-peer0.org1.example.com-basic_1.0-3cfcf67978d6b3f7c5e0375660c995b21db19c4330946079afc3925ad7306881	42.04	21.10	12.37	9.72	36.21	17.33	0.00	0.00
dev-peer0.org2.example.com-basic_1.0-3cfcf67978d6b3f7c5e0375660c995b21db19c4330946079afc3925ad7306881	3.22	0.34	8.20	8.55	0.0546	0.0191	0.00	0.00
cli	0.00	0.00	16.8	15.2	0.000657	0.00	0.00	0.00
peer0.org1.example.com	74.33	37.34	101.1	94.5	41.5	61.4	294	0.00
orderer.example.com	1.32	0.34	36.9	37.1	0.127	0.208	294	0.00
peer0.org2.example.com	5.24	2.12	49.5	44.0	0.410	0.142	294	0.00

Fig. 6. Government affairs system with attribute encryption

within the TPS. As shown in the experiment, the mean transaction delay of the system is 565–30 ms, and the average transaction delay of the system within the TPS is 30 ms. The experimental results show that the number of successful transactions and system throughput of the system proposed in this paper are slightly lower than that of the government system without attribute base, and the transaction delay is slightly higher than it. Considering that this scheme provides the function of attribute based encryption, this slight overhead is acceptable.

6.4 Experiment

In the following experiments, we also set the number of users in the system as fixed to 8, The maximum version number is set to 2^4.

As shown in Fig. 7, In the initialization stage of the system, it can be seen that the time required to run the algorithm increases with the number of user attributes; in the range of user attributes 10–50, our scheme is better than literature [15] and literature [16], indicating the practicability of this scheme. In this scenario, when the SetUp() algorithm performs, you need to enter the parameter V (attribute range), and then for each attribute $att_i \in$ V, A random index is selected; generating the common parameter PK and master key MK requires random index corresponding to each attribute. In the SetUp () algorithm, we only used a double-line pair operation, making the algorithm more efficient.

As shown in Fig. 8, in the data decryption stage, the decryption time overhead of document [15] increases with the number of user attributes, while the scheme time overhead of our scheme and document [16] is constant, and the decryption time is about 7 ms. The CirDec() algorithm in this paper takes data ciphertext, user secret key, global public parameters, user update materials and version update materials as input. The algorithm also has nothing of the number of

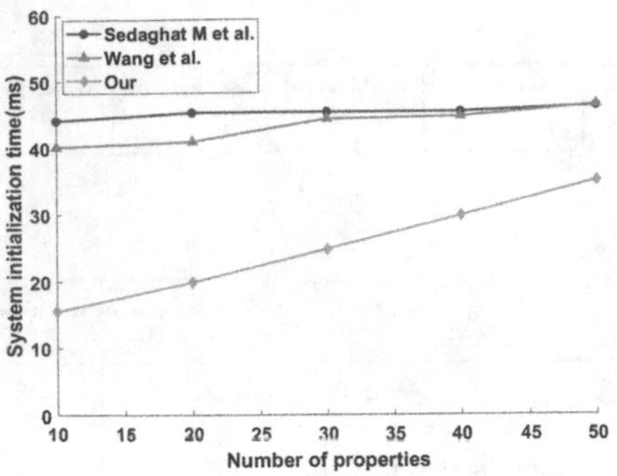

Fig. 7. Performance comparison experiment

attributes, and the computational cost of all decryption algorithms is almost constant.

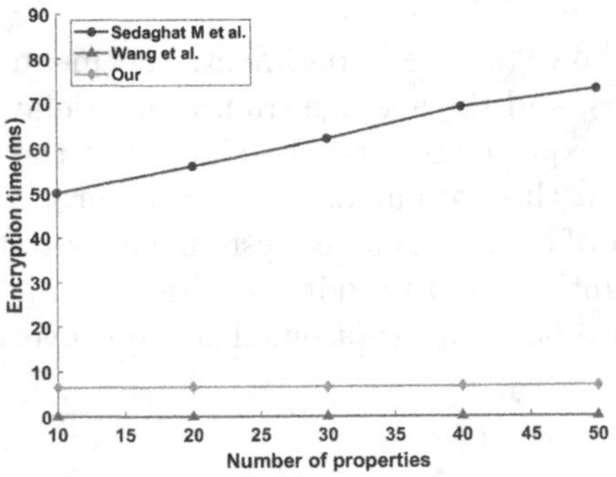

Fig. 8. Data decryption time

7 Conclusion

In order to solve the problem that traditional government data sharing systems often use centralized sharing mode, such as data privacy leakage, failure to fully consider Department privileges, single point failure, etc., this paper puts forward an encryption scheme based on revocable attributes to achieve secure data sharing in the government Federation chain. With the help of the idea of de-centralization, the key generation node (KGN) acts as a node in the Federation chain. This solves the problem that traditional key generation nodes are not trusted or semi-trusted, making highly secure communication and collaboration possible between organizations. The results of security analysis and function analysis show that this scheme not only achieves fine-grained access control and accurate management of data, but also flexibly updates and revokes user privileges, which greatly improves the security of data. Experiments show that this scheme has moderate encryption and decryption overhead compared with similar schemes, and is suitable for the certificate storage system on the government chain. Of course, there are still some areas that need to be optimised and improved, such as the flexible revocation of attributes and the design of efficient access structures, which will be the next step in the research.

References

1. Wang, S.L., Liang, K.T., Liu, J.K., et al.: Attribute-based data sharing scheme revisited in cloud computing. IEEE Trans. Inf. Forensics Secur. **11**(8), 1661–1673 (2016)
2. Zhang, L.Y., Ye, Y.D., Mu, Y.: Multi-authority access control with anonymous authentication for personal health record. IEEE Internet Things J. **8**(1), 156–167 (2020)
3. Shahid, F., Ashraf, H., Ghani, A., et al.: PSDS-proficient security over distributed storage: a method for data transmission in cloud. IEEE Access **8**, 118285–118298 (2020)
4. Zichichi, M., Ferretti, S., D'Angelo, G.: A distributed ledger based infrastructure for smart transportation system and social good. In: 2020 IEEE 17th Annual Consumer Communications & Networking Conference, Piscataway, pp. 1–6. IEEE (2020)
5. Jinxia, Y.U., Xu, H.E., Xixi, Y.A.N.: Ciphertext-policy attribute-based encryption scheme with verifiability on authority. J. Xidian Univ. **46**(4), 49–57 (2019)
6. Guo, H., Meamari, E., Shen, C.C.: Multi-authority attribute-based access control with smart contract. In: Proceedings of the 2019 International Conference on Blockchain Technology, pp. 6–11 (2019)
7. Zuo, Y.T., Kang, Z.Z., Xu, J., et al.: BCAS: a blockchain-based ciphertext-policy attribute-based encryption scheme for cloud data security sharing. Int. J. Distrib. Sens. Netw. **17**(3), 1–16 (2021)
8. Wang, H., Song, Y.J.: Secure cloud-based EHR system using attribute-based cryptosystem and blockchain. J. Med. Syst. **42**(8), 152–164 (2018)
9. Wang, S.P., Zhang, Y.L., Zhang, Y.L.: A blockchain-based framework for data sharing with fine-grained access control in decentralized storage systems. IEEE Access **6**, 38437–38450 (2018)
10. Wei, J., Chen, X., Huang, X., et al.: RS-HABE: revocable-storage and hierarchical attribute-based access scheme for secure sharing of e-health records in public cloud. IEEE Trans. Dependable Secure Comput. **18**, 2301–2315 (2019)
11. Wei, J., Liu, W., Hu, X.: Secure data sharing in cloud computing using revocable-storage identity-based encryption. IEEE Trans. Cloud Comput. **6**, 1136–1148 (2016)
12. Sheng, D., Xiao, M., Liu, A., et al.: CPchain: a copyright-preserving crowdsourcing data trading framework based on blockchain. In: 2020 29th International Conference on Computer Communications and Networks (ICCCN), pp. 1–9. IEEE (2020)
13. Kumar, R., Marchang, N., Tripathi, R.: Distributed off-chain storage of patient diagnostic reports in healthcare system using IPFS and blockchain. In: 2020 International Conference on COMmunication Systems & NETworkS (COMSNETS), pp. 1–5. IEEE (2020)

14. Macrinici, D., Cartofeanu, C., Gao, S.: Smart contract applications within blockchain technology: a systematic mapping study. Telematics Inform. **35**(8), 2337–2354 (2018)
15. Sedaghat, M., Preneel, B.: Cross-domain attribute-based access control encryption. In: Conti, M., Stevens, M., Krenn, S. (eds.) CANS 2021. LNCS, vol. 13099, pp. 3–23. Springer, Cham (2021). https://doi.org/10.1007/978-3-030-92548-2_1
16. Wang, X., Chow, S.S.M.: Cross-domain access control encryption: arbitrary-policy, constant-size, efficient. In: IEEE Symposium on Security and Privacy (S&P) (2021)

Secure Data Storage Scheme of Judicial System Based on Blockchain

Zhaoxing Jing[1,2], Chunjie Cao[1,2], Longjuan Wang[1,2(✉)], and Yulian Sang[1,2]

[1] School of Cyberspace Security, Hainan University, Haikou 570228, China
{21110839000003,wanglongjuan,19085212210035}@hainanu.edu.cn

[2] Key Laboratory of Internet Information Retrieval of Hainan Province, Haikou, China

Abstract. Nowadays, the office systems of the judicial department are disconnected from each other, which is called "data silos". Under normal circumstances, judicial data is stored in the node, and it is the possibility of malicious modification. A judicial system based on blockchain can address these challenges. However, in the blockchain systems, each judicial node has a complete ledger, which also brings challenges to the secure storage of judicial data. Therefore, how to further enhance the security of judicial data on the blockchain is of great significance. With the study of the security of judicial blockchain data, the data security requirements of the system are analyzed, and a data security storage solution for judicial blockchain is proposed to enhance the storage security and availability of judicial data. Finally, the experiment is implemented by using cryptography and smart contract technology to prove its effectiveness.

Keywords: Blockchain · Judicial data · Storage · Security

1 Introduction

With the improvement of the informatization level of the judicial department, the case evidence and other materials in the case handling process have also entered the paperless era, and the case handling efficiency of various departments has been greatly improved. However, through field research, it is found that the current judicial department systems are independent systems, the data between departments cannot be transferred electronically, which is not conducive to the further improvement of coordination and case handling efficiency of various departments. In addition, due to the complicated case processing process, and in the current traditional system, electronic evidence is stored in a centralized server, the stored electronic evidence may be tampered with.

Blockchain originated from the Bitcoin [13] system invented by Nakamoto. Due to the success of Bitcoin, blockchain technology has attracted the attention

This work is supported in part by the Hainan Province Science and Technology Special Fund (ZDFYF2020012, ZDYF2021GXJS216), the National Natural Science Foundation of China (62162020), the Science Project of Hainan University (KYQD(ZR)20021).

X. Chen et al. (Eds.): SocialSec 2022, CCIS 1663, pp. 339–350, 2022.
https://doi.org/10.1007/978-981-19-7242-3_22

of researchers. In 2014, Ethereum [3] combined blockchain and smart contract [19] technology to deploy smart contracts on the chain. Once the preset execution conditions of the contract are met, the contract can automatically perform the set operations and realize the predetermined logic [4]. Especially in recent years, blockchain technology has received great attention. Some researchers even call it the third generation Internet, which is regarded as one of the emerging forces to change the Internet. Blockchain technology has also been gradually explored and applied in many fields [2,6,10,17], such as Internet of things, energy, traceability of agricultural products, government affairs, etc.

This paper is committed to the research on the data storage technology of the storage system in the judicial blockchain, improve the degree of security protection, the development of this field, the coordination efficiency of departments, and the role of judicial departments in the construction of social rule of law. The first problem to be solved is to analyze the security storage requirements of data on the judicial blockchain, then deeply study the key technologies of the blockchain, design the data security storage scheme, finally build the blockchain network, design and implement the contract code on the chain, and test and analyze the system on the FISCO BCOS platform.

Our contributions are follows:

- We analyzed the security storage requirements and business security requirements of the evidence on the judicial chain.
- By studying the key technologies of blockchain, and using technologies such as smart contracts and consensus algorithms, we propose solutions for the secure storage of judicial data on the chain to strengthen the on-chain storage and security protection of judicial data.
- We design and build a special blockchain network, design and implement the contract code on the chain, and develop the system based on the JavaSDK of the FISCO BCOS platform to realize the security control and effective storage of data, and verify the effectiveness.

2 Relevant Work

Many experts and scholars have done relevant research on the secure storage of data on the chain. Here are some representative papers for introduction. Zhang [20]analyzed the similarities and differences of data management between traditional database and blockchain in terms of data management, and discussed the current research progress of data management on blockchain. Hou, Wang, Sun et al. [7,22,23] studied the electronic data storage system combined with electronic evidence and blockchain, the privacy data protection scheme combined with attribute based encryption and blockchain, and discussed the scalability of blockchain storage from two aspects: on chain and off chain storage. Rui, cebe, Ryu et al. [5,16,18] designed a dynamic data security storage scheme based on blockchain. The Internet of vehicles combines the post accident analysis system of license chain and the digital forensics framework of Internet of things infrastructure based on blockchain technology. Alessio Meloni, C. Martinez Rendon,

U. Narayanan and park junhoo [1,12,14–19] studied the combination of IEEE 1931.1 standard and blockchain technology, the architecture of blockchain for storing Internet of things (IOT) data, the security scheme of cloud IOT based on distributed blockchain and the framework composed of external server, data certifier and middleware for verifying contract. Ashwinverma et al. [21] proposed a blockchain-based management scheme for electronic law records (ELRs). It uses meta-hash keys to register cases in the public blockchain, links to the external interplanetary file storage (IPFS), and uses smart contracts to handle cases.

As far as we know, there is no blockchain integrated system covering the whole judicial case handling process, and there is no research on the secure storage technology of judicial data. In the judicial blockchain secure storage technology solution, through the combination of underlying blockchain data structure, hash algorithm, PBFT (Practical Byzantine Fault Tolerance) algorithm [11], smart contract and other technologies, a secure storage scheme on the judicial blockchain is proposed to realize the on-chain data protection of judicial data through the blockchain. We designed a special blockchain network and smart contracts, developed a Java SDK system based on FISCO BCOS, realized the security control and effective storage of data, and verified the validity of the data. Finally, we tested, analyzed and concluded it.

3 Requirements of Judicial Data Storage

In government systems, data security is especially important. According to the principle of information security, the data in the system should have confidentiality, integrity and availability protection. Data confidentiality requires that the system information can only be known by authorized users to prevent unauthorized users from disclosing data. The data of the system cannot exist in clear text in the system to prevent illegal users from getting information. Integrity needs to prevent illegal users from tampering with data. The data stored in the system needs to be resistant to illegal tampering. It needs to protect data integrity through distributed ledger, encryption and decryption of data, digital signature, hash pointer and other technologies, which is in line with the significance of electronic data of judicial certificate. Availability requires that the system data can be recovered after being tampered with or damaged, and the data can still run, that is, there should be a data loss recovery mechanism.

Next, we analyze the business logic security. In this system, any account should be real name system. Each account corresponds to a department staff member and a unique user number, which is created by the administrator and distributed to specific individuals. In the blockchain network, the mutual authentication between each node and other nodes shall be in the form of verification digital certificate, and the certificate shall be issued to each node by a recognized reliable and professional issuing authority. In the judicial blockchain network, it should be a committee composed of judicial departments that allows nodes to enter.

4 Judicial Data Storage Scheme

The system uses blockchain to build distributed collaboration. The data is secure and difficult to tamper with. The bottom layer is peer-to-peer (P2P) network, which meets the basic support required by the upper layer development. Each node can operate data through the consistency mechanism running in the network to ensure the data consistency of each node. The underlying network provides basic services for the upper application. The system blockchain network structure is shown in the Fig. 1 below.

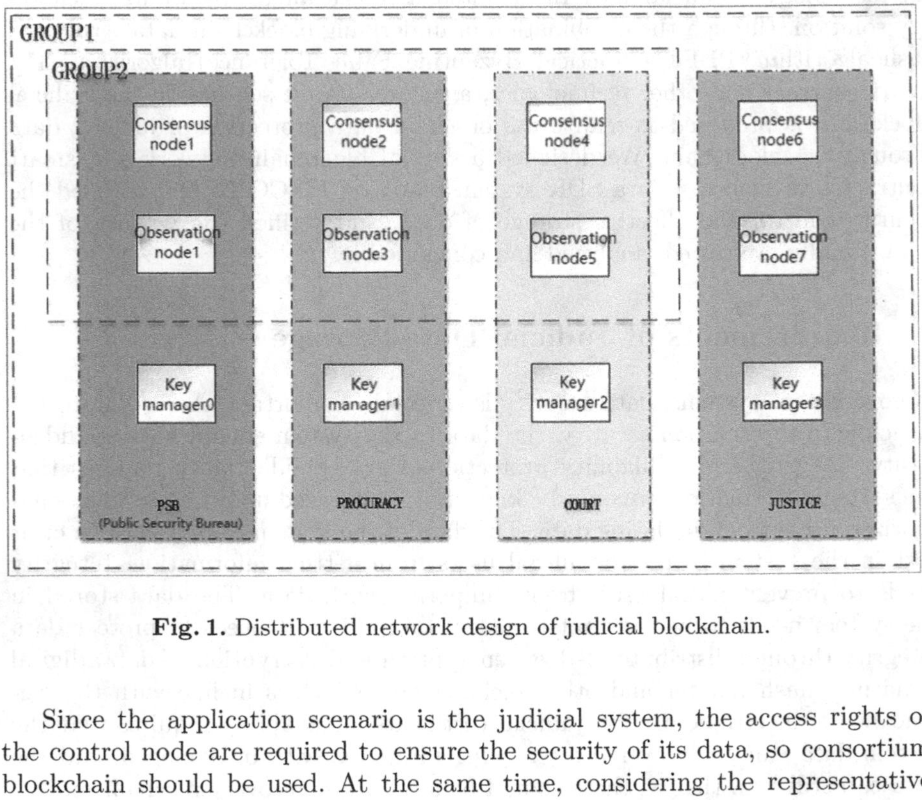

Fig. 1. Distributed network design of judicial blockchain.

Since the application scenario is the judicial system, the access rights of the control node are required to ensure the security of its data, so consortium blockchain should be used. At the same time, considering the representative purpose of the actual business role, it is abstracted into four departments here, including the Public Security Bureau (PSB), the procurement, the court and the justice. The authority that issues certificates should be jointly composed of four departments or appointed by the institution. Each department saves the copies on the blockchain and is equipped with a consensus node, an observation node and a key manager. Because the network is intended to demonstrate the cooperation of the main judicial departments, it is abstracted as four departments here, including the Public Security Bureau (PSB), the procuracy, the court and the justice. The four departments form a blockchain network, and each blockchain node has a unique node ID. The consensus node is responsible for building the consortium blockchain network with the consensus nodes of other institutions. The nodes reach an agreement through the PBFT consensus algorithm and participate in the transaction and block synchronization in the network. The observation node does not participate in the consensus process, but only participates in block synchronization. It is responsible for synchronizing data from the consensus node in real time and sending transactions to the network. Key manger is responsible for managing the disk dropping and encryption processing of all types of node data, and controlling the confidentiality of node stored data. The blockchain network is set as two groups.

As the blockchain system adopts the collaborative mode of on chain and off chain for business processing, the data in the system is also divided into up and down's data on chain. The corresponding storage schemes need to be also designed respectively.

Data Storage Based on Blockchain. Smart contract is the medium for operating blockchain data and a core point of blockchain development. The design adopts a hierarchical smart contract structure, including factory contract, storage contract and query contract. Among them, the factory contract can create new contracts. The three contracts jointly complete the functions of the contract factory model: only expose the factory contract, and the factory contract creates a new sub contract. All sub contracts are maintained by a unified factory. After agreement, all parties can call the contract to launch a new sub contract, so as to continue to expand with the progress of the project. The storage and query contracts are used in FISCO BCOS by calling the system precompiled contract kvTable. Layered smart contract design can simplify the code, reduce the impact of security vulnerabilities, and make the system more scalable (Fig. 2).

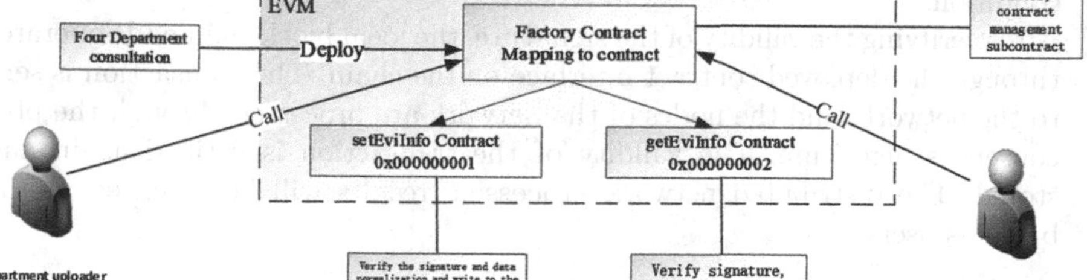

Fig. 2. Design of factory contract layered smart contract.

On chain data storage refers to the effective and safe storage of the data uploaded from off chain to on chain. Because storing data on the blockchain is expensive, and the data on the chain is difficult to tamper with, the chain has been extending over time, and the permanent storage of data increases the storage cost, so the data stored on the chain should be small and representative, decrease the expending on blockchain and increase the efficiency.

The main steps for users to store data into the blockchain network are as follows:

1) Judicial system initialization and key distribution. When the system is initialized, the data center in each institution is set as the blockchain node, the institution administrator sends the user number U_i to the business user, and the institution generates encryption, decryption and signature key pairs, expressed as

$$\{U_i, PK_\alpha^{encode}, SK_\alpha^{encode}, PK_\alpha^{sign}, SK_\alpha^{sign}\}$$

2) The Department business user uploads the certificate storage file and file information to the certificate storage system, and the user U_i structure data is sent to the blockchain node where the institution is located a construction data FR_data1 is:

$$FR\_data1 = \left\{I \parallel m2 \parallel Sign_{SK\alpha}^{sign}(m2)\right\}$$

where $m2 = \{hash(mi)||Ui||Timestamp\}$, and mi is the original data to be uploaded by U_i.

3) After receiving the data, the local blockchain node verifies whether it is a legal signature. If the business process permission requirements are not met, discard it and record the log. If it passes, proceed to the next step.

$$Design_{SK\alpha}^{sign}(m2)@ = @Sign_{SK\alpha}^{sign}(m2)?$$

Among them, the signature algorithm should ensure one-way and ensure that the original information will not be obtained in the signature verification process. Design uses PK_α^{sign} algorithm for checking the original data, @ = @ indicates that the verification of the signature algorithm passes the equivalent condition.

4) After verifying the validity of the signature, the local blockchain node operates through the deployed contract interface on the chain. The transaction is sent to the network, and the nodes of the network are processed through the pbft consensus algorithm. The validity of the transaction is verified again and stored. The distributed network processing results will be returned to the business users.

Design of Off-Blockchain Storage. Off-blockchain data storage refers to the secure storage of the original data files uploaded by business users to the system. The original files are stored in the off chain database, which is convenient for users to compare with their corresponding fingerprints on the chain when downloading files, check the file integrity, and verify whether the evidence files have been tampered with.

The main steps for users to store files in the database are as follows:

1) Judicial certificate storage system initialization and user key distribution (this step is the same as the initialization of data storage on the blockchain).

2) The business users upload the certificate storage file and file information to the storage system, encrypts the public key of the institution, and adds the user number. The system generates the index value according to the data type, the case uploaded by the file and the current timestamp. Generate stored data *Upload_data*1.

$$Upload\_data1 = \{I \parallel U_i \parallel E_{\alpha}^{PKencode}(mi)\}$$

3) *Upload_Data*1 is stored in the database of the organization and the processing results are returned to the user. When it is necessary to access data, it shall request the uploading user to decrypt the data.

Security Analysis. The judicial blockchain security storage scheme proposed in this paper can solve the security requirements mentioned above. The design of the blockchain network structure can provide basic support for the development of DAPP, a distributed application of the upper judicial depository. The blocks of the transaction are connected in series by hash pointers according to time to form a chain and stored in the node. Under pbft consensus, the network can tolerate 33% of Byzantine nodes, with high throughput, prevent double flower attacks, and strong stability. It can fully meet the business scenario of the alliance blockchain network nodes in this paper. Moreover, all operational transactions in the network need to be signed before the node can pass the verification, to ensure that the transaction data is undeniable. This scheme records the data in the judicial alliance chain, which can ensure that the judicial data can not be tampered with and security.

The disk dropping encryption control can encrypt the data storage disk of the node in the Department network through the key management server. When the hard disk of the machine where the node is located is taken away from the organization and the node is started in the network outside the organization's intranet, the hard disk data cannot be decrypted, the node cannot be started, and the data on the alliance chain cannot be stolen. The factory mode design of the smart contract is convenient for managing the sub contract, ensuring that the address on the sub contract chain is not obtained and called by external personnel, and is conducive to the expansion of contract functions in the future. The system design adopts the typical blockchain design scheme of collaboration on and off the chain. Different storage processes are adopted in the system data storage scheme. The asymmetric encryption algorithm can set the corresponding evidence files to request authorization and sharing, so as to protect the evidence files from being obtained by unrelated users in the system and meet the feedback requirements of staff during field investigation. In addition, when querying the audit evidence, the evidence file and the summary value on the chain can be mutually verified to check whether the evidence file is tampered with.

Scheme Evaluation. This section uses a comparative method to evaluate the proposed safe storage scheme. Compared with the blockchain data storage scheme [8,9]. It can be seen from the table comparison that the consensus mechanism of this paper and document [8] is the pbft consensus. Compared with the proxy Byzantine fault tolerance (dbft) used in document [8], the consensus algorithm is more decentralized than the proxy node mechanism of the former; In addition, compared with the blockchain development platform used in literature [8,9], the FISCO BCOS adopted in this scheme is a domestic open-source blockchain development platform, which can better meet the requirements of domestic independent control in the application scenario of government judicial cases in this paper; In terms of node admission control, this paper has corresponding node admission control, while literature [8,9] does not control the access of nodes to and from the network; In this scheme, the data is processed in a collaborative way on and off the chain. The encrypted ciphertext of the original evidence file is stored off the chain, and the hash digest of the original evidence file is stored on the chain. Compared with the literature [8], it can greatly avoid the rapid growth of the data on the blockchain, effectively reduce the storage cost of the blockchain system, and add a disk dropping encryption mechanism compared with other schemes, The hard disk of the data on the storage chain can be further protected; Finally, with regard to the data authorization sharing function proposed by the relevant staff during the investigation, this scheme supports the evidence request authorization sharing function. The user requesting evidence must obtain the original evidence file after the authorization and consent of the evidence uploading staff. The evidence file stored in the assurance system can not be obtained at will, and then compared with the tamperproof summary data on the chain. Compared with literature [8,9], the secure storage scheme of data on the chain in this paper is more in line with the demand scenario of the government's judicial certificate, and can effectively and safely store system data (Table 1).

Table 1. Comparison between the scheme and the other schemes

Solution	Tamper prevention	Consensus mechanism	Domestic platform	Access	Storage cost	Authorization sharing	Disk encryption
[8]	High	DBFT	No	No	High	No	No
[9]	High	PBFT	No	No	Low	No	No
This paper	High	PBFT	Yes	Yes	Low	Yes	Yes

5 Simulation

The judicial blockchain security storage scheme designed in this study includes blockchain network construction, smart contract deployment, system data storage module implementation, blockchain authority control implementation, etc. The experiment is based on Ubuntu 18.04 system and FISCO BCOS platform, using solidity language to develop smart contracts, and springboot and mybatis-plus to develop under the blockchain.

Blockchain Network Construction. Blockchain network is the foundation to support the development of upper DAPP and the safe storage of data in the system. Here are four Ubuntu 18.04 under the synchronous operation of virtual machines, install and deploy through the command line, and use the enterprise deployment tool generator to deploy the blockchain network structure designed in the scheme. Deploy the blockchain console and select the PSB-node0 node to connect. Set the node type through the console. After the blockchain network configuration is completed, observe the beginning of network consensus (Fig. 3).

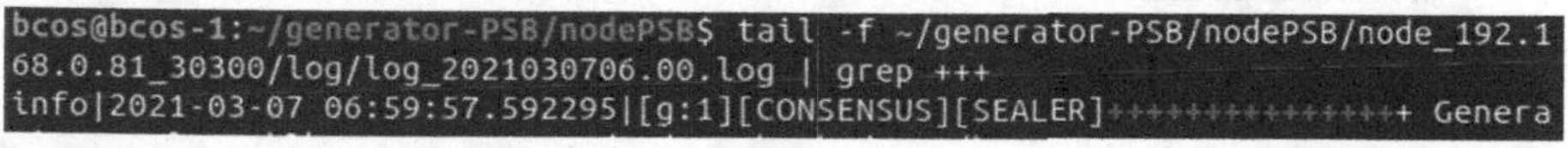

Fig. 3. Judicial blockchain network consensus a success.

Implementation of Smart Contracts. Smart contract is the special code on the blockchain of the certificate storage system on the judicial chain, which can realize the interaction between the blockchain and the SDK under the chain. The smart contracts on the FISCO BCOS platform is written using Solidity. After deployment, it is compiled into executable data and can be run on the virtual machine. FISCO BCOS supports Java SDK and other multilingual SDKs, which can be deployed on nodes Convert .sol file to Java file. The following Table 2 shows the contract name and its brief introduction.

Table 2. Smart contracts' name and description

Contract name	Description
Factory contract	Realize the function of managing sub contracts and facilitate the later expansion of the project
Storage contract	Upload case evidence related information operation
Query contract	Operation of obtaining information related to case evidence

Implementation of Data Storage. The storage of data in the judicial storage's system has two portions: the encryption storage of key for the original file data of case evidence under the chain and the chain storage of key data such as index and summary of evidence file. The user opens the evidence upload interface, selects the evidence file and writes the description and other relevant information, and clicks the operation button to upload it to the system. The system will perform encryption on it according to the idea of data storage module, generate the evidence ciphertext, and upload the summary and other information to the chain (Fig. 4).

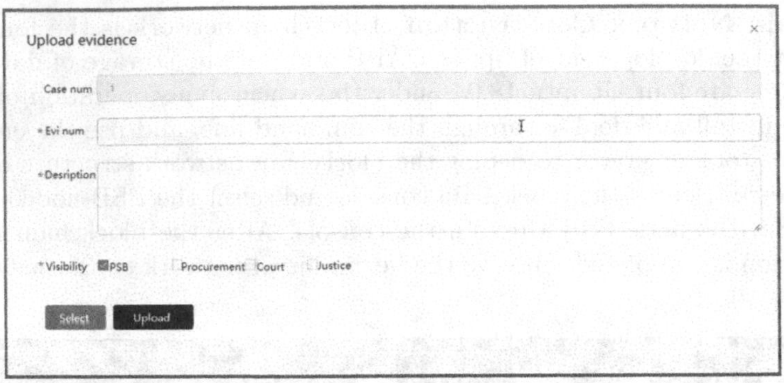

Fig. 4. Evidence upload interface.

Performance Test. Use the hyperledger caliper tool to test the performance. This tool is a hyperledger subproject. It aims to launch a set of general blockchain performance testing framework, which can support all hyperledger and other blockchain projects. Caliper can test the number of transactions per second (TPS), transaction success rate, transaction delay and other indicators in the built blockchain network in a user-defined manner. This paper mainly tests the system writing of the storage contract (the query contract does not write data to the chain). It can test the transaction processing speed on the network. The transaction volume of each round of test is 1000. From 100 tps to 700 tps, the step length is 100. Each round of test is conducted for 7 rounds.

It can be seen from the figure below that the test rate is 100%, and the relationship between the throughput of seteviinfo service and the average delay is shown in the figure. The transaction throughput of the network is about 500 tps. The sending transaction starts from 500, the average delay starts to rise sharply, and the throughput remains about 500. When the sending transaction speed is higher, the transaction will exceed the load on the chain and enter the queue to wait, resulting in an increasing delay, so there will be inflection points and bifurcation (Fig. 5).

From the figure below, the test rate is 100%, and the throughput of setEvilnfo service is about 500 tps. The average delay of sending transactions starts to rise sharply from 500, and the throughput remains unchanged at about 500. When the sending transaction speed is higher, the transaction exceeds the load on the chain and enters the queue to wait, resulting in increasing delay, so there is an inflection point and bifurcation.

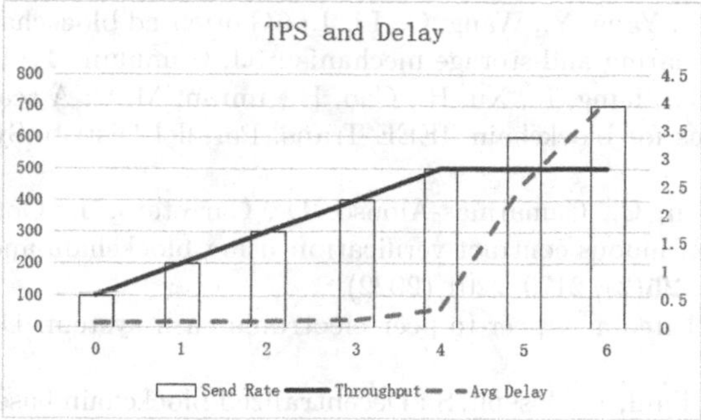

Fig. 5. Throughput and average latency of setting evidence service.

6 Conclusion

In this paper, firstly, the security requirements of judicial data storage is analyzed. Secondly, the data security storage design scheme is proposed, and the blockchain network structure is designed with data security control and data storage for different needs of the system security. Finally, the simulation experiment of the scheme is implemented according to the proposed scheme. Future work will be further in-depth research, for example, to explore adding more functional contracts, improve the current judicial blockchain system, and improve the operational efficiency and security.

References

1. Meloni, A., et al.: Exploiting the IoT potential of blockchain in the IEEE P1931.1 roof standard. IEEE Commun. Stand. Mag. **2**(3), 38–44 (2018)
2. Bonomi, S., Casini, M., Ciccotelli, C.: B-CoC: a blockchain-based chain of custody for evidences management in digital forensics (2018)
3. Buterin, V., et al.: A next-generation smart contract and decentralized application platform. White Paper **3**(37), 2–1 (2014)
4. Cao, S., Cao, Y., Wang, X., Lu, Y.: A review of researches on blockchain (2017)
5. Cebe, M., Erdin, E., Akkaya, K., Aksu, H., Uluagac, S.: Block4forensic: an integrated lightweight blockchain framework for forensics applications of connected vehicles. IEEE Commun. Mag. **56**(10), 50–57 (2018)
6. Chao, X., Yan, S., Hong, L.: Secured data storage scheme based on block chain for agricultural products tracking. In: 2017 3rd International Conference on Big Data Computing and Communications (BIGCOM) (2017)
7. Hou, Y.B., Liang, X., Zhan, X.Y.: Block chain based architecture model of electronic evidence system. Comput. Sci. **45**, 348–351 (2018)
8. Hui, W., Mingming, Z.: Blockchain-based medical information security storage model. Comput. Sci. **46**(12), 174–179 (2019)
9. Jianfu, L., Yingxu, L., Jing, L.: Log secure storage and retrieval based on the combination of on-chain and off-chain. Comput. Sci. **47**(3), 298–303 (2020)

10. Jiang, Y., Ge, X., Yang, Y., Wang, C., Li, J.: 6G oriented blockchain based internet of things data sharing and storage mechanism. J. Commun. **41**(10), 48 (2020)
11. Li, W., Feng, C., Zhang, L., Xu, H., Cao, B., Imran, M.A.: A scalable multi-layer PBFT consensus for blockchain. IEEE Trans. Parallel Distrib. Syst. **32**(5), 1146–1160 (2020)
12. Martinez-Rendon, C., Camarmas-Alonso, D., Carretero, J., Gonzalez-Compean, J.L.: On the continuous contract verification using blockchain and real-time data. Clust. Comput. **25**(3), 2179–2201 (2022)
13. Nakamoto, S.: Bitcoin: a peer-to-peer electronic cash system. Decent. Bus. Rev. 21260 (2008)
14. Narayanan, U., Paul, V., Joseph, S.: Decentralized blockchain based authentication for secure data sharing in cloud-IoT. J. Ambient. Intell. Humaniz. Comput. **13**(2), 769–787 (2022)
15. Park, J., Kim, H., Kim, G., Ryou, J.: Smart contract data feed framework for privacy-preserving oracle system on blockchain. Computers **10**(1), 7 (2020)
16. Qiao, R., Dong, S., Wei, Q., Wang, Q.X.: Blockchain based secure storage scheme of dynamic data. Comput. Sci. **45**(2), 57–62 (2018)
17. Ren, Y., Leng, Y., Zhu, F., Wang, J., Kim, H.J.: Data storage mechanism based on blockchain with privacy protection in wireless body area network. Sensors **19**(10), 2395 (2019)
18. Ryu, J.H., Sharma, P.K., Jo, J.H., Park, J.H.: A blockchain-based decentralized efficient investigation framework for IoT digital forensics. J. Supercomput. **75**(8), 4372–4387 (2019)
19. Shuai, W., Yong, Y., Wang, X., Li, J., Wang, F.Y.: An overview of smart contract: architecture, applications, and future trends. In: 2018 IEEE Intelligent Vehicles Symposium (IV) (2018)
20. Singh, M.: Blockchain technology for data management in industry 4.0. Blockchain Technology for Industry 4.0, Secure, Decentralized, Distributed and Trusted Industry Environment (2020)
21. Verma, A., Bhattacharya, P., Saraswat, D., Tanwar, S.: Nyaya: blockchain-based electronic law record management scheme for judicial investigations. J. Inf. Secur. Appl. **63**, 103025 (2021)
22. Yujiang, W., Chengtang, C., Lin, Y.: Personal privacy data protection scheme based on blockchain and attribute-based encryption. J. Cryptol. Res. **8**(1), 14 (2021)
23. Zhixin, S., Xin, Z., Feng, X., Lu, C.: Research progress of blockchain storage scalability. J. Softw. **32**(1), 20 (2021)

Judicial Evidence Storage Scheme Based on Smart Contract

Hao Wu[1,2], Xiaoli Qin[1,2(✉)], and Yuqing Kou[3]

[1] School of Cyberspace Security, Hainan University, Haikou 570228, China
20085400210077@hainu.edu.cn, xlqin@hainanu.edu.cn

[2] Key Laboratory of Internet Information Retrieval of Hainan Province, Haikou, China

[3] School of Computer Science and Technology, Hainan University, Haikou 570228, China
20085400210027@hainanu.edu.cn

Abstract. In recent years, the security of evidence storage and the efficiency of case handling in the judicial field have gradually been regarded by the government as an important issue for optimizing functions and work levels. Such as the validity certification of evidence and the timeliness and convenience of the circulation of evidence documents. Blockchain provides an effective solution for judicial evidence storage due to the immutable, synchronous and traceable properties. At the same time, as an important component of the blockchain, smart contracts provide automatic execution functions. However, as a special software, the development and management of smart contracts need an effective domain-oriented framework. In this paper, a full-lifecycle smart contract design pattern that conforms to software engineering specifications is proposed, and a scheme and framework for the design and implementation of smart contracts is introduced in the judicial field.

Keywords: Smart contract · Judicial evidence · Design and frameworks

1 Introduction

Since the blockchain technology was proposed by Satoshi Nakamoto's founding paper [9], the technology has gradually expanded from the initial virtual currency business to other fields. For example, trusted computing platform, trusted digital identity, trusted copyright protection, certificate storage solutions, etc.

Due to the properties of distributed storage, open data sharing, non-repudiation, and traceability, blockchain technology has been used in more and more application fields in recent years. In addition to public chains such as

This work is supported in part by the Hainan Province Science and Technology Special Fund (ZDFYF2020012, ZDYF2021GXJS216), the National Natural Science Foundation of China (62162020), the Science Project of Hainan University (KYQD(ZR)20021).

X. Chen et al. (Eds.): SocialSec 2022, CCIS 1663, pp. 351–363, 2022.
https://doi.org/10.1007/978-981-19-7242-3_23

Bitcoin and Ethereum, there are also smaller consortium chains, and more private chains. Different fields have different choices of blockchains with different degrees of openness. Among them, the public chain is the most extensive type of blockchain. Since the Hyperledger is shared, all nodes can freely join and withdraw from the public chain on the basis of completing the consensus. The public chain is the most representative of Bitcoin and Ethereum. Primitive blockchain type. The consortium chain is a blockchain with slightly stricter requirements than the public chain, that is, a semi-open blockchain. It only allows certain types of groups to join and withdraw from the blockchain consensus. By setting the node access threshold to determine specific Groups and alliance chains ensure the security of blockchain data and hyperledger to a certain extent. They are suitable for systems with a certain degree of trust within the group. We have noticed that the organizational relationship of the judicial department is to meet the needs of the alliance chain users characteristic organization [11]. Electronic evidence has certain particularities. Therefore, it is also necessary to strictly follow the relevant provisions of the "Criminal Procedure Law" on the nature of evidence in accordance with the first characteristic of evidence, and the legality of evidence means that it must be combined with legal forms Collecting and using evidence The so-called legitimacy of evidence refers to a formal requirement that evidence has a certain function or capability. When examining the legitimacy of electronic certificates based on blockchain, it is also necessary to follow the standards set by relevant regulations.

As an important component of the blockchain, smart contracts are the main direction for the development of functions that provide automatic execution. Step 1: Write the contract code through the Solidity programming language, reach the smart contract compiler via web3.js, and generate EVM bytecode and smart contract binary executable code. Step 2: Feedback EVM bytecode and contract binary executable code to the user front end. Step 3: Deploy the compiled content of the contract on the built node cluster, and the result returns the transaction hash of the contract packaged on the blockchain and the Application Binary Interface (ABI). Step 4: After the contract is successfully deployed, the contract account address is fed back to the front end. Step 5: The front-end calls the smart contract, and realizes the operation of interacting with the contract through the contract account address, contract ABI and nonce. Among them, nonce refers to the number of transactions, and the value will be automatically increased by one after each contract call to prevent repeated transactions. The deployment and operation process of smart contracts is shown in Fig. 1.

However, the development of smart contracts should follow software engineering specifications, that is, follow the periodic work of complete analysis, design and modeling. The existing blockchains are mainly represented by the two platforms of Bitcoin and Ethereum, so the existing smart contract design models are mainly For assets and finance [1], in other words, most smart contract designs are mainly oriented on how assets are stored and protected, or how financial markets work (transactions, confirmations, etc.). However, in the face of the need for legal evidence in the judicial field, there is no effective solution to prove

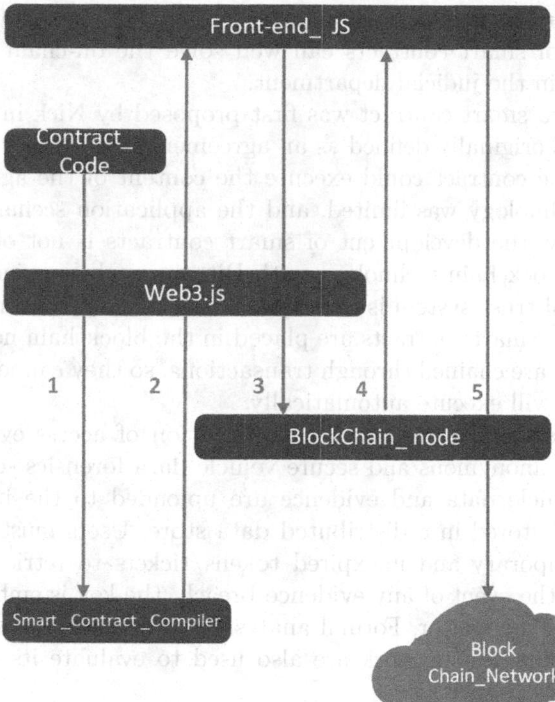

Fig. 1. Deployment and operation process of smart contract

it. In this paper a new smart contract design mode, and a full life cycle smart contract design mode are proposed in the perspective of software engineering specifications and judicial process regulations.

2 Related Work

Due to the security of the blockchain network, its application in the judicial field has always been a topic of concern to the government and application developers [6], and blockchain technology is also an important breakthrough in technological innovation that the government has focused on supporting in recent years [20]. In judicial practice, the authenticity of electronic evidence has always been controversial. Among the various reasons why judges do not accept electronic evidence, the first reason is to question the authenticity of electronic evidence. Therefore, in order to confirm whether the electronic evidence can objectively and truly reflect the facts of the case, a key is to be able to accurately determine the authenticity of the electronic evidence. The certificate deposit solution is an important part of the submission of blockchain engineering in the judicial field. Based on the certificate deposit scheme, the judicial department can complete the business process of evidence review and document approval online. As an important part of blockchain technology, the automatic execution and immutability of smart contracts can well solve the on-chain execution of business processes in the judicial department.

The concept of a smart contract was first proposed by Nick in 1994 [12]. A smart contract was originally defined as an agreement defined in a digital form. The approver of the contract could execute the content of the agreement, but the early stage technology was limited, and the application scenarios were different. Prominently, the development of smart contracts is not obvious. Until the emergence of blockchain technology with Bitcoin as the carrier, this decentralized and mutual trust system is exactly the execution environment required by smart contracts. Smart contracts are placed in the blockchain network in the form of DApps and are chained through transactions, so they cannot be changed once deployed and will execute automatically.

Smart contracts are very helpful for the solution of access evidence. Li et al. [8] proposed an anonymous and secure vehicle data forensics solution based on blockchain. Vehicle data and evidence are uploaded to the blockchain by data providers and stored in a distributed data store. Users must hold certain attributes and temporary and unexpired tokens/tickets to retrieve data from the blockchain. In the event of any evidence breach, the key is embedded in the data to track down the traitor. Formal analysis and a prototype system of the WiFi-based Ethereum test network are also used to evaluate its performance, privacy, and security properties.

However, the application of the current technical solution is only aimed at the secure storage and query of evidence data, lacking the on-chain execution of the entire business process of the Public Security, Procuratorate and Law Department, as well as the corresponding smart contract solutions, and the lack of smart contract design patterns and vulnerability detection technologies for the judicial field. Research and Application.

The smart contract design mode for judicial evidence storage system proposed in this paper, from the perspective of software engineering specifications and judicial process regulations, according to the steps of business process modeling, model sorting and standardization, and the use of smart contract design mode, proposes a full life cycle The smart contract design model of the company applies smart contract technology to the certificate deposit business of the Public Security, Procuratorate and Law Department. The idea of smart contract security detection research provides solutions and processing directions for the security of smart contracts in the judicial field. It is of great significance to the implementation of the judicial business system. As a general language for process modeling, Business Process Modeling Notation (BPMN) has been proved to be satisfactorily used for e-government service design [5]. At the same time, select appropriate design patterns and vulnerability detection technologies, and apply them to the practice of developing proprietary smart contracts for public security, procuratorial, and judicial services. It is expected to provide strong support for the safe development, safe operation and runtime monitoring of smart contracts in the judicial system, improve the security of the entire life cycle of smart contracts, and provide convenient multi-contract deployment, management, update and destruction functions.

3 Business Model of Smart Contract

Since smart contract design needs to follow software engineering specifications, the primary task of contract production is demand analysis. In this chapter the business model for judicial existence business processes will be discussed.

3.1 Business Process Modeling

According to the software engineering specification, the business model is usually sorted out from the demand analysis. For the demand analysis of traditional software engineering, the UML modeling language can be used to describe the requirements more accurately [2], and the judicial evidence requirements can be described as a unified modeling document symbol. This method can better solve the problem of smart contract development that is also applicable to the demand analysis mode.

As an object-oriented software modeling language, Unified Modeling Language plays an important role in software analysis and design. It has extensive modeling capabilities, reflecting entities, properties, relationships, structures and dynamic changes. The unified modeling language in Figs. 2, 3 and 4 can more accurately describe the business process of the judicial evidence deposit system.

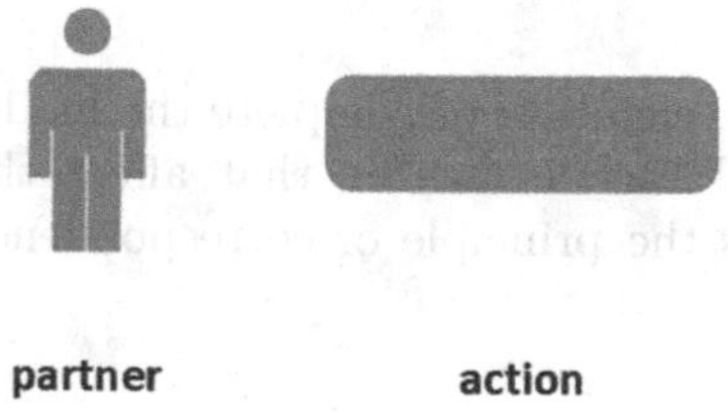

Fig. 2. Participants and behaviors

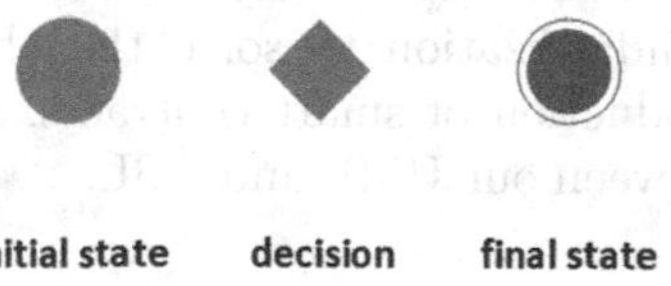

Fig. 3. State machine

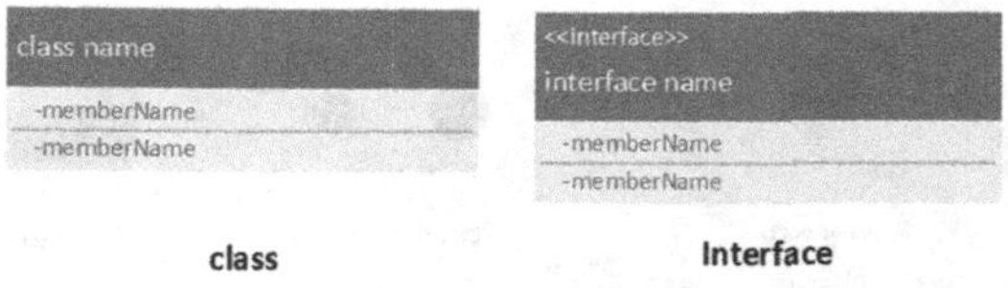

Fig. 4. Classes and interfaces

3.2 Model Normalization

However, the focus or difficulty of the design work is to accurately convert the business process into a modeling language and to enable the demand side or business domain experts and system implementers to communicate and understand each other before the modeling process, so as to achieve timely correction of demand description and improvement. The purpose of the model is the crucial puzzle.

We found that the existing solutions can solve the above problems to a certain extent [4,19], but in the process of smart contract implementation, so that it is necessary to timely discover the unfavorable security performance of smart contracts in the process of process modeling to a certain extent, scalable performance, and manageable performance factors. Therefore, inspired by the discussions of Cristian Gómez et al. [4,17], we define a Domain- Specific Language (DSL) that provides more standard model descriptions based on the Unified Modeling Language UML. Figure 5 describes the main elements in the DSL.

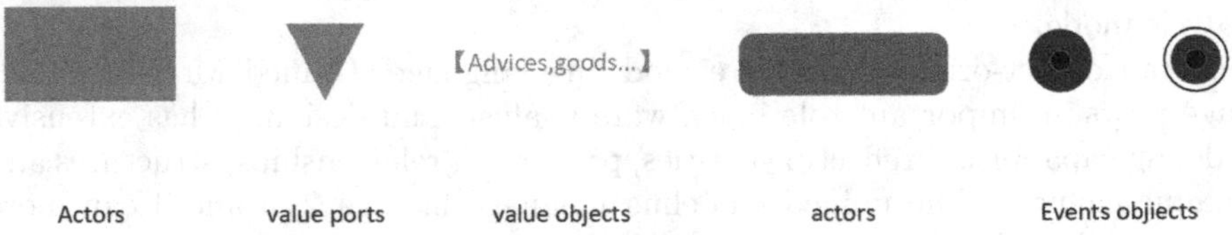

Fig. 5. DSL modeling uniform identifier

We correspond and combine DSL and UML elements to complete the model standardization to solve the above-mentioned various factors that affect the production of smart contracts. Figure 5 shows the principle of correspondence between our UML and DSL.

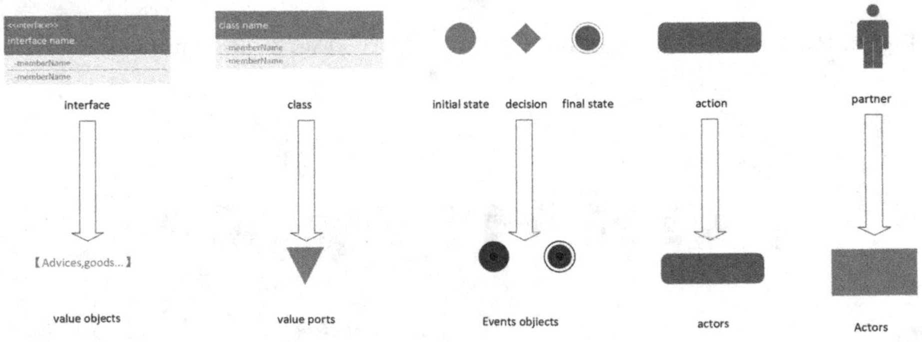

Fig. 6. Correspondence between UML and DSL elements

3.3 Multi-Contract Structure Design

The application of smart contract technology to the certificate storage business of the Public Security, Procuratorate and Law Department, the use of the non-tamperable characteristics of the blockchain and the automatic triggering of smart contracts, to explore the smart contract solutions for the entire business of the Public Security, Procuratorate and Law Department. On the premise of ensuring the security of documents and evidence data, an automated data transfer system is used to improve office efficiency and provide safe technical support for public supervision; at the same time, in order to meet the critical security of the public security and judicial department, smart contracts should be completed in the system at the same time development. It is expected to provide strong support for the safe development, safe operation and runtime monitoring of smart contracts in the judicial system. It is expected to improve the security of the whole life cycle of smart contracts, provide convenient multi-contract deployment, management, update and destruction functions, and is expected to improve the efficiency of smart contract design and development; Efficiency in reaching consensus and translating into accurate and efficient smart contract design; contributing to the realization of on-chain smart contracts that meet demand at a higher rate than ever before.

In terms of business requirements, the smart contract is automatically triggered to complete the circulation after reading the file for real-time approval. Due to the obvious life cycle characteristics of some documents, the file needs to be approved by a department before it can be transferred to the next department; after the business model is determined, it is necessary to Select the appropriate smart contract design mode, consider the smart contract design mode that meets the security and performance requirements at the design stage, and introduce an overall architecture design that can complete the full life cycle management of smart contracts. Some of the existing design patterns are suitable for the development of smart contracts in the public security, procuratorial and judicial system, and it is crucial to adopt appropriate standards in the selection process. In the process of smart contract analysis and design, communication and communication between the demander and the developer is required. How to ensure the effective communication between the two parties is one of the solutions that this research needs to provide.

This paper determines the overall structure design of multi-contract management according to the needs of judicial evidence storage, as shown in Fig. 6. All contract addresses are recorded in the contract registry, and the business process control module reads the process information from the lower-level process record contract, and then changes the status of the case, evidence and document contracts at the same level. This achieves the unification of data flow and service flow.

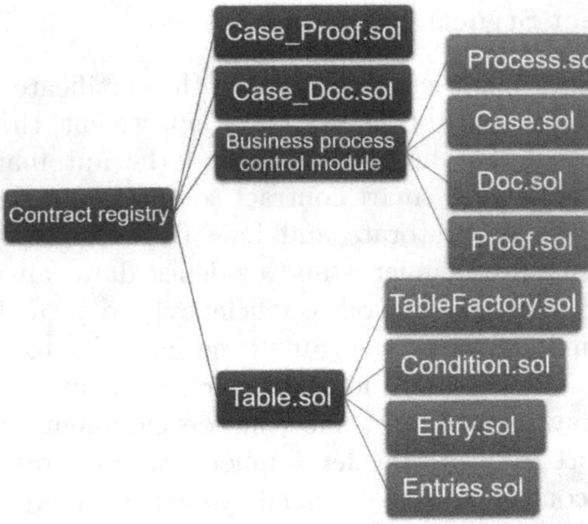

Fig. 7. Schematic diagram of multi-contract management structure

4 Design of Smart Contract

Transforming the design into a smart contract according to a complete requirement analysis is the last important work of the design pattern. In this chapter, we will take the solidity platform as an example and combines the existing Ethereum smart contract security issues [7,14,16] to give Example model descriptions applicable to the field of judicial presence.

Regular Destruction. Although due to the characteristics of Hyperledger itself, smart contracts cannot be tampered with after deployment [21], but there are a certain number of contracts with limited use time, or the old contracts need to be destroyed when the contracts are updated. As shown in Fig. 7.

Contract Registry. According to the above, since smart contracts should follow the software engineering life cycle, there is a need for software updates (i.e. smart contract updates). It is located in the same contract class. When it needs to be updated, the data and methods need to be deleted and re-chained together. The cost is high. If the data and methods can be processed separately, that is, the data will not be stored in the same contract class of the method. There is no need to update data when updating, reducing computing and storage costs. As shown in Fig. 8.

Data-Logic Separation. For contract management, due to the relatively large judicial deposit business system [13], if all the required business processes are reflected on the chain and completed automatically by smart contracts, a huge DApp is required. Therefore, it must be implemented using multiple contract

```
pragma solidity ^0.4.17;
contract AutoDeprecate {
uint expires;
function AutoDeprecate(uint _days) public {
expires = now + _days * 1 days;
}
function expired() internal view returns (bool) {
return now > expires;
}
modifier willDeprecate() {
require(!expired());
_;
}
modifier whenDeprecated() {
require(expired());
_;
}
function deposit() public payable willDeprecate {
// some code
}
function withdraw() public view whenDeprecated {
// some code
}
```

Fig. 8. Periodic destruction of solidity instances

```
pragma solidity ^0.4.17;
import "../authorization/Ownership.sol";
contract Register is Owned {
address backendContract;
address[] previousBackends;
function Register() public {
owner = msg.sender;
}
function changeBackend(address newBackend) public
onlyOwner() returns (bool) {
if(newBackend != backendContract) {
previousBackends.push(backendContract);
backendContract = newBackend;
return true;
}
return false;
}
}
```

Fig. 9. Contract registry

sub-modules. At this time, multi-contract management is particularly important. Using the contract registry, you can use one contract to manage multiple contracts. When you need to query the latest contract version, you can call the query method. To update the contract, you only need to change the contract address in the registry contract to the latest address. As shown in Fig. 9.

Post External Call. Referring to the security of Ethereum smart contracts and the previous experience of solidity development, reentrancy attacks and code injection attacks during external calls are typical smart contract security risks [10], so the external call method is placed at the end of the code and waits for the front part to complete completely. And then based on external call permissions is a critical security model. As shown in Fig. 10.

Automatic Delay. Since the smart contract conforms to the operating structure of the server-client system, there is a condition for DDoS attack in terms of security. When the server (i.e., the smart contract on the chain) continuously accepts method call applications, the operating efficiency of the system will be greatly reduced. Block confirmation may also be affected [18], so the automatic delay mode is set, and the transaction completion time is set independently, and the running delay is intentionally slowed down. As shown in Fig. 11.

Satellite. When a contract that will not be updated for a long time and needs to always run on the chain exists, and one of the methods or functions needs to be updated and upgraded normally, use this method to outsource the method

```
pragma solidity ^0.4.17;
contract DataStorage {
mapping(bytes32 => uint) uintStorage;
function getUintValue(bytes32 key) public constant
returns (uint) {
return uintStorage[key];
}
function setUintValue(bytes32 key, uint value) public {
uintStorage[key] = value;
}
}
```

Fig. 10. Data logic separation solidity

```
pragma solidity ^0.4.17;
import "../authorization/Ownership.sol";
contract Register is Owned {
address backendContract;
address[] previousBackends;
function Register() public {
owner = msg.sender;
}
function changeBackend(address newBackend) public
onlyOwner() returns (bool) {
if(newBackend != backendContract) {
previousBackends.push(backendContract);
backendContract = newBackend;
return true;
}
return false;
}
}
```

Fig. 11. Contract registry solidity instance

```
pragma solidity ^0.4.17;
contract RateLimit {
uint enabledAt = now;
modifier enabledEvery(uint t) {
if (now >= enabledAt) {
enabledAt = now + t;
_;
}
}
function f() public enabledEvery(1 minutes) {
// some code
}
}
```

Fig. 12. Auto-delay solidity instance

function that needs to be upgraded to other similar types, or in the contract code that can be updated at the same time, part of the update of the smart contract can be realized. The code is shown in Fig. 12.

Emergency Close. In the scheme, contract state is controlled by a boolean type identifier. When the identifier is not stopped, the contract run function 1. When the identifier shows that the contract has stopped, the contract corresponds to function 2. By controlling the identifier, it ensures that the contract can be executed. If necessary, changes can be made to the corresponding method. The code is shown in Fig. 13.

Mutual Exclusion Principle. The function of this method is to prevent reentrancy attacks. The contract uses the boolean type identifier as a prerequisite for method execution, and converts the value of the identifier after the method is executed. The code is shown in Fig. 14.

```
pragma solidity ^0.4.17;
contract Satellite {
function calculateVariable() public pure returns (uint){
// calculate var
return 2 * 3;
 }
}

pragma solidity ^0.4.17;
import "../../authorization/Ownership.sol";
import "./Satellite.sol";
contract Base is Owned {
uint public variable;
address satelliteAddress;
function setVariable() public onlyOwner {
Satellite s = Satellite(satelliteAddress);
variable = s.calculateVariable();
}
function updateSatelliteAddress(address _address) public
onlyOwner {
satelliteAddress = _address;
 }
}
```

Fig. 13. Satellite example

```
pragma solidity ^0.4.17;
import "../authorization/Ownership.sol";
contract EmergencyStop is Owned {
bool public contractStopped = false;
modifier haltInEmergency {
if (!contractStopped) _;
}
modifier enableInEmergency {
if (contractStopped) _;
}
function toggleContractStopped() public onlyOwner {
contractStopped = !contractStopped;
}
function deposit() public payable haltInEmergency {
// some code
}
function withdraw() public view enableInEmergency {
// some code
}
}
```

Fig. 14. Emergency close example

```
pragma solidity ^0.4.17;
contract Mutex {
bool locked;
modifier noReentrancy() {
require(!locked);
locked = true;
_;
locked = false;
}
// f is protected by a mutex, thus reentrant calls
// from within msg.sender.call cannot call f again
function f() noReentrancy public returns (uint) {
require(msg.sender.call());
return 1;
}
```

Fig. 15. Mutual exclusion example

5 Conclusion

Judicial evidence storage is studied in this paper. According to the design mode of the whole life cycle of smart contracts, along with business process modeling, as well as standard modeling language and special domain modeling language, the scheme of judicial evidence Storage is discussed by using solidity security management design mode. In the scheme, possibilities and implementation methods of smart contract technology are used to achieve automate workflow. In the future work, we will further verify the design mode, and increase the on-chain storage and automatic circulation of data such as documents and materials. Furthermore, in order to reduce the management and development difficulty of judicial smart contract applications, we will improve the security recommendations provided by the Ethereum security framework and solidity official documents [3,15] (Fig. 15).

References

1. Bartoletti, M., Pompianu, L.: An empirical analysis of smart contracts: platforms, applications, and design patterns. In: Brenner, M., et al. (eds.) FC 2017. LNCS, vol. 10323, pp. 494–509. Springer, Cham (2017). https://doi.org/10.1007/978-3-319-70278-0_31
2. Dabrowski, J., Letier, E., Perini, A., Susi, A.: Application review of analytical software engineering: a systematic literature review. Empir. Softw. Eng. **27**(2), 1–63 (2022)
3. Garfatta, I., Klai, K., Gaaloul, W., Graiet, M.: A survey on formal verification for solidity smart contracts. In: Stanger, N., et al. (eds.) ACSW, pp. 3:1–3:10. ACM (2021). https://doi.org/10.1145/3437378.3437879
4. Gómez, C., Pérez Blanco, F.J., Vara, J.M., De Castro, V., Marcos, E.: E-government design and smart contract development based on business process modeling (2021)
5. Gómez, C., Pérez Blanco, F.J., Vara, J.M., De Castro, V., Marcos, E.: Design and development of smart contracts for e-government through value and business process modelling. In: 54th Hawaii International Conference on System Sciences, HICSS 2021, Kauai, Hawaii, USA, 5 January 2021, pp. 1–10 (2021)
6. Hou, H.: Application of smart contract technology in China's e-government. In: 2017 26th ICCCN, pp. 1–4. IEEE (2017)
7. Kushwaha, S.S., Joshi, S.: A comprehensive review of Ethereum smart contract security issues. IEEE Access 10 (2022)
8. Li, M., Chen, Y., Lal, C., Conti, M., Alazab, M., Hu, D.: Eunomia: anonymous and secure vehicular digital forensics based on blockchain. IEEE Trans. Dependable Secure Comput. 1 (2021). https://doi.org/10.1109/TDSC.2021.3130583
9. Nakamoto, S.: Bitcoin: a peer-to-peer electronic cash system. Decent. Bus. Rev. 21260 (2008)
10. Sánchez-Gómez, N., Torres-Valderrama, J., García-García, J., Gutiérrez, J.J., Escalona, M.: A survey on model-based software design and examination in smart contracts. IEEE Access **8**, 164556–164569 (2020)
11. Shangtong, G., Ruijing, W., Fengzhi, Z.: Overview of blockchain technology principles and applications. Comput. Sci. **48**(2), 271–281
12. Szabo, N.: Build and secure models on public networks. First Monday (1997)
13. Tianchong, Y., Shiman, Z.: The rules of electronic evidence under the application of uniform law in my country. J. Heilongjiang Polit. Legal Manag. Cadre Coll. (6), 7 (2021)
14. Vivar, A.L., Orozco, V., García, L.J.: Security framework for Ethereum smart contracts. Comput. Commun. **172**, 119–129 (2021)
15. Wang, Z., Jin, H., Dai, W.: Ethereum smart contract security examination: surveying future research directions. Front. Comput. Sci. **15**(2), 152802 (2021). https://doi.org/10.1007/s11704-020-9284-9

16. Wohrer, M., Zdun, U.: Smart contracts: security models and reliability in the Ethereum ecosystem. In: 2018 IWBOSE, pp. 2–8. IEEE (2018)
17. Wohrer, M., Zdun, U.: Converting DSL to code: smart contracts and the submission of design models. IEEE Softw. **37**(5), 37–42 (2020)
18. XiaoYong, L., DongXi, L., DaWu, G., YingCai, B.: Research on DDoS defense and response technology. Comput. Eng. Appl. **39**(12), 4 (2003)
19. Xiong, Y., Du, J.: Digital evidences maintenance pattern based on blockchain. In: ICCSP, pp. 1–5 (2019)
20. YuJie, Z.: Judicial application of blockchain technology, system problems and innovation of evidence law. East. Methodol. **3**(99), r109 (2019)
21. Zheng, G., Gao, L., Huang, L., Guan, J.: Ethereum Smart Contract Development in Solidity. Springer, Singapore (2021). https://doi.org/10.1007/978-981-15-6218-1

Author Index

Printed in the United States
by Baker & Taylor Publisher Services

Printed in the United States
by Baker & Taylor Publisher Services